RETHINKING FRANCE

RETHINKING FRANCE

LES LIEUX DE MÉMOIRE

VOLUME 4

HISTORIES AND MEMORIES

Under the direction of

PIERRE NORA

Translation directed by

DAVID P. JORDAN

THE UNIVERSITY OF CHICAGO PRESS
CHICAGO AND LONDON

Pierre Nora is editorial director at Éditions Gallimard. Since 1977, he has been directeur d'études at the École des hautes études en sciences sociales. He is the founding editor of *Le Débat* and has directed the editorial work on *Les Lieux de mémoire* since 1984. In 2001 he was elected to the Académie Française. **David P. Jordan** is the LAS Distinguished Professor of French History at the University of Illinois at Chicago and the author of *Transforming Paris* and *The Revolutionary Career of Maximilien Robespierre*, both published by the University of Chicago Press.

The University of Chicago Press, Chicago 60637
The University of Chicago Press, Ltd., London
© 2010 by The University of Chicago
All rights reserved. Published 2010
Printed in the United States of America
19 18 17 16 15 14 13 12 11 10   1 2 3 4 5

ISBN-13: 978-0-226-59135-3 (cloth)
ISBN-10: 0-226-59135-2 (cloth)

Originally published as *Les Lieux de mémoire*, © Éditions Gallimard, 1984, 1986, and 1992.

The University of Chicago Press gratefully acknowledges a subvention from the government of France, through the French Ministry of Culture, Centre National du Livre, in support of the costs of translating this volume.

Library of Congress Cataloging-in-Publication Data

Lieux de mémoire. English
    Rethinking France = Lieux de mémoire / under the direction of Pierre Nora ; translated by Mary Trouille ; translation directed by David P. Jordan
        p. cm.
    Includes index.
    Contents: v. I. The State.
    ISBN 0-226-59132-8 (cloth, v. I: alk. paper)
    I. France—Civilization—Philosophy. 2. Memory. 3. Symbolism. 4. National characteristics, French. 5. Nationalism—France. I. Nora, Pierre. II. Title.
DC33.L6513 2001
944—dc22

                                                            2001000375

CONTENTS

℘

PIERRE NORA

T his volume, the fourth and last of *Rethinking France: Les Lieux de mé-moire*, explicitly recapitulates, in concentrated form, the internal logic of the enterprise.

Recall that this project grew out of a recognition that those brutal, historical shocks, which struck every country and contemporary society, especially during the second half of the twentieth century, as well as the accelerated transformations they brought in their wake, completely shattered the links these countries and societies had with their past. This upheaval was no doubt more clearly perceived and earlier felt in a country such as France, the model of the nation-state, whose connection with its history was of particular intensity and continuity. In contrast to other countries, history, rather than folklore, language, or the economy, took charge of memory. It would thus not be an exaggeration to speak of "memory-history," especially when history has become in France a discipline that strives for the same precision and rigor of science and at the same time the central nerve of civic and national education.

In the midst of a rapid and painful metamorphosis in this model of the nation and collective identity, a general inventory of tradition and a critical analysis of the constitutive elements of the model became indispensable. The next step was to disassemble the blocks of our national awareness and show how time had carried these familiar objects forward to us. For this reason the attempt to "rethink" the history of France included a historical dimension that went far beyond a precise, narrow, and academic definition of historiography as "the history of history." The history here presented is analytical, a kind of critical self-examination; it is a history less concerned with events and historical phenomena than with the manner by which over time these were transformed into historical memory and became *lieux de mémoire*. It was, in the last analysis, history that was totally historiographical in the critical sense.

And yet, at the heart of the enterprise, this totality of disassembled historical events and phenomena became strikingly individualized. All previous objects of memory, all the other *lieux,* had by definition a contemporary character, since their very presence in national symbols dictated our interest in them. That is not the case for the *lieux* analyzed here. The earlier ones depend on synchronous exploration. These, by contrast, depend on a diachronic exhumation. Indeed what this means is a plunge into time to identify those primary moments when a new relationship with the national and collective past crystallized. Even better, intensifying our critical effort will let the parade of these great moments of our practical, mental, and institutional apparatus stand out. These were the moments that allowed those great works of historiography to see the light of day. For the most part, they had never been studied, or studied in this sense.

Instruments of memory, moments of memory—these two sections do not lend themselves to the same treatment. One requires systematic exposition, the other illustrative sampling. First, let us look at the laboratory where, in the shadow of power, the first annals of power are hammered out: the royal chapel; the Fleury monastery, later Saint Benoît sur Loire; Saint Denis, the necropolis of the kings; Reims, city of the royal anointing; and all those sanctuaries out of which came the *Grandes chroniques de France* in the thirteenth and fourteenth centuries.

At the other end of the chain and in contrast to the arcana of sacred royalty are the Archives nationales, those "catacombs of manuscripts," "the necropolis of national monuments" in Michelet's words. They are contemporaneous with the birth of the nation and of the very source of national historiography. There is thus nothing astonishing about the position and magnitude granted to them. Nevertheless there was a limitation, for it had been possible and even desirable to shift the analytic center to the present and to show how the pedestal of France's historic memory teeters today, explodes and implodes through its material proliferation, and loses its monopoly of memory in favor of other structures of support, in particular, images and the increasing power of technologies. But this was to take as a given the actual history of the construction of the archives, something that up to then had never been done. Necessary as well was the effort to show how a form of history that is wrongly assumed to be moving away from archival work, namely the history of symbols, is to the contrary, the one that, for the first time, pushes to establish the archives' own history in depth, duration, and dignity.

Mention of the Musée des monuments français, established by the Directory and its strange creator, Alexandre Lenoir, is justified not just because of its revolutionary political meaning, nor because of the ideological importance and memories of the "moment," nor even because of its posterity of museums (particularly the museums of Cluny and Saint Germain en Laye as well as the museum of French monuments), but by the role that this museum of the Petits Augustins, situated opposite the École des beaux-arts on the rue du Bac, played in the rebirth of the Gothic and the education of historians of liberalism and the Romantic movement. It was here that Augustin Thierry acquired the taste for digging into ancient medieval chronicles. It was here that Michelet located the "primitive scene" that made him a historian of the "full resurrection of the past." Brought as a young child to visit the spellbinding labyrinth, he felt faint before the reclining statues. "I was not really sure that they still might be alive, those white marble figures stretched out asleep on their tombs. But soft, my dead sirs!"

Different though they may be, the next two *lieux de mémoire* may be linked by the utopian spirit that inspired them and the era that gave them birth. The era of the Restoration (1814–30) and the July Monarchy (1830–48), more precisely the years from 1820 to 1840, was a period of less brilliance than Napoleon's First Empire (1804–15) and of less importance than the Second (1851–70), but it was still one of the most creative and most intensely productive in national memory, as these two chapters attest.

It is François Guizot, historian and minister of public instruction, to whom we owe the creation of the major institutions of memory, still vital to us today. They include the École des chartes, the Société de l'histoire de France, and the Comité des travaux historiques. At the time Guizot believed it possible to gather together every last document of old France! As for the Galerie des batailles inaugurated in 1837 at the Palace of Versailles, that was only the remains of a commemorative project with a very different scope. King Louis-Philippe had conceived this ambitious project to give the chateau a new vocation, to enlighten: Versailles was to become a museum of reconciliation of "all the glories of France," revolutionary and Napoleonic as well as monarchical, after having been the center of government and the glory of the absolute monarchy.

Then comes Pierre Larousse and his *Grand dictionnaire universel* of the twentieth century, the ancestor of all the Larousse dictionaries. A

25,000-page monument, it was intended by Larousse to be the militant and ideological reflection of an era, straddling the Second Empire and the beginnings of the Third Republic. He was one of the giant hard workers of the nineteenth century who, following the example of Hugo, Balzac, and Michelet, could be described as "memory men." His name has become a common noun, the origin of which the user has all but forgotten.

The gathering of these disparate *lieux,* these instruments of memory from among the many possible, throws into relief what has been truly new in the *lieux de mémoire* and what has astonished and enchanted. It consisted of putting together on the same plane and viewing from the same angle the most spectacular symbols and achievements from France's national history and the most humble instruments of its formation. A classic history of France had no reason to make room for these *lieux.* Neither did a history of history.

Moments of memory? The attempt was to register those single key moments in which a total revision of the connection to the past was crystallized in an individual or collective work. These revisions are fewer than the unending flood of histories of France might lead one to believe. Each coincides with a decisive moment in the formation of France's national identity.

There are, to begin, the *romans aux roys* that Louis IX in the thirteenth century had commanded a monk at Saint Denis named Primat to draw up. These are the *Grandes chroniques de France* that extend to the fourteenth century and the Homeric equivalent of our origins. They fixed the feudal and dynastic memory of France in the French language. The narrative is essentially genealogical and mythic to be sure, but it is also the bearer of a French, Christian, and monarchical history, and for that reason, national. In the second half of the sixteenth century, during the wars of religion, there are the *Recherches de la France* created by Étienne Pasquier in response to a need to redefine the monarchy as a state. They establish the state in its *parlementaire* and Gallican version.* By substituting the Gallic origins

---

* EDITOR'S NOTE: The *parlementaire* tradition is a fundamentally aristocratic view of French history in which the absolutist assertions of the kings to rule without challenge are justified because they are descended from the Roman emperors. The aristocracy, whose rightful place in the state is to control its judicial functions, sees itself as a check on royal pretensions. The Gallican version does for the church what the *parlementaire* version does for the courts. The church is seen as national in its origins and hence not under the direct and absolute control of the papacy. Both will play an increasingly important role in French history, finally contributing to the several causes of the French Revolution.

of France for the legend of the Trojan origins of the monarchy, the *Recherches* turn France into an object to be defended and made illustrious by a powerfully legitimizing past. And especially there is the grand cycle of the nation, which brings us compelling models for understanding the past. This is the "forbidding alliance of patriotism and erudition," as Augustin Thierry says. His *Lettres sur l'histoire de France* (1827) mark the starting point, Michelet's *Histoire de France* the lyric summit, and Lavisse's history (from 1903 to 1922) the critical step in its establishment. This cycle begins unfolding right after the Revolution and continues to the beginnings of the 1930s. The *Histoire sincère de la nation française* by Charles Seignobos, in 1933, marks the culmination.

There is, finally, the decisive moment of the *Annales*, when, the crisis of the 1930s notwithstanding, the silent dissociation of history, memory, and nation occurs. Despite its declared intention to turn away from the phenomenon of the nation, discredited by the crusade against history through events, the movement inaugurated by Lucien Febvre and Marc Bloch can and must appear, in the last analysis, as the one that has most profoundly revitalized knowledge about France through its efforts to dig into the diversity and constraints of geography, to plunge into the depths of the real life of peasants in a country marked by distinct regions, and to examine that experience by extending the use of large numbers of statistics and demographics. But this revitalization of knowledge must not mislead us, for it is due to the decisive contribution of all the new social sciences (the "human sciences," as we say in France). The expression in and of itself conveys a relationship to the object quite different from the natural filiation: a distance and objectification that no longer stem from spontaneous affinity or subjective identification, especially since the outcomes from the social sciences—economics, sociology, demography, or linguistics—end up demolishing the unity of the French entity, any evidence for the national idea, and the coherence of its history.[1]

The first issue of the *Annales* review appeared in 1929, the year of the Wall Street crash. Though purely fortuitous, this coincidence may actually be significant. In the vast ideological, political, and economic crisis of the 1930s, from the standpoint of the nation, a wide-ranging metamorphosis took place: the substitution of the society-state dyad for the nation-state dyad. It was impossible for the metamorphosis involving this substitution for awareness of national identity not to have repercussions in historiographical expression.

Increasingly conditioned by the rising power of the media, this dissociation of experienced national memory from the historical sciences was again accelerated in the 1960s under the sign of the "New History" through the conjunction of two phenomena that played a crucial role in modifying the connection to the past. First was decolonization, which marked the end of a universal projection of the nation by bringing it back within the boundaries of the *Hexagone* (a term that dates from the end of the Algerian War). Then came the end of thirty years of economic growth, which had kept the entire past at a distance even as it had, by the same token, brought modernity into the smallest villages of a country so long rural and traditional. In sum, there had occurred a phenomenon, comparable to the French Revolution in its effects, for the renewal of historiography. As the France of the ancien régime had been for the postrevolutionary generation, now again the French tradition in its entirety, the totality of "Frenchness," was ready to be revisited with a critical and questioning eye and introduced for analysis through the *Lieux de mémoire.*

⚜

In this historiographical gallery the absence of Michelet and, by contrast, the disproportionate place given to Lavisse, to whom I have devoted two articles,[2] are perhaps astonishing. An explanation is called for.

Michelet is a remarkable *lieu de mémoire* unto himself. And one might even go so far as to say his is the only *Histoire de France* because it is the only one that works as an organic whole. It is one with its author, whose exceptional personality as a writer is comparable only to Chateaubriand and his *Mémoires d'outre-tombe* or to Proust and his *À la recherche du temps perdu.* His spirit animates the entire enterprise of the *Lieux de mémoire,* and perhaps he does not now show up in it as a *lieu* because he is everywhere present in it. Yet let us also say at the same time that, strictly speaking, in the historiographical stratification of national memory, Michelet, whatever his individual importance, surely does not constitute a separate layer. He is the apotheosis of the movement for which August Thierry wrote the manifesto. Lavisse, to the contrary, plays a role whose importance cannot be overestimated. He is the man who made history and its scholarly instruction the chief instrument for the creation of the national consciousness. He prepared the France of Verdun by giving its teachers a clear mission: educate citizens who love their country and soldiers who are ready to die for it. He wrote the *Histoire de France* for the two levels of education, the elementary school and the university. He set up its institutions: the degrees of the *licence* and the *agrégation* within the framework of a renovated Sorbonne. Finally, and most important, the twenty-seven volumes of his *Histoire de France* were the collective monument of the "positivist" school that passed all of inherited history memory through the sieve of a new critical science.

On all these accounts, Lavisse played the decisive and strategic role in the very conception of the *Lieux de mémoire*. If right at the outset a division of work in three sections was imposed on me—*La République, La Nation, Les France*—only later did I grasp the reason for this trisection. It is this: Lavisse's entire effort had consisted in molding three entities into a powerful synthesis in order to show the *République* as the achieved form of the nation and of France. By contrast what stood out for us in the 1980s was the decomposition, or if one prefers, the "deconstruction" of this majestic edifice. Each of these entities regained its independence, and the very mystery of their historical existence called for analysis of each of the elements that had contributed to producing them. It called for a critical analysis, the hidden aim of which was both to subvert the canonical version of the history of France and to illustrate it.

⁂

In conclusion, suppose one needed to characterize in a word the moment of memory to which the necessity for this critical inventory corresponds. One would not hesitate to say that after the royal-memory of the *Grandes chroniques de France*, the state-memory of the *Lettres sur l'histoire de France*, the citizen-memory of the *Histoire de France* by Lavisse, the structure-memory of the *Annales* school, and Fernand Braudel's *L'Identité de la France*, we now have here the patrimony-memory.

By patrimony-memory I mean not only the dramatic amplification of the idea and its recent and problematic expansion into all the objects attesting to the national past. It is rather, and much more profoundly, the transformation of what was traditionally at stake in memory itself into a common possession and a collective heritage. This metabolic action results, first, in the exhaustion of classic oppositions that, at least since the Revolution, underlay the organization of national memory: new France versus old France, secular France versus religious France, France of the Left versus France of the Right. The exhaustion of these oppositions does not lead to the disappearance of filiations or fidelities. And at least with respect to the last of these cleavages neither does it preclude the divisions that, without calling into question the very principle of this democracy, are necessary for its organization. This patrimonial transformation of memory is also expressed in the recovery of the nation's repressed past and the liberated return of its most painful episodes for the collective conscience, from the Albigensian Crusade to wartime collaboration with the Nazis, not to mention the Saint Bartholomew massacre, the War of the Vendée, and the entire colonial adventure. It is especially manifest in the ever sharper revitalization of the feeling of belonging to the nation, experienced no longer in the affirmative mode of traditional nationalism, though feeding off of its outbursts, but in the world of renewed sensibility to the nation's uniqueness combined with a necessary adaptation to the impact in France of new conditions: reduced power, involvement in Europe, widespread modern ways of life (often coming from the United States), aspirations to decentralization, contemporary forms of state intervention, strong presence of an immigrant population not easily reduced to the norms of customary Frenchness, diminution of French-speaking areas.

A decisive transformation. It is this transformation that propels the renewal of France's approach to history via memory everywhere, the approach to which this enterprise of the *Lieux de mémoire* is dedicated.

NOTES

1. I have analyzed the phenomenon and its consequences more in detail in the general introduction to *Rethinking France*, part 3, "National Memory and National History," and resume the argument here.

2. Pierre Nora, "Lavisse, The Nation's Teacher," in *Realms of Memory: The Construction of the French Past*, vol. 2, *Traditions* (New York: Columbia University Press, 1996).

CHANCERIES AND MONASTERIES

⅋

BERNARD GUENÉE

The year was 788. Charles, king of the Franks, was not yet the great Charlemagne, Roman emperor. Yet in 774 he had already forced King Desiderius to capitulate at Pavia, and had proclaimed himself king of the Lombards. In 785, after years of implacable warfare, Widukind had been obliged to lay down arms—all of Saxony as far as the Elbe was annexed to Charles's kingdom. No longer threatened from the north, Charles's armies began the conquest of what would become the marches of Spain in that same year of 785. Then, in 787, the duke of Benevento in southern Italy was forced to submit. And finally, in 788, Tassilo III, the last duke of an independent Bavaria, was toppled, so that all of Germany was henceforth Frankish. Meanwhile, even as he was accomplishing these prodigious victories, the king had spent nearly a decade establishing an institutional network, based on a solid State and an obedient Church, that would link his vast territories. In 788, then, Charles—who had just turned forty— could feel secure about the future of his kingdom. In order to secure its past, he decided to have that past inscribed in the collective memory.

THE ROYAL CHAPEL

The Frankish king had the scholarly tools needed to implement this political decision right at his own court, for he had already populated his palace school with teachers recruited from everywhere, especially from Italy and England. By 774, Peter of Pisa was teaching grammar there, as was Paulinus by 776, prior to concentrating on philosophy and later be-coming archbishop of Aquileia. In 782, Paul Warnefried, generally known as Paul the Deacon, came to teach grammar, although the deacon was also a fine poet and an excellent historian. Finally, in 786, Alcuin, mas-ter of the school at York, was summoned to Charles's palace, where he began to teach the literary liberal arts—that is to say, grammar, rhetoric, and logic—so brilliantly that Charles and his entourage came to consider Alcuin the greatest master of all. Via the court, Alcuin became *praecep-tor Galliae*, the tutor to all of Gaul. Scholars who studied at the palace school populated the kingdom's entire administration. Many also ended up in the palace chapel. The term "chapel" originally meant the king's private oratory; although it was later applied to various places of worship throughout the realm, in 788 "chapel" referred only to the palace ora-tory. The term had recently begun, however, to encompass the group of priests who conducted liturgical services there. Indeed, under Pippin the Short and during the early years of Charles's reign, the chapel orga-nized itself into a body, which therefore required a head. The number of "chaplains" grew as these increasingly learned men were asked to perform increasingly onerous tasks. They were no long expected simply to chant and pray. They had to copy all the books necessary for church services and, above all, they had to draw up all the documents required for the administration of the kingdom—certain chaplains were also clerks in the still-young chancery. Inevitably, books and documents gravitated toward the chapel in order to fulfill scholarly needs and accomplish administra-tive tasks. Archives, library, scholars: in 788, Charles had to hand, in his own palace chapel, everything required to commit the desired history of his kingdom to the collective memory.

Up till that point, neither the Franks in general nor Frankish kings in particular had been concerned with history. No Merovingian king, apparently, had prompted the writing of a single historical work. Even in that barren landscape, however, one wonderful flower had blossomed—Bishop Gregory of Tours wrote a great deal in the second half of the sixth century. By 591 he had completed, among other works, a ten-book *His-tory* that began with the creation of the world and quickly arrived at the Franks, whose story occupied the greater part of Gregory's account, from their origins up to his own day. Later, in the mid seventh century, one or several Burgundian chroniclers, now collectively known as "Fredegar," wrote a new history of the world in which a summary of Gregory's *His-tory of the Franks* was followed by an account of events up to the year 642. Then, in the early eighth century, a Neustrian historian—who probably lived in or near what is now Normandy and was ignorant of the work of Fredegar—also drafted a summary of Gregory's book, to which he added an account of events known to him up to 727. This book became known as the *Liber historiae Francorum* (Book of the history of the Franks). Finally, close relatives of Charles Martel and his son Pippin the Short later suggested to historians that they might update either the *Liber historiae Francorum* or Fredegar's chronicle with an account that, it goes without saying, would show the father and grandfather of the future King Charles in a favorable light. Thus little by little, successive continuations—arising from various initiatives and differing motives—came to constitute a kind of corpus of Frankish history from its origins to the death of Pippin in 768. This corpus was rendered even more complex, disordered, and diverse by the fact that the elements constituting it varied from one manuscript to another. As imperfect as it may have been, however, the corpus at least existed. Yet in 788 King Charles and his advisers chose to ignore it. They were not aiming to revise and extend a grand history of the Franks since their origins.

Nor were they aiming to erect a monument to the glory of the Carolingian family. Such a monument already existed, for that matter. Angilramn, bishop of Metz since 768, was summoned in 784 to head the royal chapel, where he went without abandoning his bishopric. It was probably shortly afterward that he had Paul the Deacon compose the *Gesta episcoporum Mettensium*, a history of the bishops of Metz based on the *Liber Pontificalis*, a series of brief accounts of all the bishops of Rome from Saint Peter onward. Since Saint Arnulf, an ancestor of the Carolingian line, had been bishop of Metz, Paul the Deacon's chronicle skillfully managed not only to glorify a city that was, in a way, the new dynasty's holy city, but also to tack the new ruling family's genealogy onto his list of the bishops of Metz, thereby discreetly justifying Pippin's accession to the throne.

In 788, then, Charles and his counselors were aiming neither to glorify a people nor to extol a family. Their goal was more immediate and more practical: they wanted to provide the kingdom's administrators with an accurate context for the documentation that was accumulating in archives and governing everyday operations. The need for a "collective memory" was the fruit of administrative necessity as much as political vision. All that was required were short notes that listed, year after year, the main events since 741, the year that Charles Martel died and his son Pippin came to power as mayor of the palace, prior to consolidating his accomplishments by pushing aside the last Merovingian king and becoming himself king of the Franks in 751.

The "annalistic" format was still quite recent in 788. The first requirement of Christian liturgy had been to establish in advance, for each year, the date on which Easter was to be celebrated. Thanks to learned calculations based on complex principles, an Easter calendar had been developed, which was finally adopted in the eighth century by all Western churches. One of the most precious possessions of a church or monastery was its canonical table indicating when Easter should be celebrated each year. Monasteries slowly began adopting the habit of noting, at the close of each year, one or two significant events, to serve as a record. Little by little, the annual note became an account, separate from the table itself. Thus annals were born. The first annals appeared on Easter tables in England. In the eighth century, Anglo-Saxon missionaries took Easter tables and annalistic notes to the continent where many churches and monasteries, notably in and around the Rhenish heartland of the Frankish kingdom, perpetuated and imitated these early models by commencing to keep their own brief annals. In particular, annals were kept at a monastery—the exact location of which is unclear—between Cologne and Trier, while others were composed at the Abbey of Gorze, near Metz, and still others at the Abbey of Murbach in Alsace, later continued in Swabia. Hence the chaplain to whom Charles and Angilramn assigned the task was able to collate the notes available at court with references from these easily accessible Rhenish, Moselle, and Swabian annals. That is how the court of King Charles composed the annals known to modern scholarship as the *Annales du royaume des Francs* (*Annales regni Francorum*), but which might be better called—as did ninth-century subjects of the Carolingian king— the *Annales des rois* or *Annales royales*.

Once the chaplain working under Angilramn had completed his task, the annals were regularly updated by the royal chapel itself. Every year an entry was added, summing up what had occurred in the kingdom. These *Annales royales* had all the advantages and drawbacks of a work written close to the seat of power—although well-informed, they were biased. Above all, the way they were composed reflected the vicissitudes of Carolingian culture and politics. Between 814 and 817, for example, following the death of Charlemagne, a complete revision of the *Annales royales* seemed in order, in terms of form as well as content. The scholars working for the young emperor, Louis the Pious, were no longer content with the somewhat simple and coarse Latin used by the preceding generation, and their political outlook had also changed. It was a time of great expectations. The composing of annual entries continued for some time, until tribulations and disillusion intervened—in 830, the sons of Louis rebelled against their father. The head of the chapel, henceforth called arch-chaplain, was Hilduin, abbot of Saint-Denis, who sided with the sons against the father. The work of chapel and chancery was therefore disrupted, and the entry for the year 829 was the last for a while. After a few eventful years, however, Louis the Pious regained his throne in 834, and work at the chancery became more regular. A chaplain who was not very skilled in Latin was instructed to continue the *Annales royales*. He managed to complete the years 830, 831, 832, 833, and 834, yet hardly had he begun the year 835 than the account ceased. Perhaps the arch-chaplain died, or perhaps further political difficulties arose. Whatever the case, Louis died in 840 and the empire was divided between his sons in 843 without anyone bothering to keep the *Annales royales* up-to-date.

The western part of the empire—the kingdom of western Francia—fell to the youngest son of Louis the Pious, Charles the Bald. Charles thought maintaining the *Annales royales* would help consolidate his authority and affirm Carolingian continuity. The new king therefore immediately entrusted the task to a cleric in his palace, a scholar of Spanish origin who had changed his name from Galindo to Prudentius. In return, Prudentius was made bishop of Troyes (which did not distract him from his duties at court nor his historian's task). He wrote short entries on the final, missing years of the reign of Louis the Pious, then continued to keep the *Annales* up-to-date until his death in 861. At that point a long chapter of history came to close, for King Charles was too besieged by daily troubles, and his chancery too overwhelmed by daily tasks, to find a cleric who had the time to record royal history. Things would later degrade even further, as the Carolingian dynasty declined and the royal chancery atrophied. After 861, the palace chapel was no longer what it had been for three-quarters of a century—the repository of the kingdom's memory.

Charlemagne and Louis the Pious not only insured that the *Annales royales* were written, they were also concerned with disseminating them. In fact, since the institutional ideal of those kings and their advisers was a strong State powerfully backed by an ecclesiastical hierarchy of which the pope was the uncontested head, Carolingian political constructs rested on two major historical works: the *Liber Pontificalis*, which recounted the history of the bishops of Rome, and the *Annales royales,* which recounted the history of the kingdom. Just as the *Liber Pontificalis* was owned and imitated by numerous Carolingian prelates, so the *Annales royales* were widely known throughout the empire. The limits of the annals' popularity should nevertheless be mentioned; although ninth-century laymen were not as ignorant as has long been thought—some of them were educated and had fine libraries containing a few books of history—their taste ran to works that were less austere than the *Annales royales*. In fact, there is no indication that a layman ever owned a copy of the annals. Instead, they were found in the libraries of churches and monasteries. Nor is it certain that they reached all regions of the empire, although they were widely known by the ninth century in Germanic areas, for example in Liège and Worms—where a copy was preserved—and at Salzburg, Lorsch, and Xanten, where they were copied and kept up-to-date.

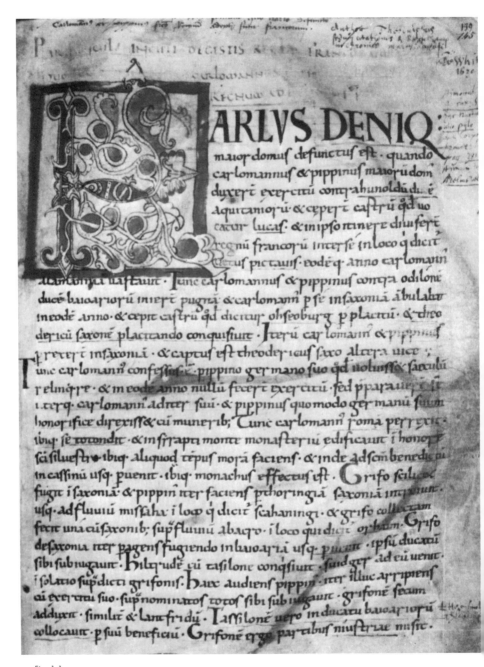

Fig. 1.1

The Carolingian *Annales royales*, continued in the ninth century by the clerks of the imperial palace, then by Hincmar, archbishop of Reims, were conserved in the archiepiscopal library of Reims, then copied in the eleventh century into a vast ensemble of historical texts kept by the Abbey of Saint-Bertin. Hence the misleading name of *Annales de Saint-Bertin* for this grand sequel of Carolingian stories.

As to Charles the Bald, early in his reign he was concerned not merely to record history; he also wanted that history disseminated. Copies of the annals kept by Prudentius were circulated. The effort was in vain, however, for not a single copy survived or was ever used. Yet there is no doubt that Charles the Bald had a copy—or perhaps the cleric's original—in his own library. And one day the king of western Francia performed an act of great import: he lent his copy to Hincmar.

REIMS

Hincmar had been a monk at Saint-Denis. When Hilduin, abbot of Saint-Denis, became arch-chaplain, he introduced Hincmar to court. The monk was highly appreciated, and Charles the Bald made him archbishop of Reims early in the reign. The ecclesiastical province of Reims was one of the most considerable in Christendom, straddling the kingdoms of Charles and Lothar. The city of Reims, meanwhile, was one of the most important administrative centers in Charles's realm. Thus in 845 Hincmar, nearly forty years old, became head of one of the key places in the kingdom and the Carolingian world. This extraordinary position enabled Hincmar's extraordinary personality to dominate the political and religious life of the West for nearly thirty years. He dominated not only through his deeds, but also through his writing, which was nourished on endless reading. In availing himself of the necessary resources, the archbishop turned Reims into one of the major intellectual centers of the second half of the ninth century. He personally supervised the activity of the school, and he created an active scriptorium from scratch, where excellent scribes copied numerous manuscripts according to strict rules—Hincmar himself read and annotated them with great care. Since the archbishop also carefully kept a copy of any document required either by his political activity or for the administration of the province, Reims ultimately housed acquired archives and a large library, of which approximately one hundred manuscripts still survive.

Hincmar was the man to whom Charles the Bald one day lent the chronicle of Prudentius. This was an unfortunate move insofar as it is not certain that the king ever got his book back. Yet it was a felicitous move insofar as Hincmar took it upon himself to continue the work of Prudentius, adopting the annalistic format into an account that was obviously well documented yet highly personal in tone—a true diary. Hincmar kept this journal until he died in 882, aged over seventy-five.

After Hincmar's death Reims, like so many other cities in the kingdom, suffered greatly from the ravages of the Norsemen. Its school went into decline. Fortunately, however, its library survived. And for several

Fig. 1.2
The manuscript of the *Grandes chroniques de France* copied around 1375–79 for King Charles V is richly illustrated. In the heading of the story of Charlemagne, two little miniatures show, respectively, the coronation of the king at Soissons in 768 and the historian Éginhard writing his *Vie de Charlemagne*. The writing scribe is a constant theme in medieval illustration.

decades the sole copy of the annals compiled by Prudentius and Hincmar remained buried at the back of a dormant library.

Once the Norse storm had passed—before the ninth century came to a close—Archbishop Fulk revived the Reims school by recruiting the best teachers. Throughout the tenth century, Reims remained an intellectual center of prime importance thanks to its rich library, supportive archbishops, and active teachers (not least of whom was the illustrious Gerbert, who would become archbishop of Reims in 991 and Pope Sylvester II in 999). It might even be argued that Reims was the sole city in the kingdom to sustain intense intellectual life throughout the entire tenth century. All the liberal arts were cultivated in Reims, both the literary trivium (grammar, rhetoric, logic) and the scientific quadrivium (arithmetic, geometry, astronomy, music). History was not among these liberal arts. Buoyed by this grand effervescence, however, and endowed with a grand library, great historians surfaced at Reims, pursuing the annalistic tradition.

Flodoard was born in 894. He studied at the schools of Reims, and was soon named canon of Reims cathedral and warden of its archives. He was thus conversant with the documents and books that had accumulated thanks to Hincmar's efforts. He was familiar with, among other works, the great archbishop's annals, which he used when writing his own *Histoire de l'église de Reims*. This man of learning, however, was also a man of action, for Flodoard had earned and retained the confidence of several successive archbishops of Reims. The archbishops of the powerful metropolis of Reims, in fact, played a major role in the realm's politics throughout the tenth century. Flodoard was thus privy to the main events of his day and knew the main characters. And, like Hincmar, he kept a "journal" year after year. Flodoard began his annals in the year 919, aged twenty-five. His accounts were complete and well-informed up to the middle of the century, when age and infirmity—the canon was now over fifty-five—kept him increasingly aloof from events. His entries became briefer and less complete. He nevertheless died quill in hand in 966, over seventy years old. Flodoard's *Annales*, without which little would be known of the tenth century, were still in the library at Reims at the close of that century when Richer, a monk at Saint-Remi in Reims, came across them.

On taking up the pen around 995, Richer expressly stated that he aspired to continue Hincmar's annals, which he openly admired. He said in the same prologue that he would also use, when he could, Flodoard's annals, about which nevertheless he had certain reservations. Richer intended to uphold the Reims tradition, but his ambitions were greater than those of Flodoard. Although Flodoard's *Histoire de l'église de Reims* had proven that he was capable of writing rather fine Latin, the language of his journal was not very elegant, and sometimes not very correct. Furthermore, it was composed of notes rather than a well-ordered account. And although it goes without saying that he referred, as events required, to the kingdom of the Franks or the kingdom of Francia, the kingdom was not at the core of his journal. Now at the close of the tenth century Reims was probably at its cultural and political zenith. The school of Reims was so renowned that Hugh Capet, duke of France, sent his son Robert there, probably around 984. And several year later, Archbishop Adalbero played a decisive role in the coup d'état that toppled the last Carolingian and made that same Hugh the new king. It was also Adalbero who crowned Hugh king in Reims Cathedral on July 3, 987. Hence when the new archbishop, Gerbert, asked Richer to keep a chronicle, the writer—nourished on Sallust and Caesar, and witness to momentous events—used Flodoard yet hoped to do better. He intended to employ a finer Latin, construct a better-ordered account, and deal with a specific subject. He announced straight away that he would recount the struggles of the Gauls (*De Gallorum congressibus*), and he began with a brief description of Gaul and its inhabitants. Richer, steeped as he was in rhetoric, should not be reproached with "padding out" Flodoard; nor is it too surprising that, faithful to Caesar and keen to establish continuity, he used the terms "Gaul" and "Gauls" when recounting the history of the kingdom and its inhabitants in the tenth century. Rather, Richer should be admired not only for continuing Hincmar, employing Flodoard, and deploying his classical learning and his political experience at Reims, but also for aspiring to write—and indeed having written—a veritable history of the tenth century kingdom in his account of the events from 888 to 995, under the title *De Gallorum congressibus*.

Richer's text encountered little success. No copy was ever made of the sole surviving manuscript, an autograph text that Gerbert, probably, took from Reims on leaving France in 998. The manuscript slumbered in a library of the Holy Roman Empire. Reims, too closely linked to the Carolingians, ceased to be the political and cultural center of the realm under the new Capetian king. It also ceased to play the role it had played for over a century—the repository of France's collective memory.

That memory would not sink, however. As early as 976, a copy of Flodoard's *Annales* had found its way to Laon. Others were made sometime later in Verdun, Langres, and Dijon, reflecting monastic enthusiasms and migrations. From Dijon, Flodoard's annals were carried to Fécamp, where they were copied in the early eleventh century, subsequently reaching all of Normandy. However swiftly and widely they may have circulated, Flodoard's *Annales* had nevertheless not reached the Abbey of Saint-Vaast in Arras by the end of the tenth century. On the other hand, the monks in Arras did possess the text of the annals of Prudentius and Hincmar (which had long been available only in the library at Reims, and therefore known only to Reims scholars). This meant that the monks of Saint-Vaast, given the *Annales royales* and subsequent additions, were able to constitute a single set of annals recording events from 741 to 882. At the same time, the monks took another initiative that confirmed what Richer's ambitions had intimated—the final generation of the tenth century would not content itself with annalistic entries. It sought a fuller vision, it wanted to anchor France to a more distant past. The monks of Saint-Vaast constituted a veritable corpus of texts on the history of France by placing Gregory's *History of the Franks* (with additions by the so-called Fredegar) in front of the Carolingian annals. The Saint-Vaast corpus was copied around the year 1000 by the monks of Saint-Bertin in Saint-Omer, at the prodding of Abbot Otbert. Thus an interest in knowing the country's entire past surfaced here and there in the north of France. Yet it was not a monastery in the north of the kingdom that would pick up the torch that had fallen from the hands of Reims. Instead, it was Fleury.

FLEURY

Fleury was a very old monastery founded in the seventh century in the Loire Valley, slightly upriver of Orléans. As early as 670–72, monks brought what they believed to be the relics of Saint Benedict from Monte Cassino, which is why the abbey was subsequently called Saint-Benoît-sur-Loire. The monks of Fleury had not merely brought precious relics from Italy, however. They also brought manuscripts, and began to endow the abbey with a fine library. In the ninth century the abbey suffered from Norse invasions, but was able to salvage many of its books. In 930, Cluniac reform at Fleury reestablished the old Benedictine traditions in all their strictness. When Hugh Capet was crowned king of France in 987, Fleury had the triple advantage of being a major religious center, having a fine library, and being located in the small domain controlled by the new king—from Senlis to Orléans—that would long remain the seat of Capetian power. Now, the following year, 988, Abbo was elected abbot of Fleury, where he had long been a famous scholar. During the sixteen years of his abbacy (988–1004), this incomparable teacher made Fleury the prime center of monastic scholarship in France. He had so many books copied that, despite subsequent catastrophes, a hundred manuscripts written at Fleury in the tenth century still survive today. Similarly, Abbo taught numerous students. Although he stressed grammar above all, he neglected no branch of learning, and was particularly interested in history. He himself composed no work of history. Yet—given that he had studied at Reims, among other places, given that he was fully familiar with the historiographical work of the Reims school, given that he was abbot of one of the largest abbeys in the royal domain, given that he was closely involved in the kingdom's political affairs, and given that Robert, who became sole king on the death of his father in 996, listened willingly to Abbo despite an earlier disagreement between Hugh and the abbot—it is hardly surprising to learn that Abbo asked one of his best disciples, Aimoin, to compose "a history of the people and the kings of the Franks" for the second king of the new dynasty.

To enable Aimoin to carry out this task, Abbo must have sent his disciple to Reims, where he himself had studied. It is inconceivable that Aimoin never sojourned in a city whose historical output he knew so well, including the most recent manuscripts. It is also inconceivable that Aimoin never knew Richer and his work: like Richer, Aimoin wanted to employ a finer Latin than his sources; like Richer, he was concerned about the confusion that might arise from so many kings with the same name; like Richer, he wanted to begin his history with a geographical introduction. Furthermore, he divided his text into four parts, like Flodoard. Aimoin knew Hincmar's annals so well that he copied them (or had them copied) for the Fleury library. He knew the extended corpus of the *Annales royales* so well that he had no intention of rewriting the history of the Franks since the advent of the Carolingian dynasty. His plan, instead, was to take up that part of the history of the Franks that was still "dispersed in various works and written in a negligent style," namely from their origins to the rise of Pippin.

This constitutes further proof that the most educated inhabitants of the kingdom in the late tenth century—a moment of major rupture, when the Carolingian dynasty was faltering—were clearly no longer content with "Carolingian memory" as conceived by Charlemagne and transmitted by clerics of the royal chapel and school of Reims. They sought more ancient roots. The monks of Saint-Vaast in Arras had done this simply by placing the text of Gregory's *History* (with Fredegar's additions) before the Carolingian annals, whereas Abbo and Aimoin started from the same idea yet harbored different ambitions and employed different means.

Indeed, once he returned to Fleury, Aimoin had access to the accumulated resources of his monastery's library. He could thus call on ancient authors like Caesar, Pliny, Sallust, and Orosius. He used Paul the Deacon's *Historia Romana* and *Historia Langobardorum*. He relied above all on works indispensable to anyone who wanted to recount the Merovingian past— the *History* by Gregory of Tours, the additions by so-called Fredegar, and the *Liber historiae Francorum*. To which Aimoin could add the lives of several saints. His documentation was therefore as complete as possible. He copied excerpts (or had excerpts copied) from all these books, then used the accumulated notes to compose the account that Abbo had requested of

Fig. 1.3

Suger, abbot of Saint-Denis during the first half of the twelfth century, played a leading role at the sides of Louis VI and Louis VII. Moreover, he restored the temporal of the abbey, made by Saint-Denis the largest historiographic center of the Capetian kingdom. He himself wrote the *Vie de Louis VI*. He's depicted here in the stained glass window of the tree of Jesse that adorns, at Saint-Denis, the chapel of the Virgin.

him, organizing his material in the best scholarly tradition. Thus emerged the first history of the Franks since their origins.

The most important and most difficult part entailed recounting those very origins. Gregory of Tours admitted his ignorance on the matter, merely reporting what he had read in the works—subsequently lost—of earlier historians: the Franks had one day come out of Pannonia (that is to say, present-day Hungary) to settle on the banks of the Rhine, and then later crossed the Rhine. They were subject at the time to dukes whose names were lost, who were known simply to be ancestors of the illustrious Merovingian kings. The eighth-century *Liber historiae Francorum*, however, shed light on this obscure point by claiming that the Franks were originally from Troy. Aimoin therefore began his account with the fall of Troy. Just as Aeneas and several companions left Troy in flames to wander far and wide before founding Rome, so Francio and his companions went to Thrace, from whence their descendents slowly crossed Europe. They settled in Pannonia, where they founded Sicambria, then conquered Germania, where they defeated the Romans. In recounting this story, Aimoin was not merely satisfying a historian's innocent curiosity, he was flattering the pride of the Franks—their ancestors had once defeated both the Germans and Romans. This pride in being Frankish was probably not yet "national," had not yet spread through the entire realm. It was as limited as the young Capetian monarchy. And it distinguished Franks from Lorrainers, as well as from Normans, Bretons, and Aquitanians. Yet thanks to the vast scholarly resources of his library and to his immense talent as a historian—one marked, like so many other inhabitants of the northern part of the kingdom, by the grave political events of the late tenth century, and one instructed by his abbot, Abbo, to uncover a distant past predating the Carolingians, for the benefit of King Robert—Aimoin nevertheless managed to give the Frankish people, for the first time, a continuous account that could serve as the collective memory of its entire past.

Politics had spurred scholarship. And politics temporarily paralyzed it. By 999, Abbo had lost King Robert's trust. The abbot thought it pointless for Aimoin to continue the project, and assigned him other tasks. Aimoin's history did not get beyond the year 654. But the ripples created by his effort were not about to die away.

That was because, first of all, several copies of Aimoin's *Historia Francorum* were made, so that the work became known beyond Fleury. More important, the material gathered at Fleury by Aimoin and his team served as the basis of further work. For example, Aimoin had returned from his stay in Reims with a copy of Hincmar's *Annales*. In 1015, meanwhile, King Robert finally won control of Sens after much effort, and made the city a fine new gem of his royal domain. Like Reims, Sens was the metropolis of a large ecclesiastical province. Although the archbishop of Sens was the traditional rival of the archbishop of Reims, the city's school of historiography was insignificant compared to Reims. In the early eleventh century, however, historians were working in the cathedral chapter and in two or three large abbeys in Sens; the city's incorporation into the royal domain and the proximity of Fleury to Sens favored contacts between the monastery's historians and those of the metropolis. Thus, shortly after 1015, Aimoin's history and its continuation were to be found in Sens, where they were recopied, revised, and adapted. In order to secure the loyalty of Sens, meanwhile, King Robert had taken care to place a trustworthy man at the head of the large Abbey of Saint-Pierre-le-Vif, namely Ingo, abbot of Saint-Germain-des-Prés. Ingo remained at the head of both abbeys until his death in 1025. It was certainly during this period that Aimoin's history, extended and interpolated, arrived at the library of Saint-Germain-des-Prés. And that is where it lay until a monk from Saint-Germain undertook to continue it, at the very end of the eleventh or start of the twelfth century. He provided a rather poor account, however, containing only what he knew of events in Paris and environs. The Parisian abbey had neither the political will, the historical perspective, nor the scholarly resources that would have enabled it to propagate the heritage that it had received, somewhat by chance, from Fleury.

It was at Fleury itself, still in the early twelfth century, that worthy successors of Aimoin were to be found. Indeed, over a century after Abbo and Aimoin, Fleury remained the kingdom's major historiographical center, as well as one of the focal points of Capetian politics. At the dawn of the twelfth century, the abbey reached the height of its glory. In 1101, when King Philip I bought the county of Bourges, the royal domain's center of gravity seemed to shift southward. In 1108, the king was buried at Fleury at his express request. In 1110, the monk Hugh, probably the greatest historian ever to work at Fleury, completed his *Histoire ecclésiastique*, which recounted the history of the world up to the demise of the Carolingian empire in the mid ninth century. And by 1115 Hugh finished his sequel, *Liber qui modernorum regum Francorum continet actus* (The book containing the deeds of the modern kings of the French), in which he recounted the history of "modern" France from the reign of Charles the Bald to the death of Philip I, who had just been buried in his abbey church. Aimoin had written the history and origins of a people, that of the Franks. A century later, in a remarkable shift that clearly indicated the consolidation of the territorial state and an historian's awareness of that fact, Hugh of Fleury wrote the history of a country, that of the kingdom of the French. Lucidly, Hugh's history began with the moment that one might indeed say the kingdom was born, that is to say the moment when the

Carolingian empire was dismembered and Charles the Bald became king of western Francia. It was at Fleury that Aimoin wrote the first history of the French, followed a century later by Hugh's first history of France.

The fact is, however, that this history of France, although remarkable in conception and scholarship, had little impact at the time. Only two copies of it now survive. Perhaps readers of the day were not pleased with the book's contents, or perhaps Capetian subjects found its outlook still too Carolingian. Or perhaps they regretted that the distant, flattering past had been amputated from the work. The explanation for the failure of Hugh's history as an autonomous work, however, probably had more to do with circumstances than with content. For in 1110 Hugh had sent a copy of his *Histoire ecclésiastique*, with a rhyming prologue, to young King Louis VI, son and heir to Philip I. He also sent another copy, with another prologue, to Adela, daughter of William the Conqueror and wife of Stephen, the powerful count of Blois and Chartres. Louis and his entourage neglected Hugh's presentation manuscript so completely that no copy was ever made of it. Adela, on the other hand, favorably welcomed the *Histoire ecclésiastique*—thanks to her, it attained a certain popularity both in France and England. In 1115, then, a resigned Hugh sent his history of modern France solely to Matilda, niece of Adela and granddaughter of William the Conqueror. Yet it was probably an impossible gamble to attempt to interest Matilda in a history of France; although the princess was admittedly of French stock, she was not only the daughter of the king of England, Henry I Beauclerc, and wife of Holy Roman Emperor Henry V, she was only thirteen years old in 1115. The initial lack of success of Hugh of Fleury's history of France was in short due to the fact that even as Hugh was writing, Fleury's moment of glory had passed. That of Saint-Denis had arrived.

SAINT-DENIS

Saint-Denis already had a long past behind it by the early twelfth century. In the fifth century, a fine church had been built just north of Paris, where it was believed that the city's first bishop had been buried. A monastic community had grown up around the church, which was regularly rebuilt. Over the centuries, the abbey had known periods both glorious and grim. Nevertheless, when Adam became abbot of Saint-Denis in 1094, the monks could boast not only that their patron saint, Denis, had long been recognized as the protector of living kings but also that their abbey church housed more tombs of dead kings than any other church in the realm—from Merovingians like Dagobert to Carolingians like Charles the Bald and all the deceased Capetians (Hugh, Robert, and Henry).

It was equally true, however, that these glorious tombs in no way saved the abbey's buildings from dilapidation or its lands from neglect. Its political and cultural influence was considerably weaker than that of Fleury. So the day when, as Suger wrote, the body of King Philip "was transported in a grand cortege to the noble monastery of Saint-Benoît-sur-Loire" according to his express wish, despite the fact that Saint-Denis was "by natural right" the "burial place of his fathers the kings," the future must have looked bleak to Abbot Adam.

Yet the moment that Louis VI became king, everything changed. Louis realized that his power base was in Paris rather than on the Loire. He turned away from Fleury, where Hugh was vainly deploying his talent. Louis showed marked affection for Saint Denis and his abbey in 1120, to the extent of giving it the crown worn by his father, Philip. Louis wanted the abbey to be more than a royal burial ground—he thought it appropriate that guardianship of the deceased king's insignia be confided to the saint and martyr who had been the king's special protector during his lifetime. Abbot Adam died a happy man in 1122.

It is known, thanks to an authentic charter, that Louis VI gave his father's crown to Abbot Adam in 1120 even though his successor, Suger, dated the event 1124—the beginning of his own abbacy—in his *Vie de Louis VI*. Modesty was not one of the great abbot's key virtues. Suger's writings glorify not only king and abbey, but also himself and his own deeds, even at the expense of his predecessor. The truth is that Suger was nevertheless a very great abbot. He pursued Adam's work with such success that he need not have elbowed his predecessor into the background. He need merely have recounted what he himself accomplished.

It was thanks to Suger's initiative that in 1124 Louis VI, before riding to confront the emperor who had invaded his kingdom, came to Saint-Denis to raise the abbey's banner, which thereby became the standard of the royal army. It was Suger who successfully promoted the idea that Denis was not only the patron saint of kings, but of the whole kingdom. It was he who bolstered a shaky royal government by erecting a pyramid of written praise, the base of which covered the entire kingdom and the pinnacle of which elevated the king. Finally, it was Suger who decided that his abbey should house not only royal tombs and regalia, but also the kingdom's collective memory.

Saint-Denis, however, did not have the scholarly resources to carry out this political decision. Its library was thin, its historiographical school inactive. Thus, for the twenty-nine years of Suger's abbacy (1122–1151), monks from Saint-Denis went to copy or have copied the books they needed at Fleury, Saint-Germain-des-Prés, and elsewhere. Their effort paid off—Saint-Denis soon had one of the richest libraries in the king-

Fig. 1.4

Guillaume de Nangis, the greatest historian of Saint-Denis at the end of the thirteenth century, composed, first in Latin then in French, a *Chroinque abrégée* or *Chronique des rois de France* to instruct the visitors at Saint-Denis, which had constant success in the fourteenth and fifteenth cent ies. The first page of the manuscript written around 1470 depicts the lily tree in the garden of France surmounted c u dais. Eight kings talk, with Charlemagne on the left and Saint Louis on the right.

dom. Once better arme , if still imperfectly trained, its historians could take up the history of France where Fleury had left off.

The Saint-Denis school clearly inherited from Fleury a concern to root French history in the distant past. It used the text of Aimoin and his followers, discovered at Saint-Germain-des-Prés, to recount not only the

Merovingian period but also the Trojan origins of the Franks. Next, the abbey's great concern was to antedate the idea of Hugh of Fleury—all the while extensively using his work—of identifying the origins of modern France with Charles the Bald. Saint-Denis was keen to base the prestige of the young kingdom on Carolingian grandeur in general and on Charlemagne in particular. It was during Suger's abbacy at Saint-Denis that the *Historia Karoli Magni* (History of Charlemagne), of unknown origin and thought to be the work of Archbishop Turpin, was acquired and revised. Thanks to Saint-Denis, this revised version became one of the most widely read books in the West.

Perhaps one should go a step further. Perhaps it should be suggested that Suger was responsible for the forged charter cited in the *Historia Karoli Magni*—dated 813 and attributed to Charlemagne—to establish the great emperor as the patron of France and Saint-Denis as the principal church of France, going so far as to make the kingdom a fief of Saint-Denis. Some people have done so. Others have rejected the idea, arguing that Suger was too great a historian and too noble a character to have done such a thing. Scholars, however, have had to admit recently that many early forgeries were well and truly the work of great historians and noble characters determined to defend and increase the privileges of their own house. Suger had already been caught in the act once, and the charter in question perfectly answered his prayers. The main point, however, is that it was at Saint-Denis, during Suger's abbacy, that kingdom, abbey, and Charlemagne were so intimately and firmly linked in French memories. Thanks to "the white-bearded emperor," that hero of chansons de geste, the history of France assumed epic proportions.

Suger was not content, however, to have his monks merely anchor the kingdom in its Trojan, Merovingian, and Carolingian past. He also wanted to glorify the new dynasty. He himself wrote the history of Louis VI's reign, and began to write that of Louis VII. Suger thus blazed the double trail that Saint-Denis would follow for the next three centuries: on the one hand, constantly recompose, in an increasingly well-documented fashion, the history of France; and on the other hand, extend that same history reign by reign. For nearly three hundred years Saint-Denis was the repository of France's collective memory, in a complex series of overlapping efforts, revisions, and additions. This period had its high points and low points, each high point contributing a new stone to an increasingly grandiose monument, lending a new hue to the overall edifice.

It was during the reign of Philip Augustus (1180–1223) that a monk named Rigord not only undertook to write a short chronicle of the kings of France as a helpful guide for visitors to the royal mausoleum at Saint-Denis, but also decided to chronicle the life of the current king. Posterity would later perceive Philip as "the Conqueror." Rigord, however, was writing prior to Philip's great victories and conquests, and he stressed above all the miracle of the late, unexpected birth of Philip "Deodatus" ("the God-Given"). Rigord surrounded the king's entire life with a miraculous aura, thereby endowing the history of kingdom and dynasty with a religious dimension.

Then there was the reign of Louis IX (1226–70), later canonized as Saint Louis. The great king was not simply concerned with reforming the institutions of the realm, but was also obsessed with justifying his legitimacy, effacing the painful rupture of "usurpation" by his ancestor, Hugh. By rearranging the tombs in the rebuilt Abbey of Saint-Denis, Louis did everything possible to stress French dynastic continuity. At approximately the same time, the historians at Saint-Denis exploited the work of previous centuries to undertake the great scholarly project of constructing a continuous history of the French from their Trojan origins up to the death of Philip Augustus. The sole drawback of this grand overview was that it was still written in Latin, since there now existed a public unable to read Latin yet interested in the past—not only the unreliable past of troubadours but the true past of historians. Louis IX wanted this vast summary to be translated at the abbey itself. The great historian Primat settled down to the task, which he only completed in 1274, after the saintly king had died. Thus the grand history of France finally emerged after five centuries of slow but steady construction that bore the recognizable mark of particular periods yet that also reflected the overriding themes that the French considered worthy of commemoration and national pride—their Trojan origins, Carolingian glory, divine favor, and royal continuity. This veritable epic was hardly the epic of an entire people (who appeared only at the beginning and a few other rare occasions)—rather, it was an epic of the bishops and barons who constantly surrounded kings, and it was above all the history of those kings. It mainly recounted "kingly deeds," and since it recounted them in French, it was first and foremost a "romance of kings."

Once Primat died, the Saint-Denis project was pursued by another grand historian, William of Nangis. William wrote a history of the reign of Saint Louis, followed by an account of the reign of Philip III the Bold (1270–85). And since he was writing early in the reign of Philip IV the Fair (1285–1314), at a time when the monarchy sought to consolidate its power further, the work of William faithfully reflected the new atmosphere—the barons receded into the background, the king was more present than ever.

When William of Nangis died in 1300, the fame of Saint-Denis was still so great that historians liked to announce what others had announced

Fig. 1.5
Grégoire, bishop of Tours, wrote in the sixth century the *Histoires grace auxquelles nous connaissons bien l'histoire mérovingienne*. In the manuscript of the *Grandes chroniques de France* copied around 1375–79 for King Charles V, Grégoire and his colleague Salvius, bishop of Albi, are depicted debating with the king Chilpéric about a heretical proposition that the king wanted to impose on the bishops of his kingdom.

throughout the thirteenth century, namely that they had relied on documents at Saint-Denis. In 1242, Philippe Mousket declared that he would recount the history of the kings of France in rhyme, according to:

> *Li livres ki des anchiiens*
> *Tiesmougne les maus et les biens,*

En l'abéie Saint Denise
De France u j'ai l'estoire prise,
et del latin mise en roumans.

[The books where authors of old
consigned deeds of evil and good,
from Saint-Denis Abbey
in France comes this story,
which from Latin to Romance I put.]

Guillaume Guiart would pick up the refrain in 1306, at the beginning of his *Branche des royaux lignages* (Branch of royal lineages):

Sont ordenées mes repliques
Selonc les certaines croniques,
C'est-à-dire paroles voires
Dont j'ai transcrites les mémoires
A Saint-Denis soir et matin
A l'exemplaire du latin
Et à droit françois ramenées
Et puis en rime ordenées.

[My lines are all disposed
following chronicles well composed,
That is to say true words
whose memory this records.
I copied, night and day,
the Latin in Saint-Denis,
put into French in time
and then disposed in rhyme.]

After Guillaume Guiart, proof of having worked at Saint-Denis became less crucial—the abbey was not long in losing its monopoly over France's collective memory.

PROPAGATING MEMORIES

Not all historical work ceased at the great abbey, of course, but after fifty years of intense activity, high points and low points recurred once again. The history of France was extended up to 1350, although in the form of simple annals kept on an almost day-by-day basis that lacked the inspiration of previous works. Then the Black Death struck in the middle of the fourteenth century, killing a great many people, disrupting a great many institutions, and briefly bringing a halt to the abbey's historiographical output. A generation later, however, things picked up again everywhere, including at Saint-Denis: Michel Pintoin, cantor at the abbey, wrote an admirable history of the reign of Charles VI in Latin. Then came civil war, foreign occupation, and the retreat of Charles VII south of the Loire, leaving Saint-Denis mute yet again. The Valois king reconquered Saint-Denis in 1435 and Paris in 1436, however, and scarcely had he made his first official entry into the capital on November 8, 1437, than he established, on November 18, the office of royal historian, awarding it to a monk at Saint-Denis, Jean Chartier. Indeed, Chartier wrote a history of the reign of Charles VII in which he carefully recorded the accounts that more or less official witnesses came to Saint-Denis to deliver orally. At Charles's death in 1461, then, the abbey was still the special repository—by royal favor—of the realm's collective memory.

It was no longer the only one, however. Even prior to 1300—and above all during the fourteenth century—the development of royal bureaucracy led to an increase in the number of servants on whom the king could count, both at court in general and in the chancery in particular. Such royal servants had bookish backgrounds, performed tasks that required them to handle archives on a daily basis, and mastered all the technical skills required to compose historical texts. At the same time, the king knew that they would faithfully reflect his own thinking. Thus, once Charles V restored royal authority—following the Black Death, the military defeats, and the disturbances that so profoundly disorganized the Saint-Denis workshop and so gravely threatened the Valois monarchy—he decided to take up the temporarily broken thread of French historical continuity; although he naturally relied on the corpus at Saint-Denis he turned to his chancellor, Pierre d'Orgemont, to extend that history by writing an account of his own reign and that of his father, John the Good (1350–64). In the preceding two centuries, the abbey had cultivated a history in which the king shared the leading role with Saint Denis. In the history written by royal officials, a gratified king henceforth had center stage to himself.

Charlemagne, the Carolingian king, had the scholarly tools for expressing his political vision close to hand, in his very court. After many vagaries during which the complex play of politics and scholarship shifted the repository of France's collective memory from one site to another, Charles V, the Valois king, found those scholarly tools close to hand once again, in his own court. Yet this apparent return to roots transpired under conditions so different that nothing was the same. Not only was Saint-Denis a long way from abdicating its role during Charles V's reign, but the social context had also evolved. Back when historical education was so limited and great historiographical centers were so few, the role of the Carolingian chancery, followed by the schools of Reims, Fleury, and Saint-Denis, had been crucial. With each shift, establishing a repository for France's collective memory required a miracle of politics and scholarship. As late as 1300, Saint-Denis was still irreplaceable. Historical awareness, however, would soon make such strides in France that although the king continued to issue his own version of events, increasing numbers of his subjects were able to learn of their past without him.

By the first half of the fourteenth century, Parisian manuscript workshops were copying the extended version of Primat's history and selling it under the title of *Chronique des rois de France*. In 1318, for instance, Thomas de Maubeuge, a manuscript dealer on Rue Neuve-Notre-Dame-de-Paris, sold a copy to one Pierre Honnorez of Neufchastel in Normandy. This copy has survived, as have several others from the same period.

The tragic events of the mid-fourteenth century put a brake on this initial propagation. Yet once Charles V had Primat's history, the Saint-Denis additions up to 1350, and Pierre d'Orgemont's history combined into two coherent volumes, a Parisian bookseller merely had to extend this royal publication up to the year 1381 to turn the *Chroniques de France* into the *Grandes chroniques de France*. Copied and illuminated in Paris, these grand chronicles encountered uninterrupted success for over thirty years during the reign of Charles VI, among a readership that was basically Parisian, noble, and rich.

At the end of Charles VI's reign, the misfortunes of the day once again put a damper on that success. As soon as Charles VII reconquered his kingdom and reestablished peace toward the middle of the fifteenth century, however, the *Grandes chroniques de France* found still more readers among a broader public in the entire northern half of the kingdom. Many subjects of Charles VII and his son Louis XI, who became king in 1461, were content with this history, which ended in 1381. Others wanted it to continue. Manuscripts therefore completed the old edition from the days of Charles VI with a French translation of Michel Pintoin's Latin history of the years 1380–1402, followed by the chronicle of Gilles le Bouvier, known as the Berry Herald, for the years 1402–22, followed by Jean Chartier's history of the reign of Charles VIII (1422–61).

This majestic collection of the *Grandes chroniques de France* from the nation's origins up to 1461 was the first book to be printed in Paris, by Pasquier Bonhomme. It would prove enormously popular. Many French readers throughout the kingdom could henceforth become repositories of France's collective memory themselves—at the very moment, moreover, when more solid scholarship was about to challenge all the major themes that the Middle Ages had steadily developed, as reflected in the *Grandes chroniques de France*. The year was 1477.

SELECTED BIBLIOGRAPHY

Primary Sources

Grat, Félix, Jeanne Vielliard, and Suzanne Clémencet, eds. *Annales de Saint-Bertin*. With notes and an introduction by Leon Levillain. Paris: Société de l'Histoire de France, 1964.

Lauer, Philippe, ed. *Les Annales de Flodoard*. Paris: Collection de textes pour servir à l'étude et à l'enseignement de l'histoire, 1905.

Richer. *Histoire de France (888–995)*. 2 vols. Translated and edited by Robert Latouche. Paris: Les Classique de l'histoire de France au Moyen Age, 1930.

Suger, Abbot. *Vie de Louis VI le gros*. Translated and edited by Henri Waquet. Paris: Les Classiques de l'histoire de France au Moyen Age, 1929.

Viard, Jules, ed. *Les Grandes chroniques de France*. 10 vols. Paris: Société de l'Histoire de France, 1920–53.

Secondary Sources

Devisse, Jean. *Hincmar, archevêque de Reims, 845–82*. 3 vols. Geneva, 1976.

Guenée, Bernard. *Histoire et culture historique dans l'Occident médiéval*. Paris, 1980.

Riché, Pierre. *Ecoles et enseignement dans le haut Moyen Age*. Paris, 1979.

Spiegel, Gabrielle M. *The Chronicle Tradition of Saint-Denis: A Survey*. Brookline, Mass., 1978.

Storiografia Altomedievale, La. Vol. 2. Spoleto: Settimane di Studi del Centro Italiano di Studi sull'Alto Medioevo, XVIII, 1970.

Vidier, Alexandre. *L'Historiographie à Saint-Benoît-sur-Loire et les miracles de saint Benoît*. Paris. 1965.

Fig. 2.1
In the National Archives, the hall of Parlement constructed under Louis-Philippe to shelter the records of the Parlement of Paris from 1254 to 1778.

CHAPTER 2

THE ARCHIVES: FROM THE TRÉSOR DES CHARTES TO THE CARAN

✿

KRZYSZTOF POMIAN

The decree of October 23, 1979, organizing the administration of the Archives of France assigns it the following mission: "To manage or to control the public archives which constitute the memory of the nation and an essential part of its historical patrimony.—To safeguard private archives that, from an historical point of view, hold a public interest.—To assure the conservation, the sorting, the classification, the inventory, and the accessibility of the public archives for administrative, scholarly, social, or cultural ends" (Article 1). The decree also applies to the Delegation to National Celebrations, which is "responsible for coordinating initiatives to commemorate events that are important for the national history and, more generally, for facilitating the organization of such celebrations" (Article 7).[1] There is no phrase in this text that makes a distinction between memory and history and yet, at the same time, fails to establish a connection between the two, which is assured precisely by the archives, both the memory of the nation and an indispensable component of its historical patrimony, and which is reactivated by the initiatives intended to commemorate events that are part of the national history—in other words, that are duly noted by scholarly history.

In what follows, we will focus on the play between memory and history as revealed in the present and the past of the archives.

Documents and Monuments

"The archives are the ensemble of documents, whatever their date, their form, or their material medium, produced or received by any physical or moral individual, and by any public or private service or organism, in the exercise of its activity." Thus are they defined in the first paragraph of article 1 of law 79–18 of January 3, 1979, on the archives.[2] First let us ask what a "document" is. The law does not address this question, although it does prohibit in advance any attempt to impose limits on the extension of the term.

The law erases any temporal limit on the term: a document may just as well be archaic as recent. The law similarly erases any formal constraint: a document remains a document, whether it be a scroll, register, bundle, isolated sheet, file, or microform, whether it be written by hand, printed, or recorded, and whatever its dimensions may be. The law also erases any material restriction: a document's medium may be papyrus, parchment, paper, ceramic, marble, bronze, a leather tablet, a disk or a plastic film, a cassette or a tape. As for spatial limits, they are not even mentioned and, truth be told, need not be, so obvious is it that a document attains its status as *document* wherever it is produced.

Let us now try other criteria. Does the law suppose that there are only written documents? Nothing authorizes such an interpretation. The verbs used with regard to documents, "produce" and "receive," are marked by an extreme generality. And archival practice replies to this question with an unequivocally negative answer. Not just because there have always been seals attached to written charters in the archives, but because oral testimonies are now collected and because it is the recording of the voice and not the transcription that is considered the original to be preserved.[3] Does every document then have a text, written or oral, fixed to whatever medium, with which it can be identified—in which case a document is only a document on the condition that it uses language? The law is silent on this subject. But archival practice replies once again in an unequivocally negative fashion: audiovisual documents and photos containing no text are collected in the archives.[4]

Last question, then: must every document be a *semaphore,* an object that carries signs attached to or incorporated in a material medium?[5] The law does not say, and with good reason, the very idea of a *semaphore* being foreign to its authors. An affirmative response is nonetheless implied. Otherwise, every human production would be a document, and the term would be deprived of its particular meaning. It is certainly true that, whatever it is, an artifact holds traces of the activities to which it owes its texture, its form, and its functions and that in this respect every artifact is a document in the etymological sense of the term: it teaches something of its origins and of the conditions in which it was made to whomever knows how to decipher the marks that it carries. That is why waste material and all traces left by humans on their environment, without their knowing, are also included among documents.

But artifacts, waste material, and traces are documents only virtually; for them to become documents in actuality, it is necessary that, rather than being used according to their function or being left for abandonment, they are removed from their context and studied as carriers of marks that are thus elevated to the level of signs, treated as visible accidents referring to something different from and outside of themselves, in this case of the cause that produced them. That is exactly what happens with artifacts included in archeological collections. It is there, and in collections more generally, that they—like waste material and other traces—acquire their status as documents, without having been produced as such.

Every document is therefore originally a semaphore. The opposite, however, is not true. There are many objects that, although originally semaphores, belong not to the category of *documents* but to that of *monuments*. The two terms maintain a complex and variable relationship with each other that has, in recent years, been studied by historians and debated by philosophers.[6] We do not intend to tell that story here. But it may be useful to make explicit the differences between *documents*, which are treated by the laws and regulations concerning the archives, and *monuments*, in the sense of the law of December 31, 1913, on historical monuments; of the law of May 2, 1930, relative to the protection of natural monuments and sites of an artistic, historic, scholarly, legendary, or picturesque nature;[7] and of the texts that apply these laws or relate to them. Such an undertaking will help us to understand better the meaning of the first of these terms and to determine the distinctive characteristics of the semaphores that it designates.

The category of *monument,* according to the juridical acts just cited, includes buildings, landscapes, grottoes, excavation sites, fossil deposits, paintings, sculptures, engravings, sketches, coins and medals, manuscripts, and rare books, as well as objects and works of art, from the art of the potter through that of the jeweler and the architect to the art of engineers, builders of machines, bridges, and factories. As such, the category of *monument* was not formulated according to criteria defined in advance. It results, on the contrary, from a history that has progressively enlarged its extension and enriched its content.[8] And the elements of this category were not all originally semaphores.

All of these elements carry signs, which is what renders them deserving of protection and interest. In all of them, these signs refer to the invisible and, first of all, to the past, whether it be the past of nature, of man as a species, or of this or that human group; but they may also refer to a beyond. And they all exemplify characteristics that make their tie to the invisible, including the past, immediately apparent—because they stand out against analogous objects produced in our day and thus manifest, to simple visual inspection, their temporal or spatial otherness. It is true that one often needs a well-trained eye to recognize their presence under the layers that cover them. And it is also true that the impression of strangeness that they create can be deceptive and that the gaze, without prior training, is not capable of situating them correctly. But it suffices to seize them as if they were arriving from an elsewhere of which they reveal the idea, however vague, in order to grant them a status apart and to consider them specifically as monuments.

Works produced in order to be recognized as monuments all have, to an eminent degree, the characteristics just enumerated: a material often rare and precious, sometimes durable; forms, colors, or textures resulting from an uncommon effort and ability; dimensions that set them apart; inscriptions that are often added and whose style of writing deviates from that of ordinary writings—so many signs that confer on them an exceptional status, manifest at first glance. Equally striking is the fact that these works, if they are not intentionally deprived of all utility, subordinate it to their first function, which is to refer to the invisible: to the past that they aim to glorify; to the beyond to which they render thanks or from which they request favors; to the future in which they must arouse admiration for the great deeds accomplished by their patrons.

Let us now move on to works that were produced to be documents in the sense of the law on the archives. Belonging to this category are certain manuscript and printed writings, certain images, maps, seals, stamps, photos, certain sound and audiovisual recordings, recordings of measurements, and computer memories. Their material may be rare but, for the immense majority of documents, it is common; like their form and their dimensions, it is generally adapted to their end, which consists in referring to perceptible or observable facts. "Perceptible" means visible or audible, as in the case of writings, which refer to persons who are supposed to have done or to have to do this or that or to objects exchanged, counted, described, modified; or in the case of maps, which represent a terrain; or in the case of images, which show figures or events whose reality lies elsewhere; or again, in the case of cassettes, which make audible again discourses that have already been pronounced. "Observable" has to do with recordings of "black boxes" or of measuring instruments of every kind, with photos made with a microscope, with graphs produced by computers, or with results of analyses and experiments.

Unlike monuments, in their reference to perceptible or observable facts documents are not immediately apparent. Since, moreover, they are most often not spectacular, if they attract the gaze, it is a gaze that is already trained to recognize the appearance of a document. Documents are identified as such only after having been deciphered and analyzed, which requires special knowledge surpassing that which a free education generally provides in our societies. This knowledge includes a mastery of specialized terminologies, notation systems particular to certain domains, diverse languages and diverse writing systems, techniques for dating and for verifying authenticity, and so on.

What is more, today there are more and more documents that require that tools produced for this purpose alter their observable characteristics—for example, magnetic configurations—so that they can be deciphered. In other words, certain documents are henceforth invisible, while nevertheless remaining documents: the eye does not perceive the difference between a recorded cassette and a blank one; hence, the growing importance of labels and other visible marks indicating that the object which carries them also carries a recording and must be treated appropriately. It is therefore even more necessary to be able to ensure that the label is correct, which is impossible without a machine equipped with the proper heads. Documents that are inaccessible to immediate sensory perception are legion in our day. But an invisible monument would be an absurdity. Because a monument is made precisely to attract the gaze.

A semaphore is therefore produced as a document when it contains an explicit reference to visible or observable facts. And a semaphore is produced as a monument when it contains an explicit reference to the invisible. Nothing prohibits these two references from being imprinted on a single semaphore, which is then simultaneously a document and a monument; it is thus with seals, coins, portraits, and certain judicial acts that are solemn and executed in an exceptional fashion. Aside from these deliberately produced documents and monuments, there also exist, as we have seen, numerous objects that have become documents or monuments without originally having been them and, sometimes, without having been semaphores, even artifacts. Some have become documents because the techniques at our disposal allow us to date them and to extract from them information about the visible or observable facts whose imprint they bear. Others have become monuments because, while they attract the gaze, they have become a reference to the invisible simply as a result of time, which in carrying us away from their origins makes them henceforth refer to the past.

This is especially true for documents. Because when the thing to which they refer disintegrates, leaving at best only fragmentary, incomplete, and decontextualized vestiges, the documents that remain henceforth reflect something that was visible but that no longer is. They thus acquire a reference to the past, that is to say to the invisible, and even while maintaining their status as document, they also become monuments, especially (but not only) when they also have an appearance that attracts the gaze. Monuments, for their part, may be approached in order to search for references to visible facts, which they contain, often without the knowledge of their authors or even their patrons: references to the work that produced them, to the events that inspired them, to certain customs of the epoch to which they involuntarily bear witness. They are then treated as documents.

Between monument and document, there is therefore no break. They are two poles of one continuum, and they need each other. The difference between the two is none the less real. The monument is made to strike the gaze of the spectator and to orient his imagination and his thoughts toward the invisible, in particular toward the past. The document, on the other hand, is made to be deciphered by a person possessing the necessary knowledge and to inform him of the visible or observable facts it refers to. A monument, which is supposed to evoke the past directly, to place it before the eyes by reactivating the souvenirs that it left and that have been transmitted to those who are looking at it, is linked to the collective memory. When the facts it speaks of are no longer visible and belong to the past, a document serves as an intermediary that allows one to reconstruct them; it is an instrument of history. The first is conceived to last, in its function as an object of admirative commemoration or as a reminder that is also a warning. The second, produced for a specific purpose, becomes an object of study when it loses this purpose (if it is not destroyed). We thus find again the opposition already present in the etymology of the two terms: *monumentum*, linked to *monere* or "to make remember"; and *documentum*, linked to *docere* or "to teach, to instruct." And we understand why the archetype of the monument remains an edifice, which by its striking features stands out from the edifices that surround it, whereas the archetype of the document remains a simple written text.

The documents affected by the law and the regulations concerning the archives are therefore semaphores, produced to carry explicit references to visible or observable facts. Even in light of this definition, however, the diversity of documents remains very large; we have already cited some examples. At first, such a wide definition of the notion of *document* in a law on the archives seems surprising. Yet an instant of reflection suffices to uncover its validity. Because one soon understands that the opportunities created by new technologies have also resulted in the creation of unpublished categories of documents, whose number does not cease to increase. And that, simultaneously, the notion of *semaphore* has changed its content.

Alongside the inheritance of a long past, already highly diversified, we thus have to contend with a present in which one still writes with pen on paper, while recordings of all kinds are multiplying and the importance of computers and of everything that is called the "new archives" is growing.[9] All of this was already apparent in the 1970s, well before the spread of data processing machines and personal computers.[10] With the progressive computerization of files, a new type of document is certainly going to have a growing place in the archives of tomorrow; it may even become preponderant. And the future threatens to modify once again the entire field of document production, as a result of the appearance of yet-to-be-discovered materials and new recording techniques.[11] The notion of *document* therefore cannot be introduced, except by tacitly assimilating it to that of every object made to be a carrier of signs referring explicitly to visible or observable facts, except by writing a law that, even if it included everything that is now found in the archives, would very quickly be outrun by future developments.

We have spoken until now of documents in general. But, what interests us most of all are archival documents taken in their specificity. This specificity can be described in few words: the characteristic feature of the archival document is that it appears alone only on statistically rare occasions; in the immense majority of cases, the archival document is an archival document because it is or was part of an archival *fund*, that is, "of the ensemble of pieces of all kinds which any administrative corps, any physical and moral individual, has automatically and organically compiled by virtue of its functions or of its activity."[12] The similarity between this definition and the definition of the archives given by the law of January 3, 1979, is immediately apparent. This similarity pertains to a specific feature of the archives, that they appear in the form of collected resources and that it is the collection and not isolated documents that, according to general rule, constitute their fundamental units. It is in the context of the collection, juxtaposed with other documents of the same origin, that a document best permits one to seize the references it contains to visible or observable facts.

Because the archives are composed of ensembles of documents, one might be tempted to draw the conclusion that they neglect memory in order to relate exclusively with history. Well, it was never this way. First, all archival documents are monuments inasmuch as they refer to facts that are no longer visible. Some are also monuments because they were created as such. The National Archives, for example, have since 1847 displayed specimens of these latter for visitors to the Sigillographic Museum,* which in 1867 became the Museum of the History of France.[13] Moreover, the archives are no longer identified as depositories for documents having lost all current utility, that is to say, any connection with memory. Such a doctrine, applied in practice until the first decades of the twentieth century, was abandoned in order to satisfy the demands of the archives that, not content in the long run with passively receiving deposits from administrations whenever these administrations wanted to make them, were obliged, in order to protect the interests of history, to manage memory itself. It is in a field organized around the two poles of history and memory that the archives situate themselves today.

THE ARCHIVES BETWEEN MEMORY AND HISTORY

Let's take another look at the first article of the law of January 3, 1970: "The archives are the ensemble of documents, whatever their date, their form, or their material medium, produced or received by any physical or moral individual, and by any public or private service or organism, in the exercise of its activity. The conservation of these documents is undertaken in the public interest as much for the needs of managing and justifying the rights of physical or moral, public or private, individuals as for the historical documentation of research." The first French law on the archives in almost two centuries, the law of January 3, 1979, is also, in France, the first normative text even to define the term *archives*. In this definition, one first notes the attribution of the capacity to create archives to any physical individual, without the slightest restriction concerning social status, cultural level, character, profession, sources of income, and so on. The capacity to create archives is attributed, similarly, to any moral individual, association, commercial corporation, industrial enterprise, bank, mutual, or cooperative. It is attributed, finally, to any public or private service or organism, without restriction, from the presidency of the Republic down to a modest provincial office. All of this seems self-evident, but appearances here are

---

* EDITOR's NOTE: The original collection of seals and medieval documents is now housed in the Hôtel de Soubise. Napoleon acquired the mansion, a splendid eighteenth-century town house, in 1808 to hold the National Archives (which have now been moved to a new building). The Museum of the History of France occupies the former apartments of the Princess de Soubise on the first floor. The documents on display are among the handsomest and most significant for the history of France from Merovingian times to the present.

deceiving, because we shall see that the law's position on this point only caps a long evolution of archival doctrine and practice, moving toward a progressive democratization of the capacity to create archives.

Let us stop for a moment over the two verbs *produce* and *receive,* not so much because of their generality, which is already apparent, but because taken together they entail the idea of a circulation of documents, of an exchange in which these documents are supposed to participate. This justifies the identification of the document with an object whose original and principal function is to be a semaphore. The semaphore always appears in the context of an exchange, whether it is made between men and gods or between human groups. But the verbs *produce* and *receive* play, in our text, a more explicit and more important role. They in effect make up part of a criterion that every group of documents must satisfy in order to qualify as *archives* in the sense given to this term by the law. This criterion stipulates that, in order to constitute archives, such a group may contain only documents produced or received by their author or addressee in the exercise of his or her activities.

This is an essential condition distinguishing archives from every other ensemble of documents, in particular from the collection—which most often develops without any connection to the activities of the collector and exists only by virtue of a conscious choice, a decision that determines the general orientation, even the details, of its composition. The archives, on the contrary, are the unintentional result of the activities of an individual, an organism, or an organization from the moment these activities are accompanied, due to their very nature, by a production or a reception of documents; no conscious decision is necessary for them to be formed; if such a decision is required, it is to destroy them. Every collection hinges on an act of will; archives are in a way automatically secreted, so to speak, by an activity, and for this reason they form an ensemble that is not artificial but organic, a fund.

As the law conceives them, the archives—and this is their distinctive trait—are accumulated in the manner of an individual memory, which retains not only what one has deliberately decided to remember but everything else, too. Yet they are an objectified memory: once secreted, in order to exist they no longer need either individuals taken in their singularity or the moral individual whose memory they originally were in order to exist. So long as the social and physical conditions are right, the materiality of this memory assures it a much longer life than that of a human, a group, or an institution. Again, it is their materiality that makes the archives an objectified memory, in the sense that multiple people can find the same documents there; this makes possible, on the one hand, the resolution of disputes concerning the past and, on the other, the reproducibility of operations that make the past an object of knowledge, at least inasmuch as they apply to documents in their material and formal character.

But this objectified memory, precisely because it is objectified, is only a virtual memory. Every material object, and notably every semaphore, may be employed contrary to its intended purpose. The vicissitudes of documents illustrate this well. When the parchment of the charters was made into packing for loading canon balls or when, closer to our own time, the administration pulped its old papers or sold them by weight, these documents did not function as memory. Pardon the truism, but to function this way, the archives must be read and understood. And even this does not suffice. Because one can read the archives as an historian does: by distancing oneself from their authors, by regarding them from the outside, by integrating them in a larger ensemble of which they are only a part. It is only when the reader identifies him or herself with the individual who secreted the archives, when he or she appropriates the latter's point of view, interests, judgments, or even emotions, that he or she arrives at a reading that is no longer the historian's—and reactivates the archives in their role as memory.

To conserve the archives is to protect them from any action liable to destroy or deteriorate them. It is also to create conditions that favor reading them. Reading for memory or in the manner of the historian, depending on the case. In specifying the purposes of the conservation of documents, the law observes that it is "undertaken in the public interest." And this interest is conceived of both as the product of particular, different, even contradictory, interests, and as the general interest, that of an abstract subject, of the human being who works at understanding his or her own past. The first interest appeals to memory; the second, to history. Such an interpretation emerges from the text itself, which assigns to conservation the objective of satisfying the "needs of managing and of justifying the rights of physical or moral, public or private, individuals"—and that assigns it the parallel objective, placed precisely on the same plane, of supplying "the historical documentation of research."

The word *management* suggests a situation in which one turns to documents that are within easy reach in order to avoid discrepancies between the decisions that one makes and those of a too recent past, or to fulfill previous obligations. Here we are in the domain of immediate memory, which is incarnated in individuals and of which documents are merely an extension and an aid. It is different with *justifying rights,* which supposes not only a conflict, a confrontation of interests, but especially, if the parties concerned are acting in good faith, an oversight of the actions that gave one rights that the other denies him and to which one must refer precisely because of this oversight. In both cases, however, the individual using the archives is supposed to be the same as the one who produced them; when it is not the same physical individual, it is a representative of the same moral "individual," which is itself the subject of memory.

This is confirmed by Article 2 of the law, which requires secrecy from "every functionary or agent charged with the collection or conservation of archives," regarding "any document which cannot be legally put at the disposition of the public." Because, in shrouding certain documents in secrecy, an individual, whether physical or moral, does nothing but appropriate them exclusively, interiorize them, treat them as one treats intimate memories, kept inside oneself or by rare confidantes. Such was for a long time the administration's policy regarding documents that it produced or received: these were elements of its memory that, as long as they remained valid, one could access only for administrative reasons. It is only since the promulgation of Law 78-753 of July 17, 1978, containing diverse measures for ameliorating relations between the administration and the public that liberty of access to administrative documents has been erected as a principle and that refusal of such access has become an exception that must be justified.

Foundation of their memorial status, the identity between the user and the producer of the archives disappears when they are made to serve "the historical documentation of research." This in effect signifies that the documents of the public archives, other than those that are anyway accessible freely or according to the conditions established by the law of July 17, 1978, are open to everyone; in other words, that no official title is necessary to conduct historical research. Thus Article 6 of the law stipulates, in paragraph 3, that such documents "may be freely consulted after the expiration of a delay of thirty years or of special delays provided for in Article 7," which run from sixty years from the date of the act "for documents that contain information compromising the private lives or concerning the security of the State or the national defense" to 150 years from the date of birth "for documents containing individual medical information."

Carrier of memory, source of history: present in the very first article of the law of January 3, 1979, the distinction between these two functions of the archives is explicitly inscribed, we have seen, in the decree of October 23, 1979, organizing the administration of the Archives of France. And it is not a purely verbal distinction that is in question. Because the law merely indicates the capacity of archival documents, in their very principle, to serve two different purposes and to sustain two attitudes that are hardly compatible, even mutually exclusive—two attitudes that integrate these documents into a memory and a history, respectively. This opposition between memory and history runs through all of the law's problematics, as well as through all of archival practice.

It underlies first of all the very idea of a date for opening documents that, because of their contents, are closed. This date in effect marks nothing less than the frontier of memory, whether short- or long-term, and implies the exclusive appropriation of memory by individuals whose memory is of a past that they believe to have been theirs. Certainly, in our day, historians are able to study documents on this side of that frontier, but such cases remain rare. It is only when this frontier is crossed that the past becomes the property of everyone and the object of history, even if there are always historians who adopt a memorial attitude toward it.

The reduction of the normal delay for opening documents from fifty to thirty years indicates, from this perspective, an acceleration of social changes, which means that documents lose their current utility and even their memorial value earlier than before: the affairs to which they refer are closed more rapidly and, as conditions vary, the role of precedent diminishes. But if institutions, policies, even customs change more quickly today, men and women also live longer; hence the lengthening of delays for everything impacting individuals, to such an extent that a grandson would not be able, except in rare cases, to study the medical files of his grandfather. The memory of moral individuals is thus assumed to be shorter, that of physical individuals longer. It remains true that, in every case and with all of the reservations that we have just enumerated, the opening of a document to public consultation signifies its passage from the registry of memory to the registry of history.

This passage is accomplished in two steps. Decree 79-1037 of December 3, 1979, taken as an application of the law on the archives and regarding the responsibilities of the various divisions of the public archives and the cooperation between administrations for the collection, conservation, and communication of the public archives, gives the administration of the Archives of France the following mission (Article 2): "a. Control of the conservation of current archives on the premises of public administrations, establishments, and organisms, including public and ministerial offices, which have produced or received them; b. Conservation or control of intermediary archives in public prearchival' depositories, according to the peculiar status of each of these depositories; c. Conservation, sorting, classification, inventory, and communication of the permanent archives after their transfer to the depositories of the national and departmental archives." The decree of December 3, 1979, thus gives force of law to the idea of the "three ages" of the archives, developed over the last thirty or so years by archival doctrine,[14] which distinguishes an "administrative age" from a "historic age," with an "intermediary age" in between. The "administrative age" is that in which the documents forming the "current archives" are conserved and routinely used by those who produced or received them (Article 12); they are handled this way, we believe, for the needs of "managing" in the sense of the law of January 3, 1979, that is to say, for the short-term memory. The "intermediary age" is that in which the documents "have ceased to be considered current archives" but preserve "their administrative interest" (Article 13), which consists, we believe, in the possibility of using them for "justifying rights" in the sense of the law of January 3, 1979, to provide support for long-term memory. The conservation of "intermediary archives" is assured by the administration of the Archives of France. The "permanent archives," finally, are made up of documents "which have been subjected to sorting and eliminations" and that "are to be conserved in perpetuity" (Article 14), in the interest of what the law of January 3, 1979, calls "the historical documentation of research."

The decree thus makes evident the distinction between history, the only thing to need "permanent archives," and memory, in its two forms of short-term and long-term memory—to which correspond "current archives" and "intermediate archives," respectively. It simultaneously makes archivists responsible for the sources of the history of France and erects them as guardians of France's public memory everywhere this memory develops. In so doing, it sanctions a practice that was established in 1952 and that consists in sending the archivists of the National Archives on missions to the ministries to oversee the conservation of current archives, to control eliminations, and to prepare the "prearchives."[15]

All of this concerns only the public archives, that is (as the law of January 3, 1979, explains): "1. Documents that emerge from the activity of the State, of local collectivities, of public establishments and enterprises; 2. Documents that emerge from the activity of private legal organisms charged with the management of public services or with a mission of public service; 3. Minutes and inventories of public or ministerial officers" (Article 3). But this law also consecrates a section to private archives. Private archives are "the ensemble of documents defined by the first article which are not included in the field of application of Article 3 above" (Article 9). Some arrive unsolicited at the archives, as a result of deposits made by the organisms that created them. Others are received "as a gift, a legacy, a transfer, a revocable deposit, or a payment in kind" (Article 10). However, private archives "may be classed as historical archives" only on the condition that they present "for historical reasons a public interest" (Article 11).

The memorial importance of private archives, the importance they may have for the individual, physical or moral, from which they emanate, obviously does not suffice to give them a "public interest" and, on this basis, a place in the "patrimony of archives" (Articles 20 and 23). In order for them to be included in this patrimony, there must be "historical reasons" (Articles 11 and 24); the documents that compose them must present a "historical interest" (Article 15, paragraph 2). The private archives that satisfy this condition, if they are classified, are classified as "historical archives" (Articles 11, 12, and 14). In other words, in order to be classified, private archives must transcend the memory of the person who created them, unless he or she played a role in the life of a collectivity, the State, or the nation. They must be capable not only of evoking memories or a sentiment of belonging, but also of informing those who did not know the past and who approach it from the outside—as historians—about that past. The law on the archives is aimed at private archives to the extent that they are sources of history. It is no longer a question of the history of the State, but of that of society in all its diverse manifestations.

Carriers of memory, sources of history: this opposition appears under other forms in the archives. Let us begin with the problems posed in theory and in fact by the necessity to satisfy both the right to secrecy, justified by the interests of the State or respect for private life, and the right to information, which is a right of every citizen and every historian. In principle, these problems are resolved by the legislative acts that regulate the communication of the public archives and among which are, alongside the two laws already cited, Law 78–17 of January 6, 1978, pertaining to data processing files and liberties, as well as numerous decrees, orders, notes, memos, and so on. Yet these regulatory texts encounter difficulties in daily application that are not negligible.

Thus, there is some discordance between the three important laws concerning accessibility of the public archives. In particular there is "a major contradiction" between the law pertaining to data processing, which sets down as a fundamental principle the right to oblivion and the law on archives of which the "raison d'être is the right to memory."[16] For the law on data processing and liberties, the archives do nothing but carry the memory of institutions; after a certain delay, information concerning individuals is eliminated, in order to protect them. But, with the law concerning the archives, the "right to memory" is in fact history's right to be able to find in the archives responses to the questions that it asks, even if they are impertinent or disagreeable. These demands are difficult to reconcile in practice.

Of the two poles, the memorial and the historical, the second is, for archivists, more important than the first: "The fundamental mission of the administration of the Archives is the conservation and the communication of all documents that may serve to write history." But, in practice, the first pole, memorial, poses many more problems. For if, in their own domain, archivists are alone responsible for the sources of history, as guardians of memory, they are also obliged to cooperate with the administrations from which these sources emanate, especially when it is a question of overseeing current archives. They may therefore see frictions, if not conflicts, emerge between two perspectives: that of the archives as memory-aid and that of the archives as sources of history, between that which sees them as a means and that for which they are also an end.

This is true notably when documents are sorted, so that only those that still hold an interest after having lost their current utility are kept and all others are eliminated. According to the decree of December 3, 1979, "the sorting of documents is the responsibility of the administration of the Archives of France" (Article 16). It is therefore the archivists who take charge of it. In proceeding with this sorting, they must balance three interests: that of the administration, which is where the documents originate and whose memory they constitute (it may need to use some of them in the future); that of the historians, who want to have as many sources as possible, so long as their mass does not keep them from working, which is in itself a difficult demand to satisfy; and finally, the interest of the archivists themselves, who must keep in mind the amount of space and staff that is available to them and that cannot increase infinitely. The sorting of documents that accompanies their passage first from short-term memory to long-term memory, then from long-term memory to history, is for all of these reasons a particularly delicate operation. Even more delicate because it determines once and for all the content of the permanent archives along with, in large part, the image that the future will have of the past. Thus the decision on which documents to eliminate is not left to the free choice of the archivist responsible for sorting. It is regulated by rules and instructions, but in the end it is the archivists who decide on the best way to apply them to concrete cases.[17]

Three other operations maintain the permanent archives as they are thus constituted in a usable condition. First of all, classification, which extends the allocation of call numbers. The rule or principle of respecting archives forbids their classification according to a grid established by the archivist himself, whatever it is, and requires that documents of the same origin be kept together, or brought together if they have been dispersed, in order to preserve the integrity of the collections of which they are a part. Easier to decree than to practice,[18] the principle of respecting collections proceeds from an attitude that is that of the historian; classifying documents according to their producers-receivers means in effect maintaining each document in its original context and each collection in that context that other collections of the same epoch have created for it, without neglecting changes that may have occurred. It means accommodating oneself to a given rather than assimilating it to one's own ideas. From the same attitude proceeds evidently the production of guides, summary overviews, inventories, tables of contents, numerical repertoires, alphabetical indexes, and so on, which are both the initial results of research and instruments allowing one to orient this research not anymore toward the documents themselves, but toward the past whose vestiges they are. This supposes that the documents are communicated to the public under conditions that permit it to study them without interference, while respecting the rules imposed by the necessity of assuring their protection.

Conserving, sorting, classifying, inventorying, communicating: all of these operations leave their imprint on the archives, which are their object. And they produce not only an entire literature (of which we have already cited—and will cite—titles), but also collections of documents, carriers of the memory of the Archives and sources of their history.[19] We have just seen how complex the relations between memory and history are in the normative texts regulating the French archives today and in the archival practice of our time. These texts, however, follow many others, from which they differ in significant ways, and archival practice has greatly evolved; it is easy to convince oneself of this, if only by reading the *Manuel archivistique* so often quoted in the present paper. If the memory of the archives that it establishes shows traces of changes in regulation and evolution in practice, its history has never been written, as if archivists have not managed to adopt toward their own institution the objective perspective required for this result. It is impossible in such an article to close a gap of this size—but also to comprehend the present of the archives without plunging more deeply into their past.

THE REVOLUTION AND THE ARCHIVES

Article 33 of the law of January 3, 1979, led to the repeal of more than fifteen texts that until then had regulated the archives. Most of these texts dated from the 1920s to the '50s, and they regulated various details, including the collection of fees for official copies and for the casting of seals. But three texts, the oldest ones, seem to have had quite another effect, judging by their heading. These are the decree of September 7, 1790, concerning the organization and the administration of the National Archives; the law of 7 Messidor, Year II, concerning the organization of the archives established for the national representative body; the law of 5 Brumaire, Year V, which ordered the collection in the departmental capitals of all the deeds and papers acquired by the Republic.* The public archives of France, in the form they have retained up to now, seem in their basic law to be a legacy of the Revolution.[20]

Convinced that they were opening a new chapter in history, the actors of the Revolution were very early on concerned with preserving a faithful memory of their works for posterity.[21] Barely two weeks after the capture of the Bastille, the Constituent Assembly voted a regulation whose Chapter 8, consecrated to the archives and the secretaryship, decided that "a safe place would be chosen for the deposit of every piece relative to the operations of the Assembly," qualified as "national deeds and papers."[22] During the famous session of August 4, the constituent found the time to elect its archivist, Armand-Gaston Camus, a well known and erudite Parisian jurist, who had for a long time been interested by the archives and was also fortified by Jansenist rigor and revolutionary firmness.[23] In May 1790, the Assembly named a commission responsible for organizing its archives, which presented a report and a proposal for a decree at the end of June. Approved September 7, this decree stipulated notably that "the National Archives are the depository for all acts that establish the constitution of the realm, its public law, its laws, and its division in the departments" (Article 1). It also defined the obligations of the archivist and proposed that the archives be opened three times a week "to respond to the demands of the public" (Article 14).[24]

Thus defined, the National Archives were the archives of the National Assembly. And the public to which they were opened was composed primarily of deputies to this assembly. A report of December 1791 observed: "The establishment of your archives must equally fulfill two objectives: the one, to assure in an inviolable depository the conservation of everything emanating from the National Assembly, or which, having been addressed to it, is considered necessary to conserve; the other, to render this treasure of enlightenment accessible to the public, and especially to the legislators, who should be able to dip into it with particular facility."[25] The differences between the National Archives of the beginning of the Revolution and the National Archives of today are striking. The two institu-

---

* EDITOR'S NOTE: These dates refer to the Republican (sometimes called the Revolutionary) calendar instituted by decree of the National Convention that declared September 22, 1792—the date of the proclamation of the Republic—the beginning of the first year of liberty. Within this new chronology was a complex new series of months (named after aspects of nature by the minor poet and revolutionary, Fabre d'Eglantine) and a ten-day week to eliminate the Christian Sabbath. The astronomical precision of the new calendar was worked out by the Jacobin mathematician Gilbert Romme. Until 1804, when Napoleon declared the Empire, this calendar was in official use. In the above text 7 Messidor, Year II is June 25, 1794, and 5 Brumaire, Year V is October 26, 1796.

tions appear, however, to be united by a line of direct continuity, attested to by the similarity of their name, which has varied only as a function of political regimes; by the presence in the latter of collections begun in the former; by the presence of these collections at the head of the classification system; and by the succession of conservators, then directors, of the archives. There is in particular no rupture between Camus, the first archivist, and Pierre-Claude-François Daunou, who replaced him after his death in 1804 and who (aside from an interruption between 1816 and 1830) remained in this post until 1840. Even their political, intellectual, and psychological profiles are similar.[26]

The continuity, we will see, is real, but it does not at all imply a project conceived in advance and put into operation all at once. The continuity is the product of a core around which were deposited successive layers yielding, in time, differences between the point of departure and the point of arrival. It results, as always in such a case, from a conjunction of circumstances and from a confrontation of forces whose stake is the institution created on September 7, 1790. Of these forces, one of the most important, and the one that triumphed in the end, was incarnated by the successive directors of the archives, first of all by Camus himself. Everything suggests, in effect, that from the beginning Camus wanted to make the National Archives the central archives of the State. It was at his initiative that the constituent decided, on August 7, 1790, to bring together in a single place the five depositories scattered throughout Paris, which contained papers relative to the finances of the realm.[27] At the time, this was not merely a minor measure. Circumstances conferred on it a significance nobody could foresee at the time.

The suppression between 1789 and 1793 of various institutions of what, after September 1789, became the ancien régime,[28] deprived many of the innumerable documents kept by these institutions in their archives—except deeds of property—of their validity. Of the deeds, certain ones were extremely interesting to the Assemblies that, in order to bring the country out of financial crisis, were looking to recuperate all national properties, including the property of the clergy—which since November 2, 1789, had been put at the disposition of the nation. On May 14, 1790, the constituent defined the means of selling these properties. On October 11 of the same year, the legislative adopted Title 3 of the decree on the administration of the national properties; its Articles 12 and 13 required that papers referring to properties whose management was entrusted to administrations of departments and districts be deposited in the archives of the district. This decree would have a determining influence on the formation of the National Archives in Paris and of the archives in the departmental centers.[29] In effect, it made the administration responsible for an enormous mass of papers of all kinds, which it had to protect from people who would have preferred simply to burn them,[30] and among which it had to separate those that seemed useful from those that, according to the ideas of the time, would never serve any purpose.

In the eighteenth century, well before the Revolution, the archives—both the word and the thing—primarily evoked not the idea of a tranquil place where one engaged in disinterested study, but the idea of a conflict. As seen by the people of the time, the archives contained deeds, proofs with which one pleaded his rights or his privileges; it happened, certainly, that these deeds were also monuments of history, but only secondarily, according to the *Nouveau traité de diplomatie*, to Camus in the *Nouveau Denisart*, and to other authors.[31] As for the conflict in question, if it sometimes involved states, it mainly concerned individuals.

According to Pierre-Camille Le Moine, archivist of the chapter of the Archbishopric of Lyon, the profession that he exercised emerged

> when Parishes, when entire Communities revolted against their
> Lords and refused to pay the dues required by the most authentic
> deeds: dues which were the vestiges of their former condition of ser-
> vitude and which humanity had converted into simple rents; when
> finally the inferior *corps*, shaking off the yoke of subordination, forced
> themselves to reinforce [*sic*] their former discipline and to place
> themselves on the level of their benefactors; then, to defend their do-
> mains, to conserve their privileges, the Lords were obliged to search
> in the Archives, to page through cartularies and Registers, and to un-
> cover papers that had long been buried in dust.[32]

The "people"—read, peasants—thought nothing else, but entirely different consequences resulted when, "in several provinces," there formed in 1789 "a type of league for destroying chateaus, for ravaging land, and especially for taking over cartularies, where the deeds to feudal property were kept."[33] To understand the vicissitudes of the archives over the course of the Revolution, it is necessary to remember the association in the eighteenth-century mind between the deeds they contained and the conflict over property rights.

On 12 Brumaire, Year II (November 2, 1793), a decree by the Convention Assembly placed the five depositories united by the Constituent Assembly, plus a sixth with papers of the same nature, "under the orders and the direct surveillance of the Archivist of the Republic" so that they formed two divisions of the National Archives (Article 1). "The first of these divisions will contain the deeds, minutes, and registers concerning the domanial and administrative part [of the Archives], that which relates

to the properties of fugitive clergy and the deeds concerning the territories of the Republic that were in the possession of the court clerks of the
former bureaus of finance of the various departments; and all of this will
be brought together in the depository of the Louvre, whose guardian is
the Citizen Cheyré" (Article 2). "The second division will contain everything that may concern historical monuments, the judicial and contentious
part, and will be formed particularly of the deposits of Sainte-Croix-de-
la-Bretonnerie and of that depository whose guardian was the Citizen
Léchevin, known by the name of *Depository of the King's Household* (with
the exception of the deeds in these depositories belonging to the first division). This second division will, in addition, unite everything relating
to it that can be found in the other depositories" (Article 3).[34]

While extending the responsibilities of the archivists, the decree of
12 Brumaire also modified the nature of the National Archives themselves
for the first time, by bringing to them funds other than those of the Assemblies, which until then had been the only archives placed there.[35] Certainly,
this measure—which was conceived as provisional since the very archives
that constituted its object were themselves supposed to disappear—was
easy to annul because it produced no displacement and affected the organization of the archives only indirectly. What preoccupied the conven-
tionals was the means of increasing the national property in order to pay
off the public debt; hence the importance of controlling relevant deeds.
The organization of the archives was envisaged here not for itself but as
an instrument of financial policy. The decree of 12 Brumaire was in any
case adopted on the initiative of the Committee of State Properties. And
the contradiction between this decree and the decree concerning disposal
of properties, which was adopted on the initiative of the Committee of
Finances on 10 Frimaire of the same year (November 30, 1793), led to the
designation of a Commission on the Archives.[36]

"The commission thus formed was soon obliged to extend its aims
far beyond the conciliation of the two decrees that had been the occasion
for its institution. It surveyed the mass of deeds and manuscript pieces
of every kind that existed in the public depositories, and searched for a
theory and a means for the sorting operation it had to accomplish." It was
to this question that Julien Dubois thus consecrated most of his report
when on 7 Messidor, Year II (June 25, 1794), he presented, in the name
of the Commission on the Archives, a proposal for a decree that would
be approved the same day. After having justified by the example of the
Romans the refusal "to deliver all deeds to the flames and to destroy down
to the smallest vestiges the monuments of an abhorred regime," Dubois
nevertheless took into account this cry of the "voice of patriotism." But
he also insisted on the "respect for public and private property" and on

the need for instruction. Hence "the general division of deeds, charters, and manuscript pieces into three classes. The first includes those which concern the national property; the second, the judicial order, that is, the judgments of the courts; the third, those which concern history, the sciences, and the arts. This last class rightfully belongs to libraries."

The first two classes had to be the object of a sorting operation whose goals were presented with all desired clarity: "One, the growth of the national property; two, the suppression of many pieces which are useless and which will be recognized as such according to the criteria that we have drawn from your decrees; three, a new reduction of federalism, to which we are delivering a mortal blow with many measures of the decree that we are submitting to you" and whose centralist spirit is summed up well in the pithy expression: "It is time that everything leads to the center and that everything brings about unity." Financial and political considerations are thus inextricably mixed here; but there is no question about the archives. And for cause, the domanial deeds are "destined to disappear to the extent that the properties they record enter into commerce"; it will be the same for judicial titles, leaving aside those that are "from long-ago times, the principal and almost the only debris remaining"; of these last, one will examine whether they deserve to be conserved "as belonging to the class of historical monuments," in which case they will find a place in the libraries.

As for the archives, they are only an emanation and an instrument of government: "In the Republic one and indivisible, there is multiplicity of department and district administrations and unity of government, from which they receive their impetus; tax collectors in the districts and a single national treasury in which everything ends up. In the same way, the national archives should be the point to which the archives of administrations of every kind, whether departmental or executive, converge." From this perspective, the archives are the depositories of official documents. They are concerned with the present and the future. The past is the responsibility of the libraries. But, in fact, the only archives treated by the report Dubois wrote and the decree he presented are those of the National Assembly itself.

"The archives established for the national representatives are a central depository for all of the Republic." From its first article, the decree in effect makes the archives depend on the legislative body, something that would be reaffirmed many more times. Article 2 defines the contents of the "central depository"; composed of the works of the Estates General of 1789 and of the national assemblies with their committees, the proceedings of the electoral corps as well as the seals of the Republic, types of coins, and standards of weights and measures, the central depository must collect documents concerning the public fortune and the public debt, international relations, the population census, and summary accounts of property deeds existing in various other depositories of the Republic, as well as "everything that the legislative corps will order deposited there." The decree moreover determines the relations between the central depository and the others (Articles 3 and 5), creates a Domanial Division of the Archives (Article 6), and maintains laws concerning their organization and surveillance in force (Article 7). At the end of the decree, in the general measures, is once again found an article concerning the archives: "Every citizen may demand in all the depositories, on the established days and times, communication of the pieces that they contain; this communication will be granted to him without cost and without displacement, with the appropriate surveillance precautions. Copies or extracts, which may be requested, will be granted for a fee of 15 *sous* each" (Article 37). The last sentence shows that the citizen in question is a buyer of national properties and that the "pieces" that he has a right to demand to see are property deeds, something the following article confirms.

Let us mention three more articles (12 to 14) devoted to "charters and manuscripts that belong to history, to the sciences, and to the arts, or which may serve an educational purpose," to maps, to printed books, and to works and objects of art, all things that do not belong in the archives. And let us note that, for the law of 7 Messidor, all of these have a different content and role than they would later acquire. The word *archives,* used alone or in the expression *National Archives,* always and exclusively designates the institution in question in the first article of this law,[37] that is to say, the archives of the National Assembly; the decree of 7 Messidor is thus in line with that of September 7, 1790. But in contrast to this latter decree, the decree of 7 Messidor only incidentally discusses the archives and devotes only one-sixth of its forty-eight articles to them. What it primarily aims at regulating is the sorting of deeds. All of this leads to the conclusion that "the essential thing about the law of 7 Messidor, Year II, that which evidently constituted the important part in the eyes of its initiators, was the programmatic destruction of the feudal archives" and that it was a question here of "a financial and utilitarian law which it would be totally mistaken to consider a law of archival organization."[38]

This mistake has however been committed by numerous French and foreign writers who have traced the origins of the National Archives, and it became rooted to such an extent that the law of 7 Messidor peacefully survived all of the changes that occurred over the next 185 years. How is this possible? And by what paths did the archives of the legislative body, with their content and their role defined by this law, become a profoundly different institution, without there ever having been an obvious rupture?

The two questions are connected, as we will see. Both of them refer primarily to the contradictions[39] in the attitude of the revolutionaries (including the members of the Convention) confronting the old papers for which they had to assume responsibility, and therefore confronting the past itself, of which these papers preserve the traces and that they enable us to read: in other words, confronting the memory of the ancien régime.

The Republic had long been proclaimed, the king guillotined, and the rupture with the past pushed as far as the adoption of a new era and a new calendar, but the public debt was nevertheless still there, and with it, the necessity of managing the properties of the former Crown and of the former clergy. While repudiating the ancien régime, the new regime still wanted to recover debts and everything that it had illegally disposed of. And, respectful of private property, it needed to know the juridical situation of the properties destined for sale. Called to preserve property deeds for national as well as private properties, it could not allow the destruction of all the old papers indiscriminately: property is inseparable from memory. These papers therefore received a reprieve, while the government waited for the time when a new memory would supplant the old one, when only the new deeds would remain in force.

Another reason argued strongly against indiscriminate destruction: the need to preserve everything that might serve an educational purpose or that belonged to history, to the sciences, and to the arts, a need all the more imperative because, already on October 24, 1793, the convention had broken with the policy of encouraging iconoclasm by adopting a decree forbidding the destruction of works of art.[40] Even though it appeared in the middle of the Terror, the law of 7 Messidor was thus approved at the stage of the Revolution when the indiscriminate destruction of objectivized memories of the ancien régime was already being repudiated as a counterrevolutionary act. It therefore introduced the obligation to conserve everything that belonged, as Dubois said, in the "class of historical monuments." It was this respect for both property and history that led to the idea of sorting. "The recovery of national properties being one of the principal and most essential objects of this operation, the administration of the department will always scrupulously see to it that, from the beginning, sorting takes this direction." But this should not occur to the detriment of history, the sciences, and the arts.[41]

Thus conceived, sorting without a doubt causes enormous damages, and one is right to judge it with horror. But it is nevertheless necessary to distinguish it clearly from pure and simple destruction. The principal difference between the two is that sorting presupposes that there exist documents that must be preserved. Now, in order to recognize them in a mass, one must be capable of reading and understanding them. The decree of 7

Messidor thus stipulates: "To accomplish the prescribed sorting, citizens possessing knowledge of charters, laws, and monuments will be chosen." These citizens—former *feudistes*,★ archivists, librarians, court clerks—were brought together in a Temporary Agency of Deeds and they were given six months to finish sorting (Articles 16 to 18), a time limit that was impossible for them to respect, given the quantity of documents accumulated over the centuries, even if they had arduously destroyed them by fire, which manifestly was not the case.[42] They had in effect to sort the documents of 392 depositories, archives, or charter houses, of which 142 belonged to the administration, to courts and jurisdictions, and to colleges; 124 to convents, congregations, and monasteries; 100 to parishes and manufactures, chapters, chapels, and seminaries; and 26 to hospices and hospitals.[43] A decree by the Directoire on 5 Floréal, Year IV (April 24, 1796), reorganized the agency and changed its name to the Bureau for Sorting Deeds (*Bureau du triage des titres*), while also subordinating it to the Archivist of the Republic (Article 10),[44] who returned at the end of 1795 from the captivity in which he had found himself since April 1793. Subsequently stabilized, the bureau pursued its activities for another five years.

If the members of the agency did not sort documents quickly enough for the authorities charged successively with controlling and hastening their work, it is because—in the political and cultural climate following Thermidor—they had reorientated their work in conformity with their professional habits: the research and the protection of papers "belonging to history" had bit by bit become their principal objective. Already in the *Compte général* of the end of October 1795 they emphasized the importance of deeds and charters for history. After generalizations on the subject, they recalled d'Aguesseau's project for the *Trésor des chartes*, the *Recueil des historiens*, the *Gallia christiana*, and other erudite publications, then condemned the vandalism to which the archives had been victim and valorized what they had done to protect them.[45]

Later, the members of the Bureau for Sorting Deeds offered veritable courses in archival practice and history for the official readers of their reports. They explained to them that "seeking to undertake the sorting and ordering of a depository of archives without knowing the elements, without having at least a general knowledge of the particular history of the corporation or the families to which they belonged is to engender difficul-

---

★ EDITOR'S NOTE: An ironic provision. The *feudistes* were among the most hated functionaries of the ancien régime. In the final decades of the old monarchy these men were employed by landlords—noble, ecclesiastical, and lay—to discover in the old charters and estate archives feudal obligations perhaps long moribund, and reimpose them on the peasantry, as a means of enhancing their income.

ties and do a very bad job." Convinced of this principle, they presented in detail the history of the Accounting Office of Blois. Demonstrating to what exactly the exceptional importance of the archives of religious orders was due, they rejoiced in "the unification of the deeds of the Abbey of Saint-Denis with those of the *Trésor des chartes* in the same place, [. . .] fortunate effect of the Revolution, which only it could bring about. [This unification] made the collection of Monument-Deeds, which began only toward the end of the twelfth century, go back to the sixth in an uninterrupted line. And certainly in no depository does such a precious ensemble exist." Although they did not forget their duties toward the administration, serving history seemed manifestly more important to these officials.[46] In their *Compte rendu* of 25 Thermidor, Year VIII (August 13, 1800), to which is joined an *État des titres et objets recueillis jusqu'à ce jour pour l'histoire*, the same attitude is expressed even more forcefully.[47]

As for the tutelary authorities, they were especially concerned with the recovery of national properties, and their spokesman criticized the agency for its slowness. Camus' position seems for a long time to have been the same,[48] something that only aggravated even more his conflict with the Bureau for Sorting Deeds, which, taking advantage of the incoherence of the laws, wanted to liberate itself from the surveillance of the "archivist." To justify their attitude, the members of the agency, then of the bureau, constructed in the autumn of 1794 an interpretation of the law of 7 Messidor that saw it as a law on the protection of the archives: "Our archives, dispersed in a multitude of depositories, entrusted to guardians who are either inept or negligent, have necessarily experienced the decadence of our former government. Already they were in a deplorable state and they have suffered a lot from vandalism during the course of our revolution. It is to stop the progress of this evil that the law of 7 Messidor was promulgated," one reads in a *Mémoire sur la loi du 7 Messidor an II*. The *Compte général* is just as clear: "It is to save the precious remains of the charters and the archives, and to stop the brigandage which has been directed against these riches, that the Convention rendered its decree of 7 Messidor, Year II." And the *Compte rendu* of 25 Thermidor, Year VIII, invokes "this salutary law for deeds of public and private fortune, as well as for monument-deeds, this law whose conception cannot be praised too highly."[49]

One thus sees here a veritable change in purpose of the sorting operation, which, from "purge" (the word is Dubois's) moved to salvaging documents that have historical value according to the criteria of the epoch. And one sees simultaneously a change in the meaning of the law of 7 Messidor, which of course ordered that certain documents be preserved but that considered this only a secondary effect of the search for estate deeds.

At the same time, due to the actions of the Bureau for Sorting Deeds or
of Camus, certain clauses of this law feel out of use even before they had
begun to be applied. Thus, in Frimaire of Year VI (November–December
1797), in the report on the *Trésor des chartes* that it had just put together, the
members of the bureau proposed that there be created a depository that
would unite around the *Trésor des chartes* all of the old archives and that
would be entrusted to them, thereby liberating them from the surveillance
of Camus.[50] This led to the abandonment of the idea of depositing at the
National Library (Bibliothèque nationale) the "charters and manuscripts
that belong to history, to the sciences, and to the arts," and first of all the

Fig. 2.5
Charles Braibant, direc-
tor of the Archives of
France from 1948 to
1959.

Fig. 2.6
André Chamson, general
director of the Archives
of France from 1959 to
1971.

Fig. 2.7
Jean Favier, general
director of the Archives
of France from February
1975 to 1994.

Trésor des chartes itself, something that the law of 7 Messidor, however, explicitly ordered. On his side, the official responsible for estate archives, already in conflict with the Bureau for Sorting Deeds, also sought to obtain his autonomy; hence a conflict that would survive Camus and with which Daunou would still be concerned.[51]

This conflict seems to be behind the message from the Directoire of the Council of 500 of 14 Pluviôse, Year VII (February 2, 1799), obviously written by someone who was familiar with the archives. "The archives," it begins, "are the collection of acts produced by different authorities, and the pieces that may relate to them. Their aim is double. They must, in the first place, provide each authority with documents on past transactions, indispensable for regulating its present and future progress. In the second place, they provide the public with depositories in which all citizens may occasionally obtain information concerning their fortune, their civil status, or even, with the appropriate precautions, their mere instruction." After this promising debut, the message draws, from the separation between legislative and executive powers, the conclusion that the archives must also be separated. From this perspective, it criticizes the laws of 12 Brumaire and 7 Messidor, especially the latter. "It seems that in establishing such a short time limit [for sorting deeds], one had ceded rather to the desire to destroy much, than to the utilitarian reasons that could have encouraged one to conserve much. It is easy to see, moreover, that the articles of this law, by which the Convention attributed to itself the administrative surveillance of all the archives, were once again based entirely on the unification of all the powers assembled in its hands." Starting from these premises, the message proposed a dismemberment of the National Archives: they would keep only what pertained to the legislative power; the territorial archives would become the responsibility of the minister of finance, the judicial archives that of the minister of justice.[52] But the Legislative Commission of the Council of 500, in its session of 1 Nivôse, Year VIII (December 22, 1799), did not follow these conclusions.[53]

A few weeks later, the State Council's Department of the Interior prepared a proposal for a decree concerning the National Archives, the stake of a battle between those who wanted to dismember them and Camus, who triumphed in the end.[54] The decree of the consuls on 8 Prairial, Year VIII (May 28, 1800), radically modified the status of the National Archives. It detached them from the legislative body and placed them under the first consul, who reserved to himself the right to name and to revoke the archivist and place the latter "under his immediate authority" (Article 8). It reiterated that the National Archives belonged to the two divisions "known by the name of *judicial archives* and *territorial archives*," stipulated that "all pieces, acts, and other objects deposed in the Archives before last 4 Nivôse [December 25, 1799] will remain there, without any of them being misappropriated" and announced that "a law for determining the nature, the form, and the epochs of the deposits that must be made to the National Archives by the diverse constituted bodies of the Republic will be proposed to the legislative body" (Articles 1, 3, 4).[55]

The proposal for such a law was effectively presented to the legislative body on 3 Frimaire, Year IX (November 20, 1800), and it set off a lively debate that, due to lack of space, will not be described here.[56] The negative vote that concluded this debate for a long time put an end to the attempts to get a new law on the archives adopted; Daunou sketched a few more of these proposals, which seem never to have left his files.[57] The decree of 8 Prairial, Year VIII, therefore defined the status and the composition of the National Archives until the ordinance of January 5, 1846, relative to the organization of the Royal Archives, and the decree of December 22, 1855, organizing the Imperial Archives. The decree of December 14, 1911, reorganizing the National Archives still referred to this decree.[58]

The decree of 8 Prairial did not stop the members of the Bureau for Sorting Deeds from returning to the attack. But their rear guard combat only accelerated things: the bureau was suppressed and, from October 1801 on, part of its personnel entered the National Archives to form the Bureau of Historical Monuments, which later became the Historical Division.[59] Before these developments and even before the decree of 8 Prairial, Camus had asked the Minister of the Interior to take the necessary steps for placing the *Trésor des chartes* and other papers that should be returned there in the National Archives. A consular decree of 4 Thermidor, Year VIII (July 23, 1800), gave him satisfaction on this point.[60] There followed a new attempt to dismember the National Archives, undertaken by the appellate court of Paris in order to obtain restitution of the judicial archives; a proposal for a decree moving in this direction was even drawn up. But Camus' counterattack was once again victorious.[61] Other alerts under the Empire[62] and at the beginning of the Restoration, even if they caused certain papers to be returned to their former proprietors, did not have the same grave effect.[63]

In 1804, upon Camus' death, what remained of the law of 7 Messidor, which was then barely ten years old? Apparently, almost nothing. All of the articles on sorting deeds were obsolete, as were all of the general measures except one. Of those that defined the fundamental bases of the organization of the archives, certain ones remained a dead letter, others were modified by later regulations; even the content of the National Archives changed in relation to the stipulations of the law and it was no longer the legislative body that ordered deposits in the archives and that assured surveillance of them. Everything happened as if the law of 7 Messidor was no longer in force, and such was in effect the position of the appelate court of Paris in the litigation that opposed it and Camus.[64]

However, what remained of the law of 7 Messidor was the National Archives, which would not have been able to become what they have become without a return in the law to the essence of that of 12 Brumaire, Year II, and without a reaffirmation of the position of the archivist as it had been defined on September 7, 1790. Because it was by supporting himself on these texts that Camus succeeded in acquiring responsibility for overseeing the sorting of deeds; in uniting at the National Archives the domanial and judicial deposits, later the *Trésor des chartes*, along with deeds belonging to history; and in protecting the unity of the ensemble against all those who wanted to dismember it. Moreover, from the law of 7 Messidor there remained several powerful ideas that henceforth would work on people's spirits. The idea, first of all, that access to the National Archives was not a grace, a privilege, or a good deed, but the right of each citizen. Even if this idea resulted from a contested reading of Article 37, it nonetheless moved efficiently toward an always wider access of the archives. The law of 7 Messidor was also behind the idea of the National Archives as the "common center" of a system in which all of the public archives in France would take part. Finally, the idea of the National Archives as "central depository for all of the Republic" would be used by their successive directors to justify the obligation of the ministries and other government offices to deposit their archives after they had lost their immediate utility. We will later show that all of these ideas materialized in the nineteenth century in the legal measures regulating the archives, something that will permit us to evoke the law of 5 Brumaire, Year V, the last of the three laws overturned by that of January 3, 1979.

Along with the division into departments, the metric system, the national museums, the tricolor flag, the *Marseillaise*, the Republican motto, and the Republic itself (among other innovations), the National Archives are effectively a legacy of the Revolution. But their roots are much more profound.

FROM THE *TRÉSOR DES CHARTES* TO THE *ÉCOLE DES CHARTES*.

Camus, we have just seen, succeeded—not without effort—in incorporating the *Trésor des chartes* into the National Archives. And Daunou, we will see, did not want anyone to touch it, out of respect for all those who had consulted it and for the "inventory of Dupuy," that is, the detailed inventory of the *coffres*★ and *layettes* of the *Trésor* compiled by Pierre Dupuy and Théodore Godefroy at the beginning of the seventeenth century and still used today. But the *coffres* and *layettes*, which became just *layettes*, formed only one division of the *Trésor des chartes*. The second division is that which has been called, since 1836, the *supplément* and that before the Revolution was called the *sacs*: documents of the same nature as that of the *layettes* but certain of which, kept at that epoch in sacks, had not been inventoried by Dupuy and Godefroy, whereas others had been restored to the *Trésor* at the end of their work. The third division is that of the *registres*.[65]

The difference between the *layettes* and the *registres* dates from the origin of the *Trésor*, in the first decades of the thirteenth century. It results from its very operation: in the beginning, the *registres* contained especially cartularies. From the reign of Philip the Fair on, they became *registres* of the chancellery that, with few exceptions, recorded there in chronological order "royal acts with perpetual effect, often presented in the form of charters and sealed with green wax."[66] The *coffres*, *layettes*, and *sacs*, for their part, contained original documents: deeds of hommage and service, testaments, marriage acts, treaties and other diplomatic acts, papal bulls, and so on. The separation between what was leaving and what was arriving, between the *registres* and the *layettes*, is indicated immediately by a difference in call numbers. This difference goes back to the second half of the fourteenth century. It bears the mark of the labors of Gérard de Montaigu, guardian of the *Trésor des chartes* from 1370 to 1391, who created the two divisions: that of the *registres* and that of the *layettes*, while giving the *registres* a numbering system that the current numbering system preserves and extends.[67]

The very idea that a document that is supposed to have perpetual

---

★ EDITOR'S NOTE: Rather than using inexact English equivalents the French words of art— *coffres, layettes, registres,* and *sacs*—which refer to the several ways of holding archival materials have been retained.

effects can one day cease to be valid was completely foreign to the medieval mentality; it remained difficult to accept for a long time afterward. Rights and privileges could certainly be lost through forgetfulness, but once they were recalled and their legitimacy established, nothing prevented one from benefitting from them as before. Their ancient origin only conferred more dignity and more strength on them. Certain documents therefore always remained valuable as proof; others established precedents or furnished examples. And the current archives, precisely as such, were also permanent; the distinction between the two made no sense. In the epoch of its splendor, the *Trésor des chartes* operated according to these principles. One conserved everything that had been deposited there. At the same time, one borrowed documents from it that one sometimes forgot to put back or that, on their return, did not necessarily find their former place, and one also deposited new documents that had to be integrated and inventoried. That is why the history of the *Trésor* consists primarily of a series of attempts to reestablish order, broken by long periods in which disorder reigned.

One of these periods of disorder extended from the death of Gérard de Montaigu until the end of the fifteenth century. In 1474, then in 1482, Louis XI ordered a collection and an inventory of the *Trésor des chartes*, which was carried out but with much delay. In 1539, François I noted the impossibility of finding the deeds one needed, when one needed them, in the *Trésor*. There followed a new ordering of them, which did not last. In 1562, François II in turn complained of the difficulty of finding the necessary documents in the *Trésor* and charged Jean du Tillet with putting them in order and with transcribing those papers that had become almost illegible. Du Tillet fulfilled his mission. But Dupuy, who left a pathetic description of the disorder he found in the *Trésor des chartes* in 1615, accused du Tillet of having contributed to it. Even worse, du Tillet did not return to the *Trésor* the documents that he had borrowed from it—and certain of which have never been returned. Likewise, Pierre Pithou created his celebrated collections with the documents of the *Trésor*; only part of them were recuperated, long after his death.[68]

Without ever having been the sole depository of the French monarchy—the archives of Saint-Denis also played such a role[69]—the *Trésor des chartes* nevertheless had a central and privileged position. Depending in certain regards on the Chamber of Accounts that was responsible for managing the royal properties and tied directly to the chancellery, it was in this capacity the memory of the king, immortal being, personification of the State, for everything that pertained to the properties and the rights of the Crown. But, beginning in the second half of the sixteenth century, it began to lose this role: the *registres* of the chancellery end in 1568, under the reign of Charles IX, and out of approximately a thousand articles in the *layettes* and their *supplément* only twenty or so are posterior to 1600; most of them treat France's external relations and dynastic affairs. From this epoch on, the *Trésor* is thus composed mostly of collections that today one would call closed collections.[70]

It was also at the end of the sixteenth century that the *Trésor* became an object of interest for historians. Certainly, Jean de Montreuil had access to it in his capacity as secretary to the king and, later, Guillaume Budé, whose father and uncle were charged with putting it in order again.[71] It was Jean du Tillet, however, who made the members of learned circles understand the importance of the *Trésor des chartes* for the study of France's past. He used the documents that he had found there for his works on French public law: on the age of majority of the king, on the rights of the Crown, on the privileges of the Gallican Church.[72] And even before he had published his own collections, he put these documents at the disposal of du Haillan, who made use of them for his history of France.[73] The same subjects—age of majority of kings, rights of the Crown, rights and liberties of the Gallican Church—were later the object of the research of other personalities tied to the *Trésor des chartes*, Pierre Pithou and Pierre Dupuy. Dupuy not only inventoried the *layettes* but also published several documents and a history of the *Trésor des chartes*.[74] In the second half of the seventeenth century, Carcavy and Baluze, under orders from Colbert, transcribed extracts from the *registres* of the *Trésor*; somebody also transcribed some historic documents for Achille III du Harley. Bit by bit, the *Trésor* distanced itself from the present and the future and became a monument of the past. Its ties with the administration were loosened. It drew closer to history.[75]

Mathieu Molé, royal public prosecutor and guardian of the *Trésor des chartes*, like all holders of the title since 1582, did everything he could to stop this evolution. In June 1626, a decree by the King's Council ordered the seizure of documents relative to the properties and rights of the Crown, which had passed to private parties. "If this may accomplish its aim," noted Peiresc in regard to the decree, "it will be a very good thing. But I doubt it a little."[76] He was right. An edict of Louis XIII on September 23, 1628, thus ordered in turn that the originals of all acts concerning affairs of state "in the past as well as in the future" be included in the *Trésor des chartes*. Molé worked hard to see that these decisions did not remain a dead letter. And the efforts he made to restore to the *Trésor* documents that had been removed from it produced some effect. But he did not succeed in reestablishing the *Trésor* in its role as central archive of the French monarchy.[77] The reign of Louis XIV, after Fouquet's fall had put an end to his attempt to make the *Trésor des chartes* a machine of the administration, witnessed the great development of the Royal Library where were deposited documents that at one time would have been sent to the *Trésor*,[78] which was slowly sinking into its decline.

The future chancellor d'Aguesseau, who was then the royal prosecutor, noted this in 1711: "Before, one was very careful to place in this depository all acts that it was appropriate to conserve there; but in the last century, one has begun to lag in the accuracy that is so necessary to this endeavor, with the result that at present one would have more trouble finding acts from the last century, which has barely ended, than finding monuments from far more distant centuries." Convinced that "nothing can ever equal the security of a public depository, which is perpetual, immobile," d'Aguesseau thus proposed that one return to the practice of depositing in the *Trésor des chartes* all peace treaties, as well as "the originals of the king's edicts and declarations, the originals of the papal bulls demanded by His Majesty, the originals or at least the official copies of marriage contracts received by Messieurs the Secretaries of State, the testaments, the inventories, the partitions, the sales, exchanges, bequests, and other acts that concern the king's domain."[79]

But it was too late. The restructuring of the administration of France, begun in the sixteenth century, had notably conferred a greater role on the Parlement de Paris and, consequently, on the public prosecutor, who was the king's representative to this body. So that the prosecutor could, in the exercise of his responsibilities, have easy access to the documents of the *Trésor des chartes*, Henri III made him guardian of the *Trésor*: "Given that such responsibility and protection of our deeds and papers is more appropriate and relevant to our public prosector than to anyone else, to be the true agent and defender of the rights of the domain and patrimony of our said crown, and given that without these deeds and papers, he could not have total enlightenment and cognizance nor undertake such research and pursuit of the said laws as his said status as our public prosecutor requires."[80] This decision ratified the rupture of ties between the *Trésor* and the chancellery, which had taken place fourteen years before. And it provoked a conflict between the public prosecutor and the Chamber of Accounts, which demanded of the former that in his capacity as guardian of the *Trésor* he swear allegiance to it; this conflict did not end until 1697, with the victory of the prosecutor. Victory without future. The destiny of the *Trésor des chartes* had already been sealed for a long time.

Beginning in the second half of the sixteenth century, there arose in all European countries in which absolute monarchies reigned—and espe-

cially in Spain—a tendency to replace archives such as they were incarnated in the *Trésor des chartes* with archives that, emanating directly from
government offices, would be used daily as a political instrument of the
State.[81] The French administration thus secreted new archives, beginning
with the chancellery and the secretariats of state, which, beginning in the
1570s, kept the documents they generated.[82] Later on, the king decided
to give himself a depository for his papers at the Louvre and Richelieu
envisaged the creation of a new *Trésor des chartes*, which would have in
common with the old one only its name and that would be reserved exclusively for the royal power, independent of the public prosecutor, who
was henceforth suspected of ceding too much to Parlement.[83]

A similar tendency led the administration to treat papers connected
to the maintenance of an office of the State as the property of the State,
not of the holder of the office. In France, during the Wars of Religion and
the regencies shaken by troubles up to the time of the Fronde, this was
especially difficult to put into practice because it went against secular customs. There were certainly precedents; witness the presence in the *Trésor
des chartes* of Nogaret's papers and of the "coffers [*coffres*] of the chancellors," documents that were seized in the sixteenth century from several
holders of this title.[84] But in general the papers of the various offices were
considered private property; the holder of the office kept them with him
and left them to his inheritors, without eliciting any sort of reaction. Following the example of their predecessors, all of the great figures of the
French administration in the seventeenth century, from Richelieu to Colbert, proceeded in this fashion.[85]

The idea that the State was not identified with the king as a visible
individual was ancient and well established in the mind of theologians.
And in that of jurists, whose ranks provided the majority of high functionaries. But the idea that each embodiment of the State also existed independently of the persons who were responsible for it and that this embodiment must consequently have its own memory seems to have been
accepted more slowly. The big shift in this domain occurred under Louis
XIV. In August 1671, after the death of Hugues de Lionne, secretary of
state for foreign affairs, his official papers were seized by order of the king.
They would be transferred to the new holder of the office and the same
thing would occur at the next change in powers in foreign affairs. "From
now on, one may take the archives of Secretaries of State for depositories
of public archives."[86]

In effect, the first measures aiming to create a depository for foreign
affairs, which would receive its definitive form in 1710–11, date from
1688. In 1699, the Archives of the Navy, the Colonies, and the Galleys

were established. The year 1701 witnessed the beginnings of the War Archives. Between 1703 and 1708 those of the general comptroller were put in place, whose organization would be achieved around 1715. It was then the turn of the Archives of the Council of Finances and of the Council of Extraordinary Affairs in 1716 and that of the Archives of the King's Household in 1717. Simultaneously, over the course of the first decades of the eighteenth century, numerous decisions aimed at ensuring the protection of the different archives dispersed throughout the realm and at putting them in order.[87] One sees that from then on any attempts to restore to the *Trésor des chartes* its status as central archives for the monarchy were destined to fail, even if some diplomatic documents were deposited there and if occasional deposits were made to it until the eve of the Revolution. Each branch of the administration henceforth had its own archives and a dissociation in fact occurred between these archives that, in today's terminology, were current archives and the *Trésor des chartes*, which had essentially become a depository for permanent archives.

Nothing demonstrates this better than the contrast that exists between the secrecy that surrounds the archives of the administration and especially the ministerial archives, which are accessible only to individuals on official business, and the openness of the *Trésor des chartes*. Relative openness, certainly; "it is impossible," wrote Boulainvilliers, "to penetrate there without permission, which is granted only with very great precautions and difficulties, in addition to the money it costs."[88] But real openness, nevertheless, which would expand with time.[89] Because the *Trésor des chartes* would become in the eighteenth century a center of historical research: works on the *registres*, begun on the initiative of Pontchartrain and launched again by d'Aguesseau, were pursued, and materials for the *Ordonnances des rois de France de la troisième race* and other learned publications were compiled.[90] In fact, whoever was interested in history could learn, without even entering the *Trésor*, what it contained; manuscript inventories, including that of Dupuy and Godefroy, were found in several libraries, as were extracts of *registres* and copies of documents; of these latter, a large number appeared in diverse publications.[91] This relative openness of the *Trésor* to history alone sufficed to prove its new status: that of permanent archives.

But this change in status led to no rupture in continuity. And it was not recorded by those who treated the archives as an institution. The *Nouveau traité de diplomatique*, drawing support from legal advisors, made the archives serve to demonstrate proof before a court, while underlining their importance for history; thus were cartularies "monuments capable of spreading great lights on the history of the most distant times and on the rights or pretensions under litigation." A position that is more juridical but that nevertheless does not forget that history is adopted quite naturally through collections of law or jurisprudence.[92] This is not only a particular case of the direct link established between law and history by the thought and the juridical practice of the ancien régime; witness theoreticians of the law, such as Montesquieu, and certain historians, especially those who studied French institutions. All of the debate surrounding the constitution of France is both a historical and juridical debate, whose two components cannot be separated from each other.[93]

It is the same with private law:

> The very term *custom*, which designates the particular laws of our provinces, indicates that these are not laws established by the absolute will and the proper action of the sovereign but habits to which continuous practice has, through the passage of time, given the force of law. In general, in order to understand thoroughly what has been established only by habit, it is necessary to go back to the origin and try to discover what was practiced in the beginning. It is therefore very advantageous to understand the monuments of ancient habits and first statutes, which preceded our customs and which gave birth to part of their measures.

And Camus—because it is he who is speaking—advised a young lawyer to read, among other works, the *Capitularia regum francorum*, the *Établissements de Saint Louis*, and the *Coutumes de Beauvaisis* by Beaumanoir, as well as, among the sources of public law, the *Ordonnances des rois de France de la troisième race* and the *Remonstrances* of the Parlement de Paris.[94]

Place where law and history meet, the archives belong to both. And those who conduct research there, rather numerous in the seventeenth century,[95] combine the attitude of the jurist, for whom documents are deeds, and that of the historian, for whom they are sources to different degrees, and insist on one or the other, depending on the case. In theory, the jurist justifies, the historian notices. But when certain documents from the distant past are supposed to have a perpetual validity or when certain customs draw their strength from their age, to notice is often to justify. That is why in du Tillet, Pithou, and Dupuy, these two attitudes coincide; for them history is principally an auxiliary of public law. If the research of Peiresc and later of the Mauristes or of du Cange reveal a history that is autonomous with respect to the law, it is because it pertains to ancient practices, in Peiresc; to the monastic past of the provinces and of Paris, in the Mauristes; and to medieval Latin, in du Cange among others. But when Colbert had research done in the archives, it was principally juridical questions that interested him, as they would later interest Pontchartrain or d'Aguesseau.*

The two attitudes of erudite history—that which put history in the service of public law and that supposed continuity between the past, however distant, and the present and that which, on the contrary, presumed a big gap if not a rupture between past and present and that was astonished by the "bizarre" habits of ancestors—these two attitudes thus were adopted throughout the eighteenth century, often by the same people and without the difference between them being clearly perceived. Also uniting them was the imperative to prove what one asserts by referring to original documents, which demanded research in the archives. Nevertheless, one privileged national history more and more. This was true at the Academy of Inscriptions and Literature, where the connection between jurisprudence and national history was reaffirmed by d'Argenson and by the Mauristes, who abandoned the history of their order to consecrate themselves to the religious and civil history of France.[96]

In 1762, Jacob-Nicolas Moreau, guardian of the Library of Finances, asked his minister, Henri-Léonard Bertin, to gather a collection of copies of medieval charters—that is to say, as it would later be specified, of charters anterior to the fifteenth century—dispersed in the archives and charter houses of the realm, so as to form a depository that could serve both public law and history. Created in 1763, this Depository of the Charters was in some ways an emanation of three institutions: of the power that patronized and financed it; of the Academy of Inscriptions, several members of which had been associated with it since the beginning of its work; and of the Benedictines of the Congregation of Saint-Maur and of that of Saint-Vanne, who would provide Moreau with the bulk of his collaborators.[97] The depository operated until 1790 in its double capacity as effective center of historical research and virtual center of French archives, public and private, to which Moreau worked to establish a "general map" and to illuminate the contents, while simultaneously gathering together the copies collected in "the different depositories that contain the charters

---

* EDITOR'S NOTE: Nicolas Claude Fabri de Peiresc (1580–1637) had studied astronomy with Galileo and was a scientist of note. He also collected old manuscripts and coins. Charles du Fresne du Cange (1610–88) was the compiler of two important dictionaries: one of the Latin language, another of medieval Greek. He was one of the earliest historians of the Byzantine Empire and wrote several deeply learned works. The Maurists, or more correctly the Benedictine monks of the Congregation of St. Maur, were devoted to scholarship, particularly of the Middle Ages, and refined the study of diplomatics, the science of reading complicated medieval manuscripts.

[. . .]: the curio-cabinets, the archives of gentlemen and lords, those of States, provinces, royal seats, sovereign courts, bishops, churches, monasteries, and religious communities, and of towns and secular communities."[98] At the time of the Revolution were found there notably 400 boxes and approximately 50,000 copies of charters coming from 350 collections, according to one source, and 394, according to another.[99] The depository participated as an institution in almost all of the great works of erudition conducted during this epoch.

The *Trésor des chartes* originally contained the objectified memory of the king, personification of the State. Beginning in the sixteenth century, a sort of progressive slide detached it from the memory of the administration and pushed it toward erudite history. But this history, since it studied the foundations of law, was itself inseparable from memory, even if this was no longer the memory of the administration but the long memory of the monarchical institution itself and of other institutions of the realm, certain of which—the peerage, the *parlements*, the Church— supposedly limited the monarchy. It was the Revolution that introduced a break between the history and the memory of institutions, because it dissociated law from history and founded it henceforth on sovereign will and reason. And the Revolution condemned the memory carried in the old law and the ancien régime, even as it pretended to respect history. The rescue of the archives, in particular ecclesiastical and seigniorial archives, could not be accomplished otherwise than by demonstrating that they were indispensable to history.

The representatives of the milieu that provided the Depository of the Charters with its foundation were found during the Revolution in all the institutions responsible for monuments and deeds; later on in the National Archives and in the Institute. They wrote instructions concerning the conservation of the archives and made efforts to save them. Thus, taking up an idea sketched by the *Nouveau traité de diplomatique*, Dom Poirier introduced to this effect the distinction between "common, active deeds" and "monument-deeds," between documents that serve always to justify rights and those that have value only for history.[100] This distinction between memory and history, which is laid out by the law of 7 Messidor, Year II (among others), led to a distinction between archives that are the instrument of an institution or a family and archives that can be only an object of study pertaining to a revolved past—a distinction between current archives and permanent archives.

Dom Poirier, however, conceived this distinction rather confusedly, not in terms of archives or funds, but in terms of deeds, which led him to recommend sorting and separating between monument-deeds and active deeds, something that surprised no one at the time. It is nevertheless true that this distinction, coupled with the idea that documents concerning history merit protection due to this very fact, was at the foundation of all the efforts made to save the old papers and to organize the archives. And it is true that this distinction was a seedbed for thinking about delays, at the end of which a collection preserves only historical value. Double delays, as one discovered rather quickly, occurred because the date on which a collection must leave the current archives does not generally coincide with the date on which it may be opened to the public. This latter was legally defined only in the decree of January 12, 1898, which stipulated that in the absence of reservations on the part of the administration that had deposited them, "documents more than fifty years old will be freely communicated to the public by the National Archives."[101] In other words, they would then pass from the domain of the management and justification of rights to the domain of historical research.

The Revolution interrupted works of erudition for a long time, and it destroyed the very institutions that made them possible: the Benedictine religious order and the Academy of Inscriptions.[102] In the new circumstances, the former members of these institutions quickly became conscious of the fact that the knowledge of charters they possessed threatened to disappear with them, in the absence of establishments that would ensure its transmission. In its report on the *Trésor des chartes* in Frimaire Year VI, the Bureau for Sorting Deeds underlined that

> it is essential that persons to whom care [of these deeds] will one day be given are instructed equally in diplomatics, in history in general, and particularly in that of the French government. It would even be appropriate for [the members of this Bureau] to prepare themselves in advance for this work, by undertaking the study of a language which no longer exists today, and by educating students chosen from the class of young people instructed in ancient languages. The Bureau for Sorting Deeds will not cease to express the wish that one avoid the evils which would result from abandonment of the study of diplomacy.[103]

This is the first notion of what twenty years later would become the École des chartes.

Under the Empire, de Gérando, then secretary general of the Ministry of the Interior, presented to his minister, who submitted it to Napoleon, a proposal for a "sort of new Port-Royal" called to bridge the gap created by the disappearance of the Mauristes: there some great erudites would teach research methods to young people. At the same time, the minister, concerned by the decadence of erudition, submitted to Napoleon a proposal for encouraging learned societies in the provinces, for continuing the *Histoire littéraire de la France* begun by the Benedictines, and for creating at the Collège de France four new chairs, one of which would be consecrated to the history of France. But Napoleon had his own ideas on the subject and the affair did not go any further.[104] It was the ordinance of Louis XVIII on February 22, 1821, that created an École des Chartes whose students, numbering twelve, were to learn "to read diverse manuscripts and to explain the French dialects of the Middle Ages" (Article 3).

This first École des Chartes lasted only two years. Reactivated with an extended program beginning in January 1830, it acquired a new organization in 1846. One would henceforth teach: "The reading and the deciphering of charters and written monuments;—figurative archaeology, encompassing history of art, Christian architecture, sigillography, and numismatics;—the general history of the Middle Ages applied particularly to chronology, to the art of verifying the age and authenticity of deeds;—linguistics applied to the history of the origins and formation of the national language;—the political geography of France in the Middle Ages;—summary knowledge of principles of canon and feudal law" (Article 8 of an ordinance of December 31, 1846). The decree of January 30, 1869, modified this measure. Beginning on this date, the school's curriculum in effect included the following courses: "Paleography.—Romance languages.—Bibliography, classification of libraries and archives.—Diplomacy.—Political, administrative, and judiciary institutions of France.—Civil and canonical law of the Middle Ages.—Archaeology of the Middle Ages" (Article 1).[105]

Through the intermediary of its first two professors, once members of the Temporary Agency of Deeds, then of the Bureau for Sorting Deeds, a tie—very tenuous it is true—united the École to prerevolutionary erudition. But this was true only in the very beginning. As it appeared after 1830 and especially after 1846, the École des Chartes was the result of a rupture. The Catholic Church excepted, institutions that might presume to be rooted directly in the Middle Ages no longer existed. Charles X tried hard to reestablish ties, across the Revolution, with the former traditions of the French monarchy. July 1830 put an end to these vague reactionary desires. Public and private law was no longer the same as under the ancien régime, nor were the distribution of property, the social hierarchy and mores, and even the visual environment that had been fashioned by centuries of demolition of "gothic" architecture, a demolition intensified by the sale of national properties. It was this rupture that made possible the new historical interest in the Middle Ages and the new taste for the vestiges of this epoch.

What is more, although certain members of the former Academy of

Inscriptions and of the religious orders where erudition had been culti-vated joined the Institute and once again picked up certain works begun under the ancien régime—the *Histoire littéraire de la France* or the *Receuil des ordonnances*—it was not their knowledge, aside from paleography and diplomacy, that the École des Chartes dispensed. In spite of Guérard's re-spect for Daunou,[106] the questionnaire structuring the former's research on the Middle Ages owed nothing to him. And Quicherat found his in-spiration in Michelet.[107] Reading the course titles of the École des Chartes as they were defined by normative texts, one sees that teaching there was inseparable from the "romantic" tendencies of the 1840s to 1860s and the "positivist" ones of the 1870s on. Located at the crossroads between archi-val practice and historical research, the École des Chartes was an institu-tion emblematic of the new age of history, that in which history claimed the status of science.

Classifications and Deposits

Viewed with the eye of an archaeologist, archives in general and the Na-tional Archives more particularly look like a succession of alluvia that were left by different epochs and that, superimposed on one another, together form a stratified architecture. Let us take as our starting point that which is the most superficial, that which literally jumps out at the eyes: the com-plexity of the call numbers—with their letters, doubled letters, two differ-ent letters, capital and lowercase, Arabic numerals, Roman numerals, to the left of the letters, to the right of the letters, as exponents, with diverse diacritical marks, too. That the National Archives have nevertheless suc-ceeded in becoming computerized is a kind of miracle.

The extreme diversity of codes identifying classes, collections, or groups of documents at the National Archives betrays the absence of a single principle presiding over their construction and rendering them in-telligible; how should one know from a single glance, for example, that a doubled letter designates a subseries of the series designated by that letter alone, as in the case of the J, K, L, M series, where JJ, KK, LL, and MM designate *registres* as opposed to *layettes* or cartons. But BB does not desig-nate a subseries of the B series; it is a series of equal rank containing the deposits of the Ministry of Justice, whereas the B series brings together documents relative to the elections and votes of the revolutionary period as well as popular votes down to 1946. It would be only too easy to mul-tiply analogous examples.

The lack of a single principle in the construction of the codes refers in turn to the history of the classification of the funds. They are today divided into three divisions: the Ancient, containing prerevolutionary funds; the Modern; and the Contemporary. This last fund was added in 1947, first as a subdivision, to make room for documents posterior to July 1940. Before that, there were only two divisions: the Ancient and the Modern. "Logic would have it that the National Archives be divided into two main Divisions: one containing all of the ancien régime, the other the new; certainly it is that organization which will one day prevail."[108] The minister of public instruction who, in 1897, made this prognostic greatly overestimated the power of logic.

Let us open the *État général des fonds*. We will note, among other things, that the order of the divisions does not correspond to that of the series: the volume consecrated to the ancien régime begins with the E series and continues with the G, after which one finds the habitual sequence of letters, with the exception of I and W. Second anomaly: some series belong both to the Ancient Division and to the Modern Division (O and Q series). Then, in the series belonging to the Ancient Division, there are documents posterior not only to 1789 but also to the first years of the nineteenth century. They are rare, it is true, and their presence is generally justified by the continuity of the institutions they emerge from; but there are exceptions to this rule. Moreover, sometimes for the same reason, sometimes for no apparent reason, documents anterior to 1789, certain of which go back to the seventeenth century, are relatively numerous in the Modern Division, principally in the F series, consecrated to the general administration of France. Finally, special funds, the funds of the Ministries of the Marine and of the Colonies as well as the Minutier central are not divided between the divisions; there the date 1789 marks, where need be, only an internal frontier.★

The division into series therefore does not coexist very well with the classifications into divisions defined, each one, by a period in the history of France. The reason is that these two divisions have different origins and proceed from a different logic. The first will be considered later. As for the second, it is only after the decree of December 14, 1911, reorganizing the National Archives[109] that they replaced the classification into divisions in force since the decree of December 22, 1855, which essentially followed an ordinance of January 1846 on this point. Aside from the division of the Secretariat, the National Archives were then composed of the following divisions: Historical, Administrative (in 1846, it was called Administrative

---

★ EDITOR'S NOTE: There is no English equivalent for either the *Minutier*, an index or guide to notarial records, or the person who creates these records, the *notaire*. Notarial records are often inventories of the possessions of a decreased (required by law) and inventories made in property disputes, divorces, and so on. As a general rule those pertaining to an estate cannot be consulted before a century has elapsed.

and Domanial), Legislative, and Judiciary.[110] Two principles manifestly predominated in these divisions: the distinction between documents whose sole interest is historical, that is, the study of former times, and those that might be useful for the State; the distinction, among these latter, is not their provenance but their nature. Hence the Historical Division, whose very name demonstrates that it was different from the two others, just as the past is different from the present. Hence also the attribution of the first group, which deals with the management of men and property, while the second deals with the production and application of laws.

Obviously, such a classification does not proceed from the principle of respecting holdings. It requires, on the contrary, that a collection be dismembered when it contains documents belonging to different fields of the State's activity. In this sense, it does not take into account history, whose successive contributions are recorded by each archival collection up to the moment when the institution from which it emanates disappears. It replaces history by a preestablished framework. The principle of respecting collections did not definitively impose itself on the National Archives until the end of the nineteenth century.[111] But since the end of the 1860s, one had attempted to reconstitute the collections—not materially but on paper—which led to the *Inventaire sommaire* of 1871, the first to categorize them by period. In effect, "the reconstitution of primitive collections naturally highlights the profound separation that exists at the National Archives between the old and new regimes, because the classification adopted in the depositories [. . .] melded the different regimes, and, through assimilations that were inexact and often arbitrary, brought together institutions that were absolutely distinct and of a very different nature." It "thus made apparent the necessity of dividing the summary inventory into two parts, of consecrating the first to the ancien régime and the second to the period dating from 1789."[112]

Such were, it seems, the roots of the new divisions introduced in 1911. Let us now return to the divisions that preceded it. The form in which they appeared from 1846 on was not luminously clear. Where was the frontier between the Historical Division and the others, given that it was certainly not 1789? According to what criteria were these divisions divided? One might think that the distinction between the three powers—legislative, executive, and judiciary—was being referred to. But then why was the legislative united with the judiciary? And what was the term *domanial* doing in the name of the Administrative Division until 1855? To find answers to these questions, it is necessary to refer to the *Tableau systématique des Archives de l'Empire au 15 août 1811*, written by Daunou and dating in fact from 1809. The state of things observed in 1846 appears then to be the result of a reduction in the number of divisions and of an alteration in the original classificatory framework, which, concerned with the "French Division"—there were others—, was organized as follows:

Legislative Division:
A. Collection of laws
B. Proceedings of the national assemblies
C. Pieces appended to the minutes of the proceedings of the national assemblies
D. Papers of the committees and deputies sent on an assignment

Administrative Division:
E. General administration. Government. Royal Household
F. Ministries
G. Special administrations
H. Local administrations

Historical Division:
J. *Trésor des chartes*
K. Historical monuments
L. Ecclesiastical monuments
M. Historical mix

Topographical Division:
N. Geographical division and population of France
O. Maps

Domanial Division:
P. Chamber of accounts
Q. Territorial deeds
R. Estates of the princes
S. Formerly ecclesiastical properties
T. Sequestrations, confiscations, and sales

Judiciary Division:
V. Great chancellery and councils
X. Parliament of Paris
Y. Châtelet
Z. Diverse courts and jurisdictions
&. High criminal courts[113]

Six divisions, then, with the Legislative Division at the summit, beginning with collections of laws; the first contains the "Edicts, Declarations, Royal Patents in chronological order from 1160 to 1789" and the second the "Originals or Official Copies of laws passed in 1789 and over the following ten years." Then come the proceedings of the national assemblies, from the Assembly of Notables of 1787–88 to the Tribunat and the Legislative Corps. This classification thus reveals a vision of history in which the Revolution opens a new epoch, which both breaks with precedent and continues it. The rupture is signaled by the role assigned to 1789 as pivotal date; the continuity is indicated by the leading position given to the monarchy's documents, which Daunou could have overlooked, because it concerned printed volumes, stored in the library. But he obviously considered it important to underline the continuity of the history of France.

Why then did he not expand his classificatory framework to the Historical Division? We do not know. One can say only that he thought about it. In 1812, he in effect sketched a project for a new organization of the Archives of the Empire. He proposed "to establish at the head and outside of the three or five great divisions [French, German, Italian, Spanish, Dutch], a General Treasury of Charters that would be composed of: 1) the former *Trésor des chartes* of France such as it now exists; 2) the other charters on parchment, collected in the old and new departments and all reassembled in one and the same chronological series. This preliminary or frontispiece of the Imperial Archives would be the richest depository of the kind that one had ever had the means or even the idea to form." Similarly, the French Division would have the Historical Division, "composed of the oldest elements," at its head.[114]

This proposal, which no one ever even began to apply, is nonetheless significant. It demonstrates, in effect, that the question Daunou was asking concerned the starting point for the history of the French archives: *Trésor des chartes* or National Archives of 1789? A question that seems fruitless to us today, on the one hand because we treat classifications in a purely instrumental fashion and, on the other, because we place the Revolution itself in the continuity of the history of France. In this respect, we are the inheritors of the historians of the nineteenth century, principally of Tocqueville. Daunou, who himself emerged from a period in which the relationship between the ancien régime and the Revolution was seen as a radical rupture, wondered, in reflecting on the classification of the archives, if he was going to make the Revolution a new beginning (in which case he must place the acts of the revolutionary assemblies at their head), or a prolongation of the ancien régime (which would require him to place the *Trésor des chartes* at the top). That the decision on this subject was perceived not as technical, but as ideological, is attested to by a successor of Daunou, the Marquis de Laborde, more than a half century later. Proposing a new classification of the National Archives, which began with an Ecclesiastical Division, he wrote, "I know the effect that the word *Church* placed at the head of the historical documents conserved in the archives would have had on Daunou's spirit, because I experience the same repulsion in seeing the acts and papers of the Committee of Public Safety filling the same spot, even today."[115] An exaggeration, because these papers never appeared there.

In the end, Daunou arrived at a compromise solution. In the Legislative Division, the Revolution followed the ancien régime, while simultaneously opposing itself to it; hence, the two dates 1160 and 1789. In the Administrative Division, the documents of the executive power bridged the frontier between the old and new regimes; proof is the inclusion of the Royal Household in the E series and of the General (Tax) Farm in the G series. (These two series, redefined, today belong to the Ancient Division.) But the significance of these continuities is limited. The position of the Historical Division after the Administrative Division underlines the break between the present and the past by demonstrating that, with regard to the executive power, the present is not a prolongation of the past but a new departure.

The play between continuity and rupture is also found in the interior of the Historical Division, in the opposition between the *Trésor des chartes* and the collections of documents formed during the Revolution. Daunou seems to have been conscious of this. "Although the order established a long time ago in this precious collection," he wrote of the *Trésor des chartes*, "is not very methodical, one has scrupulously maintained it, because it is to this order that both Dupuy's inventory, of which there exist many manuscript copies, and the citations which various authors have made from the pieces of the *Trésor* correspond." And he noted with regard to the K series: "These Monuments, collected in the Archives of several suppressed establishments, make up a second *Trésor des chartes*, which one abstained from melding into the first one." A meritorious abstention because the Bureau for Sorting Deeds proposed exactly the opposite approach.[116]

After time came space, as a prelude to the documents concerning the management of the property of the State. And it all ended, in conformity with theory, with the Judiciary Division. One will note that the distinction between the powers is underlaid by the opposition between Paris and the departments, the first three divisions being those of the central power whereas, of the last three, two referred explicitly to the ensemble of the territory and the third would have, too, if Daunou had succeeded in uniting all of the archives of France, as he had planned.[117] We note again that the order of the series, which in its ensemble corresponded to the hierarchy of the three powers and to that which places Paris above the departments, also corresponded, inside each division, to the hierarchy of institutions. The order of the alphabet, which the series follow and in which the absence of the letters I and W requires the use of the ampersand, lost as a result its purely artificial character and an accord was established between the signs and the things themselves. Daunou's classificatory system thus proceeded from a truly "philosophical" spirit, not only because it depended on Montesquieu, but also because it fully conformed to what one demanded from such a system during the Enlightenment.

All of this did not come from Daunou's mind alone. In 1809, when he put the last touches on his classificatory system, twenty years had passed since the Constituent Assembly's vote creating the first kernel of the National Archives—and since the first classification of the papers that belonged to this Assembly were published by Camus shortly after his nomination.[118] This classification, later extended, divided the National Archives (which at that time, let us recall, were only those of the constituent) into five series designated by the first five letters of the alphabet,[119] a division since maintained, with one significant change: the number of series was reduced to four, and the letter E received a new allocation. The decree of 12 Brumaire, Year II, had added to this initial kernel the Domanial and Judicial Divisions; that of 7 Messidor, a map depository as well as the Temporary Agency of Deeds and its successive reincarnations. At the end of these expansions, in 1804, at the time of Daunou's nomination, the Archives included: "One: the papers deposited by the national assemblies since 1789, inventoried and in very good order; Two: the *Trésor des chartes* inventoried long before, and other historical documents which were collected by the Bureau for Sorting Deeds and to which M. Camus had a summary inventory compiled; Three: a collection of geographical and topographical maps, along with the proceedings of the Division of the Territory and of the State of the Population; Four: a domanial division whose general order was not at all established, the works prescribed by M. Camus having not at all been executed; Five, a judiciary division, the most considerable of all the divisions, in perfect order and summarily inventoried".[120] As we have seen, Daunou imposed on all of this an elegant and logical classification, a product of the Enlightenment spirit. But Daunou's classification had a major flaw: with regard to the past, he replaced real history with a history that was rational or, if one likes, "philosophical," with the result that the collections already entered in the archives could be distributed among its rubrics only at the price of dismemberments and recompositions, from which only the *Trésor des chartes* was excepted. And, with regard to the future, this classification created a framework that one could maintain without changes only in the absence of any new deposit or, alternatively, only on the condition that the institutional system remained in conformity with its rubrics and remained immutable, and that the requests presented to the archives remained thus as well.

But the archives—and Daunou himself—wanted to receive new deposits. In 1810, after a visit to the Hôtel Soubise where the National Archives had just moved, Napoléon asked the minister of the interior to come up with a "proposal for a general decree on the Archives" that would see to it that the administration would deposit all documents anterior to the reign of Louis XIV; fifty years later, it would be the turn of documents from the reigns of Louis XV and of Louis XVI and then from the following epochs.[121] In the proposal that he wrote at the time, Daunou went much further: he proposed the deposit of all documents anterior to 1800 followed, beginning in 1820, by deposits made every ten years.[122] But since the general decree was never promulgated nor even drawn up, the affair ended there.

It returned in the decree of December 22, 1855, but the form retained gave the depositors complete liberty to decide which documents of public interest they considered useful to conserve and which were no longer necessary to them. Certain offices, such as the Ministry of the Interior (after 1811), deposited their papers rather regularly, others deposited them according to a more unpredictable rhythm or not at all. In addition, changes in political regime, followed by the suppression of private organisms henceforth deprived of their raison d'être, or even by administrative restructurings, which made other organisms disappear, resulted in the deposit of their papers at the National Archives. The archives thus received deposits throughout the nineteenth century, whereas institutions were transformed, as well as their public and the questions it addressed to the documents. Hence the growth in number of series, which went from twenty-five under Daunou to thirty-five in the *État sommaire* of 1867.[123] Hence also the modification of the very framework of the divisions and the series: reduction of the number of the first and, in a few cases, redeployment of the second. Hence, finally, the division into subseries of already existing series and the introduction of even smaller subdivisions, especially in the F series, which was the best supplied while also being the most sensitive to political and administrative shake-ups, because it had to account for the fact that new ministries separated themselves one after another from the common trunk that was the Ministry of the Interior.[124]

During this whole period, the National Archives and the departmental archives followed different paths. The departmental archives were born later, following the decree of 5 Brumaire, Year V (October 26, 1796)—third of the revolutionary laws repealed by the law of January 3, 1979—which suspended the sorting of deeds over the quasi totality of the territory and ordered the collection in every departmental capital of "all the deeds and papers dependent on the depositories belonging to the Republic."[125] These archives emerged from the former Royal Archives, but also from ecclesiastical and seigneurial archives. How many of them were there in France at the end of the ancien régime? One thousand two hundred twenty-five, of which four hundred and five were in Paris? Ten thousand?[126] To facilitate the collection of copies destined for the Depository of the Charters, Bertin, himself fortified with history and following Moreau's advice, decided to draw up a "general map" of the archives and charter houses of the realm; in 1769, he launched an investigation to this effect among the governors of the provinces.[127] The responses, collected at the Depository of Charters, must however be treated with extreme prudence, and they justify no numerical conclusion without prior qualification. Let us content ourselves with remarking that the mass of ecclesiastical and seigniorial archives was very large, which is not surprising; there were probably several thousand collections.[128]

Placed under the responsibility of the general secretaries of the prefectures by the law of 28 Pluviôse, Year VIII (February 17, 1800), the departmental archives, inheritors of the part of the ancient deposits that had survived the destruction of the Revolution, long remained depositories for old papers that no one knew what to do with; they suffered greatly from this.[129] The only person interested in them was the minister of the interior, who demanded information about them from the prefects, without ever getting any response.[130] After 1820, they seem to have been abandoned to the point that, according to Guizot in 1834, "the very memory is erased, in several places, by these [revolutionary] translations operated negligently and without formalities. Hence the generally established opinion, become so to speak a tradition, in a large number of departments, that everything perished in these agitated times. It is nevertheless certain that one may still find a considerable part of the ancient archives."[131]

Under pressure from Guizot, especially after the passage of the law of May 10, 1838, which included in the obligatory expenses of the departmental budget the protection and conservation of the archives, the archives excited a growing interest, in particular among learned societies. They were thus the object of several reglementary texts, of which only one will be recalled here: the circular of April 24, 1841, the work of Natalis de Wailly, who introduced into archival practice the principle of respecting funds, strictly opposed to the very idea of methodical classification that Camus and Daunou defended and that led to the practice of sorting, resulting in these collections of documents of diverse origin that are, in the National Archives, the K, L, and M series. This idea betrayed an attitude toward the past that aimed if not at destroying it at least at transforming it so as to make it conform to reason. The principle of respecting funds adopted a conservative attitude toward the past. But must we emphasize this? In the two cases, the past is not presented in the same way: at the end of the eighteenth century, it was incarnated in a system of institutions; sixty years later, there remained only monuments to protect and old papers in the process of decaying.

What the circular of 1841 recommended was "to collect the various documents by *funds*, that is to say, to form a collection of all the deeds coming from a *corps*, an establishment, a family, or an individual, and to arrange the various funds according to a certain order." And de Wailly explained that "it is necessary to understand thoroughly that the mode of classification by funds consists in uniting all the deeds that were the *property* of a single establishment, of a single *corps*, or of a single family, and that the acts which are only related to them must not be confused with the funds of this establishment, of this *corps*, of this family."[132] The classification of the departmental archives thus differed from that of the National Archives in its very principle. In particular, from 1841 on it introduced a split between those documents anterior to the division of France into departments and those that are posterior to this epoch, by imposing a rigorously historical point of view on the archives.[133]

Let us skip over the numerous juridical acts relative to the departmental archives and mention only the decree of March 21, 1884, which united them, as well as the communal and hospital archives, with the National Archives under a bureau of the Ministry for Public Instruction, thus realizing the idea that had already been expressed in the law of 7 Messidor, Year II.[134] This bureau would give way in 1897 to the administration of the Archives of France. Simultaneously, at the turn of the century, the deposits became more regular, following the decree of January 12, 1898, which stipulated that "dossiers, registers, and pieces recognized as useless for the current operations of offices will be released by the ministries and administrations to the National Archives during the first semester of each year, either directly or after staying for a while in a provisional depository." In relation to the previous situation, this was progress. But the lack of any sanction deprived this decree of constraining force, and deposits thus still depended on the good will of the administrations.[135]

Significant changes began to occur only in the 1920s. The law of March 14, 1928, authorized notaries to deposit at the National Archives in Paris and at departmental archives in the provinces minutes that were more than 125 years old, something that led to the creation of the Minutier central.[136] And the decree of July 21, 1936, resolved the problem of deposits from state administrations. The ministers, who all signed this decree, finally recognized the principle of obligatory and periodical deposit in archival depositories of the papers they generated, as soon as these papers had become useless, in order to be conserved or destroyed with the approval of the departments concerned. They forbid any destruction of documents other than "waste paper" without a visa from the administration of the Archives of France.[137] It was in forcing the letter of this decree a bit that Charles Braibant, director of the Archives of France, succeeded in 1952 in installing at the Ministry of the Interior the first Mission on the Archives, charged with establishing a permanent liaison between the two institutions and with ensuring deposits.[138]

A pivotal period in their history, the second half of the nineteenth century also saw a change in the relations between the French archives and the public. Beginning in the 1840s, the creation of a reading room by Letronne, Daunou's successor, greatly ameliorated working conditions; before, one had been obliged to use the office of the division whose collections one was consulting.[139] However, despite Article 37 of the law of 7 Messidor, Year II, access to the National Archives remained limited; according to the regulation of 1856, in order to have rights to immediate communication of the requested documents or to an explicitly justified refusal, it was necessary to be a public functionary, member or honorary of the Institute, doctor of a university faculty, paleographical archivist, or student at the École des Chartes. Thus in his report Ravaisson proposed to divide the National Archives into ancient and modern archives, the first having "their own special rules of communication, rules dictated by the most open and liberal spirit."[140]

This wish was satisfied only by the texts promulgated as a result of the decree of May 14, 1887, which accorded to anyone the right to obtain access to documents conserved in the archives provided that they were more than fifty years old and were not reserved by the administration that had deposited them. Access was granted, it is true, in a reading room that, "low, narrow, [and] poorly arranged [. . .] dishonors the establishment of the Hôtel Soubise."[141] This did not prevent the number of communications from rising from about 590 on average between 1847 and 1853 to more than 20,000 in 1888. The same year, there were more than 57,000 at the departmental archives.[142] Let us add the appearance of numerous research tools in the departmental archives, since the 1840s, and the multiplication of these tools by the National Archives, beginning in the 1860s. And let us end with the opening of the ministerial archives that, without ever having been hermetically sealed, were nevertheless very difficult to access. Even in the 1880s, those of the Ministry of Public Works remained out of reach and it was still necessary to have an authorization from the minister in order to penetrate into those of the Ministries of Foreign Affairs, of the Navy, or of War, where only the ancient collections could be studied. In 1874, the year they were opened, the Archives of Foreign Affairs communicated documents only from before 1774, and again only under certain conditions; moreover, the frontier fell in 1814. But already, during the following decade, the delays in access were everywhere reduced and a rule of fifty years was adopted by the National Archives.[143] The frontier between memory and history thus became, for all public archives, an internal frontier whose location is determined by regulatory texts and that tends to move ever closer to the present. The time of memory shortens, while the time of history continues to expand.

THE ARCHIVES TODAY AND TOMORROW

Lack of space obliges us to leave aside the long gestation of the integral connection between historiography and the archives, institutions whose relations were, until the beginning of the nineteenth century, unstable as well as factual. At the base of this connection is the conviction that history is produced with sources and that there are only written sources, a conviction that would be erected as a fundamental dogma of scholarly history in the second half of the last century, only to be abandoned, at the beginning of this century, as new sources acquired value: first of all, objects and landscapes; then, over the course of the last fifteen years, words and images; this is another subject that merits more ample study. Here it will suffice to note that the repudiation of the fundamental dogma by scholarly history in no way broke its privileged connection to the archives. The geographer-historians of the Vidalian school assiduously frequented them. Later, the *Annales* of Marc Bloch and Lucien Febvre, even as they tried to direct historians toward nonwritten sources,[144] displayed a sustained interest in the archives and the work of archivists, by examining notarial archives and company archives and by reporting on inventories, repertories, catalogues, the *Gazette des archives*, and notices on particular collections.[145] As for the historians of this school, from Bloch and Febvre themselves, continuing through Ernest Labrousse and Fernand Braudel, and up to today, they have extended and deepened archival research in comparison with their predecessors. This fact is inscribed in the increased demands on scholarly history, which have significantly impacted the choice and the treatment of documents used.

Today, history is no longer made exclusively in the archives. It is also made—sometimes even primarily—on archaeological digs, in museums and laboratories, in the course of investigations in the field and of collections of oral testimonies, if not on an editing table. The archives nevertheless remain the locus par excellence for the production of history. First of all, because the renewal of the questions that history asks and of the methods that it applies leads it to search for new information in funds that have already been used and to value other funds that no one has yet employed. Secondly, because technical improvements permit the historian to exploit better and better the very numerous sources of medieval and early modern history; the computer henceforth renders it possible to examine large documentary series that, until now, could only be partially studied. In addition, the displacement of the center of gravity of history toward the nineteenth and twentieth centuries, including the present time, has reinforced historians' dependence on the archives, which preserve most of the sources from this epoch.

History thus always needs the archives. And the archives, on their side, have known how to satisfy the successive demands of historians by making accessible documents that are likely to answer their questions. The first step in this direction was made, we have seen, at the end of the 1920s with the creation of the Minutier central. But notaries are ministerial officials and their papers thus possess the status of public papers.[146] The inclusion of these papers in the archives did not therefore call into question the doctrine according to which the archives must conserve only documents "whose official origin is a guarantee of authenticity," a doctrine that remained in force until the time of Langlois.[147] However, it was necessary to find a place for documents deposited in the archives not by the administrations, but—and the very expression is evocative—"by extraordinary paths," that is by gifts, bequests, or purchases. Thus, in 1856, one opened the series AB XIX, in which were found, in the beginning, personal and family papers. But the arrival of more and more numerous collections emanating from institutions and business enterprises has shown the limits of this solution. In 1917, one therefore opened the series AJ for them.[148]

The rupture with the traditional doctrine that prevented the National Archives from following an active policy of protecting private funds, and in particular the archives of business enterprises, came only in the years immediately after the war, under the direction of Charles Braibant, inspired by Robert-Henri Bautier.[149] In 1949, with the creation of the Office of Economic Archives, Private Archives, and Microfilm, four new series were opened: AP (personal and family archives), AQ (archives of business enterprises), AR (press archives), and AS (archives of associations); numerous funds that had previously been classified in the AB XIX and AJ series were divided up among these new funds.[150] In 1952, the budget of the National Archives included, for the first time, a sum devoted to the purchase of private archives.[151] The distinction established in the nineteenth

Fig. 2.8
Saint-Chapelle, seat of the charters Treasury from the eighteenth century
until 1783. Engraving from *La Géométrie classique* by Desargues, around
1703.

Fig. 2.9
The Hôtel Soubise, rue des Francs-Bourgeois, in Paris, seat of the National
Archives since 1808.

century between private papers and public papers was thus erased bit by
bit, which brought about an enlargement of the repertory of documents
conserved in the archives and, in time, accessible to researchers.

This also modifies the very character of the Archives of France, which
ceased to be devoted exclusively to the conservation of the official memory
and to serve a history that was merely a tributary of documents expressing
the official point of view, even if it did have to submit them to criticism.
Certainly, the private funds that the archives acquired were supposed to
hold a "public interest," a fluid notion that has been condemned to see
its content vary. It is nonetheless true that since the '50s the Archives of
France have stopped identifying the memory and history of the nation

with the memory and history of the State, by putting into effect a policy
of acquiring private archives. The law of January 3, 1979, only consecrates
this change, which also affected the very content of this memory and this
history—which are no longer, as they long were, limited to political,
diplomatic, military, and administrative facts. The papers of notaries, of
families, and of business enterprises permit this memory and this history
to embrace economic and social life, as seen in cooperation and conflict
between groups and individuals.

The second act of the expansion of the repertory of documents conserved in the Archives of France began in the 1980s. It was then that oral
testimony collected by the archivists themselves for the needs of the ar-

Fig. 2.10

The Caran, 1988, work of the architect Stanislas Fiszer: the façade on the rue des Quatre-Fils; on the right, the magazines constructed under Napoleon III.

chives, and no longer gathered only by others, made its appearance.[152] Hence a new attention accorded to voice recordings, which at that time had nevertheless already been present in the archives for more than twenty years.[153] Likewise, it was in the 1960s that one became conscious of the importance of figurative documents and that one began to make note of photographs in the inventories. But it was necessary to wait again until the 1980s in order for their specificity to be recognized and the problems that they pose for archivists to be discussed in the framework of reflection on the "new archives."[154] The same thing happened with audiovisual documents: from the 1960s on, their importance was no longer in doubt, but it was only in the course of the last decade that they appeared in the center of the archivists' horizon.[155]

Until the end of the last century, an archival document was almost always a manuscript. Then, following the spread of typing, of mechanical reproduction and photocopying, following also the promotion of printed archives by economic and social history,[156] a document was identified with a written text. The developments that we have just described, crowned by the arrival in the archives of electronic recordings that only machines can decrypt,[157] end by in fact dissociating the notion of document not only from writing, but also from natural language. The extreme generality that the law of January 3, 1979, gives to the notion of document and, consequently, to that of the archives only records the mutations that have affected the content of the archives over the course of the preceding years, even while anticipating those that are certainly to come. Provoked by technical innovations and by changes in administrative work, these mutations also reveal the influence exercised by the scholarly historian on the archives and their capacity to adapt themselves to his or her particular demands.

The growth and the diversification of funds only profits history, however, if it is followed reasonably quickly by the creation and publication of research instruments that permit their exploitation. It is impossible to present here the entire production of inventories, repertories, and guides pursued since the middle of the nineteenth century.[158] Let us therefore limit ourselves to indicating the appearance of research instruments in the computer age. One illustration, among others, is the database ARCADE, which "concerns documents coming from the funds of the archives of the Administration of Beaux-Arts (orders, acquisitions of art works by the State in the nineteenth and twentieth centuries) conserved in the National Archives in the sub-series F^{21}" and that permits notably the publishing of an index or the compiling of statistics according to different criteria.[159]

Final element of the adaptation of the archives to the demands of the times: a renovation of architecture and a perceptible improvement in working conditions both for the personnel itself and for users. The great number of new buildings for departmental archives erected between 1948 and the 1960s contrasts with the quasi stagnation of the years between the two world wars. And the new generation of these buildings, which date from the last twenty-five years, distinguishes itself from the preceding generation by an increase in surface area open to the public and by an improved consideration for the physical constraints imposed by the conservation of documents and the needs of personnel.[160] The symbol of these changes, the Center for the Reception and Research of the National Archives (*Centre d'accueil et de recherche des Archives nationales*, or CARAN), inaugurated on March 23, 1988, and opened to the public on June 6 of the same year, was immediately hailed as a success. By providing a large reading room with 360 seats, a reference room with 72 seats, and 100 seats in the microfilm consulting room; by also giving visitors the capability of ordering documents by computer and the opportunity of reserving them in advance from home via Minitel, the *État général des fonds*, and the instruction "3616 CARAN" at hand, the CARAN in effect breaks with the miserable tradition of the libraries and archives of Paris and signifies the entry of these libraries and archives into modernity. In the history of the National Archives, the CARAN is the greatest event, if not since their very creation, at least and very certainly since 1847, when the first reading room was opened.[161]

Today, the French archives are not what they were even half a century ago. The repertory of documents that one conserves, sorts, classifies, inventories, and communicates there has been so profoundly modified that the very idea of a document has been affected. The number of documents of every kind has undergone a dizzying growth. And the container has followed the content. How to qualify all of these changes? Mutation?

Revolution?[162] The two terms are used: one speaks of the "documentary revolution," of the "archival revolution," of "mutations of contemporary archival practice."[163] But behind these discrepancies in terminology there emerges an accord on the essential issue. And the essential issue is the observation that over the course of the last fifty years the archives have entered a new world, with the positive effects that we have just rapidly evoked. But, with regard to the contemporary archives, this new world is accompanied by problems that are sufficiently serious for one to wonder—and to wonder in the *Gazette des archives*—if the archives still have a future.[164]

Among these problems, one of the most important is the inflation of the contemporary archives, that is to say the growth of documentary masses that are produced by institutions and that attain such enormous dimensions that one hence wonders not how to conserve them, but how to destroy them. What remains of them after initial eliminations is still so voluminous that the archives risk being rapidly swallowed up, whatever the size of the storage space, and it seems very unlikely that there will ever be historians with the desire and the means to explore these mountains of paper whose significance is not always obvious.[165]

With inflation there is also fragility. The new materials are in general more difficult to conserve than paper, especially the good paper of centuries past. Such is the case with films of highly flammable and unstable substances, produced until the middle of this century; with photographs, especially in color, which cannot tolerate light; with voice and computer recordings, which are very sensitive to dust, to variations in temperature and hygrometry, to magnetical fields.[166] The growing use of electronic mail, which is not always transcribed on paper, combined with the possibility of easily erasing the content of a computer memory, moreover threatens to result in a situation in which the archives will be submerged under a flood of relatively insignificant papers, whereas the documents that are truly important for citizens and for historians will disappear without leaving a trace.[167]

And these are far from the only problems posed by the new materials. There is another, which is tied to their great diversity. Computer technology uses disks, cassettes, videodisks, optical numerical disks, CD-ROMs; and nothing allows us to suppose that this list is exhaustive. It is the same with regard to sound. Documents recorded with new technologies can be read only by machines that age quickly and disappear rapidly from the market. "What will we do when we have a computer memory which is readable with a type of machine that no longer exists?"[168] The question was asked fifteen years ago. Today, since the appearance of personal computers and the proliferation of machines that treat text—products that are produced by different firms and that are generally incompatible—the question is even more dramatic. Is it thus necessary "to reform patent law to require producers to deposit all of their models and to maintain them in working order for all eternity?"[169] And will it be necessary, in order to have access to documents, to preserve also specimens of every type of machine ever produced, in a way combining the archives with museums of computer technology? It is also easier to collect machines than to employ all the software needed to run them.[170] Since computer technology is always progressing, it is highly probable that, in the coming years, the archives—and especially the contemporary archives—will experience a revolution even more radical than that which transformed them over the course of the last half century.

Alongside this revolution, the very institution of the archives has witnessed an expansion that has profoundly modified its position in France. This expansion stems first of all from the appearance and multiplication of the archives of business enterprises. Let us cite as examples Saint-Gobain, which constructed a building for its archives at Blois; Rhône-Poulenc, which did the same at Besançon; or again Total and E.D.F.-G.D.F. By dispatching graduates of the École des chartes to take charge of the management of these depositories, the Archives of France demonstrated the importance they attribute to them. But the big firms are not the only ones to concern themselves with their archives.[171] The Archives du monde du travail (Archives of the World of Work) plan to collect the documents of patrons and workers in five depositories, of which (at the moment) only that at Roubaix is up and running.[172] And the Centre rhénan d'archives d'entreprise de Mulhouse (Rhine Center for the Business Archives of Mulhouse), the only private organization of this type in France, collects the archives of enterprises that have disappeared as well as of enterprises that still exist.[173] The expansion of the archival institution also means the creation of editorial and audiovisual archives, notably those of the Institut national de l'audiovisuel (National Institute of Audiovisual Materials), of the Établissement cinématographique et photographique des armées (Cinematographic and Photographic Organization of the Armies), and of the Service des archives du film (Office of Film Archives).[174] It means, finally, becoming conscious of the importance of scientific archives in establishments that have possessed them since their beginnings—and creating new ones.[175]

The expansion of the archival institution does not stop there. In order to convince oneself, it suffices to inventory the papers of a statistically representative French family. The following would be approximately the result: national identity cards, often passports too, voter registration card(s), professional card(s), family record book, birth certificates, marriage certificates, school certificates and diplomas, affidavits, pay stubs, retirement fund statements, social security card(s), checks, bank account statement(s), savings account book(s), credit card(s), property deeds or rental agreements or both, insurance paper(s), rent or mortgage receipts, electric bills, telephone bills, radio and television taxes, income declarations, tax forms, property tax statements, driver's license, grey cards, discount cards, warranty statements for different appliances, bills. In sum, more than thirty types of documents, many of which one is required by law to keep for years, or forever, along with copies of some of them, which grow over time, yielding some hundred if not some thousand items.

And that is not all. The documents that we have just enumerated proceed only from relationships with the State and with local powers, administrations, banks, and national and private enterprises. To these we must add relationships with the medical establishment, especially since they are becoming more frequent, and the list of documents to take into account is supplemented by X-rays that one must bring to the next exam, electrocardiograms, test results of all sorts. Private life is not to be neglected either, producing its lot of letters, journals, souvenirs—old school books, old calendars—hundreds of photos, as well as (more and more often) films or video recordings, cassettes, diskettes. Let us not forget, finally, alongside these domestic or personal papers, family papers received as an inheritance, which sometimes go back several centuries to a distant past.[176]

Taken together, all the documents that thus accumulate in our homes are produced or received by physical individuals in the exercise of their daily activities as citizen, spouse, parent, child, worker, welfare recipient, proprietor or renter, client, taxpayer, driver, patient, consumer—I stop there. These documents do not result from a deliberate decision, as is the case with a collector of old papers. They are secreted in an organic fashion by the deeds and gestures that fill our daily lives. These documents therefore form the archives in the strictest sense of the term, that is to say, in the sense of the first article of the Law 79–18 of January 3, 1979, and of archival doctrine. It follows that with the exception of individuals from the "fourth world" who often have neither a fixed residence nor papers, all households in France are containers of archives. And all of us, without even knowing it, are archivists. Amateur archivists, but archivists all the same.[177]

Documentary inflation is therefore not a malady only of public archives. Everyone can discover its symptoms without leaving home. As for the countless commissions charged with simplifying relations between the administration and users and with curbing, even with decreasing, the flood of papers, until now they do not seem to have obtained spectacular results. In this domain, it is rather technical innovations that, for several years now, are beginning to yield their effects: thus the propagation of credit cards has provoked a decrease in the number of checks and therefore of check registers that one must keep; the possibility of making certain payments monthly and of authorizing deductions from one's bank or postal account reduces the number of bills; the use of personal computers and of Minitel replaces letters or forms in certain cases and is becoming more and more frequent. May we see in all of these facts a foreshadowing of a society without paper, which would be supplanted by electronics? Such a society is difficult for us to conceive. But, in the eleventh century, a clerk would certainly not have imagined a society without parchment. And, in the fifteenth century, the Humanists did not think that the development of printing would little by little confine the manuscript to a role as rough draft, note, personal letter—in short to a private sphere. Without subscribing to visions of a society without paper, one can nevertheless not deny that paper will see its uses transformed in relation to what they are today, something that will have repercussions for the content and operation of public and private archives.

Eight centuries separate us from the Battle of Fréteval (1194) in which Philippe Auguste lost his travelling archives, something that led him, it seems, to create the *Trésor des chartes*. And two centuries have passed since the decree of 7 Messidor, Year II. The memory that the archives preserve, the history that they inspire, and the relationship between the two changed first slowly, under the ancien régime, and then in a dramatic fashion, following the Revolution. Originally dynastic, memory became connected to the State (even while remaining dynastic), whereas history simultaneously changed from chronicle to erudite treatise. But it still did not distinguish itself from memory by a difference of perspectives; so much did the guardians of the one and the practitioners of the other—they were often the same—identify themselves with the past of the dynasty and the State. Yet memory—in this case, the archives—remained the property of the individual whose memory it was; from the moment it was published, history belonged to all. Thus, contrary to memory, history was worked out through controversies.

The Revolution began by instigating two types of archives: those that it was in the process of producing and those of the ancien régime; their union at the heart of one and the same establishment was not at all destined in advance. Once realized, the Revolution made the dynastic and State past, which before then had been an object of memory, a virtual object of history. As for the Revolution itself, it nourished the new State memory, which was erected as national memory. That is why, at the end of the Revolution, the French past found itself at the center of a double controversy. On the one side, between a history-continuity, prolongation of the dynastic and State memory, and a history-rupture, which actively rejected all identification with prerevolutionary political institutions. On the other side, controversy between the new State memory and the memory of the people, both of which claimed to represent the national memory. This latter conflict also manifested itself in history, where those who examined it by identifying themselves with the State opposed themselves to those who adopted the popular perspective in one of its varieties. The supposed common ground between the two—the continuous existence of the same moral individual, motherland, or nation—would be contested only in the twentieth century with the illumination of the divisions or rather the conflicts internal to the State or the nation, and especially with the idea that the State and the nation are not the substrata of events but the works of forces that vary according to time and place, which cooperate and that confront each other.

This trip through the French public archives during the eight centuries of their existence may be summed up, in an initial approximation, by the expression: first from memory to history, then the coexistence of the two. From memory to history, to a scholarly history, inseparable from the memory of the monarchy: this is illustrated by the trajectory of the *Trésor des chartes*, from Pierre d'Étampes, the first guardian of the *Trésor* whose name we know, to Moreau and Bréquigny, passing by du Tillet and Dupuy. From memory to history but this time to a scholarly history inseparable from the memory of the nation: this is illustrated by the trajectory of the National Archives, from Camus and Daunou to Guizot and Michelet, and later to Langlois and Lavisse.

Beginning in the 1830s, the archives were made to serve historical research; they would need more than fifty years truly to adapt to this role but, in the end, it would happen. During this time, the problem of deposits not having been resolved, the archives were only secondarily depositories of the memory of the administration. Things changed only beginning in the middle of this century, when the decree of 1936 began to make its effect felt with, notably, the creation of missions to the ministries and the opening at Fontainebleau in 1969 of the Cité interministérielle des archives (Interministerial City of Archives), which seventeen years later became the Centre des archives contemporaines (Center of Contemporary Archives). Beginning in the '50s, therefore, the archives belong both to memory and history; the problems that they have to resolve in their daily operation result largely from the necessity of reconciling the demands of the one and the other.

But there is another dimension, just as important, to the temporal trip through the French public archives. The evocation of three emblematic buildings brings it to light: Sainte-Chapelle, which sheltered the *Trésor des chartes* from the thirteenth century until 1783; the Soubise Palace, where the National Archives were installed in 1808; and the CARAN, opened 180 years later. The archives thus pass, so to speak, from the sacred to the profane. But this expression, too general, demands deciphering. Supposed to possess a perpetual validity, the documents deposited in the *Trésor des chartes* are removed from alteration and corruption. They exist in the *aevum*, which—contrary to the *aeternitas*, reserved to God alone—has a beginning and an end but that—contrary to the *tempus*—experiences no substantial changes; it is the domain of continuity, of duration. These documents are therefore not thought of in terms of relations between the past, present, and future. They are exterior to time. Hence their sacred character, which means that they are in their proper place in Sainte-Chapelle.

They still preserved this sacredness in the seventeenth and eighteenth centuries, when the *Trésor des chartes* became essentially a closed fund. Certainly, for those who make these documents an object of study, they belong henceforth to a more or less distant past. But this past is supposed to run into the present without rupture; it is not a past accomplished and achieved; it begins but does not finish. The temporal interval that separates them is filled, in effect, only by accidental variations: the kings succeed each other but the dynasty remains, and even if the institutions change, the French monarchy continues in its essential identity. Everything happens as if the monarchy were always situated in the *aevenum*, and the *Trésor des chartes* with it. This continuity, which is the basis for the identification between each king and all his predecessors and between each generation of state servants and the ensemble of the monarchical tradition, makes the royal and state past an object of memory and prevents scholarly history from treating the documents it studies simply as sources, because they always preserve their normative value. History in the service of law is history in the service of memory.

The modern archives are not inscribed in the division between *aeternitas*, *aevum*, and *tempus*. They exist in time. In a time that accepts and even supposes substantial changes, of which the Revolution supplies the privileged model. And a time in which the present differs from the past not superficially but in its profound nature, just as the future in its profound nature will be different from the present. Without having been dictated by such elevated considerations, the installation of the National Archives in the Soubise Palace after the revolutionary (mis)adventures testifies to this game of continuities and ruptures; it underscores the link between the archives and the past—a past that, although in certain respects continuing into the present, is in others terminated, achieved, revolved, and that inevitably will remain entirely this way in the future, becoming then an object of history.

Today, the archives conserve, sort, classify, and inventory the documents of the present in order to be able, when the moment arrives, to communicate them to the historians of tomorrow, of the day after tomorrow, and of a time as far into the future as one wishes. This fact materializes in the architecture of the CARAN; its interior setup and its computerized equipment show, alongside many others (in particular the Center of Contemporary Archives at Fontainebleau), that the archives are in no way a constitutionally outdated institution. The link that they maintain with the past is subordinated to their orientation toward the future. Contrary to appearances, the modern archives are, like museums, a futurocentric institution.

NOTES:

1. The text of the decree is found in *Nouveaux textes relatifs aux archives*, 3rd ed. (Paris: Archives nationales, 1988). All texts regulating the archives are cited from this work. Due to lack of space, references are reduced to a strict minimum: to the sources of citations or information given in the text. The following abbreviations are used: A.N. (Archives nationales), B.N. (Bibliothèque nationale), Bordier (Henri Bordier, *Les Archives de la France* [Paris, 1855]), Duchein (Michel Duchein, *Études d'archivistique 1957–1992* [Paris: Association des Archivistes français, 1992]), E.G.F. (*Archives nationales: État général des fonds*, 5 vols., under the direction of Jean Favier [Paris: Archives nationales, 1978–88,]), Laborde (Marquis de Laborde, *Les Archives de la France: Leurs vicissitudes sous la révolution, leur prospérité sous l'empire* [Paris, 1866]), *Manuel* (*Manuel d'archivistique: Théorie et pratique des archives publiques en France*, work compiled by the Association of French Archivists [*Association des archivistes français*] [Paris: Archives nationales, 1991; reprint of the 1970 edition]).

2. Concerning this law, see Ariane Ducrot, "Comment fut élaborée et votée la loi sur les archives du 3 janvier 1979," *La Gazette des archives* 104 (1979): 17–33. The text of the law is found in the same issue, 34–41.

3. See Christine de Tourtier-Bonazzi, *Le Témoignage oral aux archives: De la collecte à la communication* (Paris: Archives nationales, 1990), 28.

4. See *Manuel*, 540 sq. *Les Archives audiovisuelles*, Actes du 27e congrès national des archivistes français, Limoges, September 27, 1987 (Paris: Archives nationales, 1988).

5. On the notion of *semaphore*, see my "Pour une histoire des semaphores: À propos des vases des Médicis," *Le Genre humain* 14 (1986): 17–36; and *Collectors and Curiosities: Paris and Venice, 1500–1800*, trans. Elizabeth Wiles-Portier (Cambridge: Polity, 1990).

6. See Paul Zumthor, "Document et monument: À propos des plus anciens textes de langue française," *Revue des sciences humaines* 97 (1960): 5–19; Michel Foucault, *The Archaeology of Knowledge*, trans. A. M. Sheridan Smith (New York: Pantheon, 1982), especially 6ff.; Michel de Certeau, "L'Opération historique," in *Faire de l'histoire*, under the direction of Jacques Le Goff and Pierre Nora (Paris: Gallimard, 1974), 1:3–41, especially 20ff.; Jacques Le Goff, "Documento/monumento," in *Enciclopedia Einaudi* (Turin, 1978), 5:38–48.

7. See also Paul Léon, *La Vie des monuments français* (Paris: Picard, 1951).

8. "Les Monuments historiques demain," colloquium held at La Salpêtrière, November 1984 (Paris: Ministry of Culture and Communication, 1987), especially 63ff.

9. See *Les Nouvelles archives: Formation et collecte*, Actes du 28e congrès national des archivistes français, Paris, September 29–October 1, 1986 (Paris: Archives nationales, 1987).

10. See the articles collected in *L'Histoire et ses méthodes*, vol. 11, under the direction of Charles Samaran (Paris: Gallimard, Encyclopédie de la Pléiade, 1961), especially Robert-Henri Bautier, "Les Archives," 1120–66.

11. See Jean Favier, "Les Archives de l'an 2000," report made to the Academy of the Navy on October 22, 1976 (Paris: Académie de Marine, 1977).

12. *Manuel*, 22–23.

13. See Jean-Pierre Babelon et al., *Centenaire du musée de l'histoire de France: L'Oeuvre du marquis de Laborde aux archives nationales* (Paris: Archives nationales, 1968).

14. *Manuel*, 103ff.

15. See *La Gazette des archives* 137–38 (1987), consecrated entirely to the missions.

16. Jean Le Pottier, "La Communication des documents publics contemporains: Synthèse des comptes rendus des réunions régionales de l'association des archivistes français," *La Gazette des archives* 130–31 (1985): 213–24, here 217. See also Jean Favier, "La Communication des archives contemporaines en France: Droit et pratique," ibid., 202–9. This issue of the *Gazette* contains the proceedings of the colloquium "Droit à l'information, droit au secret: La Communication des archives contemporaines."

17. *Manuel*, 66 (citation), 112, 161ff.

18. See Duchein, "Le Respect des fonds en archivistique: Principes théoriques et problèmes pratiques" (1977), in Duchein, 9–34.

19. The most important collection for the history of the National Archives is the AB series, but there are also sources for the history of the archives in the J, M, and F series. There are sources, moreover, in the collections of the Manuscript Department at the National Library (B.N.). See Lucien Auvray and René Poupardin, *Catalogue des manuscrits de la collection Baluze* (Paris, 1921); Léon Dorez, *Catalogue de la collection Dupuy*, 2 vols. (Paris, 1899); Suzanne Solente, *Table alphabétique*, 2 vols. (Paris, 1928); Auguste Molinier, *Inventaire sommaire de la collection Joly de Fleury* (Paris, 1881); Henri Omont, *Inventaire des manuscrits de la collection Moreau* (Paris, 1891); R. Poupardin, *Catalogue des manuscrits des collections Duchesne et Brequigny* (Paris, 1905).

20. Duchein, "Requiem pour trois lois défuntes" (1979), in Duchein, 81–84.

21. Armand-Gaston Camus, *État des archives nationales au premier octobre 1791* (Paris, n.d.), 6. See also Bronislaw Baczko, *Une éducation pour la démocratie: Textes et projets de l'époque révolutionnaire* (Paris: Garnier, 1982), 17ff.

22. See *Archives parlementaires*, 8:302; and François Furet and Ran Halévi, eds., *Orateurs de la Révolution française* (Paris: Gallimard, Bibliothèque de la Pléiade, 1989), 103–4.

23. See his notice in M. Michaud, ed., *Biographie universelle* (Paris, 1854–65), 6:521–22. The papers of Camus are at the A.N. in 163 AP and AB Vᵃ1ᶜ. See also Pierre Géraudel, "A.-G. Camus, garde des archives nationales (1740–1804)" (thesis of the École des Chartes), in *Positions des thèses soutenues par les élèves de la promotion de 1942 pour obtenir le diplôme d'archiviste-paléographe* (Nogent-le-Rotrou, 1942), 61–67. On Camus' archival interests before the Revolution, see Amédée Outrey, "Sur la notion d'archives en France à la fin du XVIIIe siècle," *Revue historique du droit français et étranger*, 4th series, 31 (1953): 277–86, especially 280ff.

24. *Archives parlementaires*, 16:561ff.; 18:572–74 and 648–49.

25. *Rapport présenté au nom des commissaires aux archives par M. Blanchon, l'un d'eux, le 20 décembre 1791* (Paris, 1791), 1.

26. On the changes in title of the director of the National Archives, see Eugène Lelong, *Archives* (an extract from vol. 5 of the *Répertoire alphabétique du droit français*) (Paris, 1889), § 101; On Daunou, see M. A. H. Taillandier, *Documents biographiques sur C.-F. Daunou* (Paris, 1847), and infra, note 106. Daunou's papers are found at the B.N.: n. acq. fr. 20567, 21566, 21880–21933, 22199. On the ressemblance between Daunou and Camus, see Bordier, 15.

27. *Archives parlementaires*, 17:652; Bordier, 4–5.

28. François Furet, "Ancien Régime," in *Critical Dictionary of the French Revolution*, under the direction of François Furet and Mona Ozouf, trans. Arthur Goldhammer (Cambridge: Belknap, 1989), 604–15.

29. *Archives parlementaires*, 19:544.

30. On the burnings of the papers see Bordier, 327ff.; for the opposite point of view, Laborde, 21ff., 217ff. See also the excellent article by Edgar Boutaric, "Le Vandalisme révolutionnaire: Les Archives pendant la Révolution française," *Revue des questions historiques* 12 (1872): 325–96.

31. Dom C.-F. Toustain and Dom R.- Tassin, *Nouveau traité de diplomatique* (Paris, 1750), 1:64ff.; Outrey, "Sur la notion d'archives," 282ff.

32. Pierre-Camille Le Moine, preface to *Diplomatique-pratique ou traité de l'arrangement des archives et trésors des chartes, ouvrage nécessaire aux commissaires à terriers [. . .] et à tous ceux qui veulent s'adonner à l'étude des Monuments de l'antiquité* (Metz, 1765), 2.

33. Duc d'Aiguillon, "Motion sur les privilèges particuliers et sur les droits féodaux et seigneuriaux," August 4, 1789, in *Les Orateurs de la révolution française*, 3.

34. The text of the decree is in *Réimpression de l'ancien Moniteur* (Paris, 1847), 18:330–31, here 330.

35. The anonymous author (whom I believe to have been Cheyré) of a *Rapport général sur les archives*, written between the end of 1808 and 1809, notes in this regard: "The Archives of the Assemblies became in this moment General Archives, because the Archivist responsible for protecting these acts made himself Archivist of the Re-

public and acquired the direct surveillance of all the Archives of Paris," A.N., AB V^A 5–11, ff^os 60–61.

36. For everything that follows, see *Archives parlementaires*, 92:177–80 (report of Dubois) and 180–82 (decree).

37. Pierre Santoni, "Archives et violence: À propos de la loi du 7 messidor an II," *La Gazette des archives* 146–47 (1989): 199–214. This important issue published the acts of the colloquium organized by the Association of French Archivists, *Archives et révolution: Création ou destruction* (Châteauvallon, March 10–11, 1988).

38. Duchein, "Requiem," in Duchein, 82–83, note.

39. See Duchein, "La Révolution française et les archives: La Mémoire et l'oubli dans l'imaginaire républicain" (1987), in Duchein, 59–66.

40. Édouard Pommier, *L'Art de la liberté: Doctrines et débats de la Révolution française* (Paris: Gallimard, 1991), 132ff.

41. *Instruction préliminaire arrêtée par le comité des décrets, procès-verbaux et archives. . . .* Neither place nor date of publication is given on the title page, but the work is dated (11) 24 Prairial, Year 3 (June 12, 1795).

42. On the personnel of the Bureau for Sorting Deeds, see the biographical notices in Bordier, 75ff. On the criticisms that the bureau received from authorities, see Laborde, 133ff., 354–55.

43. *Tableau indicatif des dépôts, archives et chartriers existant à Paris* [1794 or 1795], A.N., AB V^C 1.

44. The manuscript text of the decree of 5 Floréal, Year 4, can be found in A.N., AB V^C 3–3.

45. *Compte général rendu par l'agence temporaire des titres aux membres composans le directoire exécutif* (not dated, but from the end of Brumaire, Year 4 [end of October 1795]), A.N., AB V^C 2.

46. [Villiers de Terrage], *Compte rendu par le Bureau de triage des titres ou [deux] comptes des travaux du Bureau du triage des titres* (one report from the establishment of the bureau up to the month of Ventôse, Year 7 [end of March 1799]; the other from this month up to the first of Vendémiaire, Year 8 [September 25, 1799]), A.N., AB V^C 3–1.

47. *Compte rendu par les membres du Bureau du triage des titres du département de la Seine*, printed (dated 25 Thermidor, Year 8 [August 13, 1800]), A.N., AB V^C 2.

48. Laborde, passim, and A.N., AB V^C 2.

49. A.N., AB V^C 2.

50. *Rapport fait en frimaire an VI, par le Bureau de Triage des Titres, sur le dépôt connu sous le nom du Trésor des chartes*, f° 162ff. Several copies of this report exist. I have used the AB XIII 2.

51. A.N., AB II 5 and especially AB V^A 3.

52. *Le Rédacteur* 1155 (27 Pluviôse, Year 7 [February 15, 1799]).

53. *Journal des débats et lois du Corps législatif* 38 (Nivôse, Year 8).

54. A.N., AB V^A 4–13.

55. The text of the decree is in Bordier, 391–92.

56. *Archives parlementaires [. . .] de 1800 à 1860* (Paris, 1862), 1:669–70, 673, 687ff., 703ff., 723ff.

57. See these proposals in A.N., AB VI 1.

58. See Gabriel Richou, *Traité théorique et pratique des archives publiques* (Paris, 1883), with a chronological tool, 279ff.; E. Lelong, *Archives*, and infra, note 109.

59. Bordier, 12.

60. All of the documents referred to are in A.N., AB V^C 3–3.

61. A.N., AB V^A 4–2 and 4–17; AB II 5.

62. A.N., AB V^A 5–9 (letter from Daunou to Regnaud de Saint-Jean d'Angély of March 1807).

63. Bordier, 22.

64. *Demande du tribunal d'appel séant à Paris, tendant à ce que les anciens registres des tribunaux de Paris soient remis sous garde du Greffier. Observations de l'archiviste sur cette demande. Réponse du tribunal d'appel* (Paris, 11 Thermidor, Year 12 [July 29, 1804]), 15.

65. E.G.F., 1:185ff.; H.-François Delaborde, "Étude sur la constitution du trésor des chartes et sur les origines de la série des sacs dite aujourd'hui supplément," in *Layettes du trésor des chartes* (Paris, 1863–1909), 5:181ff.

66. E.G.F., 1:218; on the colors of wax used to seal the royal acts and their meaning, see Octave Morel, *La Grande chancellerie royale et l'expédition des lettres royaux de l'avènement de Philippe de Valois jusqu'à la fin du XIVe siècle (1328–1400)* (Paris, 1900), 192ff., and especially R.-H. Bautier, "Le Sceau royal dans la France médiévale et le mécanisme du scellage des actes," in *Chartes, sceaux et chancelleries* (Paris: École des Chartes, 1991), 2:537–62, especially 542ff.

67. E.G.F., 1:212; Delaborde, "Étude," 166.

68. Delaborde, "Étude," 167ff.

69. See Morel, *Grande Chancellerie*, 343.

70. Calculated from E.G.F., vol. 1; according to Delaborde ("Étude," 200–201), the *Trésor* contains 300 pieces posterior to 1628, all deposited in the series of the *sacs*.

71. On Jean de Montreuil, see Bernard Guenée, *Histoire et culture historique dans l'occident médiéval* (Paris, 1980), 99; on Budé, see Donald R. Kelley, *Foundations of Modern Historical Scholarship Language, Law and History in the French Renaissance* (New York: Columbia University Press, 1970), 58ff.

72. Jean du Tillet, *Recueil des roys de France, leur couronne et maison. . . .* (Paris, 1580); Kelley, *Foundations*, 215ff.

73. Bernard de Girard, seigneur de Haillan, *De l'état et succez des affaires de France . . . depuis Pharamond . . . jusques au roy Loys unziesme. . . .* (Paris, 1570), 1005ff.; Kelley, *Foundations*, 214ff.

74. Pierre Dupuy, *Traitez touchant les droits du roy très chrestien sur plusieurs estats et seigneuries possédés par divers princes voisins. . . .* (Paris, 1655), 1005ff.; Kelley, *Foundations*, 241ff.

75. Léopold Delisle, *Le Cabinet des manuscrits de la Bibliothèque nationale* (Paris, 1868–81), 1:440; ibid., 2:101.

76. Peiresc to his brother, August 2, 1626, in *Lettres de Peiresc*, ed. Tamizey de Larroque (Paris, 1896), 6:593.

77. The edict of 1628 is in Armand Baschet, *Histoire du dépôt des archives des affaires étrangères* (Paris, 1875), 26–27.

78. Delaborde, "Étude," 203ff.; Boucher d'Argis, "Trésor des chartes du roi," in *Encyclopédie, ou dictionnaire raisonné des sciences, des arts et des métiers*, 16:599.

79. The text of the brief is in Félix Ravaisson, *Rapports à S. Exc. le ministre d'état au nom de la commission instituée le 22 avril 1861* (Paris, 1862), 251–58, here 252–53, 255, 257.

80. Ibid., Royal Letters of January 1582, 231–33, here 232.

81. R.-H. Bautier, "La Phase cruciale de l'histoire des archives: La Constitution des dépôts d'archives et la naissance de l'archivistique (XVIe–début du XIXe siècle)," *Archivum* 18 (1968): 139–49; Duchein, "L'Histoire des archives européennes et l'évolution du métier d'archiviste en Europe," in Duchein, 67–80.

82. Hélène Michaud, *La Grande chancellerie et les écritures royales au XVIe siècle (1515–1589)* (Paris, 1967), 366ff.

83. On the new *Trésor des chartes*, see Mathieu Molé, *Mémoires* (Paris, 1855–57), 1:388–89 and 525ff. See also cardinal de Retz, "Mémoires," in *Oeuvres* (Paris: Gallimard, Bibliothèque de la Pléiade, 1983), 292.

84. Delaborde, "Étude," 111ff. (Nogaret), 171ff. ("coffres des chanceliers," or "chancellors' coffers").

85. Baschet, *Histoire du dépôt*, 29ff.; Duc de Saint-Simon, *Mémoires*, ed. A. de Boislisle (Paris, 1906), 19:359ff.; Duc de Saint-Simon, *Addition de Saint-Simon au journal de Dangeau* 932:439; Duc de Saint-Simon, *Journal du marquis de Dangeau*, ed. E. E. Saulié and L. Durieux (Paris, 1858), 12:119.

86. Baschet, *Histoire du dépôt*, 63ff.; Bautier, "La Phase cruciale," 144.

87. Baschet, *Histoire du dépôt*; *Les Archives du ministère des relations extérieures depuis les origines: Histoire et guide*, 2 vols. (Paris: Imprimerie nationales, 1984); Étienne Taillemite, "Les Archives et les archivistes de la marine des origines à 1870," *Bibliothèque de l'école des chartes* 217 (1969): 27–86; Paul Laurencin-Chapelle, *Les Archives de la guerre, historiques et administratives (1688–1898)* (Paris, 1898); foreword to *Correspondance des contrôleurs généraux avec les intendants des provinces*, vol. 1, ed. M. de Boilisle (Paris, 1874) (archives of the general comptroller); Outrey, "Sur la notion d'archives," 279–80.

88. Cited from Renée Simon, *Henri de Boulainviller* [sic], *historien, politique, philosophe, astrologue, 1658–1722* (Paris, n. d.), 50.

89. B.N. MSS Joly de Fleury 1005–1008: *Demandes, communication et expédition de pièces au trésor des chartes, rangées par ordre alphabétique du nom du demandeur.*

90. See Xavier Charmes, *Le Comité des travaux historiques et scientifiques (Histoire et documents)* (Paris, 1886), 1:259ff.; Pierre-Nicolas Bonamy, "Mémoire historique sur le trésor des chartes et sur son état actuel," in *Mémoires [de littérature tirés des registres] de l'Académie royale des inscriptions et belles-lettres* (Paris, 1764), 30:697–728.

91. See Jacques Lelong, *Bibliothèque historique de la France*, vol. 3, ed. Fevret de Fontette (Paris, 1771), nos. 29485–29526.

92. Toustain and Tassin, *Nouveau traité de diplomatique* 1:64ff., here, 87; Outrey, "Sur la notion d'archives," 280ff.

93. See Élie Carcassonne, *Montesquieu et le problème de la constitution française au XVIIIe siècle* (1927; repr., Geneva: Slatkin reprints, 1978).

94. Armand-Gaston Camus, *Lettres sur la profession d'avocat. . . .* (Paris, 1777), 96–97 and 105–6.

95. Krzysztof Pomian, "Les Historiens et les archives dans la France du XVIIe siècle," *Acta Poloniae historica* 26 (1972): 109–25.

96. Pierre Gasnault, "Les Travaux d'érudition des Mauristes au XVIIIe siècle," and Henri Duranton, "La Recherche historique à l'Académie des inscriptions: L'Exemple de l'Histoire de France," in *Historische Forschung im 18. Jahrhundert,* ed. Karl Hammer and Jürgen Voss (Bonn, 1976), 102–21 and 207–35.

97. See Delisle, *Le Cabinet,* 1:559ff.; Charmes, introduction to *Le Comité,* 1:iv–lxxxiv, as well as the documents collected in this volume; Dieter Gembicki, *Histoire et politique à la fin de l'ancien régime: Jacob-Nicolas Moreau (1717–1803)* (Paris: Nizet, 1979), especially 85ff.

98. Charmes, *Le Comité,* 1:63.

99. Ibid., 440; Omont, *Inventaire,* 159–66.

100. Dom Germain Poirier, "Observations sur les archives des établissements ecclésiastiques," in E. Boutaric, "Le Vandalisme révolutionnaire," 344–47; and, on Dom Poirier, see Léon Deries, "Un Grand sauveteur de documents historiques, l'ancien bénédictin dom Poirier," *Revue Mabillon* 19 (1930): 50–67, 260–81.

101. *Manuel,* 307.

102. An inventory of fixtures can be found in Bon-Joseph Dacier, *Rapport à l'empereur sur les progrès des sciences, des lettres et des arts depuis 1789,* vol. 4, *Histoire et littérature ancienne (1810),* ed. François Hartog (Paris, 1989), especially 168ff.

103. *Rapport fait en frimaire an VI par le Bureau du Triage des Titres,* A.N., AB XIII 2, f° 97.

104. Auguste Vallet de Viriville, "Notes et documents pour servir à l'histoire de l'École royale des chartes," *Bibliothèque de l'École des chartes,* 2nd series (1847–48): 4:153–76; Abel Lefranc, *Histoire du Collège de France* (Paris, 1893), 313ff.

105. See these ordinances in *École nationale des chartes: Livre du centenaire (1821–1921)* (Paris, 1921), 1:315ff., and Richou, *Traité,* 279ff.

106. Benjamin Guérard, *Notice sur M. Daunou* (Paris, 1855).

107. See Robert de Lasteyrie, "Jules Quicherat, sa vie et ses travaux," in Jules Quicherat, *Mélanges d'archéologie et d'histoire: Antiquités celtiques, romaines et gallo-romaines* (Paris, 1885), 2, 5–6.

108. *Manuel,* 50ff., 137 (citation).

109. *École normale des chartes: Livre du centenaire,* 1:252–53.

110. Richou, *Traité,* 304, 311–12.

111. Charles-Victor Langlois, introduction to *État sommaire des versements faits aux archives nationales par les ministères et les administrations qui en dépendent* (Paris, 1924), 1:lxxxii.

112. Alfred Maury, preface to *Inventaire sommaire et tableau méthodique des fonds conservés aux Archives nationales,* part 1, *Régime antérieur à 1789,* iii.

113. [-C.-F. Daunou], *Tableau sytématique des archives de l'empire au 15 août 1811* (Paris, n. d. [1811?]); and letter from Daunou to his subordinates from June 25, 1809, A.N., AB XVI 1.

114. [Daunou], *Archives de l'empire 1812,* A.N., AB VI 1.

115. Laborde, 169–70.

116. [Daunou], *Tableau*; *Rapport fait en frimaire an VI* [. . .], f° 90, and *Trésor des chartes: Reconnaissance faite en fructidor an VIII et vendémiaire an IX*. Both in A.N., AB XIII 2. One has even begun to unite the two "Trésors des chartes." Cf. E.G.F., 1:186.

117. [Daunou], *Observations générales sur les archives de l'empire*, A.N., AB VI 1.

118. [Camus], *Ordre pour les archives de l'assemblée nationale* (Versailles, n. d. [1789?]).

119. [Camus], *État des archives nationales, au premier octobre 1791; et dépenses de cet établissement du premier octobre 1790 au premier octobre 1791* (Paris, 1791).

120. [Daunou], *Exposé des accroissements successifs que les archives de l'empire ont reçus depuis 1804 et de l'état actuel du matériel et du personnel de cet établissement*, A.N., AB VI 1.

121. Letter from February 15, 1810, in *Correspondance de Napoléon*, 20:255; Laborde, 155.

122. [Daunou], *Minute d'un projet de loi sur les Archives*, A.N., AB VI 1.

123. *Inventaire général sommaire des archives de l'empire* (Paris, 1867) (edition reserved to archivists); *État sommaire par séries des documents conservés aux archives nationales* (Paris, 1891).

124. Langlois, *État sommaire*, 74ff., 94ff.

125. Richou, *Traité*, 36ff., 291.

126. The first two numbers come from Charmes, *Le Comité*, 1:90. The third comes from Laborde, 9 and 209–10.

127. Charmes, *Le Comité*, 1:74ff., 113.

128. B.N.: Moreau, 361, *État des envois faits par les intendants*; 365, *État général des chartriers*; 366, *Table générale des chartriers contenant les titres du Royaume*

129. Richou, *Traité*, 292; Ch.-V. Langlois and Henri Stein, *Les Archives de la France* (Paris, 1898), 116, 150, 195, 198, 219, 249 (examples of fires and destructions of the archives in the first decades of the nineteenth century); Jules Michelet, *Journal*, ed. Paul Viallaneix (Paris: Gallimard, 1959), 1:165–217; id., "Rapport au Ministre de l'Instruction publique sur les bibliothèques et les archives des départements du sud-ouest de la France," in *Oeuvres complètes*, ed. Paul Viallaneix (Paris, 1973), 3:539–64. This essay was already finished when I learned of the article by Françoise Hildesheimer, "Des triages au respect des fonds: Les Archives de France sous la monarchie de Juillet," *Revue historique* 580 (October–December 1991): 295–312.

130. Bordier, 341ff.; *Tableau de situation des dépôts d'archives des départements de l'ancienne France au 1er novembre 1812 contenant les réponses aux 16 questions adressées aux préfets par la circulaire ministérielle du 22 septembre*, A.N., AB V^F 1*. Only forty-one prefects responded.

131. Charmes, *Le Comité*, 2:14–15.

132. *Manuel*, 207ff.; Bordier, 50–51.

133. Françoise Hildesheimer, "Archives et périodisation," in COLLECTIF, *Périodes: La Construction du temps historique, actes du Ve colloque d'histoire au présent* (Paris: Éditions de l'E.H.E.S.S., 1991), 39–46.

134. See Langlois and Stein, *Les Archives*, 3, and Gustave Desjardins, *Le Service des archives départementales* (Paris, 1890).

135. Langlois, *État sommaire*, xivff.

136. *Manuel*, 380ff.

137. The text of the decree is in Henri Courtault, *Les Archives nationales de 1902 à 1936* (Paris, 1939), 74ff.; *Manuel*, 66ff., 134ff.

138. Daniel Farcis, "Un Cas exemplaire: La Mission des archives nationales auprès du ministère de l'intérieur," *La Gazette des archives* 137–38 (1987): 113–31.

139. Bordier, 24 and 58.

140. Ravaisson, *Rapport*, 200ff., 204.

141. Langlois and Stein, *Les Archives*, 9–10.

142. Mean calculated according to Bordier, 61; for the rest, see Langlois and Stein, *Les Archives*, 10 and 69.

143. Langlois and Stein, *Les Archives*, 46, 51, 54, 58; *Les Archives du ministère des relations extérieures*, 1:258; *Manuel*, 307.

144. See our "The Era of the *Annales*," chapter 11 in this work.

145. Maurice-A. Arnould, *Vingt années d'histoire économique et sociale: Table des "Annales," 1929–1948* (Paris, 1949), 319, 320, 454–94.

146. *Manuel*, 24ff., 32; "L'Étude du notaire" by Jean-Paul Poisson.

147. Richou, *Traité*, 3; Lelong, *Archives*, §2, 72; *Manuel*, 147ff.

148. E.G.F., 4:212; *Manuel*, 150ff.

149. Charles Braibant, introduction to *Un Demi-siècle aux archives nationales et départementales 1900–1950*, Exposition catalogue, Palais Soubise, October 18–November 18, 1951 (Paris, 1951); *Huit siècles d'histoire de France: Nouvelles acquisitions des archives nationales* (1950–56), Exposition from February 21 to March 21, 1957, Palais Soubise (Paris, 1957), especially R.-H. Bautier, "Les Acquisitions des archives nationales," 13–17; Ibid., "Présentation," in *Chartes, sceaux et chancelleries*, 1:xiii–xiv.

150. E.G.F., 2:495, and 4:145 and 212.

151. Braibant, in *Huit siècles d'histoire de France*, 8; *Manuel*, 82ff.

152. Tourtier-Bonazzi, *Le Témoignage oral aux archives*, 13.

153. R.-H. Bautier, "Les Archives," in Ch. Samaran, *L'Histoire et ses méthodes*, 1153–154.

154. Michel Quétin, "Introduction à l'atelier images fixes," in *Les Nouvelles archives*, 23.

155. *Manuel*, 540ff.; *Les Archives audiovisuelles*; *Les nouvelles archives*, 61ff.

156. *Manuel*, 502ff.

157. *Les Nouvelles archives*, 123ff.

158. *Manuel*, 243ff.; Duchein, "La Clef du trésor: L'Évolution des instruments de recherche d'archives du Moyen Âge à nos jours d'après des exemples français" (1986), and "Les Guides d'archives" (1976), in Duchein, 105–22 and 123–38.

159. *Base de données ARCADE*, Archives nationales, Service de l'informatique, 1987 (pamphlet distributed by the Archives of France October 22, 1987). Brigitte Labat-Poussin, "'Arcade': Traitement par l'informatique d'un fonds des archives nationales," *La Gazette des archives* 125–26 (1984): 249–56.

160. Duchein, "Vingt ans de constructions . . . et l'avenir" (1986), in Duchein, 151–56.

161. Jean-Pierre Babelon, *Du Palais Soubise au C.A.R.A.N.: Le Siège des archives nationales* (Paris, 1988); Jean-Pierre Rioux, "Les Visiteurs du C.A.R.A.N.," *Vingtième siècle: Revue d'histoire* 19 (1988): 107–8; Frédéric Edelmann, "Inauguration dans le Marais du Centre d'accueil des Archives: Variations néo-subjectives," *Le Monde*, March 25, 1988.

162. Duchein, "Les Archives en France, 1945–1984: Mutation ou révolution?" *Archives et bibliothèques de Belgique* 55 (1984), 84–111.

163. Favier, *Les Archives de l'an 2000*; Duchein, "La Révolution archivistique: Le Défi des archives modernes à l'archiviste," *La Gazette des archives* 80 (1973): 11–25; Georges Weill, "Les Mutations de l'archivistique contemporaine," *La Gazette des archives* 149 (1990), 107–17.

164. Bertrand Joly, "Les Archives contemporaines ont-elles un avenir?" *La Gazette des archives* 134–35 (1986): 185–94.

165. See *L'Archiviste et l'inflation des archives contemporaines*, Actes de la vingt-deuxième conférence internationale de la Table ronde des archives (Bratislave, 1983) (Paris: Archives nationales, 1984); Joly, "Les Archives contemporaines," especially 189–91.

166. *Manuel*, 545ff.; Anne Cartier-Bresson and Michel Quétin, "La Préservation des photographies: Notes sur un colloque récent," *La Gazette des archives* 128 (1985), 17–49; see also the articles of Favier and Weill, cited above.

167. "L'Historien, la Maison-Blanche et le courrier électronique," *Courrier international* 81 (May 21–27, 1992): 29.

168. Favier, *Les Archives de l'an 2000*, 8.

169. Michel Melot, "Des Archives considérées comme une substance hallucinogène," *Traverses* 36 (1986): 14–19; here, 17.

170. Joanna Pomian, "Archives: Vers les musées de l'informatique?" *Quaderni* 17 (1992): 45–50.

171. Louis Bergeron, oral communication.

172. Usine Motte-Bossut, *Centre des archives du monde du travail*, pamphlet published by the Ministry of Culture and Communication and the Nord-Pas-de-Calais Region, March 1987.

173. Florence Orr, "Le Centre rhénan d'archives et de recherches économiques," *La Gazette des archives* 134–35 (1986): 222–26; Id., *Guide du centre rhénan d'archives et de recherches économiques (CERARE)* (Mulhouse, 1991).

174. "Les Archives de la télévision: Quand le passé se conjugue au futur," *Problèmes audiovisuels* 22 (November–December 1984); Hélène Eck, "L'Informatisation et la consultation des archives de l'I.N.A.," *Vingtième siècle: Revue d'histoire* 7 (1985): 172–74.

175. *La Gazette des archives* 145 (1989), entirely consecrated to scientific archives.

176. Philippe Joutard, "Bilan d'une expérience: La Vie d'autrefois dans les Cévennes à travers les papiers de famille," and id., "Un Nouveau sondage à travers les archives des famille cévenoles: Les Vallées du Gardon à travers l'histoire," *Bulletin de la Société de l'histoire du protestantisme français* (1972): 200–205 and 738–49.

177. See Claudine Dardy, *Identités de papier* (Paris: Lieu commun, 1990); Gérard Noiriel, *La Tyrannie du national: Le Droit d'asile en Europe (1793–1993)* (Paris: Calmann-Lévy, 1991), especially 37ff., 155ff.

Fig. 3.1
Marie-Geneviève Bouliard, *Alexandre Lenoir*, 1793. Oil on canvas glued to wood. Paris, Musée Carnavalet.

CHAPTER 3

ALEXANDRE LENOIR AND THE MUSEUM OF FRENCH MONUMENTS

DOMINIQUE POULOT

The Museum of French Monuments reopened in September 2007 in Paris after a disastrous fire and many long years of work, within the City of Architecture and Heritage that brings together a center of contemporary architecture (Ifa) and a school of training in restoration (École de Chaillot).[1] This revival, and the success encountered since with the public, has caused many to forget how many of the collections have long suffered from a scant affection, contrasting with the surges of republican eloquence surrounding its establishment in 1879. Initially a "museum of comparative sculpture," its new name, bestowed in 1937, proved powerless to resuscitate the vaunted charms of the first museum of monumental French art, opened in 1795 by Alexandre Lenoir in the former monastery of the Petits-Augustins. It is true that the meager remains of the latter, whether in situ at the École des beaux-arts or at the Père-Lachaise cemetery, could hardly further such an unlikely revival.

But, if their successors seem bereft of both patriotic and aesthetic urgency, this is not solely due to institutional wear and tear: much of the responsibility must be borne by recent changes undergone by the "modern cult of monuments." It was under this rubric that, in 1903, the eminent art historian Alois Riegl developed a history of the "increasing generalization of the concept of the monument" articulated in three successive stages. These corresponded to "three types of monument . . . according to the degree to which they foster memory": intentional monuments, deliberately intended by their makers to "commemorate a specific moment or a complex past event"; historical monuments "that refer to a particular moment, but one determined by our subjective preferences"; and ancient monuments, which is to say "all human creations that have manifestly suffered from the ravages of time."[2] According to Riegl, this process is accompanied by corresponding shifts in approaches to restoration, briefly discussed by him, as well as by the appearance of museums, a phenomenon that he does not address.

In these new institutions devoted to the illustration of historical value, which in France date from the Revolution and thus were dominated by patriotic and nationalist agendas, commemoration was still bound up with history.[3] The deputy Armand-Guy Kersaint affirmed in 1791 that "monuments are irreproachable witnesses to history," and categorized them as either "straightforwardly commemorative" or "of mixed public function" ("commémoratifs simples" or "publics mixtes").[4] This is effectively to maintain that all monuments, even when used to write history, are dominated by the recollective function. Such a conflation is apparent in the Museum of the Petits-Augustins, simultaneously the first refuge of France's historical monuments and a privileged site of memory during the Directory.

Under the Third Republic, Cluny and the Trocadéro, the only museums administered by the Service des monuments historiques,[5] served as both memorials and sanctuaries for cultural artifacts. Unlike the other French historical museums established in the nineteenth century at Versailles and Saint-Germain, these two institutions were shaped by a museological model conceived by Lenoir. At once "lesson-promenades" into national history and art studio annexes, in any case resolutely didactic in their ambitions, they were very different from the Louvre, the seat of universality and the province of amateurs, dilettantes, and idlers.[6] It would seem that the image—largely mythic—of the Petits-Augustins set the program in advance for every museum of large-scale artifacts until the threshold of the twentieth century. Doubtless the persistent oral tradition relating to the Petits-Augustins is a function of the edifying literature that sprang up around the name of Alexandre Lenoir: only specialists can now list from memory the names of curators from the last century, but that of Lenoir, when uttered in educated company, evokes a host of commonplaces about the savior of our monuments and a man smitten with medieval culture.[7]

AN EXEMPLARY CRITICAL FORTUNE

Aside from autobiographies published in successive editions of the *Description du musée des monuments français*, the first account of Alexandre Lenoir's life, by one Monsieur Allou, appeared in *Mémoires de la Société royale des antiquaires de France* in 1842. This text was largely derived from Lenoir's own image of himself, for the author acknowledges having used "a manuscript in which most of the important facts in the life of Monsieur Lenoir are recounted by himself and written in his own hand." The introduction establishes the tone for the whole, which is that of a panegyric: "In vain were [all records of] the good that was done wiped out, in vain have cruel insouciance and blind prejudice tried to efface even the last traces of the Museum of French Monuments: the name of Lenoir will live forever, honored as that of a zealous citizen, an artist devoted to the glory of his country who lived only to make it known and admired."[8] His titles to posterity, three in number, are then listed: that of a "simple artist" who "saved, through his persistence, a part of what is most curious about old France"; that of the "skillful enchanter who so well arranged these marvels and added to them, to assure that nothing was lacking, the charm of an attractive promenade, a pretty garden"; and finally that of a man of science whose "words will never be forgotten." After a century and a half, these generous predictions have become fragile.

Lenoir's convictions concerning the origins of "Gothic" art and the nature of the "hieroglyphs" on Roman gates, like his many iconological readings, are esoteric musings in the eighteenth-century tradition; they constitute the dead part of his writings. The scientific prestige of the curator's books and articles quickly evaporated: his many scholarly publications—extended excursuses on such matters as the meaning of the animals on twelfth and thirteenth century tombs, the solar cult celebrated by the church, and the feast of the dragon of Metz—have been allowed to sleep undisturbed. To be sure, when they first appeared they exerted considerable influence on the members of scholarly societies and provincial academies: to cite one example, it was thanks to Lenoir that, in 1804, one Dr. Rigollot deciphered "secrets" in Amiens Cathedral antithetical to the Catholic faith![9] Very early in the nineteenth century, however, the first "medievalists" grasped that their new discipline was foreign to the Chevalier Lenoir. He was either ignorant of or misunderstood the groundbreaking publications of national archeology, and his work held no interest for young researchers in the field.[10] The limitations of his knowledge and intellectual outlook even led him to oppose Champollion's decoding of Egyptian writing in the name of an outdated theory of sacred symbols. In short, the direct legacy of the Petits-Augustins to historical knowledge was virtually nil, save for its having perpetuated errors and reinforced the authority of false attributions and dubious anecdotes, to the considerable benefit of the Romantic generation.[11]

Lenoir's strictly museological contribution has also been somewhat neglected, in this case unjustifiably. François Furet and Denis Richet are virtually alone among contemporary historians of the Revolution in insisting on the man's genius, for having established the "first European museum of Medieval and Renaissance sculpture" as well as having formulated "principles of chronological classification that are the foundation of modern museography."[12] But the persistent fame of the establishment is based on extramuseological considerations, first and foremost the engaged historiography pertaining to Revolutionary vandalism.

In effect, Lenoir's reputation rose and fell throughout the century in tandem with assessments of his museum's having safeguarded national monuments or functioned more equivocally. Georges Lefebvre, in his *La France sous le Directoire*, rehearses the republican vulgate: "Grégoire did not protest against vandalism in vain. The assemblies did their best to preserve what remained: the Convention established the Museum of French Monuments."[13] From this school's perspective, Lenoir was "often heroic."[14] An opposing tradition rails bitterly against his mistakes and dubious reconstructions but praises his determination. Louis Dimier, after indicating the "ridiculous antiquarian and befuddled critic," concedes that "Lenoir, by becoming director of the museum, nonetheless saved from almost certain destruction many monuments of incalculable value to history and the education of taste."[15] No such indulgence was forthcoming from Pierre Espezel, however, who in 1932 unequivocally condemned the republican museums: "Stalls and ciboria are made for churches, furniture for houses, tombs for cemeteries. The only government to adopt a sensible approach to museums was the Restoration: it dismantled the absurd Museum of French Monuments and restored its component elements to their legitimate destinations."[16] About the same time, Jacques Vanuxem, in his thesis, set out to demonstrate that "Lenoir's depot, transformed into a museum, was to the very end a site for the disorderly dispersion of religious sculpture," maintaining that "it is very difficult to forgive such carelessness."[17] Insofar as this historiography reflects a debate over the extent of Revolutionary destruction and the attribution of culpability for it that still rages, it is more or less openly political. In the Petits-Augustins, both heirs and adversaries of the Republic find an exemplary case, a pretext for arguments and demonstrations. And the museum also figures within a strictly artistic historiography, as a locus of what Paul Léon dubbed "the quarrel between the classics and the gothics."[18]

The role of Lenoir's museum as a popularizing "cultural relay" was emphasized by Henri Jacoubet: "Lenoir was not, nor did he want to be, a mere technician who materially reconstituted ruined monuments. He resuscitated their legends in a style that was fashionable, thereby attracting the interest even of the most profane."[19] Marcel Aubert remarked at about

Fig. 3.2

Pierre-Joseph La Fontaine, *Alexandre Lenoir Defending the Tomb of Louis XII and Anne of Brittany at Saint-Denis from the Furor of the Sans-Culottes*. Drawing. Musée Carnavalet, Paris.

the same time that it furthered the incursion of neo-Gothic elements into collections, literature, theater, and historical writing.[20] Louis Réau viewed the museum as a site where painting of the first Empire, with its emphasis on the evocation of national history, came into being: "All things considered, the effect of the Museum of French Monuments on the Davidian school was no less beneficial than that exercised [by the Louvre]. It was in the rooms of the Elysian Gardens of the Museum of French Monuments that so-called troubadour genre painting was born, which was to develop with Romanticism and rid us of Greeks and Romans."[21] The museum's critical fortune was henceforth established, despite refinements introduced by René Lanson and recently repeated by Pierre Barrière: "The works of Lenoir and Chateaubriand, who have too often reaped glory for having discovered the Middle Ages, resulted from the work of two generations." According to this reading, Lenoir is but an "intermediary between the generations of 1775 and the followers of Thierry, Michelet, and Romanticism."[22]★ But the view of Lenoir as the discoverer of an art, the man of a fashion, persisted to such an extent that he became an exemplum for sociologists. For Roger Bastide, "there are inventors of taste who know how to choose among the hypotheses proposed by creators and who, due to their prestige and thanks to barrier-and-standard mechanisms, end up disseminating their type of aesthetic pleasure more broadly. Some of these inventors are well known, for example Alexandre Lenoir, founder of the Museum of Historical Monuments [*sic*]."[23]

Today, almost all histories of the Revolution and the Empire discuss the Museum of French Monuments, emphasizing its influence on troubadour art—which has recently returned to favor[24]—or its contribution to the religious revival of the century's early decades.[25] But beyond the rediscoveries of kitsch taste and scholarly curiosity, the museum's posterity now seems linked to the constitution of national archeology, which is to say to the history of the French patrimony. Such is the essence of the judgment previously voiced by Ferdinand Brunot: "I readily concede that the Museum of French Monuments, sketch of the present museum, occasions considerable sadness and legitimate regrets. But it is just possible that this heteroclite assembly of so much magnificent debris fostered historical syntheses and gave birth to fecund ideas about the [sense of] unity emitted by so many juxtaposed fragments. The result was a great lesson, a revelation of the degree to which French taste and intelligence manifest themselves even in such a motley array."[26]

As early as 1886, an article by Lenoir's first historian, Louis Courajod,

---

★ EDITOR'S NOTE: See chapter 9 of this volume, "Augustin Thierry's *Lettres sur l'histoire de France*," by Marcel Gauchet.

made a case for "the museum's influence on the development of historical studies."[27] Half a century ago, the large *Manuel d'archéologie* edited by Joseph Déchelette dispensed with the classic opposition between preservation in situ and shelter within a museum. Monument museums, one reads there, "were and remain an indispensable element of archeology in general and of national archeology in particular."[28] Henceforth all histories of archeological research were obliged to acknowledge Lenoir's importance; as a consequence, his name gradually disappeared from histories of art but became a regular feature in those of the auxiliary sciences of history. The index of *L'Histoire et ses méthodes*, published in December 1960, identifies Alexandre Lenoir as a "French archeologist,"[29] as does the *Dictionnaire des noms propres* by Paul Robert. Only Bénézit still describes him as both "painter and archeologist."[30] More recent historical publications tend to describe him as the inventor of the historical monument. The 1980 exhibition *Hier pour demain* affirmed that "the same desire to preserve, inventory, and study lost monuments, or those on the verge of becoming so, finds expression in the enterprise of Lenoir, in the museum, and in that of the Académie Celtique."[31] The title selected by Pierre de Lagarde for the first chapter of his book *La Mémoire des pierres* is telling in this regard: "Alexandre Lenoir ou l'idée du monument historique."[32]

Even so, none of these studies truly acknowledges how this eminently political institution functioned in its own time as the guardian of a certain "philosophical" and national memory. Only an investigation into the precise circumstances of the museum's foundation, a study of the catalogues and programs Lenoir wrote for it, and, finally, an examination of the spectacle of the monuments themselves will cast light on all aspects of its function in French society under the Directory and Consulate.

THE ELABORATION OF THE SPECTACLE

The story of the museum's genesis is fairly well known and can be summarized quickly. Everything began with the Constituent Assembly's decision, on November 2, 1789, to "place the goods of the clergy at the disposition of the nation."[33] The next year, the Commission des monuments decided that the old convents of the Capuchin friars on the rue Saint-Honoré, the Jesuits on the rue Saint-Antoine, and the Cordeliers (Franciscans) would serve as depositories for books and manuscripts and that the Hôtel de Nesle and the convent of the Petits-Augustins would serve the same purpose for statues, marbles, and metal artifacts from religious foundations. At the instigation of the painter Gabriel-François Doyen, an appraiser for the commission, his student Alexandre Lenoir was appointed guardian of the last named of these depositories on June 6, 1791. His job consisted of delivering "feudal" paintings to the bonfires of the sansculottes sections and bronze liturgical furnishings to the Mint to be melted down; in addition, he was to auction all objects rejected by the advisory committee and preserve the others, destined for the future Musée de la république. All indicators suggest that Lenoir, who more than any other individual was responsible for the survival of Parisian artworks in this period, sometimes in defiance of iconoclastic instructions issued by his superiors, hoped to join the conservation staff of this museum. He was to be disappointed, however, being nominated neither to the first museum commission, formed by Roland de la Platière, minister of the interior, nor to the curatorial staff that succeeded it in 1794, in the wake of attacks mobilized by Jacques-Louis David. Thus excluded from the Louvre project, Lenoir set about remounting the disassembled tombs and incorporating sculpture and statuary into the walls. So successful was this campaign, in fact, that as early as July 1793, to the great surprise of the Commission des monuments, the church and cloister of the Petits-Augustins resembled a museum more than the depository it was meant to remain. Thanks to the support—in all likelihood decisive—of Barrière, Lenoir obtained authorization to open his depot to the public in August and September 1793, on the occasion of the arrival in Paris of delegations of *fédérés*, or "departmental representatives." Finally, on October 21, 1795, the Committee of Public Instruction officially approved the program for a "historical and chronological museum where the periods of French sculpture will be found in specially allocated rooms, each having been given a character and physiognomy precisely appropriate to the century it represents."[34]

The museum was to last slightly longer than twenty years, adapting itself to successive political regimes. When it closed in 1814, elements of the eastern façade of the Château d'Écouen as well as the portals of the Château de Gaillon were on display in its entry court. From there, visitors proceeded via a gallery of the cloister to an "introductory room" housing pieces of all eras, from the Gallo-Roman period to the seventeenth century.* The heart of the museum was a series of rooms devoted to a single century, from the thirteenth to the seventeenth. Daylight, almost completely absent from the thirteenth-century room, was increasingly allowed to penetrate the subsequent ones, such that the seventeenth-century room was flooded with the clarity of virtue triumphant. In effect, Lenoir had composed this sequence in a way analogous to certain "Egyptian" Masonic rites inspired by Dupuis's *L'Origine de tous les cultes*, an extravagant history of religion. Finally, the former convent gardens, rechristened in

---

★ TRANSLATOR'S NOTE: Judging from the plan, one entered directly into the *salle d'introduction*, not from the cloister (as one does today when attending exhibitions there).

1799 the Elysian Fields, had been transformed into an attractive pantheon of evocative *fabriques* of which the "Tomb of Abelard and Heloise" is only the most famous. At the museum one could purchase a descriptive catalogue that, in addition to entries on the exhibited statues and artifacts, boasted a generous helping of ancillary information and anecdotes that made it a kind of cultural handbook, incorporating brief discussions of stained glass, the wearing of beards, the clothing of different periods, and so on. It ran to twelve editions, and the last, dating from 1815, appeared in both French and English.

The museum was never integrally recast, but several partial remodelings and complementary projects were proposed. In 1800, Lenoir envisioned the establishment of "a theoretical curriculum and a practical drawing school," for in his view the examples in the collection were appropriate to "shape taste and constitute [a basis for] reasoned study." This project, doubtless modeled after the drawing classes of the *écoles centrales*, with which the departmental museums were meant to be affiliated, was never realized. Ten years later, the curator proposed to build a new room, to be named either the "Room of heroic deeds of Napoleon the Great" or "Nineteenth century: the Egyptian voyage of Emperor and King Napoleon I," that was to feature plaster models of all the State-commissioned statues and reliefs commemorating the ruler's many glorious actions.

Vigorously opposed by adherents of classical taste (who could not forgive him for this museum of *magots*, or "grotesqueries"), by Catholics (who insisted that the scandalous placement of tombs in a museum be rectified), and by Royalists (who had never forgotten certain turns of phrase in the early editions of his catalogue), Lenoir was obliged to close his museum in 1816, not without first having proposed installing within the Petits-Augustins an "expiatory chapel" dedicated to the memory of the dead whose sleep had been disturbed by the Revolutionary displacements.

THE PANTHÉON AND THE FAMILY CEMETERY

The selection of works exhibited at the Petits-Augustins, like the texts about them in the museum's descriptive catalogue, incited visitors to funereal meditation of a kind fostered by all the "fields of rest" conceived in this period.[35] In effect, to realize his plans for a gallery of national glory, Lenoir initially tried to assemble widely dispersed busts of famous men, supplemented when necessary by new ones commissioned from sculptors of his acquaintance. His crucial sources were Saint-Denis and Parisian churches, whose funerary monuments in the end proved sufficient to fill the exhibition rooms. As for the new monuments solemnizing ancient and contemporary figures, Lenoir did not present them as simple works of art or artifacts filling out a chronology but insisted on their commemorative function. From this point of view, the museum was primarily a pantheon, one designed to rehabilitate old regime "pariahs" whose genuine talents had been denied by "fanatics" or "despots." Thus Lenoir saw to the completion of the tomb of Crébillon, "which had been left incomplete and homeless. It was originally meant for the church of Saint-Gervais where he was buried, but the vicar refused to authorize its erection, saying that a profane monument should not decorate his church" (no. 342). The text about the urn containing Molière's ashes served as a pretext for this anecdote: "The archbishop of Paris having refused to accord him burial, the widow of this great man cried out, her eyes overflowing with tears: 'They deny a tomb to this man to whom Greece would have raised altars'" (no. 508).

The overtly polemical intent of some of the monuments in no way compromised the prevailing rhetorical tone, which was one of respect: "The French Senate has issued several decrees in favor of individual tombs, and these monuments, erected to my own designs and containing the bodies of Descartes, Molière, La Fontaine, Mabillon, Monfaucon, and Turenne, are a series [expressing] its gratitude for talent" (ibid.).★ Most of them, however, resulted solely from the curator's own initiative: the busts of Goujon and Montaigne for the sixteenth century, Fabri de Peiresc for the seventeenth, and Rousseau, Winckelmann, Chamfort, and Gluck for the eighteenth (p. 305). Regarding one of them, that of Peiresc by Francin fils, Lenoir noted simply: "I was obliged to have this marble executed by the memory of this great man" (no. 273). The bust of Winckelmann occasioned a somewhat longer text: "The respect that this sublime man inspired in me, the gratitude owed him by artists, all this compelled me to erect a monument to him" (no. 401).†

The choice of individuals reveals the philosophical and artistic preferences of the man in charge: Abbé Guillaume Raynal, historian and philosopher, and the astronomer Jean-Sylvan Bailly were included (nos. 416–18), along with, in the Elysian garden, Jacques Rohault, "disciple of Descartes . . . the most zealous partisan of his friend's system, founded on natural phenomena and not on speculation" (no. 314). For the series of famous men from the seventeenth century, Lenoir commissioned four statues whose subjects are indicative of the period's tastes and aesthetic

★ EDITOR'S NOTE: Mabillon and Montfaucon are the two French Benectine monks/scholars who created the scholarly science of diplomatics, the rational study of medieval documents.
† EDITOR'S NOTE: Johann Wincklemann (1717–69), the German art historian and theorist—*Laocöon* and *History of the Art of Antiquity* are his most famous works—was one of the first to consider works of art from the point of view of style and its development in history.

Fig. 3.3
Proposed restoration of the portal of the residence of Diane de Poitiers at Anet, presented by Alexandre Lenoir to the minister of the interior in the year VIII. Intended for the principal entrance to the Musée des monuments français, leading from the entry court into the introductory room, it differs slightly from the realized design.

preferences. Poussin ("the philosopher's painter"), Eustache Lesueur ("the French Raphael"), Jacques Sarrazin, and, finally, Pierre Puget ("the French Michelangelo"; nos. 236–39). This artistic roll of honor was supplemented in the sixteenth-century room by their predecessor Jean Goujon ("the French Phidias," no. 107).

Thus the Museum of the Petits-Augustins was an important source of commissions during the post-Revolutionary years, when patrons as well as large decorative projects were scarce. Several artists were so interested in this permanent and much frequented exhibition that they donated examples of their work. Pajou reacquired his bust of Vaucanson from the marble dealer Teuret for exhibition there (no. 505). "Citizen Foucou, esteemed artist, wishing to have an authentic monument of his talent in this museum, composed a relief . . . I will not hold forth regarding this work's distinction, leaving that solicitude to posterity" (no. 384). Lenoir sometimes bowed to friendship and accepted monuments to familial piety. The widow of the architect De Wailly donated a bust of him "made by Pajou his friend" (no. 504), and from citizen Dulongbois, in February 1802, "a life-size relief representing Madame Élisa Joly, celebrated actress, his wife, whom he had interred on his property."[36] The cenotaph of Marie-Joseph Peyre, "erected at the expense" of Lenoir himself "after a design by his son," combined filial gratitude with a disciple's admiration: "Peyre the son, wanting to honor the memory of a good father and an artist of distinguished gifts . . . , consecrated to him this monument to his tenderness and the recognition he owes his master" (no. 494).

Such gestures of homage, commingling friendship and respect, paid by "sensitive men" to their peers found its most complete expression in the monument to Jean-Germain Drouais, the brilliant David student who had tragically succumbed to malaria at the French Academy in Rome in 1788 (Lenoir commissioned a copy of the original Santa Maria in Via Lata from its sculptor, Claude Michallon): "Unable to follow him into the tomb, I felt obliged, for his contemporaries and for the comfort of my own soul, to erect to him, amid monuments to our history, the same monument consecrated to him by his worthy rivals" (no. 355). The funereal character of this memorial prevailed over all other considerations, and Lenoir closed his text, quite logically, with a veritable appeal to the cult of the deceased: "Oh Drouais! Tender son, faithful friend, receive the incense of he who erects to you today this monument in surroundings devoted to the fine arts. Sensitive mother, and you, cherished relatives, take comfort! Those whom he loved will come here to honor his memory, and leave flowers at the feet of his image; and already immortality has consecrated his name in centuries to come."

The Petits-Augustins was coming to resemble both a pantheon of early neoclassicism and a prestigious double of artists' family cemeteries. The entries stressed these aspects, combining descriptions of the tombs with extended accounts of the life and works of the deceased. The pages on Peyre were penned by his son; Lenoir himself wrote the text on Drouais, casting it as an archetypal creative apprenticeship narrative (pp. 335–41). In the 1810 edition of the guidebook, Lenoir explained his use of the name "Elysian" for the gardens by invoking the "magic attached to this word, which is current in artistic language and is used every day to signify the idea of happiness: by and large, it is reserved for the lot of virtuous men after they have ceased to live in this visible world" (p. 285). The description that follows evokes "a majestic landscape" decorated with "monuments that a timid hand dares consecrate to famous men." The curator states that this spectacle was meant "to instill in the souls of [his] readers and those who visit this Elysian the same holy respect for enlightenment, talent, and virtue with which [he himself] was penetrated in fashioning it" (p. 293). The garden was a site of poetic immortality: "Let it be supposed that these inanimate remains have taken on new life in order to be seen and understood, to enjoy a universal and unchangeable felicity." Far from being an addendum inconsistent with the museum's basic project, the Elysian reveals in an exemplary way its close ties to the cult of the dead. A detail of the projected disposition is telling: "In front of the building's circular portion, in the entry court, a Corinthian column surmounted by a [figure of] Fame will bear this inscription: 'To the memory of artists celebrated in France.' Their busts will adorn the nineteen niches composing the entirety of the decoration of the court" (p. 215).

All of the individuals showcased in the museum were presented as both historical figures in an unfolding chronology and national heroes outside the passage of time. On the one hand, they functioned as so many dated exempla from the past evidencing the stages of historical evolution; on the other, as the *membra disjecta* of a great universal man signifying the immortality of French virtue. Lenoir summed up this idea in a single phrase when he referred, using language typical of the period, to these "figures who exemplify their century through their talents and who have honored the French nation by their morality."[37]

THE VISITOR'S GAZE

A breakdown of the monuments cited in the large corpus of visitor's accounts makes it possible to list the names of the most popular figures in order of descending interest. Most often mentioned are Francis I, Diane de Poitiers, and Richelieu, with Abelard and Heloise being *hors concours*.[38] They are followed by Mazarin, Henri II and Catherine de Médicis, Leb-

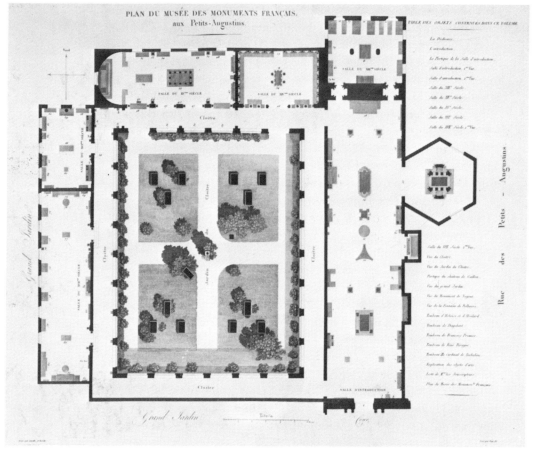

Fig. 3.4
Plan of the Musée des monuments français, etching by Jean-Baptiste Réville and Jacques Lavallée after a drawing of Jean-Lubin Vauzelle for B. de Roquefort, *Vues pittoresques et perspectives des salles du Musée des monuments français* (Paris, 1816).

run, Corneille, Henri IV, and, from the medieval period, Duguesclin, Clovis, and Clotilde. A group apart consists of St. Louis, Philippe le Bel, Louis XII, and Anne of Brittany, whose monument was remarked by visitors primarily because, "although it still has a Gothic feeling, it is noteworthy as filling the interval between the first advances of art and its perfection." The other figures mentioned with particular frequency are Jean Cousin, Chancellor L'Hôpital, Admiral Coligny (a pretext for nonbelievers and Protestants to evoke the St. Bartholomew's Day Massacre), Le Tellier, Colbert, and finally Pibrac, whose moralizing quatrains had become a part of traditional culture.[39] The most often cited eighteenth-century figures are Maupertuis, Montesquieu, Dubois, Voltaire, and Piron.

The names of monarchs and statesmen are those most often cited in these visitor's accounts, especially those offering pretexts for historical and sentimental anecdotes, for example Francis I (his artistic patronage; his passion for Diane de Poitiers) and Richelieu (Lenoir's having saved his tomb from Revolutionary iconoclasts armed with bayonets). Their authors often paraphrased Lenoir's guidebook. Before the tomb of Philippe d'Orléans, for example, visitors tended to recall his chansons, while Charles of Anjou prompted musings on the Sicilian Vespers, Valentine of Milan on his device ("Nought is left me, I am myself nought"), Frédégonde on his cruelty, Charles VI on his madness and the conduct of Isabel of Bavaria, and King John on his English captivity. Among less prominent figures, Mary Queen of Scots held a trump card in the poem written to her dear France on departing for England (and eventual death), Sanède in her writings on her mortal distress upon learning of the assassination of Henri IV, and so on.

To a certain extent, then, the museum created its own celebrities, exaggerating the historical importance of many figures in tandem with the serendipities of its collection and Lenoir's own preferences. The extended biographies—more like picturesque epitaphs—contained in the guidebook only intensified this effect.[40] Nonetheless, prevailing tastes and the visitor's cultural predispositions remained the primary determinants of their responses to the monuments. The extraordinary success of the monument to Abelard and Heloise, to cite only the most obvious example, was fostered by literary recollections. The Englishman John Carr claimed that when he approached "this treasurable antique, all those feelings rushed in upon me, which the beautiful, and affecting narrative of those disasterous lovers by Pope, has often excited in me."[41]

In order to evoke these figures as effectively as possible, the museum supplemented the tombs with a multitude of texts: inscriptions in the rooms as well as rhymes, witty remarks, and other "historical" phrases published in the guidebooks. The cults of these great men and women were sustained by a formulaic recollection of their exalted deeds, both during tours of the museum and afterwards. According to Arago, "it was quite unusual for visitors not to complete their day with a careful reading of several chapters from our history."[42] Apparently he was not exaggerating, for in many accounts of the Petits-Augustins personal observations and commonplaces are embellished with citations and copied passages. For example, that by W. D. Fellowes, dating from 1815, opens with a description of the violation of the royal tombs at Saint-Denis taken from Burke and the account of the exhumation of Henri IV published in Lenoir's guide. These citations are followed by descriptions of the monuments of three great ministers—Richelieu, Mazarin, and Sully—and an excerpt from the verses penned by Mary Queen of Scots upon leaving France (displayed in the museum's introductory room). He then cites the epitaph of Agnès Sorel, an extended passage from Voltaire's *La Pucelle d'Orléans*, and Lenoir's text on the bust of Joan of Arc. Having entered the Elysian Garden, he rehearses Kotzebue's description of Heloise and then copies all the inscriptions on her "tomb." Of the eight pages he devotes to the museum, one is reserved for Henri IV, one and a half for Joan of Arc, and three for Heloise, in each case consisting of transcribed inscriptions or literary citations or both.[43]

Such evocative textual compendia were not the only sort of garrulous commentaries for which Lenoir's museum served as a pretext: followers of Lavater saw in the faces of its gallery of famous men opportunities to determine, after careful deciphering, the keys to their personalities. Visitors tried to ferret out the truth of these physiognomies, to discover through them the expressive or banal character of the sitters.[44] Charles of Anjou disappointed the "physiognomist" Niemeyer, who could not make out "the pitiless man who had ordered that the young, sixteen-year-old Conradin be decapitated in the market of Naples."[45] On occasion, such corporeal scrutiny could degenerate into fetishism: the dispersion of the remains interred at Saint-Denis led to the development of an underground traffic in royal relics that soon became a profitable business (some of the guidebooks even provide dealers' addresses).

The museum of the "sensitive man" at the Petits-Augustins was part of a larger trend, paralleling for example the taste for epitaphs and funerary keepsakes that even Chateaubriand embraced.[46] A fear of becoming lost to memory was inextricable from a concern for permanence, from the desire for immortality that haunted orators of the period, notably Robespierre, and of which Michelet provides the best account.[47] In short, the monuments erected by Lenoir, like those donated to the museum by artists concerned about the judgment of posterity, manifest "a humanist conception of glorious immortality that blossomed" with the democratic and bourgeois values of the nineteenth century.[48]

A REVOLUTIONARY MUSEUM

This homage to well-known figures inaugurated an attempt to establish republican memory, but what is most significant about it is not the selection of this or that individual but rather the very miscellany of the panorama of French glory that it proposed. The radical novelty of the Petits-Augustins consists in its juxtaposition of royal monuments from Saint-Denis with the tombs of statesmen from Parisian churches and garden *fabriqués* erected by Lenoir to commemorate artists and other "picturesque" personalities.

The museum's conception was contemporaneous with the elaboration of a "new" national history by a commission of scholars—"the likes of Bréquiny and Barthélemy"—whose periodical organ was Puthod's *Les Monumens ou le pélerinage historique*: "Everything portends the most beautiful days for History. They will belong to he who enters this career and encircles his forehead with its crown." Puthod, in fact, envisioned the establishment of a monument museum in Sainte-Geneviève (now the Panthéon) that would effect a fusion of aristocratic memory with the republican community. "Now that the Revolution has happily abolished the grievous difference between the titled and untitled classes," he wrote, "it is the truth of history that must henceforth be our primary concern, and not familial vanity. Men of equal rights no longer have need of ancestors." He thought the establishment of such a museum would make it easier for the nobility to give up its monuments, for "pride in seeing a family inheritance become a national inheritance [will accomplish] what patriotism could not."[49]

Such proposals cast light on Lenoir's practice, as does the indignation with which the keepers of traditional memory responded to his museum. The sculptor Deseine, who in fact had donated works of his own to its collection, summarized their views in his *Opinion sur les musées* (year XI): "It is praiseworthy to save artistic monuments from the furor of vandalism, to be sure, but such [an action] would be useful to the public good . . . only if these same monuments were preserved like sacred objects that, belonging entirely to the history, morality, and politics of different periods of an Empire, merited deep respect. . . . It would be necessary to preserve these same monuments just as they were before the Revolution, as opposed to democratizing them, so to speak, by giving them in succession the character of the different factions dominating public opinion." The same author denounced the novelty, hence the scandal, of a place of democratic memory antithetical to all former places of official remembrance, whether monarchical or aristocratic, whether images of the State or of an individual family: "We will not let our attention linger over a rabble of monuments erected at the Petits-Augustins, which, being the result of an individual will, cannot enter into the same system of the progress of art, nor serve the history of the antiquities of France. . . . One cannot permit oneself to raise monuments to suit one's fancy, to anyone at all. . . . *An individual who thinks he is honoring someone's memory by erecting a monument to him is exactly like a commoner who foolishly sets out to bestow a nobility he lacks on his equals* [my emphasis]."[50]

From this perspective, the Petits-Augustins appeared to be a site where memory was laid waste, one that consecrated a rupture in dynastic continuity and bankrupted familial remembrance for the sole profit of a national chronology. The monuments themselves were preserved but their function as reference points was not, with the result that memory, insofar as it is premised on a knowledge of spatial relationships, simply vanished. Deprived of meaningful connections, these "remains" were but mutilated signs reorganized in a discourse foreign to them, that of the history of art. At the end of his description of the Petits-Augustins, Richard Boyle Bernard regretted "this violation of tombs whose mortuary emblems once inspired a salutary terror," lamenting that so many "formerly consecrated places" had been abandoned.[51] On 16 Ventôse year X (March 7, 1802), the *Journal des débats* published an article entitled "A Promenade at the Musée des Monuments Français" that rehearsed some of the ideas prevalent at the time:

> What reflections take hold of us upon seeing the instability to which man is subject even beyond the tomb! Someone who thought he would surely sleep in peace where his ancestors slept, there awaiting the day of judgment, is wrested from his fathers. The beauty of a tomb that had flattered the Great Man's vanity when he was alive proves baneful to his ashes. The columns, statues, and reliefs with which he had himself surrounded are removed and carefully carted away. The fate of his remains is of no consequence; they are neglected and dispersed. One has eyes only for his tomb: what is taken into consideration is not his own name but that of the sculptor.

Others adopted an opposing view, praising the museum precisely for having transformed private memorials into historical and stylistic landmarks. The traveler Schultes lauded such institutions for preserving artistic productions: "It is in the interest of architects and sculptors for their clients to expect of them, of their hands, the perpetuation of their existence. That is why I do not want well-conceived, well-executed monuments to be dispersed haphazardly; I want them to be exhibited in a place safe from the ravages of time."[52]

This dissociation of what is remembered—the remains—from that which reminds—the monument—found surprising partisans, for example Lieutenant Hall, who, in the name of Christian piety, judged it beneficial to distinguish between two classes of monuments, those perpetuating the memory of loved ones and those proclaiming to posterity the greatness of the deceased. He considered this to be a return to the distinction drawn by the ancients between the statues of emperors or heroes and cemeteries reserved for the common people.[53] According to this view, the separation of monuments reserved for the Panthéon from those assigned to churches seemed advantageous to both religion and philosophy. Its adherents held

that museums were necessary to the new society, for they satisfied an authentic need for places of remembrance.

Even the most circumspect conceded that such institutions had been
rendered necessary by the outbreak of iconoclasm: "To be sure, one can
say that these monuments, separated from the remains they formerly contained, no longer inspire the respect they previously commanded; one
might even say that their contemplation [now] occasions less pleasure;
but it must not be forgotten that there was no other way to save them."[54]
A few, enchanted by their visits, went so far as to express satisfaction at
the threat of vandalism that had resulted in such a spectacle. At the close
of his description of the Petits-Augustins, the Prince de Clary remarked:
"It is said that, crammed together as they are, these tombs are not half as
effective as they would be in their original sites in the churches. Granted,
but who would see them if they were scattered throughout France? As it
stands the collection is of the most intense interest, unique in the world,
and something that could only have been created in circumstances of
revolutionary upheaval."[55] Finally, a few observers realized that such a
museum display, in addition to being convenient, conferred a new interest
on the objects within it simply by bringing them into proximity with one
another. J. F. C. Blanvillain noted in 1807: "Despite the displacement,
educated men take great pleasure in these monuments, which otherwise
they might not have had either the time or the means to see. Their very
assembly adds interest of a kind, by facilitating comparison."[56]

All of the debates and polemics surrounding memory as it operated
at the museum focus on the value, preserved or not, of the *monument*. Lenoir himself provided an excellent summary of the dispute, indicating his
own position in the process, during a conversation reported by Schultes:
"When we came to speak of the different impressions occasioned by a
monument in its original placement and in a museum, Monsieur Lenoir
did not dispute my contention that a monument awakens greater interest
in the place for which it was initially intended, especially when this was
immediately above the remains of the deceased; but he maintained that
when fate intervenes so brutally, and everything is wrested from its place,
a historical collection can offer just as much interest, as well as better protection against destruction and the ravages of time" (p. 111).

A SITE OF NATIONAL MEMORY

Like all of his contemporaries, Lenoir subscribed to the—etymological—
definition of the *monument* as architecture meant to establish and preserve
a mnemonic imprint. The primary referent was ancient precedent: "After
a battle, it was rare for a monument not to be raised in memory of the citi-

zens harvested by the war, and such perfectly appropriate reminders were spurs to glory; their names were inscribed on marble tablets, pyramids, and columns; and it was in this way that grateful peoples transmitted to the most distant posterity the striking deeds of their victories, and the precious names of those whose blood had been shed for the public good" (no. X). When all other traces have been effaced and human memory fails, monumental works of art remain, the sole witnesses to extinguished lives: "I cite in this regard the examples of Jean Goujon and Germain Pilon, the most accomplished of French sculptors living in previous centuries. These artists might be claimed by any nation, for we know neither where they were born nor where they died; and without parish death registers we could not even determine the dates of their decease. Fortunately . . . a way has been found to transmit to posterity, one might say everlastingly . . . historical facts, allegories, etc. that have come down to us as fresh as if they had just left the artist's hands, without time's having overtaken them" (p. 379). Given the terms in which Lenoir couched this encomium of the monument, it is not surprising that he modeled his museum after the most famous collection of tombs of his day: not the Panthéon, which only recently had been rededicated to this purpose and was all but empty, but Westminster Abbey, the perfect image of a national memorial.

The opinions of foreign visitors—especially English ones—confirmed this identification of the Petits-Augustins as a French Westminster. They never compared the Panthéon with this unique English church: the Constituent Assembly had decreed that "the new church of Sainte-Geneviève will henceforth become the French Westminster, that this edifice be consecrated to the remains of our great men," but it was empty of monuments and all its visitors left disappointed by this. At the Petits-Augustins, by contrast, they found quite a large number, both the royal tombs from Saint-Denis and those of ministers, generals, and artists taken from various Parisian churches. Ann Plumptre even thought that the purely museological character of the Petits-Augustins made it more conducive to reflection than melancholy Westminster, where the chain of associations was less calculated and more often severed.[57] Without exception, all visitors found the Museum of French Monuments superior to the basilica of Saint-Denis, preferring chronological sequence to dynastic crypts. In the words of A. H. Niemeyer, "All the same, this is a different sort of spectacle than the one to be had at Saint-Denis; there the imagination discerns only the shades of royalty and princes, many of them long since forgotten, hovering about their empty sepulchers. Here one also stands before the monuments of their subordinates, both noble and common, their courtiers, and their immortal contemporaries. The whole great book of the Annals

Fig. 3.5
First view of the large garden, etching by Jean-Baptiste Réville and Jacques Lavallée after a drawing by Jean-Lubin Vauzelle for B. de Roquefort, *Vues pittoreques et perspectives du Musée des monuments français* (Paris, 1816).

of France is here open to our gaze, not in letters, to be sure, but in brass and marble" (A. H. Niemeyer).

This ideal of a pantheon-museum that was simultaneously affecting and didactic, customary and official, religious and national, persisted until the Third Republic—along with the almost mythic authority of Westminster. This is made clear by the peregrinations of the remains of the Molière and La Fontaine. Exhumed on July 6, 1792, from the cemetery of Saint-Joseph, they were delivered to Lenoir by the municipal administration of the third arrondissement on 18 Floréal year VII (May 7, 1799) and placed in caskets in the museum on 17 Thermidor year VII (July 5, 1800) and 17 Vendemiaire year VIII (October 6, 1799), not without the curator's "having considered tenderly for some time the august debris of these two illustrious philosophers that so honored France."[58] When the museum

Fig. 3.6
Jean-Lubin Vauzelle, *The Thirteenth-Century Room in the Musée des Monuments Français*, watercolor from the Lenoir Album. Paris, Musée du Louvre, Cabinet des dessins.

closed, they were presented for a time at the church of Saint-Germain-des-Prés and then moved to the cemetery of Père-Lachaise (March 6, 1817). In 1875, the Académie Française lodged a complaint about the poor condition of their tombs; the matter was subsequently taken up by the press, and Minister De Cumont wrote to Philippe de Chennevières that it would be appropriate "to erect monuments to Molière and La Fontaine worthy both of these great men and of France, who counts them among her most illustrious children." On March 1, 1875, de Chennevières wrote to the minister deploring the absence of a site of remembrance in terms virtually identical to those used at the beginning of the century: "It is vexing that France does not possess a Campo Santo like those devoted by the smallest of old Italian states to its famous dead; England has its Westminster, Florence its Santa Croce, but by law we are no longer permitted to commit the remains of our great men to churches, and it is in cemeteries that one must seek their resting places." When he published his memoirs, the author added the following note: "I would never, either in the past or today, have proposed the basilica of Saint-Geneviève for this purpose.

Attempts were made in 1791 and 1830, and it must be conceded that they failed. Proud'hon is in agreement on this point with Michelet . . . and all republicans of good sense."[59]

The question would be resolved, however, in precisely this way, in the name of republican fidelity. But the model of Westminster was not abandoned, as is indicated by a continuing nostalgia for the Petits-Augustins, even in the early twentieth century. In 1908, a Harvard academic, Barrett Wendell, drew the following parallels between various European memorial sites: "You evoke with regard [to the Panthéon] the profound gravity of Westminster Abbey, the immensely competitive atmosphere of Santa Croce, where great men rest. . . . Quite different despite their apparent similarities, all these edifices are nonetheless animated by a persistent life. The French have enriched theirs with artistic marvels, perhaps evidencing more intelligence than in all the manifold assemblies in the other buildings. But in an indefinable way, this temple seems strangely, dreadfully devoid of life. . . . You find yourself in a sanctuary from which the soul has fled."[60] The tone here is quite similar to that of the average post-Revolutionary English visitor, adding to the sense that a viable French site of recollection was an impossibility. The Petits-Augustins might have played this role, thanks to the eclecticism of those it solemnized, in other words to the fact that it mobilized the entirety of French history, but such a strategy is impossible in the context of a pantheon limited to the great men of the *patrie républicaine*.

THE BIRTH OF THE "HISTORICAL MONUMENT"

To put it somewhat differently, Lenoir gave his blessing to the appearance, still tentative, of historical value at the heart of an artistic category hitherto the exclusive province of homage and recollection, namely the *monumental*. His interest in tombs was not exclusively religious, nor was it that of a man of sensibility or a specialist in Gothic sculpture; rather, he approached these artifacts as a historian whose goal was to compose "a veritable monumental history of the French monarchy." Hence his belief that "the monuments thus brought together should be regarded as no more than an assembly of mannequins wearing the clothing of the epochs to which they belong and accorded placements consistent with those occupied by [the individuals] they represent." Such an attitude was the sole viable response to a Revolutionary iconoclasm sympathetic only to the "value of intentional recollection." If old regime monuments were to survive the campaign of condemnation and appropriation mobilized in the name of the Revolution, in short the entire machinery of "vandalism," there was no alternative to such a strategy. To frame the question in Riegl's terms, either "contemporary values" linked to the monument's original significations would remain, condemning them "inexorably to ruin and destruction . . . from the moment those for whom they were destined and who had never ceased to attend to their conservation disappeared," or their historical value from a national and patriotic perspective could be affirmed, thereby guaranteeing their protection because "the people as a whole [would] consider the works of their putative ancestors as a part of their own creative activity."[61]

Both the Museum of French Monuments and the Cluny Museum (see below) played an essential role in the transition from one set of criteria to the other. The considerable "posthumous" success of the Petits-Augustins with the generation of 1830–40, whose members had visited it as children, testifies not only to the singular gifts of its originator but also to his fundamental sympathy with a pervasive shift in sensibility. In the context of an evocation of analogous provincial archeological installations in 1872, the curator of the museum in Pau recalled his frequent visits to Lenoir's museum in exemplary terms. The monuments

> arranged chronologically under its cloister and within its rooms formed a sculptural survey of the history of France . . .
>
> As children we came to know all these marble personages intimately: kings, warriors, prelates, writers, poets, artists. Scarcely had we learned to read before we became familiar not only with their features but their histories. We avidly deciphered the interesting entries and anecdotes that Monsieur Lenoir had incorporated into his learned catalogue.
>
> I have never heard of a more striking way of teaching history. . . . What a fine preparation it was for reading Augustin Thierry, de Barante, and the galaxy of historians that shortly thereafter shed light on hitherto obscure parts of our national history.[62]

Michelet felt similarly, affirming that he had received a "vivid impression of history" in Lenoir's museum: "Even now I recall the emotion, still quite vivid and still the same, that made my heart beat fast when, as a child, I entered beneath those dark vaults and contemplated those pale faces, when I went searching—ardent, curious, fearful—from room to room and age to age." Seat of the Académie Celtique and then of the Société des antiquaires de France, the museum was also the center of a network of scholarly sociability that perpetuated its memory. J.-P. Brès, in the introduction to his *Souveniers du Musée des monuments français* of 1821, wrote as follows: "Most enlightened nations could present their history through their monuments . . . France is perhaps the country in which the visual arts have been most varied in their phases, most diverse in their character." This language anticipates, almost word-for-word, Guizot's "Report to the King" of 1830, which led to the establishment of the Inspection générale des monuments historiques.

CLUNY, OR THE VIRTUE OF RELICS

The great French historical school of the early nineteenth century, then, was closely linked to museums: under the July Monarchy, some of its representatives even encouraged the establishment of the Cluny museum based on the Du Sommerard collection, and in accordance with a plan drafted by the son of Alexandre Lenoir, who followed the example established by his father. "Jovial, truculent, and given to punning," Alexandre Du Sommerard "had in 1821, like Quatremère de Quincy, joined the Société Royale des Bonnes-Lettres, which attributed to history an essential role in the formation of national consciousness." A fixture of society, especially artistic and literary circles, he was the French antiquarian best known to the public: "While the Du Sommerard collections are recommended to visitors in the Paris guidebooks of 1830, they say nothing about the other cabinets devoted to national antiquities."[63] In order "to revitalize the past *more majorum*, to cite the Latin expression he adopted as his device," he organized his collection in the Hôtel de Cluny as suggestively and picturesquely as possible. Describing himself as "an old maniac smitten with the most distant eras, huddling beneath smoke-blackened, half-Romanesque and half-Gothic ruins," he maintained that his goal was "to encourage the appreciation of everything that our old arts have to offer in the way of science and poetry" by means of an "exhibition," a "free spectacle," that was strange and "unexpected."[64] Jules Janin left an enthusiastic description of this installation that makes it easier for us to understand its popularity:

> One first entered the chapel (1490), which was admirably preserved, and there, amidst daisies, garlands, grape clusters, vines, and coats-of-arms of Charles VIII and Louis XII, one suddenly found oneself surrounded by the Middle Ages. . . . So powerful was the illusion that one breathed the old incense of this oratory, a lost incense revived by all this Christian art . . .
>
> From the chapel, one proceeded to the chamber of Francis I, or rather of Queen Blanche, and this time one had before one's eyes a complete picture of the royal and popular magnificence of centuries past. The door of this Francis I room came from the Château d'Anet; it brought to mind Diane de Poitiers and Henry II. The chess board was the very one used by King Saint Louis.

Adopting a more measured tone, the *Notice sur M. Dusommerard*, published in 1845, went beyond straightforward description of this collector's lair to attempt a definition of the museographic method reflected by it. Thanks to the "scattered debris" assembled there, Cluny, one reads, "unfolds before our eyes twelve centuries along with their outmoded mores, their customs, their furnishings, their costumes, their arms, in short all their relics." Its founder "has cast light on this chaos of ancient remains" by classifying them "according to their period and their value." By doing so, "he has neither written nor reproduced history, he has recomposed it with his own spoils."[65]

This anonymous specialist in collections discerned that, despite apparent similarities, this undertaking was different from that of Lenoir's. The latter represented each century by a heteroclite assemblage of *specimens* in accordance with the figure of metonymy, of a "reductive rhetorical strategy whereby the part does duty for the whole in a purely mechanistic way, without implying reference to any organic totality."[66] Du Sommerard, by contrast, brought together *relics*, seeking to revive the past by displaying them within integrating historical ensembles in special rooms. In our view, the contrast derives largely from the particularities of each collection: monuments and architectural fragments in the one case, precious artifacts, utilitarian objects, and furnishings in the other. According to Stephen Bann, it is to be explained by a break between two epistemes, with the Cluny museum corresponding to the structure of Romantic history and its aim to mythically reconstitute a period's everyday life. In any event, the disparate effects produced by the century rooms in the Petits-Augustins and the "chamber of Francis I" at the Cluny museum should not be allowed to obscure their common ambition to present history as it "really was." The virtuosity of the first attempt generated memories of such strength that transformation of the Du Sommerard collection into a public museum could not help but proceed, in some fashion, under Lenoir's auspices.

In 1883, a twelve-page pamphlet appeared, signed "Lenoir, architect, student of the painter Debret, and disciple of David," that called for conversion of the entire Cluny baths complex into a vast "national museum." The proposal's authority was buttressed by a long tradition of similar projects that had never proceeded beyond the planning stage. According to this text, a series of preliminary "Druidic rooms" and another devoted to the conquest of the Gauls would be followed by the large room of the baths, to contain an evocation of the Roman era. A wing devoted to the early monarchy, "dark like the historical epochs it represents," would house Romanesque and Gothic sculpture. A cloister given an eastern aspect would evoke the crusades, while the ground floor of the Hôtel de Cluny would

Fig. 3.7
Jean-Lubin Vauzelle, *The Introductory Room of the Musée des Monuments Français in the Former Church of the Petits-Augustins*, watercolor from the Lenoir Album. Paris, Musée du Louvre, Cabinet des dessins.

be devoted to the fourteenth and fifteenth centuries. Finally, in the last three rooms, by way of a postlude, a collection of historical portraits and a library would render "homage to the genius of writers." This scheme is a scarcely altered repetition of a proposal for expanding the Petits-Augustins that had been drafted by the elder Lenoir.[67]

After many administrative and financial vicissitudes, a bill calling for the establishment of such a museum was brought before the legislative chamber on June 17, 1843, by Arago. In his speech, he evoked the disappearance of "a similar establishment" that had met with "popular success, which is to say the most honorable kind. . . . With a few exceptions," he insisted, "the large rooms of the Louvre are frequented only by those with nothing better to do; the Museum of French Monuments, by contrast, was visited by studious and meditative crowds." The simultaneously democratic and didactic intentions of the proposed establishment were emphasized again in the Chambre des pairs, on July 4, by the Baron de Barante: "The Hôtel de Cluny would replace . . . the museum of the Petits-Augustins that was mistakenly destroyed. . . . The Société des Antiquaires de France has already requested to hold its meetings there, as it previously held them in the Musée des Petits-Augustins. Clearly the Hôtel de Cluny would be a site of study and research. . . . What the Musée de Louvre is for the artist, the Hôtel de Cluny would be for the worker."

Some forty years later, in the *Revue des arts décoratifs*, its editor Alfred Darcel underscored "the serious education" offered by Cluny and its interest for "the art industries": "It must not be forgotten that the museum was created in the past by the individual taste of an *amateur* who could not have been as preoccupied with useful application as we are today."[68] As early as 1847, in the museum's first catalogue, its founder's son, Edmond de Sommerard, used a two-tiered classification system, categorizing the collection first according to production type and then, within each subdivision, by date. This procedure was at odds with the program that had been the foundation of the Du Sommerard collection's initial fame as well as with the idealized model of the Petits-Augustins. As a result, the public seems to have been somewhat disappointed when the museum first opened.[69]

Subsequently, at the behest of the superior commission of the Monuments historiques, it acquired the architectural and sculptural remains of countless demolitions and restorations as well as plaster casts of many famous pieces. It rapidly took on the character of a lapidary depot juxtaposed with a store of artifacts "evoking" famous names and everyday life of the past. At the beginning of this century, Edmond Haraucourt, a member of the Monuments historiques commissions responsible for the museum, published *L'Histoire de France expliquée au musée de Cluny*, "an annotated guide organized by room and by series" that was divided into two parts, titled respectively "Centuries and Souls" and "Furnishings and Mores."[70] By then, lovers of monuments could compare this installation, so evocative of the models established by both Lenoir and Du Sommerard, with a parallel institution at the Trocadéro conceived along more scientific lines, namely the Museum of Comparative Sculpture.

THE TROCADÉRO, OR THE LESSON OF PLASTER CASTS

The idea for this museum dates back to a petition drafted by Parisian cast makers and presented on April 24, 1848. "The national museum," they wrote, "possesses a gallery of antiquities that is extremely rich in originals and casts, but the ancient world is not the only source of masterpieces. France, more than any other country, is covered with sculptural monuments of the greatest beauty, rightly admired by all. These monuments, being situated far from the large study centers, cannot easily be drawn." The petitioners proposed that this situation be remedied by "forming a collection of national sculptures available for study and research."[71] This proposal did not bear fruit, but a report written by Viollet-le-Duc and sent to Jules Ferry, then minister of public instruction, and Antonin Proust in 1879 initiated a process that resulted in the establishment of such an institution.

In a funeral oration delivered on November 8 of that same year, Jules Ferry noted that the architect had wanted "the many great things sown in our soil between the tenth and sixteenth centuries to constitute a new museum. . . . For this great soul, both artist and scholar, was above all a great French soul. Monsieur Viollet-le-Duc cultivated a passion for France, a France that can only be loved as it deserves when one knows it entirely, admirable not only in the great things it has accomplished over the last hundred years but in the imperishable works scattered by its genius in the course of past centuries."[72] Such a didactic vocation worked in tandem with the political stakes. This republican museum effectively set out to demonstrate, through a systematic comparison of ancient and medieval sculpture, "that the one is not inferior to the other," for the greater glory of the French people.

It succeeded totally in realizing this goal, for in 1907 the curator, Camille Enlart, stated that "the revelation of the beauties of Gothic statuary surpassed even the organizers' expectations, especially where artists were concerned. . . . The demonstration was so expeditious and so eloquent that further action was rendered superfluous; we had carried the day."[73] Beginning in 1933, casts of ancient art were excluded from the collection, which has henceforth been devoted to French monumental art in the form of sculpture casts, copies of mural paintings, and architectural models. Here the value bestowed upon the exhibited monuments is exclusively historical, whereas at the Petits-Augustins as well as, to a somewhat lesser degree, at Cluny, they had retained something of their original commemorative function.

The three monument museums examined here seem to have played a decisive role in the "democratization" of national memory. The earliest of them still adhered in some sense to the tradition of the commemorative monument, in the form of the composite memorials that Lenoir dedicated

Fig. 3.8
Photograph of the eighteenth-century room as formerly installed in the Musée des monuments français in the Palais du Trocadéro.

to great men. The two others favored the emergence of the "historical monument" as testimony to a reconciled history. The twentieth century has seen the triumph of what Riegl termed the "value of antiquity," which privileges the "traces of age," in short "the past in itself," whereas "historical value isolates a moment of historical development" to consider its "objective singularity" (*Le Culte moderne,* 50). Such sensitivity to "ancient monuments" favors the preservation of original sites and states as opposed to museum displays.[74]

NOTES

1. Léon Pressouyre, ed., *Le Musée des monuments français : Cité de l'architecture et du patriomoine* (Paris: Nicolas Chaudun, 2007).

2. Alois Riegl, *Le Culte moderne des monuments: Son essence et sa genèse* (Paris: Seuil, 1984; French translation of *Der moderne Denkmalkultus*, 1903), 47. English translation: "The Modern Cult of Monuments : Its Character and Its Origin," *Oppositions* 25 (Fall 1982), 21–51. See also André Chastel, "Le Patrimoine," *Encyclopedia universalis: Supplément I* (Paris, 1980), 43; and, by the same author, "Le Problème de l'inventaire monumental," *Bulletin de la Société de l'histoire de l'art français, année 1964* (Paris: F. De Nobele, 1965), 137–45.

3. It was especially prevalent in Revolutionary festivals. See Mona Ozouf, *Festivals and the French Revolution*, translated by Alan Sheridan (Cambridge, Mass.: Harvard University Press, 1988), 166ff.

4. Armand-Guy Kersaint, *Discours sur les monuments publics* (Paris, 1792), vi.

5. Paul Dupré and Gustave Ollendorf, *Traité d'administration des beaux-arts: Historique-législation-jurisprudence* (Paris: Paul Dupont, 1885), 2:487.

6. See the collection of studies on idleness edited by Adeline Daumard, *Oisiveté et loisirs dans les sociétés occidentales au XIXe siècle*, proceedings of an interdisciplinary conference sponsored by the Centre de recherche d'histoire sociale de l'Université de Picardie, Amiens, November 19–20, 1982 (Abbeville, 1983).

7. Although it does not altogether satisfy the expectations raised by its title, see the article by Bruno Foucart, "La Fortune critique d'Alexandre Lenoir et du premier musée des monuments français," *Information d'histoire de l'art* 5 (1969), 223–32.

8. Monsieur Allou, in *Mémoires de la société royale des antiquaires de France* (1842), 16:4–5.

9. Dr. Rigollot, *Lettre à M. Rivoire sur sa description de la cathédrale d'Amiens* (Amiens, 1806), 24.

10. See the letter by Gerville to Le Prévost dated December 18, 1818, cited by Jean Mallion, *Victor Hugo et l'art architectural* (Paris: Presses Universitaires de France, 1962), 30, n.103.

11. On the literary and scholarly reception of Lenoir's publications, see the study by Brian Juden, *Traditions orphiques et tendances mystiques dans le romantisme français (1800–1855)* (Paris: Klincksieck, 1971), 561–63, 663, and the anthology edited by B. Feldman and R. D. Richardson, *The Rise of Modern Mythology 1680–1860* (London, 1972), 276–78.

12. François Furet and Denis Richet, *La révolution française* (Paris: Fayard, 1973), 473.

13. Georges Lefebvre, *La France sous le directoire, 1795–1799* (Paris: Éditions Sociales, 1977), 577–78.

14. Albert Grenier, *Archéologie gallo-romaine* (Paris: Picard, 1931), 61.

15. Louis Dimier, *Les Impostures de Lenoir, examen de plusieurs opinions reçues sur la foi de cet auteur, concernant plusieurs points de l'histoire des arts* (Paris: Sacquet, 1903).

16. *Cahiers de la république des lettres, des sciences et des arts* (Paris, 1931), 13:7.

17. Jacques Vanuxem, "La Sculpture religieuse au musée des monuments français," thesis submitted in 1937, summarized in *Positions de thèses des élèves de l'École du Louvre de 1911 à 1944* (Paris: École du Louvre, 1956), 203.

18. Paul Léon in *La Revue de Paris*, issues of July 1 and July 15, 1913.

19. Henri Jacoubet, *Le Genre troubadour et les origines françaises du romantisme* (Paris: Les Belles Lettres, 1928), 48.

20. Marcel Aubert, *Le Romantisme et l'Art* (Paris, 1928), chap. 2, 23.

21. Louis Réau, *Histoire de l'Art*, series edited by André Michel, vol. 8, bk. 1, 38 and 84–85.

22. René Lanson, *Le Goût du moyen âge en France au XVIIIe siècle* (Paris: G. Van Oest, 1926), and Pierre Barrière, *La Vie intellectuelle en France des origines à l'époque contemporaine* (Paris: Albin Michel, 1961), 394. Lenoir rates a brief mention in the compendium edited by Paul Frankl, *The Gothic: Literary Sources and Interpretations through Eight Centuries* (Princeton: Princeton University Press, 1960), chap. 4, 564.

23. Roger Bastide, *Art et société* (Paris: Payot, 1977), 97.

24. Marie-Claude Chaudonneret, *La Peinture troubadour: Deux artistes lyonnais: Revoil (1776–1842)–F. Richard (1777–1852)* (Paris: Arthéna, 1980); François Pupil, *Le Style troubadour* (Nancy: Presses Universitaires de Nancy, 1985), esp. 117–27. See also the groundbreaking article by Francis Haskell, "The Manufacture of the Past in Nineteenth-Century Painting," *Past and Present*, no. 53 (1971): 110–20, now republished in the same author's *Past and Present in Art and Taste: Selected Essays* (New Haven: Yale University Press, 1987), 90–116.

25. Louis Bergeron, *L'Épisode napoléonien* (Paris: Seuil, 1972), 222.

26. Ferdinand Brunot, *Histoire de la langue française des origines à 1900* (Paris, 1943), 10:2, 93.

27. Louis Courajod, "L'Influence du musée des monuments français sur le développement de l'art et des études historiques," *Revue historique*, no. 30 (1886): 107–18.

28. Albert Grenier, *Archéologie gallo-romaine,* vol. 5 of *Manuel d'archéologie préhistorique, celtique et gallo-romaine,* edited by J. Déchelette, 62–64.

29. Charles Samaran, ed., *L'Histoire et ses méthodes* (Paris: Gallimard, Encyclopédie de la Pléiade, 1961).

30. *Le Petit Robert 2,* 5th ed. (Paris, 1981), 1067; E. Bénézit, 1952, 5:512.

31. *Hier pour demain: Arts, traditions et patrimoine*, catalogue of an exhibition held at the Grand Palais in Paris, June 13–September 1, 1980, 65.

32. Pierre de Lagarde, *La Mémoire des pierres* (Paris: Albin Michel, 1979), 13–20. See also two erudite articles by Françoise Arquié-Bruley: "Un Précurseur, le comte de Saint-Morys, collectionneur d'Antiquités nationales, 1772–1817," *Gazette des beaux-arts* VI/XCVI and XCVII (1980–81): 109–18 and 61–77; "Les Monuments français inédits (1806–39) de N. X. Willemin et la découverte des 'Antiquités nationales,'" *RACAR* 10, no. 2 (1983): 139–56.

33. Michel Vovelle, *La Chute de la monarchie, 1787–1792* (Paris: Seuil, 1972), 150.

34. The primary sources and basic secondary publications relating to Lenoir's Musée des monuments français are as follows:

    ❧ Archives of the Musée des monuments français, Archives nationales, series F. 21. A selection of these documents is published at the beginning of *Inventaire général des richesses d'art de la France,* 3 vols. (Paris, 1883–97).

    ❧ Lenoir papers in the library of École nationale supérieure des beaux-arts (Department of Manuscripts).

    ❧ Dossiers Lenoir in the Archives du Musée du Louvre (Z 62 Lenoir).

    ❧ Three bound volumes containing approximately 250 drawings relating to the museum and its collections in the Cabinet des dessins of the Musée du Louvre (RF 5279, 5280, 5281).

* Lenoir's *Journal*, published in the first volume of Louis Courajod, *Alexandre Lenoir et le musée des monuments français*, 3 vols. With complete bibliography on Lenoir (Paris: 1878–87).

* Alexandre Lenoir, *Description historique et chronologique des monuments de sculpture réunis au musée des monuments français* (Paris, twelve editions between 1794 and 1815).

* The eight volume catalogue of the museum's collections: *Musée des monuments français ou description historique et chronologique des statues en marbre et en bronze, bas-reliefs et tombeaux des hommes et femmes célèbres, pour servir à l'histoire de France* (Paris, 1800–1806).

* L. de Lanzac de Laborie, *Paris sous Napoléon: Spectacles et musées* (Paris: Plon, 1913), 330–64.

* Critical bibliography of subsequent publications in Dominique Poulot, *Musée, nation, patimoine, 1789–1815* (Paris: Gallimard, Bibliothèque des Histoires, 1997), as well as in various later articles, such as "Pantheons in Eighteenth-Century France: Temple, Museum, Pyramid," in *Pantheons: Transformations of a Monumental Idea*, edited by Richard Wrigley and Matthew Kraske (London: Ashgate, 2004), 123–46; and "Gloires et opprobres politiques au musée," *Sociétés et représentations* 2008, "La gloire politique."

35. On this point, in addition to the general studies by Philippe Ariès, *Essais sur l'histoire de la mort en Occident du moyen âge à nos jours* (Paris: Seuil, 1975) and Michel Vovelle, *La Mort en Occident de 1300 à nos jours* (Paris: Gallimard, 1983), see the documents collected by Pascal Hintermeyer, *Politiques de la mort* (Paris: Payot, 1981) and especially Lionello Sozzi, "I Sepolcri e le discussioni francesi sulle tombe negli anni del direttorio e del consolato," *Giornale storico della litteratura italiana*, 1967, 567–88.

36. *Inventaire général des richesses d'art de la France*, op. cit., vol. 1, piece ccxlv.

37. Ibid., piece clxi. On Drouais, see the exhibition catalogue *Jean-Germain Drouais 1763–1788*, Musée des beaux-arts de Rennes, June 7–September 9, 1985.

38. Computations made in conjunction with the author's thesis on Revolutionary museums. Thesis published as Dominique Poulot, "Surveiller et s'instruire: La Révolution française et intelligence de l'héritage historique" (Oxford, Voltaire Fondation, 1996) (Studies on Voltaire and the Eighteenth Century, 344).

39. See the selections from the so-called *Bibliothèque bleu* republished under the editorship of Daniel Roche by éditions Montalba.

40. See especially the discussions of Chevart and Brizard.

41. John Carr, *The Stranger in France* (London, 1803), 224.

42. *Rapport fait au nom de la Commission . . . pour l'achat de l'hôtel Cluny, par M. Arago (June 17, 1843)* (Paris, 1843), reprinted in Albert Lenoir, *Le musée des Thermes et de l'hôtel de Cluny: Documents sur la création du musée d'antiquités nationales. . . .* (Paris, 1882), 68–75.

43. *Paris during the interesting month of July 1815, a series of letters addressed to a friend in London, by W. D. Fellowes, Esq.* (London, 1815).

44. Martine Dumont, "Le Succès mondain d'une fausse science: La Physiognomie de Johan Kasper Lavater," *Actes de la recherche en sciences sociales* 54 (1984): 2–30.

45. August-Hermann Niemeyer, *Beobachtungen*. . . . (1824), 2:89 (Paris, Bibliothèque Nationale, G.27.190).

46. Claude Mouchard, "Deux secondes vies," *Le Temps de la réflexion* (Paris: Gallimard, 1982), 3:170.

47. Jules Michelet, preface to the 1868 edition of *La Révolution française*.

48. See the analysis of Claude Lefort, op. cit., 193–95.

49. *Prospectus*, 15–16. Note, by contrast, "the small role allotted research into national origins by the commission of departmental statistics" (Marie-Noëlle Bourguet, "Déchiffrer la France," thèse de troisième cycle, typed manuscript, 2 vols., Bibliothèque de la Sorbonne, n.d., 554).

50. On the ultimate fate of the monuments, see Geneviève Bresc-Bautier, "Tombeaux factices de l'abbatiale de Saint Denis ou l'art d'accommoder les restes," *Bulletin de la société nationale des antiquaires de France*, 1980–81, 114–27.

51. *A Tour through Some Parts of France, Switzerland, Savoy, Germany and Belgium, during the Summer and Autumn of 1814 by the Hon. Richard Boyle Bernard, M.* (London, 1815), 65.

52. I. A. Schultes, *Briefe über Frankreich auf einer Fussreise im Jahre 1811* (Leipzig, 1815), 2:395.

53. Francis Hall, *Travels in France in 1818* (London, 1819), 72 and 97.

54. John Dean Paul, *The Journal of a Party of Pleasure to Paris* (London, 1802).

55. Prince de Clary, *Trois mois à Paris lors du mariage de l'Empereur Napoléon Ier et de l'archiduchesse Marie-Louise* (Paris, 1914).

56. J. F. C. Blanvillain, *Le Pariseum, ou tableau actuel de Paris* (Paris, 1807), 122.

57. Ann Plumptre, *A Narrative of a Three Years Residence in France*, 3 vols. (London, 1810), 1:31.

58. *Inventaire général des richesses d'art de la France*, op. cit., vol. 1, pièce cclxxxvii.

59. Philippe de Chennevières, *Souvenirs d'un directeur des beaux-arts (1820–1899)* (new edition, Paris: Arthéna, 1979), 68–71.

60. Barrett Wendell, *La France d'aujourd'hui* (Paris, 1909), 273–76 (in the "Petite Collection Nelson").

61. Alois Riegl, op. cit. (see note 2), 43, 47–48, 51.

62. Ch. C. Le Coeur, *Considérations sur les musées de province* (Paris: Vignancourt, 1872). See also Ernest Vinet, "Les archives pendant la Révolution," *Journal des débats*, April 23, 1867, in which he wrote, "Lenoir not only created, in the midst of tempests, a museum full of poetry, a refuge for old French art; he gave us Augustin Thierry: it was during visits to the Gothic halls of this picturesque museum, whose loss is so much to be regretted, that the eloquent, penetrating, and patient interpreter of the old chroniclers conceived the idea of disentangling the chaos of the origins of our history."

63. Pierre Marot, "Les Origines d'un musée d''antiquités nationales.' De la protection du 'Palais des Thermes' à l'institution du 'Musée de Cluny,'" *Mémoires de la Société nationale des antiquaires de France*, 9th series, vol. 4 (1969): 259–327. Unless otherwise specified, all of the following quotations are cited from this article.

64. Alexandre Du Sommerard, *Les Arts du moyen âge* (Paris, 1838), 1:402–3.

65. *Notice sur M. Dusommerard, avec explication et détails de son musée* (Paris, 1845), offprint from *La Renommée, revue politique, parlementaire, littéraire. . . .* The text by Jules Janin is cited on 8–12.

66. Stephen Bann, "Poetics of the Museum: Lenoir and Du Sommerard," chapter 4 of *The Clothing of Clio: A Study of the Representation of History in Nineteenth-Century Britain and France* (Cambridge: Cambridge University Press, 1984), 85.

67. "Observations sur le musée des monuments français," following "Ordre à suivre dans le placement des monuments" (in Mousseaux), published in the *Inventaire général des richesses d'art de la France*, op. cit., vol. 1, piece clxxxii.

68. Alfred Darcel, "Les Art décoratifs au musée de Cluny," *Revue des arts décoratifs* 7 (1886): 97–111.

69. Alain Erlande-Brandenburg, "Le Musée des monuments français et les origines du Musée de Cluny," in Bernward Deneke and Rainer Kashsnitz, eds., *Das Kunst und Kulturgeschichtliche Museum im 19: Jahrhundert* (Munich: Prestel-Verlag, 1977), 49–58. See also *Le 'Gothique' retrouvé*, an exhibition catalogue (Paris: Caisse Nationale des Monuments Historiques et des Sites, 1979), 75–78. Charles Morice, in a discussion of the Cluny Museum, had already noted that "Alexandre Lenoir, his son Albert Lenoir, and Du Sommerard are the true founders of this precious museum," in *Pourquoi et comment visiter les musées* (Paris: Armand Colin, n.d.), 31.

70. Edmond Haraucourt, *L'Histoire de France expliquée au musée de Cluny* (Paris: Larousse, 1922), 6.

71. The petition is reproduced in its entirety in Louis Courajod, "Le Moulage—principales applications—collections de modèles reproduits par le plâtre. Conférence à la 9e exposition de l'Union centrale des arts décoratifs," *Revue des arts décoratifs* 8 (1887): 254.

72. Cited in Paul Deschamps, "Le Musée de sculpture comparée," *Congrès archéologique de France*, 97th session, Paris, 1934 (Paris: Picard, 1935), 1:388–89.

73. Camille Enlart, "Deux musées historiques de l'art français: Petits-Augustins et Trocadéro," *Bulletin de la Société historique du VIe arrondissement*, 1907, 76.

74. *Le Musée de sculpture comparée—Naissance de l'histoire de l'art moderne*, Collectif (Paris: Editions du Patrimoine, 2001).

Fig. 4.1
François Guizot.

CHAPTER 4

GUIZOT AND THE INSTITUTIONS

OF MEMORY

❧

LAURENT THEIS

A HISTORIAN IN POWER

François Guizot, on becoming minister for public instruction in October 1832, was a mature, almost elderly man. By then prominent in the world of politics for more than fifteen years, he had already completed most of his intellectual and historical works, begun twenty years earlier. He would hardly take them up again to finish them, even after having moved away from the sphere of public affairs. Only his *Mémoires*, published around 1860, would in another way crown these and give him all his later import, as was no doubt intended.

It was not so much the political theorist as the historian that first entered government. In the chamber and in the press it was this quality that was first recognized in him, this quality that even his opponents admired. It set him apart from the politicians over whom he held sway, for the most part from on high. His activity as a historian was carefully distinguished from his political practices. The latter may have undergone criticism, the former has scarcely ever been disputed, certainly not during his time as minister of the public instruction, which came to an end in 1837.[1] His contemporaries do not seem to have realized to what extent the two are one and the same in Guizot's case. It is true that they themselves were almost all in the same situation, and that one seldom notices in oneself that which one does not find in others.

The Ministry of Public Instruction was the one in which Guizot's double identity as politician and historian could best come to fruition.

Foreign affairs, in later years, undoubtedly did not provide him with the same satisfaction. "His ministry," wrote his wife a few days after he took office, "pleases him. He delights in once more being among the companions and works of his youth. Public instruction affords him a rest from ordinary politics."[2]

Guizot liked it all the better since he could tailor the department to his own specifications. In 1832 it did not really exist as such. Separated from the Department of Ecclesiastical Affairs in 1828 to become a ministry in its own right, it would bring all denominations under its auspices from July 1830 onwards. As regards public instruction, the briefs of Guizot's predecessors did not go beyond those of the grand maître de l'Université, which in reality had changed in name only. Guizot asked for and received a considerable extension of the jurisdiction of his ministry. Apart from educational establishments and the Université, institutions that had previously had various statuses, or indeed none, were attached to his department, namely the Collège de France, the Muséum, the École des chartes, École des langues orientales, libraries, and, most important, the royal library, and, to top it all, the Institut. In short, Guizot would find himself at the center of an enormous range, a vast constellation of previously disparate institutions of learning, where he was to put his ideas into practice and make the most of his authority. As is well known, he lacked neither ideas nor authority.

Among the qualities that Guizot readily acknowledged in himself were an alertness and determination to act upon a decision as soon as he had established that such a decision was necessary. Indeed in less than two years he would provide the impetus for, or create, two capital institutions, essential in the advances that they sanctioned and the developments that they contained: the Société de l'histoire de France, and under another name, what would become the Comité des travaux historiques et scientifiques. Both still exist today. Guizot the historian and Guizot the statesman came together and complemented one another; the Société de l'histoire de France for the former and the Comité for the latter, to which other more minor but nevertheless significant actions can be added. In all these matters it was a case of rediscovering, preserving, and bringing to light the archives of France.

Neither Guizot the teacher nor Guizot the minister can be seen unequivocally as the instigator of this project.

THE CABINET DES CHARTES

There is no need to go back to the Middle Ages, let alone earlier, because in the West as elsewhere State archives have no precise origin. The French archives achieved a particular status, which was not yet public yet was no longer wholly private, when the kingship became identified with the State, sometime between the reigns of Charles V and Louis XI. It was then that the documents, which founded and maintained the State's legitimacy and that kept a record of activities relating to public power, were collected and held in store. Such documents therefore became of enormous value, as is demonstrated by, for example, the name Trésor des chartes, such was the extent of power, significance, knowledge, and tradition held in these parchments, soon to be papers, with their wax emblems attesting to their authenticity. Even as early as the Middle Ages, only that which was historical was of worth. More that anything else, the memory of the king and everything about him and around him deserved to escape the erosion of time. The State was also born from paperwork.★

This soon became widespread with the extension of royal authority, and, from the sixteenth century onward, with the propensity to codify everything, to put in writing all laws, customs, title deeds, judgements, decisions, instructions, enquiries, and so on, manuscripts and printed matter accumulated, often with no order or classification, sometimes unusable but nonetheless invaluable. Without records that could be consulted, the State would lose some of its effectiveness, continuity, and even legitimacy. Fouquet was one of the first to be concerned about this state of affairs.† He contemplated the classification of, and the making of an inventory of, papers necessary for the smooth running of the State, which were also matters that concerned him. But it was not until the second half of the eighteenth century that a serious, and in many ways productive, attempt took shape.

Jacob-Nicolas Moreau had been an *avocat des finances* since 1759.[3] This forty-five year old lawyer, a mediocre polygraph but an active and capable organizer, was entrusted with the documentation of the Ministry of Finance, the most modern department of its time in terms of structure and operation. It was his task to procure for the minister texts, many of which were ancient, which justified and founded the king's right to collect revenue of any kind, notably in the face of seigniorial claims and the resistance of the *parlements*. In 1762, Moreau, quickly promoted to the position of "keeper of the archives and the library of finance," proposed to Controller-General Bertin, an open-minded man who took pride in

---

★ TRANSLATOR'S NOTE: As the names of many institutions and societies have no direct English equivalent, or are particularly "French" institutions, I have chosen to leave many of them in the original French form.

† EDITOR'S NOTE: Nicolas Fouquet (1615–80) became the superintendent of finances in 1653. He accumulated an immense fortune by dubious means and was ruined by Louis XIV in 1661. His famous chateau, Vaux-le-Vicomte, was confiscated by the king, along with all Fouquet's worldly goods. He was the first notorious prisoner in the infamous Bastille.

his knowledge of history, the constitution of public law, and the history archive. When Bertin became secretary of state the following year, the library of finance, and Moreau with it, came back under the auspices of the library of the king. It was in these circumstances that Moreau started to execute his project: making copies of all deeds written before the fifteenth century, attaching to each explanations, describing it exactly, and giving an outline of the contents. And, firstly, making an inventory of the available texts and drawing up a list of documents already printed. It would take 107 years and eight enormous volumes.

The Dépôt des chartes, masterminded by Moreau, lacked human and material resources. Moreau took on the assistance of Bréquigny, an eminent scholar, already responsible for publishing the *Ordonnances des rois de France de la troisième race*, and who would carry out the essential cataloging and publishing work that Moreau had envisaged. Apart from scholars such as Bréquigny, Foncemagne, and Sainte-Palaye, the realm of palaeography and familiarity with medieval texts still belonged to the Benedictines of Saint-Maur, heirs of Mabillon and Montfaucon, who had regenerated historical study by submitting sources to rigorous criticism, imposing even then the rules of modern scholarship. It was the guardians of this inheritance, in fact six to eight monks, whose collaboration was sought by the Dépôt des chartes. The fact that they were churchmen meant that they did not have to be paid. This meeting of the most erudite minds of the age, the *antiquarii*, and the State archives was of considerable impact for the future. In their precise methods, the creations of Guizot followed exactly the path traced by Moreau, Bréquigny, and the Maurists under the auspices of Bertin, and thus of the king.

However, the purpose of the Dépôt des chartes, despite the scale of the project, was the result of a concept of historical information as an instrument. It was not a matter of granting access to the monuments of the past but of procuring an efficient tool through which the administration could act. There was never any question of opening the collected treasures to the public—quite the opposite. As a lawyer, Moreau believed that history was at the root of law and that a knowledge of history justified the founding and legitimization of laws, in this case those of the monarchy. The royal decree of March 3, 1781, which combined the library of finance and the Dépôt des chartes and linked them to the chancellery of France, in other words, to the Ministry of Justice, gave this institution the significant title of Bibliographie et dépôt de législation, histoire et droit public. It is known that during these years many nobles, driven by a similar desire for recovering the past, took on specialists in feudal law, like small-scale Moreaus, to sort out their papers and revive the memory of their families, their long history, and all their rights, rooted more often than not in a Middle Ages they hoped to rediscover. This unearthing of archives to support the law led to an interest in history that was no longer philosophical or purely narrative, given over to reflection, instruction, and even education, as it had been in the first half of the century, but that now took account of the exercise of authority and the institutions that were the basis of that authority, of relationships between groups, of material goods, and of defined spaces, whether it be a field, an estate, or France itself. From then it was understood that the search for origins necessary to protect established situations required the classification and exploitation of written documents, a process that led for the most part to the Middle Ages and the genesis and infancy of modern society.

At the end of the ancien régime, private archives, now combined, ordered, and used—a result of the need to organize the new—carried the faintest acts of the still scattered memories that carried France high on the shoulders of its past. The importance of these documents as a pillar of the State's identity did not escape the notice of the protagonists of revolutionary movements. This either involved spontaneous or deliberate destruction, or the removal of such documents from the hands of those they supported and their transfer to a nation that was finally its own mistress, the possession of archives constituting a powerful assertion of existence. Estate, seigniorial, and royal archives, on becoming national archives, changed their role. Formerly instruments of domination, they became the providers of a collective identity; the past was no longer something for a select few, but entered into the heritage of all. This is the reason why the archives of the *Assemblée* were the first to be granted the status of *national* archives, and why the law of 7 Messidor, Year II, introduced a distinction between historical documents and administrative documents. The former, the only ones of concern here, were themselves the object of a selective system, according to whether or not they echoed earlier tyranny. The national memory needed to be purified if its virtues were to flourish fully. At the same time, however, access to them was made public. Everyone had the right to consult them. In the same movement that gave the nation back its history, every Frenchman was in a position to become aware of the pieces upon which that history was based. The citizens of France revelled in this knowledge, which was widely exercised. Eventually the law of 5 Brumaire Year V organized the gathering of all departmental archives at the prefecture.

On the one hand interrupted, as inventories and publications were postponed for more propitious times, the enterprise begun by Moreau, thanks to a new organization and above all a new way of thinking, nevertheless received the means to develop when the will was there to meet the need.

FROM ONE REVOLUTION TO ANOTHER

Under the Empire and the Restoration, it was chiefly the Institut that was the holder of the combined heritage of the ancien régime and the Revolution. This was no thanks to the institutions, for the national, or royal, library and the archives fell under the auspices of the Ministry of the Interior. The former members of the Cabinet des chartes, Moreau's collaborators, were called to sit in the Institut, bringing with them the erudite tradition of the antiquaries, and the will to constitute the collective memory of France through research in the documents. One of the most active and conspicuous men in the Institut was Daunou, who had been curator of the National Archives since 1808 and provided a link between eighteenth-century philosophy, the pieces of which were being picked up by the ideologists, and traditional historical science. It was he who in his important report to the convention in October 1795 had raised the plan for the Institut to become a "national temple." In 1818 he was elected to the chair of history and ethics at the Collège de France. This conjuncture of philosophy and scholarship personified by Daunou, under the auspices of the revolutionary patriotism symbolized by the former member of the convention, was to a large extent the basis of Guizot's culture, who was himself a loyal friend and to some extent a disciple of Royer-Collard, professor of the history of philosophy at the Sorbonne in 1811 and very close to Daunou.

The role of the Institut in producing a national memory, in classifying its available material, and especially in synthesizing the traditions of the ancien régime and the spirit of the Revolution was vital in the early decades of the nineteenth century. There was nobody more closely associated with this than Guizot, not only because it was his domain as minister, but because he was a member, and an active one, of the Académie des sciences morales from 1832, which he had just reconstituted and where Daunou once again held the highest office; was a member of the Académie des inscriptions et belles-lettres from 1833; and of the Académie française from 1836, a very rare example of one man with so many offices.

The Institut, which had not been very active under the empire when reflection on the nation and its history was scarcely encouraged by the spread of a conquering France, all the more so because the protagonists of the Revolution were keeping very quiet or were in exile abroad, found new life under the Restoration. In an attempt to develop a national history and collect the various elements thereof, the Académie des inscriptions et belles-lettres produced a report on the "ancient buildings and historic monuments" of France in late 1818 on the initiative of the Comte de Laborde, an important personality in the efforts to unearth and preserve

French heritage. The report states that "what France has always lacked has been to attach to these treasures the importance they deserve, to assure their conservation, and to endeavour to put them to good use for both our edification and our national history." Laborde's plan to complete an inventory of the archaeological treasures of France came to nothing. It was Guizot who was to take it up at a later date.

Another initiative in the same vein met with more success. In 1820 the Baron de Gérando, member of the Council of State and of the Académie des inscriptions et belles-lettres, suggested to Comte Siméon, minister of the interior, the creation of a school where the students would learn to read old manuscripts, for that skill once held by the Benedictines and the associates of the Cabinet des chartes was being lost. Instigated by Gérando, who had made a similar but unsuccessful effort as early as 1806, Siméon wrote to the king: "A branch of French literature, that relating to the history of the nation, is going to be deprived of a group of associates, without whom it cannot exist." And so on February 22, 1821, the bill was passed creating the École des chartes to "revive a type of study essential to the glory of France." After a sluggish start, the École was to be given a new vigor, thanks to Guizot.[4]

THE NEED FOR HISTORY

Torn and shaken by decades of internal strife, defeated by a coalition at the heart of which the growing power of Prussia represented a renascent German national spirit aided especially by philosophical and historical study, France had to find reasons to believe in itself that its present was unable to offer, but could be obtained by a knowledge of its past. From the end of the Empire to the beginning of the Republic a feeling existed throughout France that the building and regeneration of a national memory was both a political and cultural necessity. Among the more obscure and more eloquent of the numerous adherents to this obsession was the Comte du Hamel, an ultraroyalist *député* from the Gironde, who intervened thus in the budgetary debate of 1827, "I would like our young people to be educated in a manner more French than is customary in our schools . . . Rome, Sparta and tales of the legendary or heroic age that are used there are far less suitable for the formation of French hearts and minds than examples drawn from French annals and charters."[5] In fact history as a subject in its own right, taught by specialist teachers, had only been officially introduced in schools in 1818 and was significantly overshadowed by the study of classical antiquity. However, the call for history, and above all a national history, whatever idea people had about the nation, was both pressing and considerable. Chateaubriand, describing the historiographical activity of the preceding decades, in the astonishing and perspicacious preface to his *Études ou discours historiques*, published in 1831, observes, "The times we are living in are so strongly historical that they are leaving their mark on all forms of work. Ancient chronicles are being translated, old manuscripts published . . . everything today abounds with history; polemics, theatre, novels and poetry." At the heart of this movement to actualize the past were numerous voices who, often in order to justify their own undertakings, observed the absence of a real national history. The new historical school, which was active from 1810 onward (of which Guizot, according to Chateaubriand one of the great reformers of French collective history, was soon one of the most conspicuous representatives), was slow in producing the works whose necessity was so keenly felt. Augustin Thierry regrets the "lack of a national history,"[6] an issue that Henri Martin, whose first volume of *Histoire de France* appeared in 1833, raised once more: "France has no national history."

This was because the French nation and the people that constituted it were a new subject of study, one still being formed. It was no longer a case of looking at kings and their reigns, in the manner of the historiographers of the ancien régime, but at an entity hitherto neglected, the nation, which arose in 1789 and whose origins needed to be found and its development traced. The political commitment to history was, essentially, the source of the revival of historical study, the materials and method and even the object of which changed completely.[7] It was not merely the clamor of Frankish war cries that ensured Augustin Thierry's vocation as an historian. It was also the "ardent desire to contribute to the triumph of constitutional ideas," which, in 1817, led him to "search the history books for evidence and arguments supporting my political beliefs."[8] In 1821, Sismondi, first to be disgusted by the "prejudices of the compilers" and declaring his wish to take history back to its source, dared to entitle his work *Histoire des français* (History of the French). Even this history, praiseworthy and innovatory as its conception may have been, remained strictly political. The new historical school only realized its full potential when the concept of "nation" met that of "civilization." Launching his course in modern history at the Sorbonne in 1812, Guizot took that as his aim. It was in France, he argued, that this concept was best represented. In the *Histoire de la civilisation en France* he writes, "Civilization is the sum of all histories; all of them are needed as elements thereof." However, the elements were lacking; hence the undertaking of publishing sources not only of charters, but also of annals, written accounts, and chronicles that led to an appreciation of the widest possible aspects of a people's existence, which recounted not only politics and law but the social, cultural, and moral realities that form the identity and originality of a civilization.

Between 1819 and 1826 Petitot published the 52 volumes of his *Collection complète des mémoires relatifs à l'histoire de France depuis le règne de Philippe Auguste jusqu'au commencement du XVIIe siècle* (*Complete collection of the memoires relating to the history of France from the reign of Philippe Auguste to the beginning of the seventeenth century*). Buchon followed closely behind: 46 volumes (1826–28) of the *Collection des chroniques nationales françaises, écrite en langue vulgaire du XIIIe au XVIe siècle* (*Collection of French national chronicles written in the common tongue from the thirteenth to the sixteenth century*). These undertakings can be joined with those of Guizot himself, whose *Collection des mémoires relatifs à l'histoire de France depuis la fondation de la monarchie française jusqu'au XIIIe siècle* (*Collection of memoires relating to the history of France from the foundation of the French monarchy to the thirteenth century*) formed 30 volumes of Guizot's thought between 1823 and 1825. Historians then had something to work on, and a public curious for knowledge about the ancient history of France could find something to satisfy its demand. For scientific necessities and ideological preoccupations form a close pair with similar goals: the reestablishment of the ties of history to understand that otherwise inexplicable event, the Revolution; integrating it into a continual evolution; looking for precedents within it to make it intelligible; and ensuring the appearance throughout their successive changes of a unity of the French people and French history that the Revolution had seemed to call into question, and that the Restoration threatened in its turn with a diametrically opposed movement. Writing history meant taming the recent past. For Guizot's generation to understand the revolution was to draw all that was good from it to prevent it happening again. And to understand it they had to go back to the beginning, in order to place the present under the security of an unimpeachable national memory that would provide identity, certainty, and reason. Albeit with their own personal views, Fauriel, Augustin Thierry, Mignet, Quinet, and Michelet shared this belief with Guizot, at least up to 1840.[9] For them the study of national history, to which they all devoted themselves to a greater or lesser extent, was the indispensable propadeutic of the construction of the present, not to learn lessons from history but to know and understand history's idea of the nation and its interests. The incredible events of the last few decades threw new light on former revolutions, of which it was important to be well aware to appreciate the state of France and how it had become what it was. The Middle Ages were also a favored field of study. It was then that French civilization was moulded by a succession of events, then that the systems and instruments of government were forged, and then that the middle classes, the bourgeoisie, the people—those forces that constitute the substance of the nation today—developed and emerged. According to Augustin Thierry, "The largest and most forgotten part of the nation deserves to take its part in history once more. One must not imagine that the middle classes or popular classes were born yesterday as far as patriotism and energy are concerned."[10]

The search for the bases of national identity, the historical legitimization of the third estate, the demands of recent history—these preoccupations were precisely those of Guizot the professor, and later the statesman.

THE TIME OF THE PROFESSORS

According to Guizot and his intellectual allies, the principal characteristic of modern societies was the government of minds, a belief that was embodied in the representative system.[11] Even before coming to power the future men of July had already exercised this government of minds thanks to their roles in universities. The new generation, which had not participated in either the revolutionary adventure or the imperial epic, which was not weighed down by their failures but instead looked to penetrate the reasons behind them, found in higher education a means to confirm its ideas, perfect its knowledge and, already, to test and feel its power. Faced with a political establishment tied by memories and personal experience, these (at least in those respects) free-spirited men were free to confront the real questions posed by the contemporary world. By excluding them from the political sphere and from any say in matters, the Restoration gave them a field of influence that established their reputation. Augustin Thierry notes that through the courses of Guizot, Villemain, and Cousin, "the academic world rose to become a social power."[12] The suspension of these courses by the minister Villèle in 1822—a wonderful tribute paid by vice to virtue, by power to thought—was to ensure the prestige of these professors. Guizot's return to the chair in 1828 brought forth such clamors of triumph that he had to appeal to his listeners for calm. Under the Restoration the political activities of Guizot were conveyed for the most part by the development of his writing as a historian.[13] The rediscovery and constitution of a national memory were fundamental for a modern society as he understood and conceived it. The present is all the more safe in the knowledge that the chains of the past are more securely tied. There are numerous statements to this effect in his work. He comments in his *Mémoires* about the reinstitution of his courses in 1828, "Whilst serving the cause of our present day society, I had it in mind to bring back to us a feeling of justice and sympathy toward the memories, the mores of old, towards that French society of old that lived laboriously and gloriously for fifteen centuries to build the civilisation whose fruits we all now enjoy. It is a serious folly and a great weakness for a nation to show such neglect and disdain for its past."[14] And Guizot adds, providing us with the key to his action as minister and underlining with good reason the perfect unity of his career, "The same idea which had led me, the same hope that had driven me when I outlined in my lectures at the Sorbonne the development of our French civilisation, followed me to the Ministry of Public Instruction and in my efforts to revive and spread a love for and study of our national history."[15] It was indeed a case of continuing, albeit by other means and on a larger scale, the government of minds.

The July régime had all the more need to turn to history and the recesses of a national memory as it lacked a certain legitimacy. The Restoration had claimed to revive the ancien régime while making allowance for change. It had been in a position, with some semblance of reason, to admit its direct descendance from the most ancient and glorious French monarchic tradition. The July monarchy, brought about through force, could have appeared as a government of chance. The name it has been given demonstrates precisely this circumstantial nature. The king of the French had not acceded to the throne by any of the known and recognized methods; not hereditary, not election, nor divine right. The principle of conservatism that was at the very heart of Guizot's intellectual and political system required that a tradition be quickly established. Louis-Philippe, even if he did not derive power from any particular principle, personified a reality: the nation. This king was "national" par excellence, swathed in the three national colors, and symbolized the alliance finally agreed between royalty and the Revolution, finishing after numerous trials and tribulations a process begun forty years earlier. The end product of a process almost lost in the mists of time, the July régime, concerned for its legitimacy, called the national memory to its aid, in which nothing could be opposed to it and that would act as a counterweight to its fragility. The middle classes, instead of being ashamed of themselves, should take pride in their origins, when the first communes lent their alliance to the king in the twelfth century.

This is why Guizot's very conservatism gave rise to an intellectual undertaking that was both ambitious and innovatory. It was to take shape in two different institutions, which were in fact closely linked.

The Société de l'histoire de France

"Some of my friends," Guizot recalls, "came to talk to me about their idea of founding a society, the society of the history of France, which would be dedicated to the publication of original documents pertaining to our national history"[16] This approach addressed as much to the minister as the historian could just as well have been made by Guizot himself. In any event, at the official establishment of the society on June 27, 1833, in the conservatoire of the royal library, he was quite naturally named head of this enterprise, and his name appeared at the top of the list of the first committee of twenty who co-opted themselves on that day. Among them were many of Guizot's political allies such as Molé, Thiers, and Pasquier (at that time president of the Chambre des pairs), historians close to him, including Barante, Mignet, and Beugnot, and personal friends such as Fauriel and Vitet. These names will appear again, and to these can be added those of specialists and scholars such as Champollion-Figeac, curator of manuscripts at the royal library;[17] Letronne, director of that library; Crapelet, member of the royal society of antiquaries; and Le Ver, representative of the very considerable Normandy society of antiquaries, founded twenty years earlier by Arcisse de Caumont and that needed to be won over.[18] In brief it consisted of liberals, especially doctrinaires, linked by the common struggles of the Restoration, historians, and scholars, all representatives of a well-defined circle to which Guizot belonged from the beginning and of which he was the hub.

On January 23, 1834, in the rue Taranne, the society gave itself a definitive constitution and began its work. A governing body of thirty, yearly renewable by thirds, was set up, with the addition of eleven new members, among whom were Jules Desnoyers, librarian at the Museum of Natural History;[19] Hippolyte Royer-Collard, then head of the literature and science department at the Ministry of Public Instruction; and Charles Lenormant, assistant curator of the Département des médailles at the royal library.[20] Guizot had noticed and appreciated the talents of the latter at an early stage, and in 1835 chose him as his stand-in at the Sorbonne. The marquis Fortia d'Urban was elected honorary president of the society by prerogative of age—he was born in 1754—rather than by talent. Prosper de Barante, the successful author of the *Histoire des ducs de Bourgogne*, a political ally and personal friend of Guizot for more than twenty years, chaired the society until his death in 1866. Guizot himself succeeded him. A year after its foundation the society numbered over one hundred members, among whom was Henri Beyle, French consul in Civitavecchia.

The aim of the society, according to its first bulletin that appeared in 1834, was to "popularise the study and love of our national history through sound criticism and especially through research into and use of original documents." Indeed the members of the society observe, like others before them, that the French "still await a true history of their country." For this to be achieved, the society decided—it was indeed its raison d'être—to start up a collection of documents pertaining to the history of France. The pedagogical, even ideological, intentions of the society were apparent from the format of each of the volumes published. The documents were not destined for scholars but for those interested in their national history and who wanted to be given access to its masterpieces. The collection was therefore produced in a "comfortable and portable" format, often octavo, a novelty compared to the folio or quarto volumes of previous centuries and contemporary academic editions such as the *Monumenta Germaniae historica*, an undertaking with which the Société de l'histoire de France had more than a little in common, especially as far as its origins were concerned. Indeed in 1818, Stein, who had retired from active political life after the Congress of Vienna, remained motivated by a feeling for the German nation and maintained the patriotic feelings that he had put to such good use in the service of Prussia in the previous decade. He also had a pronounced penchant for historical study. Now pursuing his politics of old by new means, he devoted himself to collecting and editing the sources of German history, in particular the medieval documents that proved that Germany had existed long before the contemporary system of small states would seem to testify. To this end Stein collected together a group of scholars for which he obtained support from both lay princes and clerics, as he could demonstrate that this idea went beyond Prussian borders and was shared by the whole of the German nation. On January 20, 1819, the Society for Research and Publication of Documents of Early German History was founded on this basis. A periodical began in the same year. It took five years to develop the general publication scheme. The scientific management of the enterprise was left in the hands of Pertz, certainly the greatest medieval philologist of his time. He was to remain in this role until 1873, which ensured the *Monumenta* an unrivalled continuity of inspiration and achievement.

The first volumes were, naturally, devoted to medieval narrative sources. Three had already appeared by the time that the bulletin of the Société de l'histoire de France started to take note of its illustrious elder in 1835. Jules Desnoyers paid it careful attention without entirely being aware of the scale of the institution, because he compared it to the Recueil des historiens de la France,[21] founded by the Benedictines under the ancien régime and continued thereafter under the auspices of the Institut. Whatever the intentions had been at the launch of such an operation, its size and, above all, its scientific nature were unlike anything that had previously existed in that field. Böhmer, formerly linked with Pertz, had launched the series *Regesta* in 1831, a catalogue of royal and imperial documents that, alongside the *Monumenta,* formed an indispensable reference work. Unlike the Société de l'histoire de France, whose activity, as we will see, gradually ebbed away, the *Monumenta* was continually growing in different directions, substantially increasing its rate of publication and taking on the leading specialists such as Waitz, who succeeded Pertz and

Mommsen. From 1875 the *Monumenta* became a state organization, had its head office in Berlin, and considerable means at its disposal, but never lost its very scientific nature.

The objectives of the two societies already differed slightly in 1834. For example, publication of texts by the Société de l'histoire de France were to include new translations as well as necessary notes and introductions. This collection was to some extent consistent with a wider perspective, continuing in the vein of a series of *Mémoires* edited by Guizot in the previous decade.[22]

As might be expected, the first volumes depicted the better side of the Middle Ages: Aimé du Mont-Cassin, Grégoire de Tours, and Villehardouin all appeared in the first four volumes, where the modern era's sole representatives were Mazarin's letters to the queen. Furthermore, the dual role, scholarly and popularizing, of the society, can be seen in this first choice of publications: two texts more or less hitherto unpublished and two texts already printed on numerous occasions, the *Histoire des Francs* and *Conquête de Constantinople*. During its first twenty-five years the society produced 70 volumes, as well as a bulletin, and from 1836 a substantial yearbook. For a long time the Middle Ages were granted the most page space. The monumental publication, from 1841, of the trial of Joan of Arc, scrupulously edited by Jules Quicherat, was a well-judged combination of scientific demand and national necessity. In 1833 Pertz had likewise discovered the sole manuscript of Richer de Reims's *Histoire de France*, published in the *Monumenta* in 1839. The society decided that the French public should have access in France to this unique source about the end of the tenth century when, perhaps, the French nation was born. The two volumes of this history appeared in 1845, thanks to Pertz. It was actually not difficult to edit and included a mediocre yet indispensable translation by Guadet. During the same period Auguste Leprévost, champion of traditional and strict erudition, was undertaking the publication of Orderic Vital's *Histoire ecclésiastique*, a very difficult read and this time with no translation, and Teulet the publication of the works of the Carolingian, Eginhard.

In the first two decades of its existence, the society's publications undoubtedly owed much to individual initiatives, or someone's particular interests and availability. However, although with hindsight it seems that most were chosen judiciously, a tendency for replacing the more scholarly and confidential medieval publications with more recent and more accessible texts can be observed, as Philippe Contamine has pointed out.[23] Benjamin Guérard, an expert in medieval studies who was at that time editing, quite impeccably, a number of precious and austere cartularies under the auspices of the Comité des travaux historiques in the society argued nevertheless in favor of "less serious and more modern documents," as well as inventories, registers, and accounts, all a novelty at that time. The *Journal de Barbier*, which was published in four volumes between 1847 and 1856, printed some of the latter two, as did the *Mémoires du comte de Coligny-Saligny* in 1841, the various accounts of the royal silver edited by Douët d'Arcq, and the *Registres de l'Hôtel de Ville de Paris pendant la Fronde*.

Ten years after its foundation, the society numbered nearly four hundred members, which made it the largest scholarly society of its time. Its beginnings, considering its ambitions and the size of the task that it set out to accomplish, were laborious, as even its founders admitted, including the most illustrious of these, Guizot. The society received very few subsidies, and the sale of its publications produced very little income at all. Indeed each volume, sold at nine francs to nonmembers, was given free to members, who between then took about half of each print run of between 300 and 750 copies. The sale of publications for the society's income came to less than half the amount raised by subscriptions, which were fixed at thirty francs a year per member according to the 1834 constitution. Any development of the society's activities was therefore severely restricted by lack of funds.

A Matter of State

Guizot was aware of this from the start. The Société de l'histoire de France, although it may have been the most active and intellectually rich, was merely one of the many scholarly societies that already existed in Paris and the provinces. The unearthing and publishing of the national memory was too large an undertaking, the risks and achievements involved too considerable, to be abandoned to private initiatives, no matter how dynamic and competent these were. In Guizot's eyes it could only be a matter of State, and the July government, as has been seen, had many reasons besides the personality of Guizot himself to make it its own.

The creation of the Société de l'histoire de France thus emerged as the first stage of a much larger project that was carried out soon after, as if the whole had long been premeditated. From 1833 Guizot asked all prefects to search their public libraries and departmental archives for "manuscripts which purport to our national history," as there was widespread ignorance and lack of classification of the riches held in these institutions and public archives. So, seventy years after Moreau, but with a quite different purpose, Guizot sent a report to the king on December 31, 1835, on his ministry's budget for that year, in which he expounded the considerations according to which it was the government's task to "accomplish the great task of a general publication of all important and hitherto unpublished material relating to the history of our nation." Firstly, only the government had the financial means at its disposal to guarantee the success of this enterprise. Furthermore, the State held or owned a very large proportion of the documents to be published, which were in the royal library, Archives des royaume, or the ministries, in particular that of foreign affairs. Documents relating to governments before Louis XV could thus be made public at no disadvantage to the country's people or its interests. "The publication which I have the honour of proposing to Your Majesty," Guizot concludes, "will be a monument entirely worthy of itself and of France," which fully justified the extraordinarily large sum requested.

Guizot was also prompted by a sense of urgency shared by all those affected by the destruction of the Revolution. The material remains of the ancien régime, especially those from further back in time, were threatened with disappearing entirely or risked becoming unintelligible. The nation's instinct for self-preservation, as well as intellectual and scientific curiosity, demanded that these be preserved. This is why professional *conservateurs* took pride of place during the July government, in which a profound tendency not to restore, but to conserve in order to progress, is revealed. The committees created by Guizot, just like the central committee of the Société de l'histoire de France, were full of them.

To launch the operation, the minister of public instruction asked the députés during the budget debate for a special allowance of one hundred and twenty thousand francs for 1835,[24] forty times the amount produced by subscriptions to the Société de l'histoire de France for that year. Opposition was largely on financial grounds, but that of the left-wing was purely political, expressed by Garnier-Pagès in particular: was it not a question, in the opinion of the minister himself, in using them in a learned work to distract some young people from reading such things in the popular press judged vicious or seditious? Guizot developed his argument accordingly, "Our history before 1789 is, to some extent, ancient history in our eyes. . . . Speed is of the essence if we are to gain enjoyment and use from these great works. Our knowledge of them will soon be lost, just as the works themselves will disappear."[25] The project was fervently supported by the Vicomte de Sade, *député* from the Aisne department and noted author of the 1822 *Réflexions sur les moyens propres à consolider l'ordre constitutionel en France* (*Reflections on the means needed to consolidate the constitutional order in France*) "There has been much discussion recently of the greatness of the nation. Well, nothing contributes so much to that greatness as the monuments dedicated to it, and among these masterpieces literary works hold pride of place." Perhaps alluding to the Cabinet des chartes under the ancien régime and without a doubt to some of the initiatives of the Restoration, the speaker continues, "You will not leave incomplete the work begun by a government which was not entirely national . . . I dare to hope that you will not hold back in your generosity when it comes to conserving our family deeds, our chronicles, our origins."[26] This was the spirit, liberal and national, that prevailed in the debate. Guizot got his way. He comments in his *Mémoires* with an uncertain humor, "the Chamber trusted me in such matters and delighted in measures of a liberal nature which would not change in the slightest the policy of order and resistance." In fact, far from changing it, a decision of this kind reinforced it by inviting the nation to discover its past, the source of a solid consensus. As the educational science of knowledge and reason, history once again came to sustain and intensify political action. It now fell to the minister of public instruction, especially when his name was Guizot, to create a national memory, not only through remembering the past but through the use of a scientific mentality.

He gave himself the means to do so in a decree of July 18, 1834, which established "a committee with the task of overseeing the research into and publication of hitherto unpublished documents pertaining to the history of France." This was the birth of what became better known as the Comité des travaux historiques et scientifiques (Committee of Historical and Scientific Works), the name still used today.[27] The eleven members who supported the minister in this task, among whom the most conspicuous were Villemain, the vice-president, who had shared Guizot's and Victor Cousin's disgrace at the Sorbonne in 1822, and Daunou, general curator of the Archives du royaume whose origins and intellectual career we know, were all men with varying titles and qualifications, all knowledgeable and competent. The Université as an institution was kept out of the way, while the Institut, with five representatives, had a strong presence thanks to its persistency in supporting the upkeep of scholarly traditions. The Institut provided the link between the new institutions and the old Cabinet des chartes, to which Guizot referred explicitly in his report to the king of November, 1834, about the creation and first acts of the Comité. Jules Desnoyers, outlining the history of the government's plan in the *Bulletin de la Société de l'histoire de France*, comments, "This vast plan to publish our historical treasure, in its aims and its execution, can and therefore must become an entirely national work, and all the activities and effort of the Société de l'histoire de France must work towards this goal." Establishing a close association between two authorities now with a common purpose, the general secretary of the society and five members of its central committee were appointed to the Comité: Guérard, Champollion-Figeac, Mignet, Fauriel, and Vitet. The last three of these were particularly close to Guizot. Mignet, who had published his *Histoire de la Révolution* with considerable success in 1824, had been appointed to the important post

of director of the Dépôt des archives diplomatiques, from which Guizot
expected much for his project. In 1834 he published an *Établissement de la
réforme à Genève*, more than one part of which was of interest to Guizot.
The following year he had the honor of unveiling a series of previously
unpublished documents on the history of France: the *Négociations relatives
à la succession d'Espagne sous Louis XIV.* Guizot's links to Claude Fauriel,
fifteen years his elder, were even closer.[28] Very close to the idéologues,
Fauriel had collected up the remains of the philosophy of the eighteenth
century, frequenting the salons of Suard, Cabanis, Mme de Staël, and
Mme de Condorcet, whose lover he became. Guizot, who revolved in
these circles at the time, met him in 1811. It was the then novel concept
of civilization as a focus for historical study that undoubtedly brought
them together for a long and close friendship; while Guizot was starting
his university career on the theme of European and French civilization,
Fauriel was involved in a project to trace the history of southern civilization, which would form the basis of his œuvre. Fauriel, applying the
most rigorous scholarship to new subjects, and a skilled philologist, was
praised by Augustin Thierry in 1829 as "the father of historical reform,
the first who conceived and wanted what has actually happened in the last
few years."[29] Guizot was without doubt more indebted to him intellectually than he would have us believe. Deputy curator of manuscripts at the
royal library, Fauriel quite naturally put himself forward to translate and
edit the history of the Albigensian crusade, which was indeed published
under the auspices of the Comité in 1837. After a short period teaching,
Ludovic Vitet, born in 1802 and hence one of Guizot's youngest associates, had taken part in the ventures of the newspaper *Le Globe* and that of
the society called Aide-toi, le ciel t'aidera (Help Yourself, Heaven Will
Help You), of which Guizot had been one of the instigators. The latter
was very close to Vitet too, and created the post of general inspector of
historic monuments for him in 1830, which he held until 1834 when he
was succeeded by Mérimée. General secretary of the Ministry of Trade,
he was *député* of the Seine-Inférieure from 1834 to 1838.

The relations between the society and the committee were not just
on a personal level. Even before the decree of July 2, 1834, Guizot had
outlined to the society's board what he expected of it. According to the
minutes of June 2, "the minister made known his intention that the Société de l'histoire de France in particular should unite and work towards
this vast plan to publish original manuscripts relating to the history of
France. . . . He would take pleasure in seeing that the Society could combine its plans for publication with those that he himself envisaged undertaking on behalf of the government, so that together they could one day
form one great historical monument."[30]

To this end Guizot set himself to mobilizing the institutions that could lead to his project being accomplished. He appealed to the École des chartes to supply him a contingent of specialists. One "pupil" of this École, Fallot, was chosen as secretary of the Comité. In order to give his associates in the Comité a reliable guide, Guizot commissioned a manual of palaeography from Natalis de Wailly, attaché to the archives. The *Éléments de paléographie*, published in 1838, long remained an irreplaceable guide. Guizot was also the first to entrust the care of departmental archives, whose riches he hoped to mine, to archivist-palaeographers who were consequently given the task of classification and publication. The École des chartes thus took on a new impetus, and its mission to research, study, and conserve the original monuments of French national history, as defined by a report sent from the Société de l'École des chartes to the minister of public instruction in 1839, found itself defined precisely in those terms.[31] Guizot above all attempted to mobilize the scholarly societies, many of which had been stagnating. From July 20 he sought their assistance, while assuring them of the active support of his ministry in publishing their own works. The minister expected to find correspondents of the Comité among the scholarly societies, experienced men who would have a good knowledge of local history and archival resources. These correspondents, of whom there were eighty-nine at the end of 1834, received a circular in December giving them precise instructions as to how to research, survey, classify, and describe these documents. In these scholarly societies Guizot was looking for the associates Moreau had found on a smaller scale in the Benedictines. Indeed, one of the tasks of the Comité was the reawakening and even management of scholarly societies.

THE IMPETUS GIVEN

The initiative launched by Guizot had an immediate and considerable impact. As we have seen, it came exactly at the right time. Guizot himself acknowledged the debt he owed to the overall intellectual situation: "Public opinion came to my aid. Even if the teaching of history in higher education had suffered serious losses"—no doubt he was thinking primarily of himself, now a minister—"the desire for historical research and thought became increasingly widespread."[32] The will to serve the national memory, finally with the means necessary to do so, met with an almost universal approval. The same movement saw the middle classes shown the long-standing nature of their origins and how their evolution gradually became the very history of the nation; this temporarily at least sealed the alliance between the historians (for the most part of the Guizot school anyway), and the July monarchy. How could one not endorse a regime in which the greatest historian of the time was also its most conspicuous statesman, a man who transformed the château of Versailles into a museum of national treasures, who created the inspectorate of historical monuments, restored the Institut, who in truth founded primary education, transformed higher education and lavished favors and money on people and institutions serving learning in general? As for the two men who were later to distance themselves from Guizot both intellectually and politically, Quinet offered his services willingly, and Michelet, formerly Guizot's stand-in at the Sorbonne and thanks to him named head of the history section of the Archives du royaume, was entrusted with reporting on the libraries and departmental archives of the Southwest. In 1841 he edited the trial of the Templars for the collection of previously unpublished documents. Even Eugène Sue, then writing his maritime novels, contributed to this great work with the three volume publication in 1839 of the correspondence of Henri de Sourdis, head of Louis XIII's navy. Of course Augustin Thierry also played a crucial role in this scheme, even if he was not a member of the first Comité. Guizot gave him the great responsibility of overseeing the collection of charters granted to towns and medieval communes, as well as "early charters and constitutions of the various guilds, *maîtrises*, and private societies established in France so that his collection may bring together and show in their full, true light the numerous and diverse origins of the French bourgeoisie, in other words the first institutions which helped to liberate and build the nation," as the minister wrote in a report to the king on November 27, 1834.

Guizot's overall plan to find and publish all documents that could contribute to a knowledge of French national history, seen on a human scale, was too much to undertake. The instigator of the plan was naturally the first to be aware of this. But, he notes, "in the intellectual world just as in the political world it is through great hopes and great demands that human sympathy and activity are stirred into decisive action."[33] In one respect he met with great success in this project during the early years. The Comité soon had to apply itself to channelling the flood of help offered spontaneously by many of the kingdom's towns, often with more enthusiasm than enlightenment. A second Comité established on January 10, 1835, was entrusted with "working towards the research into and publication of hitherto unpublished documents of literature, philosophy, science and the arts considered in the light of their relationship to the general history of France." "Such research," underlines a ministerial circular of May 15, "is the natural complement of that previously undertaken; it is of vital importance to the knowledge of our national history." Victor Cousin, who previously held no precise position, was named vice-president of this second Comité. He was therefore Villemain's opposite number, and with Guizot at the head of the two committees reformed the famous university truimvirate of the 1820s. Vitet and Lenormant were also members of this Comité, where they sat alongside Mérimée and Victor Hugo, who was particularly active in pointing out and protecting any medieval monuments threatened by local officialdom, or uncultured or less than scrupulous individuals.

This veritable activism of the early days predictably waned somewhat thereafter. On March 10, 1837, in a report to Guizot about the progress made in collecting the historic monuments of the Third Estate, Augustin Thierry regrets that "of the 120 correspondents you named to take part in the research and conservation of our historical monuments, only forty have replied to the request I made them on your behalf." The government was also becoming less generous, and credit allowances lowered. So Champollion-Figeac, to whom the Comité gave the task of supervising the analytical survey of the manuscripts of the royal library, was at first aided by a staff of twelve, and during the first half of 1835 they were able to catalog forty thousand items. But the pace of such analysis was soon to slow due to staff reduction and, no doubt, a lack of enthusiasm and qualification among them. In 1846 this undertaking was stopped, after two hundred and fifty thousand items had been cataloged.

The double Comité set up by Guizot was reorganized several times. At the end of 1837 Salvandy, who succeeded Guizot,[34] reunified the Comité and divided it into five sections, each in principle based on one of the five sections of the Institut. Salvandy did much for the royal library[35] and the École des chartes, a task made easier by the fact that as executor of Daunou's will, he became trustee of the latter's thoughts, and those of his associates. Under the Second Empire, going directly against Guizot's project, Rouland tried to link the scholarly societies to the Université. It was under Jules Ferry that the Comité, under its present name of Comité des travaux historiques et scientifiques, was to find a definitive organization. Of course the task that Guizot set it never was and never will be completed, although about 5,000 volumes now exist. But Guizot gave historical study a formidable impetus that lasted at least until the beginning of this century. The historians of the Republic, scholars and patriots, owed a great deal to the minister of Louis-Philippe, as far as both the material they worked on and the now solid institutions were concerned, institutions now comparable, although not equal, to their German colleagues and, sometimes, rivals. This history of the French nation in its various successive forms, and the reasoned formation of a national memory can trace their origins to a large extent to 1834–35, when the State made historical works a political act.

The conditions that had allowed Guizot's concepts and plans to take shape without doubt soon lost much of their force. From 1850 onward, the fields of investigation, just like the intellectual and ideological game itself, were shifted. Universal suffrage beat any other form of the State's legitimization. The Middle Ages therefore had nothing in particular to offer either the Empire or the Republic, which is why that period, previously so sought after, was somewhat abandoned in favor of the Revolution (Tocqueville, Quinet, and Taine) and, as in Germany, of antiquity in particular; Duruy, Renan, Fustel de Coulanges, and Jullian provided classical texts, the movement strengthened by archaeological discoveries in which France held an eminent position and to which she lent a new reading and interpretation, due especially to the Athens School, which owed much to Guizot. The men mentioned, especially the latter two, were both thinkers and scholars. Indeed at the same time as historical subjects changed, there was considerable progress in knowledge and methodology. The strengthening of the role of the École des chartes, the restructuring of the Université, and the creation in 1867 and subsequent rapid development of the École des hautes études produced good results, brilliant as well as solid subjects, and sound publications. The senior civil servants, peers of France and figures who were sometimes more prominent than knowledgeable and who formed a large part of the Société de l'histoire de France and the first Comité des travaux historiques, gave way to real experts, for the purpose of publishing and studying documents, who were more concerned with developing, in a new spirit, their rigorous, personal works rather than becoming involved in the process of unearthing old material that Guizot had devised and begun, but that was increasingly running out of steam. The manifesto with which Gabriel Monod led the first issue of the *Revue historique* that he created in 1876 showed the extent of this development, even though it somewhat exaggerated the situation for the sake of his cause.

As paradox would have it, Guizot, who had done so much to enable the nation to become aware of itself, was promptly removed from the national history and memory, where he is making a belated comeback, and even in his lifetime he did not appear to the most punctilious to be "French" enough. Renan, reviewing the early parts of the *Mémoires* in 1859, notes this and regrets that "the austere thinker who sought to raise himself above the prejudices of his age and his century, met with the most serious reproach possible; that of not being national." And Taxile Delord concludes a cutting article in *Le Siècle*, "He sometimes seemed to himself to be a man naturalised amidst his compatriots."[36] This is because the minister of foreign affairs at the end of the July monarchy had followed in the footsteps of the minster of public instruction from the beginning, of whom Camille Jullian, more equitable than most of his contemporaries, wrote in 1897, "Even though it may seem a paradox to state it in these days too hostile to Guizot, it was he who, without always succeeding, made the most reasonable effort never to be anything but a historian."[37]

NOTES

1. Guizot was minister of public instruction from November 11, 1832, to February 22, 1836, and from October 6, 1836, to April 15, 1837.

2. *Mémoires*, 3:52

3. On Moreau, see Dieter Gembicki, *Histoire et politique à la fin de l'ancien régime, Jacob-Nicolas Moreau (1717–1813)* (Paris: Nizet, 1979).

4. On the École des chartes, see Martial Delpit, "Notice historique sur l'École royale des chartes," *Bibliothèque de l'École des chartes* 1 (1839–40), and *Centenaire de l'École des chartes,* 2 vols. (Paris, 1921).

5. *Archives parlementaires* 51:677.

6. *Lettres sur l'histoire de France*, 2nd ed. (Paris, 1829). On Thierry, see in particular R. N. Smithson, *Augustin Thierry: Social and Political Consciousness in the Evolution of a Historical Method* (Geneva, 1973).

7. On the renewal of historical studies, see Boris Réizov, *L'Historiographie romantique française* (Moscow, n. d.), and Stadler, *Geschichtschreibung in historisches Denken in Frankreich, 1789—1871* (Zurich, 1958).

8. *Lettres sur l'histoire de France*, foreword.

9. See Yvonne Kniebiehler, *Naissance des sciences humaines: Mignet et l'histoire philosophique au XIXe siècle* (Paris: Flammarion, 1973).

10. *Lettres sur l'histoire de France*, 7.

11. On this point, see Pierre Rosanvallon, *Le Moment Guizot* (Paris: Gallimard, 1985), in particular chaps. 6 and 7.

12. *Considérations sur l'histoire de France* (Paris, 1840), 190.

13. See Charles Pouthas, *Guizot pendant la Restauration* (Paris, 1923).

14. *Mémoires* 3:337.

15. *Mémoires* 3:171.

16. *Mémoires* 3:177. On the beginnings of the Société de l'histoire de France (hereafter SHF), see Ch. Jourdain, *La société de l'histoire de France de 1833 à 1884* (Paris, 1884), and Charles-Olivier Carbonell, "La Naissance de la société de l'histoire de France," *Annuaire-Bulletin de la SHF* (1983–84).

17. See Charles-Olivier Carbonell, *L'Autre Champollion: Jacques-Joseph Champollion-Figeac* (Toulouse, 1984).

18. Caumont was himself admitted to the society on May 5, 1834.

19. On Desnoyers, see Marot, "Le Premier secrétaire de la Société de l'histoire de France," *Annuaire-Bulletin de la SHF* (1962–63).

20. At their meeting on May 5, 1834, Lenourmant presented a proposed model for the society's seal, representing one of those ancient torches "which will be the symbol of a mutual exchange of shared knowledge."

21. *Bulletin de la SHF* (1835), 2:154.

22. Robert de Lasteyrie, *Bibliographie générale des travaux historiques et ar-chéologiques publiés par les sociétés savantes de France* (Paris, 1901), vol. 3.

23. This argument owes much to Philippe Contamine's paper at the confer-ence entitled "Le Temps où l'histoire se fit science," organized to mark the 150th anniversary of the revival of historical science by the *Comité français des sciences histo-riques*, held in Paris from December 17–20, 1985. We thank Philippe Contamine for having sent the text of his paper entitled "La Société de l'histoire de France et son programme de travail, 1834–1851." We also note the very rich opening address given by M. Robert-Henri Bautier, president of the *Comité français des sciences historiques*, and for this reason focal point of the conference, and the exposé by M. Charles-Olivier Carbonell, "Guizot et le renouveau de l'histoire."

24. The complete text of this report, along with many other documents, can be found in Xavier Charmes, *Le Comité des travaux historiques et scientifiques*, 3 vols, (Paris, 1886).

25. *Le Moniteur universel* (May 11, 1834)

26. Ibid.

27. Apart from Xavier Charme, see Charles-Olivier Carbonell, "Guizot, homme d'États, et le mouvement historiographique français du XIXe siècle," in *Actes du colloque François Guizot* (Paris: Société de l'histoire du protestantisme fran-çais, 1976).

28. On the interesting Fauriel, see Jean-Baptiste Galley, *Claude Fauriel* (Saint-Étienne, 1909).

29. Cited by Galley, *Claude Fauriel*.

30. *Bulletin de S.H.F* 1 (1834): 51.

31. See Martial Delpit, "Notice historique," op. cit.

32. *Mémoires* 3:176.

33. Ibid., 178.

34. On Salvandy, see Louis Trénard, "Salvandy et son temps, 1795–1856" (the-sis, Lille, 1968).

35. See Jean-François Foucaud, *La Bibliothèque royale sous la monarchie de Juillet* (Paris: Comité des travaux historiques et scientifiques, Bibliothèque nationale, 1978).

36. Cited by Michel Richard, "Guizot mémorialiste," in *Actes du colloque Fran-çois Guizot*, 294.

37. Camille Jullian, *Notes sur l'histoire en France au XIXe siècle* (Paris, 1897), 31.

THE HISTORICAL MUSEUM
AT VERSAILLES

∾

THOMAS W. GAEHTGENS

I

Versailles played a central role in the history of France for only about a century. Whereas Paris has represented the political and cultural center of the country ever since the Middle Ages and definitively since the eighteenth century, Versailles only temporarily deprived the capital city of its preeminence. Nevertheless, this era of French history was so formative that Versailles signifies more than a mere *lieu de mémoire* [place of memory]. The political and cultural radiance that emanated from there to embrace all Europe still influences the present. Centralization as a principle of political activity continues as the everyday experience of France. The absolutist system of government introduced by Louis XIV, which raised this insignificant country seat to a center of power and illuminated all of Europe with the splendor of its court, has left its imprint upon the current administration of the country.

Yet Versailles is more than a chapter in the history of France. It is therefore important for the cultural history of the country to examine how the political past of this place continued to inscribe itself within history and has continued to remain vivid to this day. Although at present all decisions about the future of the country fall to Paris, the French people will always have a need to recollect the past of Versailles. Versailles is a noteworthy example of how a historical locale preserves its past and how we must give ourselves up to this "place of memory" in order to reexperience history.

The effect of Louis XIV's policy upon everyday life of present-day France, however, is to be distinguished from the necessity of entering into the past of Versailles. The political consequences of his reign have been discussed often. Even though their importance has been variously evaluated, the consequences of the Sun King's policies for the administration of the country remain essentially uncontested. Yet why Versailles preserves its power of attraction today is a more complicated question to answer. The splendor of the royal palace and the artistic treasures within are only part of the answer. The fact that the court of Versailles from the period of Louis XIV to Louis XVI is still considered one of the most splendid sites of artistic creation in the service of the monarch's glory may also account for the countless foreign visitors. For the French, on the other hand, Versailles embodies more than a tourist attraction. For this place represents to each individual, in his own way, his own political conviction.

In the nineteenth century, Louis Philippe was able to perceive, recognize, and exploit this circumstance in political terms. The Citizen King thus stood at the beginning of the historicization of Versailles. We shall attempt to trace this process by means of his historical museum and its Galerie des batailles in the south wing of the palace of Versailles.[1] Utilizing the historical location of Versailles, the July Monarchy rendered French history in pictures, interpreted it, and made it into an object of contemplation with clear political intent. The objective, implementation, and foundering of this enterprise illustrate that the aura of a place can survive over the centuries only when history is actually made there. Simply gathering memorabilia in a specific place, however, will not survive the changing times or escape oblivion.

II

From the departure of Louis XVI in the spring of 1789, the palace at Versailles was threatened with demolition. Whether it was the costs to be incurred by the destruction or the protest of the town's citizens that saved the edifice from this fate is difficult to say.[2] In any case, the French Revolution ushered in a change in the way that the fate of Versailles was conceived. Soon those voices demanding preservation and even restoration carried the day. The edifice had been recognized as a monument, independently of its artistic merit—which only a few valued very highly—because it possessed a certain symbolic aura. The protests by the population of Versailles against the demolition plans are eloquent testimony of a new conception. In this situation the conviction emerged that the palace had to be preserved in order to introduce the place of tyranny to the young and to succeeding generations. Blind hatred of feudalism had transformed

destructive rage into a didactic conception. Out of the former royal palace
there grew a monument.

This decisive step was accomplished at the end of the Age of the
Enlightenment. A place where politics were formulated for more than a
century was suddenly robbed of its role as a seat of princely government.
It was given a new function. Formerly, citizens were drawn to Versailles
to submit petitions or to witness the absolute ruler in his natural milieu.
Now, in that same place, they were called upon to accept the empty shell
as the whole. The edifice became an object by which to contemplate by-
gone history.

The late eighteenth-century conception of history differed from ours,
however. The past was not an object of research; rather, reference to history served as a political argument. The didactic intention mentioned
above was fused with the hope that citizens would contemplate history
in a place of memory, a *lieu de mémoire*, and thereby gain insight into their
present-day political situation. Versailles as a monument and a historical
place that elucidated the present—these two elements put their stamp
upon the future of the royal palace.

III

"The Power of History" showed itself stronger than all the attempts to
restore the palace to its original signification. Napoleon, who thought to
remodel it completely, foundered. He failed in the financing of his plans,
and his policies led to his abdication before he could finish a new residence in keeping with his inclination.

Yet it is possible to imagine how remorselessly he would have remod-
eled the former royal palace of his greatest predecessor. The following
passage from the *Mémorial de Sainte-Hélène* is instructive:

> I damned the very creation of Versailles . . . but in my often vast ideas
> for transforming Paris, I dreamed of including Versailles and, in time,
> making it into a kind of suburb, an annex, a vantage point for the
> great capital I envisioned. To accomplish this goal I had conceived
> a unique idea whose realization was clear to me. I would drive all
> those silly nymphs out of the beautiful garden glades, get rid of all
> that cheap, sentimental ornamentation, and replace it with sculpted
> panoramas of all the cities we had entered as victors, all the cele-
> brated battles that had proclaimed our might. These would have been
> so many eternal monuments to our triumphs and our national glory,
> erected at the very gateway to the capital of Europe, which would
> have been visited by the entire universe . . . ![13]

The emperor clearly had monstrous notions that fortunately were never acted upon. Versailles would have perished; the artistic unity of its park would have been destroyed.

The intentions Napoleon expressed on Saint Helena are instructive about more than just his thinking on the arts. The idea of commissioning powerful panoramas depicting victorious battles would have bequeathed monuments to the nation's glory. Although he complained that the palace was too small and that it did not measure up to his dignity, the place itself still evoked historical grandeur in his mind. The emperor, too, wanted to exploit the "solemnity of the place," and for the same reason that the revolutionaries had refrained from leveling the palace.

The restoration of the palace at Versailles has Napoleon to thank, this despite his actual ambitions. The notions he expressed on Saint Helena served to champion Versailles as a national commemorative site and pointed clearly to future developments. E. Cazes has convincingly shown the intellectual relationship between the National Museum of Louis Philippe and the plans of Napoleon:

> Fortunately we were spared this massacre of Le Nôtre's gardens, and it was Louis Philippe who realized the transformation, happily confined to the interior of the chateau, by creating a museum dedicated to all the glories of France, and where the Napoleonic epoch came to have so important a place.[4]

Louis Philippe was familiar with the *Mémorial de Sainte-Hélène* that appeared in 1823. Nevertheless, the creation of the National Museum at Versailles was not simply a belated realization of the emperor's plans. An essential precondition for the future history of Versailles was already operative around 1800. In the collective consciousness Versailles was, as it were, a possession of the nation. Because this was so, the projected return of the Bourbons to Versailles during the Restoration signified no more than an interlude. To be sure, rehabilitation and other work were undertaken. But for political as well as financial reasons the intention never became reality.[5]

IV

It was Louis Philippe who first gave the former palace its new significance. He never thought of taking up residence in Versailles. Rather, he understood that the idea of the French Revolution ought to be carried further. His decision in 1833 to transform the palace into the historical museum implemented the idea first voiced during the Revolution and then went beyond it.

Fig. 5.1
View of the Galerie des batailles.

In one point, however, his undertaking differed fundamentally from the considerations of the French Revolution. After the expulsion of the Bourbons, the building was intended to serve as a document of these feudal lords. But Louis Philippe gave the monument a different sense. In the memorandum signed by him on September 1, 1833, he determined that all the memorable events that comprised the glory of France were to be on view at Versailles:

> This beautiful edifice which testifies to much of the brilliance and grandeur of France, and to the splendor of the crown that the will of the nation has called upon you to wear, has fortunately not suffered excessively from the neglect to which it has been consigned for so long. It has escaped the deplorable madness that has deprived France of so many monuments, whether destroyed to extract the paltry value of their raw materials, or to save the expense of their upkeep. Your Majesty has realized that the best way to preserve the monuments that still remain was to give them a purpose which would prove by the advantages offered that destruction of these monuments would have been a national calamity.
>
> Versailles, which joins to the most sumptuous physical setting art treasures that could not be moved without destroying them, as well as historic significance so precious to preserve, presented enormous difficulties. The new destiny for the edifice was not fixed until now, despite the many proposed projects. And it was reserved for Your Majesty to provide the best and most worthy solution.
>
> At the time of your last visit to Versailles, Sire, you deigned to reveal, before all those who accompanied you, the plan you had formed. You told us that, without depriving the Louvre of its masterpieces of painting and sculpture and the objects both ancient and modern that the Crown currently has deposited there, you hoped that Versailles might offer France a repository for the artifacts of her history, and that the monuments to all our national glories would be deposited here, to be surrounded by the magnificence created by Louis XIV.[6]

With this decision the former royal palace and monument to feudalism became a museum of French history. Thus, Louis Philippe's undertaking went far beyond the ideas of the Revolution. It was no longer only the "monument value" of Versailles that was exploited; now, in the representation of French history from its beginnings up to and including the July Monarchy, the Age of Absolutism was conceptualized as one of the high points.

Versailles was not an accidental choice for such a conception. Obviously, a historical museum could have been erected elsewhere; however, in that case it would not have had the same special character or measurable effect that Louis Philippe expected. For Versailles represented not only absolutism but also its downfall and the beginning of a new epoch. The place was not only a commemorative site for royalists. The Revolution with its Oath of the Tennis Court had also accomplished a historical act that ushered in a new age of emancipation. By establishing his museum in this place, Louis Philippe acknowledged the hope that these differing political conceptions could be joined together. The rhetoric of the Revolution would not be taken to absurd lengths but, in the sense of his own politics, be set in a broader context. Uniting all Frenchmen—the aim of the July Monarchy—was to be the serviceable principle deduced from history itself.

As a common but too superficial view would have it, the image of history that Louis Philippe wanted to convey in the galleries of Versailles was designed to do no more than show the glory of the French nation by means of the country's history. In the pediments of the two pavilions of the palace, the appropriate dedication greets the visitor: "À toutes les gloires de la France." This connotes more than the idea that France's history can demonstrate numerous praiseworthy deeds, however. Such a reminder would not have been necessary at all. For these deeds had often been recorded as individual events. And, historically, the gallery exhibits of French palaces also upheld a tradition of putting outstanding examples of virtue before the ruler and his court.

Louis Philippe's intention differed from all earlier undertakings in that he wished to demonstrate that these praiseworthy deeds had been possible only because they had been *national*. By means of history it was to be proven that beyond differences of estate, and beyond the resulting political conflicts, there is a common bond uniting all Frenchmen. The history museum appealed to the citizens' sense of community. Even though—and this is controversial—many citizens supposedly suffered during the Age of Absolutism, Versailles now belonged to everyone. All those who nourished a sense of French national pride felt part of the glory to which history stood witness and participated in the grandeur of the country. Contemporaries recognized this intention and, according to their political conviction, approved or rejected it as an illusion. One of Louis Philippe's closest confidants, his librarian, Jean Vatout, grasped the aims of the Citizen King particularly clearly and approved them:

> We naturally leave to others the task of appreciating the implications
> of the idea that a palace consecrated to the apotheosis of a single man

has become the palace of national grandeur, and that rather than having the majesty of this monument circumscribed within the limits of
a single reign, it embraces all the epochs of our history, thus uniting
in one place of homage the France of all ages, adopting all her glories
and gathering them in the same sanctuary, since they are all part of
the same country.[7]

Among the historical galleries that the Citizen King began to establish
in 1833, this intention is most clearly visible in the Galerie des batailles in
the south wing of the palace.

V

From the first draft, the king's plans involved the installation of a Galerie
des batailles. Louis Philippe's most significant and expensive construction
at Versailles was undertaken for the realization of this gallery.[8] The king
spared nothing in the way of costly ornamentation. The most important
element of the decor is the sequence of the thirty-three paintings on the
walls. They portray events chronologically from the battle of Tolbiac (496)
to that of Wagram (1809). The scenes in large format were, with few exceptions, produced specifically for the gallery.
     Naturally, it would be of extraordinary interest for the understanding
of the ensemble if the principles by which the themes were selected were
known. However, in light of the available sources, only a few inferences
concerning this are possible. There is no doubt that the Citizen King
himself took a decisive role in choosing the battles. From earliest youth
he devoted himself to the study of history under the influence of Madame
de Genlis; later in life he surrounded himself with historians—Guizot,
Thiers, Mignet, Thierry, Michelet, and Barante were among his guests in
the Palais royal. The private notes and occasional communications of his
advisors have not been preserved. Presumably they were destroyed in the
fire at the Tuileries in 1870. However, from the memoirs of the Count de
Montalivet, the minister responsible for the execution of the project, we
know that the king not only participated in the plans but also attended
closely to their implementation. Louis Philippe paid nearly four hundred
visits to Versailles, and used every free moment to seek out the painters
in their studios at the Louvre to check on their progress.

VI

In the absence of primary documents confirming the original pictorial
program of the Galerie des batailles, it is through an analysis of the in-

dividual paintings as well as of the entire cycle that we can arrive at certain conclusions. Contrary to the intention of the original memorandum, nothing representing the period of the Restoration and the July Monarchy is to be found in the Galerie des batailles. The north and south walls of the gallery are occupied by Clovis at Tolbiac and Louis XIV at Valenciennes (1677), the founder of the nation facing its foremost ruler who united France and led it to European greatness. The four sections of the long wall, set off from one another by triumphal columns and arches, accommodate the following events: the first section of the wall on the east side is devoted to the Middle Ages. Two important aspects of the battles selected from this epoch can be noted. On the one hand, the engagement of the French monarchy in the defense of Christianity is emphasized; on the other, by depicting the personal intervention of the king in battle, the common struggle of king, nobility, and people is expressed. The defense of Christianity stands at the center of the battles of *Tolbiac* (496), *Poitiers* (732), the *Baptism of Widukind at Paderborn* (785), and also [the battle of] *Bouvines* (1214). In *Eude's Defense of Paris* (886), the battles of *Taillebourg* (1242), *Mons-en-Puelle* (1304), and *Cassel* (1328), the notion of the common struggle for the greatness of France is more strongly emphasized.

The large format of the painting showing the Battle of Bouvines in the middle of the east wall carries a special significance. The picture, painted by Horace Vernet in 1828, found its fitting place in the Galerie des batailles. Instead of a battle scene it portrays an event that took place before the battle. According to the legend, Philip Augustus laid his crown upon the altar, putting it at the disposal of anyone found more worthy than himself. However, he attached to this offer the condition: "as long as you are ready to preserve it in its entirety and not let those excommunicates dismember it."[9]★ The painting portrays the general jubilation as the king is reconfirmed in his office. It is hardly an overinterpretation to suggest that this scene ought to be understood as a clear reference to the political situation of Louis Philippe. The sovereign also owed his crown to the assent of the people—the same people who had been lately added onto the left side of this painting in order to better suit the purpose of the Galerie des batailles. While it originally portrayed only the assent of the knights, the work was intentionally modified to respond to the general program of the historical gallery at Versailles. References to contemporary events as clear as this one are quite rare.

The center of the gallery holds three paintings of important individu-

---

★ TRANSLATOR'S NOTE: "Excommunicates" in the quotation refers to Philip Augustus's opponents at Bouvines: King John of England and the Holy Roman Emperor, Otto IV, both of whom had been excommunicated by Pope Innocent III.

Fig. 5.2
H. Vernet, *Philippe-Auguste avant la bataille de Bouvines* (1214), Versailles, Galerie des batailles.

als whose virtue and daring made them exemplary figures in French history: du Guesclin, Joan of Arc, and also a great enemy, the English Lord Talbot, who is depicted at the moment of his death, at once an homage to the man's achievements and commemoration of the end of the Hundred Years' War.

It is certainly no accident that the *Entrance of Joan of Arc into Orleans* (1429), a painting by Henri Scheffer, stands in the center of the Galerie des batailles. Initial plans for the gallery show that an equestrian figure was envisioned for this position.[10] Doubtless, this was to have been a portrait of the reigning king, Louis Philippe. This significant change of plans followed a long debate over the decoration of the southern room adjacent to the end of the wing. Because, as we will discuss later, that room was to be dedicated to the events of Louis Philippe's assumption of government in July 1830, and because the king would be at the center of these events, his representation in the Galerie des batailles could be dispensed with.

That the initially planned equestrian image of the king was replaced by a representation of Joan of Arc can also be interpreted as of programmatic significance. For in this way the saint who represented the nation, according to Michelet, could be made the focal point. There are many indications that Louis Philippe sought to associate himself with this legendary figure. It was scarcely accidental that his daughter, Marie d'Orleans, created a statue of Joan of Arc for Versailles. It has been frequently copied and belongs to the devotional art found in French churches and other public places, in various sizes, in marble or bronze. In a painting of Louis Philippe, which shows the king in the Galerie des batailles, the sculpture (of Joan of Arc) appears in reduced form.

The second section of the long wall in the Galerie des batailles portrays the period from the Renaissance to Louis XIV. The *Entrance of Charles VIII into Naples* (1495) and the *Battle of Marignano* (1515) indicate the growing European significance of the French monarchy. The *Expulsion of the English from Calais* (1558) shows the courageous and skillful capture of the town, the last bastion the English held on French soil. At the center of this section of the wall is once again a painting executed during the Restoration, François Gerard's *Entrance of Henry IV into Paris* (1594). As in the painting of Philip Augustus, a ruler surrounded by a jubilant and welcoming people also stands at the center point of this section of the gallery. This painting was also designed to represent the total harmony and concord between people and monarchy. This message, deemed appropriate during the Restoration, was still valid for the July Monarchy. Mounting the painting in the Galerie des batailles was thus a programmatic decision.

Proceeding chronologically through the Galerie des batailles, we come now to the sequence of paintings devoted to the famous commanders of the century of Louis XIV: the battles of *Rocroi* (1643) and *Lens* (1648), devoted to the Duc d'Enghien; the *Battle of the Dunes* (1658), to Turenne; the *Battle of Marsaglia* (1693), to Catinat; the *Battle of Villaviciosa* (1710), to Vendôme; and the *Battle of Denain* (1712), to Villars. In the center on the southern façade of the gallery is the Sun King himself, as commander at the *Taking of Valenciennes* (1677).

We now find ourselves in the center section of the wall on the park side where the large format painting of the *Battle of Fontenoy* (1745) by Horace Vernet is especially striking. In this case also, it is not actually the battle that is depicted but rather the moment afterwards when Marshal de Saxe presents Louix XV with the battle standards captured from the English. The following *Battle of Lawfeld* was also won by Marshal de Saxe. In the center of the picture, however, Louis XV stands facing the captured English general, Ligonnier. The depiction of the council before the *Battle of Yorktown* (1781) demonstrates the French role in the American War of Independence. There follow the battles of *Fleurus* (1794), *Rivoli* (1797), *Zürich* (1799), and *Hohenlinden* (1800)—victories won against the allied rulers of Europe by troops of the French Revolution led by Jourdan, Bonaparte, Masséna, and Moreau. The last four battles, those of *Austerlitz* (1805), *Jena* (1806), *Friedland* (1807), and *Wagram* (1809), are devoted to the greatest of the commanders, Napoleon.

VII

To deduce an exact program from the paintings of the Galerie des batailles is only partially possible. A more precise understanding can only be established by taking the surrounding rooms and their relationship to the central palace complex into consideration. But before discussing these relationships, a few more observations concerning the gallery itself are in order.

In contrast to earlier programmatic galleries that were mostly devoted to individual rulers, typically the patron himself, the graphic realizations of the Galerie des batailles encompass the glorious deeds of the entire past of France. While Rubens's Luxembourg Gallery or the Hall of Mirrors by Lebrun lionized a single ruler, the Galerie des batailles commemorates the great victories and sovereigns of many centuries and many conflicting political points of view. Presented side-by-side and given equal weight are medieval kings, Renaissance princes, Louis XIV, and Revolutionary generals, including Napoleon. At the basis of this unusual conception was an idea that differed from the baroque rulers' wish simply to decorate their palaces with sumptuous galleries. The decorative purpose of earlier galleries was to render visible and thereby confirm the power of the ruler.

Fig. 5.3
Marie d'Orléans, *Jeanne d'Arc*, 1837, Versailles, Galerie de Pierre.

Louis Philippe's historical museum summoned visitors to feel that they were bound together by a common history. Each of them, despite differences in social status, was to participate in the victories of the national commonality.

No contemporaneous visitor to the gallery would have missed the point. Nonetheless, one could not ignore the fact that no battle per se was actually depicted in the Galerie des batailles—an observation that did not fail to trigger ironic comments from sharp critics. The great majority of pictures followed a scheme of composition in which the ruler or general in question stood in the foreground, issuing commands, while the battle, if depicted at all, was pushed into the background. Only a few of the paintings deviated from this principle, and in no case to the point where an important personage was not clearly visible at the center of events. In this manner, a Revolutionary general was elevated to the same plane as a medieval king. Thus, the patron sought to communicate clearly that the two were of equal rank in so far as their historical significance was concerned.

Further, it is repeatedly emphasized that the personages were sustained by popular participation in these national events. A ruler without a people is of as little value as a commander without an army. Putting the prince or general in a painting at the center of the action, of course, has the effect of displaying him prominently. But it should be noted that doing so also shows him as participating in battle like any ordinary soldier. The rows of busts displayed in front of the paintings and the memorial plaques naming those fallen in war testify to the great number of sacrifices made for the nation, first and foremost from among the nobility.

Thus, just as every battle depends on the participation of all, so, too, does history demonstrate how common effort in the previous centuries created the nation's greatness. That is the programmatic message of the Galerie des batailles.

VIII

To all appearances, the program of the Galerie des batailles represents past history exclusively. Its patron, Louis Philippe, seems not to be included. The Galerie des batailles thus is distinguished from the Hall of Mirrors, which glorifies the deeds of the Sun King.

This distinction has been explained by pointing out that the Hall of Mirrors was the center of the seat of the Baroque residence. It was the social and representational focal point for the king's fêtes, ceremonies, and state receptions. Because Louis Philippe no longer lived in the palace but wanted to create a museum there, it was only to be expected that representations of his person and his monarchy could be dispensed with.

This explanation, however, misconstrues the Citizen King's intention with regard to his museum. Within the historical museum Louis Philippe did not renounce the representation of his person. Quite the contrary. Walking through the museum we come, at the end, to the graphic depiction of his own era presented as the political apogee. But before we turn to this room, it must be pointed out that even in the Galerie des batailles, the programmatic message that we have sketched above contains direct references to the reigning prince. Again and again the paintings emphasize the close relationship between people and ruler in the history of France. Thus precedents from the past are made to point to the present. This theme is especially visible in the event depicted by the *Battle of Bouvines*. Here, the monarch is confirmed by the army and the people, who see in him the sole guarantor of national unity. This is a typical scene that could not have failed to evoke, to the eyes of contemporaries of the July Monarchy, a clear parallel with Louis Philippe, the reigning king. The *Entrance of Henry IV into Paris* with its enthusiastic welcome from the citizenry was but another happy representation of the harmony between king and people.

Louis Philippe owed his crown to a revolution, and he accepted it in order to rescue the nation from party strife. Only politically, by the representation of historical precedents, could he legitimate his dominance (which did not rest on legal succession to the throne). For this reason, the sequence of paintings in the Galerie des batailles represents more than a vicarious nostalgia for earlier heroic events. Specific past occurrences were selected and brought to view in characteristic ways in order to justify current political conditions. In this way the Galerie des batailles symbolized a political program to which the king repeatedly gave expression in his speeches:

> The unwavering goal of a sovereign's efforts ought to be to maintain the most intimate harmony between all the powers of the state. It is by this harmony that we are able to find the strength that all public functionaries, all depositaries of authority, need in order to fulfill the responsibilities that they have been called to exercise. It is only from this harmony that can spring the moral force which, in guaranteeing the stability of institutions, inspires in the nation this confidence in its future, which is the first guarantee of its repose, its happiness, and the maintenance of its liberties.[11]

IX

The position of the patron is elucidated in the south wing of the National Museum of Versailles. Anterior to the Galerie des batailles lies the Salle

Fig. 5.4

F. Gérard, *L'Entrée d'Henri IV à Paris* (1594), Versailles, Galerie des batailles.

de 1792, dedicated to the campaign of 1792 in which the Revolution
defended itself successfully against the dynastic houses allied against it.
Léon Cogniet's *The Parisian National Guard Leaves for the Front in September 1792*, which depicts the French going off to war to defend their country, lends the room a programmatic meaning. Independent of whether or
not all (the volunteers) supported the aims of the Revolution uniformly,
they nonetheless exhibit patriotism. Among them was the young officer,
Louis Philippe, who played a decisive role in the victories of Jemmapes
and Valmy, as depicted in two large paintings in the room. A further portrait of Louis Philippe is displayed with the portraits of officers who particularly distinguished themselves in this campaign. In the Salle de 1792,
contemporaries of the July Monarchy were reminded of a campaign in
which the combined loves of liberty and patriotism battled against the
ancien régime. The patron of the historical museum and the reigning
king had actively participated in this struggle and taken the side of liberty
and France. It was this engagement that had qualified Louis Philippe to
assume the government after the July Revolution of 1830. And for this
reason the proclamation of July 1830, which favored the Duc d'Orléans,
contained the sentences:

> The Duc d'Orléans is a prince devoted to the cause of the Revo-
> lution. The Duc d'Orléans never fought against us. The Duc
> d'Orléans was at Jemappes. The Duc d'Orléans carried the tricolor
> under fire. The Duc d'Orléans alone can still carry the flag. We want
> no others. The Duc d'Orléans has declared himself. He accepts the
> letter and the spirit of the *Charte*. It is from the French people that he
> will hold the throne.[12]

X

Traversing the Galerie des batailles, the visitor reaches the Salle de 1830,
the last in Louis Philippe's gigantic historical museum. The pictorial program of this room shows most clearly that the almost overwhelming
number of artworks that the king gathered at Versailles were intended to
present an image of history in which the current regime appears as the
happy and logical consequence of historical experiences. The Salle de 1830
contains five paintings, all of which show the Citizen King standing at
the center. They depict the various stages in his rise to power: *The Duc
d'Orléans, Lieutenant-général of the Kingdom, Proceeds to the Hôtel-de-Ville;
The Reading of the Deputies' Declaration; The Lieutenant-général Received at
the Barrière du Trône by the First Regiment of Hussars; The King Takes the Oath*

in the Presence of the Chambre; The King Distributing Battalion Standards to the National Guard. The paintings illustrating the head of state's acts are complemented by the ceiling fresco representing the fundamental principles of government: liberty and public order. National unity above all party-political conflicts is to be guaranteed by acknowledgement of the *Charte* and the obligation to defend it.

It has already been pointed out elsewhere[13] that the spatial sequencing of the three rooms, the Salle de 1792, Galerie des batailles, Salle de 1830, and their thematic interconnection, bear a striking resemblance to the central core of the palace. The Salon of War, the Hall of Mirrors, and the Salon of Peace correspond to the political program of the nineteenth century in the disposition of the rooms and their iconography.

But there is an essential difference between the works of the seventeenth and the nineteenth centuries. The pictorial content of the Baroque era serves to glorify the legitimate ruler, lending expression to the unfolding of his grandeur and the fullness of his military and political power. The south wing is dedicated, on the other hand, to the nation. The Salle de 1792 expresses this national awareness, yet the Salle de 1830 shows it was only realized fully when the Duc d'Orléans received the call. Thus, the Galerie des batailles could no longer be dedicated to just one ruler but to all those who had contributed to the glory and greatness of this country throughout its long history. Not the victories of individuals but collective glory was rendered heroic; the hope was that recalling the glorious deeds of the past would bring unity in the present.

XI

Interpretation of the pictorial program of the Galerie des batailles and its surrounding rooms is incomplete without a thorough analysis of the other halls in the historical museum. Nevertheless, interpretation of the south wing, for which the most extensive constructions and expensive decorations were devised, shows rather clearly what intentions motivated the Citizen King in the erection of the history gallery at Versailles. It made obvious references to Louis Philippe's policies. As its patron he sought to make the history of the country accessible to the people, while simultaneously presenting his own actions in a favorable light. Recalling the great deeds of the past was supposed to unite the fractious parties of his era. The Program of National Reconciliation demanded that the citizens put the interests of the nation before their own.

The museum's political character was recognized by contemporaries and commented upon accordingly. The *Journal des débats* expressed the

Fig. 5.5
Engraving by L. Cogniet, *La Garde nationale part pour l'armée* (1792), Versailles, Salle de 1792.

hope that the king might succeed in transforming the programmatic message of the historical museum into social and political reality:

> All the great families of France, those gloriously established in our
> Revolution of 1789 and those whose origins are lost in the mists of
> time, those who rallied around the July Monarchy and those whose
> sense of honor or passionate conviction force them into retirement,
> will they not all have their representatives, their escutcheons, their

Fig. 5.6
Engraving by E. Devéria, *Louis-Philippe prête sement de maintenir la Charte en 1830*, Versailles, Salle de 1830.

titles, their trophies, their history, in this vast Pantheon of all the exploits and all the heroes of the *patrie*? The king has excluded no one.
He has gathered the great historical family of France, he has reunited
the various epochs, reconciled everyone, whatever their origins. May
he rally all men of sincerity and good will to the true interests of
France! May he, in consecrating the ruins of Versailles to the glory of
the country, also raise a temple to Peace and Harmony![14]

In this way, Versailles became, as the article put it, a "vast Pantheon of all the
exploits and all the heroes." The historical museum represented the locus
in which the various events deemed worthy of remembrance were brought
together. This conception of a museum that Louis Philippe implemented
at Versailles is thoroughly unfamiliar to modern understanding of such institutions. It was in no way his intention simply to put valuable objects on
public view; rather he sought to assemble events. Their selection and form
of representation were surely subordinated to his political intentions.

The Historical Museum of Versailles was thus a place of memory, a
lieu de mémoire, in which past heroes and heroic deeds were used to uphold
a political program of the present. Just as he wanted to unite compatriots
of the most diverse political views, so did he bring together in Versailles
outstanding historical events and their protagonists.

Louis Philippe was quite right that the place itself was alive with history. The parallels between the provision of rooms in the main building
and in the south wing certify that the Citizen King wanted his conception of things to appear in contrast with that of the Baroque age. *Versailles
ancien et moderne* reads the title of a richly illustrated book by Alexandre
de Laborde that presented the historical museum and all its rooms.[15] The
medal issued at the opening of the history galleries in 1837 places Louis XIV
and Louis Philippe in apposition. Thus, homage is paid to the creator of
Versailles and its consummator. Louis Philippe was able to exploit the
"solemnity of the place" in the nineteenth century. Indeed, it was Versailles' aura that allowed him to realize his conception. Versailles of the seventeenth and eighteenth centuries was one of the most significant princely
residences in Europe; then the Revolution recast it into a monument of
feudalism. Louis Philippe transformed the palace into a history museum:
he joined to the place of memory of an epoch the heroic deeds of all the
past—together they were to bear witness to the nation's greatness.

XII

Louis Philippe's gigantic and expensive undertaking at Versailles was illusory. Social problems and class conflicts could not be solved by an ap-

peal to national greatness or a sense of community. His hope of making Versailles a place of national pilgrimage failed. To be sure, the museum drew thousands, especially on the weekends, but the hoped for didactic effect remained elusive. Practical politics ignored the ideal represented by the museum. Moreover, historical research during the nineteenth century rendered the representation of historical events ever more questionable. When we visit Versailles today, we expect to gain an impression of the Sun King and his successors' style of life. The aura of the ruler who made the place memorable has shown itself stronger than the attempt to use that place for the solving of political problems. A nation has many places of memory. A policy that seeks to overcome political conflicts with an appeal to national commonality must fail. Similarly, a representation of history subjected to the needs of practical politics will also grow stale.

This failure was predictable and was already being expressed in the contrasting judgments of Victor Hugo and a commentator writing for the *Siècle* in 1837. Hugo welcomed the undertaking as a deed of national importance: "What King Louis Philippe has done to Versailles is good. To have accomplished this work is to have been great as a king and impartial as a philosopher. It is to have made a national monument from a monarchical one, to have enclosed a huge idea in an immense building, to have joined the present and the past: 1789 juxtaposed with 1688, the emperor with the king, Napoleon with Louis XIV. In a word, it is to have given this magnificent book that is the history of France, a magnificent binding, that we call Versailles."[16] According to the *Siècle*, on the other hand, the nation did not feel itself represented:

> The July Monarchy, which has invited so many to its celebrations at Versailles, has forgotten to invite the people, to whom it owes its existence and fortune. . . . [These are] insincere, empty words, inflated predictions, which were not absent from the celebrations of the Republican period, nor the solemnities of the Empire, nor the anniversaries of the Restoration, and which did not give any of these regimes a single additional hour of existence![17]

In our own day, this conflict in views has lost its relevance. Versailles draws its strength from the history it has embodied. The works gathered there by Louis Philippe are today only documents that allow us to better situate the July Monarchy in its historical context. Their meaning, the program that they obey no longer appears to be anything more than a favor bestowed from one era upon those prior—the favor of a reconstruction of the past accompanied by historical commentary in good and due form. Meanwhile, this episode in the history of Versailles has removed not a whit of the historical presence of Louis XIV from this place.

NOTES

1. For a broader presentation and more detailed analysis of the Galerie des batailles with citation of sources and further literature, see Thomas W. Gaehtgens, *Versailles, De la résidence royale au musée historique* (Antwerp: Mercatorfonds, 1984).

2. Pierre De Nolhac, *L'Art à Versailles* (Paris, 1930), 205–81; Gaehtgens, *Versailles*, 47–50.

3. Comte E.-A. Las Cazes, *Mémorial de Sainte-Hélène* (Paris, 1823), 5:189–90; Gaehtgens, *Versailles*, 55.

4. E. Cazes, "Napoléon à Versailles et Trianon," *Revue des Études Napoléoniennes* 4 (1913): 169.

5. Compare Gaehtgens, *Versailles*, 56–57.

6. Gaehtgens, *Versailles*, 391.

7. J. Vatout, "Palais de Versailles," in *Souvenirs historiques des résidences royales de France* (Paris, 1837), 22.

8. Gaehtgens, *Versailles*, 87–111.

9. F. E. Mézeray, *Histoire de France* (Paris, 1830), 3:236–37; Gaehtgens, *Versailles*, 139.

10. Compare the plans of Frédéric Nepveu from 1833 in Gaehtgens, *Versailles*, 101.

11. G. Boissy, *Les Pensées des rois de France* (Paris, 1949), 372–73.

12. Cat. Louis Philippe, *L'Homme et le roi, 1773–1850* (Paris: Archives nationales), 78, no. 300.

13. Gaehtgens, *Versailles*, 320–22.

14. *Journal des débats*, June 10, 1837.

15. A. de Laborde, *Versailles ancien et moderne* (Paris, 1839; 2nd ed., Paris, 1841).

16. Victor Hugo, *Choses vues, 1830–1846* (Paris, 1972), 1:133.

17. *Le Siècle*, June 16, 1837.

CHAPTER 6

PIERRE LAROUSSE'S GRAND DICTIONNAIRE: THE ALPHABET OF THE REPUBLIC

✦

PASCAL ORY

Mediation rests at the heart of culture. Unfortunately, apart from the press and the educational system, the third great sphere of these activities, popularization (libraries, museums, scientific magazines, lexicography, etc.), has been ignored by researchers till the last decades. However, during the last third of the nineteenth century, when republican culture in French society was developing in a decisive way, republican action in the domain of popularization was perhaps the most constant and productive. Indeed this development suited democratic ideology and the necessities of universal suffrage. Similar to our rereading of political texts, it is not possible to write the history of the "republican mind" without carefully reevaluating the *Dictionnaire de la langue française* by Émile Littré (1863–72) or, at the tail end of the period, the *Grande encyclopédie* sponsored by Marcelin Berthelot (1885–1902).

This essay will concern only the *Grand dictionnaire universel du XIXe siècle*. The tireless Pierre Larousse (1817–75) directed and did most of the editing[1] of this work between 1863, the date of the first subscription (exactly contemporary with the first fascicle of the *Littré*), and 1876, the point at which the 524th and final fascicle appeared. The last volume appeared two years before the publication of the first *Supplément*, which has been integrated into the dictionary; the second *Supplément* was published in 1890. This truly monumental work—20,700 quarto-sized pages, four columns per page, 483,000,000 characters—was influenced by the upheaval of 1870–71. The events of the Paris Commune seem to have debilitated

Fig. 6.1
The tireless Pierre Larousse.

Larousse, who greatly curtailed his activities beginning in 1872; in lexicographical terms, these events occurred around volume 6, letter D.

This fact is even more important given that the personality of Larousse and the project he executed lend themselves to speculation.[2] Beginning in 1849 the former republican teacher devoted himself to producing scholarly studies and documentary collections; he turned his entire corpus into a pedagogical work in the interest of free thought and democracy.[3] When he edited the *Nouveau dictionnaire de langue française*, his other great success that helped to transform his personal name into a generic name,[4] he was still constrained by discretion, due to both technical necessity and prudence. Many years later the heavily used copy, which belonged to the Empress Eugénie (the wife of Napoleon III), was found.* The *Grand dictionnaire*, presented as the nineteenth century's version of Diderot's *Encyclopédie*, crowns the enterprise by giving the dictionary, in contrast to the earlier work, clear ideological significance. Victor Hugo understood this very well when he accorded his patronage to Larousse. The author saw Larousse's works as a potential counterattack against lexicographic literature, which Hugo, exiled by Napoleon III for his republicanism, perceived as having been written "with hostile intention towards the century." Those who collaborated with Larousse were chosen from the most "intellectual" milieus, from the logician Louis Liard to the classicist Alfred Naquet, two future republican notables, and including Louis Combes, the great champion of Gambettism to whom the majority of articles on the French Revolution are attributed.[†] The preface of 1865, however, marked by a certain restraint, proclaims Larousse's regret at not having been able to secure Pierre Joseph Proudhon's collaboration on the articles "God" and "Propriety" before the author's death. He describes Proudhon as "the most daring and profound thinker of the nineteenth century." The insolence of the first words of the article "Bonaparte" is well known:[5] "The greatest, most glorious, most brilliant name in history, not to omit Napoleon's.—General of the French Republic, born on August 15, 1769, in Ajaccio on the island of Corsica, died near Paris at the chateau of Saint-Cloud on the Eighteenth

---

★ EDITOR'S NOTE: The example of the Empress Eugénie here is offered as evidence of the prudence and discretion of Larousse's work—characteristics for which the Empress, long suffering under the notorious infidelities of her husband, was known—as well as its popularity, even among those who were not republicans.

† EDITOR'S NOTE: Léon Gambetta (1838–82) was an outspoken republican opponent of the Second Empire. When the French were defeated at Sedan by the German army Gambetta participated in the "revolution" on September 4, 1870, that proclaimed the Third Republic. He later sat on the extreme Left after the Commune had been destroyed and was kept from leading the Republic by politicians of the Center and Right in coalition with the moderate republicans.

of Brumaire in the Eighth year of the French Republic, one and indivisible (November 9, 1799)." History dictated that the article "Napoleon"
appear in December of 1873, which explains the tone.★

This example, provided as such, nonetheless gives an idea of the plas-
ticity of the formal channel in which the master's discourse flowed; for
example, the length of the articles was very dependent on the polemic use
to which the author subjected it.[6] The lexicographic procedures that Bayle
or Diderot[7] explored in order to divert the censors were used crudely: the
references, the biased citations, the unpredictable digressions, and so on.[8]
Bibliographic and iconographic appendices satisfyingly complement all
of the important articles.[9] In the body of the entry itself, value judgments
are omnipresent, through an intentionally informal lyric tone (anecdotes,
witty remarks, confessions), like a faint echo of Hugo or Quinet's style.
Personification makes an appearance at important moments, as in the surprising eight column diatribe at the end of "England as seen by Jacques
Bonhomme" (1866, 1:374–76), which until that point is quite impartial.
The author proceeds candidly and uses the reader as a witness, as in the
article "Bouillon (Rose)" (1867, 2:1085), which begins, "Forgotten, unknown name, misunderstood by historians who, engaged in seizing, in
understanding events as a whole leave the consideration of individual
scenes and details to the writers of memoirs and chronicles." The author
interrupts himself at one moment to address the *Grand dictionnaire*: "Now,
now *Grand Dictionnaire*, which style are you using here? It seems that you
are dipping your pen into the ink bottle of Monsieur Michelet or more
likely that of Madame Michelet.—To be sure, reading, I do not deny what
you say; the style is lyrical and feverous and proceeds by leaps and bounds.
But with respect to the woman . . ."[10]

With such investment, we must ask if there is sufficient representiv-
ity in the *Grand dictionnaire*. The personal quality of the work has sparked
a great deal of criticism, even from the left wing,[11] and it is clear that as
early as the 1870s,[12] the successors of Pierre Larousse noticeably glossed
over the master's ideology. But beyond the naïveté in considering these
and the later articles as paradigms of impartiality,[13] it is clear that his readers did not allow such small details to impede the success of such a rich
compilation of material. In a speech at the unveiling of the statue of Larousse in his native town of Toucy, the politician Eugène Spuller said that

---

★ EDITOR'S NOTE: Napoleon III died January 9, 1873, in exile in England. Early in Larousse's article on "Napoléon" we read: "It must be understood at the moment when the
article 'Bonaparte' was published, we did not have a great deal of liberty. The regime in
power was the object of the article and it is well known what brutal measures were taken
by the rulers of the day against independence and sincerity."

within the republican pantheon, Larousse is perhaps the most "powerful popularizer of Science and Virtue." The *Grand dictionnaire* can be considered one of the original forms of republican popularization at the end of the nineteenth century both by its date and by its context, scholarly manuals, popular literature, prize-winning books, popular didactic literature, and so on.

SYNTAX

Located thus at the heart of a historical movement, the *Grand dictionnaire* boldly lays claim to its role as a spring of memory. Even though Pierre Larousse appreciates history, he mistrusts historians in the same way that a fervent, slightly mystical believer would mistrust the clergy. His systematic mind, colored by the writings of Auguste Comte, leads him to conclude that "the sixteenth is the poetic century, the seventeenth is the classical century, the eighteenth is the philosophical century, and the nineteenth is the historical century" ("French literature" 1872, 8:711–15). When this free thinker avows that "today one would say that history has become a universal religion," it is not to devalorize it, but rather to prophesize that "for modern civilization, history is destined to become what theology was for the Middle Ages" ("History" 1873, 9:300–303). But from this prestigious position, history draws closer to philosophy, in the sense of the seventeenth century, than to erudition. The beginning of "Bouillon (Rose)" gives proof to this and is confirmed eleven years later (after Larousse's death) in the vitriolic review of *Henri IV and Marie de Médicis* by Berthold Zeller (*Supplément* 1878, 947): "Mr. Zeller went astray as many people have. We now acknowledge that it is possible to write only 'from unpublished sources'; published information does not count."

This publication, contemporaneous with the first issues of *Revue historique* (1876), is in character with a work edited for the most part by those who, to use a word from the period, I will call "publicists" (a mix of journalist, essayist, and activist) who continued to exist in the succeeding years albeit under different names. At a deeper level, this work recalls a notion of history akin to "the queen and the moderator of the conscience" ("History"). When the article "Educator" (1873, 9:725–26) vigorously denounces academic history as battle history and the history of monarchic "subjects" while "we need to understand the history of man, the history of the common people," it concludes simply by demonstrating the importance of a morality of substitution. This classic contradiction of this generation was greatly criticized by the contributors to *Revue historique*, before the "new history" unveiled its new hatchling, et cetera ad infinitum.

In fact, in this case dogma explains all since it is a question of progress, the philosophical justification of historicism. The *Grand dictionnaire* is the sum of a robust progressivism that at the same time engendered Michelet's gospels or the aptly named *Profession de foi* (*Avowal of Faith*), an absolute rationalist faith, by Eugène Pelletan, the father of the left-wing politician Camille Pelletan. We must take the religious metaphors literally in the article "Middle Ages" (1873, 11:657–58) when the author writes about the "dogma of the indefinable perfectibility" and, in the key article "Progress" (1875, 13:224–26), the following tautological premises: "Faith in the law of progress is the true faith of our epoch. This is a doctrine which has few disbelievers."

A similar premise is clearly at the core of each entry, from zoology to metaphysics. It justifies the encyclopedia's hostility toward the past, its optimism concerning the future, and its acknowledgment of societal hierarchy; there is of course a "Savage" (1875, 14:275–76) and a "Civilization" (1869, 4:366–70). The former is still in its infancy by virtue of the "analogy between the ideas, the language, the customs, and the character of savages and that of children." Civilization is the "state of a people who demonstrates cultivated intelligence, delicate customs, prosperous arts, and active industry." In this regard, the theories of the "distinguished ethnologist," Joseph-Arthur de Gobineau, are treated favorably, along with those of François Guizot, Charles Fourier, and above all Henry Buckle, an English historian/philosopher whose perspective is that of a culturalist. These theories lead the "Aryas" (1:736–37) to be known as the "generic name of one of the most noble branches of the great Aryan family or the white race."

This being said, the *Grand dictionnaire* is the first to insist that its credo be verified via the "scientific method" ("Middle Ages") and not remain trapped in the "religious and mystical breath" of the "illuminated" style of someone like Pelletan ("Avowal of Faith in the Nineteenth-Century" 1875, 13:219). The authors of the articles are ready to embrace the delicate problem of "Decadence" (1870, 6:206–7), which is finally resolved by acknowledging a certain discontinuity in the details of evolution. The Middle Ages are an example of one of several periods of "obvious retreat" that become, from the point of view of Sirius, "periods of incubation" ("Middle Ages") wherein "science and liberty" germinate. The word *liberty* holds the key to the enigma: history contains decadence, but only within alienated peoples ("Decadence"). This liberal voluntarism would remain a tautology if it were not akin to the doctrine that justifies all of the work of Larousse—faith in the education of all people. This is the ultimate response to the ultimate argument: if humanity progresses in the same way as the individual, then it will one day deteriorate and finally

Fig. 6.2
The Larousse printing house in the 1890s.

become extinct. The 1878 supplement to the article "Progress" sounds strange from this perspective and its very existence is difficult to justify. In this addendum the hypothesis of a negative reversal of these tendencies is theoretically not excluded even though in practice it is rejected in the name of progressivist work. However, the *Grande dictionnaire* is, in one way, the best example of precisely this.

Language

There remains one last internal contradiction unique to the Third Republic, this moment between the wars: how do we reconcile universal progress, a unifying movement par excellence, and the defense of national values? Larousse's political radicalism led him to present a rather negative image of colonization ("Colonization" 1868, 4:646–53; note that this was

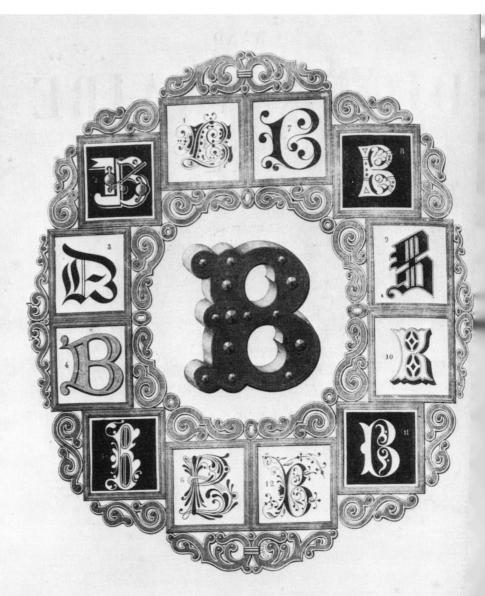

1 — Tiré d'un manuscrit de la Bib^{que} royale de Munich. — XIIe siècle.
2 — Alphabet lapidaire de Turin. — XVe siècle.
3 — Tiré du missel du cardinal Cornelius. — XVIIe siècle.
4 — Tiré d'un manuscrit du XVIe siècle.
5 — Lettres bullatiques d'Italie. — XVIe siècle.
6 — Tiré d'un manuscrit de Venise. — XVe siècle.

7 — Tiré d'inscriptions sépulcrales de Vienne (Autriche). — XIVe siècle.
8 — Tiré d'un évangéliaire de la Bib^{que} royale de Munich. — XIe siècle.
9 — Écriture d'église du XIVe siècle.
10 — Tiré d'inscriptions sépulcrales lapidaires de Naples. — XIIIe siècle.
11 — Tiré de la Bible du surintendant Fouquet. — XIIIe siècle.
12 — Alphabet vénitien du XVIIe siècle.

Fig. 6.3
Original edition of the *Grand dictionnaire universel du XIXe siècle*, 1863–76.

B — n. flei et mieux, suivant le nouveau système d'épellation, be — du gr. **η**, lequel n'est lui-même que le *beth* phénicien et hébreu. La deuxième lettre de l'alphabet et la première des consonnes dans presque toutes les langues anciennes et modernes. Cependant, dans l'alphabet éthiopien, il occupe la neuvième place, et la vingt-sixième dans les anciens arméniens. Dans l'ancien alphabet irlandais, le *b* est la première lettre, et l'a la six-septième : *Un B majuscule*, *Un grand B*. *Un petit b*. *Un b mal formé*. *La panse, le boudin d'un b*. *Un b initial, médial, final*.

— La figure de cette lettre est empruntée aux Latins, qui la tenaient des Grecs. On a dit qu'elle représente la forme que prennent les lèvres avant l'articulation de cette consonne, mais il est facile de sentir combien de pareilles explications sont hasardées.

— Cette lettre, l'une des plus fréquemment employées dans notre langue, fait défaut dans plusieurs idiomes du nouveau monde : ainsi, la langue aztèque manque des trois labiales *b*, *p*, *f* et de la liquide *r* ; la langue totonaca manque des deux labiales *b*, *f*. — La dentale *d*, de la liquide *r* ; au mexicain manquent trois labiales, *b*, *f*, *v* ; une gutturale ; une dentale, *d* ; la palatale *j* ; la liquide *r* ; la sifflante *s*.

— B, surtout lorsqu'il est placé au commencement du mot, exprime fréquemment une sorte d'explosion, un bruit ou un mouvement soudain, comme dans *bruit*, *bondir*, *bourder*, *bombe*, etc., etc. Nous sommes cependant tout disposé à accepter un millier d'exceptions, et notre prétention se borne ici à formuler une remarque plutôt qu'une règle. C'est une lettre qui appartient surtout au langage mal formé des enfants, et alors il y a souvent redoublement de syllabes : *bébé* (en arab.), *babij), bebé*, *bonbon, bobo*, etc.

> Balbutié bientôt par le bambin débile.
> Le *B* semble bondir sur sa bouche bibiatile.
>
> De Piis.

— B est la première et la plus douce des labiales ; il a beaucoup d'analogie avec les lettres du même ordre, *p*, *f* ou *ph*, *v*, et avec la liquide *m*. Cette labiale, ainsi bien que le *p*, se produit par une sorte d'explosion de l'air vivement chasse des poumons, et ne diffère du *p* que par une moindre énergie de l'action de cet organe (comparez *Bertha* et *perle*). Toutes ces lettres, d'ailleurs, se permutent les unes avec les autres, ainsi qu'on va le voir par des exemples. L'alphabet sanscrit, le *Devanagari*, qui, de tous les systèmes graphiques connus, est celui qui rend le mieux compte de la formation phonétique des sons, et qui les classe selon la méthode la plus rationnelle et la plus logique, donne au *b* la troisième rang dans l'ordre des labiales. Le *b* et le *h* aspiré ou bh constituent ce qu'on appelle en grammaire comparée les labiales douces ou sonores, et ont pour antécédents immédiats le *p* et le *p* aspiré ou ph, qui forment les labiales fortes ou sourdes. Ajoutons encore qu'à l'ordre des labiales se rattache immédiatement encore la nasale spéciale *m* et la semi-vocelle *v*, que les Indous l'habitude des hautes

spéculations philosophiques, et permet de constater d'un seul coup d'œil les diverses modifications que la lettre *b* est susceptible d'éprouver. à 1° B devenu *b*. Voici des mots latins et les mots français qu'ils ont donnés : *Astrolis*, *Anima; volataria*, *boulanger*; *Avalbera*, *boutique*; *braia*, *braie*; *carer*, *carer*; *caraln*, *cisaule*; *durira*, *double*; *quadraim*, *tomme*. L'italien surmonta à donné le français *amoureux*. Dans les manuscrits, on trouve fréquemment *Betrus* et *baubu* pour *Petrus* et *Paulus*. à 2° F devenu *b* : *Fiver*, nom latin du castor, a donné *bièvre*, ancien nom français du même animal. Le grec *bread* a donné le latin *fremo*, d'où le français *fremir*. D'après Plutarque, les Lacedemoniens changeaient ph en *b* et disaient *Bilippe* au lieu de *Philippe*. De même, le grec avouai (lons deux) a donné *anus* en latin. à 3° V devenu *b*. Le latin *corvus* a donné *corneau*; *curvus, courbe*; *vervax, avons*; *vervace, brevis*; *vessnita, Bo*. *eneen*; et le *tudesque barbara* ou *bierme Ason; wepen, bappor*. De plus, on trouve fréquemment dans les manuscrits *neeus* pour *veeus*, etc., et, de nos jours, les *bipaigants* et les Français du Midi prononcent encore le *b* et le *v* réciproquement. Ainsi, les uns disent *bive* pour *vive*, les autres, *vibon* pour *bibon*. De là l'exclamation de *bangre* : *bieles papudi quibus letres vir et biere* ! (Heureux le peuple pour qui vivre c'est boire!) Un grand nombre de mots latins ont passé dans le français avec le changement inverse du *b* en *v* : *au-avis*, *avant*; *caverculum*, *certain*; *corvana*, *chauvre*; *cavallus, chaval; caballa*, *cheval*; *coluvere*, *couleuvre*; *cunare*, *couver*; *deuaro*, *devoar*;

fava, *fève*; *febris*, *fièvre*; *februarius*, *février*; *hibernum* (tempus), *hiver*; *gaumare*, *gouverner*; *havere*, *avoir*; *ravir*, *ravir*, *rive*; *labrum*, *lèvre*; *liber, livre*; *libaram, lèvre*; *primare*, *prouver*; *ruivr*, *rouvre*; *luberna*, *taverne*; *corvena*, *cervena*; *Vervaum*, *Vervax*. L'espagnol semme à donné le français *mervare*, *moreure*. Les anciens Arabes semblent avoir également connu le changement de *m* en *b*, car, à côté du mot *Mekka*, qui est le nom de la célèbre ville sainte que nous écrivons *Mecque*, on trouve une autre forme archaïque *Bekka*. Du reste, *b*, aussi bien que *p*, a beaucoup d'affinité avec la lettre *m*, de là vient qu'il s'est intercalé entre cette lettre et l'une des liquides *l* ou *r*, dans plusieurs mots tirés du latin : *Camuter*, *comble*; *cu-mular*, *chambre*, etc., à devenait aussi *m* : *Samíti dies, samedi*; *noram, corme*. Pour cette raison *encore*, *a* devant *b*, dans un même mot, se change presque toujours en *m* : *Encharger* pour *enbarger*, *emballer* pour *embal-ler*, *embu* pour *enbu*, etc., etc. Nous ferons remarquer à ce propos, avec M. DeMéry, que l'insertion d'un *b* euphonique entre la labiale *m* et la liquide *r* est également une des règles fondamentales de la dérivation espagnole, comme on peut voir les exemples suivants : *hombrau*, *hombre*, *homme, comhrau, hombre*, *femme, hembre*, etc. L'addition de *r* euphonique, après *b* euphonique lui-même, est également très-caractéristique dans la formation de ces mots. Le grec lui-même n'est pas exempt de cette loi euphonique, c'est ainsi qu'il écrit *gamuros* pour

during the reign of Napoleon III); this radicalism, in conjunction with the historical period in which his work appeared, allowed Larousse to dare to expand his affirmation of the biased unity of human history. The article "Conquest" (1868, 4:960) celebrates this situation while aligning itself with democratic condemnation by thoroughly denouncing the conquerors and the respect they are given. The progressive and progressivist fusion of the races is announced; the first sign of this is the disappearance of "indigenous" races (the extinction of the "negro race" is already underway) when faced with "more civilized" races. "Humans comprise an ideal family" ("Progress") and the lexicographer is already concerned about the single language to be created for this humanity, already linked by railroads and philosophy ("Language" 1873, 10:144–45). As a federalist, this admirer of Proudhon hardly believes in the disappearance of national entities, despite nonetheless regretting them, but positive science leads him to recognize the progress of mixed races: "It is possible that the continual mix of races which has occurred in Europe since the beginning of our era, will allow us to escape destruction" ("Nation," 11:854–55).

A progressive of 1870 and even 1871 must finally agree on the model from which the fusion will be made; that which is essential for the *Grand dictionnaire* is that it be largely of French inspiration and that it persists in using lexicographic methods. Thus with respect to language in the article devoted to "French" (1872, 8:708–11), the supposed length of time taken in the development of the national language allows him to conclude that there is, as in a living being, a relation between the growth and longevity of an organism. Nowhere else does this intertextual approach better reveal its function than in the citations chosen to illustrate this word. Out of the four entries, three are devoted to the people, which begin gallantly, "Grace of movement and liveliness of spirit never abandons French women" (De Ségur). Then there are two maxims by little-known contemporaries chosen for their content rather than their form: "The French people have always been God's instrument for changing the earth" (Butain) and "French intellect does not appreciate confusion; it is always positive when surrounded by disorder" (Aristide Dumont). As for the citation reserved for the language itself, it is obvious that "all that is not clear is not French" (Rivarol).[14]

Pierre Larousse's generous and impulsive spirit is such that the hegemonic potential of these sorts of presumptions come to light where we would expect them. The article "Gallic" (1872, 8:1081–84) begins: "There exists in our time a people who distinguishes themselves from others through the universality of their genius and by the marvelous variety of their talents." It ends, "It is possible to affirm, without being too Gallic, that no more talented race has ever populated a more beautiful country." The beginning of "France" (1872, 8:719–43) needs only to trumpet, "*France* (formerly *Gallia*). State of western Europe whose fortunate geographical harmony, history, literature, arts, and industry have established it at the pinnacle of civilized states." The mystery of the cultural formula's structure is raised in the following lyric passage from the article "Middle Ages": "A nation is born. Roman in its centralization, Gallic in the audacity of its spirit, Frankish in its indomitable sense of freedom, and finally universal in its genius, France is a complete civilization."

There is nothing surprising, given this context, that French excellence naturalizes genius. "*Rousseau* (Jean-Jacques). One of a number of eighteenth-century philosophers who exerted the greatest influence on France and Europe. Born in Geneva, June 28, 1712, died at Ermenonville, near Paris, July 3, 1778. Although born in Switzerland, he belongs completely to France."[15] In an analogous way, adversaries within the nation's history must be associated with foreign blood. Of course Marie-Antoinette is Austrian, and Eugénie, to whom she is explicitly connected, is Spanish. But a mischievous pleasure is taken in suggesting that Napoleon III's natural father was Dutch and in the citation of Michelet's diatribe concerning Louis XVI that "by his race and through his mother he was completely German." "Napoleon" (1874, 11:804–14) himself is a "foreigner by his race and his ideas," later expanded to "foreigner, of uncertain race" and then he suddenly finds himself greatly influenced by Oriental despotism. "Far from being a continuation of the French Revolution, his reign was, despite its splendor, a malignant backlash against the Revolution and was a pure imitation of Byzantine Caesarism in terms of its political coalitions." Those who would be tempted to attribute these associations to excessive enthusiasm should refer to the article "Bazaine" in the astute *Grande encyclopédie*, where Camille Pelletan attributes the vile deeds of this monster who "barely knew France" to the Orient.★

This patriotism, which dates back to "Bouvines" (1867, 2:1166–67), "the dawn of our nationality," is even more jubilant because it has not yet admitted all of the consequences of its 1871 arrival in the era of relativism. The *Grand dictionnaire* furnishes us with a rather unrefined version of the event in which Germany is still a geographical expression dating from 1865, Russia is, from all points of view, disagreeable but remote, and the

★ EDITOR'S NOTE: François Achille Bazaine (1811–88) was a French Marshal. He was commander-in-chief of the army in Lorraine during the Franco-Prussian War. After the fall of Napoleon III Bazaine tried to negotiate with the Prussians. When his machinations were rejected he surrendered himself and the city of Metz. In 1873 he was condemned to death for treason, which was later commuted to twenty years imprisonment. He escaped to Spain, where he died.

United States are agreeable but remote. Only England rises arrogantly to
its role as hereditary enemy, but this is so imbued with aristocratic prejudice that its future seems quite dark. One must only compare London and
Paris to know which side the scale of civilization will tip.

Republican progressivism is a centralizing system of thought—it places
France squarely at the articulation point of cultures and then it swiftly becomes the capital, "the center of the whole world" ("Paris" 1875, 12:226–
81). The incontestable cultural brilliance of France thus becomes the principal argument in favor of its universalist ambitions. In the eponymous
article "Paris," the long rhapsodic section entitled "The Role of Paris in
Modern Civilization" constitutes no less than thirteen columns. The cult
of the City of Lights was never so intense as within the republican milieu during these years, in part due to the power of the Assembly, which
was suspected of wanting to "decapitalize" Paris. By virtue of this article
"Paris" is fifty-six pages long—double that of the article "France."

It would be a serious anachronism to think that such a well-anchored
conviction corresponds to aggression against minority cultures within
France; condescension is enough. It is clear that, for example, "The Basque
people will resist modern ideas for a long time yet" ("Basque" 1867,
2:317); there is indeed nothing to worry about since "in the middle of
the nineteenth-century, [they] still are at the midpoint between a state of
simple nature and a civilized state." Brittany, a Celtic country, enjoys the
sympathy that the romantic conception of the nation's history authorizes—
as a battle between the old Gallic roots and the successive invaders—and
Breton literature is seen through the rose-tinted glasses of Hersart de la
Villemarqué. It is not only the "Chouan uprising"★ (1869, 4:199–200) that
is treated with moderation as an aberrant moment for the "ignorant and
lost country folk." Granting the honors of war to adversaries is easy since
history will always condemn them.

The final word is in the articles devoted to the different provinces, all
of which conclude with the regions' ties to the kingdom or to the events
of 1789. "The Breton and the Normand people are still very different from
the people of Gascony and Languedoc. Even the names of these ancient
provinces are still used in everyday language; nonetheless, the nation is
still *one*" ("Province" 1875, 13:329). Since the inauguration of the National

---

★ EDITOR'S NOTE: The Chouans were peasants of the extreme west of France—present-
day Brittany, more or less—who rose in rebellion in 1793 against the French Revolution's
new laws on army recruiting. The rebellion, the most serious and brutal in the Revolution, lasted for years, its last embers finally extinguished by Napoleon. Their rallying
cry was "King and Church."

Assembly, democracy, at once universal and modern, has destroyed any inclination whatsoever toward autonomous expression.[16]

Vocabulary

Larousse often positions himself as an originator; as a lexicographer-turned-mythographer he systematically reevaluates the historic French imageries transmitted by the two great monarchic interpretations against which he battles. His historical vision uncritically borrows François Guizot's and Augustin Thierry's* accounts while erecting a pleasant representation of Gallic civilization ("Gaul" 1872, 8:1079–80); unlike "Germanic" society, Gallic society is exempt from the barbarous fate that is considered from afar as a big, dark, incomprehensible object (1872, 8:1220–22). Larousse also limits the article "Gallo-Roman" (1872, 8:968) to an overview of the Merovingian period in the style of Augustin Thierry. The same intellectual genealogy initiates a silent condemnation of "Nobility," which, it can be said, is already "thoroughly destroyed as is the odious inequality which was its result" (1874, 11:1036–39).[17]

Larousse's originality is clearer in his determination to remove from their pedestals the exalted men whose reputations could be exploited by the supporters of the ancien régime. The most popular figures are held at a distance: Louis IX showed concern for the meek but his religious obsession drove him to take part in a disastrous expedition overseas; if Louis XI (1873, 10:701–2) "did some good, it was unbeknownst to him"; "*Henri IV.* . . was an *important king* rather than a *good king*." The heroes of absolutism are disparaged. In the article "François Ier" (1872, 8:772–73), the central image of "defender of the arts" is suspect because the collective of the Enlightenment is more important than the individual monarchs: "We honor him for the restoration of literature and we identify his reign with that admirable movement known as the Renaissance, but others hold that religious reform was the most important element in this resurrection which had already taken place much earlier in Italy."

The articles on the last Louis are brutal: the inconsistent Louis XIII, in the style of *The Three Musketeers*; the foul Louis XV, pretext for sinister anecdotes; and the weak Louis XVI, guilty of complicity with the enemy. But the important Other is Louis XIV (1873, 10:705–8) whose presence also dominates the historical part of the article "France." The entry on him underscores his "immense conceit" and shows the disastrous conse-

---

★ EDITOR'S NOTE: See chapter 4, "Guizot and the Institutions of Memory," by Laurent Theis, and chapter 9, "Augustin Thierry's *Lettres sur l'histoire de France*," by Marcel Gauchet.

quences of this original sin committed during his lifetime. This technique is modeled on a style common to biographies of despots (through the example of didactic Catholic literature that, beginning in 1870, built upon Napoleon III's fate). Like a psychological analysis of morals in the style of Auguste Comte's work, Louis XIV becomes a stock character. Dominated by "one single motion—the most despicable of them all: egotism," he personifies absolutism, "of which he offers the most complete and sometimes the most extravagant example."

Confronted by this gallery of autocrats, the *Grand dictionnaire* knows how to manipulate the multiple avatars of Michelet's "common people." From the cult of the bourgeoisie the dictionary inherits the "Commune," to which a long article is devoted (1869, 4:739–49). Even more radically, the son of humble Burgundy folk from the town of Toucy waxes poetic about the long-despised "Jacquerie" (1873, 9:871). But this man who mistrusts traditional icons is, of course, the first to offer up other exemplary figures, which are united under the same democratic teleology. The nineteenth-century judges and acquits Marcel (Étienne) (1873, 10:1134–35) who "during the fourteenth century, far ahead of his time, dreamed of establishing parliamentary institutions in France." Confronted with Colbert (1873, 4:1134–35), the jury of "democratic opinion remembers that he loved the weak and the humble and that, entrusted with complete power, he counseled reforms which were so radical that even seventy years of revolution have not been able to produce them." "Reform" is the important historical password. This alone justifies the existence of people like "Sully" or "L'Hospital (Michel de)" (1873, 10:458–59), credited with "much earlier reforms which prepared the way for the great reform of the eighteenth century."

The Revolution itself poses many problems. Certainly not all of the cases are as desperate as that of Carrier (Jean-Baptiste) of whom the writer acknowledges extenuating circumstances: "This article is the most difficult, maybe the most delicate, and certainly the saddest of the *Grand dictionnaire*, whose opinions, although progressive, are honest," (1868, 3:451–52).★ But even if the article "French Revolution" proposes without entering into details the continuity "up through present history" of the event, the complexity of the stakes leads to choices based on the interests of the period.

★ EDITOR'S NOTE: Jean-Baptiste Carrier was perhaps the most notorious of the terrorists in 1793–94. Charged with subduing Nantes, a city that had welcomed the Chouans, Carrier inflicted a terrible and sadistic reign of terror, most notably the *noyades* mass drownings in the Loire River of those suspected of Chouan sympathies. He was tried and executed after Robespierre's fall.

From this it emerges that the cult of Danton does not date back to the work of historian Alphonse Aulard but, ambiguously, according to "informed" opinion and influenced undoubtedly by the work of Auguste Comte, it is said to be at its zenith as far back as 1860: "*Danton* (Georges-Jacques), illustrious member of the Convention, born in . . ., died on. . . . We are here in the presence of one of the most important figures of the Revolution" (1870, 6:92–95). "Robespierre" bears the brunt of the confrontation. Criticism is once again absent from the entry that is coldly enumerative and focused on accounts of "*French Revolution (Essay on)*" by Lanfrey (1858) or on the biography of Ernest Hamel (1865–67), itself judged as too accepting. However, a comment by Adrien Hébrard, contributor to the perceptive review *Temps,* saves "Marat" in the name of "the demon of patriotism" (1873, 10:1121–23) and Saint-Just is recognized as a "rare and exceptional soul" ("*French Revolution (Essay on)*"). Robespierre is and remains the Tyrant; on this point Larousse's liberal logic is without fault.

For those who would doubt the coherence and the goal of the project there is the ostentatious treatment reserved for Jean "Darc" (such is the degrading spelling in the *Grand dictionnaire*), a long piece (thirty-five columns with the appendices; 1870, 6:106–11) that strives to cut the heroine down to human dimensions ("Jean Darc's greatness is above all the domain of history and history sees only human realities"); this downsizing allows a strictly patriotic interpretation, highly anticlerical in tone, to be substituted through lexicographical means. The process, originating with the article "Bonaparte/Napoleon," consists in addressing the heroine's biography twice in a row; the tone of the first is that of a narrative while the second is similar to a rational survey, separating the elements of Christian hagiography from that which at the time was not even considered respectable. The rationalist version credits the young girl with a strongly calculating intellect, of having "used the beliefs of her time with great reflection and efficacy," while the second biography exists in order to "assemble in one package all of the facts which will show that the role of this peasant girl was completely nationalistic and that this important figure, transported into the world of visions, is purely and simply an example of legend stealing from history."

There still remains the deifications in the *Grand dictionnaire* that are not always under the authority of such an erudite group of people. Always on the edge, Larousse is a proselyte whose day-to-day fight against Bonapartism or the moral order clarifies, in the end, his relative indifference to the Vercingetorix (1876, 15:894–95), too recently reclaimed by Napoleon III, or to Henri IV, whose 1873 demystifications were entirely directed against

Fig. 6.4
Monument to Pierre Larousse erected in 1894 in Toucy, the village of his birth.

the legitimist enterprise. In both cases time would allow the Third Republic to accept its heritage without danger. There is no doubt that in this respect someone like Ernest Lavisse,★ touched by Bonapartism and distinguished by a completely different academic baggage than that of the son of a cooper/wheelwright from Toucy, would have been clearly better prepared to fashion a historical synthesis suitable for an established republic. Within the power structure he became the nation's greatest teacher while Larousse was only an approximation: limited throughout most of his life to the opposition and compelled to be a commonplace mediator.

Pierre Larousse thus had no other choice than to get his own way and he did not deprive himself of this. It is not completely by accident that this linguistic centralizer, who devoted his life to the cult of an essential language, nonetheless credited "Patois" (1875, 12:399–403) and "Dialect" (1870, 6:704) with the virtue of flaunting their vivacity before the dominant languages; they are "the real life, the elementary and natural life of language." His ideology and culture are dialectal. His posthumous renown is as much owing to his other, less fiery didactic works, which he initiated and which were managed very conservatively by his successors, than to the *Grand dictionnaire* itself—a noisy, flamboyant, and somewhat compromising object, even if it was, for a third of a century, the principle source for many journalists and politicians on either side of the political spectrum.[18]

In reality, was it not analogous to Victor Hugo's situation: lionized during his lifetime despite the independence of his political convictions? As in Hugo's case, the text devoured the writer. But if a myth takes shape somewhere between the man Larousse and the encyclopedia *Larousse*, it can be explained only through the success of his pedagogical project, in turn replaced by a thousand others. The collective nature of the endeavor and the progressive elimination of the old warrior, crushed by the two events of 1871 (the defeat of France in the Franco-Prussian War and the commune), encourage the myth, even during his lifetime. Thus, Pierre Larousse resolved for himself the contradiction between the hero and the common people that was left open in his work; the name of this partisan popularizer has become synonymous with the term "reference work."

★ EDITOR'S NOTE: See chapter 10, "Ernest Lavisse's *Histoire de France*: Pietas erga patriam," by Pierre Nora.

NOTES

1. Since there are no archives that allow distinctions to be drawn between the true contributions of the director and those of his collaborators (the names of twenty-seven contributors appear in the preface of 1865 but there were many others), the subject of this chapter, "Pierre Larousse," is the collective writer. All evidence at hand confirms that the ideological articles were either written or carefully edited by him.

2. This chapter grounds itself in several fundamental texts. First, the pioneer study of Larousse, André Rétif, "Pierre Larousse, républicain," *L'Esprit républicain*, conference at Orléans, September 4 and 5, 1970 (Paris: Klincksieck, 1972), 273–78, augmented by *Pierre Larousse et son oeuvre* (Paris: Larousse, 1974); then Gilbert J. Maurin, *La Critique du second empire dans le Grand dictionnaire* (Paris, 1975); finally Évelyne Franc, *La Mémoire nationale dans le Grand dictionnaire*, mémoire de DEA from the IE (Paris, 1980).

3. Letter published in the July 2, 1864 issue of *L'Illustration*; quoted by Rétif, *Pierre Larousse et son oeuvre*.

4. The first edition was published in 1856. Five million copies were sold in fifty years. Larousse therein initiated the *pages roses,* which were lists of Latin and foreign language expressions commonly used in French, printed on pink paper. In reestablishing the publication in 1905, Claude Augé entitled it the *Petit Larousse illustré.*

5. *Grande dictionaire* (1867), 2:920–46. (Subsequent citations in this form refer to the *Grand dictionaire.*) According to Rétif, the publication dates of the articles and his seventeen "Laroussiana" have been established from the review *Vie et langage.* These were found in the archives of the publisher. In general, it is impossible to know the date of their composition.

6. For example, eleven columns, plus the appendices, make up "Jesus" (1873, 9:966–68) but the article "Jesuit" (9:958–65) is comprised of thirty columns.

7. "Diderot" (6:764–73): "The most commanding genius, the most distinctive character, the most powerfully constituted athlete, philosopher, thinker, critic, and artist of the eighteenth century . . . after, or rather alongside, Danton." Thereafter ensued eighteen and a half columns plus appendices, more than double that for Voltaire.

8. For example, the article "Concours" (1869, 2:856–61) is riddled with malicious allusions against the regime.

9. "Henry IV" (1873, 9:185–86): three columns of biography but six columns of appendices.

10. Another example, in the article "Loan" (1870, 8:482): "Today, March 15, 1870, the Tunisian loan has dropped to 160 francs. Here it is appropriate to say: 'what a slump!'" Or, in a completely different tone, the agonizing exclamation at the end of the article "Damiens (Robert François)": "Atrocious! Atrocious!" (1870, 6:47).

11. Here is the opinion of the radically oriented *Grande encyclopédie* in the article "Encyclopedia": "This enormous compilation was very popular due to its anecdotal character and the material which it offered to journalists writing their commentaries. It is a humorous dictionary but its lack of methodological organization and balance between the entries, and the almost complete absence of analysis, makes it dangerous for laborers [*sic*]."

12. Compare the indulgence of "Flourens (Pierre-Jean-Marie)" (1872, 8:508–10)—a friend of Larousse's—and the relatively harsh judgment of the Paris Commune in the articles "Hugo" (1873, vol. 9) and especially "Commune" in the *Supplement.*

13. Ironically, Émile Moreau (1841–1919), one of the editors around 1900, joined the Action française of which his son Lucien was one of the founders.

14. It would be interesting to compare the citations used in the dictionaries of all countries in order to characterize their peoples. It is enough to note here that the greater number of citations found in the *Littré* of the same period moves in the same direction.

15. Similarly the dictionary Gallicizes the greatest patriots; for example, the name "Carnot" (1867, 3:426–28) "derives from old Gallic dialects . . . and there reigns in the region a tradition of affectionate respect towards this family."

16. This is the same reasoning used in "Jew" (1873, 9:1083–88). "Jews who want to make a name in literature today should understand, as most do, that it is necessary to relinquish that incomplete, outmoded, antiquated tool"—which is to say Hebrew.

17. Intertextuality reinforces devalorization; the citations in the *Littré* for this same word support this analysis.

18. In this respect it would be interesting to study the successors to the *Grand dictionnaire*: the second *Supplément* (1890), the *Nouveau Larousse illustré* (1896–1906), the *Larousse du XXe siècle* (1927–33), the *Grand Larousse encyclopédique* (1958–75), and the *Grande encyclopédie* (1971–78).

CHAPTER 7

THE GRANDES CHRONIQUES DE FRANCE: THE ROMAN* OF KINGS

(1274–1518)

✎

BERNARD GUENÉE

Phelippes, rois de France, qui tant ies renommés
Je te rens le romans qui des roys est romés.
Tant a cis travaillé qui Primas est nommez
Que il est, Dieu merci, parfais et consummez.

[Philip, King of France, you who are so renowned,
I present to you this account of kings written in French.
So carefully has it been prepared by one named Primat
That it is, thanks be to God, perfect and complete.]

It was in such terms that, in 1274, the historian Primat, a monk at Saint-Denis, in the presence of his abbot, Mathieu de Vendôme, presented to King Philip III (the Bold) of France the historical work that Louis IX had asked him to write some years earlier. Did such a scene really take place? However it may have occurred, the scene was painted in a luxurious presentation manuscript known to have been in the royal library in the fourteenth century.[1] Certainly the monk and the abbot had reason to

---

★ TRANSLATOR'S NOTE: In modern French, *roman* is most often used to mean "novel," in the sense of an extended work of fiction, but in the thirteenth century it designated either the French vernacular as opposed to the Latin (still the first definition given in most French dictionaries; hence the appearance of the verb *romer*, "to write in French," in the lines at the head of this article) or a narrative in French verse (e.g., the *Roman de la rose*).

savor this momentary triumph, which had been amply prepared by the venerable history of their monastery.[2]

Crowds had begun to gather at the tomb of St. Denis, the first bishop of Paris, soon after his decapitation in the third century. A religious community flourished there beginning in the sixth century. In the seventh century, King Dagobert was generous with donations to the institution, and the "foires du Lendit," or "market faires," on the nearby plain also began to flourish. Henceforth, Saint-Denis, supported by those in power and enriched by advantageous economic developments, was to prosper. In 1274, it was a rich and powerful Benedictine monastery where some two hundred monks resided in the shadow of the abbey church begun by Abbot Suger (1122–51)—a structure completed by his eventual successor Mathieu de Vendôme (1253–86).

Other communities devoted themselves to prayer and to the study of scripture and theology. While neglecting none of these pursuits, Saint-Denis made a specialty of historical research. (Rather late in the day, it should be said.) The historical school of the monastery of Fleury (the present Saint-Benoît-sur-Loire) produced many remarkable works long before anything of the kind was undertaken at the scriptorium of Saint-Denis. The earliest, rather feeble attempts at historiographical activity there date from the late eleventh century. Several historical compilations were produced at Saint-Denis in the first half of the twelfth century; such work predated Suger's abbacy, but he enthusiastically supported it, for he was himself a historian, having written a long history of King Louis VI. By way of preparation for this synthetic project, the monks copied, or had others copy, at Fleury, Saint-Germain-des-Prés, and other important historical repositories of the day, all the texts they deemed essential. Their enterprise proved fruitful. Saint-Denis soon became one of the richest libraries in the realm and an indispensable resource for researchers. About 1175, Count Hainaut Baudouin V, fascinated by the history of Charlemagne, dispatched clerks to Cluny, Tours, and Saint-Denis in search of documentation. About 1180, a monk from the Abbey of Saint-Foillan in Rœulx, Hainaut, then preparing a vast historical compilation, may have traveled as far as Fleury to take notes; Saint-Germain-des-Prés was certainly on his itinerary, and he also made a long stop at Saint-Denis.[3] Thanks to this library, by the reign of Philippe Auguste (1180–1223) the historical school of Saint-Denis had become the most active in the realm, and it remained so in 1274.

The natural vocation of Benedictine historical centers was the production of hagiographic works, universal histories, and regional histories in which the monastery itself played a leading role. Certainly the scriptorium at Saint-Denis devoted considerable energy to the glorification of

St. Denis but, otherwise, its most original contribution was its work on the history of the kings reigning over the *Franci*: in other words, first the Franks and then the French. This novel enterprise came to fruition in the thirteenth century in two great Latin syntheses. By the early years of the century, a history of France from its origins to the death of Louis VI (the Fat) had been compiled at Saint-Denis.[4] Fifty years later, another Latin compilation had been assembled narrating the history of France from its origins to the death of Philippe Auguste (1223).[5] From the beginning, the orientation of Saint-Denis historiography was royal and national.

This is because of the longstanding close ties between French kings and the abbey. In the early seventh century, Clotaire II acknowledged St. Denis as his "special patron." All of his successors, whether Merovingian, Carolingian, or Capetian, had done likewise. Suger went further, making Denis the patron saint of the realm. Furthermore, some Merovingian and Carolingian kings were interred in the abbey church, also the burial site of all but two of the Capetian monarchs. By the thirteenth century, Saint-Denis had become the "cemetery of kings." Finally, not far from the royal tombs, in its treasury, the monastery preserved the crowns and other regalia used for each new *sacre*, French monarchs having abandoned the custom of being buried with them. It was only natural for the Saint-Denis school to devote itself to the history of the kings whose remains were so close by.

French royal authority accrued additional glory and prestige from the Saint-Denis historiography. But the latter also had need of royal authority. For the principles of historical criticism were not the same as they are today. When it came to distinguishing truth from falsehood, medieval historians did not dispose of the critical arsenal that, whatever problems attend its use, is available to us. The credibility of an account—what they termed its "authenticity"—was understood to be a function of the prestige of its author, or of the power of the individual who had sanctioned it. And what lay person in the realm possessed greater authority than the king? The dream of French historians was to write a "trustworthy" history, in other words, one that would be authenticated by royal approbation. At the beginning of the thirteenth century, Rigord, a monk at Saint-Denis, undertook to write, at his abbot's bidding, a Latin history of Philippe Auguste. Upon its completion, the author, now styling himself "chronographer of the king of France," humbly submitted his work to the very Christian king "so that it might become, by the king's sole authority, a public monument." In 1274, Primat repeated Rigord's gesture in hopes of having his history likewise authenticated.

Benedictine monks had always written their scholarly histories in Latin. But in the twelfth century, princely and seigniorial courts began to enjoy hearing long, rhymed historical recitations performed in the vernacular by *jongleurs*.* Beginning in the thirteenth century, however, a consensus emerged that, as verse distorted the truth, serious history should be written in prose. And an increasingly large and well-informed lay public clamored for such serious history. Historical works in French prose proliferated. But the monks remained faithful to Latin. Until, that is, Louis IX invited Primat to write this history in French, to *romer* this *roman* that, perfect and complete, was presented to the saint-king's son and successor in 1274.

⁂

Initially it was thought that Primat was only the copyist of the presentation manuscript. Later he was believed to have done nothing more than translate into French a Latin compilation prepared at Saint-Denis toward the middle of the thirteenth century. In reality Primat was a true historian and his work is more original than it was long acknowledged to be. True, he made extensive use—as he himself admitted—of the "chronicles of the abbey of Saint-Denis in France, where the histories and deeds of all the kings are written."[6] In other words, his primary task had indeed been to translate the authors successively copied into the mid-thirteenth-century Latin compilation, including for example Aimoin, the great historian active at the Fleury monastery around the year 1000 and author of a history of the Franks that he completed only as far as the seventh century; Éginhard, who knew Charlemagne and wrote an account of his life; and Suger, who wrote a life of Louis VI. But when he had managed "to find worthwhile chronicles in other churches," he profited from them. Furthermore, neither the French words used in his translation nor his interpolations (in the forms of small phrases and even entire passages written by himself) were innocent. They are quite revelatory of the perspectives and ambitions that shaped his work.

Primat clearly set out to provide his readers with examples to avoid and to imitate. True, this was a longstanding preoccupation of medieval historians. But Primat gave it much greater emphasis than did many others. He insisted on it in his prologue: "May everyone find good and evil, beauty and ugliness, wisdom and folly here, and derive profit from the examples of [this] history."[7] And he included periodic reminders of his intention in the account itself: "All princes should follow this example."[8] Primat's *roman* was first of all an extended lesson in ethics.

---

* EDITOR'S NOTE: Wandering minstrels who chanted or recited verses usually accompanying themselves on a plucked string instrument.

hclippos tois de frice q tar tes renoines.
Ge te rei le romar q tes tois or tume.
Tat a eritalhe q pmaz est notne.
Que il est dieu men pfaiz 7 asimie.

uolem 7 tois tes lorante soutenir.
Cat anat selairoter par lespee ferir.
Z il ferlsei chose dor maus dart tienir.

Fig. 7.1
In 1274, in the presence of his abbot, Mathieu de Vendôme, Primat, a monk at the abbey of Saint-Denis, presents King Philip II (the Bold) of France with his *Roman des rois*, which Louis IX had commissioned him to write.

The examples were drawn from the lives of kings. But this is not to say that Primat limited himself to a few stories he found especially instructive. His aim was to compose a continuous narrative of kings, to "make known . . . the actions of kings,"[9] to write "the *roman* . . . of kings" in French.

To be still more precise, his aim was to rehearse "the genealogy of the kings of France, whatever their origins and line of descent."[10] Everyone knew "that three generations [i.e., "dynasties"] have been kings of France since it was established"[11]: that of the Merovingians, that of the Carolingians, especially prestigious, and that raised to the throne by Hughes Capet in a highly dubious coup d'état. But, correctly, in a passage that might be considered the key to this work, Primat explains that Philippe Auguste had deliberately married a descendent of Charlemagne and that his son, "the valiant king Louis [VIII] was descended from the great Charlemagne, having recovered his lineage."[12] The notion that in 1223 the realm had reverted to the line of Charlemagne was fundamental to the political thought of St. Louis. He constantly repeated this, especially to those obsessed with the great emperor's memory. In 1263, the king rearranged the royal tombs in the abbey church at Saint-Denis with the intention of making it clear that, beginning with Philippe Auguste and Louis VIII, Capetian and Carolingian blood had been joined to make a new dynasty. Was it a matter of chance that this same idea subtends the work from Primat commissioned by the same king, and that Primat considered his history complete when, in 1223, with the death of Philippe Auguste and the accession of Louis VIII to the throne, the Carolingian return that he had been announcing since the advent of Hughes Capet was finally consummated?

Primat states in his prologue that he had set out to write the "geste des rois," the deeds and genealogies of kings. His first chapter, however, is entitled "How the French Descended from the Trojans." As this wording indicates, Primat's history is as national as it is royal. According to him, the Trojan origins of the French, maintained by historians since the eighth century, should be the very foundation of their national pride: "French *seigneurs*," he has Clovis say, "you who are descended from the exalted line of the Trojans, take pride in your high name and your lineage."[13] And Saint-Denis historians were always careful to evoke the presence, behind the kings, of proud Frenchmen. In Aimoin's account of the battle of Tolbiac, the Alamans "abandoned victory to Clovis," but Primat's "translation" of this passage reads: "Victory reverted to the king and the French."[14]

Behind the king were Frenchmen. Above the king and the French were the crown and the realm. The rebirth of Roman law had gradually imbued these pale abstractions with reality. At the end of the thirteenth century, the most educated of Frenchmen declared themselves ready to defend the realm, to die for their country. And Primat echoes the sentiments of this cultivated elite when, in his account of the invasion of Emperor Henry V in 1124, based on Suger's treatment, he describes the reactions of the French combatants in phrases absent from his basic source: they came "richly appareled to aid the king their lord and defend his reign"; they were "ready to die to defend the throne wielding their swords"; "and in any case [they] had come there because of the realm's struggles with foreign nations."[15]

At Tolbiac, victory had fallen "to the king and the French," and Primat insists, in a phrase all his own, that this did not happen by chance but "was divinely ordained."[16] Indeed, the conviction that God afforded special protection to the kings and the realm of France is ubiquitous in the work—God and St. Denis, that is; generally known to be "after God the special defender of kings and of the reign."[17] A constant presence, this divine aid was never more evident than when Louis VII, having previously sired only daughters of his three wives, after ardent prayer beseeching God to grant him a male heir who might be a "noble governor of the realm of France, to the confusion of [its] enemies," was finally vouchsafed a son, Philippe, whom Primat sometimes calls "Auguste" but prefers to describe as "Dieudonné," or "God-given." But there is more. Louis VII was not simply blessed with a son. He was also favored with a vision in which he saw his son Philippe holding a chalice in his hand, "and from this chalice brimming with human blood he administered and gave drink to all his princes and all his barons."[18] An audacious dream indeed, one in which the king of France is not simply protected by God but almost becomes God.

The French, however, were not overwhelmed by this divine royalty postdating them. For, faithfully echoing—like Jean de Meun, author of the *Roman de la rose*—the contemporary teaching of Parisian doctors, Primat interpolates into Aimoin's text an important passage in which he shows the French living simply at the beginning, without a king and doing whatever they pleased, until they designated Pharamond their "lord and king."[19] After which point the French as a population virtually disappear. In his father's dream, Philippe Dieudonné gives drink only to his princes and barons. Only this elite of princes and barons plays a role in Primat's history. But its role is crucial, sometimes taking precedence even over that of the king. Following his sources or improving on them, Primat shows how "the barons of France and Burgundy . . . received their lord," the young Clovis II;[20] how Louis the Stammerer "gave the barons what they wanted so as to win their favor";[21] "how the barons of France crowned the two sons" of Louis the Stammerer;[22] and "how the prelates and barons assembled in Orléans . . . to crown" the young Louis VI.[23] Throughout the history of France, the "barons" carry much weight. Primat's work is the *roman* of kings, the history of the realm, but it is also the epic of the barons of the realm.

Texts were not so rapidly disseminated in the Middle Ages as they are today. A quarter century elapsed before Primat's history began to be read and copied by visitors to Saint-Denis. The earliest copy dates from about 1300[24]; another was made around 1320,[25] and there are a few others. But only rarely was it merely copied, for medieval thought maintained that a history was never complete, that it should be continued as time passed. The school of Saint-Denis continued to flourish after Primat's disappearance from the scene. At the beginning of the reign of Philip the Fair, shortly after 1285, a monk composed a short life of Louis VIII. More important, Guillaume de Nangis, the monastery's archivist from 1285 to 1300, was feverishly active as a historiographer. In addition to a universal chronicle, he composed a Latin life of St. Louis, a life of Philip III, and a short chronicle of the kings of France. Translation of these Saint-Denis productions would suffice to continue Primat's work.

The life of Louis VIII was translated first; thus a few rare manuscripts narrate the history of France from its origins to 1226.[26] Then, sometime before the end of the thirteenth century, the life of St. Louis by Guillaume de Nangis was rendered into French. But, in fact, only one of the manuscripts dating from the early years of the fourteenth century appends this translation of Guillaume's life of the saint-king to Primat's text.[27] For Primat's work was soon continued by another means. Having written his short chronicle of French kings for the benefit of visitors to the royal tombs at Saint-Denis, Guillaume de Nangis quickly translated it into French himself. It is this short chronicle that was known and continued, and since the scriptorium of Saint-Denis was becoming less active, allowing Primat's work to recede from view and limiting itself to the production of brief Latin accounts of recent events, Parisian book dealers diffused a *Chronique des rois de France* tracing it from its origins to the present day that was none other than Primat's work followed by Guillaume de Nangis's short chronicle, itself brought up-to-date. One such example is a *Chroniques des roys de France* that "Pierre Honorez of Neufchâtel in Normandy had had written and arranged, in accordance with the order of the chronicles of Saint-Denis, by Master Thomas of Maubuege residing on the Rue Neuve Notre Dame in Paris the year of Our Lord 1318."[28] The same plan was followed in three other manuscripts copied in the second quarter of the fourteenth century, two of them probably in Paris[29] and the third in northern France.[30]

By the end of the first half of the fourteenth century, then, the diffusion of Primat's work had escaped Saint-Denis's control, but it nonetheless proceeded on a modest scale. In all, only ten manuscripts survive from this period; most were produced in Paris, but one originated in northern France and another in Brabant.[31] Their known owners are a diverse lot, including a king (of France), a count, a bishop (of Cambrai), and the aforementioned Pierre Honoré, about which we know only that he was from Neufchâtel-en-Bray. But as far as we can tell even after three quarters of a century the dissemination of Primat's history was limited to Paris, northern Normandy, northern France, and the Brabant.

Richard Lescot became a monk at the Abbey of Saint-Denis in 1329, while still a young man. For more than thirty years he was prodigiously active as a copyist and historian; doubtless he would appear even more so if all the manuscripts copied by him had been identified and if most of his own historical works had not been lost. In any event, we know that the young Richard Lescot, soon after becoming a monk at Saint-Denis, began to contribute to what remained the collective project of its scriptorium by writing a Latin account of events transpiring between 1328 and 1344. He then abandoned the task of contemporary chronicler to devote himself to more erudite work, notably a revision and updating of Primat's text. Between 1340 and 1360, several projects were begun at Saint-Denis that he must have initiated and sponsored.

To continue Primat's narrative after the death of Philippe Auguste, the life of Louis VIII that had been appended to it before the end of the thirteenth century was retained, but beyond 1226 the short chronicle of the kings of France by Guillaume de Nangis was abandoned and the translation of the life of St. Louis by the same Guillaume de Nangis, also written before 1300, was restored. After which many additions were introduced on the basis of accounts, especially hagiographic narratives, found in the libraries of various churches in the realm. The text resulting from this first process of revision was copied in a luxurious manuscript presented to Jean, duke of Normandy, prior to his accession to the French throne in 1350.[32]

At the same moment a modification was introduced, probably at royal initiative, but it was carried out at Saint-Denis. It was decided that the translation of the life of St. Louis by Guillaume de Nangis gave far too much prominence to the abbey. Accordingly, a second translation was prepared in which references to Saint-Denis's role in certain events were either shortened or suppressed completely. It is this second version that was copied into the manuscript of Primat's work that Primat himself had presented to Philip the Bold and remained in the royal library. And it is this second version that prevailed at Saint-Denis itself, where the first revision was definitively abandoned.

There followed the dark years of the Black Death (1348–350); of the disaster at Poitiers, where King Jean was taken prisoner (1356); and of the Parisian revolt and peasant uprising (1358). To aid a collapsing throne and a tottering country, Richard Lescot redoubled his learned activity. He wrote a short genealogy of French kings in which he was the first to invoke the salic law as justification for Philip of Valois's accession to the throne in 1328. Then, in a time of increasingly rigorous standards of historical exactitude, he revised Primat's text by comparing it with the Latin sources that Primat himself had used. Since Primat had suppressed many passages, this revision resulted in numerous additions which were inscribed in the margins of the manuscript prepared for Jean of Normandy. In the end, these marginal notes were never incorporated into the text and Primat's efforts were wasted. Another initiative, by contrast, proved decisive: that of continuing the narrative until the death of the last king to die, Philip VI of Valois (†1350). To do this, one uses what historians like Bernard Gui and Jean de Saint-Victor had been able to write. But, as seems only natural, productions of Saint-Denis were used in this undertaking: the universal chronicle of Guillaume de Nangis was translated, bringing the account to 1300; subsequent contemporary Latin chronicles, including that written by Richard Lescot himself, were also translated, advancing the narrative to 1344; to which was added an original French text covering the final years of Philip VI's reign, as there was no Latin account of this period to serve as a model.

The atmosphere pervading this revised and updated text differed somewhat from that of Primat's original history. While less dominated by the spirit of Saint-Denis, it was just as royal. It remained firmly if discreetly baronial, stating directly, for example, that upon the death of Charles IV in 1328, "the barons and nobles assembled to negotiate the government of the realm."[33] It remained just as Christian, noting at the close "how good King Philip was a true Catholic," and maintaining that his defeats were proofs of divine favor every bit as strong as Philippe Auguste's successes: "Our Lord willed him pain and tribulation in this world so that he might reign everlastingly with Him after death. Amen."[34] But it was decidedly more French, as is indicated by the work's new title. Primat wrote in his text of "the actions of kings," of a "*roman* of kings," but he did not indicate a precise title for it. Furthermore, many of the fourteenth- and fifteenth-century manuscripts lack titles. When manuscripts dating from the first half of the fourteenth century do carry one, they always, like Primat himself, showcase the role of the kings: *Chroniques des roys de France*,[35] or *Chroniques de tous les roys de France crestiens et sarasins et toz leur fais*.[36] But when the new editions produced at Saint-Denis bear a title, it is simply *Chroniques de France*. From *Roman aux rois* to *Chroniques de France*: the emphasis has shifted considerably over the course of a century. But this somewhat vague new formula was used in different ways: one manuscript—and only one—speaks simply of the *Grans croniques de France*,[37] whereas several others specify the origins of the work at Saint-Denis: *Chroniques de France selon ce qu'elles sont composées en église de Saint Denis en France*.[38]

Richard Lescot lived until the very end of the fourteenth century. The historical school of Saint-Denis continued to produce important works after his death. But the *Chroniques de France* perfected at the monastery around 1360 thereafter definitively abandoned their cradle at Saint-Denis. This was not due to the scale of its success in this form. It was still poorly disseminated, as evidenced by the existence today of only four manu-

uatre cens z iiii ans a
uant que romme fuft
fondee vernoit pudoit
en troie la riant il en
uoia paris laisne de ses
fils en grece pour rauir la royne hele
ne femme au roy menelaum pour soy
venetier dune honte q̃ li auer eu orent
la faute li gregois qui moult furent
courouciez de ceste chose s'esmurent z
emptrent affegier troie z ce fiege qui
·v· ans durer furent occis tous les fils
le roy priant il z la royne ecuba sa

feme z plusieurs autres la cite fu arse
z destruite le peuple z les barons occis
mais aucuns est'haperent de celle pe
stilence z plusieurs des princes de la cite
qui s'espandirent en diuerses parties
du monde pour querir nouuelles ha
bitacions come helenus eneas z athenor
z maint autre cilz helenus fut li uns
des fils au roy priant si ert poetes z
bons clers auf. or. en mena auec lui
des essilliez de troie en grece s'en alaou
royne pandrare de liu yssi puis crut
lutyne Eneas qui refist des plus truo

Fig. 7.2

It is not uncommon for manuscripts of the *Grandes chroniques de France* to be decorated with quadripartite frontispiece miniatures recalling the Trojan and Christian origins of the French people. Here, the first compartment represents
the departure from Troy and the one immediately below it the *sacre* of Clovis, the first Christian king of France.

Fig. 7.3
Chapter four of the *Grandes chroniques de France*, continuing its account of the Trojan origins of the French people, narrates "how and when the city of Paris was founded," then how Pharamond, the "first king of France," changed its name from Lutetia to Paris in honor of his ancestor Paris, son of King Priam of Troy. This miniature, an illustration of this chapter from the manuscript for Charles V circa 1375–79, shows Pharamond ordering the construction of a monument in the city henceforth known as Paris.

scripts.[39] But the destiny of the *Chroniques de France* was soon transformed by the will of Charles V.

*·ɔ,**

This prudent ruler understood the importance of the word and the pen as well as of the sword. He wanted to see written, under his supervision, a history of the reign of his father Jean le Bon, in which he had played such an important role, as well as that of his own reign. But he broke with tradition, confiding the task not to the monks of Saint-Denis, where Richard Lescot would have been well qualified to undertake it, but to his chancellor Pierre d'Orgemont. Laymen, and especially jurists, had now assumed a primary role in the king's service. And Charles V himself was too much the jurist not to prefer their manner of writing. The work produced by his chancellor satisfied his expectations. Instead of a national and Christian epic, it was a kind of cold official journal in which events at court, armed combats, and diplomatic initiatives were carefully entered, an extended brief in which all recorded facts and public documents underscored the king's legitimacy, in which everything was designed to convince the reader that the king was indeed, in his realm, the sovereign lord.

In 1375, Charles V had his scribe Henri de Trévou copy the text of the *Chroniques de France*, which he enriched with many illustrations. He worked from the last of the Saint-Denis revisions, introducing a few changes meant to emphasize the subjection of the kings of England and the dukes of Guyenne to the authority of French kings, a subordinate status also given striking visual expression in several of the miniatures. And to this volume, which traced the history of France from its origins to 1350, the king added another, copied by his scribe Raoulet d'Orléans and likewise richly illustrated, containing the work composed by Pierre d'Orgement. The result was a history of France from its origins to the present day, which Charles V had bound in 1377: "For the spines and covers of the Chronicles of France and those prepared by our faithful and loyal chancellor, in two volumes for ourselves, a piece of *baudequin* leather, twenty-six francs."[40] After which, on a few sheets left blank, the narrative was continued until April 1379, at which date it came to a definitive close.

Copied (at least in part) by the same scribe Raoulet d'Orléans and decorated with the same cycle of illustrations, another manuscript of this compilation was executed at the same time, doubtless for a member of the royal family.[41] More important, several years later, after the death of Charles V (1380), the same text came into the hands of Parisian book dealers, who added a few chapters extending the narrative to the death of Charles V and the decision of the dukes, the dead king's brothers, in the coronation and crowning of the very young Charles VI.[42] Several manuscripts emerged from this mold containing two new chapters, recounting "How King Charles VI was crowned" and "How the Jews were plundered"[43]; the latter short chapter closed with an invasion of English cavalrymen and their subsequent defeat outside Nantes.[44]

With or without the last two chapters, very few of these manuscripts covering the history of France from its origins to 1380 carried titles. Some of those that did bore a variant of the earlier one: *Croniques des roys de France, Gestes des roys de France, Geneologie des roys de France*. But the title most frequently used for this compilation is that first ascribed to the Saint-Denis text in the years prior to 1350: *Croniques de France*, or in a few exceptional cases, *Grans chroniques de France*.[45]

The success of the *Chroniques de France* was immediate and extensive. Only twenty manuscripts of the work produced by Primat and his successive avatars over the century preceding 1375 survive, but some fifty manuscripts of the 1380 text produced over a period of forty years, during the reign of Charles VI, have come down to us. They have several features in common. All were produced in Parisian workshops. All were prepared with considerable care, having been transcribed on parchment with a high degree of accuracy. Given their considerable scale (each consists of 500 sheets of large or very large formats bound into two or three volumes, with text on both recto and verso), we can scarcely speak of inexpensive exemplars. But these simpler ones, still costly, represent only a minority of the Parisian production, constituting one-fifth of the surviving corpus. The remaining four-fifths are lavish manuscripts decorated with numerous and often quite beautiful miniatures.

That was due to the specific clientele for which these Parisian productions were made: the king, the princes, and rich nobles in their service. Beautiful manuscripts of the *Chroniques de France* were cherished gifts, often presented by wealthy familiars to their prince or by princes to their faithful servants, for example as New Year's offerings. That is how the Duke of Berry; the Duke of Burgundy; the Duchess of Orléans; the Countess of Armagnac; Aimeri de Rochechouart, lord of Mortemart, advisor and chamberlain to the king, the seneschal of Limousin;[46] Regnault d'Angennes, chamberlain to the king;[47] and still others became happy owners of *Chroniques de France* manuscripts. They may have circulated outside this narrow circle of princes and their familiars, but it is quite clear that the manuscripts were owned by the nobles whose arms were painted on the first sheet of each exemplar.[48] Parisian book dealers were so confident of the status of their eventual clients that a space was systematically left blank on these pages to accommodate the arms of future purchasers.[49]

The reader might be tempted to speculate that exemplars unknown to us might have been owned by individuals of different social status. But such reasoning would be hazardous. Indeed, the evidence tends to refute it. Many library inventories survive, and they indicate that not a single *conseiller* in the Parlement of Paris had a copy of the *Chroniques de France* in his library, nor did a single academic. And the few ecclesiastical libraries to possess one, for example the cathedral chapter at Chartres, the cathedral chapter at Reims, and the Abbey of Saint-Bertin, in fact owned transcriptions copied at some point during the fourteenth century into old manuscripts consisting of Primat's work and the life of Louis VIII, to which they appended their own continuations.[50] Versions of Primat's account updated to 1226 were disseminated to ecclesiastical foundations in the fourteenth century, but the 1380 text of the *Chroniques de France* was not. It is not even clear that Saint-Denis owned a copy. Everything suggests, then, that under Charles VI possession of the *Chroniques de France* was the exclusive privilege of wealthy nobles.

It would be overly glib to maintain that these nobles contented themselves with looking at the beautiful illuminations. This in itself would be quite an admission, for they are never innocent. But the reality is that these nobles knew how to read and took the time to read, and that the text met with their approval because it corresponded to their tastes and inclinations. The *Chroniques de France*, then, allow us to deepen our understanding of noble culture, so distinct from those of clerics or jurists. Above all, this public was passionately interested in history, which counted for little at the University of Paris. Those with university educations who were historically inclined preferred universal or Roman history. But the nobles, while not neglectful of Roman annals, were interested primarily in their national history. The nationalist sentiment that sustained France through its tribulations during the fourteenth and fifteenth centuries was certainly not an exclusively noble prerogative, but there can be no doubt about the vigorous nationalist sentiments of the nobility, whether sustained by knowledge of national history or not. A national history, but also a resolutely royal history, and oft-repeated images of the royal *sacre*, appearing at the beginning of each reign in some manuscripts, further accentuated the royalist character of the text. But these images of the *sacre* also show, almost always, the king surrounded by prelates and barons; indeed, in some cases his crown is supported by a prelate and a baron. The chapter titles—not always precise duplicates of those used by Primat and telling indicators of the interests of both the scribes and their readers—never miss an opportunity to underscore how the king of France owed his crown to the French barons, who paid him homage and were accorded "great gifts"[51] by him. The images, titles, and text of the *Chroniques de France* all insisted that the king of France was nothing without the barons of France.

The work had indeed found the public for which it was intended, the very "vaillanz gens,"[52] or valiants, for whom Primat himself had written.

It is not always easy to determine where these nobles, possessed of so many dispersed seigneuries, kept their books. But to the best of our knowledge, under Charles VI copies of the *Chroniques de France* were still concentrated in the Parisian region and northern France, where the 1380 text was even recopied on paper around 1410.[53] Beyond this, we know that there were two exemplars in Burgundy.[54] There may have been one at Chaumont-sur-Loire, if Anne de Beuil, the wife of Pierre d'Amboise, Lord of Chaumont, kept her copy there.[55] There may have been two others at Moulins, if the manuscripts of the Duke and Duchess of Bourbon were kept there.[56] And that is all. While the success of the *Chroniques de France* under Charles VI was considerable, its geographic diffusion was as limited as its social diffusion.

The hardships of the era suffice to explain that the history of the *Chroniques de France* during the second quarter of the fifteenth century remains a complete blank. But after Charles VII reentered Paris, inaugurating a period of monarchical dominance and peace, the success of the *Chroniques* continued and even increased. For in the second half of the fifteenth century, the almost seventy exemplars previously copied and still read were joined by, at least, some thirty new manuscripts. To which we can almost certainly add a half-dozen manuscripts mentioned in fifteenth-century inventories that, while impossible to date with certainty, seem to me to have features placing them, too, in the second half of the fifteenth century. Furthermore, the first book to be printed in Paris, by Pasquier Bonhomme, in January 1477, was a three-volume edition of the *Chroniques de France*, reissued in a second three-volume edition by Antoine Vérard in 1493. We do not know how many copies of these incunabula were printed. Fourteen copies of each of these two editions are now in French libraries. It seems likely that both ran to at least a hundred copies. All in all, over the course of this fifty-year period, printed and manuscript versions of the *Chroniques de France* reached a much larger readership than during the first seventy-five years of the text's existence.

This readership still included princes and nobles. Of extant manuscripts, more than ten are on vellum or parchment, and most of these, decorated with abundant miniatures by excellent artists, for example Jean Fouquet, were costly productions intended for the same clientele that had made the success of the *Chroniques* under Charles VI. Even some of the copies on paper, those featuring large miniatures as frontispieces, were intended for nobles and other wealthy purchasers. And even the beautiful exemplars of the Bonhomme and Vérard editions, some of which were augmented with miniatures on parchment, were not unworthy of princes

Fig. 7.4

The *sacre*, or "French coronation ceremony," is illustrated time after time in manuscripts of the *Grandes chroniques de France*. The repetition of these images accentuated the royalist tenor of the text, for example in the exemplar copied and illuminated for Charles V around 1375–79. An illuminated sheet later interpolated at the beginning of this manuscript represents another *sacre*, probably that of Charles VI, which took place on November 4, 1380.

and nobles. Jean de Derval, the great noble bibliophile, owned all three volumes of the Bonhomme edition.[57] The small library of the Molé family, prosperous nobles residing in the environs of Troyes, contained all three volumes of the Vérard edition.[58]

But princes and nobles were now a minority among owners of the *Chroniques*. Most manuscripts dating from this period, written on paper and offering a more rapidly transcribed text—sometimes even shortened—without enlivening images, were intended for a clientele of lesser means, or a more intellectual one less fond of beautiful books. And *Chroniques* manuscripts of both old and new vintage thus came into the hands of writers, jurists, and merchants who would not have possessed them fifty years before.[59] For example Robert, abbot of Mont-Saint-Michel and former chancellor of the Duke of Bedford, who in 1438 acquired in Paris a manuscript copied in the same city at the beginning of the fifteenth century. Or Pierre de Taise, future notary and secretary of King Louis XI, who copied the entire text of the *Chroniques* in 1460, when he was at the side of the Dauphin Louis in Genappe and presumably found himself with much time on his hands.[60] Or the historian Nicole Gilles, another royal notary and secretary, who in 1499 included the Bonhomme edition of the *Chroniques* in a list of the sixty-three most valuable titles in his library.[61] Jean de Courcelles, *conseiller du roi* to the Parlement between 1439 and 1495[62]; Jean Le Féron, still a lawyer at the Parlement in 1548,[63] Jean Blondeau, *procureur* at the Parlement[64]; Étienne Le Boucherat, merchant in Troyes in 1485[65]: such were those who had the *Chroniques de France* in their libraries during this period.

This expanded social diffusion was accompanied by an expanded geographic diffusion. Doubtless many copies were still in Paris, where many must also have been copied. But production of the *Chroniques de France* was no longer a quasi-exclusive monopoly of Parisian workshops. Professional and amateur copyists transcribed the text in Flanders and Hainaut around 1455,[66] in Genappe (Brabant) in 1460,[67] in Callac (Brittany) in 1467,[68] in Calais in 1487,[69] and elsewhere as well. And this dispersal of production was consequence and cause of an even more widely dispersed success. Exemplars of the *Chroniques de France* were then numerous in the northern part of the realm and in the Low Countries. While less densely distributed, there were also copies throughout the northern half of the realm and north of the Loire, from Normandy to Champagne and from Burgundy to Brittany. There were even two or three copies south of the Loire, and a few found their way to London. Doubtless it would be a mistake to rush to the conclusion that the *Chroniques de France* could be found everywhere. To the best of our knowledge, there were practically no copies south of the Loire, and even to the north we know, for example, that not a single

library in Amiens possessed a copy. Nonetheless, by contemporary standards it is permissible to speak of a widespread success.

Some manuscripts dating from the second half of the fifteenth century reproduce the pre-1380 text. To cite one example, around 1455 Guillaume Fillastre, bishop of Toul and abbot of Saint-Bertin, arranged for a
Chroniques exemplar in the library of his abbey to be copied, richly illuminated, and presented to his master Philippe le Bon, duke of Burgundy.
The result was a manuscript containing Primat's text up to 1223, followed
by the life of Louis VII, followed by the first translation of the life of St.
Louis by Guillaume de Nangis, followed by the *Istoire et chronique de Flandre*, which had enabled the late fourteenth-century compiler of the Saint-
Bertin manuscript to continue his account as far as 1370.[70] Such exceptions
aside, many manuscripts copied in the second half of the fifteenth century
contain only the 1380 text. Toward the end of the reign of Charles VII,
however, it began to seem unacceptable for the narrative to conclude with
the death of Charles V. Hence, with the aid of several chronicles, one
manuscript was continued up to 1453,[71] two others until 1458,[72] and still
others as far as the death of Charles VII in 1461.[73] One of the latter was
reproduced by Pasquier Bonhomme in his 1477 published edition, which
also contains, after the 1380 text, a chronicle by Gilles le Bouvier, known
as Le Héraut Berry, covering the years 1402–22, to which was added a history of the reign of Charles VII (1422–61) written by Jean Chartier, monk
and chorister at Saint-Denis and chronicler of France, the last production
of the Saint-Denis school of historiography. For his own published edition
of 1493, Antoine Vérard used an improved version of Bonhomme's text.
Bonhomme had retained the title *Chroniques de France*. Vérard, too, used
Chroniques de France on his title page. But in his prologue and in the title
of the first chapter he reintroduced an inflated title found only in a few
manuscripts: *Grandes chroniques de France*. Unfortunately, this rare and late
title was the one adopted by modern editors of the *Chroniques de France*.
As a result, it must be retained today to avoid confusion.

At the very moment the *Chroniques de France* began to reach a wider
public, scholars began to find it wanting by modern standards of erudition.
It said nothing of the Salic law, now generally accepted as legitimately
justifying the exclusion of women from the French throne. It maintained
the Trojan origin of the Franks, now doubted by several historians. And
there was more. When, in the early sixteenth century, an attentive member of the Molé family came across the passage in the Vérard edition
interpolated by Primat and maintaining that, at the beginning of their
history, the French had lived simply, without a king and doing whatever
they pleased, he noted in the margin: "This is false."[74] By the early sixteenth century it was apparent even to nonerudite readers that the *Grandes*

chroniques de France was an outdated text. Other histories of France were more consistent with prevailing views. In 1513 and 1518, two more Parisian editions appeared, duly continuing the narrative. Then the text fell into oblivion.

⚘

Given the survival of 106 manuscripts of excerpts or abbreviated versions, it is fair to say that the *Chroniques de France* were quite successful in the Middle Ages. It will be useful here to situate this success. Between the fourth and eighth centuries, several major works were written presenting histories of the world, of Rome, and of new nations in a Christian light. These works met with long-lasting success, providing a common pool of historical culture for the whole of the medieval West over a millennium. The number of these manuscripts to survive far exceeds that of the *Chroniques de France*: nearly 250 for Orosius's universal *History*; more than 150 for Bede's *Ecclesiastical History of the English People*. In the sixth century, Gregory of Tours wrote his *Histoire des Francs*, but its success was extremely limited. The same must be said for other histories of France subsequently written in some of the great Benedictine abbeys of the realm. To sum up, in the thirteenth century there was no national history of France with a national readership, a situation indicative of the youth and fragility of this political entity. Primat's work was meant to fill this gap.

The history by this monk at Saint-Denis was not the only synthesis produced in its time. The twelfth century saw considerable advances in the historical science, especially in terms of research. It was followed in the thirteenth century by a period of synthesis, of encyclopedias and compendia. The enormous *Miroir* of Vincent de Beauvais predated Primat's history by several years, and the short *Chronique* by Martin le Polonais is its exact contemporary. Vincent's *Mirroir*, Martin's *Chronique*, and Primat's history are among the syntheses that, with the great works of the fourth to the eighth centuries whose success had not slowed, marked the historical culture of the fourteenth and fifteenth centuries. But Vincent and Martin wrote universal histories in Latin that won an international readership and were far more successful than the *Grandes chroniques de France*. More than 150 manuscripts of Vincent's enormous *Miroir* survive.

Finally the success of Orosius, Bede, Vincent de Beauvais, and Martin le Polonais persisted long after 1500, whereas the history of France by Robert Gaguin and the *Annales et chroniques de France* by Nicole Gilles, while largely based on the *Grandes chroniques*, "modernized" its style and spirit by omitting errors and incorporating new information, thereby rendering their model superfluous from the beginning of the sixteenth

Le premier chappitre parle cõ
ment les francois descendirẽt
des tropens.

Vatre cens et qua
tre ans auant que
Romme fust fõdee
regna priant en
trope la grant. il
enuoia paris laisne
de ses fil. en grece
pour rauoir la royne helaine la femme
au roy Menelaus pour soy venger du

ne honte que les grecz lui auoiẽt faitte.
les greiois qui moult furent couroucez
de ceste chose sesmeurent et vindrent
assieger trope. a ce siege qui.v.ans du
ra furent occiz tous les filz au roy pri
ant. mais que vng appelle elenus il et
la royne ecuba sa femme. la cite fut ar
se et destruicte le peuple et les barons
occis.mais aucuns qschapperent de ceste
pestisence et plusieurs des princes sespa
girent en plusieurs et diuerses partes
du mõde pour querre nouuelles habita
cions cõme elenus eneas anthenoret

Fig. 7.5

Like many manuscripts of the *Grandes chroniques de France* produced in the preceding century, copies of the edition printed by Pasquier Bonhomme (1477) were often acquired by wealthy nobles. The one owned by the great bibliophile Jean de Derval (d. 1482) survives. He had a piece of vellum painted with his coat of arms glued to the first page of its volume.

century. The entire history of the *Grandes chroniques de France* encompasses
only 250 years.

To be sure, during this short period it dominated the history of France.
But it would be imprudent to affirm, even with regard to this period, that
its success was unique, that the *Chroniques de France* functioned "as the
Bible of France,"[75] and that it exists in "countless manuscript copies."[76]
For, on close examination, what is most striking is the limited extent of
the text's diffusion. Written in 1274, it had to wait nearly a century and
submit to many avatars before finding true success. The "massive" diffusion of the *Chroniques de France* began only in the late fourteenth century
and came to an end in the early sixteenth century. A history of France
written in French, it virtually never left France, save to be read and copied
in Brabant and Hainaut. A Parisian production, it was indeed "massively"
disseminated in Paris and in northern France, but elsewhere its diffusion
was belated and less concentrated, and in any event it scarcely extended
beyond the Loire. Even north of the Loire, the *Chroniques de France* were
never read at the university and clerics were almost completely unaware
of it, for only one monastic library and three cathedral libraries possessed
copies, and very old ones at that. The first readership of the *Chroniques*
consisted of princes and nobles, to whose tastes and opinions it catered.
They were later joined by a larger readership of writers, jurists, and merchants who had the time to read as well as the means to acquire this enormous and costly work.

That is not to say that other Frenchmen were uninterested in the
history of France. But they could learn about it from other sources. Men
of the cloth still read the Latin histories translated by Primat, Vincent de
Beauvais, Guillaume de Nangis, and Bernard Gui. For those without Latin
or who preferred to read in French, there existed countless works—long
and short, more or less amply illustrated, in book or scroll format—from
which they could learn about the history of their country, depending on
the time and money at their disposal. And not all of these works derived
from the *Chroniques*; they were not all informed by the same spirit.

Knowledge of the French past played a fundamental role in the development of French nationalist sentiment at the end of the Middle Ages,
and the historical component of this sentiment was essential. The *Chroniques de France* were certainly the most fully elaborated and prestitious,
and perhaps the most widely disseminated, history of France in this period.
But there were also other histories, handbooks, and compilations through
which Frenchmen came to know and love the history of their country. In
the tangled skein of late medieval French history, still inadequately known
and understood, the *Chroniques de France* doubtless constitute the most visible thread, but it is far from the only one in this powerful net.

SUMMARY BIBLIOGRAPHY

Modern Studies and Editions

Delanchal, Roland, ed. *Les Grandes chroniques de France: Chronique des règnes de Jean II et de Charles V.* 4 vols. Paris: H. Laurens, 1910–20.

Lemoine, Jean, ed. *Chronique de Richard Lescot, religieux de Saint-Denis (1328–1344) suivie de la continuation de cette chronique (1344–1364).* Paris: Renourd, H. Laurens, successeur, 1896.

Paris, Paulin, ed. *Les Grandes chroniques de France, selon que elles sont conserves en l'église de Saint-Denis en France.* 6 vols. Paris: Techener, 1836–38.

Reinach, Salomon. *Un Manuscrit de la bibliothèque de Philippe le Bon à Saint-Pétersbourg.* Vol. 11 in *Monuments et mémoires publiés par l'Académie des Inscriptions et Belles Lettres.* Paris: Fondation Eugène Plot, 1904.

Viard, Jules, ed. *Les Grandes chroniques de France.* 10 vols. Paris: Société de l'histoire de France, 1920–53. Referenced in the notes as *G.C.F.*

Recent Studies

Bodmer, Jean-Pierre. "Die Französische Historiographie des Spätmittelalters und die Franken: Ein Beitrag zur Kenntnis des französischen Geschichtsdenksens." *Archiv für Kulturgeschichte* 45 (1963): 91–118.

Capo, Lidia. "Da Andrea Ungaro a Guillaume de Nangis: Un'ipotesi sui rapporti tra Carlo I d'Angio e il regno di Francia." *Mélanges de l'École française de Rome, Moyen Âge–Temps modernes* 89 (1977): 811–88.

Du Pouget, Marc. "Recherches sur les chroniques latines de Saint-Denis: Édition critique et commentaire de la *Descriptio clavi et corone Domini* et de deux series de texts relatifs à la légende carolingienne." In *Positions des theses de l'École nationale des chartes.* Paris, 1978, 41–46.

Erlande-Brandenburg, Alain. *Le Roi est mort: Étude sur les funérailles, les sepultures et les tombeaux des rois de France jusqu'à la fin du XIIIe siècle.* Paris, 1975.

Guenée, Bernard. "État et nation en France au Moyen Âge." *Revue historique* 481 (1967): 17–30.

———. "La Culture historique des nobles: Le Success des *Faits des Romains* (XIIIe–XVe siècles)." In *La Noblesse au Moyen Âge, XIe–XVe siècles: Essais à la mémoire de Robert Boutruche,* edited by Philippe Contamine. Paris, 1976, 261–88.

———. "Les Genealogies entre l'histoire et la politique: La Fierté d'être capétien, en France, au Moyen Âge." *Annales, Économies, Sociétés, Civilisations* (1978): 450–77.

Libraire de Charles V, La. Texts by François Avril and J. Lafaurie. Catalogue of an exhibition held at the Bibliothèque nationale, Paris, 1968.

Spiegel, Gabriele M. *The Chronicle Tradition of Saint-Denis: A Survey.* Brookline, Mass.: Classical Folia Editions, 1978.

NOTES

1. Paris, Bibl. Sainte-Geneviève, 782, fol. 326v.

2. Over the last two centuries much excellent scholarship has been devoted to the *Grandes chroniques de France*. Even so, a definitive study of the text's elaboration and diffusion would require several years of additional work. The present essay, the fruit of several months of research, is a preliminary effort in which hypotheses—and probably errors—abound.

During its preparation I profited from the knowledge and generosity of Bernard Bligny, Raymond Cazelles, Henri Dubois, Marc Du Pouget, Sylvette Guilbert, Michael Johnes, Gillette Labory, Michel Pastoureau, and, above all, François Avril. I am deeply grateful to all of them.

It did not seem feasible to document here all of the sources on which I have based my conclusions. I have, however, referenced all textual citations as well as all manuscripts specifically mentioned in the text.

3. Paris, Bibl. nat., lat. 12710.

4. Vatican Library, reg. lat. 550.

5. Paris, Bibl. nat., lat. 5925.

6. Jules Viard, ed., *Grandes chroniques de France,* 1:2 (hereafter abbreviated as G.C.F.).

7. Ibid., 3 ("Ci pourra chscuns trover bien et mal, bel et lait, sens et folie, et fere son preu [profit] de tout par les examples de l'estoire").

8. Ibid., 104 ("A cestui doivent tout prince prendre example").

9. Ibid., 3 ("fere cognoistre . . . la geste des rois").

10. Ibid., 1 ("la geneologie des rois de France, de quell original et de quel lignie ils ont descendu").

11. Ibid., 3 ("que III generacions ont esté des rois de France puis que il commencierent à ester").

12. Ibid., 5:1–2 ("Li vaillanz rois Loys [VIII] fu du lignage le grant Challemaine, et fu en li recovrée la lignie").

13. Ibid., 1:69 ("Seigneur François, qui estes descendu de la haute lignie des Troiens, vous devez ester remembrable de la hautece de vostre non et de vostre lignange").

14. Ibid., 66 ("Laissent la victoire à Clovis"; "la victoire demora au roi et aus François").

15. Ibid., 5:238, 240, 241 ("richement aparelié por le roil or segnor aidier et por son regne defender"; "prest de morir ou de la corone defendre aux espées tranchanz"; "et totevoies estoit-il là veuz por le besoing dou roiaume contre les estranges nations").

16. Ibid., 1:67 ("Au roi et aux François"; "fu par divine ordenance").

17. Ibid., 5:237 ("Estoit après Dieu especiaus defenderres des rois et dou regne").

18. Ibid., 6:89–91 ("Et de ce Kalice qui estoit touz plains de sanc humain, amenistroit et donoit à boire à touz ses princes et à touz ses barons").

19. Ibid., 1:18–19 ("Seigneur et roi").

20. Ibid., 2:184–85 ("Li baron de France et Borgoigne . . . recurrent à seigneur").

21. Ibid., 4:260 ("Dona aux barons ce qu'il leur plesoit pour acuerre leur grâce").

22. Ibid., 285 ("Comment li baron de France firent coroner les II fiuz").

23. Ibid., 5:145 ("Comment li prelate et li baron asemblerent à Orliens por . . . coroner").

24. London, British Library, add. 38128.

25. Brussels, Bibl. roy., 4.

26. Cambrai, Bibl. mun., 682.

27. Paris, Bibl. nat., fr. 2615.

28. Paris, Bibl. nat., fr. 10132 ("Pierre Honnorez du Neufchastel en Normandie fist escrire et ordener en la maniere que elles sont selonc l'ordenance des croniques de Saint Denis à mestre Thommas de Maubuege demorant en Rue Neuve Notre Dame de Paris l'an de grace Nostre Seigneur mil CCC et XVIII").

29. Brussels, Bibl. roy., 5; Paris, Bibl. nat., fr. 2600.

30. Brussels, Bibl. roy., 14561–14564.

31. Brussels, Bibl. roy., 5.

32. London, British Library, reg. 16 G VI.

33. *G.C.F.*, 9:71–72 ("Furent assemblez les barons et les nobles à traictier du gouvernement dy royaume").

34. Ibid., 329 ("Comment le bon roy Phelippe fu vray catholique"; "pourquoy Nostre Seigneur voult que il eust paine et tribulacion en ce monde, afin qu'il peust avecques lui regner après la mort pardurablement. Amen").

35. Paris, Bibl. nat., fr. 10132.

36. Paris, Bibl. nat., fr. 2600.

37. Paris, Bibl. nat., fr. 23140.

38. Loyon, Bibl. mun., 880; Paris, Bibl. nat., fr. 10135.

39. Grenoble, Bibl. mun., 1004; Lyon, Bibl. mun., 880; Paris, Bibl. nat., fr. 17270 and 23140.

40. Roland Delachenal, ed., *Chronique des règnes de Jean II et de Charles V*, xiii ("Pour les hez et chemises des Chroniques de France et de celles que a faittes nostre amé et feal chancellier, pour deux volumes pour nous, une piece de baudequin, XXVI frances"). The contents of the two volumes prepared for Charles V are now bound in a single volume: Paris, Bibl. nat., fr. 2813.

41. Great Britain, private collection; cf. *La Librairie de Charles V*, no. 196.

42. End of the text: "Which recommendation was reported to the said dukes, who deemed it acceptable and consented to it."

43. Lyon, Bibl. du Palais des arts, 30.

44. "Comment le roy Charles six fu couronné"; "Coment les juifs furent pilliés." The text ends as follows: "But in the end they withdrew without gaining anything, a great many of their people and horses having perished. And others surrendered, bringing an abundance of goods" ("Mais finalement il s'en partirent sans y aucune chose prouffiter, et y mourut grant foison de leur gens et de leur chevaux. Et s'en alerent aucuns et en menerent grant foison de biens"). Variant: "abundant priso-

ners" ("grant foison de prisonniers"). In four manuscripts, scribal perplexity about textual inconsistency led them to stop short, ending the passage with "great abundance" or "great abundance of" ("grant foison"; "grant foison de").

45. Chantilly, Musée condé, 867; London, British Library, Sloane 2433.

46. Paris, Bibl. nat., fr. 2608.

47. Paris, Bibl. Sainte-Geneviève, 783.

48. Unidentified coat of arms: Paris, Bibl, de l'arsenal, 5223; Paris, Bibl. mazarine, 2028.

49. Brussels, Bibl. roy., 1.

50. Chartres, Bibl. mun., 271; Reims, Bibl. mun., 1469; Saint-Omer, Bibl. mun., 707.

51. Paris, Bibl. nat., fr. 6466, fol. 200v ("Grands dons").

52. G.C.F., 1:3.

53. Paris, Bibl. nat., fr. Nouv. Acquis. 6225.

54. Brussels, Bibl. roy., 4; Saint Petersburg, Public Library, F v. IV 1.

55. Paris, Bibl. nat., fr. 10132.

56. Paris, Bibl. nat., fr. 2608; Paris, Bibl. de l'institute, 324.

57. Paris, Bibl. de l'arsenal, Hist. 1582; Rouen, Bibl. mun., 7.

58. Paris, Bibl. Sainte-Geneviève, OE XV 468.

59. Paris, Bibl. nat., fr. 73.

60. Paris, Bibl. nat., fr. 4955; Aix-en-Provence, Bibl. méjanes, 426.

61. Roger Doucet, Les Bibliothèques parisiennes au XVIe siècle (Paris: A. et J. Picard et Cie, 1956), 83.

62. Vatican Library, reg. 744.

63. Paris, Bibl. nat., fr. 4956; Doucet, op. cit., 129.

64. Paris, Bibl. nat., fr. 2611–2612.

65. Vatican Library, reg. 725.

66. St Petersburg, Saltykov-Shchedrin Library, erm. fr. 88.

67. See note 60.

68. Paris, Bibl. nat., fr. 4984.

69. London, British Library, reg. 20 E I.

70. St. Petersburg, Saltykov-Shchedrin Library, erm. fr. 88.

71. Glasgow, Hunterian Museum Library, 203.

72. Madrid, National Library, vitr. 24–12 (E 242); Paris, Bibl. nat., fr. 2611–2612.

73. Dijon, Bibl. mun., 288; Paris, Bibl. nat., fr. 20355.

74. Paris, Bibl. Sainte-Geneviève, OE XV 468 ("Cecy est faulx").

75. G.C.F., 1:xxxii.

76. Auguste Molinier, Les Sources de l'histoire de France des origins aux guerres d'Italie (1494), 6 vols. (Paris, 1901–6, no. 2530).

*É*TIENNE *P*ASQUIER'S *L*ES
*R*ECHERCHES DE LA *F*RANCE:
*T*HE *I*NVENTION OF THE *G*AULS

CORRADO VIVANTI

In his *Account of the Affairs of France*, written in 1512, Machiavelli, who had been sent several times by the republic of Florence to the court of the very Christian king, noted that "the Crown and the King of France are at this time more flourishing, rich, and powerful than they have ever been."[1] And he gave three reasons for this: the crown had become rich following several heirless successions; the king's authority was no longer contested by powerful "barons," as it had been in the past; and the enemies of France could no longer count on the support of the great feudal lords, as they did when there was a Duke of Brittany, of Burgundy, or of Guienne. A half century later things had changed a great deal: 1559 had been a dark year for France. The accidental death of Henry II from a jousting wound and the beginnings of a regency that, for better or worse, was destined to go on a long time, marked the beginning of an internal crisis that ended in the wars of religion. But before that, the peace of Cateau-Cambrésis had been concluded, according to the French, "with great advantage" for Spain "and shame to them."[2] The loss of all the conquests in Italy indicated a historic defeat, while Spain, by assuring its dominance over the peninsula, asserted its hegemony over Europe. Fifty years later, the historian Jacques-Auguste de Thou deplored the "unjust conditions" of that peace.[3]

France fell into disorder: the great "barons" reappeared with their claims and divided up entire provinces among themselves, often seeking the support of Philip II of Spain; the monarchy, in the hands of the Italian regent, Catherine d'Medici, and her children, was so weak that the very unity of the kingdom was threatened, and the house of Guise had the audacity to challenge the Capetian line with its own earlier lineage from Charlemagne. In addition, the religious schism divided the consciences of the French people, when it didn't set them against each other.

It was in this environment that Étienne Pasquier chose to publish *Les Recherches de la France*, or at least a preview of the work (the first book did in fact appear in 1560), but the entire project was outlined in the first chapter. According to Pasquier, in these difficult years, France needed to be studied: it was a sign that the country existed rather than a bunch of fragments. Its unity, its personality could not depend on political motives that were likely to change. Its unity and personality were to be found in its very distant past. To say that the Gauls were the ancestors of the French was not a complete novelty, but in *Les Recherches* that heritage was asserted with complete assurance, allowing for no argument. Thus for Pasquier it was the French nation that for centuries was the guarantor of its own existence, regardless of chance vicissitudes, and shocks that would only be temporary.

Therefore, the legacy to be defended was above all the historical memory, and beginning in the first chapter, Pasquier stresses the need to "recommend in writing" the virtuous actions of a people "to posterity." The choice between oral tradition and the written word is raised in these terms: "Whether it is more appropriate for the public's use to communicate one's concepts through writing to the people, or, without communicating them, give them to one's successors by word of mouth to hear."[4] It was not just a matter of transmitting a reminiscence of the past: it was also necessary to set forth the fact that knowledge was to be shared, and not kept like *arcane imperii*, as an instrument of power for scholars. By speaking out clearly in favor of sharing knowledge Pasquier was revealing his confidence in the virtues of an education that would be as widespread as possible, thereby conforming to the principles of the most open currents of humanism.

The immediate consequence of this was that the author had to make a linguistic choice: Pasquier decided to write his work in French. If the historical memory was not to be locked up for use only by a privileged circle of scholars, then Latin should not be used, for it prevented texts from being explored by the vast majority of the public. "For my part," he declared to one of his friends, "in writing in my vernacular, at least I write in the language with which I was nursed at my mother's breast" (II, 3 B). The scholar who, in the seventh book of the *Recherches* sketches a general portrait of French literature by proposing to raise the value of great medieval poetry while stressing the progress made in its time by literary production, concluded that the French language was as capable as Latin or Italian of reaching the summits of great poetry, and creates no myths about the classical languages: his penchant for history taught him that "Greek was the vernacular of Hippocrates and Plato, and Latin was that of Cicero and Pliny" (II, 3 A). And he had no trouble reminding Turnèbe, the great Hellenist of the Sorbonne who had advised him against "writing our ideas in our vernacular": "The very objection you are making today was once made to Cicero to dissuade him from writing in his language" (II, 3 BC).

Therefore, through his linguistic choice Pasquier was proposing to assert the national identity of France, convinced that "just as no land, however rich, will bear any fruit, nor will any language thrive, if it isn't cultivated" (II, 5 C). For Pasquier resorting to Latin was only a remnant of times past, those of "the great figures whom past centuries have born, such as Valla, Politian, Pico della Mirandola, and in our own time, Erasmus, Budé, Alciat." Aspiring to an equally noble culture, but one adapted to his time and to the needs of France, he declares: "We will bring the golden age back to life when, not allowing bastard opinions to affect strange things, we employ what is natural and believe to be part of us without external intervention" (ibid.). Furthermore, his arguments against Latin were only a consequence of his attitude toward a certain idea of classicism, one that was in vogue among the Italianist currents, which he considered to be an obstacle to the development of a French national culture.[5]

Pasquier's interest in history came directly out of his intellectual training, which was carried out in the most advanced intellectual centers of the French Renaissance:[6] at the school of legal experts such as Cujas, Baudoin, Hotman, and Alciat he had learned to think of the law and political institutions as so many products of the times, closely connected to the progress of a society. If we look closely at *Les Recherches*, less as the work of a specific author than as the work of a qualified representative of a group of intellectuals led to study the fate of a country, we will see that this penchant for history did not come out of a desire to escape the stormy present in order to take refuge in a nostalgic contemplation of the past. Nor was it the reflection of a scholarly or academic mentality. To recover the collective memory as a historical memory meant rooting out the political structures of the French monarchy in the national life. Thus, beyond "great history," Pasquier was enlarging the domain of the historian— which we will see better in what follows—to include popular traditions, the history of the language, proverbs, and sayings. It has been noted that "the phenomena of memory, both in their biological and psychological aspects, are only the result of dynamic systems of organization."[7] If one might extrapolate this principle to the phenomena of collective memory, we will better understand the vitality of this "dynamic system of organization" that was French civil society in the sixteenth century, despite the internecine struggles and the defeat suffered in the prolonged duel against the house of Habsburg.

We must also remember that the displacement of the great axes of political and economic power from the Mediterranean to the north of Europe gave the French losses much less importance than that which contemporaries attributed to them; if, during the forty years that followed the peace of Cateau-Cambrésis, the kingdom of the last Valois was no longer active on the international stage, it was less a consequence of the "injustice" of that treaty than of civil wars that tore it apart. The sudden revival of the kingdom after Henry IV's accession to the throne and the reestablishment of internal peace reveals the strength of its structures. People were aware of this situation at the time: on the solidity of the kingdom—noted a historian at the height of the civil wars—"the best account and the surest proof of what had been so well established is the present ruin: for although our misfortunes have for a long time come from our opinions and divisions do all that they can to ruin and demolish [the kingdom's] edifice . . . its structure is such, its laws so strong, the cement of its government so hard and the foundation of its fine laws and constitutions so good, that it can only succeed."[8]

It was the solidity of French civil society that explained that sort of historical compensation thanks to which France, precisely during the most troubled times, experienced a cultural explosion that turned it into one of the major centers of the Renaissance. In fact, a great period of intellectual life was opening at that time: after Rabelais, whose literary invention Pasquier admired, Ronsard and La Pléiade—of whom he was the friend and disciple—showed the extent of their new art; Montaigne and Bodin renewed moral and political thought; finally, "quasi Musarum secessus,"[9] philological and historical studies seemed to disappear from Italy, while France, thanks to Budé and his disciples, became the heir of the great humanist tradition. "Budé took the first step," recalled Pasquier at the end of his *Recherches*, in evoking the beginnings of the new scholarship in France—"in his Annotations on the Pandectes . . . in the year 1508." He is the one who introduced "beautiful Latin, scattered with lovely flowers of stories and sentences" in France and who denounced "the barbarism of the early doctors of law." After him there was the Italian André Alciat who taught at Avignon and Bourges. But "things were not very successful for him among his peers"—this is Pasquier's own remark—"for I do

Fig. 8.1

Étienne Pasquier.

not see that the Italians, who came after him, were very concerned with becoming humanists like him." And in this regard he adds a memory from his youth: "Having traveled from the town of Tholose to the land of Italy, to conclude my legal studies there, I had listened to three or four of [Alciat's] lessons in the town of Pavia. From there, having traveled to the city of Boulogne, where Marianus Socinus, the nephew of Bartholomaeus, taught, all the Italian students were much more impressed with him than with the other . . . for this single reason—they said—that never had he lost time in the study of human letters, like Alciat." The success of "our Budé in our France" was completely different, Pasquier proudly stresses, and he mentions the "infinite number of strong minds who follow his teachings, both in our universities of legal studies, and in all manner of other studies" Corras, Du Ferrier, and Forcatel in Toulouse, Ferret in Valence, Govéan in Cahors, Jean Robert and William Fournier in Orléans, and finally Gregory of Toulouse and Godefroy of Paris, whose "writings seem to be the height of this new jurisprudence." But above all Pasquier wanted to point out that the University of Bourges "in our century had seven great figures who made the reading of civil law shine: Alciat, Baron, Duaren, Balduin, Hotoman, le Comte, and, above all, the great Cujas." At the same time he recalls the eminent jurists "who it pleases me to name humanists" Budé himself, as *maître de requêtes*, François Connan, Charles du Moulin, Pierre Pithou, Pierre du Favre, Louis le Charond, and Guy Coquille, among others.

In a cultural context that was profoundly involved in national life, the new doctrine was enriched with content and goals that were very close to the political sensibilities of the times. "The intellectual force of French humanism," Marc Fumaroli has noted,[10] "was, in the movement of William Budé, the *mos gallicus*, the French method of interpreting the law, enlightened by philology and history." Historical criticism, while highlighting the layers of the judicial heritage, managed to deepen the knowledge of the connections between the law and society. We are not concerned here with stressing the differences, compared with the origins of French law, between the "Romanist" thesis of Budé and Alciat, the "Germanic" one of du Moulin and Hotman, or the "Gallic" one of François Connan: what interests us is indeed the common method of research that, in law as in history, explored literary sources and inscriptions, numismatics, and archeological data in order to understand the past in its totality and to enlarge the field of observation beyond classical antiquity, to the centuries of the late empire and of Byzantium and up to the Middle Ages.

The centers out of which this scholarship radiated were, as has just been noted, the universities of Bourges, Toulouse, Orléans, and Valence, which Pasquier attended: a "new history" was born out of "the alliance between the history of the law, the history of institutions, and humanist philology."[11] For all of those who, in that period of adversity, sought foundations for the kingdom that were less fleeting than the figure of a king, history showed the complex heritage that had been transmitted through a distant past, able to indicate the deep connections between the nation and the State. In periods of crisis, when the immediate future revealed dark unknowns, an analysis of the collective entity to which one belonged enabled a better grasp of the specificities, the leanings, and the antecedents, and thus to have a wider and more detached view of the present. In this regard, it is possible to note a common attitude both in the great historians of Italy of the time—Machiavelli and Guichardini—as in those who, in France, gave life to the new studies of the past. But with this difference: through their works, the former studied above all the causes for the ills of the present time, by striving to envision the potentialities of an Italy that didn't yet exist; the latter wanted to bring out the consistency of the national heritage, approaching in their work the different realities of a State that had been there for centuries.[12]

It is this distinctive feature of French scholarly research that makes it one of the most important contributions of the sixteenth century, even if it has generally been underestimated: more attention has often been paid to the great works of immediate political significance—Hotman's *Franco-Gallia*, Bodin's *République*—than to these cultural contributions that bore witness to certain aspects of the civil society and of a country in the process of transforming itself. Furthermore, only those works by the most traditionalist authors had been considered works of history: the classic history textbook of the historiography of Eduard Fueter—in speaking of French humanist output—mentions only Paul Émile, Le Feron, and Du Haillan; in other words, the annalists. Such prejudices have skewed the consideration of this cultural output by ignoring the fact that in this period history was enlarging its borders in space as well as in time, and was succeeding in encompassing geography, law, and political theory, which "joined up with it, sometimes disjointedly but always in a natural, necessary and vital way."[13] It was in this shaking up of the very concept of history that we can discern one of the original traits of French culture of the period and find the roots of the critical reflection that ultimately brought down outmoded ways of thinking: the fact that the restoration of Aristotelianism—so distant from all historical reasoning—at the end of the sixteenth century did not have the success in France that it had in other countries is not a coincidence. Indeed, what pushed history beyond pragmatic narration and led it to become in a certain sense a way of thinking that grasped institutions and customs, in short, the life of the society, was, once again, the pressing urgency of the interior political scene in France.

It is true that, in the vast amount of historical material produced in this period, it was traditional history that represented the lion's share. Out of the more than two hundred and seventy history books that were first published between 1550 and 1610, seventy dealt with general history, fifty with local history, and as many with biographies and royal genealogies or tales of heroic deeds.[14] At the same time, there were also some fifty more original works on the history of magistratures, offices, and political and civil institutions, and the growing discrepancy between reprintings for these works as compared to other first editions also shows the penchant of readers for the "new history." Although there was strong interest in regional frameworks as seen in the publication of works devoted to the history of towns and provinces, it must be noted that this local specificity did not manage to threaten the unity of the kingdom, and all of the history texts that were published appeared to be marked by an awareness of the nation as a whole: as proof of this, there were countless histories of France that followed the royal succession—these biographies of rulers, these chronicles grouping the reigns of the various Charleses, Henrys, and François, were the foundation around which the very notion of the country was built.

We have already mentioned that we are witnessing the development of a collective memory, one that was renewing the vision and the judgment that French society fashioned of its past and of itself. But we should also note that out of the three hundred and nineteen authors mentioned by La Croix du Maine in his *Bibliothèque Françoise* for the period 1540–89 whose professions we know, George Huppert has calculated that one hundred and seventy-eight (at least) were magistrates, judges, or lawyers, and this number grew even more when one considers the social position of the families of many other writers.[15] This immediately brings to mind the verses cited by Lucien Febvre regarding the fortune of the great Comptoise bourgeoisie, which came out of the offices:

> Vive la plume magnifique.
> Le papier et le parchemin . . .[16]

> [Long live the magnificent pen,
> paper, and parchment . . .]

These men of the robe, secure in their knowledge and in their economic and social prestige, playing an intermediary role between the monarchy and the upper levels of the Third Estate, attempted to find an ever broader role in French society. The book, the printed word, which enabled them to reach all the keepers of culture, gave them the possibility of presenting themselves almost as interpreters of social groups that hoped to be involved in the political life of the kingdom. Thus these jurists, to whom the fortunate nature of their class had assigned them an important position, managed to assume an active, leading role in the struggle that was to decide the fate of their country. The history of the magistracies and institutions gave value to their role in the French monarchy and justified their political ambitions. It is perhaps a bit simplistic to believe that the historiographical choices of these scholars was suggested by class interests, which would have influenced them to favor research into the political and administrative structures of the kingdom instead of following the path of "old" history. The traditional tale of battles, lineages, and miracles would have been of no interest to them, because "these powerful and rich magistrates were neither warriors nor priests" and "they would have sought in vain for mention of one of their ancestors in the *Grandes Chroniques*."[17] It is nevertheless true that their works were often inspired by their discontent with the existing state of affairs and by an awareness of the necessity of supporting, through their scholarly work, a political and religious activity whose goal was the restitution of civil peace and the reformation of the State. Henri Hauser has already noted that "talent and historical sense" belonged in this period above all to the group of those "politicians" who, in seeking the principles amenable to reforming and pacifying France, were able to express not only the demands of their own country, but those of the entire European *respublica litterarum*.[18]

In the general overview we have just presented, Pasquier's work stands out through its originality, beginning with its title: *Recherches*. It was an uncommon word at the time for a work of history, and in its striking modernity it reveals a working method and, at the same time, a new vision of history. "Do you think they are nice stories," Pasquier writes in the *Pourparler du prince*, which appeared with the first book of the *Recherches* in 1560, "all the Annales de France, in which you learn that so and so did such a thing? But how, by what means did it occur, imagine it, if you will." (I, 1035 A). He was suggesting a long-term critical work, a form of history that no one had attempted up to then. No continuous narrative, in fact, enabled it to be grasped. Thus the chapters of this work, while in general grouped by subject within the different books, appear to be a succession of essays, as in a large mosaic, comprising a lively and unusual history.

Pasquier immediately departs from traditional models. He was the author of rather original, often morally driven letters, on varied subjects—questions of law, cultural life, political events, vicissitudes of civil wars—and he collected them and published them to offer "a tableau of all my ages." In his *Recherches*, as well, he felt the need to leave forms that were too defined and systematic, and adopted an often infelicitous writing style in which critical reasoning outweighed the linear narrative. The new scholarship required a new mode of expression: "Nova res novum vocabulum flagitat," the great humanist Lorenzo Valla had already noted.[19] In a period when the opening of horizons that were unknown up until then revived people's knowledge and even their vision of the world, while there developed a new way of obtaining knowledge, an appropriate expressive form was necessary that would break with the large, exhaustive treatments, or those deemed so. The content engaged the form and, from that point of view Pasquier doesn't seem so far from Montaigne whose *Essais* he so appreciated that he wrote, "I have never held a book in my hand that I've caressed as much as that one" (II, 577 C).

Aware of the novelty of his undertaking, he stressed that it was above all through the themes of his research that he distinguished himself from "most of those who have in the past used their understanding to write," having "no other subject for their eloquence than the history of the Greeks or the Romans, not casting their eyes on our own [history]" (II, 28 A). From the outset it was an argument against the traditionalist culture that was pursued in his critical attitude compared to the stylistic forms of his exposé. In noting "through occasion, not through vanity . . . to have been the first among us . . . who has uncovered several obscure ancient facts about this France" (I, 2 A), he uses this novelty to justify the use he makes of his sources, indeed his choice of them. Several of his friends, alleging reasons of style, had advised him against inserting long quotations from documents; he on the contrary considered them indispensable for proving his arguments: it was necessary "not to say anything important, without giving proof of it," even at the risk of weighing down the writing with "unwieldy" texts.

It is also worth noting that his use of sources was completely new. Usually texts and documents were used only to derive information from them and it was not common practice to report passages and to quote long pieces, which in addition had no literary quality. We can therefore understand the consternation of Pasquier's friends before this infraction of the rhetorical rules of humanist tradition. "Writing here for my France, and not for myself," he replied, he did not want to be constrained by norms that seemed to him to be true hindrances, not enabling him to document his research. Furthermore, "if those who come after me venture into the same water (as it will be very easy to do, the first ice having been broken), and do me the honor of recognizing they learned something from me, I give it to them gladly and want it to be known that it belongs to them" (I, 3 A). The generosity of the scholar was only proportional to his proud awareness of his own value.

But we must also note that already the first book of the *Recherches*, published long before the others,[20] appears as an overview of the formation of France, which goes back to the ancient Gauls, but also takes into account the successive contributions of other peoples who arrived at the time of the Germanic invasions: the Franks, the Burgondes, the Bretons, and the Normans, among others. The use of sources was a function of the method inaugurated by Pasquier. Historical and literary texts, not only from the classical age, but also from the late empire, or the accounts of the church fathers, as well as charters and diplomas, chronicles and memoirs from the Middle Ages, provided him the means of connecting the various stratifications of the past through evidence. In the process of doing so he was able to offer his contemporaries a new idea of France. Aiming to reduce the gap between the time before the conquest of Caesar and the period that followed the invasions, it was not enough to underestimate the legacy of Rome: one had to exalt Gallic civilization—disproving "our modern Italians, who believe to improve their reputation . . . when they call us Barbarians" (I, 5–6 D)—and at the same time give valid reasons for the establishment of the Franks. Other historians had evoked the Celtic origin that—according to classical tradition, up to Caesar—would have been common to the Gauls and the Teutons, and went so far as to speak of a conquest of Germany by the Gauls, who would have returned afterwards, with the name of Franks, to their earlier fatherland. But Pasquier was too good a historian to feed on those legends. He stuck to the *Commentary* of Julius Caesar, the most trustworthy source and the one richest in details, in which the conqueror of Gaul was the first to make the distinction between the Gauls and the Teutons, praising the "virtus" and the "magnitudo animi" of the former, criticizing the "feritas" of the latter. The Germanic conquest was to be considered rather as an example of the highs and the lows in the life of nations: Pasquier saw no reason for self-debasement if the peoples who had given "a thousand quarrels to the Romans" (I, 28 A) had managed to wrest Gaul from the dominators of the world. In the tracks of Machiavelli—whom he knew well, while criticizing him for his "wickedness" (II, 231 D)—he thought that kingdoms and men were subjected to "fortune" and to "advice," and he explained by this binomial France's past in pages that are among the most eminent in his work for depth of conception and patriotic passion (I, 43–46).

Of course, in the French historical memory the Gauls had for a long time been present as ancestors. To mention only a few works of the time, in the year preceding the publication of the first book of the *Recherches* Pierre de La Ramée had published a *Liber de moribus veterum Gallorum*, which was immediately translated into French, and, a few years before that, Guillaume Postel had brought out *L'Histoire mémorable des expéditions depuys le déluge faictes par les Gaulois ou François depuys la France jusques en Asie*. . . . From these two great intellectuals, both of whom were involved in an original probing into very different realms, theirs were works telling of the widespread need to connect France to a strong national tradition. But in these books, scholarly interest and the tendency for apologetics won out over a critical understanding of the continuity that was possible to show between those distant times and the history of France. Pasquier, on the other hand, by establishing that strict connection between "ancient Gaul and our new France," constantly established a precise confrontation between the past and the present. Antiquity and the Middle Ages were not conceived as periods that were in some way in the past, and he thus managed to highlight what was still living from the most distant times: institutions, traditions, laws, and customs that it was thus necessary to illustrate and to be aware of in order to discover the original characteristics of the history of France.

Traditional narratives were based on more or less imaginative reconstructions, going back to origins through successions of kings, always in the quest of the first king of France. This is where we get the legend, which had already appeared in the seventh century, of the Trojan prince Francus or Francion, who landed in Gaul after the destruction of his land by the Greeks, much like Aeneas;[21] or of the arrival of Hercules during his Mediterranean voyages.[22] In Pasquier's time the Trojan legend was still very much alive in so-called historical works, whereas the myth of Hercules remained relegated to epic tales and monarchist apologia. As for Pasquier, he devoted an entire chapter toward the end of the first book to how "our authors attribute the origin of the French to the Trojans" (I, 39–40). Not without skepticism and irony, he recalls the great deeds of the mythical heroes, noting that "to argue about the old origin of nations is a very tricky thing, because they were at first so insignificant that the old authors were not concerned with taking the time needed to deduce them, thus gradually they have been erased from our memory or converted into nice fables and stories." Furthermore, he had already declared that he had no intention of "looking for a distant line of either Trojans or Sicambrians in the Meotides Paludes [Sea of Azov], for whom we do not have any sure written sources, apart from the writings of some monks" (I, 19 C). He preferred to stick to the facts. Much more than the genealogies of kings or the accounts, also legendary, of heroic exploits, the "ancientness of our France," in its duration and its continuity, gave sufficient meaning to the image of the French nation.

It is this same "ancientness" that enabled him to speak of France independent from the existence of royal dynasties, in the time of the "Gaul republic." Of course, the word "republic" here has only the Latin meaning of "State," *res publica*; but with this expression Pasquier was able to stress the fact that there was a political system in France, a "government," without it necessarily presupposing the presence of a monarchy; for "there was no lack of well organized governors among our ancient Gauls" (I, 10 A). However strong a royalist he was, his first concern was with establishing the national identity, beyond all contingent facts. It is still necessary to add that, establishing "his" France well before Clovis, he ended up attributing only little importance to the traditional role of the "eldest daughter of the Church," exploited by so many partisans of the religious conflict in the goal of justifying the struggle against the reformers. He detested religious division and he resented the Protestants for it; but he was also concerned with distinguishing religion from politics, and he asserted this through a direct allusion to the situation of his time when, speaking of the decadence of the Roman empire and the religious pretexts advanced by the various pretenders, he wrote that God, "wishing to be adored with an inner zeal of true faith, and not through political discourses, held in his hands the sword of vengeance against them" (I, 25 A). And he showed his convictions even more firmly by speaking of the "very awful fruits" of the Crusades: "I am not convinced"—he declares—"that we must advance our religion through weapons: that of Moses was destined for such an effect, that of Jesus Christ on the contrary grew through prayer, exhortations, fasting, poverty, and obedience." Thus, having evoked several examples, when he came to speak of the wars of religion in France, he notes: "I don't see that we have contributed anything other than an atheism and scorn of both religions" (I, 618 B).

But the breadth of the past that the *Recherches* established for the history of France also showed in a particular light its relationships with the Church. This institution that, through its sacred character, tended to be considered outside the temporal order of men, was brought back into history where, compared to ancient Gaul, it could not boast such a venerable age. Thus the life of ecclesiastic institutions and their intertwining in the political and civil system of the kingdom could be considered in proportion to how new situations had been presented and imposed, and there resulted the possibility of widely confirming the validity of Gallican principles, to which the entire third book of the *Recherches* is devoted. Pasquier thus asserted the autonomy of the kingdom as opposed to the authority of the pope right at the time when the conclusion of the Council of Trent

(1563) had exalted him in almost totalitarian forms,[23] which the partisans of the holy league appeared ready to accept.

From the moment that the monarchy was not the only force of national cohesion, and the unity of France was also assured by other structures, the constitutional specificity of the kingdom raised the question of the law as a central focal point. Following his interpretation of the French past, Pasquier could not accept the preeminence of Roman law, "that mad apprehension that occupies our minds," he wrote in one of his letters, which is a true tract of juridical scholarship (II, 221–27), "through which, putting under foot that which is the true and native law of France, reduces all our judgments to the judgments of the Romans." Roman law, he noted, is not applicable to the French, who were so different from the Romans in "customs, nature, and complexion," as well as in all aspects of their civilization. "The Romans and the French seem to have established their laws on two different foundations: the former on a more economic consideration, to conserve the wills of each individual; the latter on a more political one, for the maintenance of families in their entirety." As a result there is an anthropological interpretation of the two societies, which sheds light on the different conceptions of the State and the law. It is beyond the scope of this work to establish here the extent to which this interpretation corresponds to our historical judgment: what is important is the effort Pasquier made to grasp the heart of a civilization and to understand its historical events and its needs. It was wrong, in his opinion, to assess the quality of French law by comparing it with Roman law, given their intrinsic differences; it was also impossible to replace "the cases undecided by our customs" with Roman juridical norms, for "it would be doing a wrong to our fatherland," especially since "there isn't a province in France that doesn't have its own customs, and this has been true for a very long time, as we learn from the memoirs of Julius Caesar." Again in the last book of the *Recherches* tracing the historical division of France into a "customary land and of written law" (I, 1001–2), he repeats that "Julius Caesar, in the beginning of his memoirs on Gaul, tells us that in his time there were as many different customs as provinces." Thanks to his consideration of the Gauls, "after subjugating them and having acquired over them the high point of sovereignty for his republic, he allowed them to live with their ancient customs." The same attitude was adopted by the Frankish kings and that "usage was continued on and on ever since under the name of bailliages and seneschalsies up to the present time." Having clarified that the origins of the written law in the south of France dated only from the time of the Germanic invasions, he asserts that it was "a very certain maxim that people didn't follow the Roman law except if it conformed to a general and natural reason" (I, 1008 A).

Pasquier was only tangentially interested—unlike other jurists of his time, and in particular François Hotman in his *Antitribonian*—in the issue of the historicity of Roman law, transmitted by the *Corpus juris* with an entire series of stratifications due to the evolution of Roman society throughout the centuries.[24] By completely refusing Roman law as the foundation of French laws, he wanted only to highlight the specificity of national traditions, as manifest in the "governors" of France. Out of this came his effort to push French institutions as far as possible back in time, while neglecting and almost destroying the period of Roman domination in his historical reconstruction, which was possible only because "Gaul was partitioned into factions and powers, as we now see Italy (which was truly the first defect of their republic and for which finally they were ruined)" (I, 8 A). Where, through the Italian characteristic he throws out "partitioned"—he is able to argue against the "Italian," who must "understand that we are not inferior to him" (I, 12 A)—he stresses that the end of the freedom of Gaul coincided with the end of the freedom of Rome, both of which were ruled by Caesar.

The original civilization of the Gauls, strengthened by the contribution of the Franks, can thus be recognized as the antecedent and the foundation of successive institutions. We see Pasquier's keen concern for the nation, both in his rejection of the barbarism of the Gauls and in his explanation of the conquest of Caesar or the invasion of the Franks, and his bias is also obvious when he sheds light on the originality of two essential institutions of the kingdom: fiefs, linked to the noble order, and *parlements*.

Regarding fiefs, Pasquier—differentiating himself from a scholarly tradition that included scholars such as Charles Du Moulin[25]—denied that they derived from the law of conquest of the Franks, because there would always have been, consequently, a relationship of conquerors and conquered between the nobles and the people. He believed, on the contrary, to have found in the laws and customs of the Gauls, and even the Romans, the early elements of this institution, which above all had the role of protecting and defending the common folk. Although well aware of his social status, Pasquier recognized the legitimacy of the noble prerogatives compared to those of commoners. It was not that he wished to "malign the condition of those who wore the robe" but the social order demanded hierarchies. "And I know well that every man, in every condition, whose profession is virtuous and life without reproach is noble, without exception," he remarked, recalling a novel social principle of humanism. "All the same if in a republic it is necessary to create degrees of orders, and similarly that it is required to reward men who make themselves more meritorious so that their example can induce others to do good, I would never be jealous nor upset at those who expose their lives for the salvation of us all and are attributed the title of noble, rather than those who, in their palaces, at their ease, consider themselves exempt from the affairs of justice" (I, 135 C).

In any event, Pasquier did not passively accept a tripartite division of society into warriors, priests, and workers, even if subsequently he recalled the "three types of people" who form the "State of France": commoners, nobles, and priests (I, 376 C). Men of the robe derived more advantage in fact from comparison between their role and that of the nobility, which is ultimately weakened, limited as it was to the task of the defense of the land, a henceforth debatable task in the years of civil wars. And in this regard it is worthwhile to note, in passing, that in the *Recherches*—otherwise so attentive to so many details, even the smallest, of French life and society—there is no mention of military organization or of war techniques (except for the invention of artillery). In noting a possible analogy between nobles and *parlementaires*, Pasquier thus favors the social group out of which, in the new reality of the modern State, the administrative body of the kingdom must have come. Thus, in the last book of the *Recherches*, he recalls that "under the reign of François I of that name, a Villanovanus[26] wrote a commentary on Ptolomeus, in which he said that in this France there were more men of the robe than in all of Germany, Italy, and Spain," foreseeing that this state of affairs "would take on a longer and more favorable trait" (I, 998 B). It was in fact a service of a new genre, to the benefit of an entire society (which had "banished the old barbarism"), that men of the robe were now called upon to fulfill thanks to their erudition. In the same years an English diplomat in the court of Henry IV was surprised by the fact that it was "incredible that in a beautiful country full of nobility, the State was governed and all the affairs conducted by those of the long robe of lawyers, prosecutors, and gentlemen of pen and ink."[27] For his part, Pasquier saw only in the highest titles of nobility "images of those who were of the time of Hugues Capet" (I, 116 A), and he refuted their jurisdictional claims, which would only be usurpations to the detriment of very weak kings. We mustn't forget that elsewhere, in speaking of "the state and conditions of the people of our France" (I, 373–80), Pasquier opened a chapter with a rather striking assertion. Since in his opinion it wasn't possible to broach the issue "without going beyond the limits," that is, without going back to the oldest periods of the history of humanity, he declared that "by the primitive and original law of nature, all people are born free." It was only "with the passing of time" that "there was engendered in their simplicity the desire to grow in grandeur," until conflicts and wars provoked the institution of serfdom. We will refrain from evoking the great shadow of Rousseau here, since natural law already envisioned this hypothesis; we should nevertheless note that after a rather long preamble ("someone will say that the suburbs of this chapter are much bigger than the city"), Pasquier, returning to "our France," maintains that in that kingdom "we must hold as an indubitable proposition that all people are born free." If specific customs remain in a few provinces ("those of Meaux, Troyes, Chaumont in Bassigny, Bourgongne, Nivernois, la Marche"), where "servitude on the land still exists," he wants to stress that they are exceptions. It is useless to note here that the principle of "freedom" is related less to a society of equals than to a juridical condition; and, all the same, what a difference between this assertion and that of Bishop Bossuet, more than a century later, for whom "the entire State is in the person of the prince" and "all men are born subjects"![28]

Regarding the *parlement*s, their authority is celebrated in the *Recherches* even beyond what was in principle the position of these institutional organisms in the kingdom. "All those who wanted to establish the freedom of a well-ordered republic"—this is the solemn beginning of the chapter devoted to the origin of the *parlement* (I, 45 C)—"have considered that the opinion of the sovereign judge should be tempered by the admonishments of several people of honor, being constituted into a body for this purpose." This was the role of the *parlement*, "which is the reason for which a few foreigners, talking about our republic, have considered that of this common government, which is like an intermediary between the king and the people, depended the entire grandeur of France." Here, again, is an allusion to Machiavelli, who in his writings had several times sung the praises of the *parlement*s of France in terms that Pasquier had obviously appreciated.[29]

The origins of the *parlement*s were directly connected to the Champs de mai, the annual assemblies that the palace mayors, "wanting to unite in their persons all the authority of the kingdom," introduced "so as not to be despised by the great lords and potentates," with whom they thus shared the most important decisions. This is a remark that enabled Pasquier to ennoble the *parlement* while stressing that Pépin and his sons were acting "as if, with the monarchy, they wanted to blend the order of an aristocracy" (I, 46 A), and while explaining how the kingdom of France was a "mediating governor." Since the time of Charlemagne and Louis the Pious, the Champs de mai had been transformed into regular assemblies, "where ordinary affairs were dealt with." Hugues Capet later managed to unite the kingdom under his authority—the kingdom in which "there was almost no town over which some gentleman of note was not a seigneur"—thanks to the "general body of all the princes and governors, by whose advice were settled not only the problems that arose between the king and them, but between the king and his subjects." It was thus that the *parlement* became the institution capable of "keeping France unified" and of mastering the claims of the dukes and counts, "who weakened the authority of the king" (I, 47–48).

The role of the *parlement*, to which "after several conflicts everyone submitted," was directly connected to "the custom observed by the ancient Gauls, who, however much they were divided up into leagues, came together in a general assembly for justice": this was the annual assemblies of the druids. "And following the example of the druids, who assembled every year in certain places for some time to render justice to the parties, we have almost introduced into our *parlement*s the great days" (I, 9 B), that is the sessions held by the delegations of the *parlement* in the provinces. There is nothing surprising, then, if it is to the *parlement*—issued from the order that administered religion and justice among the Gauls—that was conferred the safeguard of Gallican freedoms, by attributing to it an arbitral power in ecclesiastical politics.

Consequently, the history of the *parlement* was identified with the history of France and, in this sketch of the evolution of the feudal state to the modern monarchy, the preeminence of the *parlement* is theorized as an institution capable of checking the nobility's penchant for undermining the kingdom. This is an open allusion to the state of things in the years when Pasquier was writing his work. And we must remember that, although he often speaks of *parlement*s in the plural, it was the *parlement* of Paris that for him was "of all ancientness, the founding stone of the preservation of our State" (I, 237 B).

In this historical reconstruction there is a rigor and a coherence that gave an ideal platform to the elite of the Third Estate, aiming to consolidate its social promotion on the political level through its support of the monarchy. All the same, through his moderate attitude, Pasquier showed that he preferred the integration of legal scholars into the noble order, rather than dreaming of a shake-up or even of a modification of traditional hierarchies. Granted, he proposed reinforcing the position of the *parlement* as *Curia regis* in which, better than in the Estates General, he saw the leading classes of the kingdom represented. "It is an old fantasy that runs through the minds of the wisest Frenchmen," he confided to a friend in a letter in which he was informing him about the estates held in Orléans in 1560, "that there is nothing that can comfort the people more than such assemblies; on the contrary, there is nothing that can do them more harm" (II, 84 CD). By contrast, in another of his letters, he says of the *parlement*: "If ever the political order were healthily and piously observed

Fig. 8.2
Jean Bodin.

Fig. 8.3
Pierre Pithou.

Fig. 8.4
Claude Fauchet.

Fig. 8.5
Papyre Masson.

in whatever republic it might be, I can say frankly and it is true that it is in our Monarchy: for our ancients recognized that how much among the three main types of republic [monarchy, aristocracy, democracy] there is none that is more worthy and excellent than royalty . . . however, because it can sometimes happen that the crown falls into the hands of a weak and stupid prince, they established a perpetual and general Council for France that we call the *parlement*." And they "established it not only in Paris, the capital city of France, but, what is more, in the Palace, the former seat of our kings, to show how the effects of this company were august, sacred, and venerable." Thus the kings, "reducing by this means their absolute power under the civility of the law, guaranteed for themselves the public envy . . . making themselves in this way more beloved by their subjects than all the other princes of Europe" (I, 146 A–C).

But for Pasquier, France wasn't to be sought only in the history of her institutions or in the relationships between the different powers—king, lords, *parlements*, Church—which had determined its political life. An entire series of aspects and phenomena concerning the life of the society appeared as indispensable to an understanding of the reality of a country that was so many centuries old. Already in 1560, at the beginning of the first book, Pasquier had foreseen that he would devote the rest of his work "to some ancient history that does not concern so much the condition of the public, as it does individuals," to "the commemoration of a few notable examples that I see to be ignored by most of our chroniclers, or passed over so lightly that they are almost unknown," and also to "the explanation of a few ancient proverbs . . . and sometimes extending my text even to the origin and usage of some notable word."[30] Later this project grew and the five books anticipated at the start (the second was divided into two) became nine, one of which was devoted to the history of poetry, another to that of the language, and the last to the history of the culture, universities, and the law. At the beginning of book seven, Pasquier explains: "After having in the preceding six books looked at several specifics concerning our ancient Gauls and Franks, the government, both secular and ecclesiastic and then some ancient things that do not concern the State in general," it was time to study the "origin, ancientness and progress" of France's literary life. Similarly, history could not ignore the evolution of the French language, brought about by changes that, "depending on the diversity of the time," brought all human things, "the customs of the magistrates, indeed republics."

No one had ever conceived of such a work, enlarging the realm of research out of an inexhaustible curiosity to such new subjects. It is true that in this way the work appeared less ordered and coherent, more fragmentary: Pasquier himself apologized for this at the beginning of a chapter: "This is a mixture" (I, 671 C). Moreover, he added, "one doesn't say that a field covered with an infinity of different flowers, that nature produces without order, is not as agreeable to the eye as the gardens artistically arranged by gardeners." Thus we find chapters on subjects that today we would call folkloric: for example, the usage of the "ancient Franks" to have recourse to the books of the Holy Scriptures "to inform themselves of things that were coming in the future"; the first accounts on the arrival in France "of wandering peoples, whom some called Egyptians, others Bohemians"; or the usage of "men of the robe" to wear "great hats on their head." Clothing and style also had their history, and Pasquier reminds the reader: "Still in my youth the oldest theologians, wanting to change nothing in religion of the old clothing, wore it; and there was a small number of people who lived like that in that large street of the Cordeliers in the faubourg Saint-Marceau" (I, 396 C–D). There were other developments concerning the history of words (*assassin, compagnon, gêne, tintamarre, voleur,* and so on), still other inventions and techniques (the printing press, the "quadrant of sailors," artillery), or "some secrets of nature which are difficult to explain," and, finally, a history of illnesses, "some of which were once unknown" (among them, of course, was syphilis).

The explanation of proverbs and sayings was obviously inspired by the *Adagia* of Erasmus, offering Pasquier the opportunity to develop his reflections on various subjects in the form of essays. But whereas the great humanist had started with famous Greek or Latin words, the historian of France was inspired by sayings of his country ("Je veux qu'on me tond," "Faire la barbe à quelqu'un," "Entre chien et loup") or proverbs ("tirez de monnoyes" and so on). For example, see the chapter devoted to the saying "Laisser le monstier [monastery] où il est" (I, 783–86). Discussions of these sayings enabled Pasquier to speak of the necessity of avoiding dangerous innovations. Coming from such a curious and open mind, we don't expect expressions of conservatism such as that which opens this chapter: "There is nothing one must fear more in a republic than novelty." But that was an attitude that the troubles of the times and the wars of religion could certainly justify; let us not forget, furthermore, that at that time the authority was tradition (antiquity), and that "tradition" came out of a subjective judgment: hadn't the great reformers of the sixteenth century declared that they proposed only to restore the ancient purity of the faith and customs? It goes without saying that Pasquier was well aware of the need for change, and he cites Aristotle who "in the second of his *Politics* weighs the pro and the contra" of the issue. "For those in favor of change, he says that if in all fields one sees opinions change, depending on the variety of encounters, all the more must one do the same in a political discipline." While paraphrasing in his own way the words of the ancient philosopher, Pasquier asserts that "the laws were in the past barbaric and conformed to the customs of ancient times. . . . Those old ruffians . . . were without any civility." It would only be absurd, "customs having been polished over time, to stop with the old laws." However, those laws could be "turned into customs": hence the necessity to act with circumspection in effecting change. But if that were true "for the law," all the more "it is required in what concerns venerable religion." It is noteworthy that the arguments against the "innovators in religion" were not directed only against the reformers: they also implicated those among the Catholics who wanted to introduce into France the "innovations" of the Council of Trent. Like many other *parlementaires*, Pasquier saw in that approach an attack on Gallican tradition: it is not by chance that he was also the author of the *Plaidoyé contre les Jésuites*, which contributed in supporting the Sorbonne against the Company of Jesus, which wanted to create one of its colleges in the capital.[31]

⁂

Pasquier's *Recherches* marked a milestone in the historiography of the sixteenth century: immediately appreciated as an essential work, it contributed to propagating a specific vision of the past, as well as an entire series of *loci communes*, transmitted later in textbooks and in popular works.[32] But what should be stressed once again is that this work was not isolated in the cultural context of the period; it arrived in a favorable intellectual world, enthralled with history. As we have said, the study of the past gave value to a more articulated organization of the political life in a society in which the emerging social groups were striving to find their place. If history was capable of "bringing together, through memory, past centuries with the present," it gave a stronger cohesion to the country and, through the knowledge of national tradition—"indeed the beginnings, the institutions, the growth" of the kingdom[33]—provided the reason for and an awareness of the present.

As it is impossible to cite the vast number of historical works produced in the period, let us attempt simply to highlight them through the examples of two authors who, through writings on method, managed to propose new perspectives on research. The first was Jean Bodin, who began to be interested in history as a complement to his legal studies. His *Methodus ad facilem historiarum cognitionem* (1566) was written with the conviction that "the best of universal law is well hidden in history," because history offers a just "assessment of the laws" by transmitting to posterity a knowledge of the customs of peoples.[34] History, revealing "the origin, growth, functioning, transformations and the end of all public affairs," is the key to "the condition of republics": "It is thanks to history that the present is easily explained, that the future can be known." An instrument for political action, it gives an understanding of the destiny of men, from the moment that it can only be truly grasped as a universal history. "Those who believe they have understood specific histories before having studied . . . the order and succession of universal history throughout the centuries" commit the same error as those who draw the map of a region "before knowing the explanation of the universe and the cohesion of its various parts."[35]

Having approached history in order to obtain material for his study that ended in the *République*, Bodin attempted to master all of the empirical data by studying the temporal and natural structures of historical unfolding. All the same, he didn't want to deduce laws from universal principles: the history of mankind—the meaning of their actions—had its own autonomy, for "will is the mistress of human actions."[36] He said he was convinced that "no influence, whether of place or celestial bodies, implies an absolute necessity," for men can "rise above the law of nature . . . through a long methodical effort."

Of course, the naturalist temptation was always strong for all these scholars. Deriving inspiration from political anthropomorphism, which had already suggested more than one reflection to Machiavelli and which we find again in Bodin, Pasquier had written: "Republics are symbolic of human bodies in this: although bodies die after a certain time, that finality comes through humors that are found in every political order, each of which, having favorable beginnings and advancements, later are defeated by some misfortune, by which one can infallibly predict its end through political demonstrations, which are no less salient than those in mathematics to those who make that their profession" (I, 23 B). This naturalism thus appears as an approach toward a scientific understanding of the actions of people: the new spirit, which animated the scientific revolution of the period, acted in a way so that this knowledge was pursued not through abstract universal principles, but through experience, which was, in this case, the lesson of the past that history teaches us.

From this point of view, we find an intriguing expression in the other author that we wish to mention here, Henri de La Popelinière. In a letter sent in 1604 to Joseph Juste Scaliger, the great Italian philologist from Leyden, he informed him of his project: "In order to approach the perfection of history," he proposed "solidifying" his knowledge through "travels and the careful study of foreign lands."[37] Especially through the direct observation of different countries overseas, he thought he could succeed in understanding how "men, savages and specific recluses that are said to have existed, have gradually become social and united by various connections of human government." The formation of the first seeds of a civilization and subsequently the blossoming of fully evolved societies— he believed he could follow them in person by a voyage overseas, in the wild lands and in the empires of the Orient. It was perhaps a rather simplistic vision of the progress of civilization, but he was starting with the conviction that the human races were equal and that only the vicissitudes of history had varied the lives of peoples. He proposed, therefore, a comparative study of the customs and institutions of "civilized peoples and of those whom one calls, rather improperly, savages." Like Bodin, who was considered to be one of the fathers of modern sociology, La Popelinière's goal was to "make history, from the specific, general over the most notable things both human and natural."

The man who wrote this was moreover not without direct experience in the profession of historian. In 1599 he had published a very original book, *L'Histoire des histoires, avec l'idée de l'histoire accomplie*, in which he had provided a survey of historiography since its beginnings, in order to be able to sketch "a drawing of the new history." He had expressed his passion as a scholar by asserting the necessity of being completely detached from his own subject: "The goal of the historian is none other than to recite things as he observes them as having occurred"; he must therefore rid himself of any sentimental attitude toward his subject, for he cannot truly study it "if he fears, if he hates, or loves that of which he is speaking." The authority, the power, as well as the vicissitudes of the internal struggles could trouble his "labor," which he must however "devote and consecrate to the truth," dreaming "not of the respect of the present, but of posterity." Those were the principles that had already caused him serious difficulties with his reformed religious cohorts, who had censured his *Histoire de ces derniers troubles* (1571), written—according to the synod of Protestant Churches—"to the detriment of the Truth of God"[38]: theologians and historians, obviously, did not have the same notion of the truth. And, nevertheless, La Popelinière insisted, advising the historian: "That he not know any fear, or hope. . . . Strict, constant and without bending," he must live "under his laws and traveling among all." Like Pasquier, he, too, was wary of traditional and legendary tales, and asserts: "Nothing is more harmful to the historian than the false and the fable" (p. 48). Moreover, "to rightly express all the substance of history, without stopping at mere accidents, which are countless," one must avoid "falling into an infinite labyrinth, which accepts no learning, but stop only at the essential and formal differences" (pp. 35–36). It was truly the aim of a new form of history that he was pursuing, convinced that "knowing is understanding through causes" (p. 110): in the customs and the institutions of peoples— who live much longer than individuals—it is possible to find "the origin, progress and changing of the most notable things" (p. 83). Consequently, one must study the history of France by going back to the origins, "to know the lands from which the French emerged, the customs, laws, government" they had, and "whether they had preserved their ancient customs, languages, clothing, weapons, justice, religion, and other forms of living" (p. 111). This is the plan that Pasquier had attempted to follow. For his part, La Popelinière believed that history could not "stop with the consideration of individuals," but must not "seek to tell only of things concerning the State." In any event, his goal was universal: "It would be stupid to restrain the capacity of history, which one calls the mirror of the world, to the matters of only one session."

In another of his books, *Les Trois mondes* (1582), he had already expressed his thirst for knowing, his ardor for research, and his critical mind, open to all the innovations of the time. A work of geography and history, this book proposed to illustrate the old continent and the new, as well as the southern continent, which was considered much larger than it is, the French colonization of which La Popelinière hoped for. By bringing together the geographical discoveries and a knowledge of the past, La Popelinière hoped to achieve a unified vision of the world that was freed from the old theological and philosophical schemas. Granted, there was also a political agenda: he wanted to show the possibilities of shattering the Spanish hegemony, which was dominating Europe thanks to the treasures of America. "The earth is strangely large," he wrote, almost emotionally, and new horizons were opening, which could offer individuals and peoples different relationships. He thus notes that the countries of Asia were "so well governed, wealthy, and hardened from time . . . that the Portuguese were forced to practice other means than the effort of their weapons" to "continue their traffic in those lands."[39] What we call civilization was, in his opinion, a factor of strength and cohesion, which enabled one to envision a universe in which networks of relationships, exchanges, and knowledge would give people a higher quality of life in a community.

One should note that, especially in the second half of the sixteenth century, the aftermath of the great discoveries unleashed in France a fever of curiosity with regard to new lands and an entire series of reflections on the possibilities that they were going to offer. It is true that in often seeing works of ancient history, books of travels, novels of adventure, and medieval poetry arranged side by side in the libraries of the great bourgeois of the time, we can imagine that the tragic vicissitudes of those years were not foreign to the fortune of such readings, which enabled the reader to cross—with the help of the imagination—the bloody borders of the kingdom.[40] We have already stressed the meaning of the studies on antiquity; in all that travel literature, there is much more than a stylish curiosity or the desire to escape: there is also news and remarks that would work deeply in consciousnesses, contributing to transform not only geographical knowledge or cultural traditions, but the mental workings, the religious problematics, the very foundations of morality and civil life. The Mediterranean world henceforth appeared small—as La Popelinière noted—compared to the huge expanses of recently discovered lands and seas at the time when the balances of the ancient *Respublica Christiana* were upset not only by religious struggles, but also by the awareness of causes that were at the origin of Spanish power. New worlds were presented to the minds of readers of these books: they discovered the Far East, very ancient civilizations that were perfectly governed, other religions, and above all the coexistence without conflicts of believers of different faiths, which took on the value of myth in the formation of the idea of tolerance in the age of Enlightenment.

The path leading to the deep changes in the vision of the world would be long, as Paul Hazard writes in his *Crise de la conscience européenne.* We nevertheless find the distant foundations of this crisis in the sixteenth-century works we have just looked at. Indeed, the great transformations of feelings and beliefs required an entire stratification of knowledge, experience, and reflections that did not only know favorable circumstances and pushes toward the future, but also moments of stagnation and even of reflux. The passage from conservatism to innovation, noted by Hazard, between the end of the seventeenth century and the beginning of the eighteenth century, had been as abrupt, but in the opposite direction, a century earlier. If some forty years had been enough so that up until then an unknown way of considering the relationship between one's own country and time, in short, a new vision of history, was asserted in the sixteenth century, proposing to blend into a single perspective the past of men and the new worlds, moral life, and nature from the beginning of the following century, a reflection on the past as well as on the interests concerning the State and society changed directions. The alert and knowledgeable curiosity toward everything that a living relationship between the past and the present offered in meaning to history lost in intensity. History returned to an annalist narrative, scholarly research was an end in itself, philological analysis no longer had the same innovative ardor; it was only in the realm of ecclesiastical and religious antiquity that one dug to the depths of tradition and the origins of institutions and beliefs, but that was dictated first by the demands of controversy.

It is not our purpose here to seek to penetrate this change in cultural and intellectual climate; it is clear, nonetheless, that the "new history" no longer had a place in the France reorganized by the monarchy of the Bourbons. Despite the political crisis, French society in the sixteenth century had been open and dynamic and the possibilities of transformation, linked to the search for a national identity, had stimulated the construction of a vast and complex historical memory. By contrast, the more fixed social structures contributed to isolating the present in seventeenth-century France, which no longer appeared so concerned with seeing in the past the scansions of an uninterrupted temporal process, projected toward innovative goals. Moreover, the interest in institutions, which had inspired Pasquier in his *Recherches* and, like him, other historians, could no longer feed the work of scholars, from the moment that the person of the monarch, exalted and almost divinized, must appear, without any alternative, as the image and the guarantor of the continuity of the nation as a political whole. And then, it was to the tale of his great deeds that one had to return, to the tale of wars that the king led, to the illustration of his political acts and of his sovereign decisions. At the same time, the role that the nobility played in the court required the return to genealogies, to evocations of the exploits carried out by the great figures of the past. And customs, which concerned only popular interests, could be of only minor interest to those who—like Bossuet, and unlike Pasquier—felt that all men were born subjects.

We must add that an important change also occurred in the intellectual milieux: among the men of the robe, the connection between political involvement and cultural effort was no longer the same. Beginning in the first years of the seventeenth century, they sought and found other paths to consolidate their position in the kingdom, and those means involved less the advantages of their order than their aspirations as individuals. It was no longer a question of asserting the central role of the *parlement* in the monarchy, as Pasquier had done: the great families of the elite of the third estate multiplied their alliances with the nobility, thanks to the venality of the posts and to buying noble land, which ended by upsetting the sense of solidarity that we find asserted in so many works and correspondence of the sixteenth century, showing the common interests of the social and intellectual life.

But it is not only the changes in mental attitudes that reveal the decline of the problematics of the "new history." Returning to Pasquier, the history of the editions of his *Recherches* is already in itself significant, as opposed to the almost uninterrupted chain of their reprintings, continuing into the first decade of the seventeenth century. Beginning in 1621 the book reappeared only three times, at a distance of twelve, ten, and twenty years. If one must recognize the natural aging of the work, one must also note that no comparable undertaking ever took its place. After 1665, only the scholarship of the eighteenth century proposed, in its way, to pursue the work of which the great historian was so proud, knowing they had gathered

> ce que j'ay veu par ma France passer
> pour l'engraver au temple de la mémoire (II, 876 C).

> [what I saw pass through my France
> to engrave it on the temple of memory.]

NOTES

1. Nicolas Machiavelli, *The Historical, Political, and Diplomatic Writings of Niccolò Machiavelli*, trans. Christian Edward Detmold (Houghton Mifflin, 1882), 404.

2. Letter from the Duke of Alba to Philip II of Spain, sent from Paris, July 8, 1559, cited in R. Romano, "La pace de Cateau-Cambrésis e l'equilibrio europeo a metà del secolo XVI," *Rivista storica italiana* (1949): 539.

3. *Jacobi Augusti Thuani Historiarum sui temporis pars prima*, Paris, Veuve de Mamert Patisson, 1604 (but I am citing from the Frankfurt edition, Kopff, 1614, 1:1010).

4. *Les Recherches de la France*, chap. 1 (I, 3 B): Pasquier's texts are cited from *Les Œuvres d'Estienne Pasquier* . . . published in Amsterdam, paid by the Compagnie des libraires associez, 1723 (anastatic reprint by Slatkine Reprints, Geneva, 1971). The Roman numeral in parentheses indicates the volume number, the Arabic numeral the column, the letters from A to D indicate the cited passage's position in the column.

5. The "oral transmission/written word" question was associated in this period with the issue of the art of memory and with hermetic philosophy (in favor at the court of the last Valois, especially among the Italianist groups); see Frances A. Yates, *The Art of Memory* (London: Routledge and Kegan Paul, 1966); and from the same historian: *French Academies of the XVIth Century* (London: Warburg Institute, 1947; reprint, Kraus, 1973); *Giordano Bruno and the Hermetic Tradition* (London: Routledge and Kegan Paul, 1964); *Lull and Bruno: Collected Essays* (London: Routledge and Kegan Paul, 1982).

6. Étienne Pasquier, born in Paris into a family of jurists and lawyers, was destined very early on for a career at the Bar, and studied law at several universities in France and Italy. He became a lawyer in 1549, and was well known above all for his *Plaidoyé contre les Jésuites* of 1564. A lawyer in the Chambre des comptes in 1585, he gave up his post as lawyer to the king to one of his sons in 1603. He died in Paris in 1615. See Clark L. Keating, *Étienne Pasquier* (New York, 1972); Paul Bouteiller, *Un*

historien du XVIe siècle: Étienne Pasquier (Abbeville, 1945); Robert Bütler, *Nationales und universales Denken im Werke Étienne Pasquier* (Basel, 1948); and Margaret J. Moore, *Étienne Pasquier: Historien de la poésie et de la langue françaises* (Poitiers, 1934).

7. Jacques Le Goff, "Memoria," in *Enciclopedia Einaudi* 8:1069.

8. Bernard de Girard du Haillan, preface to *De l'estat et succez des affaires de France* (Paris: Olivier de l'Huillier, 1570). On the consequences of the peace of Cateau-Cambrésis, less serious than the French of the time had believed, and on the new political and economic balances of Europe in the second half of the sixteenth century, one immediately refers to the henceforth classic work *La Méditerranée et le monde méditerranéen à l'époque de Philippe II*, by Fernand Braudel (Paris: Armand Colin, 1949 and 1966).

9. Petrus Crinitus, *De honesta disciplina*, ed. C. Angeleri (Rome, 1955), 317; see Donald R. Kelley, *Foundations of Modern Historical Scholarship: Language, Law and History in the French Renaissance* (New York: Columbia University Press, 1970), 12.

10. Marc Fumaroli, "Aux Origines de la connaissance historique au Moyen Age: Humanisme, réforme et Gallicanisme au XVIe siècle," *XVIIe siècle* (1977): 114–15.

11. Ibid., 16.

12. Donald Kelley, op. cit., 12.

13. Alberto Tenenti, "La Storiografia in Europe dal Quattro al Seicento," in *Nuove Questioni di Storia Moderna* (Milan: Marzorati, 1963), 5; see also the offprint, and more generally, Claude-Gilbert Dubois, *La Conception de l'histoire en France au XVIe siècle, 1560–1610* (Paris: Nizet, 1977).

14. For all these data I refer to my article, "Paulus Aemilius Gallis condidit historias?" *Annales E.S.C.* (1964): 1117–24.

15. See George Huppert, *L'Idée de l'histoire parfaite* (Paris: Flammarion, 1973), 193–95. The *Bibliothèque Françoise* of François La Croix du Maine was published by Abel l'Angelier in Paris in 1584.

16. Lucien Febvre, *Philippe II et la Franche-Comté* (Paris: H. Champion, 1912), 351.

17. See G. Huppert, op. cit., 40–41.

18. See the preface by Henri Hauser to *Sources de l'histoire de France* (Paris: A. Picard, 1912). On these issues see also my book, *Lotta politica e pace religiosa in Francia fra Cinque e Seicento* (Turin: Einaudi, 1974), specifically 139ff.

19. Lorenzo Valla, *Recriminationes in Facium*, cited by D. R. Kelly, op. cit., 78.

20. The history of the editions of the *Recherches de la France* is not simple, and there has still never been a critical edition of the work. In 1560 Pasquier published the first book with V. Sertenas in Paris, and in the same volume there appeared *Le Pour-parler du prince*. There was a second edition in 1567 from Trepperel of Orléans, who, in the same year, also published the "Second Book." Two years later l'Huillier brought out "Books I and II." Several editions followed, always enlarged with new chapters or new books, but it was only in 1607 that Pasquier published the work in seven books. The final two books of the *Recherches* appeared only after the author's death, but in the editions that followed the organization of the added books is not always the same. Two volumes of selected works (following the Amsterdam edition) were published by Léon Feugère with Firmin-Didot in Paris in 1849.

21. See Colette Beaune, *Naissance de la nation France* (Paris: Gallimard, 1985), 19ff.

22. See Marc-René Jung, *Hercule dans la littérature française du XVIe siècle* (Geneva: Droz, 1966).

23. "The followers of the pope," wrote Paolo Sarpi, historian of the Council of Trent, to one of his French friends, the *parlementaire* Jacques Gillot, on September 15, 1609, "now aspire not only to his primacy, but they dream of a 'totat' ["totatus" in the original Latin], if it is allowed to create a new word to define a situation in which, all legal order suppressed, all power is conferred upon one person." See Paolo Sarpi, *Lettere ai gallicani*, ed. B. Ulianich (Wiesbaden, 1961), 134.

24. Pasquier deals with this issue only once, in a letter to Pierre Robert: II, 575–82 (especially 580–81).

25. Charles du Moulin, *Commentarii in consuetudines Parisienses* (Paris: M. Somnium, 1576), 2: "Merito priore loco ponitur hic materiae feudalis titulus, quum feuda sint proprium et peculiare inventum veterum Francorum."

26. This concerns the famous anti-Trinitarian heretic Michel Servet, who was burned at the stake in Geneva in 1553, and who in 1535 had published in Lyon with the Trechsel brothers the work of Ptolemeus, *Geographicae enarrationis libri octo* (another edition was published in 1541).

27. Robert Dallington, *The View of Fraunce* [sic]: *Un Apercu de la France telle qu'elle était vers l'an 1592*, translated from the English by E. Émerique (Versailles: Cerf, 1892), 167.

28. Jacques-Bénigne Bossuet, *Politique tirée des propres paroles de l'écriture sainte* (Paris: Cot, 1709), 248, and see esp. p. 1, first article, first sequence.

29. The fact that Pasquier once again appealed to the writings of the "republican" Machiavelli to sing the praises of the institutions of his own country—G. Procacci has noted—shouldn't be surprising. His familiarity with the writing of the Florentine secretary was very great and, in spite of the usual invectives against his impiety, he felt a deep admiration for him. See Giuliano Procacci, *Studi sulla fortuna del Machiavelli* (Rome: Istituto Storico Italiano per l'Età Moderna e Contemporanea, 1965), 118. Pasquier alludes here in particular to chapter 19 of *The Prince* (see Machiavelli, *Complete Works*, op. cit.).

30. I am quoting from the edition of the *Recherches* (first and second books) published by Claude Micard in 1571, 8.

31. The argument between Pasquier and the Jesuits went on for a long time and degenerated into a true war of words on the part of the Company of Jesus. In his collected letters, Pasquier published the response that he wrote to the general of the company, Father Acquaviva; among other things he specified that "in our France" one must say, "He is a true French Catholic, therefore an enemy of the Jesuits" (II, 637 B).

32. The history of the fate of the *Recherches de la France* remains to be done. One can read in a biography of Pasquier that "all of that has become commonplace for having been copied into all the books that have been written ever since," and indeed from the accounts of friends and correspondents of Pasquier we can see that the first books were imitated in the cultural world, so much so that after their publication works on antiquities in Gaul multiplied. The Trojan legend disappeared from history books, whereas the Gallic origin of the French appeared, henceforth, as an

indisputable fact. We should also note that Hercules also now became a "Gaul": Lucien's story on this particular figuration of the Greek hero created by the Gauls, as a symbol of persuasion, had been translated by Budé in 1508, but it became widespread especially in the monarchist propaganda of the second half of the sixteenth century (see my article, "Henry IV, the Gallic Hercules," *Journal of the Warburg and Courtauld Institute* (1967): 176–97, and the book by M.-R. Jung cited above). One day, textbooks will speak quite naturally of "our ancestors, the Gauls." It is difficult to say whether Pasquier is also the direct source of Uderzo, whose Gallic heros fear only one thing: that the sky doesn't fall on their heads. Indeed, this according to the response the Gauls had given to a legendary emissary sent by Alexander the Great, who is mentioned in the beginning of the *Recherches* (I, 7 A).

33.   Bernard du Haillan, *De l'estat et succez des affaires de France*, op. cit.

34.   Jean Bodin, *Methodus ad facilem historiarum cognitionem,* in *Oeuvres philoso-phiques*, text assembled, translated, and published by Mesnard (Paris: Presses Universitaires de France, 1951), 276 B.

35.   Ibid., 178 A.

36.   Ibid., 287 B.

37.   See *Épistres françoises de personages illustres et doctes à M. Joseph Juste de la Scala*, published by Jacques de Reves, Harderwyck, Veuve de Thomas Henry (Amsterdam, 1623), 303–7. The letter, which I have reproduced in the appendix of my article, "Alle origini dell'idea di civiltà: Le Scoperte geografiche e gli scritti di Henri de La Popelinière," *Rivista storica italiana* (1962): 23–25 from the offprint, was republished by G. Huppert in the appendix of the book cited above.

38.   See Jean Aymon, *Tous les synodes nationaux des églises réformées de France,* vol. 1, part 2 (La Haye, 1710), 151ff. XI Synod . . . La Rochelle, 28 June 1581.

39.   Henri de la Popelinière, *Les Trois mondes,* part 1 (Paris: Pierre l'Huillier, 1582), folio 53.

40.   See Geoffroy Atkinson, *Les Nouveaux horizons de la Renaissance française* (Paris: Droz, 1935). See also Alphonse Dupront, "Espace et humanisme," *Bibliothèque d'humanisme et Renaissance* 8 (1946).

CHAPTER 9

AUGUSTIN THIERRY'S *LETTRES*
SUR L'HISTOIRE DE FRANCE

"The Austere Conjoining of Patriotism and Science"

∾

MARCEL GAUCHET

"For some forty years now, ever since Augustin Thierry, publishing his first letters in a periodical, drew the public's attention to the origins of our nation, our ancient society has been subjected to a labor similar to that carried out by geologists on the earth we inhabit. From the visible surface where the full power of life prospers and struggles, we have delved back into the debris hidden in its entrails; and just as we push back from one stratum to the next into the first ages of the globe, we have explored from century to century the layered epochs of our history." This is one of many possible testimonials: Rémusat's 1860 tribute to the path-breaking quality of the ten *Lettres sur l'histoire de France* published in 1820 in the *Courrier français*.[1] They inaugurated the in-depth exploration of the national past: this is the "event" that they were here to crystallize. They provide a marker for "the revolution which since 1820 has completely changed the aspect of historical study, or rather, which established history for us," as Renan put it in *L'Avenir de la science*.[2] Renan's formulation in fact echoes the very phrase Thierry used in 1827, when his first manifestoes were being reworked and merged into a volume on the subject of works that had signaled "a real revolution in the writing of French history," the writings of Sismondi, Guizot, and Barante.[3] We wish here to do justice to the historical revolution of the 1820s that so deeply impressed those who carried it out and witnessed it—"we are the first to understand the past," one of them bluntly put it[4]—which was still memorable and starkly visible to those like Renan who came right after it, but has gotten blurred and even buried by later developments in the discipline. For once, indeed, against the usual disqualifying slant of history, the historian's task is to requalify and justify the perspective of participants in and witnesses to the event, in the eyes of a posterity that has gradually lost the sense of their initiative. Between 1820 and 1830 took place a transformation in the relationship to the past, one that laid the groundwork for today's "scientific" historical research as we still practice it—in ways, of course, which today seem strange, and with limitations that mask the true achievement and make us aware only of the tentativeness or waywardness in that discourse. We need to recover it in all of its sharpness and depth. We must travel beyond surface appearances in order to recapture the meaning of this seminal rupture.

I

While signposting this memory of origins, Rémusat also shows us the path that led to its recovery: in a word, its conquest by politics. Where did this intense, imperious interest in the nation's annals come from? From the need to find an answer to the question: "Why did the French Revolution happen? I have never imagined," says Rémusat, that "one could read the history of France without constantly having in mind the French Revolution." And the great reward, "the bright light" that he sees as the outcome of patient excavation by the "gifted historians of our time" is that once they had finished their investigations the Revolution "had become the natural outcome of a drama lasting ten or eleven centuries."[5]

Not that this statement was wrong. Even leaving aside the resounding works devoted to it (Thiers's in 1823, Mignet's in 1824), the huge shadow of '89 and '93 loomed over this period. There can be no doubt about the need that was felt to situate oneself in relation to the legacy and the results of the Revolution; within the context of the Restoration, this was the basic condition defining political attitudes. Under the Napoleonic regime, actors remained trapped within the very consequences of the great event, unable to reach a thoughtful distance from it. The immediate effect of its collapse, along with the urge to link up with monarchical tradition by jumping over an extraordinarily eventful quarter of a century, had the effect of freeing up the Revolution as a problem, to pose that problem in all of its freshness and acuity, as the event suddenly needed to be apprehended in its entire scope and judged in light of its full consequences.

In an aside from an article of 1820, Thierry eloquently describes the new sense of openness, which he likens to a reawakening: "in 1814 the French nation suddenly awakened. Having dug itself out of the imperial slime, liberal France was to be seen again in all its youth and radiance, like

Fig. 9.1
Augustin Thierry.

those cities we find unaltered after centuries by breaking through the coat of lava which covered them."[6] And it is true that, on a purely intellectual level, understanding the rupture of '89 by reinscribing it within a long span of centuries was the quintessential exercise through which a new awareness of the depth and power of historical time became self-assured. From Guizot in 1820 evoking in famous terms the "decisive battle" that was the Revolution in the struggle "for over thirteen centuries" by the defeated people "to cast off the yoke of the conquerors,"[7] to Thierry in 1827 honoring in the "municipal revolutions of the Middle Ages" the anticipation of "constitutional revolutions of the modern age,"[8] there are numerous instances of this search for an understanding and legitimation of present developments through the link to an impetus coming from the dawn of time. Still, it is through this association between the reform of historical studies and the revolutionary object and cause that the discovery of the past played out at that moment in time has since disappeared from sight. Once progress in erudition and the demands of positivist criticism starkly exposed the shortcomings of our romantic and liberal historiography, only the political side of their endeavor was remembered.

It must be said that the authors had provided a whole battery of quotes that can be used to bolster the cliché. Just listen to Thierry, as he relates with admirable candor, the utilitarian origins of his vocation: "In 1817," he writes in the foreword to the *Lettres*, "seized with an intense desire to play my part in the triumph of constitutional beliefs, I began to search history books for proofs and arguments which would support my political beliefs." Even though the following lines proceed to make clear how he moved from this to a passion for history itself, emphatic statements of this sort bequeathed a suspicion that at this initial moment the concern with a righteous cause overwhelmed scholarly concerns. "Let us do justice to the historians of 1820," wrote Camille Jullian in a burst of sympathy, "they did everything they could to keep from making truth a hostage to freedom."[9] Some justifications only add to the charges! And so, this phalanx of militant Restoration historians have left the image of bourgeois advance troops intent on providing both their party and their class with a clearer sense of themselves, their origins, and their mission. This happened before history became a real science, after 1830, thanks in part to the fortunate effects of the "Historians' Revolution," so conspicuously illustrated by the career and works of Guizot at the head of the enterprise (see chapter 4 by Laurent Theis, "Guizot and the Institutions of Memory"). From Michelet's methodical collecting of documents, both fully nationalistic and truly archivistic, through the surge of Chartist [royalist?] scholarship, we owe to the July monarchy the flowering of a truly scholarly knowledge of the past, of which the embattled romanticism of Thierry, Barante, or Mignet would offer only vague or sentimental premonitions—the statement of a social need, in other words, and the creation of a public awareness, both of which were satisfied better, in later years, by other historians.

Our authors did not lose out completely in exchanging, in the eyes of posterity, their scholarly credentials for an ideological and political role. They even won one of the most eminent claims to fame, that of inventing class struggle, awarded them by the very founders of dialectical materialism. Marx took pride in stressing how much he owed, on that score, to the bourgeois historians, especially Thierry and Guizot; Engels joined him in acknowledging the crucial nature of their debt to the French Restoration school, and their disciples, of course, followed suit.[10] It is to this filial devotion to the discoverers of the conflictual understanding of historical development that we owe the only recent overview of the period, B. Reizov's *L'Historiographie romantique française, 1815–1830.*[11] These first explorers may have lacked philological precision, perhaps, but they still played an outstanding role in shaping the intellectual tools for a materialist and scientific analysis of social change.

Even those willing to credit the work of these liberal historians with contributing in crucial ways to bringing about modern historical science, at least modern historical consciousness, even they feel a need to play down this contribution by always reducing it to the status of aftereffect of the Revolution. This might indeed have been a cultural event, they concede, but only as an extension and translation of political events. "The upheavals of the Revolution and the Empire," writes for instance Philippe Ariès, "in sweeping away the past had interrupted the normal course of history. From now on there was a 'before' and an 'after.'"[12] In the shadow of this immense fracture a new sense of becoming takes shape, marked by distance and discontinuity. It is in the shadow of this gaping hole that the discovery of "differences of human color over time" takes place. The more or less skillful quest for "local color," for the distancing detail (such as, in Thierry's work, the rash restitution "of Frankish names, following the Teutonic spelling"), the concern with lively narration, all speak to this new awareness. It is through all of these preoccupations that the historians' project feeds into the aesthetic mutation of romanticism. "My ambition was to produce art along with science," Thierry later wrote about his first book, *L'Histoire de la conquête de l'Angleterre par les Normands* (1825).[13] Let us just say that artistic resources made it possible to compensate for the gaps in uneven erudition. "The concern with foreignness which now made historians look to living images was," writes Ariès, "just a rough sense of differences over time."[14] And so, in this romantic historicism and its naïve dramatic portrayals, we might be dealing with a literary transition between two different epochs in historical consciousness. In this reading, the principle of discontinuity introduced by the revolutionary earthquake would be expressed in poetic terms, in the absence of other means, before the systematic use of sources and documentary criticism came to inaugurate a real cognitive mastery of our distance from the past.

Here again, what makes this reading plausible is its convergence with contemporaries' understanding. They too read the cultural transformations they witnessed in terms of *the* exemplary rupture, that of the Revolution. Here is Stendhal, for instance, in 1825: "By the end of the next two or three years, all of the old literary absurdities will perish in a general Saint Bartholomew's Day. Literature will experience the effect of the Revolution."[15] And how they went on about their superiority as men of the nineteenth century, "endowed with the experience of political life which is one of the privileges of our era with its surfeit of great events," over even the best minds of the old regime. "There is not one of us," bluntly states Thierry, "who does not know more than did Velly or Mably, more than Voltaire himself, about the dismembering of empires, the death and resurrection of dynasties, democratic revolutions and the reactions which follow them."[16] How would it have been possible for those bringing about innovation not to understand it in terms of the great earthquake they had just experienced?

It may behoove us, however, to understand it differently. It seems difficult to cast doubt upon the magnitude of the revolutionary rupture, in France and abroad, whether as to its concrete effects, or as an unavoidable intellectual problem. But must we for all that reduce the transformation in the understanding of the past that becomes apparent in the 1820s solely to the effect of the break with the past brought about by the fall of the old regime? We do not believe so. The precariousness of the scholarly basis of this history is what leads one to do so. That precariousness gives credence to the notion that this is a shift in sensibility, hostage to its era, rather than a true pursuit of knowledge framed by a deliberate purpose, on the basis of a mastery of its own tools. But can the pursuit of knowledge not be conceived of along other lines? This seems to us, in this context, absolutely necessary. Is not the fruitful, decisive moment that when new assumptions gel, opening up both new empirical routes and new frameworks of understanding? Ideally, of course, and in practice, most often, it is impossible to separate a new epistemic framework and the technical means necessary to achieve its instantiation. But things can sometimes happen differently, as the case at hand perfectly demonstrates. Where history is concerned, as a matter of fact, the paths leading to the constitution of the discipline as a science do not fit very well into this classic pattern. At the end of the seventeenth and the beginning of the eighteenth century, the scholarly and critical means for restoring exactly data from the past took shape, independently of an urge toward a global understanding of the continent of the sort first apprehended in all of its factual truth.[17] In sum, the raw materials were there, but not the means of exploiting them (or even the means of presenting them, since the alphabetical order of the glossary or dictionary compensated for the inability to produce an organically linked presentation). What happened here is the exact opposite: the emergence in the abstract, as it were, that is in a literary or philosophical mode quite removed from any new work that underlies and dictates our understanding of the past, right down to our own time. One could therefore describe this, by contrast, as a premature exploitation of available knowledge, but without a real material basis.

The reasons for this disjunction can be found in the peculiarities of the French context. The interruption occasioned by the Revolution, as well as gaps in prior knowledge, combined to enlarge further a gap that was already less pronounced elsewhere, especially in Germany—but also, in doing so, to make manifest a set of intellectual factors that a closer alliance of scholarly training and vindictive ambition would have hid, and in fact did hide, elsewhere. The [French] movement comes essentially from outside the academy, and no institution was in a position to provide it with either information or controls: this, in short, is the problem. Camille Jullian does exaggerate when he writes: "History was born anew, not from quiet labor in the study, but from the struggle between parties,"[18] but he does point to one of the most striking characteristics of this renaissance: its removal from the "natural environment" of historical study. Technically, all of our authors were self-taught. All of them came to history on their own, albeit building upon a solid classical education, and sometimes, as in Guizot's case, a remarkably cosmopolitan culture, but without any practice reading documents, nor any exposure to an antiquarian tradition. For all of them, the turn to scholarship came second, deriving from some other impulse—political, philosophical, or aesthetic—to which it became necessary as an instrument. When Guizot is named to the Sorbonne in 1812, he has to begin by learning most of the modern history he is required to teach. Now in Restoration France there were no channels through which to acquire the intellectual baggage these men had not started out with. As Dacier notes in 1808: "Of all the branches of literature, medieval and diplomatic history are those most likely to suffer from the ravages of the Revolution."[19] "The suppression of monastic orders and of learned academies," he explains, has suspended the activities of the two live centers for "the study of ancient charters and manuscripts from different centuries," the Benedictine congregations of Saint-Maur and Saint-Vanne, and the Académie des inscriptions et belles-lettres. The gap they left could hardly begin to be filled by the timid continuation of their great endeavors started under the empire.

Although the École des chartes was created in 1821, it only began to be active and productive after 1830. There was, for sure, Daunou's teaching at the Collège de France after 1819.[20] As a former oratorian as well as a onetime member of the revolutionary convention, he was indeed steeped in the tradition of monastic scholars (as a contributor to the *Histoire littéraire de la France* and the *Recueil des historiens* he is one of those carrying on their monumental collections). His case is interesting, and deserves closer attention. It is revealing in two ways. To begin with, his case alone suggests that the facile equation between liberalism and the new history needs to be qualified. Daunou does more than hold opinions, he is one of the representatives for the liberal opposition on two occasions, in 1819 and 1828; for all that, he strongly opposes, from an intellectual standpoint, the innovations of younger writers to whom he is politically close. This standoff between two generations emphasizes the old-fashioned and narrow historical perspective to which the scholarly tradition belatedly represented by the older man remains attached, as opposed to the new demands of his younger colleagues. (Daunou is fifty-eight when he obtains his chair in 1819, Thierry twenty-four, Guizot thirty-two, Mignet twenty-three, and Michelet twenty-one.) One needs only dive into the twenty volumes of his majestic *Cours d'études historiques* to understand his teaching's lack of influence, even as the genre itself was on the rise. The volumes relate, literally, another history than the one being written at that time in response to the concerns and interests of the age. And this is where we may guess that far more than the lack of a sufficiently developed and institutionalized discipline, offering an example and imposing norms, is the key to our puzzle. What is at stake is the reinvention of the very purpose and foundations of scholarship.

Now France, in this respect, remained outside of the renovation of methods that culminated, in nineteenth-century Germany, in the triumphant flowering of the philological method. At the very moment when "the science of Antiquity" is gaining ground, with the publication of the work of men like Wolf, Niebuhr, and Boeckh, in France Latin and Greek studies are reduced to the lowest status.[21] Furthermore, both the seminar format and the documentary technique of philologists played a well-known role as matrices for the entire field of history. Niebuhr was Ranke's master. Neither solid ongoing links with the older scholarship, nor a close relationship with the new: this initial lack of substance will leave a lasting mark on French historical science, even when it was taken over by the universities and the École des chartres, and critical accuracy will remain an elusive and often-invoked goal until the advent of Gabriel Monod and the positivist school. In 1820, all this has yet to be created or recreated. The reforming movement starts pretty much from nothing. Hence the ingenuousness that will mar its first products. For its initiators brandish the standard of a return to the strict truth of sources as against the legends retailed by a fanciful literature. They are certain to be finding at last, in the "dust of chronicles," the authentic basis for a national literature heretofore hidden by "faulty compilations."

Thierry touchingly related his journey of initiation as he worked through different strata of historical works accumulated, since the sixteenth century on "the old French monarchy and the institutions of the Middle Ages," until his electrifying contact with "original documents." In the first months of 1820, as he tells it, having made his way through "the entire range of secondary works," from Fauchet and Pasquier to Montlosier through Mably,

> I had begun to read the great collection of original historians of France and the Gauls. As I proceeded with my reading, I felt both intense pleasure at the contemporary account of the men and objects of our ancient history, along with a muffled anger against our modern writings who, far from faithfully reproducing this vision, had disguised the facts, twisted the characters, and imposed on all of it a false or misleading color. My indignation increased each time I had occasion to compare the real history of France, as I faced it in the original documents, and the shoddy compilations which had usurped that title.[22]

On the strength of this discovery he unfurled the diagnosis, in his first ten *Lettres*, of a glaring deficiency—"we do not yet possess a history of France."[23] Along with this irresistible indictment, which sounded the death-knell of a tradition, came the memory of a revelation: that of the precious material for national memory, an unknown treasure waiting to be reclaimed by its heirs. It was, then, within the chasm thus revealed— we were rich and did not know it—that the tide of publications rushed in, offering the "original monuments" of the French past to a reappropriation.

This gigantic excavation—from 1820 to 1840 an array of collections of memoirs and chronicles will launch onto the market some 500 volumes (see Pierre Nora, "Memoirs of Men of State," chapter 11 of *Les Lieux de mémoire*, vol. 1)—gives the measure of a hungry demand. However, it is also true that there were scientific shortcomings to this scientific "invention" of sources testifying to the authentic origins of the nation. The "truth of

history" invoked with such passion tolerates a dangerous ambiguity. It connects better with lively recreation than with scrupulous verification; it fits
within the framework of the "prodigious intelligence of the past," which in
Thierry's view differentiates the work of Walter Scott from "the cramped
and drab erudition of the most famous modern historians."[24] Hence the
privileged place granted to the sort of document that was supposed to best
reflect "local color" and the picturesque substance of olden times. This is
why Petitot, a pioneer among editors of the great documentary collections
of the Restoration, could write at the head of his *Collection*: "People com-
plain of the dryness of French history, and this is what makes memoirs,
with their wealth of those missing details, so appealing. Our historians,
unfortunately, have drawn less from this precious source than from the
charters, ordinances, and diplomas recording great events without delving
into their causes."[25] Hence also, under the empire, an appetite for poetic
rather than factual truth, and a definite ignorance of the problems posed
by the critical use of the documents thus collected. That quest for truth
found a better outlet in the popular project of letting the writers of the past
speak directly, as if one could touch the raw truth of their time through the
words of these narrator-witnesses. This is the basis for Barante's *Histoire des
ducs de Bourgogne*. It inspired Thierry's plan, along with his brother Amédée
and Mignet, for a "grand chronicle of France"; the plan went nowhere, but
the articulation of it reveals its illusory ambition: to obtain, on the basis of
a series of "unadorned testimonials, uninterrupted by philosophical reflection or modern additions . . . the *unmediated representation* of the past which
produced us, along with our habits, manners, and civilization."[26] It is as if
an unmediated contact with the past were really possible, without the re-
constructive operations that are the very essence of historical criticism.

   In the absence of other means, the urge to recreate differences in
time led to the taking of voices from the past as models, in the hope their
archaic flavor would produce the desired sense of distance: "As for the
narrative," writes Thierry in the introduction to the *Histoire de la conquête
de l'Angleterre*, "I kept as close as possible to the language of the historians
of old, either contemporaries of the events or close to the time in which
they occurred."[27] In a striking about-face, this new sense of temporal difference leads to a reprivileging, at least in artistic terms, of the status of
those who were eyewitnesses to the events, or nearly so; in traditional
historiography, this privileged status stemmed logically from an epistemology of unmediated knowledge, which implied a basically continuous
understanding of time. In the older view, to "know" an event is to revisit
it through the eyes of a witness to it, with the implicit understanding that
the knowing agent belongs in the same temporal sphere as the witness—
this common belonging is necessary to identify with the witness's point of

view, and to preserve the integrity of his attestation from a distance.[28] The newer recourse to the same strategy is inspired by exactly opposite reasons. What is expected of voices from the past is that they will make manifest the distance which separates us from them. All of which logically leads to the insight that knowledge of the past can only be indirect, resulting exclusively from the work of reconstruction carried out by the historian from contemporary documents treated not as fragments of truth but as indices, mute in themselves and speaking only through the inferences that their appropriate treatment makes possible. Hence the contradiction our historians get sucked into: their "naïve" manner of using sources contradicts the implications of their sense of the past's strangeness.

This contradiction will soon be realized and progressively resolved.[29] The technical treatment of historical materials will soon fall in line with the norms dictated by the distancing of the past. French singularity remains captured in this foundational path leading to science through poetry. As late as 1835, Augustin Thierry hails Walter Scott as "the greatest master ever of the art of historical divination."[30] Legend has it that Ranke, by contrast, came to his calling as the result of reading the same Walter Scott's *Quentin Durward*, but on the basis of a very different reaction, a mixture of indignation at the liberties the novelist took with the facts with faith in the superiority of scientific results over artistic products, even with regard to the satisfactions to be derived from the exotic. This contrast is as good as any as an example of the way in which the two traditions parted ways. More seriously, the gap can be exemplified by the two men's different attitude at the outset when dealing with original documents. Thierry uttered in 1825 the statement we quoted about his use of ancient historians; just the previous year, Ranke had published, along with his first book, *Geschichten der romanischen und germanischen Volker von 1494 bis 1514*, a technical appendix to the latter entitled *Zur Kritik nuerer Geschichtsschreiber*, in which one sees the very first instance of Niebuhr's philological criticism being applied to modern sources, to the texts of contemporary historians treated as sources.[31] And we find this same discrepancy with respect to technical standards and consistency between the great collections of documents published in France under the Restoration, and the *Monumenta germaniae historica*, whose first volume appears in 1826.

In part, it is true, the achievements of seventeenth-century scholarship serve as bait for militant champions of historical nationalism in the Restoration. Those achievements feed into the latter's inconsistencies. If the Restoration historians did not have the earlier methods and instruments, they had at least inherited the products. They were very much, it must be stressed, the heirs of this earlier tradition. Without this prior accumulation, their own work would not have been possible. They drew upon it for all that is solid in their understanding of this or that point. What they called going back to the sources was really a reappropriation of the material unearthed and published by their scholarly predecessors. Thierry did not take on the manuscripts of the oldest medieval chronicles in 1820. He could devour the texts as they had been edited in Dom Bouquet's *Recueil des historiens*. And in the same way, Barante could build his own *Histoire* upon the *Histoire générale et paritculière de Bourgogne* undertaken by Dom Plancher in the context of his provincial history of the Benedictine order.[32] Once the euphoria of rediscovery had worn off, they inevitably became aware of the limits of a procedure that consisted of exploiting the riches of a science to which nothing is added and that therefore becomes confining. Whether in reaction to methods involving a contradiction between the end and the means, or to the inevitable sense that the documentary base was insufficient, the first wave of liberal and romantic history in the French style begins around the late 1820s to reach the end of both its resources and its self-confidence.

And so it was certainly the case that, when Benjamin Guérard, future presiding genius of the École des chartes, articulates in 1829 on the subject of Guizot's teaching a stinging critique of all recent historical work, his attack, harsh as it is, is meant to be heard by the very writers he discusses. Guérard stigmatizes, and rightly so, their lack of curiosity with regard to new sources. "Since the end of the work by Benedictines," he notes severely,

> no work which has appeared has been really *progressive* for the history of our country. Leaving the difficult but safer road that these learned men of the cloth had taken, the historians who followed them instead of going forward rushed to the left or to the right or even retreated back, discovering nothing, conquering nothing of the past: they were content with the wealth accumulated for a century and a half by the illustrious congregations of Saint-Maur and Saint-Vanne, and without even attempting to follow up on the immense task these men had taken on and left unfinished, they did nothing but scrape and dig in the old stuff.[33]

This indictment is so much on the mark and it pinpoints so exactly the difficulties facing the development of the "historical reform" that it could just as well have been formulated internally.

Whereupon takes place the July Revolution. It resolves and changes everything by creating the employment opportunities to meet the glaring and urgent need for scholarly establishment and development. Guérard is named in 1831 to the École des chartes, which had started up again in 1829 but to which he will give the decisive push. Mignet and

Michelet, however, had begun to work in archives in 1830. And 1832 saw the beginning of Guizot's decisive work, beginning with the Ministry for Public Education. Barante becomes president of the Société de l'histoire de France when it is founded. And the Comité des travaux historiques, created in 1834 with a mission to seek out and publish the "unpublished documents concerning French history," includes, besides familiar names such as Daunou, Guérard, and Mignet, other luminaries of the previous decade's historical reawakening, whether they inspired it, like Fauriel, or popularized it, like Villemain.[34] It was in the context of the committee's work that the blind Thierry, named in November to head the Collection des chartes, directed by speaking and listing his edition of the *Recueil des monuments inédits de l'histoire du Tiers-État*, a venture closely connected to the writing of his last book, the *Essai sur l'histoire de la formation et des progrès du Tiers État*, 1853.[35] It was Mignet, however, who inaugurated the committee's publication series by bringing out in 1835 his *Négociations relatives à la succession d'Espagne sous Louis XIV.* Whether from near or afar, directly or indirectly, whether they made the decisions or implemented them, all of the protagonists of the movement in the 1820s thus wound up within the network of institutions that established history as a science.

From the perspective of this second wave and its work of professional consolidation, the preceding wave is generally seen as a preliminary phase whose glaring uncertainties had to be concealed. A number of actors' statements contributed to popularizing this view. First up is the greatest, Michelet, whose preface to his *Histoire de France* carried great weight in fixing this genealogy. Organized around the retrospective redefinition of his own endeavor as a point of origin—"I saw France . . . first, I saw her as a soul, as a person"—the distinction he posits between before and after became a canonical turning point: "until 1830 (until even 1836) none of the remarkable historians of this period felt the need to go looking for facts outside of printed books, to go to the as yet unpublished primary sources, the manuscripts in our libraries, the documents in our archives."[36] What this reconstruction conceals is the general, unanimous conversion to the quest for "primary sources" of which Michelet's is only one among many (and suffers, it must be said, from the same deficiencies as the others). The rupture of 1830 is not in doubt. But for it to be fully understandable, it must be replaced within a continuous process, the biographical continuity of a generation that, in devoting itself to scholarly research, completes its conversion to history, as well as the intellectual continuity of an approach that came within its internal development to need wider and more accurate access to facts.

The transformation of polemicists into scholars does not fall from the skies; it is not dictated by urgent political agendas or a sudden shift in the zeitgeist; nor is it a surrender to external constraints, whether a foreign example or the reimposition of the norms of a venerable tradition. It is also the internal culmination of the digging of self-taught scholars, whose meandering speculations did more than prepare for the solemn reinstatement of the program and rules for sound criticism. For scholarship drew from this liberal and romantic detour a radical renewal of its point of view. For if the severe seventeenth-century pioneers set down its foundations, the belated and groping nineteenth-century converts immeasurably enlarged its range. On this point the criticism of Guérard, however true, should be qualified. It was not a matter of going back, around 1830, to a forgotten discipline, but of linking anew with a tradition after a damaging interruption. The reappropriation of a critical apparatus is meaningful only with respect to the uncovering of an object whose power and range was specifically defined by the angry young men of 1820.

Thierry gave an excellent explanation of this in his *Considérations sur l'histoire de France,* which appeared with his *Récits des temps mérovingiens,* as a sort of complement and double of his *Lettres* of 1820–27. By 1840 the battle has been won, political polemics are no longer the order of the day, and the narrative history of the classical ages, which had the public's favor in 1820, is now out of fashion. Putting aside diatribes for a more popular genre, Thierry calmly draws up an overview of the "fundamental theories and great systems of the history of France"—a summing-up that is solid and systematic enough to be considered a foundation of its genre, the first real history of the history of France.[37] He stresses forcefully, in passing, the debt of the "new historical school" and his own to "the great tradition of pre-revolutionary scholars." This leads him to characterize the difference in viewpoints he describes, in a favorite simile, to "the prodigious transformations in power and society which have taken place before our very eyes." "The unprecedented events of the last fifty years," he writes,

> have led us to see the essence of things between the lines of chronicles, to extract from the writings of the Benedictines what those learned men did not see, or what they saw in a partial and incomplete fashion, unable as they were to reach conclusions, or grasp the scope of it. They lacked the knowledge and understanding of great social transformations. They poured over laws, public actions, judicial forms, and private contracts with great curiosity; with surprising wisdom they discussed, classified, and analyzed texts, sifting truth out of falsehood; but the political meaning of it all, what comes alive to the imagination from all of his lifeless writing, society's own self-understanding, all this escapes them, hence the lacunae in and limits of their work.[38]

Fig. 9.2
Ary Scheffer, *Mort de Gaston de Foix à la bataille de Ravenne*. The painting accompanies the "discovery of the past"
called for by historians. Ary Scheffer was the intimate friend and a Charbonnerie companion of Augustin Thierry. At
the Salon of 1824, his picture is alongside *Les Massacres de Chio*, by Delacroix. It was the object of a war critique
by Thiers in *Le Constitutionnel* of September 2, 1824.

Renan will later take up this same argument in defense of Thierry against
attacks on his method by persons "exclusively concerned with the search
for historical sources." There is more than the publication of texts, says
Renan in substance, there is also the lessons to be learned from them. "To
recognize the value of a text is in some sense to discover it. Testimonials
to which former scholars were indifferent have become shafts of light. A
mass of information considered secondary in the seventeenth and eighteenth centuries have taken on, to enlightened critics, unexpected meaning." Following this is the Parthian shot aimed at Guérard and his disciples
in the École des chartes: "How can it be, for instance, that the scholars of
Saint-Germain-des-Prés who have published so many texts of mediocre
value left it to a scholar of our own time [Guérard himself] the task of
editing one of the most precious sources for Frankish history, Irminon's
Polyptique, which they possessed in their library and were perfectly aware
of?" Renan closes with a dictum that sums up our very point: "To open

up a new series of historical insights almost always means creating a series of texts that were previously neglected, or to show in those which were already known what had previously not been seen."[39]

This is the neatest condensed expression one could desire of the dimensions of the problem. No doubt the historians of 1820, more or less improvising their craft, did not advance our exact knowledge of the past by bringing sources to light; but they set up the intellectual program on the basis of which the analysis of sources took off to an extent that cannot be compared to the achievements of its initial phase—right down to us, for we will venture to suggest that later revolutions in the historical discipline proceeded in fact with reference to these original programmatic schemes as opposed to understandings of historical practice judged incomplete and unsatisfying in comparison. When in this respect a writer like Michelet, looking back on his itinerary, dates his beginning, almost, from the archival beginnings of his program, we should not be fooled by this. The beginning is in fact a culmination. It is up to us to recover the conditions in which the discovery of France, which led him to the archives, took shape. Why Cousin? Why Vico? What leads a person to take a sudden turn from the philosophy of history to historical work? What can be learned from history through contact with the constraints of didactic ordering? How, in what sense, does one become a historian by writing a modest *Précis d'histoire moderne* for use in the classroom? Between the theoretical trigger and the pedagogical fallout, this particular course has dual exemplary value. It could not be more representative of the more general conversion experience that led a generation to the practice of the factual via the logic of feelings and ideas.

There is the originality of those "ten years of which France had seen no equal," as Thierry puts it. This originality resides entirely in the circumstantial lag between the level of the technical approach to history and the level of interpretation. Thanks to this lag we are in possession of the unique corpus of a prelude to history as science that starkly reveals the intellectual conditions for the approach to the past within which we still function. Thierry's *Lettres* may stand for the memory of this entire movement. They start things off in the summer of 1820—at the end of that year, Guizot begins his course on the origins of representative government, which marks the real beginning of his career as a historian; the next year sees the publication of the first three volumes of Sismondi's *Histoire des français*; the commemoration machine has been started up. The *Lettres* remain the central manifesto making clear what was intended and at stake in this movement. They stress the central phenomenon of this epistemic transformation, which is also its main paradox: the subordination of outlooks to national ambitions, and the apparently unnatural alliance of "patriotism and science" that results—for that is the problem we face in the rise of history as science over the course of the nineteenth century. Far from being ushered in by the disinterested quest for truth, critical rigor, and the positivistic quest for certainty, the rise of history as science is on the contrary closely linked to the passions of national spirit; knowledge is conquered here over the concerns that underlie it and make for its existence. Thierry, after all, made himself into the human memory of the movement to which he was the first to lend his voice. From the preface of *Dix ans d'études historiques* to the *Considérations sur l'histoire de France* he made himself the historian of this memorable quest for the key to the past. But while it is perfectly legitimate to consider his book as the emblematic monument of a fertile period in the history of history, it would be absurd to consider it in isolation. It makes sense only as part of a vast sequence of works whose end point and fermata is Michelet's *Introduction à l'histoire universelle*, written right after the July Revolution. The revelation of the nation—begun in 1814, brought to fruition in 1820—attains its final form and full, if speculative, expression in this 1831 breathless celebration of "our glorious fatherland" becoming "the pilot of the ship of humanity." With the full development of the idea of a national individuality and personality the phase of preliminary work comes to an end. A mechanism is now in place for a fully effective articulation of "narrative" and "system," to use the terms of the 1833 preface to the *Histoire de France*. This brings to completion the operational synthesis that organically links the three operations: establishing, presenting, and understanding events. The new understanding of the past is given form by and is founded upon the conjoining of these three activities. Thierry's book remains the best instance of this cauldron gradually melting into a single substance of discourse and strategy the contributions of literature, the demands of scholarship, the resources of philosophy, and the lessons of politics. This is only a link, but the most solid link in the chain. We wish to consider the whole process through these twenty-five letters *to serve as an introduction to the history of France*, as the subtitle has it. At one end, the renewal of the power of narrative thanks to the historical novel; at the other, the renewal of critical perspectives thanks to the philosophy of history; in between, as a condition of their coming together, the rise of a new way of presenting collective embodiments, a rise dictated by historical circumstances but which continues today to produce the symbolic framework from which jointly proceed both our view of political legitimacy and our understanding of change: these are the axes of the field we must map out.

We can only account for the emergence of the idea of *total history*— for that is another term for this history written from a national point of view—in the very terms of *total history,* by grasping at one end the shift in structure that underlies social and political events, and at the other the most elaborate intellectual products within the depth of collective experience. To such an extent are we the heirs of what happened during those ten fruitful years, that we can only make sense of it by reinventing the interpretive framework of which they witnessed the emergence, and then applying it back onto that period. Today, the key to total history is political—now that politics has been rediscovered as the deepest level of organization of human communities, having once been confined, and dismissed, as the foam at the surface of events. At the heart of the process of which our historians are such an intrinsic part lies the irresistible triumph and definitive installation of the national form as basis of and framework for the operation of democratic societies—a form within which the irreversible triumph of democracy will proceed over the course of the century. The preface to the *Introduction à l'histoire universelle* is dated April 1, 1831. That very same month de Tocqueville sets sail for America, convinced of the inevitability of the drive toward social equality. And indeed, something had happened, a crucial transformation that cannot be equated with tangible effects, not even with the July Revolution, which for contemporaries stood as unquestionable proof of change. Certainly, the July Revolution capped the reshuffling of symbolic markers of political identity with which 1789 began. Certainly, in this respect a crucial step was taken in the shoring up of democratic forms, inasmuch as form always precedes and determines function. Once the implicit evidence of the subjective structuration of social consciousness was taken for granted, political struggle consists for the most part in the laborious, groping, but irresistible alignment of explicit rules of collective existence with their hidden foundations. Only once this focus has been identified is it possible to shed direct light, without oversimplifying one level or another, upon the origins of the reorientation of meaning that made this revolution a revolution in the view of the past—whether in the case of the perception (and conservation) of the past through the monuments and documents that bear witness to it, of its critical reconstruction, or of its evocation or restoration in the appropriate terms. The creation of archives as we understand them, the constitution of a historical corpus, a new approach to deciphering texts, and a new form of presentation—all of these march forward in lockstep. These are all intimately related—neither as consequences nor as causes but as other aspects of a single phenomenon—to the subterranean but central political mutation of the 1820s and 1830s through which society came to understand itself solidly and totally in the guise of a nation. This is the original nexus of scholarly history as we practice it, the commemorative tangle of memory, which the name and writings of Thierry offer us a chance to untangle.

II

1820: Thierry is twenty-five. His young age must be noted. The reform of history can in some ways be equated with a generational upsurge. Thierry belongs to the youngest stratum, made up of those born in the waning or the aftermath of the Revolution (Mignet in 1796, Thiers in 1797, Michelet in 1798, and Quinet in 1803), as opposed to the doctrinaire elders born before the Revolution (Barante in 1782, Guizot in 1787; the Genevan Sismondi, who will remain a somewhat marginal forerunner, is older, born in 1773). The two future greats of the famous academic year 1828 (besides Guizot)—the literary critic Villemain and the philosopher Cousin—provide a link between the two cohorts (Villemain was born in 1790, Cousin in 1792). To some degree their ability to break new ground derives from the freedom their age allows them with respect to the haunting foundational event: they are the first to be able to consider the Revolution and its consequences from a distance, to locate themselves as the heirs of its causes and consequences.

In 1820 Thierry had been an independent polemicist for three years, having distanced himself from the comte de Saint-Simon, whose secretary and collaborator he had been since 1814, to the point of earning the title of "adopted son."[40] With his newly minted *licence* in letters, he had been named for the school year starting in 1813 seventh-grade (*cinquième*) teacher at Compiègne. Thanks to the new École normale meritocracy (Thierry belonged to its second graduating class while Cousin, the eponymous *normalien*, graduated first in the first class in 1810), this brilliant child of the lowest provincial bourgeoisie had access to academic training.[41] Thierry kept completely silent in later life on the subject of his work in collaboration with the eccentric prophet of industrialization. But it should be taken account of if only to correct the overly one-sided impression of the man as he described himself, the folksy historian. Thierry's interest in history initially came out of the philosophy of history, of speculations about the destiny of European societies, and "the direction so clearly inscribed in the course of events over the last six centuries" and its culmination in the new "order of things" characterized by "commercial government."[42] In fact he is often held responsible for the initial turn to economic thought taken by the author of *Mémoire sur la science de l'homme*, along with his new liberal orientation. And it is in fact the case that his writings in this period are clearly marked with the influence of economistic assumption, which he drew especially from the work of J. B. Say.[43] This will completely disappear in later years. But it has a lot to tell us about the conceptual genesis of the new history. One of the latter's most original aspects is its vision of the productive aspects of the future that it implies. The new history understands productivity as a "spontaneous movement," one "whose principle resides in the mass which moves freely, propelled by its own force," as Thierry writes in an article in *L'Industrie*.[44] History is in this manner linked to the liberal revolution in conceptions of society. As he comes to depict the struggle for freedom of "the greater and most overlooked portion of the nation," Thierry has not forgotten what he learned from his intellectual exposure to utopian socialism.

While he breaks with Saint-Simon, he remains in similar circles by joining the editorial staff of the *Censeur européen*, a highly visible vehicle for the liberal and industrialist opposition, which had noisy clashes with censors and the governing establishment.[45] Thierry may have come into contact there with Auguste Comte, who replaced him at Saint-Simon's side, and who was on the newspaper's staff when it became a daily in 1819. It was in this newspaper that Thierry published his first historical essay, highly typical of Restoration-era interests: "Vue des revolutions d'Angleterre." Its originality is its attempt to demystify the English model, the famous "mixed government" praised by the many authors who were pushing a liberal "English"-style reading of monarchy based on the charter. And Thierry does relate that he felt at the time "some disgust for English institutions which seemed [to him] at the time to lean more to aristocracy than to liberty."[46] This is why he also takes the trouble in 1853 to rebut retrospective suspicions that he was a Republican. He says that he was "without prejudice in favor of any form of government," and describes as his political beliefs "aversion for military government along with hatred for aristocratic pretensions, but with no real revolutionary inclinations. I looked forward with enthusiasm to the future, though I knew not what it would be, to a form of freedom whose definition, if I had to give one, would be as follows: any government with the greatest number of individual safeguards and the least possible governmental power."[47] In sum, radical liberalism, but prudent on the subject of government, which places him alongside the "La Fayettists," to the left of the Doctrinaires and Guizot with whom, it is said, he nearly had a falling out because of politics.[48] From the start he appropriates from one of his favorite fields of study, English history, and one of his great themes, the seminal theme in his work, conquest. This is the idea that gives him critical instrument to use against the worshippers of the English constitution with its checks and balances. It was not the result of a political plan. It came out of protracted struggles following a primal event: the taking of land and men by the Normans in the eleventh century.

This idea comes from the opposite side of the spectrum, from the comte de Montlosier, an original and independent intellectual warrior whose blunt feudal-sounding positions, reviving the old theme of inva sions and conquests and bringing them back to the center of public debate, will paradoxically bestow upon the liberal party one of its main polemical tools. It could be argued on several grounds that it was Montlosier's *Monarchie française* of 1814 that triggered the Restoration's renewal of history writing.[49] There are striking passages in the *Considérations* of 1840 in which Thierry ponders the mechanism of appropriation whereby the repression of 1816 imposed Montlosier's harsh views pitting the old and new people of France against one another: "It was there that you could see, from one age to the next, reflections of the current division between parties . . . this view of France condemned by its own history to form two opposing, irreconcilable rival camps, struck the imagination as something grave and prophetic. The theory of national duality stoked both of the opposing camps, that of the Revolution and that of the Charter, with allusions and phrases."[50] The main lines of Thierry's oeuvre are present in seed in the work of this nonconformist member of the party of tradition, a man whose very hatred of modern society bestowed on him a visionary understanding of its origins and components, thus allowing him to escape the narrowness of his intellectual clan. Montlosier read French history not only in terms of social antagonisms rooted in ethnic differences, but also in terms of the importance of the freeing of *communes* (towns), which he places at the heart of his story, and more generally of the pivotal role conferred on the continuous rise of the Third Estate. "He was the first," Thierry writes, summing up, "to have a sharp understanding of the origins of the modern social order, and the first to understand the true importance of the twelfth century as the time of a revolution which engendered all of those which followed."[51] Having experienced 1789, Montlosier radicalizes the stance of previous exponents of aristocratic reaction, especially Boulainvilliers. He does not stop at sharply denouncing the leveling of activities of the monarchy; he categorically states its responsibility in the origins of the Revolution: "Let us not condemn too bitterly the sovereign people," he writes for instance, "it only completed the prior work of the sovereigns. It followed faithfully the road laid out for two centuries by the kings, parlements, and men of law."[52] He thereby introduces a theme that will run through two restorations, culminating as we know in Tocqueville's treatment of it: the intrinsically revolutionary nature of the absolutists' program.[53]

But that which in Montlosier is conceived of and expressed in the language and the spirit of the eighteenth century gets filtered in Thierry's work through the new perception of social dynamics he owes to his liberal background. Where his aristocratic initiator and adversary relates, from a distance, a centuries-long war, explaining its different incarnations, he gropes through the history of the conquerors and the conquered in search of the very motor of historical change. This search colors his later studies in the same vein, extending this first attempt. It inspires, for instance, some telling remarks on the key problem of the "great man" in his review of Villemain's *Cromwell*. He takes advantage of his defense of and thoughts upon that work to launch a significant attack upon those who dote upon "great characters," who weep at "royal misfortunes," and otherwise celebrate the genius of "empire buildings." "The English Revolution is not about Charles Stuart and Oliver Cromwell," he writes, "it is about the English people and freedom . . . what are the personal misfortunes of the English people? What is Cromwell's cunning, compared to the great idea of freedom?"[54] "Cromwell," he writes elsewhere, "is not the hero of his own story."[55] History makes great men; in other words, great men do not make history. In 1820 he will reassert the need to stand things on their head, fully aware of what this break with tradition implies: "It is a singular fact that historians persist in granting no spontaneous agency or independent thought to the mass of humanity. If an entire people emigrates and makes a new home for itself, chroniclers and poets will say that some hero took it in his head to found a new empire; if new customs come about, some legislator will have dreamt them up and imposed them; if a town takes shape, it was brought into being by a prince: always the people, citizens, are the stuff of which a single man's thought is made."[56] Instead of idealizing origins, he suggests, let us realistically consider interests. "Do you really want to know who created an institution, inspired a collective undertaking? Look to those who needed it." Instead of assuming the designs of a single man, let us plumb the depths of the human masses. In this design, political and intellectual interests come together. Making sense of historical change involves giving ancestors to the common people, bringing back to historical life, as he puts it in the first *Letter* in the *Courrier Français*, "the largest and most overlooked part of the nation."

This is where one grasps the extent to which the new historical consciousness belongs to the liberal-democratic phenomenon, understood not as the basis for a party but as a dynamic agent, the axis along which modern societies develop. What is at stake in this self-interested change in scholarly focus from the top to the bottom of society is the shift from one system of thought to another, which itself cannot be separated from a change in social perspectives. The assumption that innovation proceeds from an exceptional person is neither class prejudice, poetic convention, nor myth-hungry innocence; rather, it fits into the logic of an understanding and mapping of the world in which the ordering principle comes from outside and above humanity—dictated by the gods, expressed through tradition, inscribed in nature. In terms of politics, this means that collective being inheres ideally in the person in power, uniting in his body both invisible legitimacy and visible power, and thus linking the chain of the living to divine wisdom through the ruler's command. This means, in terms of an understanding of the course of events, that there is no history in the sense that humans do not shape their world but, when great events affect the state of empires—that is, when vicissitudes within an unchanging order alter or displace elements of its configuration—such events are understandable only when fully related to the designs of an individual who founds, designs, or legislates. Within a universe whose substantial economy is neither produced nor affected by humankind, change can only be understood as the product of the will of men who are causal agents, set apart from the common run of humanity.

This is the principle giving coherence of the familiar history of events focused on great men, which historical reformers have tried periodically to exorcise since the 1820s. And with good reason, since its legacy will weigh heavily long after its basis was undermined by democratic revolution. Not that the latter should be considered an absolute beginning. One could trace back to the sixteenth century the succession of shocks opening cracks in this understanding of human temporal affairs, and that enriched the latter with contributions increasingly in tension with its basic economy. It is, however, a revolution in understanding when the idea of power as the keystone of society, keeping the latter closely united with its intangible ordering principle, is irrevocably replaced in people's minds with an idea of power as the embodiment and instrument of society, itself launched on a quest for progress. The political revolution consecrating in people's minds the legitimacy of representation must sooner or later give birth to a retrospective historical revolution—the very one that Thierry's work announces. What we perceive at the top proceeds from the bottom of society, expressing its tendencies. Far from being an originator, the "great man" is an end point, the quintessential reflection of his era and his people. Alongside deliberate, thoughtful political action is a whole level of activity taking place in the depths of civil society as the result of a convergence of private initiatives. The pattern of change is much broader than the transformations explicitly pursued in the context of public political institutions; it proceeds at least as much from the slow and humble gestation to which each one of us contributes.

It is clear that this change in political outlook carries the seeds of a dramatic widening and deepening of historical analysis. This movement has nourished, down to our own time, periodic restokings of the knowledge of the past. The bourgeois historians of the Restoration, involved in celebrating the saga of the middle classes, will only make a shallow dent in the mines they opened. Their own criticism of their predecessors' narrow-mindedness will be turned against them by their successors.

Drawing on their very initial intuitions, others extend their scope beyond the overexposed theater of political life, delving deeper into the depths of the material existence of the masses, descending to the darkest level of the slowest, least tangible evolutions to look beyond the elite of "industry and talent," which Thierry claimed as his own, to those actors who have been forgotten, neglected, or rejected. It must be stressed that this reconfiguration of historical projects, which we ourselves have not yet exhausted, goes hand in hand with the advent of liberal and representative values whose effects begin to be noticed around 1820 in connection with a new understanding of the relationship between power and society. In very broad terms they yield an increasingly accurate account: a deeper and broader understanding of society as a productive power, and the greatest possible inclusion of historical actors. In other words the same dynamic broadens and democratizes the object of history, both carried by the rising tide of democracy and contributing to it.

But however fruitful the consequences of this liberal shakeup, it is not alone in creating the new history. It transforms the understanding of historical forces; it does not change either its rhetoric or its standard of proof. It remains compatible, at least in its first incarnation, with a classically philosophical style that consists in "abstracting from the narrative a corpus of coherent proofs and arguments in order to lay out a summary demonstration rather than to narrate in detail."[57] The hegemony of this philosophical style of exposition is indeed striking in the first wave of historical reform, in the works, say, of Sismondi or Guizot. And in fact Guizot initially publishes his *Essais sur l'histoire de France* in 1823 as a preface to one of the classics in that genre, Mably's *Observations sur l'histoire de France*. These are works whose argumentative orientation leaves little room for local color. The tenor of the analysis, on the other hand, fully reflects his new course. The work is even perfectly clear as to its central point: the historian's task is to explain institutions in light of social arrangements they derive from, not to explain society as resulting from institutions. "Research on the status of lands," writes Guizot, "must precede that on the status of persons. A knowledge of different social conditions and relationships is necessary in order to understand political institutions. To understand different social conditions one must know the nature of property and property relations."[58] The same cannot be said of Sismondi, in whose work the weight of the philosophical legacy is heavier, including in the understanding of society. What is new in his book is the plan to study *the French*, all of the nation's components beyond the "kings, lords, and prelates" of traditional historical narrative, while working to draw out the unity, the "life principle" connecting facts to one another.[59] At the same time, despite this goal, he remains hostage to a political context he understands within a new framework, but to which he remains faithful for a basic, and quite traditional, reason: he continues to believe that the "condition of peoples" is a "great outcome of public institutions."[60] These striking ambiguities make him interesting as a transitional figure, while illuminating the intellectual stakes of this transition.

One additional factor was needed to crystallize Thierry's militant plans for a recasting of the historian's task in its conception, object, and presentation; we will call it, for want of a better term, "the discovery of the past as past." This was a double discovery, taking place via both scholarship and fiction: on the scientific side the discovery of the poetry of sources, and on the artistic side of the truth of narration. As we have seen it was in the first months of 1820, as he tells it, that Thierry encounters the great Benedictine collections. The novel scholarship in his articles at the time testifies to this encounter. In contemporary political warfare, the theme of "the social antagonism of the Franks and the Gauls" is at its zenith. And in this same year 1820, Guizot will produce one of its most brilliant orchestrations in his oppositional manifesto, *Du Gouvernement de la France depuis la restauration et du ministère actuel* (Paris, 1820).[61] The powerful reasons impelling the "plebeian champions of the people's rights" to appropriate the ultra-aristocratic theme of the two peoples, in either Boulainvillier's or Monlosier's version (forget their differences), becomes ever clearer. When wielded against a static, hierarchical representation of relationships of domination, which allowed for only those masters with a great name to rule over the mixed, confused, and indifferent mass of the servile, the thesis of subjection through conquest awards the vanquished not only the dignity of a people in its own right, but also, and especially, the energy and collective agency of a historical actor able to sustain a plurisecular struggle. The two-nations theory does more than just answer the need to represent concretely the political struggle by awarding it a substance and a rationale drawn from the very sources of the nation; it also provides, eminently, the means of conceiving of social action on the bases of autonomous agency and of the specific strengths and interests of its different components.

Thus it was Thierry's effort to add to his panoply of polemical arguments that led him back from the classic historians to the primary documents. A series of references to Du Cange's *Glossaire*, to Dom Bouquet's *Recueil des historiens*, to the collections of charters and diplomas of Brequigny, which he marshals in support of an allegorical "Histoire de Jacques Bonhomme" published in the spring of 1820, testify to this delving into the sources.[62] Thierry's curiosity is in step with a growing interest among the public, since at the same time the Petitot collection begins to publish a translation of part of the very texts he went looking for in the Benedictine collections. But scientific progress radically alters the neophyte's point of view; it leads to a conversion. Thierry finds his calling as a historian by discovering the past's difference, the interest it presents in itself in all of its aspects, independently of the inductions that can be derived from it, and the intrinsic pleasure to be gotten from its very strangeness.

This feeling born from having truck with original relics of the past is all the more effective if it can be buttressed by the sort of writing that can evoke this perceived strangeness. The historical novel is at hand to reveal a technique allowing one to explore what the sources suggest. The "Histoire veritable de Jacques Bonhomme," an allegory of the conquest, is published in the *Censeur européen* on May 12, 1820; soon following it on May 27 is an enthusiastic review of a novel about the conquest, *Ivanhoe*. "A man of genius, Walter Scott, has just given us a real look at the events disfigured by modern phraseology. . . . It is a novel he has chosen to shed light on this major historical event, and to represent the Norman conquest in a fresh, living manner, after the scholarly narrators of the last century, less accurate than the illiterate medieval chroniclers, had elegantly buried it under such banal formulations as *succession, gouvernement, mesure d'État*, of *conspirations reprimées, pouvoir*, and *soumission sociale*."[63] A whole run of Walter Scott's novels had been translated since 1816, but only with *Ivanhoe* did he become *the* fashionable writer, dragging in the wake of his success a massive vogue for historical novels culminating, according to its best historian, in 1827, the year when the planned *Lettres sur l'histoire de France* attains its completion.[64] This parallel trajectory should be noted, although we should not read too much into it. It is a fact that the credibility of the science of the past in the eyes of a broad public cannot be separated, in this period, from the avid fascination triggered by the literary recreation of the past. A history one wants to know is a history one likes to imagine.

It is in this respect that the reform of historical study goes hand in hand with romanticism's aesthetic transformation (for which the year 1820 also provides a conspicuous marker: the March publication of Lamartine's *Méditations poétiques*). On a more intellectual level, it would not be out of line to argue that the "Scottian" novel was a vehicle through which the traditionalist current discreetly left its mark on liberal historiography, which was otherwise ill disposed to welcome it explicitly and ill informed of its scholarly implications, as was the case in German juridical Romanticism.[65] Whether or not there was an influence, in any case what matters is the convergence of sensibilities revealed in the ability to admire unreservedly a novelist for whom resurrecting the past is a means of evoking, in opposition to the deadly coldness of democratic geometry, a fruitful continuity over time, "the price and beauty of an organic set of traditions," the vital activity and genius of peoples over centuries that finds expression, in fact, in the irregular and picturesque aspects of history.[66] That which in France can only mean a subversive appeal to the people against a power that does not represent it elsewhere reads as a long-lived coincidence between a people and its laws and traditions, in opposition to a foreign attempt to codify or transform it (as will typically occur in Germany). These are two versions of the same upheaval that now has the motor of historical change running low, in the depths of the population, and making political legitimacy dependent upon the governors' ways of expressing popular will. A single abstract scheme, which in practical terms can result in opposite embodiments, will spawn two divergent views of the nation: one liberal and progressive, which emphasizes the conceptual difference between society and polity, and the need to bring about, and even deepen, the representative relationship between a people and its government; the other conservative and historicist, stressing both the need to develop and preserve tradition and to reinforce the organic union between sovereign and people.[67] One must keep in mind this common foundation concealed under opposing ideological expressions in order to understand how opposing cultural orientations came nonetheless to produce at the same time such similar works and, for instance, the same type of history. The divergence in political ideals does not stand in the way of a convergence in intellectual programs. Hence the strange interconnections, the misunderstandings and misperceptions on both sides, and the opposing uses of the same themes. When Thierry's close friend Fauriel, certainly one of the men best acquainted in France with German philological developments, celebrates, through the *Chants populaires de la Grèce*, a poetry "which lives in the people itself, drawing from the people's very life," and making for "a direct and true expression of national spirit," he is simply twisting into a liberal and philhellene direction a theme typical of counterrevolutionary romanticism.[68] The same goes for Guizot's use of Savigny's *Histoire du droit romain pendant le Moyen-Âge*.[69] Michelet will do no different when adapting to his own vision of the symbolic powers of the people the unprogressive *Antiquités du droit allemand*.[70] The unanimous passion of young patriots in 1820 for the author of *Ivanhoe* is a striking illustration of this singular phenomenon of double meaning in which opposite meanings are derived from the same thing: the patriots hope to draw from the past weapons against a regime that seeks to anchor its legitimacy in tradition, while the novelist exploits the wealth of tradition as a worthy follower of Burke, in opposition to equality and democracy. If he shows any interest in the little people, it is as "those who do not change," and if he shows any interest in crowds, it is in order to have them drown out the unwarranted pretensions of individuals; all the while, his Parisian admirers read into this a rehabilitation of commoners and a recognition of the historical role of the masses. But in spite of these discordances, both sides are involved in the same shift in the paradigms presiding over the perception and understanding of the past.

In Thierry's case, beyond the reasons he shared with others, enthusiasm for the novelist results from both very personal and technical causes. The poet offers what the historian is seeking. Fiction presents him with ready-made literary means for resurrecting the past at the very moment when the polemicist going over to scholarship gets a glimpse of the living truth waiting to be resurrected from the tomb of ancient texts. It is one thing to conceive of, another to recreate, to *show* these "masses of men" and these "different lives," to *make people see* the characteristics of a period, to make the details speak. Scott completes Thierry's revelation to himself by showing him a means of expression adapted both to the needs of a collective imagining of the causes of change, and to the new demand for a representation of temporal distance. By crisscrossing a series of individual destinies, the historical novel can stage the play of collective forces. Thus, in *Ivanhoe* Cedric de Rotherwood is the "representative of Saxon liberties," while other characters embody the victors, and still others, inspired by the political state of the country, "portray the beliefs of the age."[71] Alongside this ability to read the general into the particular, the dramatization makes the whole portrayal come alive by means of telling details.

What matters here is probably less the historical novel as such than the general economy of signification, and the corresponding discursive technique it entails. What appears in the context of fiction and on the subject of history is a mode of discourse based on the exemplary and the representative individual, whether around a concrete fact or an episode, the biography of one person, or the destiny of a nation; each, in its own way, can take on a universal level of meaning. In human affairs, the universal no longer derives from the decanting, the filtering of particularities: it remains attached to them, it speaks through them. The very framework of any exposition or narration is, as a result, radically changed. The appearance of the historical novel will have been the first sign of a shift in the regime of symbolicity, a change that affected the whole relationship between discourse and reality. And this is a transitional phenomenon, splitting into two separate branches. The historical novel undid itself by giving birth to, on the one hand, a new type of novelistic writing, and on the other a new form of historical exposition. It resolved its own constitutive and creative ambiguity, its recreation of the past through a fiction, its way of, to quote Manzoni, "representing through invented action the state of humanity in a past historical period,"[72] by separating out acknowledged fiction from the truth of the past pursued for its own sake. But it is precisely this effort to restore the very substance of the past that

spawned the techniques for evoking the real that make us interested in an endless inventory of places and lives in the great novels of a Balzac. But it was within fiction, and deriving from the artist's concern to speak to the imagination, that a discursive mechanism took shape that could accommodate the endless accounting through which our approach to the past gains constantly in both sharpness and objectivity. In ways that cannot be separated, both the longing and the ambition to capture the past gave rise to a new poetics, and this new poetics made possible a grasp of the real.

Not that this seminal exchange between poetry and truth should be pressed into the service of skepticism. Bringing to light the rhetorical foundations of scholarship does not in itself constitute a challenge to historical objectivity. To note the indisputable overlapping of, on the one hand, the birth of the realist novel through new techniques, and on the other, the reinvention of historical narration, in no way allows one to reduce the latter to a variant of fiction whose supreme cunning would be to claim its own status as "truth" in opposition to the imitation of truth in its novelistic homologue.[73] We are not trying to argue that the historian "borrows" the novelist's discursive tools and ends up unconsciously, and misleadingly, writing "fiction." Rather, what the historian encounters in the historical novel is a new form of storytelling that is itself but is also the most elaborate expression of a more general shift in the articulation of signs and objects. The historian is confronted, as it were, with a pristine example of a concrete and organized staging of what he knows as disorder (such as the separate, concrete data revealing differences over time), what he understands only in the abstract (the impersonal nature of the forces driving historical change), and which gives him hope in the possibility of a much broader and more evocative use of what he does and can know, giving him a chance to create the rhetorical means to enlarge the domain of scholarship to the proportions of what artists may claim. For what is going on is not a simple transformation from one domain to the other, although developments were sufficiently parallel for Thierry who, finishing his *Conquête de l'Angleterre* in 1824, inquired through Fauriel, a common friend with Manzoni, of the progress of Manzoni's *Fiancés*, writing very much like a man wondering about the future of his own work: "Tell him from me," he writes, "that I have a great desire to see his book in order to make up my mind about historical novels and perhaps even try something in that style."[74] Historical writing is being completely recast, not only with respect to narrative specifically, but also in light of this other form of expression and its double power to evoke the distance between past and present, and the presence of an entire period with its own concerns behind every actor, all behavior, and each turn of the plot.

The historical novel imitates, within the realm of art, the reconciliation of fact and idea; it will be up to the specialists to authenticate facts and establish their meaning. It offers a model to Thierry for instance when he writes, "Such and such an event, whose character was long misunderstood, once truthfully presented can shed new light on the history of several centuries . . . the uprising of Laon and the civil wars of Rheims, presented unadorned, will have more to say about the origin of a Third Estate which many believe crawled out from underground only in 1789."[75] This is also Michelet's objective, in his didactic *Précis de l'histoire moderne*, when he lays out in the preface the means to an end that, while modestly pedagogical, nonetheless implies a fundamental innovation in historical writing: "first of all to record, through a broad and simple narrative, the dramatic unity in the last three centuries; then to show all of the intermediate notions not through abstractions but through characteristic events which will speak to youthful imaginations. They should be few in number but also well chosen so as to stand for all the others, in such a way that the succession of facts will give children a series of images, and mature adults a chain of ideas."[76] And God knows, the perfecting of a means of expression capable of balancing overall meanings with discrete facts was laborious and hesitant. It would be an exaggeration to call it a battle over narrative, but it did cause divisions among the historians of the 1820s. The names of Thierry and Michelet could, for that matter, be used as symbols of the two poles around which the most revealing breach opened up: on the one hand the temptation of pure narrative, in which ideas threaten to get lost in picturesque details and the recreation of a tonality of life that is in the end superficial; on the other the temptation of excessive symbolizing, with each fact staggering under the weight of meaning it is made to bear—a "psychomania" that consists of making each fact the sign of an idea, and for which Thierry will, in fact, reproach Michelet for indulging in.[77] The Charybdis of insignificance, and the Scylla of oversignificance. Not that this problem was later resolved: the writing of history continues to feed upon this tension, and to move along its very lines. But a minimal agreement will be reached, if tacitly, to overcome the starkness of this initial dichotomy.

We will return to examine the parameters of the semiotic transformation that, by investing each singular fact with potential meaning, changed the status and range, and thereby the tenor and shape, of any factual exposition, whatever its type and purpose, and whether it's an image or story, truthful or fictional. But we should immediately emphasize the importance of what is at stake in this parallel shift in the status of a "fact" and the way its meaning is used. If one accepts, as the best authorities all suggest, that the birth of history as the discipline we know resides in the convergence of two previously separate traditions—that of antiquarian learning and that of historical narrative and philosophy—we have isolated the exact moment when this difficult union is consummated and becomes indissoluble. What Gibbon and Niebuhr never fully attained, despite their best efforts, not to mention other more timid attempts, comes about thanks to the revolution in the power of signification first attempted within the context of the novel. Within a discourse whose aim is to recreate the substance of the past in a way that makes sense, no fact can fail to take its rightful place, thereby becoming expressive and eloquent. It is up to the historian to discern those that, in Michelet's terms, can serve as "symbols of the others." He will, however, operate within the entire field of learning, with no distinction made, in principle, between specific information of use only to specialists, and general data aimed at the educated public.

This theoretical integration of all of its products within the purview of an expressive use makes for a deep change in the orientation of scholarship. Even when confined to technical work, such as the editing of sources, scholars are now concerned, consciously or not, with possible uses of them that overturn the implicit rules governing a hierarchy of interests, and kept them focused on some matters or documents deemed worthy of study, while excluding others. As a result, potential fields of investigation become prodigiously wider. But change affects no less the scholar writing history, straining to restore a coherent picture. It is no longer possible to abandon to antiquarians the jumbled, detailed knowledge of a period's memorabilia to focus only on that which stands out—great events, famous actions, eminent characters, general institutions, and high achievements—and that illustrate cultural progress and the march of civilization. The men, women, and events that automatically draw the light give access to nothing beyond themselves. Whereas the hidden detail, the fine point buried in shadows, the apparently marginal happenstance can, if their representative quality is used thoughtfully, bring to life a whole segment of the past. No "resurrection" without "critique," to use the terms Michelet brings together. The historian's art implies and draws upon a science. The greater his ambition to evoke the moving tides of the past, the more this demands that he be familiar with the humble, everyday detail, which holds within it the overall meaning.

Hence the strategic importance of problems related to artistry and narrative, in the early days of history-as-science. The seemingly secondary question of the rhetoric of history in fact touches on the very heart of how the discipline is organized, its basic orientation, and the different ways in which it is practiced. Through a "reform in the manner of writing history," what is at stake is indeed a general overhaul of it "as it is studied."[78] It is impossible otherwise to understand the impact and reverberations of a series of polemical articles attacking the most famous historians of the seventeenth century—Mezeray and Veilly—and their principal early nineteenth-century disciple, Anquetil.[79] How otherwise did a declaration of war against "the writers with no learning who saw nothing, and writers without imagination who portrayed nothing,"[80] this being the essence of the first *Letter*, come to represent for contemporaries the promise of a reinvention of both the nature and the purpose of historical knowledge? It is tempting, in retrospect, giving the terrain upon which this battle is being waged, to reduce this assault as a writers' quarrel over a change in literary style: the local color of the romantics against the elevated style of the classicists. But that would mean missing the extent to which, in this case, innovation in narrative renews both the determination and the ordering of historical facts (which facts are the ones that convey meaning?) and their understanding (in what mode does each fact convey meaning?) When Thierry criticizes the separation of narrative and commentary in the work of historians of the philosophical school (he names Robertson and Hume)—their "dissertations placed in the appendix," their "digressions about government, customs, arts, dress, armaments, etc."—and preaches the opposite (the reintegration of the whole set of data into the very body of the narrative), he is not just yielding to the dictates of taste.[81] He is laying out a demand for connections that, in tying the expression of meaning to the minutiae of facts, in effect lays the foundations for a new science— new in the facts it chooses, and new in what it asks of those facts. "It is a false method," says Thierry, "which tends to isolate facts from that which gives them their individual physiognomy and color, and it is impossible for a historian to narrate well without depicting, and to depict without narrating. Those who adopted this manner of writing almost always neglected narrative, which is the core of history, for later commentary which is supposed to yield the key to the narrative. Once you get to the commentary it does not explain anything, because the reader does not connect it to the text from which the writer separated it."[82]

The aim of this new form of narrative (inseparable from it), the aim of this demand to give life to the ups and downs of reality ordered and conveyed by the historian, is an extraordinary amplification of the historian's object. But this cannot be isolated either, since it implies an entirely changed understanding of the nature and aims represented by the narrative's data. It is true, no doubt, that concern with artistry won out, in the work of our authors, over scholarly achievements. But that should not blind us to what this artistic effort contributed to the furthering of science. The progress of science should normally have preceded or at least accompanied the creation of an instrument qualified to convey its results. As it happened, the progress came later. As a result, we can discern all that the emergence of historical understanding as we know it owes to the shaping of a rhetorical framework grafting the ideal onto the material and thus giving a second wind to the positivistic approach to the past. And let us not be misled by the beautiful simplicity of the rhetorical instrument. What we simply call "narrative" derives from a highly elaborate synthesis, bringing together three sets of components whose welding was unlikely: the illumination of history by scholarly precision along with its presentation as an overall picture and a sequential narrative, the relating of events and facts as contingent and their presentation in a graspable framework, and the imagining of history as production and restitution of things as they actually happened.

III

Let us add political circumstances to this spectrum of intellectual factors, and we will be in possession of all of the elements that determined Thierry's calling, and beyond his individual case fed into the gestation of a new science of history over the course of a decade. The passionate editor of the *Censeur européen* was carrying out his initial work in a context of great political tension. The murder of the duc de Berry on February 13, 1820, provoked both an ultrareactionary stiffening of monarchical power in a Europe of princes buzzing with rumors of the lengthening shadow of a vast conspiracy against rulers, and a sharp and irreversible polarization of opinion. "1820," Thierry later wrote, "saw the end of hope for a peaceful negotiation between the two parties created by the Revolution, that year saw all hopes being placed in the closer or more distant outbreak of a social crisis."[83] He takes a direct hit himself, since the censors closed down his paper on June 20, just as agitation spreads to the streets, and some of the liberals, including his own mentor La Fayette, start thinking in terms of an uprising. It is in the midst of this effervescence that he asks to join the *Courrier français*, which had been spared on account of its *juste milieu* stance, and publishes, from July 23 to October 18, in the face of censorship and of volleys from the ultraconservative press (they evoked Fréret's imprisonment and called for a "salutary rigor"), nine memorable articles that sketch out his program of "renovation of national history."[84] The plan never got off the ground. While he has a following of thoughtful readers, he also comes up against the indifference of a public of provincial subscribers, resistant to a science whose patriotic implications escape them. The vogue for history is only just beginning. Rather than go back to his previous bent as a polemicist covering a wide range of issues, as the editors of the *Courrier* urged him to, Thierry decides to abandon journalism. He "vowed to write only, from now on, about historical matters."[85]

But a historian has been born. From now on he devotes himself exclusively to his studies. Armed with his new insights about method, he returns to his original topic; he begins the sifting through documents and research, which will culminate four years later in the *Histoire de la conquête de l'Angleterre*. Rushing from one library to the next, he immerses himself in the evocative magic of documents with a pleasure he describes beautifully, magnified by the nostalgia and stoicism of infirmity, in *Dix ans d'études historiques*. But he does not turn away from political activism; quite the contrary. As an active member of the *Charbonnerie* he tries, after the setbacks of the summer of 1820, to provide the nonlegal opposition with the manpower of a strong secret organization. There too the plan comes to nothing. The execution of the four sergeants of La Rochelle, while it creates unforgettable martyrs in the cause of freedom, also marks the beginning of the movement's reflux. Conditions are not ripe for a victorious uprising. Impatient youths go back to their studies. For those excluded from power the political battle now shifts to the diffusion of ideas and shaping of opinions. The six years of Villèle's ministry (formed on December 14, 1821; it falls January 5, 1828), allow for a fruitful period of political latency and intellectual growth, in which plans and ideas that sprang up around 1820 will flourish triumphantly, make headway among the public, and recreate anew, so to speak, the spirit of the nation outside of the government's range of influence. As early as the summer of 1825, Stendhal notes, "France has progressed immensely in the last four years. Many a book which would have been rejected in 1820 as too difficult to understand is now disdained as superficial." He goes on to add, "We owe this change to Walter Scott, *Ivanhoe* launched the fashion for books like those of Thierry and Guizot, and today a defense of the feudal system written in sentimental jargon would be greeted with laughter."[86] When in 1827 Thierry, riding on the success of his *Conquête*, takes up the quarrel he initiated seven years earlier, sustaining his argument to the end, he wins his case. Additionally, he has sufficient stature to be awarded a pension (since July 1826), not so much to honor the historian as to support him on account of his increasing blindness.[87] His first attack of ataxia took place in the fall of 1824, as he was finishing his book. He needed a secretary to bring it to an end. He will from now on need the eyes of others in order to read, and must dictate instead of writing. He will have time for one more revision of the *Lettres* in 1828, amid a rising tide of liberalism, as his friends and fellow fighters Cousin, Villemain, and Guizot enjoy a triumph in the academy, returned to their teaching positions by the ministry and acclaimed by throngs of supporters. In September, as he ends his work, he is attacked by paralysis, and his blindness becomes complete. He will now be history's Homer—Chateaubriand hails him as such.[88] The glory days of the new historical school are bleak years for him, until the scientific organization instigated by Guizot offers him a second career. Thierry himself later gave a fine depiction of the atmosphere of this time of suspended creativity, of intellectual succession and intense study, all of which became weapons in the political struggle, "in which rest was not oppressive, and deliverance seemed certain." "And so for literature," he reminisces in 1840,

> there was a category of devoted young men to whose ambition it offered the only chance; there was a passionate literary renaissance which public opinion endowed with the same honors and popularity as political opposition. Academia rose to become a real social power, earning ovations and civic laurels, and, a sight which may never return, there were salons where success crowned the most serious speech and the most elevated questions of moral philosophy, history, and aesthetics. History loomed especially large in this intellectual work, and in worldly encouragements. There was a thirst to learn from a past whose shadow was still threatening the whole truth, and that is the origin, for historical studies, of ten years such as France had never seen before.[89]

And this was only the environment for historical reform. This exceptional context does more than just explain the social reasons for this success. It also affected the contents. The program that takes shape in Thierry's mind in the summer of 1820 cannot be understood without reference to the open break between government and society after the retrograde shift of the previous months, a gap that will only open further until the standoff is resolved in July of 1830. If Revolution reappears in 1814, the nation does so in 1820. The nation provides the integrating framework that allows for a dynamic articulation of the other sources of changes in the conception and the writing of history. An assertion of the nation underlies both the unfurling of various possibilities, which occurred to Thierry in an initial flash of understanding, and the general seepage of concern about the past into people's minds, until all of these possible insights found their full expression in Michelet in 1831, after the July illumination revealed them to him.

The *Nation*—defined as a mystical container of sovereignty, an invisible and eternal entity in whose name power is exercised—enters the stage as an independent actor, so to speak, in 1789. It asserts itself as the ultimate source of arbitration. It becomes the symbol of what lies beyond power, embodied in the king's person as he draws legitimacy from it, but sufficiently distinct from him that it can be invoked to ask for modifications in the way power is exercised. Created by the monarchy and long

nurtured in its bosom, long confused with kingship, the national principle comes to escape the monarchs and turn against them. It will end up
beheading them.

It is a dangerous business—one could get lost in it—trying to retrace
even from far above and far away a process that represents no less than
the essence of Western history's most original product over the course of
ten centuries. To do so might overturn the facile formulas whereby politics is identified as a foam on the surface of things, and hiding under its
shimmering mobility are the weighty evolutions at work in the material
depths of the foundations—such formulas come straight, we should note
in passing, from an amplification of the liberal upheaval in understanding,
as we see it entering the historical intelligence of someone like Thierry.
If any process took place over the very long range (one that concerns the
very bases of social life, since it entailed a recasting of the larger picture)
that process is the multisecular gelling of nations as a result of the consolidation of monarchical nuclei as they came out of the feudal world.
This is where a barely discernible revolution was played out, of which
modern political revolutions (but also economic revolutions) are but the
final stage. But we must keep to a few brief points that are necessary to
the understanding of the moment that concerns us. For 1820 is a crucial
moment in the long-term history of the nation. In order to understand
this one must have a basic understanding of the nature of the general phenomenon, and on the singular way it played out in the French context.
This detour is necessary to understand the cognitive effects attached to a
political schema. Without an understanding of the articulation in time of
the nation's growth, we cannot grasp the decisive effects of its unfurling
on the recapturing of the past.

If one had to put it in one sentence, this might be it: the Nation is both
the result and the expression of the transition from a society structured
by subjection to something outside itself, to a society structurally subject
to itself, given the convergence of a religious revolution, a revolution in
political space, and a revolution in social conceptions of time. The roots
of this transformation are religious: they rest upon the appropriation of a
fundamental possibility in Christianity, the uncoupling of celestial order
from order on earth; it embodies the disjunction between self-sufficiency
here on earth and dependency on the hereafter by thoroughly redefining
the relationship between the ideal essence of power and of the political
body. Concretely, this transformation unfolds along two great axes: a
spatial logic and a temporal dynamic; whence the appearance, under two
different guises, of the subjective form of the social. The monarchy will
inexorably undermine its own foundation on both sides, gradually giving
shape, via its own rootedness in space and via its settling down over time

to the two images of *representative* power that will eventually subvert any form of personal power. The history of traditional monarchy comes down to the history of the gestation of both impersonal power and a national framework, in the very bosom of power incarnate—under conditions, those brought about by French absolutism in its particular guise, which do much to explain not only why the end took place as a sharp rupture, but also the enduring difficulty in later stabilizing representative government in the country.

The Nation was born of a territorialization of power that shaped its nature, outlook, and goals. The logic of expansion, directed to a conquering unification of the world, gave way to a logic of territorial circumscription; a dynamic power gave way to a deep-seated power in which the sovereign's efforts are directed at bringing the body of the population, within the country's limits, to a full correspondence with his own. The universal form of social bonds needs particular boundaries in order to come into existence. Representative power first originates in this shift: it changes from being the symbolic incarnation of subjection to an extrinsic law to becoming the administrative agent of the internal fit between the political community and its own constitutive laws. In other words, this is where the monarchy branches off, through its own administrative apparatus, toward its own demise. It gestures, in its own activity, to a system of laws that undermines it. It brings about, against itself, the conditions for a radical conception of collective sovereignty that demands the complete return of power to the social body, and the abolition of what obligation is left to an exterior principle embodied in the king. The path from territorial nation to national sovereignty is more direct than it seems.

But a second source for the creation of collective subjectivity was no less decisive in bringing about the shape of the nation and the redefinition of power as representative: the injection of religious time into human institutions. Timelessness was among the most basic aspects of Western identity. It is one of the most important factors shaping our understanding of public affairs, and has weighed heaviest on our understanding of collective behavior. The secret behind its effectiveness resides in a strange alchemical formula: time gives birth to persons. The indefinite continuity of the function in contrast to the persons who fulfill it in succession tends to make that function into a self-sustaining entity, more real in its own way than the people serving it precariously, who are secretly marked as anonymous despite the honors their role confers. In the same way, the permanence of a collective body in contrast to the persons composing it, who are born and die, makes for its recognition as a transcendent reality endowed with its own consistency. The investment of timelessness in

public roles and social bodies thus casts those who hold power and authority in the role of representatives or servants of entities that, albeit invisible,
loom above them as the true and eternal driving forces of positions that
are only briefly occupied. The mortal king is but the temporary incarnation of a royal dignity that itself never dies. And similarly, while the
mortal members of the political body appear and disappear in a continual
renewal, the political body itself lives on, unchanging in its invisible same-
ness to itself. There appear, as a result, beyond creatures of flesh and blood,
angelic or rather angelomorphic beings, the State or the Nation, virtual
persons since they are endowed with a quasi presence to themselves by
the permanence of their intangible identities over time, and that gradually
assert themselves as the real holders of a legitimacy that can be delegated
to mortals, but that the latter can never really possess. The personification of legitimacy through its timelessness secretly brings about a shift of
power at the origin of the representative principle: power among humans
can be exercised anonymously, but not held personally.

What we have here in its temporal dimension is the same act of self-
divestiture that also derives from the symbolic rooting of power in space.
Within the most typical form of personalized power, the monarchy, appears the shape of radically impersonal power exercised in the name of
those transcendent powers, the State and the Nation, which are its true
possessors. In other words, the king embodies in his political body that
which precisely leads him to his doom as an incarnation. Democratic
revolution represents the triumph of the abstract personification of the
community, over the singular individuality that tied it to a concrete body.
Only then does the Nation, by becoming disincarnate, by breaking with
any holder of personal legitimacy, acquire full subjective transcendence.
Only through regicide does the eternal body of the nation become fully
personal: no longer appropriated or made flesh, it remains only represent-
able. The representation of the political community of the living through
its own will is also the visible representation of the invisible and eternal
Nation. Power is no longer simply the organ through which the political
body that produces it takes deliberate, all encompassing, hold of itself. It is
also the instrument through which this national "person" of which temporary political actors are but representatives of a sort appears and acts. The
rule of the Nation as agent is impossible without a fictional personification. This aspect of democratic sovereignty is both obvious and obscure,
a spectral face both familiar and unacknowledged, without which the
political function of history cannot be understood. The secret key to the
effectiveness of the scheme as a cognitive scheme resides in its temporal
basis. Our science of the past would not exist without this strange melting

Fig. 9.10
Ary Scheffer, *Les Femmes souliotes*. The support of the cause of Greek independence is one of the great sources of inspiration for the culture of the Restoration. In 1826, Ary Scheffer had already proposed a *Missolonghi*. In the 1827 salon (year of the battle of Navarin), he illustrates another famous episode of the war against the Turks: the women of Souli throwing themselves on top of rocks in the Adriatic to escape the Turks, commanded by the pasha of Janina.

pot in which the rock of permanence is born from universal change, and the flow of becoming generates and sustains a subjectivity nobody sees, but that governs us nonetheless.

Within this general framework, we must still determine the specific path through which the years around 1820 became the time when the Nation unleashed its potential as a sign and a science, when thirty years of political activity in its name had not brought about this effect. This means returning to the central originality of this genesis in the French case: its focus on the figure of the monarch. "The Nation has no corporate existence in France. It resides entirely in the person of the King"[90]: Louis XIV's maxim says it all. Instead of taking place as a gradual transition (despite violent conflict at some crucial junctures) as was the case in English parliamentary rule, the transition to modern representation in France meant the breaking of absolutism, the silencing of traditional organic-hierarchical representation, of the Nation as a body whose sovereignty brought together king and grandees (since social superiority included and stood for social inferiority). The English revolution paradoxically produced continuity, one might suggest, by having the modern developments of the expression of the political body extend the ancient formula for sovereignty, "King in Parliament," snatched from the absolutist menace. The French Revolution inherited, by contrast, one and a half centuries later, the main discontinuity introduced by victorious absolutism. It had to deal with the consequences of the change in the principle of power created thanks to the monarch's single-handed appropriation of sovereignty. The thorough recasting of the economy of representation took place, in this context, through a repudiation of ancient forms. In France it was through an extreme individualization of absolute power that the political body regained its constitutive power. And it was the intense personalization of the sovereign's role that ushered in the reign of the State as an abstraction and of the Nation as impersonal. Hence the intensity of contradictions when things came to an end, and the inevitably brutal and radical nature of that ending. Hence also, as has been suggested, the attraction to regicide as a resolution, and the inevitable need to get rid of an embodiment (the king) whose attributes could not easily be restricted. Hence also, given what was tacitly at stake, the extraordinary reverberations of this execution, which cannot really be compared to the English precedent (it signifies the death of a whole world while the English event is a transgression that authorizes, maybe even calls for, a return to the proper order of things). Hence a whole series of consequences that, while they may explain nothing by themselves, like the previous considerations cast a more direct light upon the political process of the Revolution and after.

The weight of origins, the will to create anew, to reconstruct ex nihilo, none of this will keep the dead regime from pursuing and haunting the living one. The foundational legacy of the monarchy will constantly encumber all attempts to set up the opposite form of government whose shadow kingship projected before itself, and will lastingly impede the stabilization of representative government in France. It is as if, in the grips of the seminal model making the impersonal personal and abstraction into embodiment, the sovereign Nation could not manage to shed its body and free itself as invisible and personal difference. Whereas if a distance had been maintained between the body of the Nation and that of the king, this would have introduced some slack between power and society, making it necessary to grasp and ensure a representative fit between them by virtue of their very separation; the unavoidable image of a king carrying in his person the entire Nation will keep political representations confined within the powerful myth of an identification between power and society.

In practice, this need to merge the Nation with its governing institutions will take the shape of two great rival programs, one parlementary, the other authoritarian, programs whose differences should not conceal their common conceptual roots. An attempt could be made, in opposition to monarchical personification, to have the Nation take the king's place, thereby rigorously bringing about the impersonality of power; but while royal sovereignty is beheaded its organizing principle lives on, namely the idea that the entity representing the community *is* the community, which only exists politically, only has a voice and a will through that entity. The consequences of this are very far reaching: the virtual alienation of sovereignty delegated in this manner, since in any procedure to control the fit between the actions of representatives and the wishes of those represented is unthinkable. Hence the danger of parlementary usurpation, which the Revolution will demonstrate constantly, and in many forms. (There were multiple versions of this development, from usurpation in the name of the people to usurpation in the name of Enlightenment and reason, from the fiction of direct democracy to the cynical resorting by the ruling elites to property qualifications: here again, the differences between these expressions should not conceal their common origin.) Or else, at the opposite extreme from this republican route, whether it be radical or moderate, if no internal mechanism can be found to stabilize it, the resigned resort to a repersonification of power, the only way of effectively giving concrete form to the people's sovereignty in a way that makes its operation fully identifiable and readable by seeming to hand it over in its entirety to the sole authority of a providential trustee. In reaction to the headless drifting of an assembly, with its removal from the community's control, the reign of a perfectly individualized will seems the only way to establish, by means of a coercive fit, an explicit marriage between the Nation's will and the government's action. It is thus that Napoleon's dictatorship is profoundly implicated in the Revolution's politics, if one sees it as an attempt to embody exactly the mysterious, uncontrollable sovereignty of the Nation. One could in fact show the ways in which expansionist warfare and revolutionary imperialism are also part of the frenzied unleashing of the national principle, which calls for the realization of the universal in the particular, led astray in this case by the return of the classic tool of universalism, the conquering overflow out of the particular once stability cannot be found within.

Because of representative usurpation or autocratic substitution, in 1815 the Nation has not attained political existence even after a quarter of a century of struggles in its name and efforts to bring it into being. Its development is still arrested by the weight of a constricting lack of separation between sovereign and people, between the instantiation of power and the principle of power, which stands in the way of a balanced, normal form of delegation. It is with respect to this roadblock that, paradoxically, the Restoration's turning back the clock will have a liberating effect. Many writers have rightly pointed out the extent to which this period, in which 1789 was at the center of public debate and partisan struggle was channeled into parlementary procedure, was a constructive moment in the country's democratic apprenticeship. The argument above allows us to go further. The dissociation of power and society that resulted from the reestablishment of the monarchy from above, which occurred within a context of a legitimacy that does acknowledge the representative principle along with the return to tradition, frees the assertion of national principle from the shackles holding it captive, and lets it, this time, fully work itself out. Whereas the Revolution reappears in 1814 and 1815, brought back to life by its very extensions and consequences, the confrontation of a new society to the pretensions of the former legitimacy brings about a situation, a context thanks to which the Nation's acquisition of its own identity, separate from power but in relation with it, becomes possible through reflection about what the Nation should be but happens not to be. The political shift of 1820 is the crux of this process. The backward-looking reorientation of the monarchy following the liberal laws of 1818–19, its terminal inability to grasp either the trends or the spirit of the era in which it keeps itself imprisoned, just as movements and ideas are particularly eloquent and urgent, brings home irrefutably the divorce between society as it really functions and its image for a government that is blind to the evolution undermining it. The four great works published in rapid succession by Guizot from October 1820 to June 1822 mercilessly diagnose this imprisonment in an illusion—"Power is often the victim of a curious error. It believes itself to be self-sufficient"—noting with remarkable acuity both the novelty of the age and the transformations in the state of society.[91]

Nonetheless, and this is the fruitful originality of the situation, the antagonism between these two forces headed in opposite directions remains sufficiently limited to fit within a space tacitly governed by common rules, and to play itself out in symbolic clashes. Old-fashioned arbitrary power is not despotism, to begin with, and the methods that this reactionary government allows itself permit it neither to nip collective expression in the bud nor to shut down the legal means of protest. "We had faith in our institutions," Guizot will later say.[92] While it is not necessary to believe that everyone shared that faith, the statement does have general import: it does indeed remain possible to invoke the legal bases of power against the ways in which it is exercised, and to contrast the true spirit of institutions with the way that spirit is interpreted. Even if it is a purely tactical move, invoking the principles of the charter against the government's conduct, a leitmotif of the period, it lays down a rule with important implications. Even as it claims to be to the death, the "struggle between two races" still acknowledges implicitly a common frame of reference. Hence, after the conspiratorial and preinsurrectional rash of 1820–22, a remarkable movement takes place in which civil society secedes, with learning, ideas, and books becoming the privileged means for public action, and the independent expression of thought becoming a political instrument in a battle whose object is not, in the immediate, power itself, but the foundations of the latter's legitimacy. Everything that speaks to the gap, the dissimilarity between the Nation and the government, adds to the indictment and delegitimation of the latter, shows how disconnected it is from the direction in which society is spontaneously moving. And this is how, through the playing out of dissidence against a background demand for resemblance, the central articulation of the representative process takes shape, namely the separation of the Nation as an essence from its expression in a specific theater of power.

History is both an agent and a product of this process. The deepening and the spread of historical consciousness are salient vehicles for national expression. They contribute in central ways to the individuation of this collective sovereign that transcends the labor of centuries while concentrating it within itself. At the same time, the virtual emergence of this distinct entity as separate from the actual people opens up a new, immense purview to the historian's labor, while bestowing on him an urgent task. Everything he can wrest from the past has weight in the present as a contribution to the rights of the public so long ignored by the masters in power. The historian is creating the political subject upstream, alongside those trying to give the public a voice in the here and now. But above all, beyond this laudable patriotic mission, the reinterpretation of the past in light of the national "person" entirely changes ways of perceiving, treating, and restoring the past. The political advent of the Nation within the singular conditions of the French case does more than invest the historian with the civic mission of revealing to both his compatriots and the world the authentic possessor of sovereignty. It also establishes the historian as a man of science, whatever the circumstances, and recenters his work upon an organizing nucleus whose critical understanding of the data governing change will take off in an unprecedented way. History as a science, as we understand it, comes from investing the whole of the past in this virtual subject that continually presents itself as the personal core of the passage of time, and that governs under the name of Nation. The most technical part of the historian's operations has its source there, just as his perspective and presentation depend upon it, and it provides the basis of his very relationship with the past.

Such is the combination of the essential and the contingent that makes the teaching of those years into a fight for history. The degree to which the scholarly agenda is involved with the political process is what allows both of them to shed so much light. For the deep political process brings about, as it turns out, a first symbolic solution to the special difficulty of getting the Nation's government to embody the French tradition—a difficulty that will reappear after this brush with a resolution, but it will no longer be possible to undo this first rooting of difference without which no representative correspondence is possible. For furthermore, thanks to the close association between the development of scholarship and the unfurling of the Nation as principle, we can follow down all of its meanderings the appearance out of nowhere (or almost out of nowhere) of a whole system for appropriating the past thanks to the initial push given by the subjective agenda taking over the political order. The congenital link between science of the past and knowledge of the Nation will remain blatant over the course of the entire nineteenth century, at least until 1914. But it will never again appear as clearly as in the form that was bestowed upon it by the situation of 1820–30—that clarity being decisive since it allowed for a distinction between ideological purpose and structural model. Once political innocence had evaporated, the subjective structure supporting it remained. Long beyond the cult of the Nation, the model that was built within the framework of the Nation remains seminal. We are certainly witnessing a foundational moment.

The two striking outlines Thierry sketches out in the summer of 1820 thus should be read on two levels: they are connected to an explicit political polemic, significantly displaced onto the terrain of history; and at the same time they speak, in an embryonic but evocative fashion, to the ways in which national formation recasts historical questions and historical presentation. The restored monarchy establishes its legitimacy on its historical titles and traditional roots. The constitutional charter of 1814 explicitly mentions "linking back to the chain of time." And the need to conceal behind august precedents the concessions wrested in the shadow of what the charter calls "tragic errors" had led that document's authors to produce a "theory of French history" that combined motley recollections and clichés in the service of the great cause. "Silences and historical errors all serve the same purpose," Thierry will later write, "they want to prove that kingship was always in France the only constitutive power."[93] These are the stakes, this is the power. If there is any bone to pick with eighteenth-century writers, it is only because the theories of Dubois and Mably pervade this document that needs to be undermined, and more profoundly because classical historians have the same bias as the authors of the constitutional document—they only want great actors to appear on

stage. Tying each legislative innovation to the name of a king is but a particular instance of the general principle that the march of events proceeds
from heroes. A reversal of this point of view must be invoked. There must
be a demand for a history based on a consideration of "the entire mass of
the nation," which is usually behind the finery of courts.[94]

The charter evokes the "ancient assemblies in the fields of Mars or of
May"—an allusion, via a vague memory of Mably as Thierry explains it,
to the Frankish origins and alleged fourteen-century-long existence of
the French monarchy. In the face of this legendary legitimation Thierry
endeavors to bring under scrutiny "the real period in which the monarchy was established." A hot topic, since it exposed him to the "red pencil
of censorship."[95] As an example of the initiatives of "the kings who preceded us" the charter finally brings up the creation of free townships: "The
communes owed their emancipation to Louis Le Gros, the confirmation
and extension of their rights to Saint Louis and Philippe Le Bel."[96] To
which Thierry responds in his letter of October 18, 1820, the last in this
first series: "The creation of the first communes in the north of France
thus came out of a fortunate convergence . . . the oldest and greatest arose
spontaneously in the course of uprisings against seigneurial power."[97] The
three great themes he will play out again in 1827 and beyond are already
in place: criticism of conventional historical method, the shaping of the
French nation, and the revolution of the communes. All three derive from
the very text of the charter to which they provide a counterpunctual refu-
tation. But the wonder of the moment makes an ad hoc polemic into a
reform of a basic framework of understanding.

It is not just that political struggle, thanks to the cunning of reason
that mobilizes passions in the service of truth, goads people to articulate
accurate ideas where a facile lack of curiosity allowed for the perpetuation of inaccurate ones; this is not just a matter of one thesis displacing
another within the same frame of reference—the frame of reference itself
is transformed. Mably was equally concerned with the rights and the authentic claims of the Nation, but this did not stop him from thinking and
writing in the same spirit as those who believe in royal prerogative. The
clash here is not just about contents. It is first and above all between two
approaches to the past. What is important is that the assertion of the nation
through history not be separated from the recasting of history under the
influence of the nationalist agenda. What matters is not so much that the
axiom maintaining that Clovis founded the French monarchy is proven
to be absurd, as the change in relation to the past that made that demonstration possible.

Previously, the means whereby past legitimation was possible derived
from a system of meaning in which such things were determined from

without. This system demanded the identification of a beginning that would be valid inasmuch as it could be related to the action of a pristine, individual will shaping events from without, preferably from very far— then it would only be a matter of observing this transmission, unaltered and uninterrupted. The weight of the past is here measured with reference to the internal development of an individual whose point of departure must be assessed from the vantage point of the past, through an attempt to circumscribe it. The problem is no longer to attach the origin of the French monarchy to the actions of some distant founder, but to "determine the specific point at which the history of France takes over from the history of the Frankish kings,"[98] the monarchy then being no more than one piece of the development of a much vaster entity. "All which we have read and heard," Thierry writes with reference to the ups and downs of kingship, "would have us believe in fixed, unvarying, immemorial entities. That is not, and never could have been. Nothing is, in truth, ancient: new things lurk under old names, and if the letter remains, the spirit changes."[99] The perspective that posited a continuous transmission from an immemorial origin is thus displaced by the notion of a discontinuous, limited genesis—which implies a separation between "the history of France itself and the history of Frankish Gaul"—and of the instability of the meaning of words, even words like "kingship," that are determined solely by the context.

We are back, of course, to the intellectual effects of the liberal upheaval with respect to ideas about change, but they are here integrated into a comprehensive framework that is both broader and more precise, focusing and intensifying the implications of those effects. They could have been integrated into a classic, eighteenth-century style narrative, as Thierry himself pointed out. But we now hold the key to the ways in which those new ideas were recruited in the service of a discovery of the past on its own terms. The approach to history "from below," as a dynamic that results from the push and pull of anonymous collective forces, is now given meaning in the context of the rise of this global subject, present in each accident and particularity that it nonetheless transcends, and whose unwavering presence unto itself must now be chronicled by recording in detail the infinite number of expressions and incarnations it has taken on. We see here that total history must also be a history that demands the most rigorous precision of detail, the restoring of past entities to their real place, in all of their characteristic color. Not only liberal understanding, but also the demand for new scholarship and expressive narration, take on for their own purposes the framework of a national permanence. This is indeed total history in that no fact among those that can be documented, whatever its range, can fail to be included among the components building up to the creation of this transcendent being, which is all the more solid in itself if its sources are numerous. This totality is by nature an open one; it can and must be indefinitely completed. But it still carries within itself a unifying principle: all of the elements it takes in indiscriminately and equally can be made into a unit, in ways that are to be defined. But its openness does not imply indifference to the nature of the elements thus incorporated. On the contrary, the insertion within this totalizing framework calls for strict rules for defining the data: nothing has meaning if not concretely established and drawn from the life.

The cognitive framework of the nation brings about more than a global means for understanding the past. It also introduces, in connection to the latter, a principle for understanding change based on the internal coherence of discrete historical sequences, and on a framework into which scholarly data can be inserted. The seeds of all these potential developments are present in the very first of Thierry's *Lettres*, attached to the main line of argument. Thierry clearly realizes, for instance, that using the individual as a model—which he calls in plain speech "following the destiny of a whole people, just like following that of a single man"—challenges the external order commonly derived from monarchical succession. "The feeling which gives history a soul," he writes, "has until now escaped the writers who have tried to recount ours. Unable to find the internal principle which would bind together the innumerable parts of what they sought to portray, they looked to an external link, to the apparent continuity of some political entities, to the fiction of the uninterrupted transmission of an unchanging power among the descendants of a single family."[100] This is the opening shot of a lasting polemic. For God only knows that the definition of certain historical epochs through reigns and syntheses based on dynastic continuity will live on. And furthermore the effective implementation of an organizing principle based on the analogy with the internal development of an individual will prove far more difficult than is suggested by the admirable candor with which it is demanded. That difficulty is maybe linked to the model's internal dynamic, its dissemination, and its multiplying effects. It would be a mistake to confuse it with a demand for global coordination, a requirement that each element be subordinated to a totalizing law. The model basically works against hierarchy, since it requires the dissolution of artificial external links in order to bring out their internal connections. And in the same spirit, far from leading to the neglect of details for the larger picture, it allows for the decentralization and multiplication of the historian's interests by investing discrete units with their own reality, their individuality. Thierry is aware of this when he points out that the change he wishes for in the way the Nation's trajectory is presented would also affect the perception of local figures. "If there were a writer worthy of recording this truly national history," he says, "France would appear with its multitude of towns and populations, introduced to us as collective beings endowed with will and activity."[101] If the development of the whole nation must be understood by analogy with "the destiny of one man," the trajectory of each of its components must no less be conceived of as the different stages of personhood. Individuality sheds light on the entire historical object, as a result of this new conception of the total frame of reference. Hence, scholarly attention to detail and the focus on the singular acquire legitimacy, now that one is convinced that isolated segments and apparently eccentric events all feed into a general purpose. Hence the surprising alliance between monastic study and "picturesque" history.

Such ideas, under the pens of fledgling historians, or put to use in a political context, are exactly analogous to the ideas that Humboldt develops in April 1821 before the Berlin Academy of Sciences. Where the *Lettres sur l'histoire de France* invoke the identity of the whole nation, *La Tâche de l'historien* discusses "ideas which, in a dignified and peaceful mode, pervade every connection which occurs in the world, without, however, belonging to the world."[102] Whether personal or national, "each human individuation is an idea taking root in the phenomenal."[103] The concepts here are remarkable for their grandeur and speculative dignity. The framework of understanding is, however, exactly the same as to its structure and operative effects. Ideas transcend tangible data, while passing through the latter, so that one must start with the datum to extract the idea from it, without however "imposing upon reality arbitrarily conceived ideas,"[104] and so that a place must be made for the proliferation of data without ever "sacrificing the smallest part of life's wealth of particularity": the Nation, ever equal to itself beyond the infinity of concrete expressions from which it is constantly nourished, plays exactly the same role. Within very different perspectives, both texts similarly designate the crux of the same transformation of the conditions for historical knowledge. They describe along the same lines the principle that allows the determination of fact and that of meaning, the objective exploration of data in themselves and the understanding of their connection, the endless collection of testimonials to past events and the reasoned analysis of change, to run together and mingle. It is not a matter of making the language of one side of this dual operation into the "truth" of the other side's language. They complete one another, each speaking to one aspect of the emergence of an intellectual apparatus that in the course of a few years would yield another insight about history on the basis of a double move: it unblocked scholarly activity that, in its search for authenticity, had been limited in its ability to understand materials; and it disqualified philosophical history if the latter proved unable, because of a rigid outlook, to take in new facts. These prophetic texts, then, which with prescient and even visionary energy (not the least of their attributes), sketch out the program for the discipline that still lies in the future.

Fine-tuning of narrative, revision of ideas about change, reappropriation of traditional philosophies of history, establishment of the nation as a basic grid, rediscovery of the task of scholarship: ten years of attempts and efforts in all of these areas will be necessary to give the possibilities and demands of 1820 a finished form. And no sooner was there a glimpse of its totality than the program explodes into partial tasks. Thierry himself returns to the history of England, his area of predilection for developing his idea of racial struggle, but to which he will this time try to bring an exact coloring and a lively narrative. His *Conquête* will appear after another instance of this history-as-story, Barante's *Ducs de Bourgogne*. At the same time, the analysis of historical change through an understanding of society's needs and contradictions, already sketched out by Sismondi and Guizot, is spectacularly applied to the history of the Revolution of 1789. And then, as the new history begins to make headway, 1827, the year of the republication in one volume of the *Lettres sur l'histoire de France*, also sees a deepening of philosophical inquiry. Vico, Herder, and Hegel are now points of reference for the historian. But just as political triumph is in sight, the scholarly foundations of the whole enterprise enter a phase of crisis. The victorious nation will create the institutions necessary to give history-as-science a concrete foundation; concurrently, the flowering of this collective identity, which makes sense of the crazy-quilt of centuries, reasserts the necessary connection between the different components of the new understanding of the past. Those elements (philosophy, narrative, and appreciation of the sources), brought together thanks to the Nation and that had inspired in Thierry the grand design of a new form of knowledge, take on under Michelet's pen a confident form within a stable synthesis, as a result of a fully perfected individualization of the national entity.

IV

How can one grasp and convey the unity of history? This was the problem that obsessed the young Michelet. In December, 1825, he writes in his diary: "To take a very short period in the history of the sixteenth century, ten years or something even shorter, and write its authentically universal history (political, literary, scientific, artistic, religious, etc.). An impracticable plan: for a short period, no philosophical connection; for any longer period, an immense task."[105] Historical knowledge is only interesting if it gets at the heart of the whole thing, and takes on a universal point of view.

But then how can one deal with the diversity of materials that must be reckoned with? Michelet's interest was aroused by a short text by Victor Cousin, published in 1823 as an appendix to the translation of the *Histoire abrégée des sciences metaphysiques, morales et politiques* by Dugald Stewart.[106] This is yet another programmatic text, in which Cousin sketches out in a few pages the profile of what could be "the true history, the inner history of humanity." "Why," asks Cousin, "when we recount the disconnected events that make up the life of the human race as seen from outside, can we not restore between these arbitrary events the real logic that links and explains them, and connect them to the world above, of which they truly partake? That would be the essence of a true historical science."[107] Reading this text was a decisive trigger for Michelet, pushing him from philosophy into the direction of history. He meets Cousin in April 1824 and begins a close, questioning relationship with him, getting acquainted in the process with the philosophy of history. Over a few months he reads Kant, Ferguson, Vico, Condorcet, and Turgot. This is the context in which he decides to translate the *Scienza nuova*.[108] When he publishes his *Tableau chronologique de l'histoire moderne*, he solicits his mentor's indulgence in very revealing terms: "Instead of seeking history's inner coherence in the march of civilization, I introduce it superficially through revolutions in the system of balances."[109] For this is the overall difficulty in carrying out the program he has appropriated: how to convey the *inner coherence* that characterizes what Cousin sees as "truly universal history"?

Early on Michelet goes looking for this "unity in the history of the human race" in the notion of personality. In 1825 he borrows from Pascal the image of the generations of men making up "a single man who endures and continually learns"—this image derives, in a very significant way, from the bodily model that the figure of the Nation carries to its highest degree. But at this stage there is no question of national specificity; Michelet envisions the history of all of humanity. "Simple and sublime idea!" he exclaims. "Man is no longer an isolated entity but part of this collective being called humanity. . . . The individual appears for a moment, merges into the collective mind, modifies it and dies; but the species does not die, but collects forever the fruit of this ephemeral existence."[110] In practice, the *Précis de l'histoire moderne* of 1827 represents, compared with the *Tableau chronologique*, a significant advance toward the solution of the problem. The balancing system remains the frame of reference. But it is no longer there to "superficially introduce" history's cohesion. It gives access to the "dramatic unity" of the last three centuries. Revolutions in time provide a reasoned chronological framework that brings out the "unity of action and of goals" of each era. All of this fits into a broader narrative—the fusion of the northern states' system with that of western and southern states. This principle of characterization sets events firmly within a central line of argument—"the characteristic of the sixteenth century, distinguishing it profoundly from the Medieval centuries, is the power of public opinion."[111] His symbolic method allows him to represent "intermediate ideas," the interactive linking of phenomena "not through abstract notions but through characteristic facts,"[112] thus providing, through careful selection of the facts that may "serve as symbols for all others," a dramatic guiding line, where massive data and the twist and turns of events could have swamped the reader.

In parallel with the considerable advance represented by the *Précis* in the organic presentation of the past, and around the same time—the *Vico* was published in 1827—his thinking around the *New Science* offers Michelet a similar occasion for deepening his thought, this time on a theoretical level. His predilection for his Neapolitan predecessor, among all those who offered thoughts about continuity and unity in historical change, is very much, if one looks at it closely, a function of the work's unfinished quality, of the archaically theological framework in which Vico's work remains trapped. Certainly his work includes the famous "heroic principle": "Humanity is its own achievement." But all of this remains confined within a circle defined by divinity: "No doubt men created on their own the social world, that is the irrefutable principle of the new science," Michelet remarks, "but that world nonetheless sprang from an intelligence which often departs from the specific ends that men pursue, which often opposes those ends, always from above."[113] Hence the final closure of the indefinite cycle of three ages: divine, heroic, and human. What strikes and fascinates Michelet is this attribution to a transcendent being of a reality that is, however, fully the product of the creative action of humans, in such a way that the whole of men's achievements does not undermine that permanent organizing principle but feeds into it. What is contradiction in Vico comes close to being the solution in Michelet. All that is needed to complete it is to replace God with the Nation.

On February 5, 1826, Michelet notes a question to himself: "On the subject of a unified history of the human race. If God is infinite, infinitely far-sighted and wise, the world's history is a system."[114] But if both inner and global coordination is necessary for history to attain systematic universality, as Cousin would have had it, it must also be really history, that is an unplanned journey, effectively brought about by human action, so that it makes sense to chronicle its twists and turns. The *New Science* amounts to a legitimation of the dual pursuit of those two demands, a momentary balancing, if not an entirely convincing resolution, of this tension until that moment when the Nation, revealed through "the lighting of July," makes it possible to encompass both of them, and satisfy them both. History is now the history of freedom, "the account of the interminable struggles of man against nature, spirit against matter, freedom against fate."[115] But the ever ongoing struggle between self and fate does drive humanity's growth and self-assertion, embodied in the emergence of collective freedom, in the development of a social self. "Europe is the least simple, least natural, most artificial, and hence least fatalistic, most human, and most liberated area of the world; my own fatherland, France, is most quintessentially European."[116] Freedom culminates in a nation's ability to constitute itself, unify itself, and reflect upon itself. "Germany has no center, neither has Italy. France has a center. Unified and unchanging for centuries, France must be looked upon as a living, moving person. The sign, the guarantee of a living organism, the ability to assimilate, reaches here its highest degree: French France was able to draw, absorb, and give identities to the English, German, and Spanish Frances which surround her. She used them to neutralize one another, converting them all to her essence."[117]

This is the secret of universality, the subjective form of human historical creativity. From its crucible will emerge, from now on, all decisive progress toward the final achievement of the freedom and unity of humankind. "Once human connection is experienced in the limited social confines of the nation, that same idea will take over all of human society, the republic of the world."[118] But equally familiar are the famous words with which Michelet begins his *Introduction à l'histoire universelle*: "This short book could just as well be entitled *Introduction to the history of France*; it culminates in France. And patriotism has nothing to do with this. Writing in isolation, removed from the pressures of schools, sects, and parties, the author arrived, whether through logic or through history at the same conclusion: that his glorious fatherland is now guiding the ship of humanity."[119] God himself is recuperated into this earthly subjectivity that assembles and concentrates in itself a millennium's worth of struggle against determinism. In defining "the beautiful and terrible times in which we happen to live," a time of destruction and dissolution but also of transition to a configuration in which the mind looms larger, Michelet even writes, "This final step away from a preordained natural order, away from the God of the East, is a step towards a social God revealed through our very freedom."[120] And of course, he pursues as he must: "The agent of this new revelation, the mediator between God and man must be the most social of peoples. The moral world found its Word in Christianity, the offspring of Judea and Greece; France will interpret the Word of the social world which we see dawning."[121] This time, the circle is closed. The transformation of Vico's model has been achieved. The philosophical and theological reinvention of the national model that Michelet carried out for his own purpose through the *New Science* is now over. He now has the

Fig. 9.11
Jules Michelet.

means of bringing together *narrative* (of freedom as it proceeds in varied, unpredictable ways), and *system* (the coherent convergence of freedom's effects in the national person, a social and divine subject).

This framework has two advantages: on the one hand it allows for an entirely open representation of change; on the other hand the subject thus evoked—the nation—as a culmination remains a virtual subject, never closed upon itself, but feeding off the very changes affecting its parameters. In other words, while the national person is made up of the concrete actions of its members, it remains disincarnate; it functions as an ever-recurring regulating idea—but not just any idea, rather an idea of a possible totalization of all of the dimensions of change in the receding horizon of a consciousness of oneself. What we have here, fully developed since Humboldt's initial formulations, is the theoretical principle behind the split whereby historical knowledge splits away from the philosophy of history while absorbing its most sophisticated achievements. In this instance, this means the "Hegelian" element of self-reflective summary, that which truly differentiates our own idea of history as it emerges in the early decades of the nineteenth century, when the idea of self-consciousness through temporal accumulation gets added onto the "objective" idea of progress in the style of the eighteenth century. Progress is above all progress in human self-consciousness. We can see how Michelet's way of representing the Nation takes up this element while freeing it from its philosophical implications in terms of history's ends, or of absolute knowledge, or even of presentist privilege in the name of the present as theater for the awareness of a past that lacked self-knowledge. The new direction is toward more retrospective conscience, a self-consciousness that, however, never comes to an end.

The national model necessarily removes dogmatism from the representation of historical change as generating a person ever more self-aware, of which this model necessarily presents the most cutting edge. The Nation never finishes its task of self-constitution; it no more achieves than dies; its realization of full self-awareness steps back, ideally, with every step it takes forward. This introduces a "Kantian" element of limitation within the totalizing subjective thought that is otherwise mobilized. But we are not bringing up these philosophical references in order to evoke some obscure play of influences, or an abstract work at synthesis, when we have on the contrary stressed the self-taught nature of Michelet's reappropriation of the national person. These references to philosophy serve to bring out and place in context the theoretical power of a cognitive model that will serve as a foundation for the pursuit of historical knowledge. That pursuit will not require knowledge of the model in order to use it. Historians will be able to ignore, forget, or even deny it: they will be drawing nonetheless on its operative resources. Nor should one be misled by its aggressively patriotic ideological expressions: not only can it not be reduced to patriotism, it is strictly independent from patriotism in its intellectual articulation, even if it can serve as a vehicle for the latter. Nationalism is not the truth of the nation; nationalism is a historically crucial expression of it, but it remains quite secondary and rather contingent with respect to the logic of the social model that underlies the whole enterprise. Thus can we understand how works animated by explicit and ideologically perverse motives can nonetheless remain perfectly acceptable from the point of view of scholarship. The exaggeration, not to say lyrical madness, of his nation as "the guiding light of humanity" does not mean that Michelet was not, is not, a historian of genius—because there are many more different dimensions to the idea of France as a person than this oetic stretching of a particular nation to universal dimensions. Beyond the rantings it sometimes and superficially inspired, the national model gave the historical discipline both an implicit, but firm, epistemological guarantee, and an inexhaustible source of self-renewal. Its heuristic power is linked to its all-encompassing form. The latter does not, however, only call for an increasingly exhaustive consideration of all manner of data and dimensions of the historian's purview. It also implies a constructive agnosticism about the nature of the internal links within this totality. Sometimes some elements will determine others: economy, demography, and ecology can in some circumstances carry decisive weight. But the relationship between elements can be very different, without this being the result of an a priori assumption. There can be a deep unity, an essential correspondence, an intimate joining of all aspects of a society (material, geographic, spiritual) so that no level can be deemed to determine the whole thing.

Historical science's richest contribution to the understanding of change has its roots in this ever deeper digging, as a result of a basic orientation, for an ultimate connection between the levels and the modalities of collective action, a repudiation of simple forms of causality and preordained mechanisms. The history written in our own century illustrates this. When Vidal de la Blache poses the problem of "France's geographic personality," when he asks how the "illumination of its individuality" took place, how the action of men brought about "a connection between disparate elements" and substituted "a systematic concourse of forces to the incoherent effects of local circumstances," he is launching an infinitely fruitful line of inquiry not only because he calls for a broader conception of the historical object, but also, above all, because he wants us to go back to the beginning of the whole question of the internal relationships and articulations structuring a historical totality, divested from direct determinism.[122] This is why, through the vicissitudes of different schools of thought and the metamorphoses of the discipline, Michelet has remained a strangely universal point of reference and a seminal author. He was the first to conceive fully of a form of understanding in which everything is linked and the historian's highest task is to understand the means of that linkage. This task has changed means and aspects several times. It will do so again. Its initiator will remain an inspiration.

From its first complete unfolding, the effectiveness of the nation-as-person model as both a synthesis and a critique is apparent. It allows Michelet to bring together and sum up the different contributions that came in waves since 1829 and give concrete form to the great task of political remembering, of creating the national actor through an excavation of the past, and of integrating its power and legitimacy in the public mind. With the full exposition of this task comes also the explicit articulation of the programmatic notion of bringing together these axes for grasping the past, whose initial conjunction had triggered in Thierry the plan for a new history, for narrative along with philosophical analysis, for "resurrection" and "critique." In Michelet the restating and practice of this necessary alliance between erudition, interpretation, and historical restoration is expressed as a paradigmatic denunciation of his predecessors' narrowness and one-sidedness. He establishes the model of an internal appeal to the all-encompassing ideal of the discipline in opposition to the partial, limited nature of its actual achievements. Thus does he turn back against Thierry the latter's solemn protest against an exclusively political history that hid the greater part of the nation behind the doings of a few conspicuous lives. While praising his talent as an artist and a man who had "a time of daring, of high invention, of genius,"[123] he accuses him of having fallen back into his predecessors' errors and remained on the surface of things in "bringing only political history into narrative."[124] "The picturesque school was superficial; it had nothing to say about inner life, about art, law, religion, even geography which was supremely necessary to its point of view."[125]

Even more revealingly, from the point of view of the intellectual resources inscribed in the basic framework, Michelet criticizes in the name of national development the "racial fatalism" that is Thierry's favorite explanatory principle. As early as the 1831 *Introduction*, he speaks of "the intimate mingling of races which is the identity, the personality, of our nation." "The mixture," he writes, "imperfect in Italy and Germany, uneven in Spain and England, is equal and perfect in France."[126] The *Tableau de la France* explicitly places the racial factor beside the rooting in earth, of which in fact the force of history liberates man by endowing him gradually with a broader sense of belonging, bringing him to understand "instead of his natal village, town or province, a great fatherland through which he contributes to the world's destiny."[127] What Thierry misunderstands in assuming that natural differences remain fixed over time is "the work society operates on itself" and in light of which "the element of race is increasingly secondary and subordinate."[128] What he misses, in sum, is the very power of change, its recreation of the elements originally given in nature. If one wishes to produce "a formula for France," as Michelet puts it in 1833, the country must be considered "on the one hand under the aspect of its diverse races and provinces, in its geographical spread, and on the other in its chronological development, in the increasingly unified drama of national history."[129] Aside from the specific problem of race, what must crucially be stressed here is the critical potential of the model with respect to certain forms of determinism. What is played out here is not only the refusal to consider history from "special points of view," with no notion of "how difficult it is to isolate these things, how much each reacts against the others"[130]; more deeply what appears here is the limit of every notion of *fatalité*, the popular term of the 1820s.

In his 1828–29 course at the École normale, Michelet delivered a revealing critique of Thierry's ideas, a purely philosophical critique: "There is another development which must be set alongside that of races, that of ideas, where the free activity of man takes place. . . . We belong to the earth through race, but we also have within us a dynamic principle through which we endow history with movement. This is what Monsieur Thierry neglected."[131] The historian remains faithful to his initial concern to preserve an area of freedom within the confines of nature's determinism. But this needs no longer to be invoked as an abstract principle: it is now an integral part of the intellectual apparatus through which he apprehends the past. From the moment one thinks in terms of an integration of the elements of history into a unified whole endowed with the power to "work on itself," it becomes impossible to conceive of a preordained chain of development, of submitting to a network of lines of causality. If there are local constraints, they make sense only when they are replaced within a global set of interrelations which, through a capacity to turn back and reflect on itself, allows for an ineradicable openness that has to be called the *expression of collective freedom in time*. Nothing has been more important for the intellectual trajectory of the historical discipline: the discipline carries within itself, alongside this global schema with its demands for connections, a means to regulate its use by the light of reason.

NOTES

1. Charles de Rémusat, *Politique libérale* (Paris, 1860), 3–4.

2. Ernest Renan, *L'Avenir de la science* (written in 1848), in *Oeuvres complètes* (Paris, 1949), 3:834.

3. Augustin Thierry, foreword to *Lettres sur l'histoire de France* (Paris, 1827), viii.

4. Albertine de Broglie said this in an 1825 letter to Barante reprinted in her *Souvenirs* (Paris, 1890–1901), 3:248.

5. Rémusat, *Politique libérale*, 4.

6. "Sur l'ancien esprit et l'esprit actuel des légistes français," *Le Censeur européen*, May 1, 1820, reprinted in *Dix ans d'études historiques*, which we cite from the *Oeuvres complètes* (Paris, 1859) 3:477.

7. François Guizot, *Du Gouvernement de la France depuis la Restauration et du ministère actuel* (Paris, 1820), 2.

8. Thierry, *Lettres sur l'histoire de France*, 234.

9. Camille Jullian, introduction to his *Extraits des historiens français du XIXe siècle* (separately republished as *Notes sur l'histoire en France au XIXe siècle*) (Paris, 1897), xxxi. See also by Jullian "Augustin Thierry et le movement historique sous la Restauration," *Revue de synthèse* 13 (1906): 129–42.

10. The famous texts are Marx's letter to J. Weydemeyer of March 5, 1852, in *Correspondance* (Paris, 1972), 3:78; his letter to Engels of July 27, 1854 in which he calls Thierry the "father of the class struggle in French historiography," in *Correspondance* (Paris, 1974), 4:148; Engel's letter to G. Starkenburg in his *Ludwig Feuerbach et la fin de la philosophie classique allemande* (Paris, 1976), in which he writes, "Historians of the Restoration period, from Thierry to Guizot, Mignet, and Thiers see it [class struggle] everywhere as the key to all of French history since the Middle Ages" (71). This consecration is capped off by G. V. Plekhanov, "Augustin Thierry et la conception matérialiste de l'histoire," in *Les Questions fondamentales du Marxisme* (Moscou, 1965), 2:483–538. We should also cite as a curiosity R. Fossaert, "La Théorie des classes chez Guizot et Thierry," *La Pensée* (January–February 1955), 59–69.

11. Foreign language editions—Moscow, n.d., and Jean Walch, *Les Maîtres de l'histoire, 1815–1850* (Paris, 1986)—published just as this chapter was being finished, cover a broader chronological span but do not have the systematic and synthetic character of Reizov's unsurpassed book on this subject. Stanley Mellon, *The Political Uses of History: A Study of Historians in the French Restoration* (Stanford, 1958) is also limited in its outlook. See also H. O. Sieburg, *Deutschland und Frankreich in der Geschichtsschreibung des 19 Jahrhundert, 1815–1848* (Wiesbaden, 1954); Stadler, *Geschichte und Gesischtsschreiber im 19 Jahrhundert, 1789–1871* (Zurich, 1958); S. Bann, *The Clothing of Clio: A Study in the Representation of History in Nineteenth-Century Britain and France* (Cambridge, 1984); and finally notes on a little-known period in J. K. Burton's recent *Napoleon and Clio: Historical Writing, Teaching, and Thinking during the First Empire* (Durham, 1979).

12. Philippe Ariès, *Le Temps de l'histoire* (Monaco, 1954), 265. Sismondi had already written in *Introduction à l'histoire des français* (1821): "The Revolution, by interrupting the transmission of rights and privileges, put all past centuries at an almost

equal distance from us. All ages must serve to instruct us; none governs us through its institutions" (1:xxiv–xxv).

13. Preface to *Dix ans d'études historiques*, in *Oeuvres complètes*, 3:307.

14. *Le Temps de l'histoire*, 263.

15. Stendhal, *Lettres de Paris* (Paris, 1983), 80. That same year L. Vitet writes in a famous article in the *Globe*: "Taste in France is awaiting its July 14. A new group of encyclopedists has arisen to prepare for it. They are known as romantics" ("De l'indépendance en matière de goût," *Le Globe*, April 23, 1825).

16. Foreword to *Lettres sur l'histoire de France*, x.

17. The most important work on the subject is Krzysztof Pomian's unpublished book. I thank him for having graciously made available to me an as yet unpublished translation of it. In French see his "L'Histoire de la science et l'histoire de l'histoire," *Annales: Économies, sociétés, civilisations* (1975): 935–52, and "Le Passé: De la foi à la connaissance," *Le Débat* 24 (1983): 151–68.

18. Introduction to *Extraits*, xiv.

19. Dacier, *Rapport historique sur les progrès de l'histoire et de la littérature ancienne depuis 1789 et sur leur état actuel* (Paris, 1810), 182.

20. Thierry writes about this in the *Censeur européen* issue of July 5, 1819, upon the beginning of his course (he used the piece again in *Dix ans d'études historiques*). He hails in Daunou "the scholar and patriot, occupying the place of the political representative on the assembly's benches, and of the professor at the lectern."

21. C. Jullian's opinion of this can be cited: "Roman epigraphy, which was gaining an enthusiastic following in Germany, would have remained unknown to us without Letronne's reports on Imperial Egypt; as a natural reaction, Restoration France was one of the periods when (despite Naudet's careful work) the French did the least in the study of Roman Antiquity and we never made up the lead gained at this time by our rivals. While Letronne and Raoul Roquette did keep up an interest in Greek Antiquity, Germany had already caught up and overtaken us" (introduction to *Extraits*, xxxvi.) While there still exists no systematic history of French philology, it would be important to at least analyze the phenomenon whereby just at the time that Germans are looking to Greece and Rome for historical models, French erudition after 1800 turns away from this ancient world and toward the myth of Celtic roots (see on this point Mona Ozouf, "Le Questionnaire de l'académie celtique" in *L'École de la France* [Paris, 1984]).

22. *Dix ans d'études historiques*, 304.

23. "Première lettre sur l'histoire de France," *Le Censeur européen*, July 23, 1820, reprinted in *Dix ans d'études historiques*, 502.

24. Preface to *Dix ans d'études historiques*, 304.

25. Petitot, *Collection complète des Mémoires* (1819), 1:v, cited in L. Halphen, *L'Histoire de France depuis cent ans* (Paris, 1914), 48. Guizot will give the same justifications for his own *Collection*: it should make up for the dryness of "the works of modern historians, more or less accomplished scholars, often focused upon narrow or mechanical matters, and who almost never have reproduced events or men with a fidelity to their spirit, the innocent and lively directness which make history both true and appealing" (cited in Halphen, ibid.).

26. Cited in Halphen, 52. The emphasis is mine. He is equally eloquent in reminiscing about his project in 1835: "I thought that it would be possible to join together all of these materials, filling in the empty spaces, taking out repetitions, but carefully retaining the contemporary expression of facts. I thought that from this work, *in which every age would, so to speak, recount itself, speaking in its own voice* would result the true history of France" (preface to *Dix ans d'études historiques*, 312, my emphasis).

27. *Histoire de la conquête de l'Angleterre,* in *Oeuvres complètes,* 1:6.

28. On all of this see Pomian, "Le passé: De la foi à la connaissance," and his book on history in the Middle Ages, *Le Passé comme objet de foi,* which I thank him again for allowing me to consult in an unpublished translation.

29. A systematic investigation of the question would pursue the comparison with the historical novel, from Walter Scott's remarks to Manzoni's self-criticism, the strategic signification of which is examined below.

30. In the preface to *Dix ans d'études historiques,* 305.

31. In particular, Machiavelli and Gucchiardini. These two works make up volumes 33 and 34 of Ranke, *Sammtliche Werke* (Leipzig, 1873–90).

32. The *Recueil des historiens de la France et des Gaules* began to appear in 1738; 13 volumes had appeared by 1789. Dom Plancher, *Histoire générale et particulière de Bourgogne,* 4 vols. (Dijon, 1739–81).

33. His articles appeared in *L'Universel* on October 15–19, November 5 and 19, and December 31 of 1829. Cited in Jean Le Pottier, "Histoire et érudition: Recherches et documents sur l'histoire et le rôle de l'érudition médiévale dans l'historiographie française au XIXe siècle" (thesis of the École des chartes, 1979), 511.

34. As we know, it was only in fact in 1858 that this committee was named the Comité des travaux historiques, and only under Jules Ferry that it became the Comité des travaux historiques et scientifiques we know today. In January 1835 a second committee was created alongside the first. It included most notably Cousin, Mérimée, Hugo, and Sainte-Beuve. On this point see Robert-Henri Bautier, "L'Académie des inscriptions et belles-lettres et le Comité des travaux historiques sous la monarchie de Juillet," forthcoming in the proceedings of the conference *Le Temps ou l'histoire se fit science, 1830–1848.* For the full documentation, see Xavier Charmes, *Le Comité des travaux historiques et scientifiques,* 3 vols. (Paris, 1886).

35. For a detailed look at this work, see R-H Bautier, "Le *Recueil des monuments de l'histoire du Tiers-État* et l'utilisation des matériaux réunis par A. Thierry," *Annuaire-Bulletin de la Société de l'histoire de France* (1944), 89–118.

36. Michelet, *Oeuvres complètes,* ed. Paul Villaneix (Paris, 1974), 4:11.

37. We should add to this list the "Notes sur quatorze historiens antérieurs à Mézeray," included in *Dix ans d'études historiques,* to have a full overview of the work of Thierry as a historian of France.

38. *Considérations sur l'histoire de France,* in *Oeuvres complètes,* 4:121–22.

39. Renan, *Essais de morale et de critique,* in *Oeuvres complètes* (Paris, 1948), 2: 97–98.

40. On the collaboration with Saint-Simon, see Henri Gouhier, *Auguste Comte et Saint-Simon,* vol. 3 of *La Jeunesse d'Auguste Comte et la formation du positivisme* (Paris, 1970), chapters 1 and 2.

41. Thierry was born in Blois on May 10, 1795. His father was a minor employee at the Préfecture. For biographical details see A. Augustin Thierry, *Augustin Thierry d'après sa correspondance et ses papiers de famille* (Paris, 1922). More recent works are R. N. Smithson, *Augustin Thierry: Social and Political Consciousness in the Evolution of a Historical Method* (Geneva, 1973), Lionel Gossman, "Augustin Thierry and Liberal Historiography," *History and Theory* 15 (1976).

42. These phrases are from Thierry's "Des nations et leurs rapports mutuels," in *L'Industrie*, vol. 1 of *Oeuvres*, ed. Saint-Simon (Paris, 1966; reprint of 1868 edition), 111–12.

43. Whose *Traité d'économie* was republished in 1814.

44. "Des nations et de leurs rapports mutuels," 106.

45. The evolutions and misadventures of the title have been the object of three studies by Ephraim Harpaz: "*Le Censeur*, histoire d'un journal libéral," *Revue des sciences humaines* 92 (1958): 482–511; "*Le Censeur européen*, histoire d'un journal industrialiste," *Revue d'histoire économique et sociale* 37 (1959): 185–218 and 328–57; and "*Le Censeur européen*, histoire d'un journal quotidien," *Revue des sciences humaines* 114 (1964): 137–259.

46. *Dix ans d'études historiques*, 299. Only the first of the four long articles entitled "Vue des revolutions d'Angleterre" is reproduced in the 1835 volume. The others are in volumes 5 (1817), 8 (1818), and 11 (1819) of the *Censeur européen*.

47. *Dix ans d'études historiques*, 303.

48. This was reported by his brother Amédée. A. Augustin-Thierry, *Lettres sur l'histoire de France*, 63.

49. *De la monarchie française depuis son établissement jusqu'à nos jours*, 3 vols. (Paris, 1814). As is well known, Montlosier will become famous in 1826 thanks to another notorious crusade, his denunciation of the Jesuits' influence on government, in the best Gallican tradition (*Mémoire à consulter sur un système religieux et politique tendant à renverser la religion, la société et le trône*).

50. *Considérations sur l'histoire de France*, 117.

51. Ibid., 116–17.

52. *De la monarchie française*, 2:209.

53. Among analyses of this stripe is a text by the young Michelet that is little known, as it is unpublished:

> The seventeenth century in France witnessed a revolution, a peaceful revolution carried out by the King. Richelieu has every fortress not controlled by the King dismantled, except those on the frontiers. This was a revolution. The people, weary of civil wars, let royal authority have its way, and did well to do so. How great was this barely perceptible revolution! . . . If we look at civil law, this Revolution is striking: civil law under Henry III and Louis XIV, the code des Basiliques and Louis XIV's three great Ordinances are of utmost importance; France took a giant step. The Revolution carried out by the people in England is engineered by the King in France. The English Revolution does more for political freedom; the French Revolution for civil freedom. This is the beginning of equality in France. When the English spoke of 'despotic states like Turkey and France,' they put their finger on something: France was less inclined towards freedom than towards equality.

Petites leçons (École normale, 1829–32). I am citing from the typed transcription of Michelet's courses by François Berriot, which Paul Villaneix kindly made available to me, and for which I thank him.

54. *Dix ans d'études historiques*, 358.

55. Ibid., 350.

56. Ibid., 514.

57. Ibid., 303.

58. *Essai sur l'histoire de France*. I am citing from the thirteenth edition (Paris, 1872), 75–76. Daumou expressly takes exception with this idea, and his criticism is a striking instance of the tenacity of the myth of the legislator as cause: the aim of history is not to explain institutions by society, but on the contrary society by institutions. *Journal des savants*, December 1823, 703–12.

59. *Histoire des français* (Paris, 1821), i:iii.

60. Ibid., xxvi. The same idea appears in the *Histoire des républiques italiennes du Moyen-Âge* (Zurich and Paris, 1807–18): "One of the most important conclusions one can draw from history is that government is the most effective determinant of a people's character" (1:i).

61. The book is published in October. Guizot loses all his official functions in the reaction following the murder of the Duc de Berry: he leaves the Interior Ministry in February, the Council of State in July.

62. "Histoire veritable de Jacques Bonhomme, d'après les documents authentiques," *Le censeur européen*, May 12, 1820.

63. "Sur la conquête de l'Angleterre par les Normands: À propos du roman d'Ivanhoé," *Dix ans d'études historiques*.

64. The first of Walter Scott's novels to be translated into French is *Guy Mannering* in 1816. It is followed by *The Puritans* and *The Antiquarian* in 1817, *Edinburgh Prison* in 1818, *Waverley, The Soldier of Fortune*, and *The Bride of Lammermoor* in 1819 (Scott's first novel in his own language, *Waverley*, appeared in July of 1814). At his death the editor Gosselin will estimate the volumes published in Paris in the Defauconfret translation at one and a half million. On Scott's success in France see Klaus Masmann, "Die Rezeption der historichen Romane sir Walter Scotts in Frankreign (1816–1832)," *Studia Romanica* (Heidelberg, Carl Winter Universitats-Verlag) 24 (1972). Louis Maigron, in his classic study *Le Roman historique à l'époque romantique* (Paris, 1898), confirms the assessment in Pontmartin's memoirs: "this vogue, of which the year 1827 marked the highest point."

65. In spite of the efforts of *La Thémis*, recently brought to light in the work of Donald Kelley, *Historians and the Law in Post-Revolutionary France* (Princeton, 1984). One should make an exception for Guizot, who read and admired Savigny (but was more open to the results of his technical scholarship than to his guiding ideas). See note 69.

66. This ideology is well described by the abbé Brémond, "Walter Scott," in *Pour le romantisme* (Paris, 1923). See also the illuminating remarks of Jean Molino, "Qu'est-ce que le roman historique?" *Revue d'histoire littéraire de la France* 75, nos. 2–3 (March–June 1975): 195–234. See also in this same issue another important article, by Claude Duchet, "L'Illusion historique: L'Enseignement des préfaces (1815–1832)," 245–67.

67. Is it necessary to specify that we only mean to evoke, in these few lines, the logic of idea types? On this subject, see for instance Jacques Droz, "Concept français et concept allemand de l'idée de nationalité," in *Europa und der Nationalismus* (Baden-Baden, 1950), 111–27.

68. Claude Fauriel, preliminary discourse to *Les Chants populaires de la Grèce moderne,* 2 vols. (Paris, 1824–25), 1:xxv. With explicit reference to Fauriel, Thierry writes in the introduction to the *Histoire de la conquête de l'Angleterre par les Normands*: "The resurrection of the Greek nation demonstrates what a mistake it is to take the history of kings, or even that of conquering peoples for that of the whole country they dominate. Patriotic regret lives on in people's hearts long after all hope is gone of raising up the ancient fatherland . . .this is what recent work has taught us about the Greek nation, and what I have discovered for the Anglo-Saxon race by tracking down its history where nobody thought to seek it, in popular legends, traditions, and poetry" (*Oeuvres complètes,* 1:8–9).

69. Guizot hails Savigny's book, which he uses abundantly, as "perhaps the best work produced by the progress of historical criticism today." *Essais sur l'histoire de France,* 199.

70. An allusion, of course, to the *Origines du droit français cherchées dans les symbols et les formules du droit universel* (1837), in *Oeuvres complètes* (Paris, 1973), vol. 3.

71. *Dix ans d'études historiques,* 395–96.

72. Alessandro Manzoni, *Du Roman historique,* trans. René Guise with his re-edition of *The Betrothed* (Paris, 1968), 327.

73. The most suggestive piece in this vein is by Roland Barthes, "Le Discours de l'histoire," *Information sur les sciences sociales* 6, no. 4 (1967): 65–75.

74. Letter to Fauriel, Fall 1824, cited in Jean-Baptiste Galley, *Claude Fauriel, membre de l'Institut, 1772–1843* (Saint-Etienne, 1909), 302.

75. Foreword to *Lettres sur l'histoire de France,* x–xi.

76. *Précis de l'histoire moderne,* in *Oeuvres complètes,* 2:24.

77. *Considérations sur l'histoire de France,* 315.

78. *Dix ans d'études historiques,* 305.

79. Here is how Anquetil, writing in 1805, describes his approach at the beginning of his book, having reported that Napoleon urged him to produce "a history freed from the details and accoutrements which make that of France so voluminous":

> I took as guides the four general historians, Dupleix, Mézeray, Daniel, and Veilly. First, I convinced myself through my own reminiscences that nothing that offers any interest in French history was forgotten by all four of these writers, or that if one forgets it, the other one restores it; that they evaluated their sources, and therefore putting an authority's name in the margin was the equivalent of citing a proof. Then, when I had a subject to treat, I examined which one of them addressed it best, and made his account the basis for my own; then I added from the three others whatever was missing from my favorite. (*Histoire de France* [Paris], 1:vii)

80. *Dix ans d'études historiques,* 305.

81. "Sur les trois grandes méthodes historiques en usage depuis le seizième siècle," in *Lettres sur l'histoire de France,* 56–57.

82. Ibid.

83. *Considérations sur l'histoire de France*, 119.

84. The tenth of the *Lettres* of 1820, republished in 1827, is in fact an article published in the *Censeur* on February 21: "Sur quelques erreurs de nos historiens modernes: À propos d'une histoire de France à l'usage des collèges." An eleventh letter, "Épisode de l'histoire de Bretagne," appeared a bit later, in December, in the *Courrier français. Le Drapeau blanc* writes of the first letter: "This is one of the most heinous of the intellectual opposition's tactics; it amounts to a criminal slur against the sacred virginity of the throne by trying to deny it five centuries of existence, an incitement to civil war, to arm Frenchmen against one another. Fréret would have been thrown into the Bastille for far less; we demand a salutary rigor" (cited by A. Augustin-Thierry, 71).

85. *Dix ans d'études historiques*, 307.

86. Stendhal, *Lettres de Paris, 1825* (Paris, 1823), 213. Stendhal alludes to the project for a history of France by Chateaubriand who "would have described in the most elegant style the eight-hundred years of happiness France enjoyed after Clovis's conquest."

87. Smithson dates from then Thierry's change in political attitude, and his transition from republicanism to liberal and constitutional monarchism.

88. In the preface to the *Études historiques* (1831): "One cannot sufficiently lament the excessive work which deprived monsieur Thierry of his vision. Let us hope that he will for many years dictate to his friends, for his admirers (of whom I beg to be first in line), the pages of our Annals: history will have its Homer, as did poetry" (Paris edition, 1838, 37).

89. *Considérations sur l'histoire de France*, 120.

90. The maxim is known to us in this form through E. Lemontoy, *Essai sur l'établissement monarchique de Louis XIV* (Paris, 1818), 327. (He is citing the manuscript of a lesson in public law for the instruction of the duke of Bourgogne.) In 1814, the charter states, "We have considered, although all authority in France resides in the person of the king."

91. *Du gouvernement de la France depuis la Restauration et du ministère actuel* (October 1820), *Des moyens de gouvernement et d'opposition dans l'état actuel de la France* (October 1821), *Des conspirations et de la justice politique* (January 1822), *De la peine de mort en matière politique* (June 1822). The sentence quoted is from *Des moyens de gouvernement*, 128.

92. *Histoire des origins du gouvernement représentif en Europe* (Paris, 1851), 1:iii.

93. *Considérations sur l'histoire de France*, 107.

94. *Lettres sur l'histoire de France*, 4.

95. *Dix ans d'études historiques*, 107.

96. See for instance the text in the collection by L. Duguit and H. Monnier, *Les Constitutions et les principales lois politiques de la France* (Paris, 1825), 183.

97. *Dix ans d'études historiques*, 516–17.

98. Foreword to *Lettres sur l'histoire de France*, i.

99. *Lettres sur l'histoire de France*, 61.

100. *Dix ans d'études historiques*, 502.

101. Ibid., 501.

102. G. de Humboldt, *La Tâche de l'historien,* trans. A. Disselkamp and A. Laks (Lille, 1885), 86.

103. Ibid., 103.

104. Ibid., 87.

105. Michelet, *Écrits de jeunesse,* ed. Paul Villaneix (Paris, 1954), 236.

106. Dugald Stewart, *Histoire abrégée des sciences métaphysiques, morales, et politiques,* 3 vols., trans. J. A. Buchon (Paris, 1820–23). The text by Cousin is from the *Supplément* in volume 3, "De la philosophie de l'histoire," 327–36. It is reproduced with slight additions in Cousin's *Fragments philosophiques* (Paris, 1826). On the relationship of Cousin to Scottish philosophy, see the proceedings of the colloquium *Victor Cousin, les idéologues et les écossais* (Paris, 1985).

107. "De la philosophie de l'histoire," in D. Stewart, *Histoire,* 3:333.

108. We have the documents pertaining to this fascinating exchange: Michelet, *Écrits de jeunesse,* 408–10.

109. Ibid., 410.

110. *Discours sur l'unité de la science,* in *Oeuvres complètes,* 1:250.

111. *Précis de l'histoire moderne,* in *Oeuvres complètes,* 2:71.

112. Ibid., 24.

113. *Oeuvres complètes,* 1:592.

114. *Écrits de jeunesse,* 237.

115. *Introduction à l'histoire universelle,* in *Oeuvres complètes,* 3:229.

116. Ibid., 247.

117. Ibid. See the *Tableau de la France*: "The most centralized people is also the one which has most advanced the centralization of the world," *Oeuvres complètes,* 4:383.

118. *Introduction à l'histoire universelle,* in *Oeuvres complètes,* 3:256.

119. Ibid., foreword, 227.

120. *Introduction à l'histoire universelle,* in *Oeuvres complètes,* 3:255.

121. Ibid., 256.

122. Paul Vidal de La Blache, "Tableau de la géographie de la France," in *Histoire de France,* 2nd ed., edited by Ernest Lavisse, part 1, "Personnalité géographique de la France," 1:7–8.

123. Michelet, 1866 preface to the 1831 *Histoire romaine,* in *Oeuvres complètes,* 2:335.

124. Response to Sainte-Beuve, 1837, cited by Paul Villaneix, *La Voie royale, essai sur l'idée de people dans l'oeuvre de Michelet* (Paris, 1959), 216. We purposefully chose very early formulations of the sorts of statements one finds similarly expressed in later works.

125. Letter to Lenormand, 1833, cited in Villaneix, *La Voie royale,* 190–91.

126. *Introduction à l'histoire universelle,* in *Oeuvres complètes,* 3:247–48.

127. "Tableau de la France," in *Histoire de France,* in *Oeuvres complètes,* 4:384.

128. 1866 preface to the *Histoire romaine,* in *Oeuvres complètes,* 4:335.

129. 1833 preface to the *Histoire de France,* in *Oeuvres complètes,* 4:626.

130. 1869 preface to the *Histoire de France,* 11.

131. 1828–29 course at the École normale, cited by Villaneix, *La Voie royale,* 265.

CHAPTER 10

ᴇRNEST ᴌAVISSE'S ᴴISTOIRE DE ᴲRANCE: ᴾIETAS ERGA PATRIAM

PIERRE NORA

I. HISTORY AND NATION

The Advent of the New Sorbonne

One place, the Sorbonne; one name, Ernest Lavisse; one monument, the *Histoire de France* in 27 volumes: these three embody, at the turn of the nineteenth century, the national hegemony of history.

In the rapid reconstruction of higher education in a period of twenty-five years, history took the lion's share.[1] It was taught not just in the arts and humanities where in the twenty years from 1888 to 1908 the number of students increased from two thousand five hundred to nearly forty thousand. Nor was it limited to the École normale supérieure or the Collège de France or the École des chartes. It was also taught at new institutions already enjoying confirmed prestige: the École pratique des hautes études, which dates from 1872, and the even younger École du Louvre, founded in 1881.* It was this spectacular upsurge that struck a young Belgian professor, Paul Fredericq, on a visit to Paris in the early 1880s: "The École des chartes seemed to me to be an institution without peer. The École

---

* EDITOR'S NOTE: These are the prestigious institutions of higher learning in France devoted to the humanities in one form or another. The École normale supérieure trains university and secondary school teachers; the École des chartes trains those who work with
   ancient documents and manuscripts; the École Pratique des hautes études is similar to our
   Princeton Institute of Advanced Studies; the Collège de France grants no degree and the
   incumbents of the fifty-two chairs, appointed by the government, are free to offer what
   courses they choose; the École du Louvre teaches archeology, epigraphy, and museology.

329

pratique des hautes études is the place in Paris that offers the most solid, the most complete, and the most scientific education history."[2]

No other discipline came close to the status of history. It sank its roots into the base of primary education and permeated its entire spirit.[3] Abroad, it blossomed into a series of research institutes organized more or less on the model of the School of Athens (founded in 1846): Rome in 1876, Cairo in 1890. The French School of the Far East opened in Hanoi in 1901, a research institute in Florence in 1908, the School of Advanced Hispanic Studies in Madrid in 1909, the Saint Petersburg Institute in 1912, and a research institute in London in 1913. Within France itself, alongside traditional scholarly organizations, the discipline branched out and flowered into a new generation of scholarly societies born of specialized research. Some were devoted to certain periods, like the Société de l'histoire de la Révolution française (1888) and the Société d'histoire moderne (1901), and others were devoted to general questions such as the Société d'histoire d'art français (founded in 1876, reorganized in 1906), the Société d'histoire du droit (1913), and the Société d'histoire ecclésiastique de la France (1914). There were also societies dedicated to one person—a sign of further specialization—like the Société des études robespierristes (1907). Even then this enumeration, by no means exhaustive, does not take into account the vast network of local scholarly societies, flourishing but in quite a different spirit.* These local societies were often scorned by university historians but some of them, like the Société de l'histoire de Normandie (1869), the Société des archives historiques du Poitou (1871), and those societies of Saintonge and Aunis (1874), Paris and the Île-de-France (1874), have published collections of high value, issued their own journals, and for the sake of a national history created at the local level a sounding board and a reserve of good will of inexhaustible wealth.[4]

Yet introducing history to the nation did not happen so much because of its institutional flourishing as it did because of its new internal qualities. Even if the mastery of the texts had no patriotic value in and of itself, the link between philology and national sentiment was strong. Not only had the new philology modeled on German methods and furnished history with a model of true science, but philology also entailed, even more profoundly, moral austerity and intellectual asceticism. In the cloister of the new libraries, haunted by phantoms newly awakened by the great scholars of the Renaissance and by the Benedictines of Saint-Maur, a lay monasticism had retrieved clerical erudition for the benefit of republican service and its intellectual and moral reform—an ethical promotion of

---

* EDITOR'S NOTE: See Françoise Bercé, "Arcisse de Caumont et les sociétés savants," in *Lieux de mémoire*, vol. 2, *La Nation*, 533–567.

Fig. 10.1

"Hatred is blind and for that reason France must not use it as a guide on its difficult journey" (Ernest Lavisse).

the document that counted without doubt as much as its scientific promotion. "The true historian is a philologist," declared Lavisse to his students on the opening day of classes at the Sorbonne.[5] "One does history with documents"—so begins the first sentence of the breviary entitled *Introduction aux études historiques* by Langlois and Seignobos (1898). When Julien Benda later recalled his reasons for supporting Dreyfus, he attributed his actions to his "faith in the method instilled in me by mathematics and the discipline of history."[6]

"Method"—for the new school it was the master word that ruled in all of its manifestations. It was expressed in the rational organization of research, the training of students through a program of examinations, and the creation of student associations patronized and defined by the leading lights of history. One student organization in 1893 held an unfortunate dance at the Bullier café that for life-long member Gabriel Monod degenerated into a happy amusement, provoking his outraged resignation.[7] The method was expressed in the formation of a professional corps open only by initiation and the presentation of a thesis that was serious and significant. The corps was traversed by a hierarchy of careers and positions, the number of which doubled from five hundred in 1880 to more than one thousand in 1909. "Method"—the word stands for much more than a rule of work, much more than a repertory of texts, and much more than a habit of mind. What was formed at this time was the culture of the historian with its set of mental and physical tools, its work spaces, its defining structures of thought and reflexes, its sociability, its scale of values, its vocabulary, and its professional ethics imprinted by a quasi sacrificial and military spirit. When Camille Jullian wanted to do homage to his great predecessors, Thierry, Taine, or Fustel de Coulanges, he declared that they had rendered service to their country "as much as any soldier wounded on the field of battle." And when he drew up the statement of account, he noted:

> There is no country in the world or any period in history that has not been investigated in the last twenty-five years. Specialization has made such progress that each part of our history, each region of the Roman Empire and the world of ancient Greece has become a historical province with its own personnel, its legates, and its law: it has its master, its disciples, and its method.[8]

But, perhaps just because it was a corporation of historians, this immense national effort, coming as it did when France was experiencing its war and its revenge, was immediately accompanied by its own history as if the exploration, now at last scientific, into our origins was coupled with the celebration of its origins. None of the big names was immune to this self-history. A kind of saga of historical rebirth and its accession to scientific dignity was quickly solidified. One could still catch a weakened yet perfect echo of it in Louis Halphen's introduction to *Histoire et historiens depuis cinquante ans*, written in 1927:

> The War of 1870–1871, which brought such great disasters, was a stimulant for a defeated France. We have to repair the ruins, regain through work the time lost, exhibit in all domains more sustained energy and activity. Academic disciplines received a new impetus with history among them. Then France, which had thrown out the (Second) Empire on September 4, 1870, rejected every attempt to restore the monarchy and granted to itself in 1875 constitutional laws in which the republican form of government was recognized.
>
> Had not the moment come to create a *Revue historique* that would record and hasten this rebirth of history and that, while allowing its collaborators full freedom of judgment, would declare itself independent of every religious doctrine and animated by a liberal spirit? One man thought so and through his tenacity brought the enterprise to successful fulfillment.
>
> Gabriel Monod, born in Le Havre on March 7, 1844, entered the École normale at eighteen years of age.[9]

The plainly hagiographic tone here is of little importance. Whether more or less reserved, more or less lyrical, more or less debated, this patriotic-academic refrain pervaded and marked the epoch with its dense network of an enormous literature of tributes, evocations, biographical recollections, and death notices that constitutes a minor genre but a historical genre par excellence. It served as that incessant recall of memory that provided the background music for twenty-five years of collective instruction in higher education. It had its key dates, like the founding of the Hautes Études and the *Revue historique*, and its memorable events, like the struggle for the creation of the universities. It had its heroic master builders, from Duruy to Liard, from Albert Dumont to Octave Gréard. It had its commonplaces, like the comparison that had become ritual between French and German universities or like that between the old and new Sorbonne. It had its liturgy, from defense of the thesis to departure into retirement, declaimed in orations at the beginning of the academic year. It had its grand pauses, like the inauguration of the new buildings at the Sorbonne in 1889, the frescos and the paintings of which, in a vast mural inscription of memory, combined the portraits of its great ancestors, Ambroise Paré and Robert de Sorbon, with its notables for the new university culture, Claude Bernard, Émile Boutroux, René Goblet, and Ernest Lavisse.[10] Lavisse, moreover, was the one who presided over the celebrations, noting with excitement in a farewell to the foreign students the "berets of velvet, the caps with silver fringe, the birettas of red satin, the mortarboards with black tassels, the toques with plumes, sashes of all colors, age-old banners, and a thousand young faces showing the characteristics of the main human races."[11] It was a discourse in accents that were astonishingly *Boulangist*★ and reflected the moment, but at the same time it is not an exaggeration to read in it a sincere profession of Lavisse's faith and the depth of his thought:

> In the great uncertainty in which science and philosophy leave us concerning all vital questions, human activity would risk withering away if it had no tangible, visible, immediate object. I do know that if I hid from myself certain feelings and ideas, the love for the native soil, the long memory of one's ancestors, the joy of regaining my soul in their thoughts and actions, in their history, and in their legends; if I did not thrill at the national anthem, if I did not have for the flag the reverence of a pagan for an idol who demands incense and, on certain days, blood sacrifice; if I came to forget our national sufferings, then truly I would no longer know what I am and what I am doing in this world. I would lose the principal reason for living.

The Centrality of Lavisse

Lavisse the boss: a comparison between Lavisse and Gabriel Monod,[12] his alter ego in the new history, is instructive for measuring the exact place of Lavisse and his strategic role. The two men were side by side at the starting line, the *agrégation*, the competitive examination for the professoriate, in 1865, where Monod placed first, Lavisse second. But their lives, so close and so different, well illustrate the two poles of the university's triumph in the Third Republic. Lavisse did not directly participate in the scientific regeneration of history; he never attended the École des chartes or the Hautes études. He published but one article for *Revue historique*, in 1884, on royal power in the time of Charles V. His hunting ground was at the margins of the university, in politics, in publishing, and in good company. To Monod belonged the *Revue historique*, of which he was the sole director after the break with Fagniez; the Hautes études, of which he was, with

---

★ EDITOR'S NOTE: Named for the Republican general, Georges Boulanger, who almost led a coup d'état against a republic he believed had betrayed its principles. He fled for his life and committed suicide, romantically, at the grave of his mistress.

Alfred Rambaud,[13] the first of the tutors and over which he presided for thirty-five years; the École des chartes; and, finally, the Collège de France, where in 1906, on his retirement from the chair of history and morals, the chair of "General History and Historical Method"[14] was created for him. Lavisse had fiefs elsewhere: the Sorbonne, the École normale, the Académie française, and the *Revue de Paris*. The two chiefs divided the terrain. Monod was the born scholar, the man of the seminar with a reputation as a deadly boring professor, and he was the real initiator of the scientific revolution in history, which did not stop him from maintaining all his life a very intense and genuine relationship with Michelet, whom he knew well and whose papers he kept.[15] Lavisse, "that person in the nation," was the professor who enthralled his listeners and was a man at home in the ministries and the Conseil supérieur de l'instruction publique, who had a generous though generic rapport with young people and for whose jubilee in 1913 Président Poincaré of France presided in person.

But contrary to what one might assume from their careers, the real drudge was Lavisse. He was the peasant upstart who married Marie Longuet, a childhood friend from Le Nouvion-en-Thiérache, and who owed everything to a scholarship and social promotion from the École normale and the university. Right from the beginning, Gabriel Monod's horizon was much more open. Son of a well-off merchant from Le Havre and descendant of a long line of Protestant pastors, Monod was not yet at the Normale when the Pressensé, with whom he lodged in Paris, introduced him to various historians and intellectuals like Charles Gide, Paul Meyer, Ferdinand Buisson, Eugène d'Eichtal, and Anatole Leroy-Beaulieu. No sooner had he passed the *agrégation* than he fell in love, during a stay in Florence, with Olga Herzen, the daughter of the revolutionary Russian writer. He eventually married her after permission was granted by her adoptive mother, Baroness Malwida de Meysenburg, who introduced him, even before his visit to Berlin and Göttingen, to the entire intelligentsia of Germany and Wagnerian society. Nietzsche even offered, for his marriage, a piano composition for two hands. For his entire life, this liberal Protestant would remain a European and cosmopolitan spirit, the prototype of what would become, through the Dreyfus Affair in which he quickly became deeply involved, the grand "intellectual of the left." Lavisse managed his career with the caution of a peasant. He succeeded totally in obscuring the Bonapartist tilt of his youth to become the bard of the Republic, and his wait-and-see attitude in the Dreyfus Affair did not dampen the affection he enjoyed from Lucien Herr, the central personage of the intellectual left.[16] Lavisse's power, his prestige, and his moral authority, however, were never actually drawn from his knowledge or his politics but from his obsessive, vital, and tenacious identification with the national regeneration of pedagogy. It is this that made his university degree at once more banal and more fundamentally representative.

Lavisse, indeed, in almost textbook fashion, lived through all the existential university experiences of his generation. He did so even longer and more fully than all the others, since he saw the successive disappearance of his four chief contemporaries, Vidal de la Blache (1845–1918), Gaston Paris (1839–1904),[17] Alfred Rambaud (1862–1905), and Gabriel Monod (1844–1912). The four years granted him after the armistice permitted him to see, before his death, a flurry of publishing with the nine volumes of the *Histoire de France contemporaine* that would seal, with the last volume, *La Grande Guerre*, the national cycle that he embodied. His roots plunged deep into France, and his history, especially of Picardy, that land of his birth so marked by the memory of invasions, passed from emotion to intellect. At twenty-three he was apprenticed to Victor Duruy (to whom Albert, the son of the liberal minister and his comrade from the École normale, had introduced him), and was right at the heart of the first reforming effort. It was a defining experience. It gave him firsthand knowledge, for example, of the *Rapport au ministre sur les études historiques* (1867) by Geoffroy, Zeller, and Thienot; the opening sentence alone makes it worthy of posterity: "It is only the history of the past; the present belongs to politics and the future to God." He saw the *Enquête*, also issued in 1867, which revealed both the wretched state of higher education and the situation in detail of German universities. Among other documents, there is the letter in the archives from the French student Lavisse,[18] just returned from Heidelberg, that contains the key words, underscored in his own hand, that would be the leitmotiv for future action: "close relations with the masters," "the class is only an accessory, it is in the laboratory that the student is formed," "deep practical experience," "knowledge of the details," "examination focused on the facts," "under the eyes of the professor," "method, research, experimentation." Germany was where Monod had preceded Lavisse, and it took the shock of defeat for Lavisse to go there. He did not, however, go as an intellectual pilgrim, like so many others,[19] but as a professional who would bring back a doctoral thesis, which was followed by several works on Prussia. These positioned him to pass as a specialist in German studies in France until the discipline was established, with Charles Andler.[20]

When he came back from Germany in 1875, the efforts to strengthen the Republic after the May 16 crisis turned him into a confirmed republican and enabled him, within fifteen years, to move from plans to execution. At each step, Lavisse was there. The law of 1877 that set up student scholarships also provided for the professors (*maîtres de conférences*) to oversee them; Lavisse was one of those lecturers for one year at the École normale. In 1878, a group of reformers founded the Société de l'enseignement supérieur (the Society for Higher Education), that was to become, with its house organ, the *Revue internationale de l'enseignement*, a pressure group. Lavisse was a member, along with Ernest Renan, Émile Boutmy, Louis Pasteur, Paul Bert, and Marcelin Berthelot. In 1880, the undifferentiated degree became the degree in a subject. Lavisse was the one who presented a report the year he entered the Sorbonne as an academic assistant to Fustel de Coulanges—no small thing—which made him, in 1883, the director of historical studies. One year before, for the first time, the announcement of courses at the Sorbonne had used the word "student" and mentioned after certain courses "course closed." "History demands a great number of workers; we need to provide them and we need to seek them."[21] In the wooden shacks of the Gerson annex, soon to be legendary, he counted students as a miser counts his treasure: 152 in 1882, 173 in 1883! In that Sorbonne that he would not leave except to take over the direction of the École normale in 1904, each battle was his. There was the battle for students[22] and the battle for reforming the *agrégation*,[23] which attained its modern status in 1885 with tests of four to seven hours, its critical examination of texts, and its double requirement of a written and oral final examination. There was the battle for creating the *diplôme d'études supérieures* in 1886, for which Lavisse wanted the test of "creating something new" and that was to be required for all candidates for the *agrégation* in 1894. One only has to read the allocutions given by Lavisse at the beginning of every academic term, and religiously assembled by him for publication,[24] to appreciate the dramatic art with which, in the orders of the day from the Bonaparte professor to the army of students, these pedagogical innovations made their appearance and took on the stature of a national event: "Gentlemen, by virtue of a recent ministerial decision, the year we are inaugurating will be marked by an innovation for those among you who are decided on teaching." He was talking about the *diplôme d'études supérieures*. "I testify to historians that they are not to be content (I am speaking only of the best) with preparing their *agrégation* thesis, that excellent test; they will choose and receive from us subjects of short memoirs on interesting questions and deal with them from time to time in a such a way that we will be confident in their future. Those are the students who will never go to sleep."

One can hardly date the genesis of the project for a history of France from a debate over a single document. Lavisse appears fully armed from the moment of his first allocution to the Faculty of Letters on the first day of the course in the history of the Middle Ages in December 1881: "The history of France remains to be done, and it will not be done until squads of workers provided with good tools have cleared away the entire field." Only one element would be retained from this long discourse about the program[25]—the causes of "an almost entire lack of interest in the ancient history of our country"—and it would be crucial for the future realization of the program. Lavisse sees the causes even more in history's lack of influence and history's use in polemics, not to mention the Revolution that cut France off from a past that is only understood through its history:

> The Revolution left none of the monuments of old to survive for us; I understand those living monuments that have endured in other countries: royalty, the priests, classes or corporations, favored cities and regions whose privileges, contrary to reason, are founded in history. A monument of stone, a church, a manor house or house in the village is enough to bring even the ignorant traveler to stop and ask questions.

So as a result today memory passes through history:

> Indeed, our past is at the foundation of our being, forming our national temperament, but it has not left any visible traces. It is a subject of scholarship, reconstituting ancient French society, like studying Greek or Roman society. . . . The French require more effort than other peoples to recognize themselves among those old buildings of many styles with the adjacent structures and their broken lines jumbled around the main part. These structures were built without any prior order over the course of the long life of a people.

Poetry about the past, scientific scholarship, and patriotic inspiration all point to one conclusion:

> It will be asserted that it is dangerous to put a limit on intellectual work that must always be objective. But in those countries where knowledge is most honored, it is used for education of the nation. . . . What motto did those statesmen and scholars agree to engrave on the frontispiece of their work? In the belief that a humiliated Germany must be lifted up by disseminating love and knowledge of country, the motto they chose, drawn from the very sources of Germany's history, was *Sanctus amor patriae dat animum*. It is on the first page of the folio *Monumenta Germaniae*, bordered by a crown of oak leaves. . . . It is therefore legitimate to invite in advance the future legion of historians to question all the known and unknown witnesses of our past, to deliberate over and to understand their testimony well so that it becomes possible to give to the children of France this *pietas erga patriam* that assumes knowledge of one's country.

One therefore easily sees the consensus from which the *Histoire de France* grows with Lavisse as the directing intelligence: there was institutional consensus about the university as the chief motor of historical development, and no longer the peripheral institutions like the Collège de France, where Michelet was the prophet, or the École des chartes, the heir to an academic and scholarly tradition, or the Hautes études, too recent as a laboratory. There was political consensus that right after the Dreyfus Affair, the Republic would seem to have triumphed definitively over the counterrevolutionary peril without being threatened by a new form of revolution. There was a practical consensus on teaching, the factory for fabricating citizens, historians, and patriots. Also there was consensus on the professorial corps of historian specialists as well as methodical consensus on the need and nature of the traditional masterpiece of the diploma and the thesis, between archive and rhetoric. There was intellectual consensus on "Science" and on "Truth" that conferred internal independence on a system henceforth entirely dependant on the State. And, finally, ideological consensus, especially, on the nation, the ecumenical framework for receiving "the successive legitimacies of the life of a people" that would disseminate "that correct notion that the things of old did have their raison d'être," and that one could love France without failing in one's obligations to the Republic. The *Histoire de France* would be that of the nation "achieved."[26]

The Nation Realized

With respect to the historic crystallization of the national idea in the first third of the twentieth century,★ we can measure the transformation and what it represented through its literary, intellectual, and theoretical impoverishment and, at the same time, its political achievement. The historian was no longer alone, the demiurge of national identity, conjuring up that identity through his narrative or through his analysis and, by his solitary look, dominating the totality of its evolution, inspired by a patriotic and religious spirit. Nor was he the cantor for a theophanic nation or the herald of a new gospel in which, as with Michelet, the Christlike principle, the symbol becoming flesh, and the land that nourishes, came together as one. He was an academic among academics who shared with each other the tools of their common trade. From the romantic to the positivist generation, all had changed as a function of the national monument he had created: the nature of the enterprise, the breath that inspired

★ EDITOR'S NOTE: See chapter 9, "Augustin Thierry's *Lettres sur l'histoire de France*," by Marcel Gauchet.

it, the historian who realized it, the style in which he wrote. The historian was no longer the nation incarnate; rather, it was the nation that had become incarnate. What remained was to put it down on note cards; and, in a passage regarding the *Introduction aux études historiques*, Langlois and Seignobos explained how to arrange them, in what format, on what paper, how many copies, and what "very simple precautions to take to minimize the drawbacks of the system."[27] Critical and methodical history dramatically inaugurated the age of the effacement of the historian in the presence of its documents and the return to what the historians of "perfect history" used to call, in the sixteenth century, the "middle style" as it related to the style of the epic eloquence or poetry. "The most seductive history," said Camille Jullian, "is perhaps that where the historian appears less and where the reader is more directly struck by the expression of truth."[28] From Michelet, we know all, beginning with his nocturnal fantasies. From Lavisse or from any of his collaborators, we do not even know if they left an intimate journal; nor, if there were one, whether we would need it to facilitate an understanding of the *Histoire de France*. That history is, conversely, totally inseparable from the moment when it was hammered out and from the parameters that dominated it, namely Germany and the deep roots of republican democracy.[29]

The Franco-Prussian War of 1870 radically transformed, in the minds of the French, the role of Germany and the definition of its identity. Germany was no longer the Germany with its great and inspiring ancestors whose praises were sung by Michelet ("It was my Germany that made me ask the basic questions"), by Taine and Renan of the Second Empire, or by the *Revue germanique* of 1858 through which, with Littré's help, "the philological and scientific method" was already filtering in. To be sure, Germany would remain the principal factor for intellectual emulation. The Germany of the war and the annexation of Alsace-Lorraine not only provoked the emotional revitalization of patriotic sentiment, it also determined, at its most profound, a redefinition of the nation itself. Intended not as a radical break, that redefinition achieved nothing less than a body of organic doctrine that would be the bearer of a nation's new outlook on its history. It was clearly apparent in the answer given by Fustel de Coulanges (the great French historian of French origins) to Theodore Mommsen (the great German historian of the Roman Empire) to the question, "Is Alsace German or French?" (1870), and in the famous lecture given by Renan on "What Is a Nation?" (1882):

> A nation is a soul, a spiritual principle. Two things, which in point
> of fact are one, constitute this soul, this spiritual principle. One is in
> the past, the other in the present. One is the possession in common of

a rich legacy of memories; the other is mutual consent, the desire to live together, the will to continue asserting the heritage that we have received intact. Gentlemen, man is not invented. The nation, like the individual, is the result of a lengthy time of effort, sacrifice, and dedication. Worship of one's ancestors is the most legitimate of all; our ancestors made us what we are. A heroic past, great men, *gloire* (I mean the true *gloire*)—that is the social capital on which one bases a national idea.[30]

The definition echoes Michelet in many respects, but its date and pre–Maurice Barrès* accent alter the meaning and impact. If the nation maintains its identity only in the "profound complications of its history," to use Renan's words, and not in the formal membership conferred by language, race, interests, religious affinities, and military necessity, then its history in its entirety has a claim on our love and knowledge, and not just the part of history that begins with the Revolution. In the attempt by the entire nineteenth century to clarify the trauma of the Revolution, Germany introduced a shock: it dislodged decisively the borders of the legitimate identity of the nation. The formative break as a principle no longer affected what was internal to the nation, meaning the history of France occurring between a condemned ancien régime and an assumed modern France, but rather what was external, meaning what happened in the case of a nation established by its own evolution and one established through deed and might. The past found itself rehabilitated. Put bluntly, Germany's contribution was to make the geographic border sacred and to remove the curse that weighed on the historic border.

Lavisse's general outline makes this shift absolutely clear (see appendix 10.1, the outline for the *Histoire de France*), and we have only to recall from it that the first series (1901–11), the only one initially projected, goes "from the origins to the Revolution" and that the two powerful moments he chose clearly express, from the beginning to the end, the most intense images of national identification: the *Tableau de la géographie de la France* and his own *Louis XIV*.[31] A reference to Michelet? Certainly, but we must not forget that Michelet situated his *Tableau de France* in book 3 around the year 1000, after the accession of Hugh Capet. Can one say more clearly that France for him prior to that was not an organic unity? The *Tableau de la géographie* that Lavisse requested from Vidal de La Blache (see appen-

---

* EDITOR'S NOTE: Maurice Barrès (1862–1923) was a nationalist writer whose birth in Lorraine doubtless had a lot to do with his anti-German stance. He was a strong supporter of the military in the Dreyfus Affaire and one of the most articulate prophets of a strident nationalism that would exclude foreigners.

dix 10.2)—the only collaborator of his own intellectual stature—Lavisse put as the introduction, granting him an entire volume: France existed before France. This certitude was again confirmed in the second volume, on Gaul, which Michelet had dispatched in one chapter. Doubtless Lavisse intended to promote the Gauls in the national imagination, something not done since the work of Amédée Thierry, brother of Augustin (1828), and to give strong affirmation to Vercingétorix, whom the Republic had dignified as one of its founding heroes.[32] Doubtless too, with German scholarship having appropriated Gaul, recovering a centerpiece of French identity became the question for French scholarship. Doubtless, finally, that the archeological exploitation of Gaul had been scientifically inscribed into Fustel's legacy, as Camille Jullian's work was about to show.[33] The juxtaposition of the *Tableau de la géographie* and *La Gaule* was to provide nothing less than a solid point of departure to national identity: France was there at the outset, before history, in its outlines, its territory, and its character. The belief in providence was transferred, as it were, into its genetic program before being projected into its history.

The *Louis XIV* represents the other pole and, curiously, the historical counterpoint to the *Tableau*. The arc of history itself came to an end. After a very narrative, almost journalistic, beginning that brought his hero to his installation in power in 1661, there began, in nearly two volumes, a vast fresco divided into the "government of the economy," "government of politics," "government of society," "government of religion," and "government of the mind." The parallel was not purely formal. The same tension animated the two sections: in the first, tension between geographic individuality and regional divisions, and in the second, tension between deep admiration for the grandeur of the person and the epoch, in which Lavisse was seen visibly at his ease and secretly silhouetted, and condemnation of a monarch whose clearest achievement had been to obtain political obedience. Nothing could be more significant for Lavisse than reserving for himself the classical monarchy in all its radiant magnificence, but not the end of the reign. He left its wars and foreign policy to Alexandre de Saint-Léger, economic history to Philippe Sagnac, and religious and intellectual matters to Alfred Rebelliau (*Histoire de France*, 8:1). What really held and fascinated him was the great period from 1661 to 1685, the contrast between the monarch in glory and the monarch in battle, the violent play of light between the man who, in 1668, "could believe that he had responded to the expectations of the world," and the man who, in 1685, at the cost of an exhausted France, "could believe he had conquered Europe through the Treaty of Ratisbon and the Calvinist heresy through the revocation of the Edict of Nantes." Lavisse entrusted the major incarnation

Fig. 10.2
(*Top*) Alfred Rambaud.

Fig. 10.3
(*Left center*) Gaston Paris.

Fig. 10.4
(*Center*) Gabriel Monod.

Fig. 10.5
(*Right center*) Charles V. Langlois.

Fig. 10.6
(*Bottom*) Charles Seignobos.

of France to this Louis XIV, whose portrait he refrained from retouching and whom at the moment of leaving he could not leave:

> Reason may have discovered "the destructive base" of this reign, but the imagination resists, seduced by "the brilliant exterior." It feels affection for the memory of this man, who was not at all a bad man, who had the qualities, even virtues, of beauty, grace, and the gift of speaking so well. This man at the moment, when France glittered, represented it brilliantly and refused to admit "despondency" when it was overwhelmed, maintained his great role from the raising of the splendid curtain to the somber scenes of the last act, in the décor of a fairyland, with those palaces built in unknown places on inhospitable land, fountains gushing from a soil without water, trees brought from Fontainebleau or from Compiègne, that retinue of men and women uprooted as well and transplanted there to figure in the choir of a tragedy so distant to our eyes, unaccustomed to these spectacles and customs that have something of the charm and grandeur of antiquity.

The "great Lavisse" is truly Lavisse the Great. With the *Tableau de la géographie* as a bridge, the two sections express the state of the national mind at its height, expanded to the dimensions of the land and its history, the fullness of a national monument.

It was the decisive moment when, in the momentum of regeneration, history conquered for itself scientific, professional, and national legitimacy. It was the moment of the *Histoire de France*, powerfully dated, yet radically representative, at the crossroads of critical history and republican memory. In its genesis, as in its spirit, it flowed from the consequences of a defeat to the outcome of a victory. What fundamentally distinguished it from the uninterrupted flow of histories of France, making of the twenty-seven volumes a *lieu de mémoire*, was this interpenetration of scientific certainty and the obsessive cult of country. It was the crucible in which two truths were momentarily fused that seem to us to be unrelated but that the period had made indissolubly complementary: the universal truth of the archive and the particular truth of the nation.

II. ARCHIVE AND NATION

The Documentary Memory

The moment of its official birth, which all contemporaries celebrated, was the first issue of the *Revue historique* in 1876 and the lead article by Gabriel Monod.[34]

It was a major text: one of its concerns was to present itself as a history of "Progress in Historical Studies," linked with progress in scholarship. Monod, as the heir, was to take up the torch, exhuming memory precisely and arranging the links: First there were the precursors of the sixteenth century, founders of a critical method, like Claude Vignier in his *Bibliothèque historiale* or Claude Fauchet, "who was the first to submit the antiquities of the Gauls and the French to impartial criticism." Then came the scholars in the monarchist circle like André Duchesne, "at the first rank of publishers of the seventeenth century," and Du Cange, "the first to give historians the indispensable instruments for scientific study of the Middle Ages" and "to whom Louis XIV meant to entrust the supervision of a large number of historians of France." Along with this royal historiography there was the ecclesiastical historiography of the Jesuits, the Oratorians, and especially the Benedictines of Saint-Maur, to whom "our gratitude could never be sufficient" for "that combination of reverent piety and steadfast independence that gave to all their labors so much gravity and authority." Next in line was the Académie des inscriptions et belles lettres, which led to Bréquigny, "on whom was based, almost exclusively, all the work done for the collection of ordinances, the general table of charters and official documents." That brought us to Guizot and the collection of hitherto unpublished documents assembled by the Société d'histoire de France in which Monod singles out the exceptional quality of the work by Guérard, the publisher of cartularies and polyptychs. Three powerfully linked principles are thus demonstrated: the idea, affirmed at the start in the title, that "it is only with the Renaissance that historical studies properly begin"; the affirmation that "the misfortune from which historical science in France has suffered the longest is the separation, or better, the antagonism so long asserted between literature and scholarship;" and, finally, the certitude that that delay is "the fatal result of the absence of well organized higher education from which young people would come to draw both general culture and habits of method, criticism, and strict intellectual discipline."

Starting from this point, the construction and organization of documentary memory was begun and advanced by both students from the École des chartes, skilled in paleography and archival studies, and historians. We still live on their efforts, the chief lines of which can only be mentioned here in brief. There is first of all the great series of published documents, an immense and often interminable task pursued through the Comité des travaux historiques et scientifiques and the Société d'histoire de France and that, from the collection of charters and official documents by Giry, for example, to the *procès-verbaux* of the Committee of Public Safety and the Committee of Public Instruction, formed the foundation. Then there was the work on the catalog and a real bibliography, the groundwork for every possible use and the retaining structure for the galleries of the documentary mine, to which not the drudges but the stars of archival science and histo- riography yoked together were to have priority. The task was enormous, and the achievements were concurrent. In 1886, for example, when the *Annuaire des bibliothèques et des archives de France* began, there also appeared, according to Léopold Delisle's plan, the *Catalogue général des manuscrits des bibliothèques publiques de France*. In 1895, the Bibliothèque nationale began publishing its catalog of published books and user catalogs for the Depart- ment of Manuscripts. In 1888, the first model of this sort appeared when Gabriel Monod himself published a *Bibliographie d'histoire de France* with 4,542 titles, intended to provide "scholarly individuals and particularly students" with an index similar to the one his master, Georg Waitz, had created across the Rhine; he, in turn, had drawn on Friedrich Christoph Dahlmann's *Bibliographie*. That *Bibliographie* was the starting point for the collection, still indispensable and well known to historians, entitled *Sources de l'histoire de France*, systematically pursued by Auguste Molinier,[35] from the origins of France to the end of the fifteenth century and the wars in Italy (five volumes from 1901 to 1906), by Henri Hauser for the sixteenth century (two volumes, 1906), and by Émile Bourgeois and Louis André for the seventeenth century (eight volumes, 1913). This type of bibliography finds a parallel in the *Bibliographie générale des travaux des sociétés savantes*, nine volumes published between 1880 and 1907 by Robert de Lasteyrie and his collaborators, and in the *Répertoire méthodique de l'histoire moderne et contemporaine de la France* (1899) by Georges Brière and Pierre Caron, the latter noting in his important *Rapport sur l'état actuel des études d'histoire moderne en France* written with Philippe Sagnac in 1902 that "the simple possibility of doing work on any topic whatsoever in modern history is directly related to the level of organization in the archives and manuscript collections." To these purely operational signposts on the landscape, pro- viding illumination and allowing access to the users, one might usefully add the specifically historical bibliography, the index of the indexes and the science of the instruments of research. A greatly developed version by Charles V. Langlois, for example, may be found in Langlois' *Archives de France* (1891), done in collaboration with Henri Stein, or in Langlois' *Manuel de bibliographie historique* (two volumes, 1896 and 1904).[36] Another may also be found in Xavier Charmes' work on *Le Comité des travaux his- toriques et scientifiques* (1886) or in the 200-page introduction by Auguste Molinier to his *Sources de l'histoire de France*, written two months before his death and placed at the beginning of his last volume.

It is all the work of the stoker at the furnace, but it is important to put the spotlight on him. Why? Because merely evoking the person suffices to illuminate the innovation in entire sections of the *Histoire de France* in which Lavisse, notably in his own portrait of the reign of Louis XIV, which appeared before the work by Bourgeois and André, could rightly say: "There do not exist for the modern period of our history any scientific manuals that can serve as the guides for the study of institutions and mores such as one finds for the history of Antiquity and the Middle Ages." It is especially the case because critical history, if it is given the means of work for internal, professional, and general introductory use, has by definition excluded from its scope the historical in what are its own possibilities. The history of the court excluded the history of what might be called "behind the scenes." Interest in building the archives, collections, and libraries in the same way museums were built remained the speciality of scholars of scholarship; and history of memory, such as that being established today, indeed in this very essay, can only seek to bring that interest back onto the central paths of historiography. The archivist memory has weighed a little too heavily on the very formation of history and the study of history, making it impossible to take into account the particular circumstances of their union.

The Archivist Memory of the State

The archive has indeed made the historian dependent on its proper activity. It is more sensitive to conservation than to utilization, and that especially does not, in its essence and in its spirit, depend on the historian's curiosity, but on government power.[37] The meeting between the historian and the archives is therefore, in fact, the history of a slow conjunction that occurs accidentally, always contains traps, and goes in one direction. It is true that the expansion in archives was done in parallel with that of history and that it began right after 1830, affecting all of Europe within twenty years: the linkage is seen in the founding of the Archives of Bucharest in 1831, the first publications of the *Documentos ineditos* by the archivist Bofarull in Barcelona, the very important founding of the Institut für Österreichische Geschichtsforschung in Vienna in 1854, and, at the same time, the creation of schools of paleography and archival sciences in Madrid and Florence.[38] In France it occurs with the founding of the École des chartes in 1821,[39] or rather with its reorganization in 1829 and with Guizot's activities★ that came back to the original initiative.[40] But the simultaneity of trends did not preclude history and archives drawing on two profoundly different traditions. As important as the efforts by feudalists, royal historiographers, and Benedictine monks may have been and though great archivists like

★ EDITOR'S NOTE: See chapter 4, "Guizot and the Institutions of Memory," by Laurent Theis.

Muratori expressed deep concerns as historians, archives remained the private property of princes and kings, who kept them for strictly utilitarian use. It was a question of preserving the acts of their authority and their administration and providing themselves with a legal basis to their powers and their laws. The mighty of the land could have made the same witticism that Napoleon supposedly did when he launched an extravagant enterprise to bring together in Paris the complete archives of those states that had been annexed or occupied, adding, "A good archivist is more useful to the state than a good artillery general." Access, jealously controlled, remained in the keeping of the curators. The archives were "secret" weapons and true machines of war, and their ownership was at times bitterly disputed. As for the archivists, as independent as they might claim to be, they were only the faithful auxiliaries to power, in the pay of politicians and diplomats.

The notion of archives as "public" must not fool us as its development clearly shows. It does not refer to public use of documents, but to a bureaucratization of the monarchy from Philip the Fair in the early fourteenth century to the centralizing coronation of Napoleon. Here only a few of the main dates and currents can be noted. Spain furnished the first model in the middle of the sixteenth century when Charles V began transferring his treasury of the charters from Castile into the renowned fortress of Simancas. Similarly, in France official documents were no longer recorded in the registry of the *Trésor des chartes* after 1568. The move to keep the archives at the chancellery and with the secretaries of state was becoming standard and was to be generalized under Richelieu. It was in fact then, with the power of the monarchical administration of the state, that the notion of public archives underwent its first major extension. Starting in 1670, and continuing not without numerous irregularities and notable exceptions, the crown began taking possession of the archives of every major servant of the state at his death. A new phase of concentration occurred in the middle of the eighteenth century: in 1769, Maria Theresa created in Vienna the central repository of the Habsburg monarchy, the Haus-und-Hof-und Staatsarchiv, which was to serve as the model for Enlightenment Europe. The French Revolution and the Napoleonic Empire were to contribute in their turn a third wave of concentrated depositories: the Archives nationales, originally formed from a nucleus of papers from the Constituent Assembly at the Hôtel de Soubise, brought together, under the authority of Camus, not only the archival collections from the councils and high administrative bodies of the ancien régime, but also the archives of the abbeys, cathedral chapters, and churches of Paris, such as records of individual émigrés and individuals convicted by the courts. All this had to be sorted: "historical" documents would go to the Bibliothèque nationale, while items useful for the government and for litigation involving disputes over the national domains would be kept at the Hôtel de Soubise. Those papers deemed "useless" would be sold and those judged "deeds of tyranny and superstition" would be burnt. Camus' tenacious opposition limited such differentiation, and the Bureau du triage, which functioned for six years, with competent scholars in charge, fortunately limited the damage.

The contribution of the Revolution to archivist science and public archives is therefore profoundly ambiguous. In one sense, it is absolutely key. The Revolution established the very notion of archives. An ancien régime society by definition would not know such a concept, since there was no expiration date for any document. Authenticity did not establish the archive's authority, since that was already guaranteed by the possessor institution, but antiquity did. Without a doubt scholars and other learned men exchanged among themselves documents that had been pulled from the shadow of the Church and the State. The fact remains that making sources available was considered, in the France of the late eighteenth and early nineteenth centuries, in most cases a favor accorded to an individual at the conclusion of extremely long and often fruitless negotiations.[41] Mabillon himself sometimes failed to obtain from religious establishments the documents he needed. Theoretically then the ancien régime could know depositories of acts only like, at best, the one that Jacob-Nicolas Moreau created.[42] There can be archives only when authorities cease to have need of them—no archives, therefore, without the night of August 4, 1789. That was the first time, in fact, that a plan so broad was extended over the archives of an entire political, religious, and feudal regime and in one stroke extended the very notion of archives of the State to that of archives of the "Nation." The extent and systematic character of the positivist harvest would be incomprehensible without this enormous concentration of material. It put an end to the unimaginable dispersion and disorder to form true archivist capital and even went one step beyond the Archives nationales in Paris, where the Revolution instituted a depository of archives in each department and in each commune. Without that measure, and Guizot set the pace, the laws of 1838 and 1841 on the organization of the departmental archives (and, along with it, the formidable inventory of the collections, the publication of which was to begin in 1854) would have been pointless. In the end it was the Revolution that had proclaimed the fundamental principle: the archives, belonging to the nation, were to be put at the disposition of all the citizens. That principle, even if it clashed with restrictions on implementation or communication—installing a reading room in the archives began only around 1840—virtually made the professionalization of the discipline and the formation of scientific history possible.

But only virtually. Robert-Henri Bautier rightly remarked that the Revolution in no way constitutes the decisive break with the traditional conception of archives. On the contrary, it represents its crowning achievement.[43] The principle of making the archives public lay in the straight line of progression from monarchical legitimacy to national sovereignty. It in no way meant the abandonment of the State's prerogative. The authors of the law of 7 Messidor Year II (June 25, 1794) were addressing citizens; they were miles away from thinking of historians. The archives, enacted in law, remained in the meantime what they had always been, a symbol of continuity, centralization, and legitimacy. They were a theoretical right and a stock of practical material. Confirmation of that can be found inscribed in the nomenclature for the archives: twenty-four letters of the alphabet were devoted to the ancien régime and one single letter, the famous letter *F*, to the entire government collection of the last fifty years. The idea of giving flexibility to the structure did not occur to those guardians of memory, imbued merely with a protective vision and little prospective sense on what is right and proper to call, with appropriate solemnity, a heritage. Only in 1840, under pressure from the outside by historians, was the breach made—gradually, partially, and never completely—to expand with history (known as positivism). It is true that within twenty years, to use Robert Henri Bautier's phrase, "from the arsenal of authority the archives became the laboratory of history." The political stability of France had to be joined with the stability of its administrative patrimony so that the active memory of the nation might be nourished from the passive memory of the archival document. Osmosis then, not symbiosis, is what began.

The Archive Effect

The marriage of history and archive has not been quite intimate enough to impose itself as a model for the entire development of critical historiography.

The weight of memory in documents has had the initial result of forcefully shifting the center of gravity of national chronology, and the tendency has lasted as long as this kind of historiography. Marc Bloch called it the "dread of origins." The affirmation of the method, the supremacy of the text, the philosophical reflex, the Germanic influence, all contributed to hypostatizing the Middle Ages. The most contemporary issues are anchored in the most ancient archival material. Right from its start, critical history has retained—has it freed itself even in our days?—a chartist fixation. "At the École des chartes, in those distant days—that is, around 1880—," recounts Charles Braibant, whose archivist activities were deployed so effectively in the service of historians, "the medievalist experienced for the modernist something like the feeling of the cavalry-man for the infantryman. It would have done no good to come tell me that a historian occupied with events after 1453 could be anything but a poor man indeed."[44] Most of the founders of modern national history made their debut with work on the Middle Ages. Alfred Rambaud came from tenth-century Byzantium; Lavisse began with *La Marche de Brande-bourg sous la dynastie ascanienne*; Émile Bourgeois, pioneer in the diplomatic history of the nineteenth century, arrived there from the French aristoc-racy of ten centuries before; and Charles Seignobos, who in his *Histoire de France contemporaine* took charge of the whole period since 1848, began with a thesis on the feudal regime in Burgundy! One has to wait until 1880 for a thesis from the École des chartes that dared to go beyond that fateful date of 1500 and, for the teaching of modern history—a modest beginning with two lectures out of forty[45]—to be tried at the École des hautes études. Of the seventeen volumes of the *Histoire de France*, six were dedicated to the Middle Ages (more than a third).

The link between the archive and the Middle Ages is not only a prac-tical matter. It involves much more than an epistemology that connects remote times to the recent past both as cause and as beginning. It goes be-yond the embryogenic obsession natural to any exegetical concern. Marc Bloch already denounced the finalistic philosophy in it that was concealed behind that pure intoxication with far-flung erudition:

> A history centered on births was put to the service of defining
> values. . . . Whether it was the Germanic invasions or the Norman
> Conquest of England, the past was used to explain the present purely
> for purposes of justifying or condemning it such that in many cases
> the demon of origins was only an avatar of that other satanic enemy
> of true history: the mania for judgment.[46]

One can go further. In that "mania," cleverly masked by the knowl-edge of the text, the submission to the document, and the discipline of the archive to which the positivists often ended up believing that history was reduced, one cannot help but see the key to the formation of history as a corporate discipline and to the nerve of its authority. That the greatest of the chartists and the medievalists were, of all the historians, the first to throw themselves into the Dreyfus Affair is profoundly revealing.[47] Paul Meyer, Gaston Paris, Gabriel Monod, and so many others marched into the world of the journalists and the jurists as experts and moral authorities. Right after the acquittal of Major Charles Esterhazy (the actual German spy) *Le Siècle* devoted its entire first page to an article entitled "A Histo-

Fig. 10.7
Ernest Lavisse surrounded by his students in 1900 in the Dumont Library, which became the Lavisse Library.

rian Bears Witness." Arthur Giry, a member of the Institut, drew on tried
and true techniques of textual criticism to denounce the lying Henry
the very day the colonel gave evidence. At the first trial Giry, along with the
director of the École des chartes and Auguste Molinier, deposed at the
first Zola trial. Molinier's last written work before his death was the *Examen critique du bordereau*. Can their ideological engagement be separated
from their professional competence? Does not their engagement stand in
contrast to the rallying for the wait-and-see attitude of Lavisse the gen-
eralist? Working the charter, the decree, and the cartulary was for a long
time the heart of the "symbolic capital" of the historian. The archive did
not only impose a "dread of origins." It also imposed a metonymic use
of the "source."

The major impact of the archive, however, is not there, but in the
abrupt expansion that it prompted, to say nothing of the immediate explosion in the production of works of history. To rely blindly on Gregory
of Tours for a narrative about Clovis and the Merovingians, as Claude

Charles Fauriel and Jules Pétigny did, and then to add documents clearly produced later, like the writings of the seventh-century Fredegar or the *Liber historiae Francorum*, was one thing—recourse to direct accounts or to what were believed to be such, meaning close work on the narrators, chroniclers, and memorialists, had already refreshed discourse and enlarged the historical horizon.* But to grant to or to withhold credit from Gregory of Tours (he was a passionate and personal chronicler, writing his *Historia Francorum* sixty years after the death of the king) and to reestablish the exact transcription of Fredegar's manuscript to demonstrate that all those who drew from it were later inspired by it (as did, for example, Monod in 1872) was an exercise of a radically different kind.[48] And that points to a decisive threshold. In the one case, just going to the "source" does no more than return to the memory of tradition. In the other, by suspecting the source and inserting oneself deliberately into its reconstruction, one has entered the domain of criticism and science. Every history known as "positivist" has consisted in the shift from one to the other; that is, in the distinction between narrative source and archival document. In practice, the distinction took a long time to be established and perhaps it never was completely. Lavisse, and many others after him, never passed up the help memoirs provided to evoke Versailles and Louis XIV. But in theory, and that is what counts most here, the division appears sharply formulated. For example, from the introduction to the *Archives de France* (1891), in which Langlois and Stein wrote,

> What we understand by "archives of the history of France" is the collection of all *archived documents* relating to the history of France, that is, the official documents of any kind: charters, accounts, inquiries, etc., and private and political correspondence. In all, this definition excludes only one single series of old documents: literary, scientific, and historical works that have their place not in archives but in libraries.

A contrasting definition by Auguste Molinier captures the idea perfectly when in the introduction to the medieval sources for the history of France he wrote: "The complete and methodical study of the *narrative sources* of the Middle Ages in our history has not yet given rise to general works."

The simple change from narrative source to archival document ipso facto opened to history a diversification that was practically infinite. The difference in method can be compared only to the abrupt change in energy

---

* EDITOR'S NOTE: See Pierre Nora, "Memoirs of Men of State," in *The State*, vol. 1 of *Rethinking France: Les Lieux de Mémoire*.

systems, changing from the water-powered mill to the steam-powered mill, and then to the drill hole from which oil suddenly gushes forth. Some numbers, among the many possible, allow us to take the measure. In the catalog of dissertations, one single volume of 400 pages suffices for August Mourier and Félix Deltour to list all theses defended from 1800 to 1870; another volume of 600 pages for the fifteen following years (1880–95); but from 1895 to 1902, a third one just as big was necessary, listing as many in seven years as in the seventy before. After this, the volumes appear annually.[49]

Still, the quantitative change of scale was only the external sign of the expansion of history imposed and authorized by the archive when it was presented in its breadth and its immensity. As vast and interminable as discourse about the archives was, there was nothing surprising about historians long being content to have that discourse say what it was specifically saying, thereby determining the very type of history they were writing. If the historians of the positivist national generation oriented themselves first to political, administrative, military, diplomatic, and biographical history, is it unreasonable to think that it was not just from an ideological need to elucidate the origins of the nation? By suddenly taking the path of the archives, they found, in France more than anywhere else in Europe, the well-built bed of the central archives of the State. It is necessary to look closely—as did, for example, Christian Amalvi in an original article[50]—at the *Catalogue de l'histoire de France*, assembled by Jules Taschereau and Léopold Delisle, to see to what depth in the framework and nomenclature a certain type of history had been set in the basic bibliographical instruments, registered in the source materials in a neutral guise, and engraved in innocent research categories before being kneaded in the yeast of the historians. The monarchical character of the perception of the past stands out in the writing about kings who had not reigned, but one will not find the nomenclature listing names from the Revolution! There was a rapid cohesion of national history on the one side, a reunion of a heritage of long duration on the other. It was at the confluence of these two phenomena that the *Histoire de France* was forged. The Franco-Prussian War of 1870–71 and the rivalry between France and Germany, the construction of an apparatus of modern and democratic higher education, and the thorough acceptance of republican ideology precipitated the need for a national history. And yet if the type of history realized, which to later generations has seemed so shallow, was invested with the weighty responsibility of representing the nation, that was due to two major facts found in the French archival tradition: the venerable age of monarchical centralization and the scope as well as the radicalism of revolutionary reforms. The archives of power delineate a history of power, the archives of the state prefigured a history of the State.

The reason for both rupture and continuity, for this fin de siècle historiography, are contained in this intersection. Positivist national historiography is the eldest daughter of the oldest of the nation states, daughter and servant. By placing history as science on the keystone of the document, by establishing the archival document as guarantor of truth and as criterion for scientific authenticity, and by conferring on it the definitive dignity of proof, the generation of "positivists" achieved nothing less than furnishing the nation—now democratic, bourgeois, and liberal—with the titles of legitimacy and retrieving for its benefit the prestigious and subservient function that before them the feudal clerks and court historians of the ancien régime had exercised for the mighty of the land. The archive in turn furnished history the initial condition for its formation and the indispensable instrument of its dynamism by putting a definitive end to the two monologues of discourse and erudition and by allowing them to be joined. History with no other source than the texts of historians is potentially universal in its discourse, but necessarily limited in its objectives. Erudition with no horizon but its own curiosity is unlimited in its objectives but confined by the capriciousness of its own curiosity. By unifying history and erudition under the national perspective, the archive delivered the one from frivolity and the other from gossip. The archive made of positivist history the moment of a unique conjunction, one in which it would be possible for the immense capital of a traditional memory to pass "methodically" through the sieve of destructive and confirmatory scholarly memory. Conditions had converged so that a necessary history of France might become a possible history.

III. Critical Memory and Republican Nation

The Historical in the Histoire de France

Concerning the *Histoire de France*, there is certainly an interior history and an exterior history that do not coincide. The first presents a façade of beautiful unity. The second, which includes several obscure points and difficult explanations, appears largely to contradict that unity.

The adventure, to be sure, unfolded over a period of ten years, from the date of the publication of the first volumes in 1901 (Luchaire and Langlois, *Histoire de France*, vols. 1, 2, and 3), to the illustrated general publication, with its analytical tables, in 1911. It took twenty years, if one goes by Lavisse's contract of March 1892.[51] Lavisse at that time optimistically planned for fifteen volumes to be published from 1894 to 1898. Thirty years, if one includes the *Histoire de France contemporaine*. For us today, this second series seems completely tied to the first; the impression of the whole would appear very different if it lacked the Revolution and if the last volume did not illuminate the entire panorama of the heroic understanding of the Great War. That, however, was not planned. Two ways of reading this *Histoire* are therefore possible. When the first series was launched with success, the partners at the Hachette publishing house decided, in November 1904, to extend it with the idea of turning to Albert Sorel if Lavisse did not accept.[52] When Lavisse gave his consent, after three months of reflection, the contract, dated August 4, 1905,[53] envisioned again, optimistically, eight volumes to be published between 1907 and 1909. With the delays and the interruption of the war they would appear between 1920 and 1922. But the conditions were not the same: plans had to be made, in a panic, for a volume on the war and two specialists were appointed to join Seignobos: Auguste Gauvain, who was managing foreign policy for the *Journal des débats* and who had served as chief editor for *La Vie politique à l'étranger*, a yearly publication in the 1890s that Lavisse had managed, and Henri Bidou, likewise an editor at the *Journal des débats* and whom Lavisse had passed for his D.E.S. (Diplôme d'Études Spécialisées). They also had to redo the volumes on the Revolution, for Pariset never did turn in his copy. In December 1919, the editor advised breaking off from that "terrible man [Pariset]."[54] Sagnac was more understanding of the urgency, but having written the main part of the book between 1906 and 1909, he had meanwhile thrust himself into *Le Rhin français pendant la Révolution et l'empire* (1917). He saw himself obliged to do a general rewriting. "You know that my volume is based in part on unpublished documents—some of these documents have recently been published—I am proposing to take some soundings in one or two series in the Archives Nationales in order to reply to M. Lavisse's questions" (December 9, 1917). Finally, and most especially, Lavisse was getting old, and that meant that the bulk of the enterprise rested on three people: Seignobos, who was always a little eccentric and individualistic but still wrote nearly half of the nine volumes; Guillaume Bréton, who saw to daily matters; and most particularly Lucien Herr, who had been associated with the enterprise since 1912 and who had borne the weight of it since 1917.[55] Herr was now the moderator and the intermediary between Lavisse, the authors, and the publisher. It was he who corrected and revised with a keenness of mind for which the authors were grateful. Only disputes on the overall plan went to Lavisse,[56] now suffering declining health. The publisher was requesting a "resolutely optimistic" conclusion, which for the old master had become "a nightmare."

The publisher would have liked an independent volume; he would have to be content with "about thirty pages."

The historical side of this vast enterprise, analogous, to be sure, to numerous others of the same period, would thus shift the spotlight, not only at the end but right from the start, to put the enterprise in the real light of an editorial business venture. In particular, there was the rivalry between the two publishing houses, Colin and Hachette—they split the university and school market in history.[57] Colin published the *Revue internationale de l'enseignement*, founded in 1881, in which several future collaborators were to be found and that, after the primary and secondary instruction manuals, including those since 1876 by Lavisse, embarked on, notably, *L'Histoire générale du IVe siècle à nos jours* for the academic market and the wider public. It was to appear between 1890 and 1901 in twelve volumes of about 1,000 pages each with seventy collaborators of widely varying backgrounds; these collaborators already included the Lavisse core (Bayet, Coville, Langlois, Luchaire, Mariéjol, Seignobos) as well as Émile Faguet for literature and Albert Sorel for foreign political history (he was already far from Lavisse in spirit and the Dreyfus Affair would put further distance between them), and Aulard, Levasseur, Albert Malet, and Arthur Giry. Of the two directors only Rambaud was active,[58] with seventeen major contributions on the colonial, Asian, and Slavic worlds. Lavisse even left Louis XIV to Lacour-Gayet, and the strangeness of the only article signed by him rather suggests one of those last-minute lapses that obliges the directors of collective works to step into the breach themselves, in this case for "La Formation du pouvoir pontifical: L'Italie byzantine, lombarde, papale [A.D. 395 to 756]." The collective spirit was already there, as in the *Cambridge Ancient and Modern History*, but the presentation was old-fashioned, with a final bibliography of secondary works. Colin followed the same model with the *Histoire de la langue et de la littérature françaises* under the direction of Petit de Julleville (1896) and the *Histoire de l'art* with André Michel (1905). Among these enterprises of encyclopedic character, with each specialist taking charge of one chapter, and individual syntheses such as the *Histoire des peuples de l'Orient classique* by Gaston Maspero that appeared at the same time (1892–1900), the *Histoire de France* that Hachette commissioned from Lavisse just as he was being elected to the Académie française represents a mixed type. It is in the form of independent volumes but is subordinated to an overarching idea and organized as an uninterrupted progression. But if the intellectual direction belonged to Lavisse, the editorial conception and the politics of the launch accrued to Hachette, particularly under the direction of Guillaume Bréton, who succeeded his father in 1883 as head of Hachette and whom

Lavisse had as a student in 1877. He was the one who truly put his mark on the enterprise. Essentially meant for students who did not have at their disposal at this time any other advanced textbooks, it began appearing in 1901 at a rate of eight installments per volume, that is, four parts per year. But the initial print run of seven thousand five hundred per installment (eleven thousand for the *Louis XIV* by Lavisse), which per book, bound and illustrated, would reach between seventeen thousand and twenty-five thousand copies by the time the next general reprinting in 1923 found a wider public.[59] Launching the work in this form was not a trivial matter, for it necessarily involved the division and scheduling of the material. Nine tomes were divided into two volumes, which in turn were divided into "regiments" of three to five books, then subdivided into "battalions" of three to five chapters, and finally into "squads" of again as many subchapters, the paragraphs clearly differentiated by their titles in the margins. The *Histoire contemporaine*, appearing in nine volumes—half the number for the *Histoire de France*—had a well-spaced layout and was set in carefully designed and clear typography, hence its perfect regularity of impeccable classicism and handsome modernity. The volumes from the Stone Age to the age of trench warfare thus displayed an external uniformity of typeface. With twenty-four plates of simple and powerful illustration, this uniform typeface certainly contributed more than a little to reemphasize the internal unity of the contents, which had to conform it to the typeface, despite the groans of the authors. "My work will not exceed the 480 printed pages you have set as the outside limit," Henri Carré wrote docilely to Bréton, "and I will arrange the work in books, chapters, and paragraphs according to the samples that you have sent to me."[60]

    The entire architecture of the work and its originality builds on the contrast between the critical apparatus, set at the foot of the page of each chapter and subchapter with the "sources" from the "works to be consulted" clearly separated, and the text itself, which sought to integrate all the data into a concrete and linear narrative. On the one hand, it was instant history constantly overtaken by current events and out-of-date with any delay in printing, to the dismay of the authors. On the other, it was a text to which Lavisse attached the greatest importance, closely following its progress, correcting it line by line and ceaselessly modifying it to make it simple, clear, alive, and definitive. There were thus to be no explanatory notes, for a note suggested a regret, a second thought, a nuance, fastidiousness, and the risk of a variant reading. Lavisse rejected them, his history being affirmative and authoritative, and closed the door to doubt, to the debatable, to distracting curiosity, to the state of the question, to the historiography of a problem. The entire work bears the mark of this tension, between knowledge under constant revision and a text that was to leave no room for interpretation because it was intended for the general public. "I greatly desire to be done," writes Langlois, for example (January 27, 1897),

> What keeps me from finishing the work are the *major* points. The history of the period that I am to relate had to be redone from top to bottom using works I knew were in preparation. So, to write without having consulted these works would have condemned me to fruitless work. If I had written certain chapters of my book, I would now be obliged in a couple of months to rewrite them.[61]

And Luchaire:

> I have made a huge effort, as you instructed, to break with the kind of historical writing to which I am accustomed. It was necessary for me to come out of myself, and I am not surprised that I have not succeeded at every point. You are without a doubt more competent than I to know what has to be said to the general public at whom the *Histoire de France* is aimed, for you know them much better than I do; and if I knew how to talk to them the way you do, I would be in the Académie française. Do, therefore, provide me with any observations on this matter you judge useful to the success of the common enterprise without fear of offending. You have seen that I have sacrificed many of my habits as a scholarly historian. I am quite disposed to make further sacrifices, and I desire for myself, as for everyone, that everything in my work be put to advantage in the certainty that we are in agreement on the ideas and that on questions of form you will ask nothing of me that I cannot do nor anything of a nature to diminish me in the eyes of serious readers in France and abroad.[62]

It was a declaration of goodwill that the director of the enterprise, inflexible as he was, must have exploited by sending his colleague back to his work. Luchaire would write to Bréton:

> In what concerns the manuscript of my volume one, you know that I delivered it to M. Lavisse by the terms set forth in our contract. I had totally recast it according to the instructions from the director and sent it back to him. But as the printing could not begin at that time for reasons beyond my control, I had to take it back in order to keep the work current with scientific publications in France and abroad . . . which were found to be, unfortunately, very important for the subject at hand. Hence a second recasting, which is not finished.[63]

There was to be sure the possibility of maintaining relationships of cordial authority that had dictated to Lavisse the choice of his collaborators, who formed a network that is easily reconstructed (see appendix 10.2, the collaborators of the *Histoire de France*). Lavisse turned to only two of his contemporaries: Vidal de La Blache, the geographer who had already made his presence known; and for the Renaissance and the Italian Wars his old friend Henry Lemonnier, a fellow student from the Charlemagne Lycée, who had succeeded him at the Sorbonne in 1889 and whom he had named professor of art history. But the greater part of the company, twelve of twenty, were actually students of his, some as *normaliens* when Lavisse was director of classes (*maître de conférences*) at the École normale supérieure (from 1876 to 1880), for example, Seignobos, Rebelliau, or Pfister. Some were *agrégatifs* (students for the competitive teachers' examination), the *agrégation* (plain students such as Pariset, though he was the first one to take the *agrégation*), or students from École des chartes (such as Langlois, Petit-Dutaillis, or Coville) or from the École des hautes études (such as Charléty). With some, even though separated by nearly a generation, like Seignobos (graduated in 1874) and Sagnac (graduated in 1891), the tone of the correspondence demonstrates an almost paternal and constant affection of a man without any children. Lavisse made their career. But they are far from being the only ones. He oversaw their theses for all of them except for Alexandre de Saint-Léger, professor at the school of commerce in Lille, whom he did not know.[64] That one was the exception. Their doctoral work often prefigured their contribution to the *Histoire de France*: that by Pfister on Robert II the Pious (1885) was in fact a study on the origins of France; that by Langlois on Philip III the Bold (1887) situated that monarch between Louis IX and Philip IV the Fair; that by Coville on the Cabochians★ and the Ordonnance of 1413 (1889) was a study of Charles VI and the Estates General; that by Rebelliau on Bossuet, the historian of Protestantism (1892), served as a study on religious problems under Louis XIV; the thesis by Petit-Dutaillis on Louis VIII (1895) was in reality a study of the Capetian monarchy at the beginning of the thirteenth century; that by Sagnac (1898) dealt with civil legislation during the French Revolution.

There remained the periods about which Lavisse knew little or nothing. For those he turned to the established specialists, junior by six or seven years: for Gaul, Gustave Bloch, the father of Marc Bloch, "Roman" by origin and vocation, with a thesis entitled "Les Origines du sénat romain" (1884) and at the time director of classes at the École normale supérieure;

★ EDITOR'S NOTE: The butchers and flayers of Paris, nicknamed the "Cabochians" after one of their leaders, who led them on a rampage in Paris in 1413.

Charles Bayet, a former colleague of Bloch's in Lyon, at the time rector of Lille and soon to be director of primary education, whom Lavisse first considered for the entire Middle Ages but then appointed Pfister and Lein-clausz to join him;[65] and for the Middle Ages, Achille Luchaire, who had come from Bordeaux to replace Fustel de Coulanges in Paris. They were thus specialists, yet subject to monitoring, and most often they formed the second line. This arrangement explains, both for the *Histoire de France* and for the *France contemporaine*, with a ten-year gap between the two and the two parts still in the midst of revisions, the absence of Camille Jullian. One might add that around 1895 he refused all the drudgeries of follow-ing orders to devote himself to his *Histoire de la Gaule* in eight volumes.[66] Aulard too did not figure on this list probably because he was too mili-tant and at the time heavily engaged in his polemic with Mathiez.* La-visse came to prefer two of his minions over him—the loyal, and already experienced, Sagnac,[67] and Pariset,[68] little disposed to the Revolution but whose thesis, on the Prussia of Frederick William I, Lavisse had inspired. Lavisse sometimes paid dearly for his choices. This held true even for Sa-gnac, for whom he had the profoundest respect, whose volume on the Revolution, of which we possess drafts corrected by Lavisse, bears on each page and on each line corrections and annotations that deserve an in-depth study. Others, by contrast, brought him to the edge of despair and repudiation. Witness this letter to Guillaume Bréton (1908?), which deserves to be cited in its entirety:

> My dear Guillaume, I complain, but I do not scold. What has hap-
> pened is my fault. You know that I could find no one but Carré for
> the history of the eighteenth century. I never imagined that he was so
> incapable of writing that history and that I would have to put in more
> than two years of my feeble life now drawing to a close correcting it.
> I had some very difficult moments then. I no longer know what rest
> is. I am neglecting all my affairs. I am failing in my obligations. I do
> nothing good. I would like to do this and that while taking advan-
> tage of my rest. Impossible! The drafts are there, I read them, I reread
> them. With all the pains I have taken, I am troubled by the certainty
> that these two volumes will keep traces of the original sin. All that
> is very difficult. But you are not responsible for it. You are a most
> generous editor, and there are not many of those. The only thing I

★ EDITOR'S NOTE: A famous (or notorious) public debate about the French Revolution. Aul-ard believed Danton was the most representative figure of the Revolution. Mathiez, who took a line influenced by the Bolshevik Revolution in Russia, believed Robespierre was the representative figure.

ask of you is to exempt me from continuing this line of work for the contemporary history. I would not be able to do it. Let us finish the other history, and I will go plant my fields.[69]

An Authenticated National Memory

At last the work was done. What created the force behind it all and gave it the virtues of a "memory-history" was the straightforward and critical probing of the memory of tradition.

Lavisse's actual criticism concerned only the establishment of documentary *authenticity* and in no case the creation of new sources. The legends were removed, the facts were corrected. Furthermore, nothing had basically changed from the most familiar and ordinary chronological arrangement or in the narrative approach. The plan by reigns and dynasties (see appendix 10.1), which the *Histoire contemporaine* would follow, with one regime taking over from another, depended on the most archaic of divisions and even gravitated to the oldest of our medieval chronicles, bypassing classical and romantic historiography. There was nothing in the overall structure that would violate the spontaneous articulations of memory. The contrast with Michelet stands out. There were some superficial parallels—tracking the national movement in full course since the Restoration, tying national subjectivity to the national will, and the ensuing great upheavals, which Lavisse savored—were some of the elements that could and might suggest a connection between the two histories. But it would be a grave mistake to see in that of Lavisse only the scientific consequences of Michelet. The obsession with unity was the same for the two of them, but it was not the same unity. For Michelet, unity was organic; for Lavisse, it was panoramic. One called for violent choices, the other for an exhaustive vision. Michelet proceeded by periods—Middle Ages, Reformation, Renaissance—and he constructed them through intellectual effort, maintained a passionate relationship with them, embodied them with contrasting symbols according to his mood at the moment and the evolution of his political opinions. He went from death throes to resurrections, passing from the *danse macabre* of the Cemetery of the Innocents, the image for him of the waning Middle Ages, to the redemptive figure of Joan of Arc. "I need to prove to myself and to that humanity whose ephemeral apparitions I express that one does not die, one is reborn. I need to feel myself dying."[70] He interrupted himself abruptly after Louis XI when he launched into the Revolution, which represented the ultimate outcome and, in a sense, the exhaustion of the history of France, so that he could get back to the Renaissance. The *Histoire de France* is more caught up in the contemporary on the basis of which he reconstructed and ordered the entire retrospective. Michelet's relationship with the archives was of an infinite complexity. While one knows that for certain periods he consulted an incredible array of sources, he did not cite them. Aulard greatly reproached him for this. Nevertheless, when at the end of book 4, at the death of Saint Louis, he wanted to show that this volume came "in large part" from the Archives nationales, meaning the Trésor des chartes, he does so for a fantastic visit "into those handwritten catacombs, that necropolis of national monuments," where the dead emerged from the tomb, "one showing a hand, another a head, like in the Last Judgment of Michelangelo" to dance around him "their galvanic dance."[71] Michelet guessed, invented, sensed, corrected, and whenever he lacked the sources, offered to replace them: "Living spirit of France, where will I grasp you if not in myself?"[72]

Lavisse, on the contrary, never modified the traditional hierarchies, maintaining the importance of political institutions and the priorities of the state despite his interest in the economy, society, and the arts and letters, which were all quietly relegated to the last pages of each volume. The same applied to the relative importance of events that left room for individuals described at full length, for the battles that, from Agincourt to Waterloo, from Valmy to Verdun, ended up resembling each other so much that they appeared like communiqués from the general staff. These 408 pages twenty-seven times begun anew were like that famous "synthesis minute" in which Fustel de Coulanges had seen the crowning accomplishment of several years of analysis.

It was therefore a powerfully homogeneous recitative unified through the natural coalescence between the type of official sources and the underlying philosophy of the continuity of the State. Positivist historiography was the golden age of the *direct* source, that is to say, the source that says nothing more than what is explicit in it, leaving to the historian the responsibility to be sure that it was well said. These sources were the charter, the document, the cartulary, the treaty, the testament, and the transcription, all public texts charged with the purpose of memory and made solely for the record. In their *Introduction aux études historiques* (1898), devoted entirely to "operations of analysis" and "operations of synthesis," Langlois and Seignobos described, in an extravagance of detail that seems to us to be somewhat quaint, how to establish a fact from the documents, but in not one single instance did they evoke the possibility of *indirect* sources, meaning those, practically infinite in number, that allow us to draw from a document something other than what it intends to signify. But then from these sources emerges the possibility of bringing up what was problematic in this approach. Between the time of the narrative source taking priority, which the historiography of romanticism had represented, and

LIVRE II

L'INSTALLATION DU ROI

CHAPITRE PREMIER

LE ROI[1]

I. LA PERSONNE. — II. L'ÉDUCATION. — III. LE « MOI » DU ROI.

I. — LA PERSONNE DU ROI

L OUIS XIV avait vingt-deux ans et demi à la mort de Mazarin. L'ASPECT DU ROI.
Tout le monde le trouvait très beau. Un léger retrait du front,
le nez long d'ossature ferme, la rondeur de la joue, la courbe du
menton sous l'avancée de la lèvre, dessinaient un profil net, un peu
lourd. La douceur se mêlait dans les yeux bruns à la gravité, comme
la grâce à la majesté dans la démarche. Une belle prestance et l'air
de grandeur haussaient la taille qui était ordinaire. Toute cette
personne avait un charme qui attirait et un sérieux qui tenait à distance. Les contemporains pensaient qu'elle révélait le Roi :

> En quelque obscurité que le sort l'eût fait naître,
> Le monde, en le voyant, eût reconnu son maître,

1. SOURCES. Les Œuvres de Louis XIV, Paris, 1806, 6 vol.. Mémoires de Louis XIV pour
l'instruction du Dauphin, édit. Ch. Dreyss, 2 vol., Paris, 1860. Colbert, Journal fait par
chacune semaine de ce qui s'est passé pour servir à l'histoire du Roi, au tome VI des Lettres,..,
éditées par P. Clément. Lettres du P. Paulin, confesseur du Roi, au cardinal Mazarin, dans
le P. Chérot, La Première jeunesse de Louis XIV (1649-1653), Lille, 1892. Les Mémoires du
temps, notamment ceux de Madame de Motteville, de Mademoiselle de Montpensier.
Journal de la santé du Roi Louis XIV (1647-1711) écrit par Vallot, d'Aquin et Fagon, édité par
J.-A. Le Roi, Paris, 1862. Médailles sur les principaux événements du règne de Louis le Grand,
ouvrage publié par l'Académie des Médailles et Inscriptions, Paris, 1702. Saint-Simon,
Parallèle des trois premiers rois Bourbons, Les Relations des ambassadeurs vénitiens
Giovanni Battista Nani (août 1660), Alvise Grimani (1660-64), Alvise Sagredo (1664-65), au
t. III des Relazioni...
OUVRAGES A CONSULTER. Outre ceux du P. Chérot et de Lacour-Gayet : Sainte-Beuve,
Les œuvres de Louis XIV, Causeries du lundi, t. V, p. 313; Le Journal de la santé du Roi,
Nouveaux lundis, t. II, p. 360. A. Pérate, Les portraits de Louis XIV au musée de Versailles,
Versailles, 1896.

Fig. 10.8
Page 119 of *Louis XIV (1643–1685)*, by Ernest Lavisse, in *Histoire de France*, vol. 7 (Paris: Hachette, 1906), showing an eloquent typographical layout.

the "hour of the *Annales*," which expanded on the very notion of sources to make them produce all meaning, the *Histoire de France* represented the moment of perfect balance between meaning and fact because it was necessary, but also because it sufficed to establish the one correctly so that the other might emerge.

A typical example: Bouvines (1214), one of the formative events that established French national identity and a key battle that transports the heavy baggage of patriotic legend and imagination. Henri Martin, whose popular *Histoire de France* was the authority along with Michelet, relied on three principal sources, all narrative in character:[73] the chronicle of Reims, written fifty years after the battle; and Guillaume le Breton, who experienced the battle standing behind Philip Augustus and from whom we possess two different accounts—the *Philippide* in verse and the chronicle in prose. He saw a difference among these sources and preferred the last one. "The chronicle of Reims," he stated, "is a monument of much interest, less for the historical facts in it that are almost always seriously altered than for the popular traditions and sentiments that are deeply and faithfully expressed in it." But having made his choice, he recounted the battle with numerous quotations and here and there paraphrased the king's chaplain. He was quite happy to celebrate the battle with him "as a bard of ancient Gaul" and to confess frankly at the end, "This narrative is almost entirely drawn from the chronicle in prose by Guillaume Le Breton, compared with books X and XI of his *Philippide*." At the other end of the chain, there is *Le Dimanche de Bouvines* in which Georges Duby,[74] as an anthropologist of the battle and of its memory, dissected the event and reconstructed it using the traces it had left behind and then performing three different operations: he reconstituted the cultural milieu from which all the evidence had sprung, sketched a sociology of the war, and tracked down, through a series of commemorations, "the course of a memory within a fluid collection of mental representations." This was a work of an entirely different nature, using entirely different sources. It not only led to a completely revised understanding of the event, it allowed us to situate exactly Luchaire's treatment of the battle within the *Histoire de France* and his results, which were decisive and limited.

Decisive because Luchaire had identified all the documents and seen all the studies of which most of the essential ones, in Germany, had just appeared. Out of about a dozen titles in his bibliography, more than half had appeared in the previous ten years. Decisive because as the "investigating magistrate" he had uncovered the lies, checked the evidence, sorted the hypotheses. In brief, he had neglected nothing to reconstitute "what had actually happened," according to von Ranke's celebrated phrase, on the plain at Bouvines, on July 27, 1214, between noon and five o'clock in the afternoon, and to restore the day in the chain of its "causes" and its "consequences." It was a work that was indispensable, unsurpassable except for any improbable discoveries, and yet illusory, if not vain. First, because in its subjective reality this truth was inaccessible and went well beyond the range of certainties to which it could be reduced. Next, because this reconstruction, as Duby explained, was possible only at the cost of a basic anachronism "that unintentionally tended to view Philip Augustus the way Corneille saw Pompey, that is as a wish, one will facing other wills and other wishes in the immutability of 'human nature.'"

This eloquent critique, which can be generalized, points precisely to the type of memory recorded in *Histoire de France*. "Bouvines," Duby went on to say, "fits exactly into the dynamic of a history of power. That day acts like a node, more extensive than others, in a continuous chain of decisions, endeavors, hesitations, successes, and checks—all aligned on a single vector, that of the evolution of the States of Europe."

Yet it would be inaccurate to see in it only the update of a gigantic narrative. The parts of the work with which the authors felt satisfied were precisely those that were most obsolete. Either the authors were limited by lack of talent or temperament for archival work (Coville, Petit-Dutaillis), or they were dealing with periods that were too contemporary, like Charléty and Seignobos, or they did not put their best into this work on command, which would seem to be the case with Langlois. Without a doubt, Lavisse, for his part, did not perceive the intellectual revival that was taking place at the time of the publication of his *Histoire*, between the birth of *Année sociologique* of Durkheim (1896) and *Revue de synthèse historique* of Henri Berr (1900). Nonetheless, there were at least three volumes in the *Histoire* that defied the rule and that took on decidedly individualistic characteristics. First, there was the *Tableau* of Vidal de La Blache, who occupied a key intellectual position. Then there was the pressing reminder of the Michelet of the 1830s, a sign of the linkage being established between history and geography in French national education; he was at the same time the messenger for the movement in human geography that would have so much influence on the birth of *Annales* history. Finally, there was Lavisse's *Louis XIV*,[75] because the twenty-five years that Lavisse recounted were in fact an anatomy of the "century" and the description of a kind of regime, absolutism. Finally, *Le Moyen Âge* by Luchaire, for which the case is less obvious.

The titles of these two volumes do indeed denote pure chronology: *Les Premiers Capétiens (987–1137)* and *Louis VII, Philippe Auguste, Louis VIII (1137–226)*. But if one consults the table of contents, one will note that the "four first Capetians" were relegated to one chapter of thirty pages (book 1, chapter 5), and that the conflict between the Plantagenêts, Richard the Lion-Hearted, and Pope Innocent III did not occupy half of the second volume. The political flag covered a quite different kind of merchandise, in fact a vast tableau showing the formation of feudalism from the tenth to the thirteenth century. This was the fruit of the Fustelian renewal, the only true historiographical innovation of which the *Histoire de France* bore any trace. In relegating to the second rank the role of invasions, conquest, and conflicts among peoples that had dominated national historiography since the sixteenth century, the *Histoire des institutions politiques de l'ancienne France* had abruptly transformed an ethno-tribal conflict into the slow birth of the feudal regime. Achille Luchaire was a Fustelian loyalist, and the influence of Fustel de Coulanges becomes immediately perceptible in the work that opened on a large tableau of the feudal regime. Right from the first page, the tone is unmistakable:

> Within the core of the French kingdom a dynastic revolution had just been achieved (the year 987). It did not inaugurate, strictly speaking, a new era. Royal authority had been in ruins for many years; the Church and the nobles—they were all-powerful. . . . The work that had been going on for several centuries deep in society succeeded in changing the economic and social condition of the country. People would be divided into categories that had become almost fixed. . . . The feudal system, deriving from public and private patronage, included everything, penetrated everything, and threatened to conquer everything.

Hence the substitution of a Middle Ages, which Michelet saw as being "total" in scope, for Augustin Thierry's Romanesque period and even for Henri Martin's epic Middle Ages, that was purely social in nature and would be the work of a Marc Bloch, whom medievalists of today do not regard as insignificant. In the guise of an essentially political memory, the *Histoire de France* thus brought under one roof, in its best moments, two types of history.

The Making of Republican Memory

If the general arrangement of the *Histoire de France* and the procedures of positivist historiography conspire with respect to a memory spontaneously oriented toward politics and the state, its authoritarian manner embracing the republican cause bears the mark of the director of the enterprise. Indeed, on three occasions in this work, without introduction, his intentions are repeated, if not to say hammered, into the conclusions for the reigns of Louis XIV (volume 8, book 1), Louis XV and Louis XVI (volume 9), and the general conclusion to *France contemporaine* (volume 9), which, fittingly, is nothing less than his testament as a historian.

What is striking in reconciling the two is the systematic reconstruction of the ancien régime as a function of the advent of the Republic and the constituent themes of republican identity: insistence on borders in a country obsessed with Alsace-Lorraine, the failed maritime calling of royal France at the very moment of colonial expansion, the terrible finances of the kingdom in the France of the royal treasury and the *franc-or*, the lack of internal unity when the need for integrating the masses was so urgent, the absence of popular participation in the nation at a time when political education was evolving through universal suffrage and formation of parties. These were the exclusive criteria according to which Lavisse prepared the case for the final trial of the monarchy and pronounced a condemnation in which it is not easy to lay out the nature of the regime exactly or its degeneration, its intrinsic unpleasantness, and the "nullity" of the king. In the indictment it is not difficult to discern all the values of the liberal and deserving lower middle class of the 1900s. There is the lack of authority: "The king seems no longer to be master in the choice of his ministers," in whose appointments one sees the *dévôts*, the philosophes, the financiers, the coteries of the court, and the whims of the women like Madame de Pompadour, Madame du Barry, and Marie Antoinette:

> Louis XVI, to satisfy everyone, created divided ministries, as one would say today. For many of the ministers one will not find the titles they had for their function. Why did Amelot de Chaillou and d'Aiguillon become ministers of foreign affairs when they ignored each other? And what of Bertin, the lieutenant of police and controller general, and Berryer, lieutenant of police and minister of the navy? It is a strange *cumul* of offices when the office of the seals and Contrôle général or that of the seals and the navy are in the hands of Machault. Sometimes the portfolios were interchangeable and it is not clear how this operation worked to the welfare of the State.

The bad domestic economy was what really provoked astonishment and scandal:

> The king was not worried about stability in his finances. He did not have to adjust expenses against receipts, the Count d'Artois said one day to the Parlement. On the contrary, it was the receipts that had to be adjusted to the expenses. Ever since the sixteenth century, with the expenses of the Court getting added to those of war, and both always increasing, debts had accumulated and French royalty in its magnificence was perpetually embarrassed.

Yet that difficulty could have been cleared up:

> Through those reforms the king might have increased his authority
> and diminished the ills of his people; to accomplish them was simply
> the price that the abuse of royal luxury, the mistresses, the chateau at
> Versailles, and the useless wars cost.

From the economy one turns to the abandonment of centralization that
was responsible for the "incompleteness of the kingdom":

> It appears that the royal government ought to have continued the
> effort begun in the time of Richelieu to introduce into the provinces
> an administration that would have made the authority of the king
> present and effective everywhere. . . . This administration by the ac-
> tions it followed would have certainly managed to suppress the diff-
> erences (which was neither possible nor desirable) or at least to erode
> the obstacles blocking the realization of French unity.
>
> The king thus did not "naturalize the provinces of the king-
> dom," in Calonne's words; he did not naturalize them to be French.
> The kingdom was still only an "unformed aggregation of disunited
> peoples," as Mirabeau said. It is the Revolution that will make France
> "one and indivisible," the homeland for someone from Marseille,
> Dunkirk, Bordeaux, or even Strasbourg.

There was one last major accusation, but it was the most serious. "French
power was diminishing."

> The memory will never be expunged of that "stupid" Treaty of Aix-
> la-Chapelle, the shameful Treaty of Paris, fifteen years of the War
> of the Austrian Succession and the Seven Years War—without ac-
> quiring one ounce of territory; the loss of our colonies, which had
> become popular thanks to the heroism of certain officers; badly con-
> ducted operations by officers of the Court; the shameful flight before
> the upstart Prussians. The victory of Fontenoy was glorious, but even
> that day, when the king cut a fine figure, a German, the Marshal de
> Saxe, was in command. In the undermining of the monarchy, the
> France that loves *la gloire* suffered significant humiliation.

There were some changes in eighteenth-century Europe for which the
king was not responsible, "but he was fully responsible for the disorder in
the kingdom and for the incompleteness of the monarchical order." He was

a king whom Lavisse, interpreting with a sure touch for public sentiment, reproached for being too much the king and not enough. The king was inaccessible to the advice of the reformers, enclosed in an omnipotence where "he [did] no more than enjoy the vast fortune in the house that he had built at Versailles after having made that fortune." It was Versailles that concentrated the hatred, that false capital that became "the place where the king consumed the kingdom." So Lavisse concluded that "among the causes of the French Revolution, one must put the fear of Paris and the pride that led Louis XIV to erect the capital of France in a chateau that had originally been a far-off gathering place for the hunt."

That clash between the values of the lower middle class of the Belle Époque and the monarchy in its greatest brilliance gives to the personal encounter Lavisse has with Louis XIV, rough and tumble as it was, its strategic interest and its piquancy. This encounter does not have the same tone in the concluding description and judgment, a difference explainable no doubt by the choice of period for which he was personally responsible. The two volumes, which deserve a study in themselves given the exceptional range and richness of their development, link the royal majesty with such felicity of expression that one cannot but see in it personal pleasure and affinity of temperament. Lavisse wound up spending twenty years in the intimacy of Louis XIV. "He loved clashes of will," said Philippe Sagnac, "and he took pleasure in studying states at the moment when they were forming. They appeared to him like forces that, once created, spread out until they came into conflict with other states, yielded or carried the day. After Frederick II, the true creator of the Prussian state, how would he have not loved Louis XIV struggling with so many internal forces and with all of Europe?"[76] But the democrat's final sentence is severe in the extreme:

> What one would soon call "the Ancien Régime"—that composite
> of outworn and fatal ideas, a façade in tatters, rights without du-
> ties that had become abuses, these ruins from a long past over which
> stood solitary in omnipotence the one who refused to plan a future—
> would not be fair to attribute to Louis XIV alone, but he did bring it
> to the highest degree of imperfection and marked it for death.

It was a divided judgment that made of this long reign the pivot of the entire history of France. It was the summit and the beginning of its downfall.

> Louis's clearest success was to obtain political obedience, which was
> not done without some difficulty. Every year had its revolts, some of
> which were very serious. An exact history of these insurrections, the

reasons invoked for them, the insults and threats that were cried out will have to be written if one wants to see clearly the warning signs of the Revolution.

It is true that he pushed back the frontiers of the kingdom, conquered the Franche-Comté as well as parts of Flanders, the Hainaut, the Cambrésis, and Strasbourg. As considerable as these territorial results were, though, the force of France in 1661 and the weakness of Europe pushed Lavisse to think that one could have hoped for more:

> One must recall what the cost would have been for France to ac-
> quire the Spanish Low Countries, which would have put Paris, then
> too close to the frontier, at the center of the kingdom poised in the
> national unity between the genius and temperament of the North
> and the South, with its coastal areas extending to the mouth of the
> Scheldt adding Antwerp to Dunkirk, Bordeaux, and Marseille. . . .
>
> It must also be repeated that the France of Colbert and Seigne-
> lay, the France of Dunkirk, of Brest, of Rochefort, of Bordeaux and
> of Marseille, the colonizer of Canada, of Louisiana and the Antil-
> les could have become as "powerful on the sea" as it was "strong on
> land," as Colbert said.

These possibilities external to France were all spoiled by

> that policy of different and contradictory purposes grouped around
> an *idée fixe*, which was to procure *gloire* for itself by humiliating
> others. That idea was a mixture of caution and cunning as well as
> bursts of pride that destroyed in one moment an entire ancient arti-
> fice. It was an idea through which everyone was assaulted, insulted or
> duped with the result that coalitions were constantly expanding and
> eventually included all of Europe. It was the policy of perpetual wars
> led by a man who had the qualities of a good "staff officer" but not
> the head of a general nor the heart of a soldier.

Lavisse's impossible dialogue with Louis XIV led him, in a curious way, to interpose Colbert. Colbert became the "the great watchdog," to whom Lavisse never stopped returning and whom he gave all the love and attention that the *Histoire de France* never ceased to show for the great line of reforming ministers (Sully, Richelieu, Turgot) whose "revolutionary ideas" he described at length, and whom he established as the precursor to the customs and colonial policies of the republic, between the Tonkin expedition and the Méline laws. "The Colbert Offer" was the chapter subtly placed between the installation to power in 1661 and the beginnings of the personal reign. "At this unique and fleeing moment, Colbert called for a great innovation, which was that the King and France focus on what was essential: acquiring money."And Lavisse's task was to develop "Colbert's ideal France."

> He imagined an entirely different France, closed to the foreigner, unified by the removal of internal barriers and by the establishment of one law and one system of weights and measures, a tax burden "by a more judicious choice and a fairer distribution," producing and manufacturing for needs and for commerce abroad, organized for this work and for this commerce, covering the seas with its merchant marine, a large and fine military marine that would protect, and asking the colonies for all the goods that were lacking, products from the tropics and from the north. This France, separated from the wider world, would be sufficient unto itself, imposing itself on foreigners, getting rich from the gold flowing in, and, victorious in the silver war waged against all peoples, would haughtily raise itself on the ruin of others.

An ideal France presupposed an "ideal king," meaning one who was thrifty and a "friend of the merchants," a military king and a dispenser of justice, and, above all, a "Parisian king." This passage is astonishing in the purposes that Lavisse invests in it and almost makes the entire destiny of France revolve on this "unique and fleeting moment." "How did France and the king welcome the Colbert offer?" Lavisse's lapidary conclusion was, "that was the capital question for the reign of Louis XIV."

Louis XIV and Colbert: with these two one is at the meeting point of two rising lines and at the heart of the national dynamic. The first goes back through those great men who embodied national unity, beyond Henri IV and Charles VI, Louis XI and Saint Louis, right to the great founders, not Charlemagne—that man from the Rhine who dreamed of empire and "who for us remains, as it were, external"—but Hugh Capet, "duke of France, count of Paris, who was one of us. . . . He represented, above the divisions and subdivisions of our soil, the totality. In him resided the *unity* of France." But this royalty, full of sacred heroic qualities, that did not stop Lavisse from declarations of love and cries of admiration, was about to go into decline with Louis XIV, who "wore out the monarchy" in the "empty forms" that he let survive in the chaos of contradictory laws, arbitrary power, and futility, for "the principal cause of the ruin of the royalty was the lack in the king." The other line, which was embodied in Colbert, that representative of the princes' bad conscience and of the

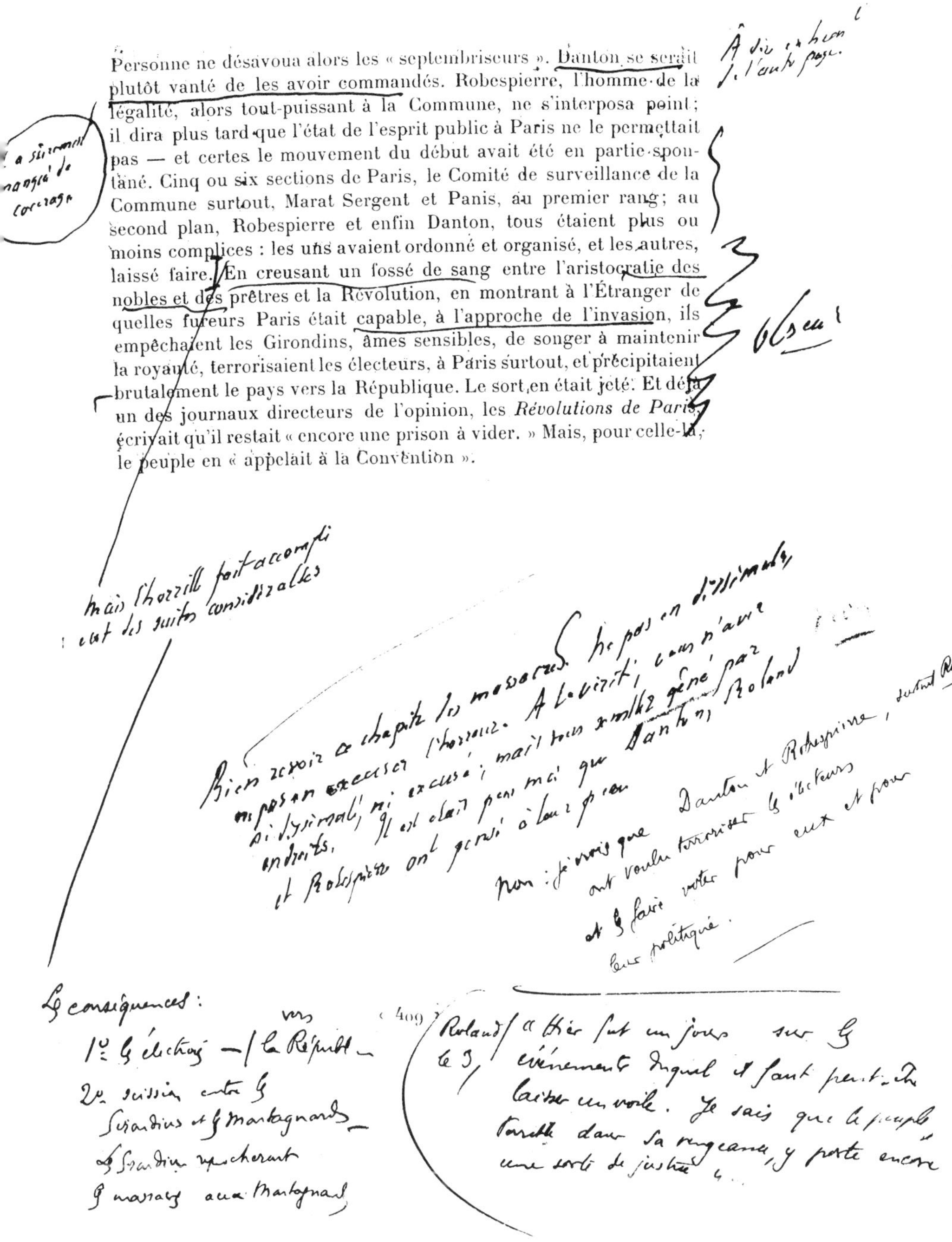

Personne ne désavoua alors les « septembriseurs ». Danton se serait plutôt vanté de les avoir commandés. Robespierre, l'homme de la légalité, alors tout-puissant à la Commune, ne s'interposa point ; il dira plus tard que l'état de l'esprit public à Paris ne le permettait pas — et certes le mouvement du début avait été en partie spontané. Cinq ou six sections de Paris, le Comité de surveillance de la Commune surtout, Marat Sergent et Panis, au premier rang ; au second plan, Robespierre et enfin Danton, tous étaient plus ou moins complices : les uns avaient ordonné et organisé, et les autres, laissé faire. En creusant un fossé de sang entre l'aristocratie des nobles et des prêtres et la Révolution, en montrant à l'Étranger de quelles fureurs Paris était capable, à l'approche de l'invasion, ils empêchaient les Girondins, âmes sensibles, de songer à maintenir la royauté, terrorisaient les électeurs, à Paris surtout, et précipitaient brutalement le pays vers la République. Le sort en était jeté. Et déjà un des journaux directeurs de l'opinion, les *Révolutions de Paris*, écrivait qu'il restait « encore une prison à vider. » Mais, pour celle-là, le peuple en « appelait à la Convention ».

Fig. 10.9

Proofs of the *Histoire de la Révolution* by Philippe Sagnac corrected by Ernest Lavisse. Coll. part., photo © Gallimard.

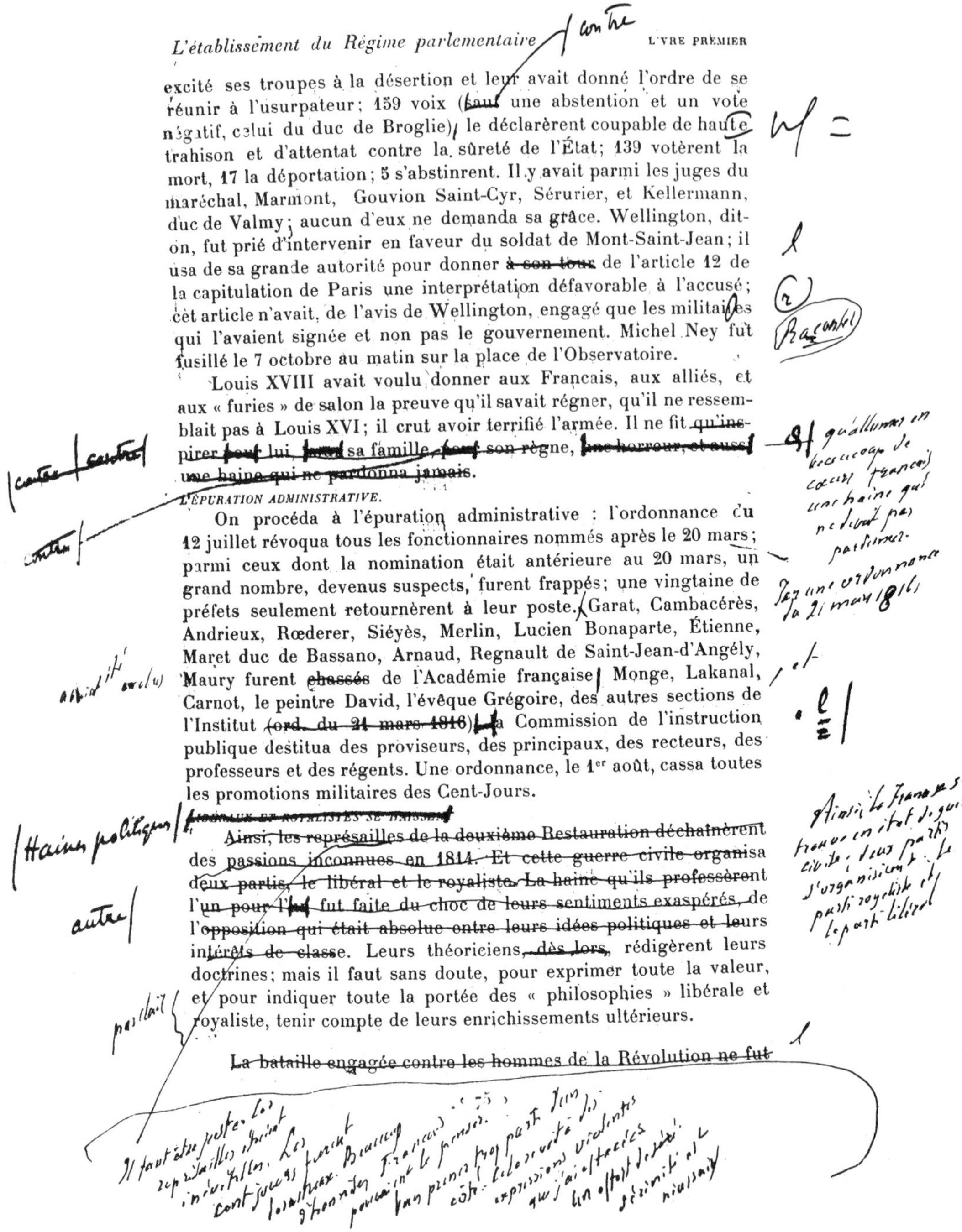

L'établissement du Régime parlementaire LIVRE PREMIER

excité ses troupes à la désertion et leur avait donné l'ordre de se réunir à l'usurpateur ; 159 voix (~~sauf~~ une abstention et un vote négatif, celui du duc de Broglie), le déclarèrent coupable de haute trahison et d'attentat contre la sûreté de l'État ; 139 votèrent la mort, 17 la déportation ; 5 s'abstinrent. Il y avait parmi les juges du maréchal, Marmont, Gouvion Saint-Cyr, Sérurier, et Kellermann, duc de Valmy ; aucun d'eux ne demanda sa grâce. Wellington, dit-on, fut prié d'intervenir en faveur du soldat de Mont-Saint-Jean ; il usa de sa grande autorité pour donner ~~à son tour~~ de l'article 12 de la capitulation de Paris une interprétation défavorable à l'accusé ; cet article n'avait, de l'avis de Wellington, engagé que les militaires qui l'avaient signée et non pas le gouvernement. Michel Ney fut fusillé le 7 octobre au matin sur la place de l'Observatoire.

Louis XVIII avait voulu donner aux Français, aux alliés, et aux « furies » de salon la preuve qu'il savait régner, qu'il ne ressemblait pas à Louis XVI ; il crut avoir terrifié l'armée. Il ne fit ~~qu'inspirer pour~~ lui, ~~pour~~ sa famille, ~~pour son règne,~~ ~~une horreur, et aussi une haine qui ne pardonna jamais.~~

L'ÉPURATION ADMINISTRATIVE.

On procéda à l'épuration administrative : l'ordonnance du 12 juillet révoqua tous les fonctionnaires nommés après le 20 mars ; parmi ceux dont la nomination était antérieure au 20 mars, un grand nombre, devenus suspects, furent frappés ; une vingtaine de préfets seulement retournèrent à leur poste. Garat, Cambacérès, Andrieux, Rœderer, Siéyès, Merlin, Lucien Bonaparte, Étienne, Maret duc de Bassano, Arnaud, Regnault de Saint-Jean-d'Angély, Maury furent ~~chassés~~ de l'Académie française ; Monge, Lakanal, Carnot, le peintre David, l'évêque Grégoire, des autres sections de l'Institut ~~(ord. du 21 mars 1816)~~. La Commission de l'instruction publique destitua des proviseurs, des principaux, des recteurs, des professeurs et des régents. Une ordonnance, le 1er août, cassa toutes les promotions militaires des Cent-Jours.

~~LIBÉRAUX ET ROYALISTES SE HAÏSSENT.~~

~~Ainsi, les représailles de la deuxième Restauration déchaînèrent des passions inconnues en 1814. Et cette guerre civile organisa deux partis, le libéral et le royaliste. La haine qu'ils professèrent l'un pour l'autre fut faite du choc de leurs sentiments exaspérés, de l'opposition qui était absolue entre leurs idées politiques et leurs intérêts de classe.~~ Leurs théoriciens, ~~dès lors,~~ rédigèrent leurs doctrines ; mais il faut sans doute, pour exprimer toute la valeur, et pour indiquer toute la portée des « philosophies » libérale et royaliste, tenir compte de leurs enrichissements ultérieurs.

~~La bataille engagée contre les hommes de la Révolution ne fut~~

Fig. 10.10

The proofs of *La Restauration* by Charléty corrected by Ernest Lavisse, adapted from Lucien Herr. Coll. part., photo © Gallimard.

fragile yet threatening general will of the people, would lead right to the *fête de la Fédération*. "The nation done by consent that the people wanted was one idea of France. On July 14, 1790, national unity succeeded to the monarchical unity, and it revealed itself as indestructible."★

This forcible identification of the Revolution with the nation, the nation with the Republic, and the Republic with "a regime that one can believe definitive" occurred but not without carefully managing some formidable difficulties. No history had ever made a similar effort to weld the monarchical past onto the republican present. The aim was to give the national adventure its coherence and exemplary range, to inject dynamism into its very depths, and to fix it in its present. As luck would have it, the history would culminate in the tragedy of war, the greatest effort to which the nation had had to consent. It emerged victorious, but exhausted, bled, divided, and depressed. Yet it was at that moment that Lavisse had to provide the recapitulating conclusion. The famous "solidity" of the French was shaken, inflation had begun, the parliament was paralyzed, the Communist party was born, and the colonial world was stirring. The place of France had changed dramatically, with Europe in pieces. Lavisse himself was at death's door.[77] "The reasons for confidence in the future," which he had to pull forth, sounded eerily hollow; his confidence in the indestructibility of democracy sounded unreal; France's aptitude for propaganda of peace, utopian. The desire for social rapprochement looked pathetic even if it did inspire in him an ending phrase that resonated like a sigh: "Is France therefore going to become bourgeois? If that were the case, there would no longer be any need to speak of the bourgeoisie—there would be the nation, complete at last."

The *Histoire de France*, and not this message, is what is responsible for inscribing Lavisse in the memory of the French, first of all, by turning this great manual into a higher form of the smaller, much more widespread book. There is reciprocal effect from one to the other in which each expanded. The two of them, which sang the same tune, mutually served each other: the "little Lavisse" energetically emphasizing the political philosophy implicit in the other, the "great Lavisse" replacing the logic of expression and the snappiness of the sentence with the ultima ratio of the source and the document. The continuity of history finds proof in the continuity of instruction through which millions of children began and a phalanx of historians concluded.

But the *Histoire de France* represents above all a rare moment of balance in the very history of the Republic and of France. It is a balance between research and teaching that gives to the magisterium of the historian the

---

★ EDITOR'S NOTE: This is the celebration, in 1790, of the first year of the French Revolution.

leadership for the national conscience and makes him the interpreter and guarantor of the myth. It is a balance of a France that took a century for the Revolution, that had not yet been replaced by the threats of another, to enter into the mores of the nation. It was a balance, finally, between fifty years, from La Fayette in 1830 to Gambetta in the 1880s, devoted to debating the Republic to another half century, from Maurras to Robert Brasillach and Jacques Bainville,★ aimed at bringing it down. Lavisse had done nothing to shatter the traditional national landscape. In regrouping the facts from which meaning is elicited, he did, nevertheless, fix the images and expand, in a definitive way, the mirror in which France will never cease to recognize itself.

APPENDIX 10.1

Plan for the *Histoire de France*

Histoire de France des origines à la Révolution

VOLUME 1

Book 1   P. Vidal de la Blache, *Tableau de la géographie de la France*, 1903

Book 2   G. Bloch, *Les Origines, la Gaule indépendante et la Gaule romaine*, 1903

VOLUME 2

Book 1   C. Bayet, C. Pfister, and A. Kleinclausz, *Le Christianisme, les Barbares, les Mérovingiens et les Carolingiens*, 1903

Book 2   A. Luchaire, *Les Premiers Capétiens (987–1137)*, 1901

VOLUME 3

Book 1   A. Luchaire, *Louis VII, Philippe Auguste et Louis VIII (1137–226)*, 1901

Book 2   Ch. V. Langlois, *Saint Louis, Philippe le Bel et les derniers Capétiens (1226–1328)*, 1901

VOLUME 4

Book 1   A. Coville, *Les Premiers Valois et la guerre de Cent Ans (1328–1422)*, 1902

Book 2   Ch. Petit-Dutaillis, *Charles VII, Louis XI, Charles VIII (1422–1492)*, 1902

★ EDITOR'S NOTE: Robert Brasillach was a writer and journalist who collaborated with the Nazis and became an important voice for the Vichy government. He was executed for treason after World War II. Jacques Bainville was a historian by craft, a disciple of Maurras, and an extreme nationalist, who wrote regularly for *L'Action française*.

APPENDIX 10.2

Historiography

Excluded from this list of authors are Lavisse himself as well as the three occasional and nonuniversity collaborators (Henri Bidou, Auguste Gauvain, and Alexandre de Saint-Léger), about whom information is given in the text.

For the professors at the Sorbonne, further information can be found in Christophe Charle's biographical dictionary, *Les Professeurs de la Faculté des lettres de Paris* (Paris: Éditions N.R.P.-C.N.R.S., 1986), of which volume 1, *1809–1908,* has appeared in print. Only the collaborator's dates of birth and death, academic background, career, and principal works will be cited here.

Bayet, Charles (1849–1918). Born in Liège, died in Toulon.

E.N.S. (École normale supérieure): *agrégé* (1868),★ 2ᵉ (1872), doctorate (1879, "Recherches pour servir à l'histoire de la peinture et de la sculpture chrétiennes en Orient avant la querelle des Iconoclastes").

Taught at the School of Rome and the School of Athens (1874–76). *Chargé de cours* (lecturer) (1876), then professor of medieval history at Lyon (1881) and dean (1886). Rector at the Académie de Lille (1891). Director of Primary Instruction (1896), Director of Higher Education succeeding Louis Liard (1902–14).

L'Art byzantin (1883), *Les Derniers Carolingiens (877–987)* (1884), *Précis d'histoire de l'art* (1886), *Giotto* (1907).

Bloch, Gustave (1848–1923). Born in Fegersheim (Bas-Rhin), died in Marlotte (Seine-et-Marne). Father: director of a primary school in Strasbourg.

E.N.S.: *agrégé* (1868), 1ᵉʳ (1872), doctorate (1884, "Les Origines du Sénat romain").

Taught at the École de Rome (1873). *Chargé de cours* (lecturer) in Greek and Latin antiquities at Lyon (1876). *Maître de conférences* (associate professor) at the E.N.S. (1887). Professor of Roman history at the Sorbonne (1904).

La République romaine (1900), *L'Empire romain* (1911), *La République romaine de 146 à 44 av. J.-C.* (completed by J. Carcopino in G. Glotz's *Histoire générale*).

Carré, Henri (1850–1939). Born in Favier (Indre-et-Loire). Father: court clerk.

E.N.S. (1870), *agrégé* (1881), doctorate (1888, "Essai sur le parlement de Bretagne après la Ligue").

Professor at lycées in Alençon (1877), Carcassonne, and Rennes. *Maître des conférences* at Rennes. Professor at Poitiers (1889).

L'Administration municipale de Rennes au temps d'Henri IV (1889), *La France sous Louis XV* (1892), *Histoire d'une lettre de cachet et d'un aventurier poitevin* (1895), an edition of *Correspondance du constituant Thibaud* (1898).

Charléty, Sébastien (1867–1945). Born in Chambéry (Savoie). Father: customs official.

E.P.H.E. (École pratique des hautes études) (1889), *agrégé* (1890), doctorate (1896, "Essai sur l'histoire du saint-simonisme").

★ Laureates of the highly competitive examination, the *agrégation*, are known as *agrégés*. The examination is normally open only to those who have completed a course of study at a university.

Professor at the Lycée de Lyon (1840). *Chargé de conférences* (assistant professor) at Lyon; professor (1901). On assignment to the Tunisian government (1908). Rector of the *Académie de Strasbourg* (1910), and of the *Académie de Paris*.

Bibliographie critique de l'histoire de Lyon (1902), *Histoire de l'enseignement secondaire dans le Rhône depuis 1784* (1901), *Histoire de Lyon* (1903), *Le Lyonnais* (1904), in the collection "Les Régions de France" in *Revue de synthèse historique* (1904), *Documents relatifs à la vente des biens nationaux dans le département du Rhône* (1906), an edition of the *Ordonnances des Rois de France, règne de François I*, vol. 3 of a seven-volume collection edited by Charléty, beginning in 1934; numerous introductions.

Coville, Alfred (1860–1942). Born in Versailles.

E.P.H.E. (1882), *agrégé* (1883), École des chartes (1885), doctorate (1896, "Les Cabochiens et l'ordonnance de 1413").

Maître de conférences in Dijon (1884) and in Caen (1885). *Chargé de cours* in Lyon (1889), professor (1891). Rector of the *Académie de Clermont* (1904). Inspector General for Public Instruction. Director of Secondary Education and later of Higher Education.

Recherches sur l'histoire de Lyon du Ve au IXe siècle (1928), *Jean Petit, la question du tyrannicide au commencement du XVe siècle* (1932), *Gontier et Pierre Col et l'humanisme en France au temps de Charles VI* (1934), *Recherches sur quelques écrivains du XIVe et XVe siècle* (1935), *La Vie intellectuelle dans les domaines d'Anjou-Provence de 1380 à 1435* (1941), *Histoire du Moyen Âge, l'Europe occidentale de 1270 à 1380*, in G. Glotz's *Histoire générale* (1941).

Kleinclausz, Arthur (1869–1947). Born in Auxonne (Côte-d'Or).

Agrégé (1881), doctorate (1888, "L'Empire Carolingien, ses origines et ses transformations").

Chargé de cours in Dijon (1897) and in Paris (1902). Professor of medieval history in Lyon (1904). *Assesseur* (assistant) to the dean (1924) and dean (1931). Director of the École nationale des beaux-arts in Lyon (1928).

Les Carolingiens (1903), *Claus Sluter et la sculpture bourguignonne au XVe siècle* (1905). *Les Villes d'art célèbres: Dijon et Beaune* (1907), *Histoire de Bourgogne* (1909), *Lyon, des origines à nos jours* (1925), *Les Pays d'art: La Bourgogne* (1929), *La Provence* (1930).

Langlois, Charles V. (1863–1929). Born in Rouen, died in Paris. Father: attorney.

E.P.H.E. (1882): *IVe section* (1882), *agrégé* (1884, 1st), École des chartes (1885, 1st), doctorate (1887, "Le Règne du Philipe III le Hardi").

Maître de conférences in Douai (1885). *Chargé de cours* in Montpellier (1886). *Chargé de cours* in Paris (1888); adjunct professor (1901); professor of the auxiliary sciences of history (1906); professor of medieval history (1909). Director of the Archives nationales (1913).

Les Archives de l'histoire de France with H. Stein (1891), *Manuel de bibliographie historique*, vol. 1 (1896), vol. 2 (1904), *Introduction aux études historiques* with Ch. Seignobos (1898), *Histoire du Moyen Âge* (1901), *L'Inquisition* (1902), *Questions d'histoire et d'enseignement* (1902), *La Société française au Moyen Âge* (1911), *Registres perdus des archives de la chambre des comptes de Paris* (1917), *La Vie en France au Moyen Âge*, vol. 1 (1908), vol. 2 (1924), vol. 3 (1925).

Lemonnier, Henry (1842–1936). Born in Saint-Prix (Seine-et-Oise). Father: former secretary of the School of Rome.

École des chartes (1865, 2nd); doctorate of laws (1866); *agrégé* (1862, 1st); doctorate (1887, "Étude sur la condition privée des affranchis sous l'Empire romain").

Attorney (1864). *Chargé de cours* at the lycée Louis-le-Grand (1873), acting professor at the lycée Henri-IV (1874), substitute (*suppléant*) at the lycée Saint-Louis (1875),
Louis-le-Grand (1881). Professor at the École des beaux-arts (1874), *maître de conférences*
at the E.N.S. in Sèvres (1884), substitute for Lavisse at the Sorbonne (1889), *chargé de
cours* and later professor of art history (1893).

 L'Art français au temps de Richelieu et Mazarin (1893), *Gros, biographie critique* (1907),
L'Art français au temps de Louis XIV (1911), *L'Art moderne, 1500–1800* (1912), edition of the
Procès verbaux de l'Académie royale d'architecture (1911–24, 8 volumes).

Luchaire, Achille (1846–1908). Born and died in Paris. Father: office head in the Ministry of the Interior.

 E.N.S. (1866), *agrégé* (1869), doctorate (1877, "Alain le Grand, sire d'Albret,
l'administration royale et la féodalité du Midi").

 Lycées of Pau (1869) and of Bordeaux (1874). *Maître de conférences* in history and the
language of southern France at Bordeaux (1877), professor of geography (1879). *Chargé
de cours* in Paris in the auxiliary sciences of history (1885), *chargé de cours* for the Middle
Ages (1888). Professor of medieval history (1889), succeeding Fustel de Coulanges.

 Histoire des institutions monarchiques de la France sous les premiers Capétiens (1883), *Étude
sur les actes de Louis VII* (1885, winner of the Gobert Prize), *Louis VI le Gros, annales de
sa vie et de son règne* (1889), *Les Communes françaises à l'époque des Capétiens directs* (1892),
Innocent III (1904–7, 4 volumes).

Mariéjol, Jean-Hippolyte (1855–1934). Born in Antibes. Father: sailor (*marin classé*)

 Agrégé (1882, 5ᵉ), doctorate (1887, "Un Lettré italien à la Cour d'Espagne: Pierre
Martyr d'Anghera, 1488–1526").

 Professor at the lycée in Lyon (1882), *maître de conférences* in Dijon (1885), *chargé de
cours* (1890), *chargé de cours* in Rennes and then Lyon (1893, professor of contemporary
history until 1925). *Chargé de cours* at the Sorbonne (1911–12).

 L'Espagne sous Ferdinand et Isabelle (1892), *Catherine de Médicis* (1920), *La Vie de
Marguerite de Valois* (1928).

Pariset, Georges (1865–1927). Born in Audincourt (Doubs), died at Strasbourg. Family
from Alsace.

 Attended school in Alsace (1874–82), *agrégé* (1888, 1st), doctorate (1897, "L'État et
les églises en Prusse sous Frédéric-Guillaume Iᵉʳ, 1713–1740").

 Auxiliary master at the lycée Henri-IV (1885), on leave from the lycée de Nev-
ers in Berlin (1888–92), *chargé de cours* in contemporary and modern history in Nancy
(1892), then adjunct professor (1897), and professor (1901). Member of the University
of the People (*université populaire*) newly established during the Dreyfus Affair. Professor in Strasbourg (1919).

 Publisher, with Georges Vallée, of the *Carnet d'étapes du dragon Marquant: Études
d'histoire moderne et contemporaine* (Strasbourg, 1929).

Petit-Dutaillis, Charles (1868–1947). Born at Saint-Nazaire. Father: chief medical officer
of the navy.

 E.P.H.E. (1887), École des chartes et agrégation (1890, 2nd and 3rd), doctorate
(1895, "Étude sur la vie et le règne de Louis VIII, 1187–1226").

 Professor at the lycée in Troyes (1891), substitute professor in medieval history
in Lille (1896). Director of the École supérieure de commerce in Lille (1899). Rector

of the Académie de Grenoble (1908). President of the Société de l'école des chartes (1925).

Le Déshéritement de Jean sans Terre et le meurtre d'Arthur de Bretagne (1925), *La Monarchie féodale en France et en Angleterre, X^e–XIIIe siècle* (1933), *L'Essor des états d'Occident,* with P. Guinard, vol. 4, part 2 of *Histoire du Moyen Âge,* in G. Glotz's *Histoire générale* (1937 and 1944), *Recueil des actes de Philippe Auguste,* under the direction of Clovis Brunel, with H.-Fr. Delaborde (1943), *Le Roi Jean et Shakespeare* (1944), *Les Communes françaises* (1947).

Pfister, Christian, 1857–1933. Born and died at Beblenheim (Haut-Rhin). Father: town hall guardian.

E.N.S. (1878, 5th), *agrégé* (1881, 2nd), doctorate (1885, "Étude sur le règne de Robert le Pieux, 996–1031").

Nancy: *maître de conférences* (1884), *chargé de cours* (1885), professor (1892), assistant to the dean (1899). Paris: substitute *maître des conférences* at the E.N.S. (1902–4), substitute professor (*professeur suppléant*) at the Sorbonne (1904–6), professor of medieval history (1906–9). Strasbourg: professor (1919–27), and rector of the Académie de Strasbourg (1927–31). Director of *Revue historique,* starting in 1912.

Le Duché mérovingien d'Alsace et la légende de sainte Odile (1892), *Les Manuscrits allemands de la Bibliothèque nationale relatifs à l'histoire de l'Alsace* (1843), *Histoire de Nancy* (1902–9, 3 volumes), *Rapport sur l'université de Strasbourg* (1917), *Histoire du Moyen Âge,* vol. 1, with F. Lot and A. Ganshof, in G. Glotz's *Histoire générale* (1928, 1934), *Pages alsaciennes* (1927).

Rebelliau, Alfred (1858–1934). Born in Nantes. Father: chief postal clerk.

E.N.S. (1877), *agrégé* (1880, 1st), doctorate (1892, "Bossuet, historien du protestantisme").

Substitute librarian at the E.N.S. (1880). *Maître de conférences* in Rennes. *Chargé de cours* in the history of ideas and of religious literature at the Sorbonne.

Editions of Bossuet, Chénier, La Bruyère, Voltaire.

Sagnac, Philippe (1866–1954). Born in Périgueux, died in a retirement home in Luynes (Indre-en-Loire). Father: business agent.

E.N.S. (1891), *agrégé* (1894, 3rd), doctorate (1898, "La Législation civile de la Révolution française").

Lille: *chargé de cours* (1899), adjunct professor (1903), professor of modern and contemporary history. Professor of history of the French Revolution at the Sorbonne (1923). Director of the *Revue d'histoire moderne et contemporaine* (1849–1914). Director with Louis Halphen of the series "Peuples et civilisations," 22 volumes.

La Chute de la royauté, la révolution du 10 août 1792 (1909), *Le Rhin français pendant la Révolution et l'empire* (1917), *Louis XIV, la prépondérance française* (1935, reworked in 1944), *La Révolution française,* with G. Lefebvre and R. Guyot (1930), *La Fin de l'ancien régime et la révolution américaine* (1941, winner of the Gobert grand prize), edition of *Cahiers de la Flandre maritime en 1784* with A. de Saint-Léger (1906, 2 volumes).

Seignobos, Charles (1854–1942). Born in Lamastre (Ardèche), died at Ploubazlanec (Côtes-du-Nord). Father: attorney.

E.N.S. (1874, 3rd), *agrégé* (1877, 1st), doctorate (1882, "Le Régime féodal en Bourgogne").

Maître de conférences in Dijon (1879). On leave in 1883; responsible for an open course on the European institutions at the Sorbonne. *Maître de conférences* in pedagogy at the Sorbonne (1890), responsible for a course on modern history (1898), and then a general course in history. Adjunct professor (1904), professor of political history of contemporary and modern times (1921).

Abrégé de l'histoire de la civilization (1887), *Histoire narrative et descriptive des anciens peuples de l'Orient* (1890), *Histoire politique de l'Europe contemporaine* (1897), *Introduction aux études historiques*, with Ch. V. Langlois (1898), *La Méthode historique appliquée aux sciences sociales* (1901), *Histoire de Russie*, with P. Milioukov and K. Eisenmann (1932, 3 volumes), *Histoire sincère de la nation française* (1933), *Histoire comparée des peuples de l'Europe* (1938), textbooks for secondary education.

Vidal de La Blache, Paul (1845–1918). Born in Pézenas (Hérault), died in Tamaris (Var). Father: professor of philosophy, Académie inspector.

E.N.S. (1863, 1st), *agrégé* in history (1866, 1st), doctorate (1870, "Hérode Atticus").

School of Athens (1866–67). Professor of history at the lycée of Angers (1871). *Chargé de cours* in Nancy (1872). Travels and special assignments to Gotha, Berlin, Switzerland, Spain, England, Algeria. *Maître de conférences* at the E.N.S. (1877), deputy director at the E.N.S. (1881). Professor of geography at the Sorbonne (1898). Founder of the *Annales de géographie*.

La Terre, géographie physique et économique (1883), *États et nations de l'Europe autour de la France* (1884), *Atlas général* (1894), *La France de l'Est* (1917), *Principes de géographie humaine*, published by E. Maitouse (1922), publisher with L. Gallois of the *Géographie universelle* in 23 volumes.

ACKNOWLEDGMENTS

Three people have been of assistance to me: Alice Gérard, who alerted me to several references in the Lucien Herr archives, notably the drafts of Sagnac's *La Révolution* corrected by Lavisse; Christophe Charle, who made available to me the as yet unpublished second volume of his *Dictionnaire biographique des professeurs de la Faculté des lettres de Paris* and over a dozen letters from Lavisse to Sagnac; and Victor Karady, who opened up his file of biographies to me of the *L'Élite universitaire littéraire au XIXᵉ siècle*. My warmest thanks to them and to M. Lanthoinette, who is in charge of the archives of the Hachette collection.

NOTES

1. Concerning the establishment of higher education, the reader may wish to begin with Antoine Prost, *L'Enseignement en France, 1800–1967* (Paris: Armand Colin, 1968) and Françoise Mayeur, *De la Révolution à l'école républicaine, 1789–1930*, vol. 3 of *Histoire générale de l'enseignement et de l'éducation,* under the direction of Louis-Henri Parias (Paris: Nouvelle Librairie de France, 1981), which is complemented by Wil-

liam R. Keylor's *Academy and Community: The Foundation of the French Historical Profession* (Cambridge: Harvard University Press, 1975). Not to be omitted is Louis Liard, *L'Enseignement supérieur en France, 1789–1893,* vol. 2 (Paris: Armand Colin, 1894).

2. Paul Fredericq, *L'Enseignement supérieur de l'histoire: Notes et impressions de voyage* (Paris: Alcan, 1899).

3. See, in particular, *Lieux de mémoire,* vol. 1, *La République,* "Lavisse, instituteur national," which analyses the "Little Lavisse" and gives a general impression of his personality. I will refer to it frequently.

4. See the introductions in the *Bibliographie générale des travaux historiques et archéologiques publiés par les sociétés savantes de la France* by R. de Lasteyrie, in collaboration with E. Lefèvre-Pontalis and A. Vidier, 6 vols. (1886–1904), three additional volumes (1901–7).

5. *Opening Lecture for the Course in the History of the Middle Ages at the Faculté des Lettres de Paris,* December 1881.

6. Julien Benda, *La Jeunesse d'un clerc* (Paris: Bernard Grasset, 1931), 196.

7. See his letter of resignation in A. Prost, *L'Enseignement en France, 1800–1967,* 242. "You seem not to realize that in so acting you will give ammunition to the enemies of the University and the Republic."

8. Camille Jullian, "Notes sur l'histoire de France au XIXe siècle," introduction to *Extraits des historiens français du XIXe siècle,* published in the Hachette classics (1897) and republished independently in 1979 (Geneva: Slatkine Reprints).

9. Louis Halphen, *Histoire et historiens depuis cinquante ans,* on the occasion of the fiftieth anniversary of *Revue historique.* See also Halphen's very useful *L'Histoire en France depuis cent ans* (Paris: Armand Colin, 1913).

10. Compare Pascal Ory, "La Sorbonne, cathédrale de la science républicaine," *L'Histoire,* no. 12 (May, 1979): 50–58.

11. Ernest Lavisse, "Les fêtes de 1884," in *Études et étudiants* (Paris: Armand Colin, 1895).

12. On Gabriel Monod, see the death notices by Charles Bémont, "Gabriel Monod," *Annuaire 1912—1913,* École pratique des hautes études, 5–27; Charles Bémont and Christian Pfister, "Gabriel Monod," *Revue historique,* no. 110 (May–August 1912); Albert Delatour, *Notice sur la vie et les travaux de M. Gabriel Monod* (Institut de France, Académie des sciences morales et politiques, 1915). See also Martin Siegel, "Science and the Historical Imagination: Patterns of French Historical Thought, 1866–1914" (PhD diss., Columbia University, 1965) and the chapter on Monod in Charles-Olivier Carbonell's *Histoire et historiens, une mutation idéologique des historiens français, 1865–1885* (Toulouse: Privat, 1976), 409–53. I was unable to consult the unpublished thesis by Benjamin Harrison, "Gabriel Monod and the Professionalization of History in France, 1844–1912" (PhD diss., University of Wisconsin, 1972).

13. On Alfred Rambaud, see Paul Vidal de La Blache, "Notice sur la vie et les œuvres de M. Alfred Rambaud," *Mémoires de l'Académie des sciences morales et politiques de l'Institut de France* 27 (1910), and Gabriel Monod's death notice, *Revue historique* (January–February, 1906).

14. See Gabriel Monod, "La Chaire d'histoire au Collège de France," opening lecture, *Revue politique et littéraire* and *Revue scientifique (Revue Bleue)* (1906).

15. See Gabriel Monod, *La Vie et la pensée de Jules Michelet,* course taught at the Collège de France (Paris: Champion, 1923).

16. See Charles Andler, *Vie de Lucien Herr* (Paris: Rieder, 1932), and Daniel Lindenberg, *Le Marxisme introuvable* (Paris: Calmann-Lévy, 1975).

17. On Gaston Paris, see Maurice Croiset, "Notice sur la vie et les travaux de M. Gaston Paris," *Bibliothèque de l'École des chartes* 65 (1904), 141–73, and Gabriel Monod, "Gaston Paris," *Revue historique* 81 (1903).

18. Lavisse papers, Bibliothèque Nationale, N.a.f. 25–165 to 25–172. Letter from Millardet to Du Mesnil, head of the ministry's Division of Public Instruction, N.a.f. 25–171^2, folio 325.

19. See Claude Digeon, *La Crise allemande de la pensée française, 1870–1914* (Paris: U.F., 1959), in particular, chapter 7, "La Nouvelle université et l'Allemagne (1870–1890)."

20. See the comparison between Lavisse and von Harnack to which Robert Minder dedicated part of his very interesting "final lesson" at the Collège de France, May 19, 1973.

21. Lavisse papers, Bibliothèque Nationale, N.a.f. 25–171^1, folios 11–19.

22. The five-year average (calculated by Antoine Prost, *L'Enseignement en France, 1800–1967*, see note 1) for the *licence de lettres* was only 296 between 1891 and 1895 and increased to 412 between 1896 and 1900.

23. See E. Lavisse, "Le Concours pour l'agrégation d'histoire," *Revue internationale de l'enseignement,* February 15, 1881, 146, and "Pourquoi il fallait réformer l'agrégation d'histoire," in *À propos de nos écoles* (Paris: Armand Colin, 1895).

24. Over a period of five years, Lavisse published, together with the publisher Armand Colin, his chief speeches, which can be found in *Questions d'enseignement national* (1885), *Études et étudiants* (1890), and *À propos de nos écoles* (1895).

25. "L'Enseignement historique en Sorbonne et l'éducation nationale," first published in *Revue des Deux Mondes,* February 15, 1882, and again in *Questions d'enseignement national* (1885).

26. By analogy to the title of the work by Lancelot-Voisin, sieur de La Popelinière, *Le Dessein de l'histoire accomplie*, which gave its name to the school of "histoire accomplie," or "histoire parfaite" in the second half of the sixteenth century. See also G. Huppert, *L'Idée de l'histoire parfaite* (Paris: Flammarion, 1973), translated by Françoise and Paulette Braudel as *The Idea of Perfect History* (Urbana: University of Illinois Press, 1970).

27. Charles V. Langlois and Charles Seignobos, *Introduction aux études historiques* (Paris: Hachette, 1898), 81ff., trans. by G. G. Berry as *Introduction to the Study of History* (London: Duckworth & Co., 1898; New York: Barnes & Noble reprint, 1966).

28. Camille Jullian, "Notes sur l'histoire de France," cxxviii.

29. See, in particular, the series of conferences at the École des hautes études sociales on *L'Éducation de la démocratie* by Lavisse, Alfred Croiset, Seignobos, Malapert, Lanson, and Hadamard (Paris: Alcan, 1907).

30. Ernest Renan, "Qu'est-ce qu'une nation?" conference held at the Sorbonne, March 11, 1882, in *Oeuvres complètes* (Paris: Calmann-Lévy, 1947), 1:997–1007.

31. The *Tableau de la géographie de la France* and *Louis XIV* were republished independently by Éditions Tallandier; the first in 1979, with an introduction by Paul Claval; the second in 1978, with an introduction by Roland Mousnier.

32. See Paul Viallaneix and Jean Ehrard, eds., *Nos ancêtres les Gaulois, actes du Colloque international de Clermont* (Clermont-Ferrand: Faculté des Lettres et Sciences Humaines de l'Université de Clermont-Ferrand II n.s. Fasc. 13, 1982), as well as the two reports by Mona Ozouf, "Les Gaulois à Clermont-Ferrand," *Le Débat*, no. 6 (November 1980) and Jean-Pierre Rioux, "Autopsie de *Nos ancêtres les Gaulois*," *L'Histoire*, no. 27 (October 1980). See also Karl-Ferdinand Werner, "Les Origines," in vol. 1 of *Histoire de France* (chapter 6), under the direction of Jean Favier (Paris: Fayard, 1981), and Christian Amalvi, "De Vercingétorix à Astérix, de la Gaule à de Gaulle, ou les métamorphoses idéologiques et culturelles de nos origines nationales," in *Dialogues d'histoire ancienne* (Paris: C.N.R.S., 1984), 285–318.

33. See Albert Grenier, *Camille Jullian, un demi-siècle de science historique et de progrès français, 1880–1930* (Paris: Albin Michel, 1944).

34. Gabriel Monod's editorial was reprinted in the centenary edition of *Revue historique*, no. 518 (April–June, 1976).

35. See Gabriel Monod and Charles Bémont, "Auguste Molinier," *Revue historique* 85 (1904).

36. The *Manuel de bibliographie historique* (Paris: Hachette, 1896) by Charles V. Langlois and H. Stein covers the principal countries. Gabriel Monod produced an analogous work just for France, "Les Études historiques en France," *Revue internationale de l'enseignement* 2 (1889): 587–99.

37. See Jean Favier, *Les Archives* (Paris: U.F., coll. "Que sais-je?" 1959; revised ed., 1976).

38. See Robert-Henri Bautier, "Les Archives," in *L'Histoire et ses méthodes* (Paris: Gallimard, Encyclopédie de la Pléiade, 1961), 1120–66, and Adolf Brenneke, *Archivkunde* (Leipzig: Koehler & Amelang, 1953). Also worth consulting is L. Sandri, "La Storia degli Archivi," *Archivum* 18 (1968): 101–13.

39. See *L'École des chartes, le livre du centenaire*, 2 vols. (Paris, 1929), and the unpublished thesis by Jean Le Pottier, "Histoire et érudition, recherches et documents sur l'histoire de la rôle de l'érudition médiévale dans l'historiographie française du XIXᶜ siècle" (École des chartes, 1979). See also Louis Halphen, chap. 4, "La Chasse aux documents," and Xavier Charmes, *Le Comité des travaux historiques et scientifiques, histoire et documents*, 3 vols. (Paris: Imprimerie nationale, 1886).

40. See *Le Temps où l'histoire se fit science, 1830–1848*, international colloquium organized on the 150th anniversary of the *Comité français des sciences historiques* (Paris: Institut de France, December 17–20, 1985). This important colloquium, the acts of which are to appear in the journal *Storia della storiografia*, took place too late for the results to be included here. I would especially like to thank Robert-Henri Bautier for having sent me his introduction, "La Renaissance de l'histoire comme science."

41. See Krzysztof Pomian, "Les Historiens et les archives dans la France du XVIIᶜ siècle," *Acta Poloniae historica*, no. 26 (1972).

42. See Dieter Gembicki, *Histoire et politique à la fin de l'ancien régime, Jacob-Nicolas Moreau (1717–1803)* (Paris: Nizet, 1979).

43. See Robert-Henri Bautier, "La Phase cruciale de l'histoire des archives: La Constitution des dépôts d'archives et la naissance de l'archivistique (XVIᶜ–début du XIXᶜ siècle)," *Archivum* 18 (1968): 139–49.

44. Charles Braibant, "Souvenirs sur Georges Bourgin," *Revue historique* 221 (1959).

45.   The two in question were "L'Histoire des idées au XVIᵉ siècle" by Abel Lefranc and "L'Alsace sous l'Ancien Régime" by R. Reuss.

46.   Marc Bloch, *Apologie pour l'histoire et le métier d'historien* (Paris: Armand Colin, 1959), 7. The work was republished in 1980 with an introduction by Georges Duby. It was also translated by Peter Putnam as *The Historian's Craft*, with an introduction by Joseph R. Strayer (New York: Knopf, 1953).

47.   See the fine study by Madeleine Rebérioux, "Histoire, historiens et dreyfusisme," in the centenary issue of *Revue historique* 518 (April–June 1976): 407–32.

48.   Gabriel Monod, *Études critiques sur les sources de l'histoire mérovingienne*, 2 vols. (Paris: Bibliothèque de l'École des hautes études, 1872–85), see in particular fasc. 8.

49.   See Albert Maire, *Répertoire alphabétique des thèses de doctorat ès lettres des universités françaises, 1810—1900* (Paris: A. Picard et fils, 1903) and A. Mourier and F. Deltour, *Catalogue et analyse des thèses françaises et latines admises par les facultés des lettres, Année scolaire 1880–1881* and *Année scolaire 1901–1902* (Paris: Delalain frères, 1880–1902). The curve would be parallel if one included the *Bibliographie générale des travaux* by Robert de Lasteyrie (see note 4). The first volume appeared in 1886, the fourth in 1904. The series lists 83,792 titles. Two supplementary volumes proved to be necessary to fill the gap between 1886 and 1900, and these listed 51,586 titles. For a fourteen year period, that was more than half of the preceding tally. For the yearly tables from 1901 to 1907, about 30,000 titles appeared.

This curve appears confirmed by another index: the *Bibliographie des travaux publiés de 1866 à 1897 sur l'histoire de la France de 1500 à 1789* by E. Saulnier and A. Martin (Paris: U.F., Rieder, 1932–38) and *Bibliographie des travaux publiés de 1866 à 1897 sur l'histoire de France depuis 1789* by Pierre Caron (Paris: E. Cornély, 1912), which lists 30,796 titles. The *Répertoire méthodique de l'histoire moderne et contemporaine de la France* by G. Brière and Caron (Paris: Société nouvelle de librairie et d'édition, Librairie G. Bellais, 1898–1965) arrives at a figure of 30,028 for the years 1898–1906; that is, as many appeared in eight years as in the previous thirty.

50.   See Christian Amalvi, "Catalogues historiques et conceptions de l'histoire," *Storia della storiografia* (1982): 2, 77–101.

51.   The 1892 contract for Lavisse cancelled a first draft, dated July 1888, that had already made provision for a "new history of France, richly and scientifically illustrated, based on contemporary documents" (Hachette Collection).

52.   Jean Mistler, *Histoire de la Librairie Hachette* (Paris: Hachette, 1954), 286. The author gathered his information from the registers of the partners' deliberations.

53.   This contract figures in the Lavisse Papers, Bibl. nat., N.a.f. 25–170, fol. 243. It set royalty payments at 7.5 percent for the author, 2.5 percent for Lavisse, and for each volume of 400 pages an advance of ten thousand francs.

54.   An echo of this quarrel appears in the correspondence of Guillaume Bréton with Lucien Herr (see note 55).

55.   Philippe Sagnac to Lucien Herr, December 12, 1912: "I heard from Bréton that Lavisse, Seignobos and you were to be in charge of contemporary history." The Lucien Herr archives, deposited at the *Institut d'études politiques de Paris*, comprise a dossier concerning *Histoire contemporaine*: some thirty letters from Guillaume Bréton to Lucien Herr, many notes from Lavisse in already deteriorating handwriting, six letters from Sagnac, five from Seignobos, and one from Esmonin (who was in charge of illustration).

The collection is very much alive. It shows Sagnac conscientious and deeply engaged in the enterprise, Lavisse in a hurry to be done, but ready to reread "all of Seignobos, at least in the delicate parts." And an unexpected side to Seignobos, who was extending his summer vacation (1917) in Ploubazlanec (Brittany) with his companion, Mme Marillier, to do some sailing: "For myself, I no longer know if it is a good thing, writing up an overview of so much abundant material, which will be difficult. No need to take oratorical precautions for corrections of form, I will accept everything you judge useful. As for beginning my sentences other than on the subject, I do not know if that will be possible. Cut out anything that appears to you unnecessary" (September 19, 1917). And again on October 23: "Do not be too cross with my laziness. We are here in the middle of flowers, fuchsias, roses, carnations, geraniums, dahlias, balsam, valerian, honeysuckle, heliotropes, sweet peas, mimosa. There are still some raspberries, but the green strawberries have yet to ripen. . . . It is therefore superfluous to add that I have not corrected the proofs, not one since I have been here."

56. Guillaume Bréton to Lucien Herr, February 25, 1920:

> I am not satisfied with Seignobos's conclusions on the history of France to 1914 (social transformations, changes in customs, culture, the arts and sciences), which would be placed after the history of the war. In that place only the results as of 1920 could be given. It is really not sufficiently brilliant for us to end on that.
>
> My opinion would be to find a way to write the summary in a much shorter way, in thirty or forty pages at the most, and to place it at the end of Seignobos's last volume, which, as an exception, would be longer. Besides the twenty pages by Lavisse, the volume on the war would comprise the conclusion, reasons for hope in the future despite the cataclysm from which we are emerging, and that would be all. The last volume would not incorporate any text and would be entirely given over to tables. You see that is worth the trouble to discuss.

He returns to the matter on March 4. "Tell me whether you find it appropriate that we challenge Lavisse on this to obtain a definitive decision as soon as possible."

Lavisse apparently responds in a note (undated, "Wednesday, 5 o'clock"), declaring, "I have asked Bidou and Gauvain for a meeting on Wednesday. Seignobos has to be there too. I am asking you to come. I will let Bréton know. Try to come meet with me Sunday afternoon. I won't be going out."

57. See Valérie Tesnière, "L'Édition universitaire," in *Le Temps des éditeurs*, vol. 3 of *Histoire de l'édition française*, under the direction of Henri-Jean Martin and Roger Chartier (Paris: Éd. Promodis, 1985), 217–27.

58. Lavisse states in his obituary notice for Rambaud that they both had the same idea but that "its realization belongs all to the honor of Rambaud, who in fact wrote it." Lavisse himself wanted to withdraw from the effort after 1891 to dedicate himself to the *Histoire de France*. See *Bulletin de l'association amicale des anciens élèves de l'E.N.S.* (1906).

59. The numbers communicated by Lanthoinette. The *Histoire contemporaine* had an initial run of ten thousand copies and reprints; between 1949 and 1956, it had a run of two thousand to three thousand.

60. No date, Hachette Collection.

61. Hachette Collection.

62. Lavisse Papers, Bibl. nat., N.a.f. 25–168, fol. 195.

63. Hachette Collection.

64. In fact, in a letter to Sagnac, a professor at Lille, on July 30, 1900, Lavisse writes some months after soliciting his participation: "I am very obliged to you for the trouble you have taken to find collaborators for me. I gladly accept the two whom you have suggested. Will you take charge of arranging things with de Saint-Léger, who presumably will be taking the period from the Peace of Ryswick to the Peace of Utrecht? . . . Have him tell me how he would understand this work and whether he has at hand the necessary books" (Christophe Charle Collection). A. de Saint-Léger, former student at the University of Lille, in 1900 defended a thesis entitled *La Flandre maritime et Dunkerque sous la domination française (1659–1789)*.

65. The contract with the three names, dated March 1902, makes reference to a 1892 contract naming only Bayet. Lavisse Papers, Bibl. nat., N.a.f. 25170, fol. 245.

66. This, at least, is the thought of Olivier Motte, who has worked on the Jullian papers at the *Institut*, for his book, *Camille Jullian, les années de formation*, to be published by the Presses de l'École française in Rome.

67. The terms that Lavisse proposed to Sagnac in April 1900 (?) are not without interest:

> You doubtlessly know that I have undertaken, in collaboration with a number of our colleagues, the publication, with Hachette, of a history of France before the Revolution. I myself will be doing the two volumes on Louis XIV. The first is almost ready, but to finish the second in time I will need help. Rebelliau has already taken over the chapters on literary, moral, and religious history. Do you want to take administrative history—politics and economy— for the same period (from the death of Colbert to the death of Louis XIV)? It seems to me that this part fits well with the work you have done. You will find in [your work] the antecedents to the questions that interest you. And then it will no doubt be pleasant to collaborate in a work that will have utility and to add your name to ours.

At this time, Lavisse was excluding recourse to the archives, since he added: "It is understood that in proposing to present the state of current knowledge on the history of France, we will only be using published documents. You therefore will not have to do archival research" (Christophe Charle Collection).

68. On Georges Pariset, see the obituary by Charles Bémont in *Revue historique* (November–December, 1927), 442, and the biography of Christian Pfister, the lead essay in a collection of posthumous articles, *Essais d'histoire et moderne et révolutionnaire* (1932).

69. Hachette Collection.

70. Jules Michelet, *Journal*, vol. 1, year 1841 (Paris: Gallimard, 1959), 359.

71. *Oeuvres complètes*, ed. Paul Viallaneix (Paris: Flammarion), 4:611ff.

72. Michelet, preface of 1847 to *Histoire de la Révolution* (Paris: Gallimard, Bibliothèque de la Pléiade, 1952), 2; translated as *History of the French Revolution* by Keith Botsford (Wynnewood, PA: Livingston Publishing Co., 1972).

73. Henri Martin, *Histoire de France* (Paris: Furne, 1844), 4:78–87.

74. Georges Duby, *Le Dimanche de Bouvines, 27 juillet 1214* (Paris: Gallimard, coll. "Les Trente journées qui ont fait la France," 1973; republished by Gallimard, coll. Folio, Histoire, 1985), 12, translated as *The Legend of Bouvines* by Catherine Tihanyi (Berkeley: University of California Press, 1990).

75. *Louis XIV,* for which it is useful to cite Edmond Esmonin. He was responsible for an important part of the documentation, but it is difficult to be precise about his contribution. Esmonin authored a thesis, "La Taille en Normandie au temps de Colbert (1861–1683)" (Paris: Librairie Hachette, 1913). Professor at the University of Grenoble, he published his dispersed contributions, upon his retirement, in *Études sur la France des XVIIe et XVIIIe siècles* (Paris: U.F., 1964).

76. Philippe Sagnac, "Ernest Lavisse," in the journal *Le Flambeau*, March, 1922.

77. His scrawled words are poignant. His wife has to have an operation; he is "worried to death." "My head is doing well, but my legs increasingly refuse to support it." "I am working very little because after an hour or two my head refuses to continue. I do not walk. My legs are always very weak." There are the appeals for help to Lucien Herr: "Thursday, the 24. My strength has crumbled. It is not without great difficulty that I sleep and get up I have to have help I have had to suspend all work. The idea of writing has become repugnant to me." To Sagnac, July 11, 1921: "I have a great service to ask of you. I am in the process of writing a conclusion to the contemporary history. It will be, in part, a summary of the volumes. Would you like to go over the part that pertains to you? Forgive me for repeating, but you will be doing me a great service" (Christophe Charle Collection). And again to Lucien Herr, September 29: "I have a relapse into neurasthenia. I am no good for anything and I feel that this state of affairs is definitive. I also think with terror about the conclusion. I embrace all of you."

CHAPTER II

The Era of the Annales

✑

KRZYSZTOF POMIAN

History reconstructs the past through the intermediary of sources, and these sources must be written ones. Put into practice as early as the sixteenth century, well before its explicit formulation, this fundamental dogma of modern historical scholarship initiated a break with the national memory as a repository of oral traditions and holy relics. This is evidenced by history's migration from the royal court, via the Benedictines of Saint-Maur, to the nineteenth-century university, where its transformation into a specialized discipline was fully realized. It is also borne out by controversies over the proper role of history, precipitated by shifts in its social placement and its constitutive relations, which left the dogma itself unchallenged. Henceforth this fundamental dogma was to determine history's boundaries as well as its temporal horizons, its spatial extension, and its content, all the more forcefully due to a replacement, in both theory and practice, of "written sources" with "texts."

"History," said Fustel de Coulanges, "is made from texts." In this usage, texts are essentially public documents, and most often official ones emanating from some recognized authority. Once a document's authenticity has been established, a historian studies its explicit content and compares it with documents of similar date and provenance to determine its degree of credibility. While not obliged to accept it at face value, he nonetheless remains dependent on its explicit content. For the process he then undertakes amounts, more or less, to reconstituting the document by studying the meanings of its words, its intended destination, the circumstances that shaped it, and so on. Described on the basis of such reconstructions, the past, from the historian's perspective, becomes identified with the ensemble of objects and changes consciously perceived by those for whom this past was the present, with the problems they set out to resolve and the goals they intended to achieve. As to forces of which the actors themselves were supposedly unaware, historians who invoked them have based their observations not on sources but on works by philosophers and theologians.

Thus the fundamental dogma determines most of history's content. It strictly limits the field's temporal horizons: everything preceding the appearance of written sources is relegated to prehistory, deemed different from history not in degree but in kind, with the present being left to memoirists and journalists until sufficient time has elapsed for it to become objectified as the past, until the day when the archives are opened and reconstruction can proceed. This criterion also delimits history's spatial extension: its purview is restricted to those peoples who have mastered writing, with all others being consigned to the attention of ethnologists. Finally, the boundaries of the historical discipline are situated so as to exclude antiquarians and archeologists, who study the material remains of the past, as well as folklorists, who record oral traditions.

Likewise, historians' adherence to the fundamental dogma leads them, in all innocence, to privilege those social groups whose members produced written documents, whose actions and deeds were recorded. When they tried, like Michelet, to abandon the colorful fêtes of the dukes of Burgundy to "explore the cellars in which Flanders was fermenting," the very texts they used constantly diverted their attention toward politics, diplomacy, war, and the individuals figuring in these enterprises. Limited by the written word, even historians of the "agrarian" and "working classes" and of industry tended to provide bookish accounts—frequently inspired solely by juridical prescriptions, often mistaken for descriptions of reality—from which everything inaccessible through reading was absent, notably work, practices, and the conditions of everyday life.

More generally, historians also fail to register longstanding invariables, things that change so gradually as to elude detection, and whatever so pervades a culture as to be considered completely unremarkable by contemporaries. Their unreflective adherence to the fundamental dogma leads them to favor short-term developments, rapid and spectacular shifts whose witnesses, duly impressed, produce paper trails directing the attention of later historians toward these same shifts: in other words, toward *events*. Hence the privileged status of chronology: the most appropriate framework within which to present sequential narrations, it is also considerably more than a literary strategy, namely an apparently natural way to conceptualize history, organize its content, and "discover" its order.

All of this seems self-evident today, thanks to the contrast between current historical practice and that which prevailed a century ago. A veritable epistemological revolution, by no means limited to France, has overthrown the authority of the longstanding fundamental dogma, and with it this conception of history as a university discipline, as a vision of the world, as a branch of literature. It remains true, incontestably, that history—scholarly history, at any rate—reconstructs the past through the intermediary of sources, but there is no longer any binding stipulation that these sources must be written ones. Of the various sources used by historians today, written documents are but one of many options. Always important and often irreplaceable, they are now considered insufficient by themselves to satisfy historical curiosity.

In the nineteenth century, the national memory celebrated primarily great events and great men: military commanders and politicians, artists and scholars, authors and benefactors. It ranked them hierarchically and arranged them in chronological sequence. After a period of disagreement, the national memory and historical scholarship again came to share a common agenda in terms of both content and organization. So much was true, at least, of the official memory endorsed, protected, and overseen by the State, which was internalized by individuals in school, doing military service, participating in public festivals and commemorations, and was reaffirmed by visits to monuments and museums. "Popular" traditions and artistic productions, orally transmitted memories, folk wisdom—everything to which only regional importance was attributed—remained outside this memory, whose boundaries coincided with those of scholarly history and its complements: the history of art and literature and the study of national monuments. But in this disciplinary trio it was scholarly history that took on the preeminent tasks: keeping watch over the memory of the nation and the State, and preserving it from contamination by legend.

The epistemological revolution that, in France, unsettled history in the first half of our century—namely the revocation of writing's monopoly and, a fortiori, that of the text—prompted historians to reconsider all aspects of their work. In growing numbers they turned toward unwritten sources and, when analyzing written ones, focused more on traces left unwittingly by their authors than on their explicit content. They began to neglect great men and events, playing down the importance of politics, diplomacy, war—and consequently of chronology. This amounted to toppling the three "idols" of the historical tribe denounced by Simiand in a celebrated article of 1903.[1] By so doing, they effected a rupture between the new historical scholarship and the national memory, for it was thanks to their efforts that the structure and content of the two diverged so sharply. This generated conflicts within historical scholarship, whose allegiances were divided between its cognitive aspirations and its social role. The outcome was a divorce between professional historians and the general public, which continued to prefer traditional history.

But this widening of the fundamental dogma of historical scholarship produced shockwaves well beyond the boundaries of its own field. The content and internal organization of today's national memory differ from those of a century ago in several respects. And the differences are not insignificant. Witness the advent of museums of altogether new kinds, or previously thought to be of only local interest: museums of popular crafts and traditions, of technology, of ecology. Witness also the appearance of new kinds of listed monuments elevated to the status of, for example, national parks, landscapes, and sites, including former workshops and factories, train stations, public markets, and peasant dwellings. Witness, finally, the recent proliferation of texts in which oral and regional traditions as well as the history of marginal groups are treated as important constituents of the national memory. No longer concerned exclusively with famous men, important political events, military exploits, and high culture, this collective storehouse is now organized along geographic and social lines as well as chronological ones.

For some time, then, historical scholarship and the national memory have been making peace with one another. On the one hand, the cleavage between traditionalists, many of whom have assimilated a number of these innovations, and the innovators, who have aged, has become much less pronounced than it was, say, forty years ago. On the other hand, and even more tellingly, the "new" history has won over the public: books formerly read by only a handful of specialists now appear in inexpensive editions, and some of them—like Fernand Braudel's *The Mediterranean*—have even become belated bestsellers. Clearly an era is coming to an end, or perhaps has already ended: that of a disjunction between historical scholarship and the national memory, both of which were undergoing transformation along similar lines but in accordance with quite disparate rhythms. Stability and harmony have now been reestablished—at least until the onset of new storms.

Relations between scholarly history and national memory from the end of the nineteenth century to the present day constitute an enormous subject, only a small fragment of which will be treated here: an innovatory, even avant-garde scholarly history in France during a period in which it prompted much debate and opposition. More precisely: history as endorsed and practiced by the group attached to the *Annales* during the first four decades of the journal's existence, from 1929 to 1968, and whose roots penetrate deeply into the human geography developed late in the previous century. Furthermore, even this story will be broached from a single perspective. The *Annales*, both the journal and the circle, will be discussed here only insofar as they set out to modify the content of French national memory, especially prevalent notions about the history of France. What were their proposals in this domain? Did they formulate a new investigative protocol for the history of France? If so, what was it, what arguments were advanced to justify it, and to what extent was it put into practice by *Annales* historians? These are the questions I will attempt to answer.

A Journal, A Circle

When the first issue of the *Annales* appeared, the *Revue historique* was more than fifty years old. The *Annales de géographie* was approaching forty. The *Année sociologique* and the *Revue de synthèse historique*, soon to become the *Revue de synthèse*, had reached thirty, and the *Revue d'histoire économique et sociale* had been appearing for twenty. Readers of all these publications would have sensed something familiar about the new journal, for here and there it featured some of the same authors. But they must have been struck even more by what was new about it. Its tone, first of all, which was quite personal, frequently polemical, and always lively. Also a pervasive feeling that what was being transacted in its pages was important, not only for one of many academic disciplines but for a world in crisis toward which historians had an obligation to "try to be useful." An openness to things outside French borders. A desire to mend the divorce between historians pouring over "documents of the past" and those, "more and more numerous," who "devote . . . their activity to the study of contemporary societies and economies." And, finally, a resolve to demolish the walls erected by historians themselves, which were "so high that they often block their views."[2]

This originality of the *Annales*, its contrarian, heterodox, and youthful character, is surprising, for its founders were not young men seeking to make names for themselves at their elders' expense. By 1929, Lucien Febvre (1878–1956) and Marc Bloch (1886–1944) had been professors for ten years at the University of Strasbourg, which they left a few years later, the first for the Collège de France (1933), the second for the Sorbonne (1936). Despite having spent four years at the front in World War I, each had produced a significant body of work. In addition to his thèse,★ "Philippe II

★ EDITOR'S NOTE: The French *thèse*, derived from the old meaning of a proposition or theory announced for public debate, most often on a theological subject, now refers specifically to the dissertation presented for a doctorate in a French university.

et la Franche-Comté" (1911), and three other books on the history of this province (1905, 1911, and 1912), Lucien Febvre had written *A Geographical Introduction to History* (1922), a biography of Luther (1928), and a great many articles, book reviews, and lecture notes, a complete bibliography of which is still lacking. Marc Bloch, for his part, had published more than a hundred articles, book reviews, and lecture notes in addition to his thèse, "Rois et serfs" (1920), and two books: *L'Île-de-France: The Country around Paris* (1913) and *The Royal Touch* (1924). Thus it was to already accomplished oeuvres, augmented by substantial books published in the 1930s and 1940s, that Marc Bloch and Lucien Febvre added their editorial responsibilities for the *Annales*, for which they also wrote almost half of the articles published during its first two decades (roughly 1,800 out of a total of 3,673),[3] establishing in the process a tone and a style that set it apart from other contemporary scholarly journals.

But the radical novelty of the *Annales* was not fully apparent until some ten years after it began to appear, by which time it had become clear that they meant to change the very idea of history as well as the way it was practiced. First of all, by manifesting a passionate and intense interest in the contemporary world that was startling in a periodical edited by a medievalist and a sixteenth-century specialist. An analysis of the contents of the *Annales* reveals that, between 1929 and 1941, articles devoted to contemporary history (that is, after 1815) occupied almost half its pages each year, and sometimes as much as 60 percent of them.[4] Closer study would almost certainly indicate that most of these texts did not deal with the years between 1815 and 1918 but rather with those through which the authors and readers of the *Annales* were living. They treated the relation between economic circumstances and the present crisis, unemployment, Taylorism and rationalism, the automobile and aviation, the League of Nations and the International Employment Office, socialism, syndicalism, the Soviet Five-Year Plan, the American New Deal, Nazism, the ideas of Marx, Lenin, and Stalin, and even, on one occasion, haute couture. And this is not an exhaustive list. During the first ten years of its existence, then, the focus of the *Annales* was largely contemporary, and its aim was to examine with "appropriate intelligence facts that tomorrow will be history."

In view of preparing today this history of tomorrow, the *Annales* fostered active collaboration between history and the social sciences throughout this period, "not in the way of articles on method and theoretical dissertations. By example and deed."[5] Responsibility for implementing this agenda fell to an editorial committee consisting of four historians, two geographers (one of them interested in political science), an economist, and a sociologist. The number of articles and book reviews pertaining to their disciplines is indeed impressive. It is difficult to tally them with precision, but the aggregate number is certainly much greater than that for contributions listed under the headings "Political Economy," "Sociology," "Psychology," "Geography," and "Archeology" in the *Annales* index (nonetheless an irreplaceable analytic tool). In the end, however, such percentage figures are less important than the *Annales*'s endorsement of the view that only by making use of all the human and social sciences could history hope to resolve all of its problems. And the fact that this idea of history was operative in every issue.

This policy presupposed a break with the deeply rooted conviction that history's only viable sources were written ones, and its implication that the basic skills of the historian were reducible to the ability to read, understood as encompassing paleographic competence. The signs of this break, to be discussed at length below, are readily discernible. Before the end of the first year, Marc Bloch and Lucien Febvre introduced the rubric "Iconography of Economic and Social History," subsequently modified to "Museums, Exhibitions, Economic Iconography." True, this was neither one of the journal's most durable category headings nor its most amply represented, but it casts light on one of the editors' priorities, likewise expressed in a collective investigation of cadastral plans and a pervasive interest in maps, atlases, and aerial photographs. Another parallel indicator is the importance accorded, on the one hand, to everything relating to landscape, and, on the other, to dwellings, tools (an inventory of ploughs figure among many possible topics recommended for collective investigation), and nourishment. In other words, the *Annales* set out to teach historians to look, to see. It encouraged them to explore visible, palpable things, showing how the words of written sources might be replaced by gestures, practices, and manipulations in view of reconstructing aspects of past life that would otherwise remain inaccessible.

To go beyond words and rediscover things in the most ordinary application of the term, one that has nothing to do with Durkheim's understanding of it. We will see that the journal's attitude toward the social sciences was a direct consequence of this ambition. For the moment, suffice it to say that the essential epistemological difference between history and the social sciences follows directly from the fact that the latter discipline studies things in many different ways, rather than only through the intermediary of sources. True, sociologists generate sources of their own by having target groups fill out questionnaires, but they can also act as observers and even conduct interviews, both of which entail personal interaction. Economists must deal with businesses, banks, and the stock exchange, with government ministries, customs offices, tax-collection bureaus, markets, corporations, and unions; like sociologists, they must also study statistics, maps, and documents, but of necessity their work entails contact with individuals, products, raw materials, money. And the same holds true for geographers. Only historians reconstruct their object of study *exclusively* through the intermediary of relevant sources, which constitute their sole tangible reality.

The *Annales* editors always upheld stringent requirements regarding historical research methods, especially pertaining to the use of sources, from the constitution of a corpus of viable evidence to the latter's critical assessment. But they also set out, from the beginning, to exploit all the social sciences in hopes of learning to read previously known sources with a fresh eye guided by new questions, and above all to expand this repertory so that it encompassed all those witnesses to the past that had hitherto remained mute, not because they had nothing to say but because historians could not understand their language, and perhaps even thought it was not worth learning.

They sought to go beyond words and rediscover things. And having rediscovered them, to proceed with comparative analysis of those seemingly drawn from a single category, or that were variations of a single type. When Henri Pirenne (1862–1935) first posited the notion of a comparative history in April of 1923, at the fifth Congrès international des sciences historiques, Marc Bloch and Lucien Febvre were in the audience, and they soon became its champions and propagandists. Of all historians then living, Pirenne seems to have been the one who most influenced the founders of the *Annales*.[6] In addition to joining the editorial board, he published two articles in the journal, and all of his books were reviewed and debated in its pages. Even more important, however, than explicit references to Pirenne's ideas and articles (whose titles contain the phrase "comparative history") is the way the enterprise was informed by the comparative spirit. This is most in evidence with regard to certain subjects, for example the feudal system, the origins of capitalism, and agrarian structures. But over time almost every subject treated in the *Annales* was discussed within various spatial and temporal contexts, such that the articles, book reviews, and bibliographic notes addressing a single topic constituted an introduction to its comparative study.

In addition to comparisons determined by the curiosity of collaborators and the occasions afforded by books under review, the editors also tried to coordinate systematic comparative projects. Such initiatives underlay investigations into land allotment, the genesis of seigneurial structures, the nobility, and prices. In this way Marc Bloch and Lucien Febvre attempted, from the first issue, to make the *Annales* something other than a letterbox journal into which "authors with nothing in common slip their manuscripts." They envisioned something more like a "crowbar journal that pries apart old constricting partitions, Babylonian accumulations of bias, routine, conceptual errors, and misapprehensions in order to demolish them."[7] They wanted the *Annales* to be the center of a collective project conceived along similar lines, a network united less by shared methodological, philosophical, and ideological premises than by complementary interests and similar attitudes, founded on a rejection of all doctrinally prefabricated solutions, and on adherence to the idea of an intrinsically problematic social world, one in which nothing is self-evident and of which no element or aspect can be understood without research into both its present and its past.

At the heart of this network, the journal's two editors were assisted by five members of the editorial board who did much to shape its character: the geographer Albert Demangeon (1872–1940), the sociologist Maurice Halbwachs (1877–1945), and three historians: André Piganiol (1883–1968), who specialized in ancient history, George Espinas (1869–1948), a collaborator of Pirenne's who specialized in urban medieval history, and Henri Hauser (1866–1946), who occupied the economics chair at the Sorbonne. The roles of Henri Pirenne, the economist Charles Rist (1874–1955), and André Siegfried (1875–1959), a geographer and *politologue*, seem to have been largely honorific. But a broader intellectual circle became visible in the *Annales* from very early on, one that provided regular as well as occasional contributors, both French and foreign, representing all disciplines of the social sciences.

The core of this larger circle consisted of sixteen individuals, each of whom, in the period 1929–48, published more than twenty texts in the *Annales*, which taken together amounts to roughly a third of all those to appear over the same span of time. First place easily goes to Paul Leuilliot (1897–1987), a historian of nineteenth-century Alsace, who was responsible for no less than 8 percent of the total. He is followed at some distance by Maurice Halbwachs, Albert Demangeon, Georges Espinas, Georges Lefebvre (1874–1959, historian of the French revolution), André Piganiol, Maurice Beaumont (1892–1981, a scholar of the nineteenth-century specializing in Germany and international relations), Jacques Houdaille (an economist), George Bourgin (1879–1958, another historian of the nineteenth century, especially the Commune), Charles-Edmond Perrin (1887–1974, a medievalist), Georges Méquet (whose specialty was Russia and the U.S.S.R), the geographer Jules Sion (1878–1940), André E. Sayous (1873–1940? a historian of business and banking), Henri Brunschwig (1904–89, whose speciality was German history), Henri Baulig (1877–1962, a geographer), and Henri Hauser.

By and large, then, the most frequent contributors of the *Annales* were in the same age bracket as its principal editors, with men in their fifties clearly predominating at the beginning. Historians for the most part, they worked on all periods, including the nineteenth century and the French Revolution, with most of their number specializing in economic and social history. The group also included at least three geographers, a sociologist interested primarily in economic and demographic questions, and an economist. Finally, apart from France, Germany was far and away the country that attracted the most of attention, followed by England, Italy, the United States, and the Soviet Union.

After the Second World War the *Annales* changed its title. For the fourth time. Initially *Annales d'histoire économique et sociale*, it became *Annales d'histoire sociale* from 1939–41 and *Mélanges d'histoire sociale* from 1942–44, reverting in 1945 to *Annales d'histoire sociale* in homage to Marc Bloch, an eminent figure of the French Resistance who had been shot by the Germans a year earlier. Beginning in 1946, however, it was known as *Annales: Économies, Sociétés, Civilisations*. Apparently, in 1939 the word "économique" had been eliminated from the title for "exclusively contingent reasons," and conditions in occupied Paris prompted the shift from the original title to the short-lived *Mélanges*. The last change, however, signaled a shift of focus. Henceforth the *Annales*, in its very title, distanced itself from the conception of history that was unified, unidirectional, uniform. The editors chose instead to broadcast their intention to take into account a multiplicity of "economies, societies, and civilizations" widely distributed in space and time, all to be accorded like status. "To clarify, we might say space equals geography, and time, history,"[8] specified the journal's editor in the manifesto inaugurating this new period. While the word "history" disappeared from the title, history itself remained more than ever the project's very heart. But a history recast in spatial terms, and thus plural.

The changes of title and orientation were accompanied by a change of editor. From 1946, his esteemed partner now gone, Lucien Febvre was seconded by Fernand Braudel (1902–85), Georges Friedmann (1902–77), Charles Morazé (1913–2003), and Paul Leuilliot. Ten years later the *Annales* published Lucien Febvre's obituary; from that point until 1968 its editor was Fernand Braudel. The pool of authors evolved in favor of younger men, but many of the older ones continued to contribute; those published most frequently between 1949 and 1968 were Georges Bourgin, Henri Brunschwig, Georges Lefebvre, Jean Lestocquoy, Paul Leuilliot, and Robert Schnerb (1900–1962). After that of Fernand Braudel, the new signatures, in decreasing order of frequency, were those of François Crouzet, Abel Chatelain, Pierre Chaunu, Jean-Jacques Hémardinquer, Ruggiero Romano, Georges Duby, Robert Mandrou, André Chastagnol, Émile James, Jean Sigmann, and Marcel Émerit. Among both veterans and newcomers, authors who published more than twenty texts in this period accounted, in the aggregate, for no more than half the total, or as much as Marc Bloch and Lucien Febvre alone had provided over the preceding two decades. The number of *Annales* collaborators had increased, but the journal had lost the personal style that was the source of its charm during the initial period.

Furthermore, it was no longer the organizational center of a collective project, for in 1946 this function was assumed by another entity: the sixth section of the École pratique des hautes études (hereafter E.P.H.E.), which translated the ideas of the *Annales* into educational and research programs. In a parallel development, heated intellectual debate became increasingly rare, for a growing number of those previously regarded as heretics, or at least as unsettling innovators, were establishing institutional power bases within the university system. By and large, however, continuity was preserved. There was the same resolve to challenge the traditional boundaries of history, encourage cooperation between history and the social sciences, and legitimize nonwritten sources and new approaches to historical research; the same desire to study things themselves; the same commitment to comparative methodologies, linked to the journal's ongoing dialogue with foreign scholars; and the same wariness of doctrines that, masquerading as research premises, in fact imposed dogmatic positions. In other words, the distinctive intellectual program of the first *Annales* period was maintained throughout the second half of its existence.

The present study will examine the forty years of history produced within the intellectual circle of which the *Annales* was the center, in other words, the work of at least three generations of historians—and not only historians. The study will examine the generation of Marc Bloch and Lucien Febvre, active prior to 1914 and encompassing most of the authors of the first *Annales* period. Then that of Fernand Braudel, which appeared on the scene in the 1920s and 1930s, reaching maturity, due to a delay caused by the Second World War, after 1945. Its members included Henri Brunschwig, Paul Leuilliot, Charles Morazé, and Robert Schnerb as well as authors who, while they published less in the *Annales*, were nonetheless associated with the journal at the beginning, and later with the sixth section of the E.P.H.E.: Roger Dion (1896–1981), Ernest Labrousse (1895–1988), Maurice Lombard (1904–64), Jean Meuvret (1901–71), Yves Renouard (1908–65), and Philippe Wolff (1913–2001). Finally, the generation that made its presence felt beginning in the 1940s; we have already mentioned several of its representatives, to whom should be added, among authors published by the *Annales*, René Baehrel, Marc Bouloiseau, Jean Bouvier, Pierre Deyon, José Gentil da Silva, Pierre Goubert, Pierre Jeannin, Étienne Julliard, Henri Lapeyre, Jacques Le Goff, Emmanuel Le Roy Ladurie, Frédéric Mauro, Pierre Souyri, and Alberto Tenenti. One special case should also be mentioned: that of Philippe Ariès (1914–84), who never published in the journal and was not affiliated with the sixth section but whose approach to the practice of history was consistent with that of the *Annales* group.

GEOGRAPHY AND HISTORY

In the couple formed by history and geography, the latter long functioned as a servant summoned to answer questions posed by her mistress. These queries tended to focus rather monotonously on two subjects: the limits of former political, ecclesiastical, and administrative divisions, and the voyages and expeditions of earlier periods, considered in tandem with the geographical ideas of older authors. This "difficult geography, one that makes use of texts,"[9] completely uninformed by curiosity about spatial realities, professed, like history, unstinting fidelity to the fundamental dogma.

The world of Vidal de La Blache originated in a resolve to emancipate geography from the cult of text and transform it into a science of things observed on the ground, one premised on establishment of the gaze instead of reading as the privileged instrument for knowledge acquisition. The gaze in question was not naïve. Aided by maps, guided by a terminology enabling description of the objects before it, prepared by a methodical apprenticeship, the gaze as used and trained by Vidal was capable of recognizing forms, inventorying their distinctive characters, assessing the traces of their previous states, and evaluating the symptoms of their subjacent determinants. This data obtained through the gaze, the geographer's raw material, is rendered intelligible by investigations carried out among the inhabitants of the country being studied, by archival research as well as firsthand observation; considered together, they make it possible to transform visible accidents of the terrain into signs of its past vicissitudes and situate present appearances within a more extended time frame. Stone and soil on the one hand, human beings on the other: Vadalian geography occupied a point at which geology converged with ethnography, aided and abetted by linguistics and history. A science simultaneously natural and human, its equilibrium was perpetually unstable because it was constantly threatened by opposing tendencies against which it had to defend its specificity.

Vidal's masterpiece, the *Tableau de la géographie de la France* (1903), was read, pondered, and assimilated not only by geographers but also by many historians, including the founders of the *Annales* and their immediate successors. The book indeed offered new perspectives on history. With consummate skill, it showed that landscape, for those capable of truly seeing and reading it, is a historical source every bit as important as texts, and sometimes more so. It explained how landscape elements indicative of frontiers between two natural regions or population zones could be identified. And it introduced the germ of a distinction that was destined to have a great future: that of *le temps court* versus *la longue durée*, or "short" versus "extended" time spans.

To be sure, Vidal did not conceptualize this distinction in terms of two dimensions of, or strata within, a single historical period. He understood it as an opposition between specifically human activities and factors imposed on human beings by nature. Translated into disciplinary terms, this schema parallels the opposition between history and physical geography, which was consistent with the accepted idea of history in Vidal's period; namely, a history squarely focused on events unfolding over relatively short temporal spans. The originality and fecundity of Vidal's contribution resided in his introduction between such a history and physical geography, with its extended geological time frame, of yet a third term: *human geography*, which, as a result of its interest oriented primarily toward factors that remain historically constant, functioned as an intermediary between the first two. It encompassed periods of time that are extended, but by human standards and not geological ones: while exceeding the temporal scale of contemporary historical practice, it fell far short of the vast periodic divisions of geology.[10]

Vidal's human geography proposed that geographers study, as geographers, the extended history of populations, economies, habitats, and techniques, even politics and the movement of ideas, insofar as these influenced the human manipulation of natural energies. To avoid the danger of falling into vague generalities, such investigations, a synthesis of physical geography and history, were best limited to clearly circumscribed regions. Like all synthetic projects, this one entailed difficulties, with some authors surrendering to a naturalist determinism and others, by contrast, insisting on the primacy of human agency. Vidal himself never clearly stated his views on this question, which seem to have evolved. In any event, regional monographs of the French geographic school generally defined their objects of study in reference to both natural conditions and human intervention, deemed the double determinants of qualities specific to a given region.

A crucial innovation whose effects can still be felt in the French social sciences, the appearance of the regional geographic monograph had considerable impact on knowledge of France, not only among geographers and historians but also among the public at large. Never had various parts of France been described so methodically as in the ensuing series of studies of human geography, some forty of which appeared between 1905 and 1970. Each resulted from several years of research on the terrain, which was surveyed in all directions and during all seasons so that its variable aspects might be grasped fully, at least to the extent they surrendered themselves to visual scrutiny and the photographic lens. These expeditions were supplemented by analysis of maps, cadastral plans, and—once they became available—aerial photographs; in other words, by images of all kinds, as well as by observation of the physical environment; presentation of data obtained in this way often took up a significant portion of these monographs.

Then came the chapters devoted to human beings. Here visually derived impressions of their external appearance and way of life were complemented by official statistics, and above all by information gathered systematically from the residents themselves, who were asked to complete questionnaires. Formulated along lines recommended by Vidal de La Blache and Gallois, before 1914 they all seem to have featured the same rubrics, adapted by their authors to the regions they were studying: agriculture (agrarian landscapes, field organization, categories of real estate, methods of cultivation, grazing tracts, the use of forests, moors and marshes, the rearing of livestock), rural industry (its resources, supplies of raw material, organization, and approach to marketing), business and communication systems, habitat (grouped villages or isolated farms, residential furnishings and arrangements), population (settlement, demographic rhythms, migration patterns), and regional divisions and their limits.

All these elements of the human environment were studied not only in their present state but also so as they were in a more or less distant period of the past. Without necessarily sharing the archival proclivities of an Albert Demangeon or a Max Sorre, or the historical curiosity of an André Allix (who concluded his study of Oisans* with an extended examination of this region in the medieval era), all these geographers assessed evidence, with regard to settlement, stretching back as far as the earliest surviving records, often dating from the medieval period but never more recent than the seventeenth century. The confrontation of two sets of statistics applying to the same region but at intervals of more than a century already adds a temporal dimension to geography, revealing what changes and what remains constant. The same could be said, with even greater reason, of comparisons collating data concerning the thirteenth, eighteenth, and early twentieth centuries, like those of Jules Sion, or of studies of human evolutionary factors covering a period between the present and the sixteenth century, or even earlier. True, according to Vidal, the variations resulted from historical factors while the constants were

---

★ EDITOR'S NOTE: Oisans is a region of the French Alps delimited by the valleys of the Romanche, Durance, and Drac rivers.

the province of geography. Such a conception of their relations, while implicitly contested as early as the 1930s, was not openly challenged until later, by Roger Dion from a geographical perspective and Fernand Braudel from that of history. Nonetheless, from early in the century the adepts of human geography provided, in their monographs, examples of work that contributed substantially to the historical literature but that, without neglecting texts, was also premised on the deployment of vision and the exploitation of nonwritten sources on a large scale. This approach proved fruitful. Hence we should not be surprised that historians subsequently began to use parallel methodological approaches in their own work.[11]

In October 1901, the Société d'histoire moderne heard a lecture by Camille Bloch on "The Organization of the Study of Local History in France," in May 1902 the same organization hosted another lecture by Pierre Caron on "The Organization of Modern Local Historical Studies," and in February 1903 Gustave Lanson delivered another entitled "The Provincial History of French Literary Life: A Program of Study." For its part, the *Revue de synthèse historique*, edited by Henri Berr, manifested intense interest in regional French studies: its first issue featured two programmatic articles on the question, one by Berr himself and another by Pierre Foncin, contributor to the *Annales de géographie* and active spokesperson for the regionalist movement with close ties to Vidal's school. In 1903 Berr published an overview of French regional studies in which he stressed the role of geographers, most notably Vidal, whose *Tableau* had just appeared, and called for a program that would "render the psychology of peoples scientific through the study of regional psychology."[12] Whatever one makes of such a project, Berr's means for realizing it had intrinsic value. He decided to publish a series of historical monographs devoted to the regions of France. The first of these appeared the same year, so that Berr's article effectively served as an introduction to the collection.[13]

This augured well for a future collaborative relationship between history and human geography, but the actual texts call for a more nuanced response. Of the ten opuscules published, seven were only bibliographic introductions to the study of a province's history conceived along very traditional lines, faithful to the sole use of textual sources, geographical publications even being excluded. A strikingly different approach was adopted in the other three titles, their young authors' first books: *La Franche-Comté* by Lucien Febvre, *Le Velay* by Lous Villat, and *L'Île de France* by Marc Bloch. All deal with the landscape of the provinces they treat: their soil, their geology, their hydrography. All exploit maps and the geographical literature, notably the *Tableau*, whose influence is discernible even in passages where it is not explicitly cited. All of these authors spent time on the terrain and made a close visual study of it.[14]

Of our three authors, the first, a disciple of Gabriel Monod and, through him, of Michelet, whose work he had absorbed since childhood, had studied with Vidal de La Blache. And Vidal—as well as Ferdinand Lot, Christian Pfister, and the geographer Lucien Gallois, author of the remarkable *Régions naturelles et noms de pays* (1908)—had also been a teacher of the third. Unlike their elders, Lucien Febvre and Marc Bloch were not only *agrégé**★** in the fields of history and geography but were true historian-geographers, or, better yet, historians who, in their capacity as historians, had been influenced by their encounter with geography. Their entire subsequent careers were striking demonstrations of just how deeply they had been affected by this "nourishing discipline," which, as Lucien Febvre put it many years later, instilled in the young Frenchmen of his generation, among other things, "a taste for the palpably real as opposed to the abstract."[15]

This is apparent in his thèse, the first example of a new type: the regional monograph similar to those written by Vidalian geographers but conceived by a historian and thus devoted to realities dating from several centuries earlier. No one, it seems, had previously treated a province as an entity that was simultaneously geographical and political, "the result of a close collaboration between natural forces and human forces" (although one in which "the human contribution remains dominant"[16]), setting out to study within this framework the unfolding of a political, religious, and social crisis.

Description of the land and its natural divisions, external influences, integrating factors (government, agricultural and industrial prosperity, demographic growth, the constitution of "nationalist sentiment"): after laying out all this, Lucien Febvre introduces the exterior event that unleashed a crisis in the Comté—the abdication of Charles V in favor of Philip II—in order to study its effect, through personal rivalry, on tensions between the nobility and the bourgeoisie. Only in the text's third and fourth parts, devoted to outbreaks within the Comté of the revolution in the Low Countries and the progress of absolutism, does the narration became chronological, presenting, in temporal order, the unfolding interplay of the many discordant factors that, taken together, determined the course of this regional crisis.

Febvre used the conceptual schema of the geographers, with its dis-

★ EDITOR'S NOTE: In the French higher education system, *agrégé* is earned by passing the *agrégation* examination and qualifies one to teach in a lycée—roughly equivalent to our high school and junior college—as well as become a member of certain faculties: law, economics, medicine, and pharmacy. It is perhaps best thought of as a license to teach issued by the state.

tinctions between the physical and human spheres and, within the latter, between slow and rapid changes. This was an important step toward integrating within history what Fernand Braudel, thirty-five years later, was to christen the *longue durée*. But geographical influence is also apparent in another aspect of his project whose importance for history cannot be overestimated: his attempt to compensate for the impossibility of the historian to see and show what he is talking about (save for the landscape, if that has not changed).

Here is an example. After studying the fortunes of nobles and bourgeois—their nature, the revenues they produce, their fluctuations (declining in the one case, rising in the other)—the author concludes:

> What separated, what opposed nobles and bourgeois was not only economic conflict: there was also a conflict of ideas and feelings. In their mode of life, their education, their general conception of the world and of action, the two classes were totally at odds, and we must describe these modes of life, analyze these rival conceptions, if we want to experience the conflict in all its sharpness.[17]

There follow two chapters on noble and bourgeois life based on family documents, wills, and inventories. The two "modes of life" (*genres de vie*, a Vidalian term) are grasped from within, as they were lived by the parties themselves, which makes it unnecessary to reduce them to economic forces and allows for the role of passionate feeling in the play of conflicting interests. As a result, the reader becomes caught up in the account rather as though he or she were watching a powerful theatrical performance.

While preparing his dissertation Febvre kept up with geographic publications, something he continued to do until the end of his life. Book reviews and bibliographic notes published in various journals show the traces of the reading. So too does the *Geographical Introduction to History*, published after a prolonged delay necessitated by the war. This is a polemical book, arguing the superiority of human geography over Durkheimian social morphology and criticizing determinist geography, notably the determinist reading of Vidal. It is also a programmatic book, offering a defense of "possibilisme" and advocating recognition of human beings as geographic agents. Finally, it is a summons to "double revolution," advocating an "expansion of history" and a "development of geography" in view of achieving a new conception of history itself:

> It is no longer exclusively the political, juridical, and constitutional armor of earlier peoples, nor their military and diplomatic vicissitudes, that we strive patiently to reconstitute. It is their whole life,

their whole material and moral civilization, the whole evolution
of their sciences, arts, religions, industries, trade, classes, and social groupings. Consider the history of agriculture alone and of the
rural classes in their efforts to adapt themselves to the soil, in their
long but discontinuous labor of clearing, deforestation, drainage, and
settlement. How many questions arise in connection with this alone
whose solutions depend in part on geographic studies?[18]

Lucien Febvre, then, was fully conscious of the amplitude of the disturbance entailed by thus challenging the fundamental dogma under the
aegis, in large part, of human geography. Marc Bloch—who had analyzed
Febvre's *Geographic Introduction* for the benefit of historians—was similarly
aware. Thus it is not surprising that, when conceiving their journal, one of
the recent models to which they turned was the *Annales de géographie*,[19] and
that geography was accorded more space in the *Annales* than any discipline
other than history. The two editors multiplied reviews and bibliographic
notes assessing geographic publications of all kinds: atlases, maps, plans,
books, articles, and so on. But that was not all: they also gathered around
them a team of some ten geographers who published extensively in the
journal's pages. Both of these traditions continued under the editorship
of Fernand Braudel.

In 1931, Marc Bloch and Lucien Febvre each published a book. In the
latter's case it was *Le Problème historique du Rhin*, to be discussed later. But
Bloch's book is best considered now. Appearing twenty years after Febvre's
thèse, *French Rural History* was the second application to historical research
of the heuristic method developed by Vadalian geographers, offering further evidence of its fertility. It was followed shortly thereafter by *L'Histoire
de la campagne française* by Gaston Roupnel, a historian instilled, like Marc
Bloch, with the geographic spirit (he never published in the *Annales* but
was sympathetic to its program), and *Essai sur la formation du paysage rural
français* by Roger Dion. These books, especially those by Bloch and Dion,
are at the origin of the quarter-century trend for geographers and historians to cooperate—and occasionally confront one another—in explor-
ing agrarian structures and the rural landscape, probing some of the great
problems of French history.[20]

The books by Bloch and Roupnel need only be compared to get a
sense of these confrontations. The first, the work of a historian, influenced
the second, but the latter, part literary work and part ideological manifesto, gives voice to a mysticism of the earth, glorifying rural civilization,
the French countryside, and the peasant soul. Marc Bloch devotes almost
half of his book to a history of seigneurial structures and land ownership
since the high Middle Ages that is also a history of social conflict. Gaston

Roupnel, by contrast, relegates these subjects to the margins. His France is a country of villages and peasants from which châteaux and large estates are absent. Marc Bloch issued warnings about such an image: "It must not be said, as is sometimes done, that [France] is a country of small properties, but rather that, in proportions which vary considerably from province to province, large and small properties coexist in it."[21]

Even so, the two books make comparable use of geographic research. Furthermore, they both ascribe considerable importance to visual evidence. For Roupnel, the latter's preeminence is almost supreme. The central portions of his book propose a visual reading of things, of the traces of old forest edges, old roads, and vanished towns as revealed by the forests, fields, vineyards, and towns of his own day. "The entire region," he writes, "is a book open to our gaze."[22] This "country walk" approach is absent from Marc Bloch's volume. But he, too, when contrasting agrarian regimes, summons the gaze, inviting his readers to imagine rural settlements and direct their look toward tilled land. He completes his data with an analysis of the sources and an inquiry into the distribution throughout France of various types of plough. Here the boundary between the historical and geographic disciplines is blurred. We should add that Roupnel asks his readers to examine maps and that Bloch's argument is based on close study of cadastral maps.

To say "gaze" is to say "present." It was from the French landscape of the present that Roupnel extrapolated that of the past, which for him was imbued with mythic colors. And it was the present state of this landscape that Bloch set out to render intelligible. "If we seek to explain the physiognomy of modern rural France, we shall find that the antecedents of nearly every feature recede into the mists of time."[23] In both cases it was assumed that the past, however distant, had not vanished, had not been defaced and destroyed; it continued into the present. History encompassed things that last—and quite a long time. This idea is implicit in Roupnel but is explicitly stated by Bloch: "In the continuum of human societies, the vibrations between molecule and molecule spread out over so great a span that understanding of a single moment, no matter what its place in the chain of development, can never be attained merely by contemplation of its immediate predecessor."[24] This assertion casts light on the French title of Bloch's book, *Les Caractères originaux de l'histoire rurale française*: to be sure, the "original characters" in question are those that distinguished the "history of rural France" from those of other countries, but they are also those that, for centuries if not millennia, provided the framework for its existence.

According to Marc Bloch, this framework consisted, in France, of three coexistent agrarian regimes: that of base land occupation and enclosed fields, and two other modes of organizing open fields, one of which, the "northern" one, invented the plough and imposed strict community standards on its settlements, while the other, "southern" one favored the swing-plough and was characterized by a less binding sense of community. Without rejecting these conclusions, Roupnel insisted above all on the opposition between south and north, which in his view was not limited to agrarian regimes: "In the south, the human community is active, urban, *citadine*. It has the animated soul of the streets. In the north it is exterior, rural, *champêtre*. It takes its theme from the silence of the fields and the daily bread. It smells of wheat and fresh air."[25] Here we are very close to Michelet.

The discovery in France of different agrarian landscapes was not the work of Marc Bloch. It dates back to Arthur Young, the late eighteenth-century British agronomist and traveler, before him to the physiocrats, and—why not?—to the author of the *Rouman de Rou*, who, about 1170, wrote of a Norman assembly to which came "Peasants and serfs / Those of the woodlands and those of the plains," a citation ritually invoked by anyone treating the subject. The first contribution of Bloch's book was the very notion of an agrarian regime, an integration of facts whose reciprocal dependence had been grasped before him by neither historians nor geographers, despite its having been well known to both farmers and administrators of the ancient régime. Then there is his account of the links between agrarian regimes, the transformations undergone by seigneurial structures, and the organization of peasant communities, with their internal divisions, prior to the convulsion of rural life affected by the nineteenth-century agrarian revolution. And finally, there is his promotion of the enclosed field, seemingly but one landscape element among many, to the rank of identifying a difference of civilization. The coexistence of agrarian regimes, which Bloch thought characteristic of French rural territory, thus comes to the fore as "problem number one," as an issue that would have to be addressed if the history of French settlement was to be reconstructed and the contrasting landscapes of its countryside rendered intelligible.

The author of a thèse on the Loire Valley, a double masterpiece belonging to both geography and history, Roger Dion could not have avoided this problem even if he wanted to. For he had discovered the distinction between open- and closed-field systems on the ground, via different approaches to the furnishing of peasant houses, the shape of cultivated fields, rural customs, the organization of rural life, habitat distribution, and so on—as well as by reading old authors.[26] Did these differences in the human sphere correspond to differences in the natural one? Marc Bloch was inclined to think so. Roger Dion, by contrast, stressed "the degree to which the influence of tradition, in these old farming systems, prevailed over that of the land."[27] Later, while discreetly eliminating Bloch's distinction between western woodlands and the "southern" regime, claiming they were variants of the same enclosed-field system, Dion extrapolated from his argument about the Loire Valley, applying it to the entire Paris basin, and even all of France:

> High mountains apart, all French rural landscapes belong to one of two fundamental category types: a northern type characterized by flat open expanses and the grouping of trees into dense blocks of forest; and a southern type characterized by the attenuation of forests and the scattering of trees over agricultural ground. We are carried irresistibly toward the east, toward the broad plains of northern Europe, when we seek to observe the most perfect forms or discern the origins of the northern type; toward Rome, when we seek to explain the principles that presided over the elaboration of the southern type.[28]

The question posed by Marc Bloch would be resolved, then, if the boundary that, in the eighteenth century, separated the collective constraints of Germanic origin from the agrarian liberty of Roman origin also passed between two types of landscape and two types of rural habitat, "with clump settlements throughout the areas north and east of this line, dispersed settlement patterns consistently to its south and west."[29]

The reality, however, was not so simple. Unless the many anomalous cases could be explained, the general thesis of France's clear division between two civilizations or rural economies would be blunted by attempts to account for them. Accordingly, Roger Dion began to study the regional variations of these two rural economies in 1934. But only twelve years later did he publish a fundamental article on this subject, which had a revealing title: "The Role of Geography and That of History in Explaining the Rural Habitat of the Paris Basin."[30]

According to this article, villages practicing crop rotation began to appear in the eleventh century at the impetus of landlords who conceded seigneurial holdings to small tenants, on condition of triennial rotation and the establishment of clustered rural settlements. In any event, the nature of the soil precluded full deployment of this system in areas that had long lain fallow or remain uncleared. Hence the appearance, in the eleventh, twelfth, and thirteenth centuries, in forested country, not of villages but of hamlets. Later, as available tracts passed into the hands of bourgeois, who acquired them from lords, isolated farms began to spring up. They proliferated during the last great period of land clearance, which extended from the late eighteenth century to the years between 1875 and 1880, when many farms were given characteristic names: Moscow, Algeria, Constantine, and Mazagran; Sébastopol, Malakoff, Magenta, and Solferino.

The article in question did not bring the history of the study of agrarian regimes and rural landscape to a close. It was continued by many publications, of which we will mention only *La Grande Limagne* by Max Derruau, comparable in all respects to the thèse of Roger Dion. In defense of this hypothesis, it is perhaps worth recalling that its explanation of the various land allotment systems and agrarian structures—apparent in configurations on the surface—in terms of conflict between the peasantry and the landed bourgeoisie was premised on the inherent natural qualities of the Limagne, apparent in the habitat, the pitches of the roofs, the form of their tiles, the dimensions of land parcels, the rates of development of a mercantile economy, even the language.[31] Which date back to the time when the Limagne, isolated by forests from northern France, was in contact only with the Mediterranean Midi, before the great land clearances of the eleventh century made it accessible to settlement by peoples from the north and to the increasing influence of Paris, an expression of the rising power of the Capetians.[32]

THE HISTORY OF FRANCE: *PATRIE* AND *NATION*

Now in its eleventh edition and translated into several languages, *L'Histoire de la civilisation française* by Georges Duby and Robert Mandrou (1958) remains the sole example, before that by Fernand Braudel, of a history of France produced within the *Annales* circle; and it begins only with the eleventh century, and the Great Invasions, treating only certain aspects of the past. But anyone construing this scarcity as evidence of a tacit *Annales* rule prohibiting the very idea of such a synthesis would be mistaken. As early as 1933, Lucien Febvre regretted the absence from the French historiography of subjects "exceeding the narrow monographic framework," and notably histories of France, proposing several principles to be followed in writing such histories in ways consistent with the new exigencies.[33]

Six years later, profiting from the leisure forced upon him by the "phoney war" of 1939–40, Marc Bloch began to write, in a notebook, a "History of French Society within the Framework of European Civilization," but he managed to complete only its first chapter ("The Birth of France and of Europe").[34] For his part, Lucien Febvre devoted his 1940–41 course at the Collège de France to analyzing the great problems of the history of France, as approached through study of its historiography. In 1943–44 he examined Michelet as a historian of France, and in 1946 and 1947, still within the perspective of a history of France, the notions of honor and *patrie*.[35] Still other texts by Lucien Febvre and Marc Bloch clarify their views about histories of France as a specific genre with its own problems and difficulties; these were given their most mature form in treatments of certain periods of French history: the last Capetians, the first French Renaissance, and the long sixteenth century, the subject of courses given by Fernand Braudel in 1953–54 and 1954–55.[36] This does not mean that the founding figures of the *Annales* school had a project or program for writing the history of France that lacked only executants to be realized. But it is fair to say that the available texts offer some indication as to their general approach to such a history, suggesting in particular what they deemed its essential chapters and how they would have organized the whole.

As conceived by Marc Bloch and Lucien Febvre, both admirers of Camille Jullian, the history of France should begin with the territory's first inhabitants, encompassing Gaul. And it should continue into the present day instead of coming to a halt a century previous, on the misguided assumption that the contemporary era was not a matter of history but rather of politics. As for the interval separating the present from the remote past, it derives its content from the bimillenarian self-constitution of France as both a territory and a people. For France is not a settled given; it is a problem. One that Vidal de La Blache had already raised in the *Tableau* and that Lucien Febvre paraphrased as follows:

> To explore *how* and why heterogeneous countries, which no Providential decree dictated should unite into a certain whole, in the end formed this whole: one that, in this instance, we encounter for the first time in texts by Caesar defining by its "natural limits" a Gaul that roughly prefigures our own France. . . . How, why, despite . . . so many failed attempts at Franco-English, Franco-Iberian, Franco-Lombard, and Franco-Rhenish nations envisioned as viable, and sometimes temporarily realized—how, why the formation of Gallia, after numberless torments, has always managed to reappear and regroup around a seed . . . the *membra disjecta* that events . . . had temporarily dissociated from the whole?[37]

The same problem could be formulated differently: to explore how and why distinct and mutually hostile ethnic groups, linguistic communities incapable of understanding one another, categories with different legal statuses (notably slaves and serfs as opposed to free men), social classes in conflict (most often latent but sometimes erupting into violence)—how and why it is that all these groups, initially heterogeneous, in the end formed a nation, the French nation, whose cohesion has proved sufficiently strong to resist victoriously wars of religion, political confrontations, internal struggles, and foreign aggression?

For Marc Bloch, as for Lucien Febvre, the history of France from Gaul to the present is one of successive solutions to the double problem of France, *patrie* and *nation*, posed by each period in its own terms, in some cases without realizing it and in others semiconsciously or in full awareness. There were four major transitional episodes in this twice-millennial trajectory: the Roman conquest; the Great Invasions preceding the establishment of the feudal order; the Renaissance and the Reformation, understood as complexly related in ways that are difficult to define with the advent of capitalism and modern civilization; and finally the Revolution, which transformed subjects into citizens and recast relations between the Nation and the State.

Preeminent among the general problems in the history of France that attracted Lucien Febvre's attention was the one posed by Vidal de La Blache, namely, the individualization of the French territory. Beginning in 1908 and for almost forty years thereafter, he was interested in the question of borders. The subject is present in his thèse, which can be read as an illumination of the factors that made "possible, easy, and desirable" the French conquest of the Franche-Comté, and with it the stabilization of an important segment of France's eastern border. And it is present in his publications of the 1920s, which show that the history of borders coincides with that of the formation of French unity, studied in terms of its political, economical, and psychological ramifications and of its basis in geography.[38]

This work culminated in the book on the Rhine, or, to use words consistent with the title of its first edition, on the historical problem of the Rhine. On the one hand was the river, a natural constant, even if its unity was the work of men, who formerly used the word *Renos* to designate certain waterways upstream from Basel, applying it to the most direct route between the plain of the Po and the northern regions. On the other hand were the variable functions and meanings with which it was invested by successive riverside settlers, which even influenced its visible appearance. Such were the givens of the problem, which could be framed as a question: How is it that the Rhine, which in its oldest history was a commercial waterway, as attested by many archeological finds of amber and salt, by toponymy, and by textual documents, also became, for a small part of its course, a border between two nations whose importance is incommensurate with its length?

In antiquity and the high Middle Ages, three cultures—Rome, Germanism, the Church—successively affected the banks of the Rhine. Their traces were superimposed over one another in the towns scattered along the river's length, from Basel to Utrecht, and that beginning in the tenth century were reborn, not from death, perhaps, but from a period of lethargy. The old Episcopal centers, expanded by the addition of commercial quarters, formed the medieval cities that are the ancestors of our own, liberated, sometimes after violent struggle, from seigneurial domination to become "crucibles of a new law, of a new morality and mentality."

"These Rhenish towns were not *within* states. They were states unto themselves. The citizen of Basel belongs only to Basel, and that of Cologne only to Cologne."[39] If they become affiliated with any larger political entity, it is the Germanic Holy Roman Empire. But they retained a distinct identity through common participation in Rhenish civilization, which was original despite its borrowings from England, Italy, and France, and whose dissemination was guaranteed by its universities, its painting, its mystical transports, its sects and religious communities—finally, by the printing press and the book, which for a time assured the Rhenish a position of dominance in the world's intellectual marketplace.

An insular civilization, the Rhineland of the cities was surrounded by a peasant sea, territory of the Rhineland of princes, which was equally fragmented and attached to its specificity. The Reformation introduced supplementary divisions into both of these entities before provoking, toward the mouths of the river, a separation between "the Catholic unity of what would become the Belgian state [and] the Calvinist unity of the Netherlandish state," while on the side of its sources "Switzerland increasingly set itself apart from everything that was not itself."[40] From the limits of Switzerland to those of the Low Countries, the Rhine axis thus appeared as the line of partition between France and the Germanies, between a nation organized as a state and a mosaic of political formations governed by dynasts whose gardens and palaces, dress and cutlery, mistresses, wigmakers, officers, language, and customs were all inspired by French models.

It was in response to this implantation of French civilization beyond the Rhine, with its cosmopolite character and universalist pretensions, that "at the end of the eighteenth century there surged forth the glorious myth of a Germanism that had generated both the Middle Ages (feudalism, chivalry, the Gothic) and the modern world (Luther, the Reformation, the prerogatives of the individual conscience)."[41] And from which coalesced, with the aid of a Lutheranism tinted with pietist sentimentality, German nationalist sentiment. France and Germany: henceforth these two nations and two cultures would face one another across the Rhine (see Jean-Marie Mayeur, "A Frontier of Memory: Alsace," volume 2, chapter 10).

In the eighteenth century the Rhine was not a border, for "there is no border when two dynasts, encamped on lands that they are exploiting, erect at common expense a few blazoned landmarks along a field, or trace an ideal line of separation through the middle of a river. There is a border when, having crossed this line, one finds oneself in a different world, amidst a complex of ideas, feelings, and enthusiasms that the foreigner finds surprising and disconcerting. In other terms: what 'engraves' a border forcefully in the earth is not guards, customs officers, or canons on ramparts. It is feelings, exalted passions—and hatreds."[42]

These were to accumulate in the nineteenth century, first after the French Revolution and then, after 1815, with the arrival on the Rhine of Prussia, the vehicle of an idea that, later, with the discovery of a coal-rich basin that gave birth to the strongest industrial complex in central Europe, transformed the state of mind of Rhinelanders, who, while remaining Rhenish, became increasingly imbued with German patriotism and took a new pride in the economic expansion of their region and its increasing prosperity. Thus it was only in the course of the nineteenth century that the Rhine became a border in the fullest sense of the term, losing this character after 1870 only to regain it after 1918.

Never republished in the half century since its initial appearance, *Le Problème historique du Rhin* is now inaccessible and unjustly forgotten.* Thus the need to rehearse its basic argument here, for it demonstrates how Lucien Febvre demythified a subject of burning contemporaneity by setting the historical facts against the image of the Rhine as a natural frontier, as the predestined site of a thousand-year struggle between a France and Germany locked in eternal mutual hostility. But the projection of present conflicts and realities into the past was not the book's only polemical target. It also took aim against the reduction of political history to a recitative of military operations and diplomatic transactions, which made it into "a history without problems, hence without obscurities."

Lucien Febvre, by contrast, was interested in the ties that guaranteed the cohesion of societies and in their relations with one another. What he set out to grasp and describe, to measure and chart, were the feelings of populations, their attachment to traditions, their ways of defining themselves through their daily behavior and of living the internal conflicts of their societies and confrontations with foreigners. Seeking out these profound attitudes, rarely made explicit (the attitudes not of individuals but of peoples) Lucien Febvre adopted the approach of a geographer, who relies not only on texts but also on the gaze that knows how to read the diversity of spectacles and images—and the approach of the archeologist, who knows how to give voice to material cultural remains. In this way he considerably expanded the repertory of sources exploitable by political

---

★ EDITOR'S NOTE: It was reissued in 1997: Lucien Febvre, *Le Rhin: Histoire, mythes, et réalités*, edition established by Peter Schöttler (Paris: Pezziz, 1997).

history, translating artifacts gathered in museums, notably paintings (portraits, architectural compositions, landscapes), into the terms of a retrospective collective psychology.

The same approach characterized Roger Dion's book on the borders
of France, whose fall into oblivion is just as unmerited as that of Febvre's
volume on the Rhine. Primitive limits, ethnic frontiers, political boundaries: all three types of separation, which emerged in different periods, left
traces on the French landscape. Hence these forests, once frontier zones
between Gallic tribes, riddled with clearings, sites of encounter and exchange, with place-names always designating sites of assembly or of judicial
courts. Hence the columns, megaliths, trees, trenches, and barriers, a few
of which have survived here and there. Hence, finally, the traces, readily
discernable in naturally homogenous landscapes, left by the existence of an
artificial frontier, for example, on both sides, from the southern border of
France, which traverses Flanders since the Treaty of Utrecht, or between
Alsace and the Rhenish Palatinate, "profoundly cut off from one another
despite the unity of their natural aspect, the similarity of their productions, and their shared language."[43]

Roger Dion used his typology of boundaries to reveal, first of all, the
work involved in substituting exact limits to forested marches, a project
begun by Roman administrators, pursued in the high Middle Ages by the
bishops, and thwarted by the feudal lords, who introduced into French
territorial divisions a deliberate lack of precision compounding the primitive one, a function of the incomplete occupation of the ground. He then
explained the circumstances that stabilized the ethnic frontier of Gaul in
the Alps and the Pyrenees, and those that conferred upon the Rhine the
contradictory roles that it has played over the centuries. There followed,
finally, a history of the political boundaries of France since the Treaty of
Verdun, from the "Four Rivers" frontier (Escaut, Meuse, Saône, Rhine)
to the modern boundaries based on perceived military advantage.

These linear limits, however conventional and artificial they might
seem, have "become, over time, real separations, and in some cases insur-
mountable barriers. The phenomenon was exacerbated as governmental
actions asserted themselves more completely and more forcefully in all
forms of economic and social life." Through governmental action, ideo-
logues can assert a greater influence and capacity to divide men than any
diversity of kinds of life: "The line across a single plain separating a democratic country from a totalitarian one can be, in 1940, more difficult to
cross than a formidable mountain range."[44] For Roger Dion as for Lucien
Febvre, boundaries become intelligible only in the light of a retrospective collective psychology.

"Rois et serfs": the very title of Marc Bloch's *thèse* announces the two directions that he explored, with equal intensity, over the barely three decades that the history of his own time allowed him to study that of the past. While it was the territorial dimensions of the formation of France that most interested Lucien Febvre and Roger Dion, Marc Bloch construed the phenomenon primarily as a series of social changes that issued in the constitution of the French nation. His book, to be sure, claims to be only "a chapter . . . in the financial history of the Capetians."[45] And in effect, after establishing the poor yield from the collection of feudal levies, or *droit serviles* (mortmain, marriage between serfs belonging to different lords), it shows how the need to reduce treasury deficits prompted the monarchy to sell serfs their liberty, on such a scale that during the reign of Philippe le Bel emancipation became "an ordinary fiscal expedient."[46] Financial history, then, but simultaneously a history of royalty's role in the disappearance of juridical differences between various groups composing the French population from the twelfth century to the early fourteenth century.

This is but a fragment of Marc Bloch's published scholarship—extending from his article on Blanche of Castille and the serfs of the chapter of Paris (1911) to a posthumous one on the end of ancient slavery (1947)—dealing with the equalization of the legal status of the French over some twelve centuries, from the Great Invasions to the Revolution. Several publications, notably *Feudal Society* (1939–40), study the destruction of the ancient social organism by repeated invasions and by the appearance, during the high Middle Ages, of a multiplicity of hierarchical legal statuses that, in the twelfth and thirteenth centuries, were distributed among hereditary classes: the nobility (originally divided into several categories), the bourgeoisie, and bondsmen, a process accompanied by the parallel edification of a clerical hierarchy whose members were drawn from the pool of freemen of all classes.

A second group of publications treats the decomposition of this system. The disappearance of slavery, at rhythms that varied in accordance with local conditions; the disappearance of servitude, never completely achieved (serfs continued to exist in the eighteenth century, even in France and on the king's properties); the dissolution of the lord-vassal relationship; communal revolution: such were the salient moments of the progressive but incomplete replacement of a motley array of statuses by the division of laymen into nobles and commoners, itself abolished by the French Revolution, a blow from which it never recovered. In France, several factors played a role in shaping this development: the Church through its condemnation of the enslavement of Christians; the monarchy through its fiscal policy, which contributed to the erosion of servitude within as well as outside the royal domains; the bourgeoisie, which after winning a place for itself

Fig. 11.7
Georges Lefebvre.

Fig. 11.8
Henri Berr.

Fig. 11.9
Yves Renouard.

Fig. 11.10
Georges Friedmann.

Fig. 11.11
Fernand Braudel.

Fig. 11.12
Philippe Ariès.

in society encouraged the tendency in the countryside to free the serfs in exchange for money, acquiring seigneurial domains on a massive scale during the crisis of the fourteenth and fifteenth centuries.[47]

The equalization of juridical conditions kept pace with the progress of individual liberty in the upper levels of society, of course, but it also kept up with parallel developments in the hierarchy's lower echelons. It is true that the "feudal reaction" succeeded in stopping "the slow apparent trend towards the emancipation of the peasantry from the clutches of seigenurial control."[48] In any case, the power of the landlords over the peasants was limited by the crown, whose provincial representative was, by the very nature of his position, "in permanent rivalry with the holders of offices," an emanation of the "Seigneurial class," as well as with individual lords, from whom he was obliged "to protect rural communities, ripe material for taxation."[49] On the other hand, the agricultural revolution, the subject of a fine article by Bloch ("La Lutte pour l'individualisme agraire dans la France du XVIIIe siècle," 1930), did not abolish but at least greatly weakened collective servitude, the submission of each individual to the village community, which was very constraining in open farm country. In this respect it exacerbated economic inequalities within the peasantry, whose importance increased proportionately with the equalization of juridical conditions.

The slow gestation of modern nations comes to a head when the bond founded on birth into a community of language and tradition, one occupying a single territory, assumes primacy over all others; when it is assimilated to blood bonds; and when, with the latter, it is the only one whose hereditary character is acknowledged by law. From this perspective, the opposition between differences in legal status and economic inequality is radical. Posited as hereditary, differences in legal status are effectively identifiable with a division of society into groups where membership determines the social identity of individuals, which slows down or even prevents the propagation of national feeling in the population as a whole. That being the case, Marc Bloch's publications on social history, insofar as they describe the equalization of juridical conditions, the movement of economic inequities into the foreground and the advent of individual liberty, can be read, among other things, as contributions to a history of the formation of the French nation from groups that almost everything initially set at odds to one another, even opposed, and whose dissolution, extending over several centuries, made possible a concomitant crystallization of language, tradition, and territory among city dwellers as well as the rural population, among rich and poor alike.

In Marc Bloch's work less space is devoted to kings than to serfs, but the former are the subject of a single book examining an important feature of the French—and English—political landscape over several centuries: the belief in their miraculous power to heal scrofula. This power is but one especially spectacular manifestation of the supernatural character traditionally attributed to royalty; the vicissitudes of the latter, then, can be reconstructed by studying the variations of the former. But Bloch's *The Royal Touch* is neither a history of ideas nor one of a liturgical ceremony. Its object of study is a collective behavior practiced over an extended period, one that seems aberrant to us and of which it attempts to establish the spatial and temporal reality, and to give an explanation. Bloch's approach here is anthropological,[50] and his brand of anthropology, placed under the sign of James Frazer and Lucien Lévy-Bruhl, is a variant of retrospective collective psychology.

In *The Royal Touch*, then, Marc Bloch produced an anthropological-psychological history of the French monarchy from the high Middle Ages to the reign of Charles X (1826–30), the last king of France to have touched the scrofulous. This is a history of the French monarchy as perceived and lived by its subjects over an extended period, allowances being made for brief variations. Initially, the king was not a man like other men; he was distinguished from his subjects by a supernatural power that inhabited him. And the sacred character attributed to his person was more important than the real power of royalty, especially under the first Capetians; it was the crucial factor that made possible the crown's retention of primacy and its subsequent affirmation, circumstances having become favorable, as a great power.

Pervasive in the final centuries of the Middle Ages, the "monarchical faith," the "royal religion," gradually declined beginning in the Renaissance. "Related to an integral conception of the universe," it was weakened by the latter's progressive disintegration and, especially, by the elimination of the supernatural. Furthermore, in the eighteenth century, "the philosophes, by accustoming public opinion to consider sovereigns as no more than the hereditary representatives of the State, discouraged belief in attempts to discover the marvelous or miraculous in royalty. One might well expect miracles of a chief by divine right, whose very power is rooted in a kind of sublime mystery; one will certainly not expect them of a bureaucrat, however exalted his rank, however seemingly indispensable his role in public affairs."[51]

Thus the history of the healing power attributed to kings tells a story that, while apparently marginal and anecdotal, is in fact an essential aspect of the equalization of legal statuses, namely the effacement of the supernatural character of royalty. Deprived of this character, the king was no longer what his ancestors were, for, while always at the summit of the political hierarchy, he did not transcend it; henceforth, the difference between him and his subjects was one of degree, not one of nature. That is why the history of the king's healing touch also describes a profound transformation of the relations between king and nation, addressing the very nature of national cohesion and its role in everyday life.

The nation had first been unified by royalty, and it was to royalty—a sacred royalty—that it believed it owed its existence. In a society composed of heterogeneous groups, the king was a group unto himself, one essentially different from all the others and hence capable of binding them together. Simultaneously secular and sacred, the liturgy of the *sacre*, or "coronation," brought together "everything that might create confusion between two almost identical rites, one of which was used for priesthood and the other for royalty:"[52] anointing oil from the sacred ampulla, descended from heaven with a fleur-de-lys–styled escutcheon, and the oriflamme, likewise of celestial origin. Thus the king of France was guarantor of the integrity and prosperity, both corporal and spiritual, of the French nation, just as God was guarantor of the integrity of the created world. It followed quite naturally that the French nation was constituted by all those who, being subjects of the king of France, profited from his temporal and supernatural power, however different from one another they might be in other—accidental—respects.

After the centuries-long process of equalization of legal statuses had run its course and the set of beliefs centering on the monarchy had disintegrated, the French nation seemed to contain within itself the principle of its own cohesion and stability. It was now composed of all those born French, which is to say that its constituents were bound by heredity, not to the monarchy but, above all, to the French language, to a specific set of traditions, to the territory of France, and to the state charged with defending its integrity and with maintaining order within its borders. It was thanks to the consent of the French that the king was king, that he represented and personified them. In short, initially the nation's existence was dependent upon the king. On the eve of the Revolution, by contrast, it was the king whose existence depended upon the nation. Hence he was no longer invested with the healing power. The royal miracle was dead, and the monarchical faith with it.[53]

Apparently anomalous within Marc Bloch's oeuvre, the book on the king's healing touch is of a piece with his investigation of the formation of the French nation, or, as he himself put it, of "the history of French society within the framework of European civilization." And comparable projects were undertaken by other authors of the first *Annales* generation. In 1932, Georges Lefebvre published *The Great Fear of 1789: Rural Panic in Revolutionary France.* Four years later, Lucien Febvre gave a course entitled "Belief and Disbelief in the Sixteenth Century: The Religion of Rabelais and a Few Others";[54] it was to serve as the foundation for three books, centering respectively on Rabelais, Des Périers, and Marguerite de Navarre but also evoking Guillaume Briçonnet, Étienne Dolet, Erasmus, Luther, and several figures of lesser importance.[55] The point of departure for all of these publications, as that of Marc Bloch, was the unintelligibility in terms of our own psychology of a collective behavior of the past: recourse to the king of France—or of England—to heal the scrofulous; the riots, peasant revolts, and panics that shook France in 1789; the coexistence of seemingly incompatible attitudes toward the sacred and the secular in the minds of certain sixteenth-century French writers, characterizable as either "pranksters or mystics, evangelists or libertines, deists or atheists."[56]

Each of these books described a supposedly aberrant behavior, determining its spatial and temporal limits, showing how it varied in accordance with shifting circumstances, and identifying the actors in social and geographic terms. Each of them made explicit the belief expressed by this behavior, one that we find difficult to comprehend, whether in the healing power of kings, ravaging thieves abroad in the countryside, an aristocratic plot, or the truth of the teachings of Christianity, especially those of the Catholic church. Finally, each attempted to explain behaviors and beliefs by integrating these into an encompassing mental framework and into lived situations. In so doing they gave them meaning, just as one confers significance on landscape elements by restoring them to the history of which they are the traces. The retrospective collective psychology of the first *Annales* generation was a historical geography of the human mind.

THE ANCIEN RÉGIME: ECONOMY AND POPULATION

The founders of the *Annales* were interested primarily in the history of societies and civilizations. Even when they turned toward economic history proper (generally in minor works), they sought to explain the facts of retrospective collective psychology, which for them, as for many historians of their generation and circle, could serve to make the past intelligible. Others attributed this role not to psychology but to retrospective economy, but psychological factors were not absent from their analyses. A case in point is François Simiand (1873–1935), whose publications were recommended to the readers of the *Annales* by Lucien Febvre and to those of the *Revue historique* by Marc Bloch.[57]

But it was a book by Ernest Labrousse, modestly entitled *Esquisse du mouvement des prix et des revenues en France au XVIIIe siècle*, that made a strong impression on historians, notably those of the third *Annales* generation. Frankly inspired by Simiand, the *Esquisse* was not only more approachable than Simiand's work (famously difficult), but also demonstrated that the study of price and income fluctuations cast light on several aspects of French history. Here the question of the influence of such movements on economic doctrines, institutions, and events was posed, with special attention being devoted to their effect on the outbreak and development of the French Revolution. So it is not surprising that a review of this work—and of three publications by Simiand—appeared in the *Annales* under the title "Price Fluctuations and the Origins of the French Revolution"; it was signed Georges Lefebvre.[58]

Labrousse did not merely pose the question, he also answered it, in terms which he himself summed up as follows: "Economic trends largely generated the Revolutionary movement."[59] The qualifying term in this sentence underlines Labrousse's desire to avoid a unilateral economic explanation of the Revolution. Nonetheless, there is no mistaking his view that any viable explanation of the Revolutionary dynamic must rest on the economy, the very foundation of human material life and, for that reason, a site where class conflict manifests itself with special acuteness. The intensity of conflict between social classes differentiated by income varied in accordance with the fluctuation of prices, revenues, and salaries, which impoverished some classes and enriched others, and it found expression in changing opinions, attitudes, and political behavior. There were three dynamics that, conjointly but in disorderly fashion, affected prices and incomes, sometimes weakening and even neutralizing one another: long-term fluctuations, cyclical oscillations, and seasonal variations. But when all three capped out at roughly the same time, as in 1789, a major social crisis poised to escalate into a political crisis was almost certain to result. Such, in schematic terms, was the reasoning that led Labrousse to his conclusion.

Eleven years after the *Esquisse*, Labrousse published a book whose very title brought together the terms "crisis" and "Revolution."[60] Hailed in the pages of the *Annales* by Lucien Febvre in an enthusiastic review,[61] this work profoundly influenced the direction of future research, regarding not only the eighteenth century but the entire period between the late fifteenth and early nineteenth centuries. Synthesizing observations in the *Esquisse* concerning, notably, cyclical variations in salaries, it effectively introduced a concept that was to prove fruitful: that of the "old type of economic crisis."

In economies "essentially characterized by high transport costs, a predominant rural sector, a generally inelastic production capacity, and vastly disproportionate expenditure for bread among the popular classes," a poor harvest triggers a cascade of consequences: the collapse of production intended for sale, falling revenues for farmers, and a precipitous rise in the price of cereal, which gives the crisis a pervasive character because it affects the entirety of rural revenues. This prompts a contraction of the rural market for goods produced in the cities, notably textiles, which in turn leads to price reductions, collapsing profits and salary levels, and rising unemployment. The consequences: reduced consumption of industrial products in urban centers, growing numbers of beggars and vagabonds, and slowed construction. In short, an economic recession that affects all sectors of production as well as the quality of life of the entire population except the very wealthy.[62]

Economies characterized by the features enumerated by Labrousse existed for centuries. And it was over a span of several centuries that crises of the old type repeated themselves, if at irregular intervals. Such long-term phenomena, which historians had not known how to treat and had largely ignored, burst into their field of vision in 1949, with the publication of Fernand Braudel's thèse. Parallel to Dion, who in the same period was integrating history and geography, reviving nineteenth century historical geography in a totally revised form, Braudel was achieving the integration of geography and history begun by the founders of the *Annales*. Fully conscious of the originality of his project, he coined the neologism "geohistory" to characterize it. He subsequently abandoned the term, but it so struck his first readers that it appeared in the titles of several reviews of *The Mediterranean*.[63]

> To make of traditional historical geography in the manner of [Jean] Longnon, devoted almost exclusively to the study of state boundaries and administrative circumscriptions without paying heed to the earth itself, to climate, soil, plants and animals, to modes of life and labor activities, . . . a veritable retrospective human geography; to oblige geographers (a relatively easy task) to pay more attention to time and historians (a more challenging task) to be more concerned with space and what it supports, what it engenders, what it facilitates and what it thwarts—in a word, to induce them to take sufficient account of its formidable permanence: such will be the ambition of this *geohistory* whose name we scarcely dare utter; such is the decided ambition of this book, and in our eyes the true reason for its existence, the justification of its action in favor of a convergence of the two social sciences, history and geography, which cannot advantageously be separated from one another.[64]

"Formidable permanence": prior to the industrial revolution of the eighteenth and nineteenth centuries, the environment scarcely changed on the scale of human time. Unfolding with relative rapidity, events seemed to bear no relation to the qualities of the space within which they transpired.

Geographic tables and geographic introductions to history did nothing but describe a scene serving as the neutral framework for the drama. The problem, which Febvre broached in his thèse without articulating it clearly or resolving it, was not raised again, for events were absent from Bloch's *French Rural History*. But was it possible to pass over them in silence when speaking of the Mediterranean of the sixteenth century, particularly its second half? Could one fail to evoke the negotiations and battles, notably the battle of Lepanto, that were essential components in Mediterranean life during this period? Their role would have to be acknowledged, along with their ties to the space that saw them develop. In short, completing the integration of history and geography meant, in practical terms, finding a means of binding together the quasi invariability of the latter and the precipitation of the former.

Braudel's solution consisted, first, in treating the natural environment like a partner in human activities, and in viewing the latter's repetitive character as an expression of the unchanging character of both the environment itself and the material and mental tools employed by men to adapt it to their needs and adapt themselves to its constraints. Despite their being repetitive, however, the activities permitting men to exist and reproduce cannot exist outside history, even if their accommodation should require us to modify our idea of history. This is exactly what Braudel did, introducing in the preface to his book the notion of "a history whose passage is almost imperceptible, that of man in his relationship to the environment, a history in which all change is slow, a history of constant repetition, ever-recurring cycles."

But the initial problem was not resolved by such an approach, despite its having brought the two terms closer together than they were at the outset. And it was at this point that demography, economy, and sociology entered the scene. For, between immobility and the volatility of events, Braudel introduced a middle term in the form of *populations*, which he divided, on the one hand, into groups that produce, consume, and exchange, and, on the other, into various hierarchies distributed among multiple linguistic and religious communities, territorial unities, and political organizations. Their conflicts participate in "another history, this time with slow but perceptible rhythms," a domain of irregular oscillations unfolding over periods of years and even decades, of demographic ebbs and flows, of rising and falling indicators of economic activity. And they also participate in "traditional history . . . on the scale not of man but of an individual" who always leaves his or her own characteristic imprint on *histoire événementielle*, or the "history of events."[65]

By proposing to Braudel that he abandon his initial thèse subject, "The Mediterranean Policy of Philip II," in favor of a "subject otherwise great,"

"The Mediterranean and Philip II," Lucien Febvre enunciated, in a form
not yet fully articulated, the problem of integrating geography and history, of coordinating an extended time span with a sequence of events.[66]
Braudel's solution was "to dissect history into various planes, or, to put it
another way, to divide historical time into geographical time, social time,
and individual time."[67] This was the point of departure for a deepening
of reflection on history that was to result in a separation of "structural
history" from "conjunctural history," and of both of them from "the history of events." In his 1950 lectures at the Collège de France, Braudel introduced all these terms and asked what methods and procedures might
make it possible "to delineate trends, then attain the structures beyond."[68]
And beginning in 1952 his lectures took as their theme the "results and
methods of historical economy" suitable for the purpose, namely the application of demographic and economic approaches—"valid above all as
regards current events"—to the past.[69]

The combined influence of Labrousse and Braudel deflected the
interest of historians toward structures and *conjunctures*, or "trends"—especially the latter, to which teachers assigned a major role as mediator
between structural history and that of events. And consequently, toward
historical economy and demography as possible bridges between, on the
one hand, geography—whether of physical space or of the human mind—
and, on the other, culture and politics. This led to a renewal of the questions addressed in the history of France. They now focused on factors
brought to light by the notion of the old type of economic crisis, onto
which was grafted a distinction between structure and trend.

According to Labrousse, such crises always began with a sudden decline in the supply of cereals, the essential component of the popular diet,
when the level of demand remained unchanged. Supply was determined
by production, which was in turn dependent on agricultural techniques
and climatic conditions. When production was insufficient to satisfy local
need, supply was also dependent on means of compensating for the deficit
(capital, waterways, transport, etc.). As for demand, that was a function
of the number of men, demographic structures, consumption habits, and,
in certain cases, purchasing power influenced by (among other things)
the availability of means of payment. By illuminating the play of factors
whose interaction was so delicate that disturbance of any one of them
might disrupt the ever-fragile balance between supply and demand, the
notion of the old type of economic crisis functioned as a kind of research
program for the economic history of France.

This program was rapidly extended to encompass population history,
for in 1944 a connection was established between "sudden price rises" and
"an increase in death rates and a simultaneous . . . lowering of conception

rates, that is of birth rates after a nine-month delay."[70] The repetition of such accidents was symptomatic of a structural relationship. It characterized the economic and demographic old regime. It could be understood only after identification of the various barriers that, for centuries, had imposed an unsurpassable ceiling on rising agricultural production, leaving the balance between cereal supply and demand at the mercy of circumstances, climatic fluctuations, and wars capable of unleashing crises. Behind trends, then, were structures; behind periodic oscillations were long-term realities.

The program laid out by the teachings of Labrousse and Braudel, then, directed interest primarily toward agricultural production, a crucial variable, with the aim of encouraging identification of its determining factors. This is what Jean Meuvret set out to do in his exemplary study of the problem of subsistence in the period of Louis XIV. He studied the technical aspects of cereal production: plowing tools and tilling methods, fertilizers and their application, sowing, harvesting. A second book, still unpublished, examined the relations between cereal production and rural society: the weight of privilege, the social distribution of arable land, agricultural enterprise, different modes of cultivation, different types of property owner. Meuvret also dealt with the grain market and fluctuations in cereal prices—it was in this context that he addressed subsistence crises—and envisioned crowning his work with a study of the policing of grain and the monarchical administration.[71]

Other research projects, which reached the publications stage long after Meuvret's death but were initiated well before, paralleled his own work on agricultural production. There was a large-scale investigation of fluctuation in production levels of the tithe, from which could be extrapolated figures of agricultural production as a whole.[72] Hughes Neveu studied grain production in the Cambrésis; inspired by both Meuvret and Braudel, he tracked long-term production trends by ten-year increments.[73] Attention was also devoted to land clearance, deforestation, grazing and livestock breeding (a principal source of fertilizer and thus an essential factor in agricultural yield), and, finally, forests, which played such an important role in old-type economies. The results of this work appeared in several volumes in the collection *Les Hommes et la terre*, published by the Centre de recherches historiques of the sixth section of the E.P.H.E.[74]

While Jean Meuvret was the man of wheat, Roger Dion became the man of wine. Not the only one, to be sure, for the subject had been treated previously by Ernest Labrousse (the eighteenth century) as well as by the authors of several less-ambitious studies. But Roger Dion raised the history of wine to a new level. Again he approached his subject as a geographer-historian. His book began with an introduction to the viticultural geography of France, which was followed by three parts. The first dealt with grapevines and wine in Gaul up to the Great Invasions as well as the survival of viticulture after the arrival of the Germans, under the triple protection of bishops, monks, and princes. The second part studied the great commercial vineyards of the Middle Ages individually, taking into account the political aspects of viticulture, technical aspects of production, the wine market, and cultural aspects of its consumption. Finally, the third part described the adaptation of wine production to the needs of modern society. This history of wine and the vine, considered in all their dimensions, was in its way a history of France, or, better, a history of the French as wine producers, sellers, and consumers that took into account the social divisions it supports, one that was spatially situated and addressed the habits created by viticulture, the sociability that it fostered, the rituals to which it gave birth, and the influence it exercised over almost all aspects of life in the country.[75]

Completed or begun between 1945 and the end of the 1960s, all these investigations of agricultural and viticultural productions were paralleled by a few more focusing on industry and still others, quite numerous in this case, dealing with commercial enterprises, the fairs, banking, and credit, reconstructing the ebb and flow of exchange on the basis of merchant letters, harbor registries, notarial documents, and toll and tariff collection records. The results filled several dozen volumes published by the E.P.H.E. under the headings "Business and Businessmen," "Ports—Routes—Trade," and "Money—Prices—Trends."

Among these publications, the work of Pierre Chaunu stands out; another example of scholarship pursued under the double influence of Braudel and Labrousse, it is devoted to the structures and trends of the Spanish and Hispano-American Atlantic. Here the sources were Sevillian. The information they provided pertained to the movement of Spanish ships, but the conclusions concerned the history of France. The book demonstrates, in effect, that trade in the Spanish Atlantic functioned as the "dominant sector" of the European economy, determining fluctuations whose repercussions were general. In particular, the decline of Atlantic trade explained a century-long trend, namely the shift from rising prices, characteristic of the sixteenth century, to the prolonged decline that continued throughout the seventeenth century.[76] Thus a shift documented in contemporary France by other *Annales* historians was shown to have resulted from a tidal wave that swept all of Europe. The same problem of integrating the French economy into a worldwide economic framework, and of clarifying their mutual relations, was addressed by Frank C. Spooner in a study of coin minting between 1493 and 1680.[77]

The subjects just reviewed were all studied individually. But they also interacted with one another and were made to speak through one another in regional monographs, where the role of the notion of the old type of economic crisis as well as the distinction between structures and trends are easier to discern. The thèse of René Baehrel on Basse-Provence begins with long-term prices trends, with the alternation of highs and lows, and looks at the symptoms causing these fluctuations. These having been described, a diagnosis is advanced. First question: What can be determined about agricultural production (harvests of wheat, wine, and oil; the area of cultivated land; the raising of livestock)? Second question: Did population levels fluctuate, and, if so, did these movements tally with those of prices or those of production, assuming the latter were discordant? Third question: What can be determined about the treasuries of both communities and individuals, in other words about saving patterns, which determine purchasing power and investment capacity?

After these three questions relating to supply and demand trends, a fourth was posed relating to structures: Did these remain the same throughout the two-century period under consideration? The structures in question were geographic (openings into the continent or toward the sea), demographic (the age pyramid, mortality rates, migration trends), economic (means of production, property distribution), social (social categories and their relative wealth), institutional (the seigneurial system above all), and, finally, mental (the monarchic faith, foundation of taxes, faith in God, foundation of the tithe, attitudes toward the social hierarchy).[78]

Published one year prior to the thèse of René Baehrel, that of Pierre Goubert implemented the same program somewhat differently. Here the accent was not on "historical statistical economy" but on demographics. "A veritable preface to knowledge of the men of the Beauvaisais, it serves to introduce economic problems and social problems . . . it can also introduce problems of mentality and even of piety."[79] In a word, its position is central. The point of departure for Goubert's history, then, was the contrast between the "natural" state of the population and the extremely violent crises to which it fell prey under the old demographic regime. Using the methods for family reconstitution developed by Louis Henry,[80] but applying it to parish registers, he established coefficients of fecundity, infantile mortality, and juvenile mortality as well as the rate at which generations replaced one another, which brought to light the fragility of the demographic balance. The latter collapsed during gusts of mortality, which were accompanied by declines in the marriage and conception rates, affecting above all children and adolescents. All these features of the old type of demographic structure, revealed by prolonged trends—demographic crises, effects of economic crises of the old type—trailed off after 1740, when they gave way to a new demographic structure.

It is only natural, then, given that the crises guaranteed their conjunction, for Pierre Goubert to proceed from demographic structures to economic structures: communications, agricultural production, textile manufacture, payments, and the role of money. There follows a detailed analysis of social, rural, and urban structures, apprehended quantitatively and as hierarchies. After the description of structures, which occupies more than half of the book, the moment arrives to address fluctuating price trends confronted with those of revenues, salaries, urban textile production, and employment. The book ends with a sketch of demographic trends.

Emmanuel Le Roy Ladurie was the first to effect a synthesis, from demographic and economic perspectives, of Goubert and Baehrel, whose importance and originality he brought to light,[81] thanks to a triple generalization of the Labroussian notion of the old type of economic crisis, as revised in the meantime by Meuvret. Le Roy took into account not only grain production but agricultural production as a whole, "pondered and corrected so as to indicate the trend of real agricultural revenues . . . integrating all types of producers and all categories of production." Second, in considering the rural economy he examined not only its commercialized sector but its entirety, including self-sufficient units of consumption, "great estates, plots independently owned or being acquired, domestics paid in kind." Third, he studied the play of supply and demand and their result: consumption, along with its effects on health and reproduction, not in the short term but over a period of several centuries.[82]

This is far from being the only contribution made by *The Peasants of Languedoc*. Le Roy began with the climate, which he subjected to an investigation of unprecedented thoroughness whose results filled an entire volume.[83] He then proceeded to plants and techniques, and finally to the men whose migrations were at the origin of the genetic and cultural brew. The whole first part of the book, then, concentrates on the articulation of the climatic and biological givens and on the contribution of history, on the actions and reactions of forces that gave the space of Languedoc its specific character. As studied in this space, however, fluctuations of produce and population levels over an extended period—from the second half of the fourteenth century to the end of the seventeenth—were constantly resituated in the French and international environments. A procedure made possible by the other work cited or evoked here, whose results Le Roy integrated into his own synthesis.

Furthermore, he stressed not only the impact of economic fluctuations on the lives of different social categories but also—and this was quite novel—the awareness among members of the "lower classes" of their own situation and on the conflicts opposing them to the beneficiaries of rents, tithes, and profits. In this context, Le Roy took religious and cultural factors into consideration: the dissemination of writing, the spread of the Reformation, local customs, popular beliefs, traditional behaviors. Thus the Braudel-Labrousse questionnaire was modified in light of interests prompted by Marxism, as filtered through the Parti Communiste Français, Labrousse's work, and Boris Prochnev's book on French peasant revolts,[84] as well as by the ideas of Claude Lévi-Strauss. As already indicated by the book's title, with its allusion to the work of Jules Sion and Georges Lefebvre, Le Roy here combined demographic and economic analysis under the triple aegis of geography, a sociology focused on social classes, and an ethnology with structuralist tendencies. In the 1960s, the promotion of these last two to the rank previously occupied by the economy fostered a revision of the questionnaire used by historians.

Birth Rates and Mentality: The Middle Ages

Under the convergent influence of Braudel and Labrousse, most third generation *Annales* historians oriented their research toward the old demographic and economic regime extending from the fifteenth to the eighteenth centuries. Between the end of the war and the end of the 1960s, this was the subject of a great many publications, probably more than any other object of study. It was also the focus of an impressive number of thèses, some of which occasioned public defenses that became veritable cultural events, from that of Braudel through those of Chaunu and Goubert to that of Le Roy Ladurie. Nonetheless, the cliché holding that postwar *Annales* historical practice is identifiable with the study of the structures and economic, demographic, and social trends of the last three centuries of the old regime is doubly misleading. For one thing, retrospective collective psychology was never completely abandoned. For another, interest in the Middle Ages and the nineteenth century never wanted. It would be impossible to provide a detailed history of these publications here, so we will limit ourselves to discussing the principal authors and most significant works.

"The birth rate is an expression of mentality."[85] The weakening of France, reflected, among other things, in its "declining fertility," must have some bearing on the development of a certain mentality, or pervasive mind-set—in this instance the bourgeois mentality, characterized by a refusal of modernity. These ideas, proposed by Charles Morazé in 1946 and subsequently developed by him in work on the history of the nineteenth-century French bourgeoisie, were premised on the conviction that retrospective collective psychology could render history intelligible.

This view was also held by Robert Mandrou, a younger man focusing on the history of mentalities and feelings during the sixteenth and seventeenth centuries.

In his *Introduction to Modern France*, Mandrou attempted to describe the structures and mental trends of this period, beginning, like Morazé in his *La France bourgeoise*, with an analysis of the "physical man" (nourishment, environment, health, illness, demography) and the "psychic man" (senses, sensations, emotions, passions, mental equipment, fundamental attitudes), then proceeding to social milieus and types of human activity.[86] *Magistrats et sorciers* studied the mental revolution that, after the epidemic of sorcery in the sixteenth century and a few causes célèbres in the early seventeenth, eventually put a stop to the judicial prosecution of sorcerers.[87] He completed this line of research by studying French popular culture of the sixteenth and seventeenth centuries through the inexpensive publications hawked by itinerant peddlers, obtaining results that made it possible to measure the distance between this culture and the learned culture of the same period.[88]

"The birth rate is an expression of mentality." Philippe Ariès, in a read of *La France bourgeoise*, revised this postulate to suit his own purposes: "Demographic statistics enlighten us about the way men live, their conception of themselves, of their own bodies, of their intimate existences: *about their attitude toward life*."[89] The book that best exemplified this program, from beginning to end, went unremarked in the *Annales*. The group became interested in its author only in 1961.[90] But Ariès had been drawn to history as practiced by Marc Bloch and Lucien Febvre from the early years of the war; both his publications and his memoirs indicate that this interest never flagged.[91] Without having belonged to the *Annales* circle, Ariès was very close to it in his work. He can scarcely be isolated from it, for he exercised an influence over its members comparable only to that of the teachings of Braudel and Labrousse.

It was the work of Ariès that opened a space within which the biological and the sociocultural could interpenetrate and interact. And that demonstrated how to study sexual practices, the stages of individual development, family life, death.[92] True, Lucien Febvre had drawn attention to these subjects and inspired Alberto Tenenti's research on death.[93] But the publications of Ariès—echoes of which are discernable, most notably, in the work of Goubert and Le Roy Ladurie—prompted the appearance of a tendency whose representatives placed historical demography in the service of a retrospective collective psychology, altering the latter's content and methods as Ariès had done. Marginal at the beginning, this tendency gained in strength beginning in the second half of the 1960s. This is evidenced by volumes in the series *Annales de démographie historique*,

Michel Vovelle's work on piety and death,[94] François Lebrun's, again, on death,[95] and that of Jean-Louis Flandrin on the family, sexuality, and contraception.[96]

We will pass quickly over the nineteenth and twentieth centuries, which were relatively little frequented by third generation *Annales* historians; likewise the French Revolution. In this respect, in this field they tended to distance themselves from their predecessors more than elsewhere; the work of Jean Bouvier, François Crouzet, and François Furet was unusual. In medieval studies, by contrast, continuity was preserved, though not without displacements. Medievalists of the second *Annales* generation were interested primarily in economic history: in rural life, like André Déléage, a student of Marc Bloch who died prematurely,[97] but also in mercantile economy. Thus Philippe Wolff focused on commerce, merchants, the fairs, fiscality, and urban economy;[98] Yves Renouard dealt primarily with large commercial and banking firms, businessmen, wine, and vineyards,[99] while Maurice Lombard devoted his attention to road networks, raw materials (wood, metals), products like textiles, and coinage.[100]

Unlike their elders, medievalists of the third *Annales* generation seem to have forsaken the economy in favor of society and, to an even greater extent, civilization. This is illustrated by two parallel if slightly staggered trajectories, those of Georges Duby and Jacques Le Goff. Duby began with a regional monograph: *La Société aux XIe et XIIe siècles dans la région mâconnaise* (1953), a typical example of retrospective sociology in the tradition of Marc Bloch. Then, while pursuing research into rural economy and life in the countryside,[101] he turned increasingly toward a history that, in addition to documentary sources, made use of both figural and literary artistic monuments, incorporating images made by man of himself and others into his study of the transformations of medieval society.[102] Jacques Le Goff, for his part, after interesting himself in the most innovative groups of urban society in the Middle Ages—merchants, bankers, intellectuals[103]—devoted most of his work to medieval civilization as seen through works expressive of the mentalities, beliefs, and feelings of the period.[104]

At the beginning of the 1960s, the Centre de recherches historiques of the sixth section of the E.P.H.E. organized an investigation into deserted villages, the results of which were published in 1965 and 1970. These austere volumes demonstrate the persistence of several features that, as we have seen, are symptomatic of what might be called the *Annales* spirit: collective research along programmatic lines, pursued not only in France but on an international scale, to assure that the data obtained will be readily comparable; interest in new techniques (aerial photography, excavation of sites dating from the Middle Ages); an interdisciplinary approach, the deserted villages having been studied in terms of demography, geography, rural history, and material culture; and a decompartmentalization of history itself, by sponsoring a collaboration between medievalists and historians of the modern period on studies of a period extending from the eleventh to the eighteenth centuries.[105] But it is the object of this enquiry—the ensemble of deserted villages—that makes the project emblematic of the approach to history in general, and to that of France in particular, characteristic of the *Annales* circle during the four decades that have just been surveyed.

This approach entailed a shifting of scholarly attention from objects very much alive in the national memory—events, institutions, individuals—to others that had been forgotten or had never even entered the level of consciousness, no one in their own time having been aware of their existence. The deserted villages—reduced to traces discernible only to those trained to look for them but that, once recognized, were counted, mapped, and excavated, yielding masses of otherwise unobtainable information about life in earlier times—can serve as a symbol of those elements of the past that had been eliminated from the national memory or had never figured in it. And that attracted the *Annales* historians, imbued as they were with the Vidalian approach to geography. By legitimizing and promoting nonwritten sources and, among written ones, those previously unexploited, as well as by fostering a new attitude toward texts of the traditional type, they effected a break with the fundamental dogma and reconfigured the relationship between scholarly history and the national memory, situating the former outside the latter.

Broaching questions prompted not by common sense but by the social sciences, setting out to find new sources and develop new techniques providing access to new objects of study, the history of France as reconstructed by the *Annales* circle assumed an unfamiliar aspect. Nothing about it was natural. Everything was a problem, including much that had hitherto seemed self-evident, notably the placement of boundaries and the very existence of the nation as it then existed. Marc Bloch and Lucien Febvre had already strayed from the narrow path laid out for them by tradition, but the work produced in the wake of Fernand Braudel and Ernest Labrousse, replete as it was with graphs, structures, trends, and models, could not help but provoke a feeling of homesickness among general readers interested in the past. Here the distance between *Annales* history and the national memory attained its maximum degree.

We now know that such was the price—probably excessive, but who could have foreseen this?—exacted for a prodigious enrichment of both scholarly history and national memory, which also greatly benefited from it. Henceforth the image of the past it conveyed would no longer be monopolized by exceptional individuals. Nor would they be banished from it. It would encompass Louis XIV, of course, but also—to cite the title of a work by Pierre Goubert—twenty million Frenchmen, all flesh-and-bone sexual beings with their own ways of being born, living, and dying, with their own familial and intimate environments, their daily bread and their feast-day wine, their beliefs, hopes, anguish. And it would no longer be a few dozen spectacular events but primarily—which is not to say exclusively—one of works and days, with all that this implies in the way of invariability, repetition, and monotony. An imminent proliferation of *Annales*-inspired histories of France intended for a general readership suggests that the moment has arrived for synthesis.

But every synthesis is provisional, at least as long as the historical discipline remains vital. Even now innovations may be taking shape in the shadows that will one day emerge to issue their challenge. Why not in these very volumes?

BIBLIOGRAPHIC NOTE

For a recent English-language study of the *Annales* school with different emphases, as well as a useful bibliography and glossary of French terms, see Peter Burke, *The French Historical Revolution: The "Annales" School 1929–1989* (Stanford: Stanford University Press, 1990). There is also a recent biography of one of the school's founding figures by Carole Fink, *Marc Bloch: A Life in History* (Cambridge: Cambridge University Press, 1989). Most of the important *Annales* historians have been amply translated (see notes below); a glaring exception is Ernest Labrousse, but see Ernest Labrousse, "The Crisis in the French Economy at the End of the Old Regime," in *The Economic Origins of the French Revolution*, ed. R. Greenlaw (Boston: D.C. Heath, 1958), 59–92. The synthetic work of French history by Braudel to which Pomian refers in passing is Fernand Braudel, *The Identity of France*, 3 vols., trans. Siân Reynolds (London: Collins, 1988–). Of the projects evoked in Pomian's closing lines, the most important is the five-volume Hachette *Histoire de France*, now available in its entirety in English: Georges Duby, *France in the Middle Ages 987–1460*, trans. Juliet Vale (Oxford, England, and Cambridge, Mass.: Blackwell, 1991); Emmanuel Le Roy Ladurie, *The French State 1460–1610*, trans. Juliet Vale (Oxford, England, and Cambridge, Mass.: Blackwell, 1994); Emmanuel Le Roy Ladurie, *The Ancien Regime 1610–1774*, trans. Juliet Vale (Oxford, England, and Cambridge, Mass.: Blackwell, 1997); François Furet, *Revolutionary France 1770–1880*, trans. Antonia Neville (Oxford, England, and Cambridge, Mass.: Blackwell, 1992); Maurice Agulhon, *The French Republic 1879–1992*, trans. Antonia Nevill (Oxford, England, and Cambridge, Mass.: Blackwell, 1993).

NOTES

1. See François Simiand, "Méthode historique et science sociale: Étude critique d'après les ouvrages récents de M. Lacombe et de M. Seignobos," *Revue de synthèse historique* 6 (1903): 1–22 and 129–57.

2. Marc Bloch and Lucien Febvre, "À nos lecteurs," *Annales* 1 (1929): 1–2.

3. Calculated from Maurice-A. Arnould, *Vingt années d'histoire économique et sociale: Table analytique des "Annales" fondées par Marc Bloch and Lucien Febvre (1929–1948)* (Paris: Association Marc-Bloch, 1953).

4. Henk L. Wesseling, "The *Annales* School and the Writing of Contemporary History," *Review* 1, nos. 3–4 (1978): 185–94.

5. Marc Bloch and Lucien Febvre, op. cit. (note 2).

6. See Lucien Febvre, "Henri Pirenne à travers ses oeuvres" (1927), in *Combats pour l'histoire* (Paris: Armand Colin, 1965), 357–69; Marc Bloch, "Henri Pirenne, historien de la Belgique," *Annales* 4 (1932): 478–81.

7. Lucien Febvre, "Albert Mathiez, un tempérament, une éducation" (1932), in *Combats pour l'histoire*, 343.

8. "En clair, l'Espace: disons la géographie. Le Temps: disons l'histoire": Lucien Febvre, "Face au vent: Manifeste des Annales Nouvelles" (first published 1946), 38.

9. Paul Vidal de La Blache, "La Conception actuelle de l'enseignement de la géographie," in *L'Enseignement des sciences naturelles et de la géographie*, ed. Le Dantec et al., lectures delivered at the Musée pédagogique in 1905 (Paris, 1905), 117.

10. See Paul Vidal de La Blache, *Tableau de la géographie de la France* (1903; reprint, Paris: Tallandier, 1979), esp. 93–94.

11. See Albert Demangeon, *Les Sources de la géographie de la France aux Archives nationales* (Paris, 1905); Max Sorre, *Étude critique des sources de l'histoire de la viticulture et du commerce des vins et eaux-de-vie en Bas-Languedoc au XVIIIe siècle* (Paris, 1913); André Allix, *Un Pays de haute montagne: L'Oisans* (Paris, 1929); André Allix, *L'Oisans au Moyen Âge* (Paris, 1922); Jules Sion, *Les Paysans de la Normandie orientale* (Paris, 1909).

12. See Henri Berr, "La Synthèse des études relatives aux régions de la France," *Revue de synthèse historique* 6 (1903): 166–81.

13. See L. Barrau-Dihigo, *La Gascogne* (Paris: Éditions du Cerf, 1903).

14. See Lucien Febvre, *La Franche-Comté* (Paris: Éditions du Cerf, 1905); Louis Villat, *Le Velay* (Paris, Éditions du Cerf, 1908); Marc Bloch, *L'Île-de-France (les pays autour de Paris)* (Paris: Éditions du Cerf, 1913).

15. Lucien Febvre, "Marc Bloch et Strasbourg," in *Combats pour l'histoire* (see note 6) (1945), 394.

16. Febvre, *Philippe II et la Franche-Comté* (1912; reprint, Paris: Flammarion, 1970), 13, 30–31.

17. Ibid., 198.

18. Febvre, *La Terre et l'évolution humaine* (1922; reprint, Paris: Albin, Michel, 1970), 69.

19. See the draft of a letter from Lucien Febvre to the publishing house Armand Colin (Strasbourg, February 29, 1928), cited in *Lucien Febvre 1878–1956*, a catalogue of an exhibition held at the Bibliothèque nationale in Paris (Paris, 1978), 27, no. 39.

20. See Étienne Juilliard, André Meynier, Xavier de Planhol, and Gilles Sautter, *Structures agraires et paysages ruraux: Un Quart de siècle de recherches françaises* (Nancy, 1957; *Annales de l'Est*, mémoire no. 17).

21. Marc Bloch, *Les Caractères originaux de l'histoire rurale française* (originally published in 1931; reprint, Paris: Armand Colin, 1976), 154.

22. Gaston Roupnel, *Histoire de la campagne française* (Paris: Grasset, 1932), 106.

23. Marc Bloch, *Les Caractères originaux*, 250.

24. Ibid., 251.

25. Roupnel, *Histoire de la campagne française*, 314.

26. See Roger Dion, "Le Val de Loire: Étude de géographie régionale (Tours: Arrault, 1933), 457ff.

27. Ibid., 490.

28. Roger Dion, *Essai sur la formation du paysage rural français* (originally published in 1934; reprint, Paris: Éditions Guy Serrier, 1981), 92–93.

29. Ibid., 93.

30. "La Part de la géographie et celle de l'histoire dans l'explication de l'habitat rural du Bassin parisien," *Publications de la Société de géographie de Lille*, 1946, 6–80.

31. See Max Derruau, *La Grande Limagne auvergnate et bourbonnaise: Étude géographique* (Clermont-Ferrand, 1949), esp. 405.

32. See Lucien Febvre, "Cadre et substance en géographie," *Annales* 5 (1950): 539–41; Roger Dion, "Réflexions de méthode à propos de *La Grande Limagne* de Max Derruau," *Annales de géographie* 60 (1951): 25–33.

33. See Lucien Febvre, "Ni histoire à thèse ni histoire-manuel: Entre Benda et Seignobos" (first published 1933), in *Combats pour l'histoire*, 82–89.

34. Marc Bloch, *Apologie pour l'histoire ou le métier d'historien* (Paris: Armand Colin, 1964), 101 (note by Lucien Febvre).

35. See *Annuaire du Collège de France*, 1943 (in fact covering 1940–41), 105–8; 1945, 125–31; 1946, 151; 1947, 167–68.

36. See Marc Bloch, *La France sous les derniers Capétiens, 1223–1328* (originally published in 1937–38; reprint, Paris: Armand Colin, 1964); Lucien Febvre, "Les Principaux aspects d'une civilization. La Première Renaissance française: quatre prises de vue" (first published 1925), in *Pour une histoire à part entière* (Paris: Service d'Édition et de Vente des Productions de l'Education Nationale, 1962), 529–603; Fernand Braudel in *Annuaire du Collège de France*, 1954, 282–83; 1955, 274–76.

37. Lucien Febvre, "Ni histoire à thèse ni histoire-manuel," 97–98.

38. See Febvre, "Frontière: Limites et divisions territoriales de la France en 1789" (first published 1908) and "Frontière: Le Mot et la notion" (first published 1928), both in *Pour une histoire à part entière*, 11ff.; Febvre *La Terre et l'évolution humaine*, 323ff.

39. Albert Demangeon and Lucien Febvre, *Le Rhin: Problèmes d'histoire et d'économie* (Paris: Armand Colin, 1935), 81.

40. Ibid., 113.

41. Ibid., 123.

42. Ibid., 129.

43. Roger Dion, *Les Frontières de la France* (Paris: Hachette, 1947), fig. 17 and 102–4, 105.

44. Ibid., 105–6.

45. Marc Bloch, *Rois et serfs: Un Chapitre d'histoire capétienne* (Paris, 1920), 10.

46. Ibid., 113.

47. See Marc Bloch, *Les Caractères originaux*, esp. 107ff., and the articles collected in Bloch, *Mélanges historiques* (Paris: S.E.V.E.N., 1963), part 4, "Le Servage dans la société européene," 261ff., and part 6, "Vie rurale," 565ff.

48. Bloch, *Les Caractères originaux*, 153.

49. Ibid., 139.

50. See the preface by Jacques Le Goff to the new edition of Marc Bloch, *Les Rois thaumaturges: Étude sur le caractère surnaturel attribué à la puissance royale particulièrement en France et en Angleterre* (Paris: Gallimard, 1983; first published 1924), esp. xxxiv ff.

51. Ibid., 359.

52. Ibid., 72.

53. Ibid., 401–2.

54. See *Annuaire du Collège de France*, 1937, 137–40; 1938, 143–44.

55. See Lucien Febvre, *Le Problème de l'incroyance au XVIe siècle: La Religion de Rabelais* (Paris: Albin Michel, 1942); Febvre, *Origène et des Périers ou l'énigme du Cumbalum Mundi* (Paris: Droz, 1942); Febvre, *Autour de l'Heptaméron: Amour sacré, amour profane* (Paris: Gallimard, 1944).

56. Febvre, in *Annuaire du Collège de France*, 1937, 138.

57. See Febvre, "Pour les historiens un livre de chevet: Le Cours d'économie politique de Simiand," in *Pour une histoire à part entière*, 185–203; Marc Bloch, "Le Salaire et les fluctuations économiques à longue période" (first published in 1934), in *Mélanges historiques*, 890–914.

58. Georges Lefebvre, "Le Mouvement des prix et les origines de la Révolution Française," *Annales* 9 (1938): 139–70.

59. Labrousse, "La Conjoncture économique a créé pour une large part la conjoncture révolutionnaire," in *Esquisse du mouvement des prix et des revenues en France au XVIIIe siècle* (Paris: Dalloz, 1932), 640.

60. See Labrousse, *La Crise de l'économie française à la fin de l'ancien régime et au début de la Révolution* (Paris, 1944).

61. Febvre, "Vignes, vins et vignerons" (first published 1947), in *Pour une histoire à part entière*, 255–64.

62. See Labrousse, *Esquisse*, 513 ff.; Labrousse, *La Crise*, 173–81.

63. See Ruggiero Romano, *Tra storici ed economisti* (Turin: Einaudi, 1982), 53–56.

64. Fernand Braudel, *La Méditerranée à l'époque de Philippe II* (Paris: Armand Colin, 1949), 296.

65. Ibid., xxiii.

66. See Lucien Febvre, "La Méditerranée et le monde méditerranéen à l'époque de Philippe II" (first published 1950), in *Pour une histoire à part entière*, 167–79.

67. Fernand Braudel, *La Méditerranée*, xiv.

68. *Annuaire du Collège de France*, 1951, 238.

69. Ibid., 1953, 251.

70. Jean Meuvret, "Les Mouvements des prix de 1661 à 1715 et leurs répercussions" (first published 1944), in *Études d'histoire économique* (Paris: Armand Colin, 1971), 95.

71. See Meuvret, *Le Problème des subsistances à l'époque de Louis XIV* (Paris: École des Hautes Études en Sciences Sociales & Mouton, 1971).

72. See Joseph Goy and Emmanuel Le Roy Ladurie, eds., *Les Fluctuations du produit de la dîme: Conjoncture décimale et domaniale de la fin du Moyen Âge au XVIIIe siècle* (Paris: Mouton, 1972).

73. Hugues Neveux, *Vie et déclin d'une structure économique: Les Grains du Cambrésis (fin du XIVe–début du XVIIe siècle)* (Paris: Écoles des Hautes Études en Sciences Sociales, 1980).

74. See Éditions de l'École des Hautes Études en Sciences Sociales, *Catalogue d'ouvrages 1986*, 48–49.

75. See Roger Dion, *Histoire de la vigne et du vin en France des origines au XIXe siècle* (Paris, 1959); Georges Duby, "Une Synthèse: Le Vignoble français," *Annales* 16 (1961): 122–26.

76. See Pierre Chaunu, *Structures et conjonctures de l'Atlantique espagnol et hispano-américain (1504–1650)*, part 2 of *Séville et l'Atlantique (1504–1650)*, 2 vols. (Paris: Service d'Édition et de Vente des Productions de l'Education Nationale, 1959); vol. 8, 2, 1 (of the whole), 19–20; vol. 8, 2, 2, 1566ff.

77. Frank C. Spooner, *L'Économie mondiale et les frappes monétaires en France (1493–1680)* (Paris, S.E.V.E.N., 1961).

78. René Baehrel, *Une Croissance: La Basse-Provence rurale (fin du XVIe siècle–1789)* (Paris: S.E.V.E.N., 1961).

79. Pierre Goubert, *Beauvais et la Beauvaisis de 1600 à 1730, contribution à l'histoire sociale de la France du XVIIe siècle* (Paris: S.E.V.E.N., 1960). This citation is from the shortened edition: *Cent mille provinciaux au XVIIe siècle* (Paris: Flammarion, collection "Champs," 1968), 104–5.

80. See Louis Henry and Michel Fleury, *Des Registres paroissiaux à l'histoire de la population: Manuel de dépouillement et d'exploitation de l'état civil ancien* (Paris, 1956); Louis Henry and Étienne Gautier, *La Population de Crulai, paroisse normade: Étude historique* (Paris, 1958).

81. See Emmanuel Le Roy Ladurie, "Voies nouvelles pour l'histoire rurale: XVIe–XVIIIe siècles," *Annales* 20 (1965): 1268–80.

82. Ladurie, *Les Paysans de Languedoc* (1960; reprint, Paris: Mouton, 1966).

83. See Ladurie, *Histoire du climat depuis l'an mil* (Paris: Flammarion, 1967).

84. See Ladurie, *Paris-Montpellier* (Paris: Gallimard, 1982).

85. "La natalité exprime la mentalicé": Charles Morazé, *La France bourgeoise XVIIIe–XXe siècles* (Paris: Armand Colin, 1952), 113.

86. See Robert Mandrou, *Introduction à la France moderne (1500–1640): Essai de psychologie historique* (Paris: Albin Michel, 1961).

87. See Mandrou, *Magistrats et sorciers en France au XVIIe siècle: Une Analyse de psychologie historique* (Paris: Plon, 1968).

88. See Mandrou, *De la culture populaire aux XVIIe et XVIIIe siècles: La Biblio-thèque bleue de Troyes* (Paris: Plon, 1964).

89. Philippe Ariès, *Histoire des populations françaises et de leurs attitudes devant la vie depuis le XVIIIe siècle* (1948; reprint, Paris: Éditions du Seuil, 1971), 15.

90. See Alain Besançon, "Histoire et psychanalyse," *Annales* 19 (1964): 237–49; Jean-Louis Flandrin, *Annales* 19 (1964): 322–29.

91. See Philippe Ariès, *Les Traditions sociales dans les pays de France* (Paris, 1943); Ariès, *Un Historien du dimanche* (Paris: Éditions du Seuil, 1980).

92. See Ariès, *L'Enfant et la vie familiale sous l'ancien régime* (Paris: Plon, 1960); Ariès, *Essais sur l'histoire de la mort en Occident du Moyen Âge à nos jours* (Paris: Éditions du Seuil, 1975); Ariès, *L'Homme devant la mort* (Paris: Éditions du Seuil, 1977).

93. See Alberto Tenenti, *La Vie et la mort à travers l'art du XVe siècle* (Paris: Armand Colin, 1952); Tenenti, *Il senso della morte e l'amore della vita nel Rinascimento (Francia e Italia)* (Turin: Einaudi, 1957).

94. Michel Vovelle, *Piété baroque et déchristianisation: Les Attitudes devant la mort en Provence au XVIIIe siècle* (Paris: Plon, 1973); Vovelle, *Mourir autrefois, les attitudes devant la mort aux XVIIe et XVIIIe siècles* (Paris: Gallimard, Julliard, collection "Ar-chives," 1974).

95. François Lebrun, *Les Hommes et la mort en Anjou aux XVIIe et XVIIIe siècles: Essai de démographie et psychologie historiques* (Paris: Mouton, 1971).

96. Jean-Louis Flandrin, *L'Église et le contrôle des naissances* (Paris, 1970); Flan-drin, *Les Amours paysannes: Amour et sexualité dans les campagnes de l'ancienne France (XVIe–XIXe siècles)* (Paris: Gallimard, Julliard, collection "Archives," 1975); Flan-drin, *Familles: Parenté, maison, sexualité dans l'ancienne société* (Paris: Hachette, 1976).

97. André Déléage, *La Vie rurale en Bourgogne jusqu'au début du XIe siècle*, 3 vols. (Mâcon, 1941).

98. Philippe Wolff, *Commerce et marchands et Toulouse (vers 1350–vers 1450)* (Paris: Plon, 1954).

99. Yves Renouard, *Études d'histoire médiévale* (Paris: S.E.V.E.N., 1968); the bib-liography is on 1121ff.

100. See Jacques Le Goff, "Maurice Lombard: Le Maître," *Annales* 21 (1966): 714–16; Maurice Lombard, *Études d'économie médiévale*, 3 vols. (Paris: École des Hautes Études en Sciences Sociales; The Hague: Mouton, 1971–78).

101. See Georges Duby, *L'Économie rurale et la vie des campagnes dans l'Occident médiévale*, 2 vols. (Paris: Aubier, 1962).

102. See Duby, *Adolescence de la chrétienté* (Geneva: Skira, 1966); Duby, *L'Europe des cathédrals* (Geneva: Skira, 1966); Duby, *Fondements d'un nouvel humanisme, 1280–1440* (Geneva: Skira, 1967).

103. See Jacques Le Goff, *Marchands et banquiers au Moyen Âge* (Paris, 1956); Le Goff, *Les Intellectuels au Moyen Âge* (Paris: Éditions du Seuil, collection "Le Temps qui court," 1957).

104. See Le Goff, *La Civilisation de l'Occident médiévale* (Paris: Arthaud, 1965), and the articles collected in *Pour un autre Moyen Âge* (Paris: Gallimard, 1977).

105. See *Villages désertés et histoire économique: XIe–XVIIIe siècle* (Paris: S.E.V.E.N., 1965); *Archéologie du village déserté*, 2 vols. (Paris: S.E.V.E.N., 1970).

CHAPTER THREE

Figure 3.1   Geneviève Bouliard, *Alexandre Lenoir*. Musée Carnavalet, Paris, photo
              © Bulloz.

Figure 3.2   P. J. La Fontaine, *Alexandre Lenoire protégeant le tombeau de Louis XII
              et Anne de Bretagne contre la fureur des sans-culottes*. Musée Carnavalet,
              Paris, Cabinet des dessins, photo © Bulloz.

Figure 3.3   Alexandre Lenoir, *Projet de restauration de la maison de Diane de
              Poitiers . . .*, year eight. Musée du Louvre, Paris, Cabinet des dessins,
              photo © Musées nationaux.

Figure 3.4   *Plan du Musée des monuments français aux Petits-Augustins*, engraving by
              Réville et Lavallée, after Vauzelle, in *Le Musée des monuments français*,
              Paris 1816. Bibliothèque nationale, photo © Bibliothèque nationale,
              Paris.

Figure 3.5   *Première vue du grand jardin*, engraving by Réville et Lavallée, after
              Vauzelle, in *Le Musée des monuments français*, Paris, 1816. Bibliothèque
              nationale, Paris, photo Jean-Loup Charmet © Gallimard.

Figure 3.6   Vauzelle, *Étude de la salle du XIIIᵉ siècle du Musée des monuments
              français*. Musée du Louvre, Paris, Cabinet des dessins, photo © Musées
              nationaux.

Figure 3.7   Vauzelle, *Le Musée des monuments français dans l'ancienne église des
              Petits-Augustins*. Musée Carnavalet, Paris, photo © Lauros-Firaudon.

Figure 3.8   Musée des monuments français, ancient palace of Trocadéro, Paris.
              Photo © Roger-Viollet.

CHAPTER FOUR

Figure 4.1   François Guizot, lithography by Delpech after Mauvin, 1830. Photo
              © N. D. Roger-Viollet.

CHAPTER FIVE

Figure 5.1   View of the Gallery of Batailles. Photo coll. of the author.

Figure 5.2   Horace Vernet, *Philippe-Auguste avant la bataille de Bouvines* (detail).
              Musée national du Château de Versailles, photo © Musées nationaux.

Figure 5.3   *Jeanne d'Arc*, statuette by Marie d'Orléans. Musée national du
              Château de Versailles, photo © Musées nationaux.

Figure 5.4   Gérard, *L'Entrée d'Henri IV à Paris*. Musée national du Château du
              Versailles, photo © Musées nationaux.

Figure 5.5   *La Garde nationale part pour l'armée* (1792), engraving after Léon
              Cogniet. Musée national du Château de Versailles, photo coll. of the
              author.

Figure 5.6   *Louis-Philippe prête sement de maintenir la Charte en 1830*, engraving by
              Devéria. Musée des arts décoratifs, Paris, photo © Bulloz.

CHAPTER SIX

Figure 6.1   Pierre Larousse, daguerreotype, not dated. Photo © Larousse.

Figure 6.2   The printer Larousse, 17, rue du Montparnasse, around 1890. Photo © Larousse.

Figure 6.3   Original edition of the *Grand dictionnaire universel du XIXᵉ siècle*, letter B. Photo © Larousse.

Figure 6.4   Monument to Pierre Larousse erected at Toucy, Yonne, in 1894. Photo © Larousse.

CHAPTER SEVEN

Figure 7.1   Primat, monk of Saint-Denis, presents the Book of Kings to Philippe the Hardy, in 1274, *Grandes chroniques de France*, fourteenth century. Bibliothèque Sainte-Geneviève, Paris, photo © Bibliothèque nationale, Paris.

Figure 7.2   History of Énée, ancestor of the Francs, *Grandes chroniques de France*, fourteenth century. Bibliothèque nationale, photo © Bibliothèque nationale, Paris.

Figure 7.3   Founding of Paris by King Pharamond, *Grandes chroniques de France*, around 1375–79. Bibliothèque nationale, photo © Bibliothèque nationale, Paris.

Figure 7.4   Coronation of Charles VI, *Grandes chroniques de France*, around 1375–79. Bibliothèque nationale, photo © Bibliothèque nationale, Paris.

Figure 7.5   The arms of Jean de Derval, miniature from the *Grandes chroniques de France*, copy in French by Pasquier Bonhomme, fifteenth century. Bibliothèque de l'Arsenal, Paris, photo © Bibliothèque nationale, Paris.

CHAPTER EIGHT

Figure 8.1   Étienne Pasquier, engraving by Pierre Gaultier, 1617. Bibliothèque nationale, photo © Bibliothèque nationale, Paris.

Figure 8.2   Jean Bodin, engraving, sixteenth century. Bibliothèque nationale, photo © Bibliothèque nationale, Paris.

Figure 8.3   Pierre Pithou, engraving by Nicolas de Larmessin. Bibliothèque nationale, photo © Bibliothèque nationale, Paris.

Figure 8.4   Claude Fauchet, engraving by Pierre Gaultier, 1610. Bibliothèque nationale, photo © Bibliothèque nationale, Paris.

Figure 8.5   Papyre Masson, engraving by Pierre Gaultier in *Clementiae isorae elogium*, Paris, Mettayer, 1612. Bibliothèque nationale, Paris, photo Jean-Loup Charmet, © Gallimard.

CHAPTER NINE

Figure 9.1   Augustin Thierry, lithography by Émile Lassalle, around 1830–40. Bibliothèque nationale, photo © Bibliothèque nationale, Paris.

Figure 9.2   Ary Scheffer, *Mort de Gaston de Foix à la bataille de Ravenne*, 1824. Musée national du château de Versailles, photo © Musées nationaux.

Figure 9.3   Claude Fauriel, charcoal drawing (by Mme de Condorcet?), n.d., Bibliothèque de l'institut de France, Paris, photo © Bulloz.

Figure 9.4   Victor Cousin, engraving by Ambroise Tardieu, 1828. Bibliothèque nationale, photo © Bibliothèque nationale, Paris.

Figure 9.5   François-Auguste Mignet, drawing by Prosper Mérimée. Bibliothèque nationale, photo © Bibliothèque nationale, Paris.

Figure 9.6   Adolphe Thiers, engraving by Bosselman, 1831. Bibliothèque nationale, photo © Bibliothèque nationale, Paris.

Figure 9.7   Edgar Quinet, lithography by Tony Toullion. Bibliothèque nationale, photo © Bibliothèque nationale, Paris.

Figure 9.8   François Guizot, engraving by Abroise Tardieu, 1828. Bibliothèque nationale, photo © Bibliothèque nationale, Paris.

Figure 9.9   Prosper de Barante, lithography by Prodhomme. Bibliothèque nationale, photo © Bibliothèque nationale, Paris.

Figure 9.10   Ary Scheffer, *Les Femmes souliotes*, 1827. Musée du Louvre, Paris, photo © Musées nationaux.

Figure 9.11   Jules Michelet, lithography by Tony Toullion, 1843. Bibliothèque nationale, photo © Bibliothèque nationale, Paris.

CHAPTER TEN

Figure 10.1   Ernest Lavisse, in Robert Kastor, *L'Académie*, etching, 1893. Bibliothèque nationale, photo © Bibliothèque nationale, Paris.

Figure 10.2   Alfred Rambaud, engraving by Navellier after a photograph. Photo © Collection Viollet.

Figure 10.3   Gaston Paris. Photo © Collection Viollet.

Figure 10.4   Gabriel Monod. Bibliothèque nationale, photo © Bibliothèque nationale, Paris.

Figure 10.5   Charles V. Langlois, photograph by Nadar. Bibliothèque nationale, photo © Bibliothèque nationale, Paris.

Figure 10.6   Charles Seignobos. Photo © Harlingue-Viollet.

Figure 10.7   Ernest Lavisse in the middle of his students, at the Sorbonne (Dumont Library, today Lavisse library), around 1900. Bibliothèque nationale, photo © Bibliothèque nationale, Paris.

Figure 10.8   Ernest Lavisse, *Louis XIV*, Paris, 1911. Coll. part., photo © Gallimard.

Figure 10.9   Proofs of the *Histoire de la Révolution* by Philippe Sagnac corrected by Ernest Lavisse. Coll. part., photo © Gallimard.

Figure 10.10   The proofs of *La Restauration* by Charléty corrected by Ernest Lavisse, adapted from Lucien Herr. Coll. part., photo © Gallimard.

CHAPTER ELEVEN

Figure 11.1   Marc Bloch. Bibliothèque nationale, photo © Bibl. nat., Paris.

Figure 11.2   Lucien Febvre. Lucien Febvre, Photo Archives familiales, droits réservés.

Figure 11.3   Henri Pirenne. Photo © Keystone.

Figure 11.4   Roger Dion. Photo © A.F.P.

Figure 11.5   Albert Demangeon. Photo © Archives Colin.

Figure 11.6   Maurice Halbwachs. Photo coll. part.

Figure 11.7   Georges Lefebvre. Bibliothèque nationale, photo © Bibliothèque nationale, Paris.

Figure 11.8   Henri Berr. Photo © Collection Viollet.

Figure 11.9   Yves Renouard. Coll. part., photo © Harcourt.

Figure 11.10   Georges Friedmann. Photo Marc Foucault © Gallimard.

Figure 11.11   Fernand Braudel. Photo © Archives Flammarion.

Figure 11.12   Philippe Ariès. Photo © Roland Allard/Vu.

Chapters translated in published or projected volumes of *Rethinking France* can be found in *Les Lieux de mémoire* as follows.

VOLUME 4: HISTORIOGRAPHY (2010)

Page numbers in italics refer to illustrations.